New Concise Maths 2

George Humphrey

Gill & Macmillan

Gill & Macmillan Ltd
Hume Avenue
Park West
Dublin 12
with associated companies throughout the world
www.gillmacmillan.ie

© George Humphrey 2001
978 07171 3184 6

I would like to dedicate this book to my three children, Jesamine, Colman and Ciana.

CONTENTS

PREFACE

New Concise Mathematics 2 completes the course for Junior Certificate Mathematics, Higher Level.

This textbook has been designed with the aims and objectives of the new syllabus and examination firmly in mind. Full account has been taken of the new approaches which should be adopted by students to solve problems in mathematics. In particular, it is crucial that students are presented with mathematics at a level that is appropriate to their abilities. The book reflects the author's experience that students learn better from worked examples than from abstract discussion of principles. For instance, all the chapters on geometry begin with numerical examples and problems, in a separate section, before students are required to tackle proofs (cuts). The ten 'formal proofs' are included separately in the last chapter of the book.

The emphasis is on clear and concise presentation of the material. Simple, familiar language is used throughout, instead of technical terms, which are not required in the examination. Long explanations are avoided, on the principle that these are best left to the teacher. A comprehensive range of worked examples, with helpful comments highlighted in colour, is included. The author has very carefully graded the exercises through testing them in class. Concepts are built up in a logical manner. Great effort is made throughout the book to ensure that the answers to the problems work out evenly. Each chapter is broken down into short, manageable sections and ends with a chapter test containing plenty of questions of the type encountered in the Junior Certificate exam.

A numbered, step-by-step approach, highlighted in colour, is used to help with problem-solving. Key terms are defined simply, and highlighted. This has been found to save valuable class time sometimes spent in copying notes from the board.

Many topics, such as area and volume, graphing functions, coordinate geometry and trigonometry, can be started directly from Book 2 without reference to Book 1. The author has found that this can save a lot of time in class, as repetition causes problems in trying to complete the course.

I would like to thank Mr Michael Dunne, Principal of Maryfield College, Dublin, who read the entire manuscript and made many valuable suggestions which have been included in the final text. I would also like to thank my colleague, Mr Geoffrey Reeves, St Andrew's College, Dublin, who helped when matters of mathematical clarification was required. Thanks must also go to Geraldine Finucane, sixth-year student, Holy Faith College, Clontarf, Dublin, who took on the task of checking my answers as well as reading the entire manuscript and also making many constructive suggestions.

Finally, I wish to express my thanks to the staff of Gill & Macmillan, and to Julia Fairlie in particular, for their advice, guidance and untiring assistance in the preparation of the text.

George Humphrey
St Andrew's College
Dublin

FACTORS

Factorising

> **Factorising is the reverse procedure to removing brackets.**

Expanding removes brackets.
Factorising does the opposite by putting in brackets.

For example:

Expanding:	$5(2a + 3b) = 10a + 15b$	Remove brackets.
Factorising:	$10a + 15b = 5(2a + 3b)$	Put in brackets.

The process of finding the factors of an expression is called **factorisation**.

There are four types of factors that we will meet on our course:

	Type	Example	Factors
1.	Take out the HCF	$12pq - 6q^2$	$6q(2p - q)$
2.	Factors by grouping	$6a^2 - 2ab + 3ac - bc$	$(3a - b)(2a + c)$
3.	Quadratic trinomials	$10x^2 - 3x - 1$	$(5x + 1)(2x - 1)$
4.	Difference of two squares	$16a^2 - 25b^2$	$(4a - 5b)(4a + 5b)$

Note: It is good practice to check your answer by removing the brackets to make sure that the factors give the original expression you were asked to factorise.

1. Taking out the highest common factor (HCF)

> **1.** Find the HCF of all the terms making up the expression.
> **2.** Put the HCF outside the brackets.
> **3.** Divide each term by the HCF to find the factor inside the brackets.

Note: To factorise an expression **completely** the HCF must appear outside the brackets.

Factorise: **(i)** $15pq + 3q^2$ **(ii)** $4x^2y - 6xy^2$ **(iii)** $ab - ac + a$

Solution:

(i) $15pq + 3q^2$
The HCF is $3q$
$\therefore 15pq + 3q^2$ (put $3q$ outside the bracket,
$= 3q(5p + q)$ then divide each term by $3q$)

$$\frac{15pq}{3q} = 5p$$

$$\frac{3q^2}{3q} = q$$

(ii) $4x^2y - 6xy^2$
The HCF is $2xy$
$\therefore 4x^2y - 6xy^2$ (put $2xy$ outside the bracket,
$= 2xy(2x - 3y)$ then divide each term by $2xy$)

$$\frac{4x^2y}{2xy} = 2x$$

$$\frac{-6xy^2}{2xy} = -3y$$

(iii) $ab - ac + a$
The HCF is a
$\therefore ab - ac + a$ (put a outside the bracket,
$= a(b - c + 1)$ then divide each term by a)
                  ↑
(There must be a 1 here)
Notice that the HCF is the same as one of the terms.

$$\frac{ab}{a} = b$$

$$\frac{-ac}{a} = -c$$

$$\frac{a}{a} = 1$$

Exercise 1.1 ▼

Simplify each of the following:

1. $\dfrac{10x}{5}$ **2.** $\dfrac{8y}{2}$ **3.** $\dfrac{15xy}{5y}$ **4.** $\dfrac{9pq}{3p}$ **5.** $\dfrac{12ab}{4ab}$

6. $\dfrac{8xyz}{4xy}$ **7.** $\dfrac{7q}{7q}$ **8.** $\dfrac{-2xy}{-2xy}$ **9.** $\dfrac{8ab}{-4b}$ **10.** $\dfrac{-20xy}{10y}$

11. $\dfrac{-5xy}{5x}$ **12.** $\dfrac{6pq}{3pq}$ **13.** $\dfrac{12x^2y}{6xy}$ **14.** $\dfrac{15pq^2}{15pq}$ **15.** $\dfrac{6a^2b}{3ab}$

Copy each of the following, and put in the missing terms in the brackets:

16. $3x + 3y = 3($ $)$ **17.** $5p - 15q = 5($ $)$

18. $x^2 + 2x = x($ $)$ **19.** $4a^2 - 2a = 2a($ $)$

20. $3p^2 - 6pq = 3p($ $)$ **21.** $-5pq - 10p = -5p($ $)$

22. $6x^2y - 4xy^2 = 2xy($ $)$ **23.** $-2x^2 + 6x = -2x($ $)$

Factorise each of the following:

24. $5x + 10$ **25.** $pq + pr$ **26.** $2x + xy$

27. $x^2 + 5x$ **28.** $4x^2 + 2x$ **29.** $a^2 - 3a$

30. $2a - 3ab$ **31.** $3ab - 6ac$ **32.** $x^2 - x$

33. $8x - 12x^2$ **34.** $x^2 - 6x$ **35.** $15bc - 3c^2$

36. $4x^2y - 8xy^2$ **37.** $ax^2 + ax$ **38.** $10p - 15pq$

39. $pq + pr + p$ **40.** $ab - 2a^2b + 3ab^2$ **41.** $8ab - 12ab^2 + 16a^2b$

42. Simplify $5(x^2 - 2x + 4) - 2(2x^2 - 3x + 10)$ and then factorise the simplified expression.

43. Simplify $(2p + 3q)(p - 4q) + (p + 6q)(p + 2q)$,
and then factorise the simplified expression.

44. Factorise: **(i)** $12pq - 6p$ **(ii)** $6q - 3$

Hence, simplify $\dfrac{12pq - 6p}{6q - 3}$ by dividing top and bottom by common factors.

2. Factors by grouping

On our course an expression consisting of four terms with no common factor can be factorised with the following steps:

> **1.** Group into pairs with a common factor.
> **2.** Take out the common factor in each pair separately.
> **3.** Take out the new common factor.

Factorise: **(i)** $2pr - 2ps + qr - qs$ **(ii)** $6a^2 - 3ab - bx + 2ax$ **(iii)** $xy + xz - y - z$

Solution:

(i) $2pr - 2ps + qr - qs$ (already in pairs with a common factor)
    $= 2p(r - s) + q(r - s)$ (take out common factor in each pair)
    $= (r - s)(2p + q)$ (take out the common factor $(r - s)$)

(ii) $6a^2 - 3ab - bx + 2ax$ (already in pairs with a common factor)
    $= 3a(2a - b) - x(b - 2a)$ (take out common factor in each pair)
    $= 3a(2a - b) + x(2a - b)$ $(-x(b - 2a) = +x(2a - b))$
    $= (2a - b)(3a + x)$ (take out the common factor $(2a - b)$)

Note: In this example, the order of the last two terms could have been rearranged to make the factorising easier.
    $6a^2 - 3ab - bx + 2ax = 6a^2 - 3ab + 2ax - bx$ and then factorise.

(iii) $xy + xz - y - z$

We will look at two ways of factorising this expression.

Method 1:

    $xy + xz - y - z$ (already in pairs with a common factor)
  $= x(y + z) - 1(y + z)$ (take out common factor in each pair)
  $= (y + z)(x - 1)$ (take out the common factor $(y + z)$)

Note: 1 or -1 is always a common factor.

Method 2:

    $xy + xz - y - z$ (rearrange order of the terms so that they are still
  $= xy - y + xz - z$ grouped into pairs with a common factor)
  $= y(x - 1) + z(x - 1)$ (take out common factor in each pair)
  $= (x - 1)(y + z)$ (take out the common factor $(x - 1)$)

Note: $(y + z)(x - 1) = (x - 1)(y + z)$

More difficult 'factors by grouping'

Sometimes rearranging is necessary.

Example ▼

Factorise: $6pq + rs - 2sq - 3rp$

Solution:

There are no common factors in the first two pairs or in the last two pairs.

Therefore, we have to rearrange the terms.

$$
\begin{aligned}
& 6pq + rs - 2sq - 3rp && \text{(rearrange order of the terms so that they are grouped} \\
&= 6pq - 3rp + rs - 2sq && \text{into pairs with a common factor)} \\
&= 3p(2q - r) + s(r - 2q) && \text{(take out common factor in each pair)} \\
&= 3p(2q - r) - s(2q - r) && (s(r - 2q) = -s(2q - r)) \\
&= (2q - r)(3p - s) && \text{(take out the common factor } (2q - r))
\end{aligned}
$$

Note: This expression could also have been rearranged into pairs with common factors in other ways, before factorising, such as:

$6pq - 2sq - 3rp + rs$ or $6pq - 3rp - 2sq + rs$

Exercise 1.2 ▼

Factorise each of the following:

1. $c(a + b) + d(a + b)$
2. $r(p - q) - s(p - q)$
3. $2x(p + 3q) + y(p + 3q)$
4. $3a(x - 2y) - 2b(x - 2y)$
5. $ax + ay + bx + by$
6. $pq + pr + xq + xr$
7. $am - an + 4m - 4n$
8. $pq + pr - 3q - 3r$
9. $x^2 - 3x + xy - 3y$
10. $x^2 - xy + xz - yz$
11. $pq - 2q + p^2 - 2p$
12. $ab - ac + bc - c^2$
13. $6x^2 - 3xz + 2xy - yz$
14. $x^2 - 3xy + 2ax - 6ay$

Copy each of the following, and fill in the missing terms in the brackets:

15. $-3p - 3q = -3(\qquad)$
16. $-5ab - 5ac = -5a(\qquad)$
17. $-2x^2 - 2x = -2x(\qquad)$
18. $-2p + 2q = -2(\qquad)$
19. $-x^2 + 3x = -x(\qquad)$
20. $-3xy + x^2 = -x(\qquad)$
21. $a + b = 1(\qquad)$
22. $x - y = -1(\qquad)$

Factorise each of the following:

23. $ab + ac - 2b - 2c$

24. $x^2 + xy - 3x - 3y$

25. $p^2 + pq - pr - qr$

26. $px + 3p - qx - 3q$

27. $ax + bx + a + b$

28. $px + qx - p - q$

29. $p(x - y) + 2(y - x)$

30. $a(b - c) - (c - b)$

31. $x^2 - 2x - xy + 2y$

32. $3p - p^2 - 3q + pq$

33. $ap - aq - qx + px$

34. $5a - 5b - 2bx + 2ax$

35. $x^2 - 3xy - 2ax + 6ay$

36. $px - py - x + y$

In **Q 37** to **Q 46**, rearranging is necessary before factorising:

37. $ac + bd + ad + bc$

38. $pq + 2r + pr + 2q$

39. $xy - zw + yw - xz$

40. $3x + yq - 3y - xq$

41. $2xa - yb + 2xb - ya$

42. $ab + 2 + b + 2a$

43. $3b - 2a^2 - 2ab + 3a$

44. $p^2 - 6q + 3p - 2pq$

45. $an - 5b - 5a + bn$

46. $3ax + 4by - 6bx - 2ay$

In **Q 47** to **Q 52**, remove the brackets and rearrange before factorising:

47. $p^2 - p(2q - 1) - 2q$

48. $q^2 - q(2a - b) - 2ab$

49. $x^2 - x(a + b) + ab$

50. $a^2 + 3b - a(3 + b)$

51. $p(10r - q) - 5qr + 2p^2$

52. $a^2 - a(2x + y) + 2xy$

Quadratic trinomials

An expression of the form $ax^2 + bx + c$, where a, b and c are numbers, is called a '**quadratic trinomial**', since in the expression the highest power of x is 2 (quadratic) and it contains three terms (trinomial).

Factorising quadratic trinomials

Quadratic trinomials can be broken up into **two** types:

1. **Final term positive**

   When the final term is positive, the signs inside the middle of the brackets will be the **same**, either two pluses or two minuses. Keep the sign of the middle term given in the question.

Middle term plus:	(number x + number)(number x + number)	(two pluses)
Middle term minus:	(number x − number)(number x − number)	(two minuses)

2. **Final term negative**

   When the final term is negative, the signs inside the middle of the brackets will be **different**.

   (number x + number)(number x − number)   (different signs)

   or

   (number x − number)(number x + number)   (different signs)

In both cases the factors can be found by trial and improvement. The test is to multiply the inside terms, multiply the outside terms, and add the results to see if you get the middle term of the original quadratic trinomial.

Factorise: **(i)** $2x^2 + 7x + 3$ **(ii)** $5x^2 - 7x - 6$

Solution:

(i) $2x^2 + 7x + 3$
The factors of $2x^2$ are $2x$ and x.
Final term $+$ and middle term is $+$.
Therefore the factors are $(2x + \text{number})(x + \text{number})$.

Factors of 3
1×3

1. $(2x + 3)(x + 1)$ middle term $= 3x + 2x = 5x$ (no)

2. $(2x + 1)(x + 3)$ middle term $= x + 6x = 7x$ (yes)

    $\therefore \ 2x^2 + 7x + 3 = (2x + 1)(x + 3)$

(ii) $5x^2 - 7x - 6$
The factors of $5x^2$ are $5x$ and x.
Final term $-$.
Therefore the factors are $(5x + \text{number})(x - \text{number})$
                    or $(5x - \text{number})(x + \text{number})$

Factors of 6
1×6
2×3

1. $(5x + 1)(x - 6)$ middle term $= x - 30x = -29x$ (no)

2. $(5x + 6)(x - 1)$ middle term $= 6x - 5x = x$ (no)

3. $(5x + 2)(x - 3)$ middle term $= 2x - 15x = -13x$ (no)

4. $(5x + 3)(x - 2)$ middle term $= 3x - 10x = -7x$ (yes)

    $\therefore \ 5x^2 - 7x - 6 = (5x + 3)(x - 2)$

Sometimes the coefficient of x^2 has more than one set of factors. When this happens write out **all** the possible factors of the coefficient of x^2 and the constant term before starting the process of trial and improvement.

Factorise $6x^2 - 5x - 4$

Solution:

The factors of $6x^2$ are $6x$ and x or $3x$ and $2x$
Final term $-$ and middle term $-$.
Therefore the factors are
$(6x + \text{number})(x - \text{number})$ or $(3x + \text{number})(2x - \text{number})$

Factors of 4
1×4
2×2

Note: The signs inside these brackets could be swapped.

1. $(6x + 1)(x - 4)$ middle term $= x - 24x = -23x$ (no)

2. $(6x + 4)(x - 1)$ middle term $= 4x - 6x = -2x$ (no)

3. $(3x + 1)(2x - 4)$ middle term $= 2x - 12x = -10x$ (no)

4. $(3x + 4)(2x - 1)$ middle term $= 8x - 3x = 5x$ (no, wrong sign)

The fourth attempt has the wrong sign of the coefficient of the middle term.
Therefore all that is needed is to swap the signs in the middle of the brackets.

5. $(3x - 4)(2x + 1)$ middle term $= -8x + 3x = -5x$ (yes)

$\therefore 6x^2 - 5x - 4 = (3x - 4)(2x + 1)$

Exercise 1.3 ▼

Factorise each of the following:

1. $2x^2 + 5x + 3$	**2.** $3x^2 + 11x + 6$	**3.** $2x^2 - 7x + 6$
4. $3x^2 + 4x - 7$	**5.** $2x^2 - 9x - 5$	**6.** $3x^2 + 8x - 3$
7. $5x^2 + 16x + 3$	**8.** $5x^2 + 9x - 2$	**9.** $7x^2 + 5x - 2$
10. $2x^2 - x - 10$	**11.** $3x^2 - x - 10$	**12.** $3x^2 - x - 2$
13. $2x^2 - 5x - 3$	**14.** $x^2 + 3x + 2$	**15.** $x^2 + 7x + 12$
16. $x^2 - 10x + 21$	**17.** $x^2 - 2x - 15$	**18.** $x^2 - 4x - 12$
19. $2x^2 + 11x + 14$	**20.** $2x^2 + 7x - 15$	**21.** $3x^2 - 11x - 20$
22. $7x^2 - 23x + 6$	**23.** $11x^2 - 19x - 6$	**24.** $13x^2 + 25x - 2$
25. $4x^2 + 8x + 3$	**26.** $6x^2 + 11x + 3$	**27.** $4x^2 + 13x + 3$
28. $6x^2 - 13x + 2$	**29.** $4x^2 - 11x - 3$	**30.** $6x^2 - x - 2$
31. $8x^2 + 6x - 5$	**32.** $10x^2 - x - 3$	**33.** $9x^2 + 2x - 7$

34. $6x^2 - 7x - 10$ **35.** $4x^2 + 5x - 6$ **36.** $9x^2 + 6x - 8$
37. $8x^2 - 13x - 6$ **38.** $24x^2 + x - 3$ **39.** $15x^2 - 2x - 8$
40. Simplify $(2x-1)(x+1) - 2(x+7)$ and factorise the simplified expression.
41. Simplify $(x-2)^2 - 2(x-2) - 15$ and factorise the simplified expression.
42. Simplify $2(x+1)^2 + 7(x+1) + 3$ and factorise the simplified expression.
43. Simplify $(3x+1)^2 - (2x+1)(x-5) + 2$ and factorise the simplified expression.

Difference of two squares

An expression such as $a^2 - b^2$ is called the '**difference of two squares**'.

The product $(a-b)(a+b) = a^2 - b^2$.

In reverse, $a^2 - b^2 = (a-b)(a+b)$.

We use this to factorise any expression that can be written as the difference of two squares.

We factorise the difference of two squares with the following steps:

> **1.** Write each term as a perfect square with brackets.
> **2.** Use the rule $a^2 - b^2 = (a-b)(a+b)$.
>   In words: $(\text{first})^2 - (\text{second})^2 = (\text{first} - \text{second})(\text{first} + \text{second})$.

Example ▼

Factorise   **(i)** $9 - 4y^2$ **(ii)** $25x^2 - 49y^2$ **(iii)** $16a^2 - 1^2$

Solution:

(i) $9 - 4y^2$
$= (3)^2 - (2y)^2$ (write each term as a perfect square in brackets)
$= (3 - 2y)(3 + 2y)$ (apply the rule, (first − second)(first + second))

(ii) $25x^2 - 49y^2$
$= (5x)^2 - (7y)^2$ (write each term as a perfect square in brackets)
$= (5x - 7y)(5x + 7y)$ (apply the rule, (first − second)(first + second))

(iii) $16a^2 - 1^2$
$= (4a)^2 - (1)^2$ (write each term as a perfect square in brackets)
$= (4a - 1)(4a + 1)$ (apply the rule, (first − second)(first + second))

Copy each of the following and fill in the missing terms in the brackets:

1. $4a^2 = ($ $)^2$
2. $9p^2 = ($ $)^2$
3. $16b^2 = ($ $)^2$
4. $36q^2 = ($ $)^2$
5. $1 = ($ $)^2$
6. $64x^2 = ($ $)^2$
7. $81y^2 = ($ $)^2$
8. $121p^2 = ($ $)^2$
9. $144q^2 = ($ $)^2$

Factorise each of the following:

10. $4p^2 - 9q^2$
11. $16a^2 - 25b^2$
12. $36x^2 - 49y^2$
13. $64a^2 - 81b^2$
14. $100 - 9a^2$
15. $1 - 25p^2$
16. $16x^2 - 1$
17. $25x^2 - 4y^2$
18. $64q^2 - 1$
19. $q^2 - 16$
20. $81a^2 - 16b^2$
21. $x^2 - 25$
22. $100 - a^2$
23. $25x^2 - 16y^2$
24. $25a^2 - 4$
25. $49 - 100m^2$
26. $121x^2 - 9y^2$
27. $144p^2 - 25q^2$
28. $1 - 196x^2$
29. $100p^2 - 81q^2$
30. $a^2b^2 - 4c^2$
31. Simplify $(3x - 1)(2x + 5) - 2(x^2 + 6x + 2) - x$ and factorise the simplified expression.
32. Simplify $(3x - 2y)^2 - y(5y - 12x)$ and factorise the simplified expression.

Expressions that have three factors

> Always look for a highest common factor first.

Sometimes we have to factorise an expression which has three factors.
Expressions which have three factors are factorised with the following steps:

1. Take out the highest common factor first.
2. Then factorise the expression inside the brackets which will be one of:
   (a) Factors by grouping   (four terms)
   (b) Quadratic trinomial   (three terms)
   (c) Difference of two squares   (two terms)

(i) Find the three factors of $20a^2 - 45b^2$

(ii) Factorise $3px^2 - 6px - 45p$

Solution:

(i) $20a^2 - 45b^2$

$= 5[4a^2 - 9b^2]$ [take out common factor 5]

$= 5[(2a)^2 - (3b)^2]$ [write the terms inside the brackets as perfect squares]

$= 5(2a - 3b)(2a + 3b)$ [apply the rule (first − second)(first + second),
              to the terms inside the brackets]

(ii) $3px^2 - 6px - 45p$

$= 3p(x^2 - 2x - 15)$ [take out common factor $3p$]

$= 3p(x + 3)(x - 5)$ [factorise the quadratic trinomial inside the bracket]

Exercise 1.5 ▼

Find the three factors of each of the following:

1. $3x^2 - 3y^2$
2. $2x^2 - 8y^2$
3. $12 - 27y^2$
4. $5x^2 + 15x + 10$
5. $3x^2 - 6x - 24$
6. $4x^2 - 8x - 12$
7. $3ax + 6b + 6a + 3bx$
8. $10ax + 10bx - 5ay - 5yb$
9. $6a + 2bq - 6b - 2aq$
10. $18ax^2 - 50ay^2$
11. $12x^2 + 42x + 18$
12. $6qx^2 + 20qx - 16q$
13. $x^3 + x^2y + 4x^2 + 4xy$
14. $20p^2q - 45q^3$
15. $8abp^2 - 2abq^2$
16. $4p^2q - 10pr - 10pq + 4p^2r$
17. $75a^3 - 12ab^2$
18. $4a^3b - 25ab^3$
19. $3x^3 - 12xy^2$
20. $50a^3 - 98ab^2$
21. $8ax^2 - 22ax - 6a$
22. $2ax^2 + 6ax - 20a$
23. Simplify $(5x - 3)^2 - 4$, and fully factorise the simplified expression.
24. Simplify $(2x + a)(4x - 2a) - (3y + a)(6y - 2a)$ and fully factorise the simplified expression.

Chapter test

Factorise each of the following:
First look for a highest common factor and take that out.
If there is no highest common factor, look for the following:
(i) factors by grouping (four terms)
(ii) quadratic trinomials (three terms)
(iii) difference of two squares (two terms)

1. $6xy + 3y^2$
2. $x^2 - xy + xz - yz$
3. $2x^2 + 5x + 2$
4. $9x^2 - 16$
5. $4x^2 - 2x$
6. $ac - 2bd - ad + 2bc$
7. $3x^2 + 2x - 8$
8. $25x^2 - 4y^2$
9. $1 - 9x^2$
10. $8a^2b - 4ab + 12ab^2$
11. $7x^2 + 32x - 15$
12. $81a^2 - 121b^2$
13. $2x^2y - 2xz - 3xy + 3z$
14. $36x^2 - 1$
15. $8x^2 - 2x - 15$
16. $2x^2y - 4xy^2$
17. $6x^2 - 19x + 10$
18. $100 - 121q^2$
19. $3xy - 12x^2y$
20. $15x^2 + x - 6$
21. $4a^2b - 3b - 6a + 2ab^2$

Find the three factors of each of the following (look for a highest common factor first):

22. $5x^2 - 20y^2$
23. $3x^2 + 3x - 18$
24. $2x^2 - 2xy + 2xz - 2yz$
25. $3px^2 - 42px + 72p$
26. $50 - 32a^2$
27. $27x^2 - 3$
28. $2p^3q - 8pq^3$
29. $12px^2 - 75py^2$
30. $12qx^2 + 24qx + 9q$

In each of the following, remove the brackets and simplify, and then factorise the simplified expression:

31. $2x(2x - y) + y(2x - 9y)$
32. $5x(5x + y) - y(5x + 4y)$
33. $(y - 2)^2 - 16$
34. $(2x + 1)^2 - (x + 3)^2$
35. $(x - 1)^2 - 2(x - 1) - 15$
36. $(a + b)^2 - 2b(a + 5b)$
37. $(a + 2b)^2 - (a - 3b)^2$
38. $(3p + q)^2 - (p + 3q)^2$
39. $(x + 2y)^2 + x^2 - 4y^2$
40. $4x^2 - (x - 1)^2$

ALGEBRAIC FRACTIONS

Multiplication and division

Operations with algebraic fractions follow the same rules as in arithmetic. Before attempting to simplify when multiplying or dividing algebraic fractions, factorise where possible and divide top and bottom by common factors. The contents of a bracket should be considered as a single term.

Example ▼

Simplify   **(i)** $\dfrac{8x^2}{14y} \div \dfrac{4x}{7y^2}$ **(ii)** $\dfrac{x^2 - 2x}{x^2 - 4}$ **(iii)** $\dfrac{4x - 2}{15 - 3x} \div \dfrac{2x - 1}{5 - x}$

Solution:

(i)

$\dfrac{8x^2}{14y} \div \dfrac{4x}{7y^2}$

$= \dfrac{8x^2}{14y} \times \dfrac{7y^2}{4x}$ [turn the fraction we divide by upside down and multiply]

$= xy$ [divide top and bottom by common factors]

(ii)

$\dfrac{x^2 - 2x}{x^2 - 4}$

$= \dfrac{x(x - 2)}{(x - 2)(x + 2)}$ [factorise top and bottom]

$= \dfrac{x}{x + 2}$ [divide top and bottom by the common factor $(x - 2)$]

(iii)

$$\frac{4x-2}{15-3x} \div \frac{2x-1}{5-x}$$

$$= \frac{4x-2}{15-3x} \times \frac{5-x}{2x-1} \quad \text{[turn the fraction we divide by upside down and multiply]}$$

$$= \frac{2(2x-1)}{3(5-x)} \times \frac{(5-x)}{(2x-1)} \quad \text{[factorise top and bottom]}$$

$$= \frac{2}{3} \quad \text{[divide top and bottom by common factors]}$$

Exercise 2.1 ▼

Simplify each of the following:

1. $\dfrac{6xy}{3y}$ **2.** $\dfrac{15a^3b}{5a^2b}$ **3.** $\dfrac{24a^2b^2}{3a^2b}$ **4.** $\dfrac{8x^3y}{4x^3y}$ **5.** $\dfrac{2xy}{2xy}$

6. $\dfrac{3x+6}{x+2}$ **7.** $\dfrac{8x+10}{4x+5}$ **8.** $\dfrac{3x+6}{4x+8}$ **9.** $\dfrac{5x-15}{3x-9}$

10. $\dfrac{-4x-12}{-2x-6}$ **11.** $\dfrac{8x^2}{5y^2} \times \dfrac{10y^2}{8x}$ **12.** $\dfrac{5a^2}{8b^2} \div \dfrac{5a}{16b^3}$

13. $\dfrac{x^2+x-2}{x+2}$ **14.** $\dfrac{x^2-9}{x-3}$ **15.** $\dfrac{3x^2-6xy}{x-2y}$

16. $\dfrac{4x-12}{x^2+x-12}$ **17.** $\dfrac{x+2}{x^2-4}$ **18.** $\dfrac{6x-4}{3x^2+10x-8}$

19. $\dfrac{x^2-2x}{x^2+x-6}$ **20.** $\dfrac{x^2-2x-15}{2x^2-9x-5}$ **21.** $\dfrac{3ab}{a^2b+ab^2}$

22. $\dfrac{2x+4}{3x-15} \times \dfrac{x-5}{x+2}$ **23.** $\dfrac{x^2-2x}{6x+9} \times \dfrac{4x+6}{x-2}$

24. $\dfrac{8x-4}{2y+6} \div \dfrac{x-1}{y+3}$ **25.** $\dfrac{y+5}{x} \div \dfrac{2y+10}{x^2}$

26. $\dfrac{x^2+2x}{x^2+3x+2} \div \dfrac{x}{2x+2}$ **27.** $\dfrac{x^2+8x+15}{x^2-9} \div \dfrac{xy+5y}{x^2-3x}$

Addition and subtraction

Algebraic fractions can be added or subtracted in exactly the same way as in arithmetic, i.e., we express the fractions with the lowest common denominator.

Algebraic fractions are added or subtracted with the following steps:

1. Put brackets in where necessary.
2. Find the LCM of the expressions on the bottom.
3. Proceed in exactly the same way as in arithmetic.
4. Simplify the top (add and subtract terms which are the same).

Note: If a part of the expression is not a fraction, it can be changed into fraction form by putting it over 1.

For example, $7 = \dfrac{7}{1}$, $3x = \dfrac{3x}{1}$, $2x - 5 = \dfrac{2x - 5}{1}$.

Example ▼

Express as a single fraction $\dfrac{3x+2}{8} - \dfrac{x}{4} + \dfrac{x+1}{2}$

Verify your answer by letting $x = 1$.

Solution:

$\dfrac{3x+2}{8} - \dfrac{x}{4} + \dfrac{x+1}{2}$

$= \dfrac{(3x+2)}{8} - \dfrac{x}{4} + \dfrac{(x+1)}{2}$ (put brackets on top)
                                      (the LCM is 8)

$= \dfrac{1(3x+2) - 2x + 4(x+1)}{8}$ (do the same as in arithmetic)

$= \dfrac{3x + 2 - 2x + 4x + 4}{8}$ (remove the brackets on top)

$= \dfrac{5x + 6}{8}$ (simplify the top)

$\therefore \dfrac{3x+2}{8} - \dfrac{x}{4} + \dfrac{x+1}{2} = \dfrac{5x+6}{8}$

LHS	$x = 1$	RHS

$$\frac{3x+2}{8} - \frac{x}{4} + \frac{x+1}{2}$$

$$= \frac{3(1)+2}{8} - \frac{1}{4} + \frac{1+1}{2}$$

$$= \frac{3+2}{8} - \frac{1}{4} + \frac{2}{2}$$

$$= \frac{5}{8} - \frac{1}{4} + 1$$

$$= 1\frac{5}{8} - \frac{1}{4}$$

$$= 1\frac{3}{8}$$

$$\frac{5x+6}{8}$$

$$= \frac{5(1)+6}{8}$$

$$= \frac{5+6}{8}$$

$$= \frac{11}{8}$$

$$= 1\frac{3}{8}$$

$$\text{LHS} = \text{RHS}$$

$$\therefore \quad \frac{3x+2}{8} - \frac{x}{4} + \frac{x+1}{2} = \frac{5x+6}{8}$$

Example ▼

Write   **(i)** $\dfrac{5}{x} - \dfrac{2}{x-1}$ **(ii)** $\dfrac{4}{2x-3} - \dfrac{1}{3-2x}$

as a single fraction in its simplest form.

Solution:

(i) $\dfrac{5}{x} - \dfrac{2}{x-1}$

$$= \frac{5}{x} - \frac{2}{(x-1)} \qquad \text{(put a bracket on the bottom)}$$
$$\text{(the LCM is } x(x-1))$$

$$= \frac{5(x-1) - 2x}{x(x-1)} \qquad \text{(do the same as in arithmetic)}$$

17

$$= \frac{5x - 5 - 2x}{x(x-1)} \qquad \text{(remove the brackets on top)}$$

$$= \frac{3x - 5}{x(x-1)} \qquad \text{(simplify the top)}$$

Note: It is common practice **not** to multiply out the expression on the bottom.

(ii) Method 1:

$$\frac{4}{2x - 3} - \frac{1}{3 - 2x}$$

$$= \frac{4}{(2x-3)} - \frac{1}{(3-2x)} \qquad \begin{array}{l}\text{(put brackets on the bottom)}\\ \text{(the LCM is } (2x-3)(3-2x))\end{array}$$

$$= \frac{4(3-2x) - 1(2x-3)}{(2x-3)(3-2x)} \qquad \text{(do the same as in arithmetic)}$$

$$= \frac{12 - 8x - 2x + 3}{(2x-3)(3-2x)} \qquad \text{(remove the brackets on top)}$$

$$= \frac{15 - 10x}{(2x-3)(3-2x)} \qquad \text{(simplify the top)}$$

$$= \frac{5(3-2x)}{(2x-3)(3-2x)} \qquad \text{(factorise the top)}$$

$$= \frac{5}{(2x-3)} \qquad \begin{array}{l}\text{(divide the top and bottom by}\\ \text{the common factor } (3-2x))\end{array}$$

(ii) Method 2:

$$\frac{4}{2x - 3} - \frac{1}{3 - 2x}$$

$$= \frac{4}{2x - 3} + \frac{1}{2x - 3} \qquad (-(3-2x) = (2x-3))$$

$$= \frac{4 + 1}{2x - 3} \qquad \text{(same denominator)}$$

$$= \frac{5}{2x - 3}$$

Note: Method 2 works when the only difference between the denominators is the sign. For example, $3x - 4$ and $4 - 3x$ or $5 - 2x$ and $2x - 5$.

$$\frac{5}{2x-1} + \frac{2}{1-2x} = \frac{5}{2x-1} - \frac{2}{2x-1} = \frac{5-2}{2x-1} = \frac{3}{2x-1}$$

Exercise 2.2 ▼

Express each of the following as a single fraction:

1. $\dfrac{2x}{3} + \dfrac{3x}{4}$

2. $\dfrac{5x}{3} + \dfrac{x}{2}$

3. $\dfrac{2x}{5} - \dfrac{x}{3}$

4. $\dfrac{x+1}{2} + \dfrac{x+5}{3}$

5. $\dfrac{5x-1}{4} + \dfrac{2x-3}{5}$

6. $\dfrac{2x+3}{7} - \dfrac{x+1}{3}$

7. $\dfrac{5x}{3} - \dfrac{1}{6} + \dfrac{2-3x}{2}$

8. $\dfrac{3x+5}{6} - \dfrac{2x+3}{4}$

9. $\dfrac{4x+3}{6} - \dfrac{6x+4}{9} + \dfrac{x}{3}$

10. $\dfrac{2x+3}{4} + 3x + 2$

11. $\dfrac{5}{4x} + \dfrac{7}{3x}$

12. $\dfrac{6}{5x} - \dfrac{3}{4x} + 1$

13. $\dfrac{2}{x+1} + \dfrac{3}{x+2}$

14. $\dfrac{2}{x+3} + \dfrac{3}{x+5}$

15. $\dfrac{1}{x+2} + \dfrac{2}{x-4}$

16. $\dfrac{3}{2x+1} + \dfrac{2}{3x+4}$

17. $\dfrac{5}{2x+1} + \dfrac{4}{2x-1}$

18. $\dfrac{2}{3x-2} + \dfrac{3}{2x+5}$

19. $\dfrac{5}{3x-1} - \dfrac{3}{2x}$

20. $\dfrac{3}{2x-5} + \dfrac{4}{x-3}$

21. $\dfrac{5}{3x-1} + \dfrac{3}{2-3x}$

22. $\dfrac{2}{x+3} + 3$

23. $\dfrac{5}{3} - \dfrac{2}{x+4}$

24. $\dfrac{2}{3} + \dfrac{5}{2x-1} - \dfrac{1}{2}$

25. $\dfrac{1}{x} - \dfrac{1}{x+3} + \dfrac{1}{4}$

26. $\dfrac{1}{x} + \dfrac{2}{x+1} + \dfrac{1}{3}$

27. $\dfrac{5}{x} - \dfrac{3}{x-2} + \dfrac{1}{3}$

28. Express $\dfrac{2x-3}{10} + \dfrac{x-2}{6} + \dfrac{1}{2}$ as a single fraction and verify your answer by letting $x = 2$.

29. Express $\dfrac{3}{2x+1} + \dfrac{2}{2x-1}$ as a single fraction and verify your answer by letting $x = 1$.

30. Show that each of the following reduce to a constant:

(i) $\dfrac{6x+5}{2} - \dfrac{9x+4}{3}$

(ii) $\dfrac{3x+5}{6} - \dfrac{2x+3}{4}$

31. **(i)** $\dfrac{6x+5}{21} - \dfrac{2x-3}{7} = \dfrac{p}{q}, \quad p, q \in R.$

Write down the value of p and q, where $\dfrac{p}{q}$ is in its simplest form.

(ii) $\dfrac{3}{x+1} + \dfrac{4}{x-2} = \dfrac{ax+b}{(x+1)(x-2)}$

Write down the value of a and the value of b.

32. Simplify each of the following:

(i) $\dfrac{3(x+1)}{(x+2)(x+1)}$ **(ii)** $\dfrac{10-4x}{(2x-5)(5-2x)}$ **(iii)** $\dfrac{-3+9x}{(3x-1)(1-3x)}$ **(iv)** $\dfrac{1-x}{(x-1)(1-x)}$

Write each of the following as a single fraction in its simplest form:

33. $\dfrac{3}{x-1} + \dfrac{1}{1-x}$ **34.** $\dfrac{5}{x-2} + \dfrac{2}{2-x}$ **35.** $\dfrac{3}{x-5} - \dfrac{7}{5-x}$

36. $\dfrac{5}{2x-3} - \dfrac{3}{3-2x}$ **37.** $\dfrac{4}{3x-1} - \dfrac{1}{1-3x}$ **38.** $\dfrac{2}{2-5x} - \dfrac{5}{5x-2}$

Show that each of the following reduce to a constant:

39. $\dfrac{1}{x-1} + \dfrac{1}{1-x}, \qquad x \neq 1$ **40.** $\dfrac{3x-5}{x-2} + \dfrac{1}{2-x}, \qquad x \neq 2$

LONG DIVISION IN ALGEBRA

Long division in algebra

Long division in algebra follows the same procedure as long division in arithmetic. The stages in dividing one algebraic expression by another are shown in the following examples:

Example ▼

Simplify: **(i)** $(x^3 + 2x^2 - 5x - 6) \div (x - 2)$ **(ii)** $(6x^3 - 13x^2 + 4) \div (2x + 1)$

Solution:

(i) $(x^3 + 2x^2 - 5x - 6) \div (x - 2)$

$$
\begin{array}{r}
x^2 + 4x + 3 \\
x - 2 \overline{\smash{\big)}\, x^3 + 2x^2 - 5x - 6} \\
\underline{x^3 - 2x^2} \\
4x^2 - 5x \\
\underline{4x^2 - 8x} \\
3x - 6 \\
\underline{3x - 6} \\
0
\end{array}
$$

$[x^3 \div x = x^2$, put x^2 on top]
$[x^2(x-2) = x^3 - 2x^2]$
[subtract, bring down $-5x$, $4x^2 \div x = 4x$, put $4x$ on top]
$[4x(x-2) = 4x^2 - 8x]$
[subtract, bring down -6, $3x \div x = 3$, put 3 on top]
$[3(x-2) = 3x - 6]$
[subtract]

$\therefore$ $(x^3 + 2x^2 - 5x - 6) \div (x - 2) = x^2 + 4x + 3$

(ii) $(6x^3 - 13x^2 + 4) \div (2x + 1)$
$= (6x^3 - 13x^2 + 0x + 4) \div (2x + 1)$
It helps in setting out the division if we put in the '**missing term**', $0x$.
All missing terms should be included in this way.

$$\begin{array}{r} 3x^2 - 8x + 4 \\ 2x+1\overline{\smash{\big)}\,6x^3 - 13x^2 + 0x + 4} \end{array}$$ $[6x^3 \div 2x = 3x^2,\text{ put }3x^2\text{ on top}]$

$\underline{6x^3 + 3x^2}$ $[3x^2(2x+1) = 6x^3 + 3x^2]$

$-16x^2 + 0x$ $[\text{subtract, bring down }0x,\ -16x^2 \div 2x = -8x,\text{ put }-8x\text{ on top}]$

$\underline{-16x^2 - 8x}$ $[-8x(2x+1) = -16x^2 - 8x]$

$8x + 4$ $[\text{subtract, bring down }4,\ 8x \div 2x = 4,\text{ put }4\text{ on top}]$

$\underline{8x + 4}$ $[4(2x+1) = 8x + 4]$

0 $[\text{subtract}]$

$\therefore\ (6x^3 - 13x^2 + 4) \div (2x+1) = 3x^2 - 8x + 4$

Exercise 3.1 ▼

Simplify each of the following:

1. $\dfrac{x^3}{x}$ **2.** $\dfrac{2x^2}{x}$ **3.** $\dfrac{6x^3}{3x}$ **4.** $\dfrac{4x}{4x}$ **5.** $\dfrac{8x^2}{2x}$

6. $\dfrac{-8x}{4x}$ **7.** $\dfrac{-10x^2}{5x}$ **8.** $\dfrac{3x}{3x}$ **9.** $\dfrac{-5x}{x}$ **10.** $\dfrac{-6x^2}{2x}$

11. $(x^2 + 3x + 2) \div (x + 2)$ **12.** $(x^2 + 7x + 12) \div (x + 4)$

13. $(x^2 + 5x + 6) \div (x + 3)$ **14.** $(x^2 + 9x + 20) \div (x + 5)$

15. $(2x^2 + 7x + 6) \div (2x + 3)$ **16.** $(3x^2 + 19x + 20) \div (3x + 4)$

17. $(2x^2 - 5x - 3) \div (2x + 1)$ **18.** $(6x^2 + 11x - 10) \div (3x - 2)$

19. $(x^3 + 4x^2 + 5x + 2) \div (x + 1)$ **20.** $(x^3 + 6x^2 + 11x + 6) \div (x + 2)$

21. $(2x^3 + 7x^2 + 5x + 1) \div (2x + 1)$ **22.** $(6x^3 + 13x^2 + 9x + 2) \div (3x + 2)$

23. $(3x^3 + 7x^2 + 5x + 1) \div (3x + 1)$ **24.** $(4x^3 + 12x^2 + 17x + 12) \div (2x + 3)$

25. $(2x^3 + x^2 - 16x - 15) \div (2x + 5)$ **26.** $(3x^3 + x^2 - 11x + 6) \div (3x - 2)$

27. $(x^3 - 2x^2 - 9x + 18) \div (x + 3)$ **28.** $(x^3 - 7x^2 + 7x + 20) \div (x - 4)$

29. $(2x^3 - 3x^2 - 12x + 20) \div (x - 2)$ **30.** $(3x^3 - 2x^2 - 19x - 6) \div (3x + 1)$

31. $(2x^3 + 5x^2 - 9x - 18) \div (2x + 3)$ **32.** $(3x^3 - 8x^2 - 41x + 30) \div (3x - 2)$

33. $(6x^3 - 17x^2 + 27x - 20) \div (3x - 4)$ **34.** $(8x^3 + 2x^2 - 5x + 1) \div (2x - 1)$

35. $(x^3 + x^2 + 4) \div (x + 2)$ **36.** $(x^3 + 11x - 30) \div (x - 2)$

37. $(x^3 - 13x + 12) \div (x + 4)$ **38.** $(2x^3 - 5x^2 + 1) \div (2x - 1)$

39. $(4x^3 - 13x - 6) \div (x - 2)$ **40.** $(6x^3 - 13x^2 + 4) \div (2x + 1)$

41. Divide $(x^3 + 6x^2 + 11x + 6)$ by $(x + 3)$ and verify your answer by letting $x = 1$.

42. Divide $(2x^3 - x^2 - 7x + 6)$ by $(2x - 3)$ and verify your answer by letting $x = 3$.

43. Divide $(2x^3 - 7x^2 - 10x + 24)$ by $(x + 2)$ and factorise your answer.

44. $(x^3 + 2x^2 - 5x - 6) \div (x - 2) = ax^2 + bx + c$.

Write down the values of a, b and c and evaluate $\sqrt{bc(b - a)}$.

Factorise $ax^2 + bx + c$.

45. $f(x) = x^3 - 3x^2 - 4x + 12,$ $g(x) = x + 2.$

$$\frac{f(x)}{g(x)} = ax^2 + bx + c.$$

Write down the values of a, b and c and evalute $\sqrt{b(a-c)}$.

Factorise $ax^2 + bx + c$.

In the following problems there is no x term in the answer.
Simplify each of the following:

46. $(x^3 + 3x^2 + 4x + 12) \div (x + 3)$

47. $(x^3 + 4x^2 - 5x - 20) \div (x + 4)$

48. $(2x^3 + 4x^2 - 7x - 14) \div (x + 2)$

49. $(2x^3 + 3x^2 - 8x - 12) \div (2x + 3)$

In the following problems there is no x^2 term and no x term.
Simplify each of the following:

50. $(x^3 + 1) \div (x + 1)$ **51.** $(x^3 + 8) \div (x + 2)$ **52.** $(x^3 - 27) \div (x - 3)$

53. $(8x^3 - 1) \div (2x - 1)$ **54.** $(8x^3 + 27) \div (2x + 3)$ **55.** $(8x^3 - 125) \div (2x - 5)$

SIMULTANEOUS LINEAR EQUATIONS

Simultaneous linear equations

An equation such as $5x - 2y = 4$ is called a linear equation in two unknowns, x and y.
Simultaneous linear equations are a pair of such equations. Two equations are necessary if
we are to be able to find the values of x and y that satisfy both equations.
For example, consider the following pair of simultaneous linear equations:

$$3x + 2y = 4 \quad ①$$
$$4x + 5y = 3 \quad ②$$

The solution of this pair of simultaneous linear equations is $x = 2$ and $y = -1$.
This pair of values satisfies both equations simultaneously (at the same time).
We can check this by substituting $x = 2$ and $y = -1$ in both equations and showing that the
left-hand side is equal to the right-hand side in each equation.

Check $x = 2$, $y = -1$:
$$3x + 2y = 4 \quad ①$$
$$\downarrow \quad \downarrow$$
$$3(2) + 2(-1) = 4$$
$$6 - 2 = 4$$
$$4 = 4 \quad \text{True}$$

Check $x = 2$, $y = -1$:
$$4x + 5y = 3 \quad ②$$
$$\downarrow \quad \downarrow$$
$$4(2) + 5(-1) = 3$$
$$8 - 5 = 3$$
$$3 = 3 \quad \text{True}$$

Therefore, our solution $x = 2$ and $y = -1$ is correct.
Equations that are solved together are called simultaneous equations.
Solving a pair of simultaneous linear equations means finding the values of x and y that
make both equations true at the same time.

Simultaneous linear equations are solved with the following steps:

1.   Write both equations in the form $ax + by = k$ and number the equations ① and ②.
2.   Multiply one or both of the equations by a number in order to make the coefficients
     of x or y the same (ignoring signs).
3.   Add or subtract (depending on signs) to remove the variable with equal coefficients.
     (a) When the equal terms have the same sign **subtract** the equations.
     (b) When the equal terms have different signs **add** the equations.
4.   Solve the resultant equation to find the value of the remaining unknown (x or y).
5.   Substitute this value in equation ① or ② to find the value of the other unknown.

Solve the simultaneous equations $2x + y = 3(y - x) + 7$ and $\dfrac{x}{3} = 2 - \dfrac{y}{4}$.

Solution:

1. First write both equations in the form $ax + by = k$ and number the equations ① and ②.

$$2x + y = 3(y - x) + 7$$
$$2x + y = 3y - 3x + 7 \qquad \text{(remove the brackets)}$$
$$2x + y - 3y + 3x = 7 \qquad \text{(letters to the left, number to the right)}$$
$$5x - 2y = 7 \quad ① \qquad \text{(in the form } ax + by = k\text{, number the equation ①)}$$

$$\frac{x}{3} = 2 - \frac{y}{4}$$

$$12\left(\frac{x}{3}\right) = 12(2) - 12\left(\frac{y}{4}\right) \qquad \text{(multiply each part by 12)}$$

$$4x = 24 - 3y \qquad \text{(simplify)}$$

$$4x + 3y = 24 \quad ② \qquad \text{(in the form } ax + by = k\text{, number the equation ②)}$$

$$5x - 2y = 7 \quad ①$$
$$4x + 3y = 24 \quad ②$$

2. Make coefficients of y the same.
Multiply ① by 3 and ② by 2.

$$15x - 6y = 21 \quad ① \times 3$$
$$8x + 6y = 48 \quad ② \times 2$$

3. Add these new equations.

$$23x = 69$$

4. Divide both sides by 23.

$$x = 3$$

5. Put $x = 3$ into ① or ②.

$$5x - 2y = 7 \quad ①$$
$$\downarrow$$
$$5(3) - 2y = 7$$
$$15 - 2y = 7$$

(subtract 15 from both sides) $\qquad -2y = -8$

(multiply both sides by -1) $\qquad 2y = 8$

(divide both sides by 2) $\qquad y = 4$

∴ the solution is $x = 3$ and $y = 4$

Solution containing fractions

If the solution contains fractions the substitution can be difficult.
In such cases the following method is useful:

> **1.** Eliminate y and find x.
> **2.** Eliminate x and find y.

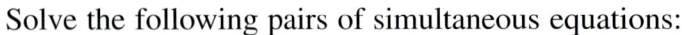

Example ▼

Solve the simultaneous equations $2x + 3y = -2$ and $3x + 7y = -6$.

Solution:

Both equations are in the form $ax + by = k$. Number the equations ① and ②.

1. Eliminate y and find x.

$$2x + 3y = -2 \quad ①$$
$$3x + 7y = -6 \quad ②$$
$$14x + 21y = -14 \quad ① \times 7$$
$$9x + 21y = -18 \quad ② \times 3$$
$$5x = 4 \text{ (subtract)}$$

$$x = \frac{4}{5}$$

2. Eliminate x and find y.

$$2x + 3y = -2 \quad ①$$
$$3x + 7y = -6 \quad ②$$
$$6x + 9y = -6 \quad ① \times 3$$
$$6x + 14y = -12 \quad ② \times 2$$
$$-5y = 6 \text{ (subtract)}$$

$$5y = -6$$

$$y = -\frac{6}{5}$$

Therefore, the solution is $x = \dfrac{4}{5}$ and $y = -\dfrac{6}{5}$.

Note: This method can also be used if the solution does not contain fractions.

Exercise 4.1 ▼

Solve the following pairs of simultaneous equations:

1. $3x + 2y = 8$
$2x - y = 3$

2. $5x - 3y = 14$
$2x + y = 10$

3. $3x + 2y = 13$
$4x - 3y = 6$

4. $x - 5y = -18$
$3x + 2y = 14$

5. $2x + 3y = 7$
$5x - 3y = -14$

6. $4x - 3y = 1$
$3x + 5y = -21$

7. $x - 2y = -2$
$3x + 7y = 20$

8. $3x + 2y = 2$
$2x + 3y = 8$

9. $2x - 5y = 11$
$3x + 2y = 7$

10. $x + 2y = 7$
$3x - 5y = -34$

11. $2x - y = -3$
$x - 2y = -3$

12. $2x - 3y = 14$
$3x + 4y = -13$

13. $2x - 5y = 19$

$\dfrac{3x}{2} + \dfrac{4y}{3} = -1$

14. $2x + 5y = 40$

$\dfrac{2x}{5} - \dfrac{5y}{2} = -6$

15. $3x - 4y = -3$

$\dfrac{x}{2} + \dfrac{y}{3} = \dfrac{5}{2}$

16. $\dfrac{3x}{5} - \dfrac{y}{4} = 8$

$\dfrac{2x}{3} + \dfrac{3y}{4} = 13$

17. $\dfrac{x}{2} + \dfrac{y}{3} = 3$

$\dfrac{x}{3} - \dfrac{y}{5} = \dfrac{11}{15}$

18. $\dfrac{x}{3} + \dfrac{y}{4} = 2$

$0.3x + 0.4y = 2.5$

19. $x = 2y$

$2(x + 3) = 5 + 3y$

20. $5x + y = 19$

$2x - y = 2(y - x)$

21. $x = \frac{1}{2}y + 3$

$y = \frac{1}{2}x - 3$

22. $2x + 7y = 3$

$x + y = \dfrac{x - 2y + 1}{2}$

23. $2(x - 5) = 3y$

$\dfrac{2x + 1}{5} + \dfrac{x + y}{2} = 1$

24. $3x - 2y = y - 6x$

$\dfrac{5x - 3y + 2}{2} = \dfrac{x - 2y + 4}{3}$

25. $3x - y = 2 = x + y$

26. $3x + 2y = 8 = 5x - 2y$

27. $5x - 2y = 9x - 5y = 7$

28. $3x + 5y = 13$

$\dfrac{2x - 1}{3} - \dfrac{4y - 5}{5} = -6$

In questions 29 to 34, the solutions contain fractions:

29. $5x + y = 10$
$3x - y = 2$

30. $7x - 3y = 6$
$3x - 6y = 1$

31. $4x - 3y = 6$
$2x + 6y = 13$

32. $5x + 10y = 11$
$2x + y = 2$

33. $2x - 5 = 0$
$3x + 5y + 5 = 0$

34. $10x + 4y = 3$
$5x - 20y = -4$

QUADRATIC EQUATIONS

Quadratic equations

An equation such as $3x^2 - 5x - 12 = 0$ is called a quadratic equation in x.

A quadratic equation has x^2 (x squared) as its highest power. In general, a quadratic equation has two different solutions (often called roots), but with some quadratic equations the two solutions are the same.

For example, consider the quadratic equation $2x^2 + 5x - 3 = 0$.

The two solutions of the equation $2x^2 + 5x - 3 = 0$ are $x = \frac{1}{2}$ and $x = -3$.

We can check this by substituting $x = \frac{1}{2}$ or $x = -3$ in the equation and showing in each case that the left-hand side is equal to the right-hand side.

Check $x = \frac{1}{2}$:

$$2x^2 + 5x - 3 = 0$$

$$2\left(\tfrac{1}{2}\right)^2 + 5\left(\tfrac{1}{2}\right) - 3 = 0$$

$$2\left(\tfrac{1}{4}\right) + 5\left(\tfrac{1}{2}\right) - 3 = 0$$

$$\tfrac{1}{2} + 2\tfrac{1}{2} - 3 = 0$$

$$3 - 3 = 0$$

$$0 = 0 \quad \text{True}$$

Check $x = -3$:

$$2x^2 + 5x - 3 = 0$$

$$2(-3)^2 + 5(-3) - 3 = 0$$

$$2(9) + 5(-3) - 3 = 0$$

$$18 - 15 - 3 = 0$$

$$18 - 18 = 0$$

$$0 = 0 \quad \text{True}$$

Therefore our solutions $x = \frac{1}{2}$ or $x = -3$ are correct.

There are three types of quadratic equations we will meet on our course:

1.	$3x^2 - 13x - 10 = 0$	(three terms)
2.	$2x^2 + 3x = 0$	(no constant term)
3.	$x^2 - 16 = 0$	(no x term)

Solving a quadratic equation means finding the values of x that make the equation true.

Quadratic equations are solved with the following steps:

1. Bring every term to the left-hand side.
   (If necessary multiply both sides by -1 to make the coefficient of x^2 positive.)
2. Factorise the left-hand side.
3. Let each factor $= 0$.
4. Solve each simple equation.

Type 1

Example ▼

Solve for x: $3x^2 - 12 = 5x$

Solution:

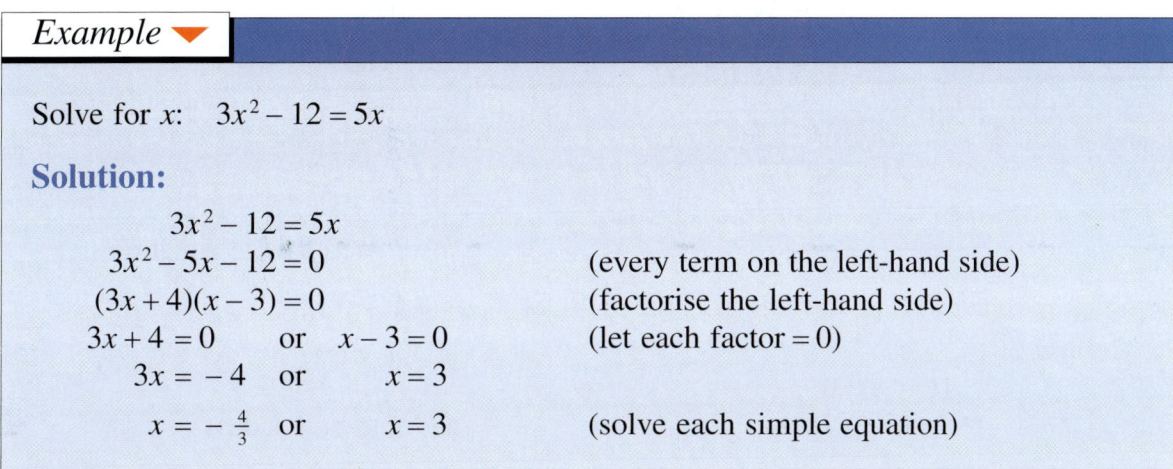

$$3x^2 - 12 = 5x$$
$$3x^2 - 5x - 12 = 0 \qquad \text{(every term on the left-hand side)}$$
$$(3x + 4)(x - 3) = 0 \qquad \text{(factorise the left-hand side)}$$
$$3x + 4 = 0 \quad \text{or} \quad x - 3 = 0 \qquad \text{(let each factor} = 0)$$
$$3x = -4 \quad \text{or} \qquad x = 3$$
$$x = -\tfrac{4}{3} \quad \text{or} \qquad x = 3 \qquad \text{(solve each simple equation)}$$

Type 2

Example ▼

Solve for x: $5x = 2x^2$

Solution:

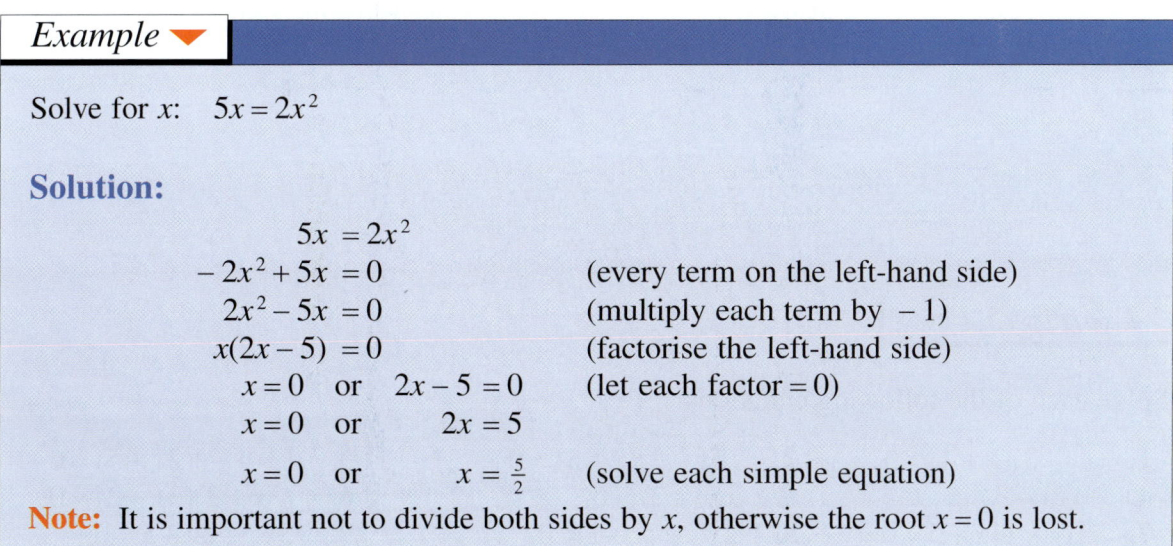

$$5x = 2x^2$$
$$-2x^2 + 5x = 0 \qquad \text{(every term on the left-hand side)}$$
$$2x^2 - 5x = 0 \qquad \text{(multiply each term by } -1)$$
$$x(2x - 5) = 0 \qquad \text{(factorise the left-hand side)}$$
$$x = 0 \quad \text{or} \quad 2x - 5 = 0 \qquad \text{(let each factor} = 0)$$
$$x = 0 \quad \text{or} \qquad 2x = 5$$
$$x = 0 \quad \text{or} \qquad x = \tfrac{5}{2} \qquad \text{(solve each simple equation)}$$

Note: It is important not to divide both sides by x, otherwise the root $x = 0$ is lost.

Type 3

Example ▼

Solve for x: $4x^2 - 9 = 0$

Solution:

We will use two methods to solve this quadratic equation.

Method 1:

$$4x^2 - 9 = 0 \quad \text{(every term is on the left-hand side)}$$
$$(2x)^2 - (3)^2 = 0 \quad \text{(difference of two squares)}$$
$$(2x - 3)(2x + 3) = 0 \quad \text{(factorise the left-hand side)}$$
$$2x - 3 = 0 \quad \text{or} \quad 2x + 3 = 0 \quad \text{(let each factor} = 0)$$
$$2x = 3 \quad \text{or} \quad 2x = -3$$
$$x = \frac{3}{2} \quad \text{or} \quad x = -\frac{3}{2} \quad \text{(solve each simple equation)}$$

Method 2:

$$4x^2 - 9 = 0$$
$$4x^2 = 9 \quad \text{(add 9 to both sides)}$$
$$x^2 = \frac{9}{4} \quad \text{(divide both sides by 4)}$$
$$x = \pm\sqrt{\frac{9}{4}} \quad \text{(take the square root of both sides)}$$
$$x = \pm\frac{\sqrt{9}}{\sqrt{4}} = \pm\frac{3}{2}$$
$$x = \frac{3}{2} \quad \text{or} \quad x = -\frac{3}{2}$$

Exercise 5.1 ▼

Solve each of the following equations:

1. $(x - 3)(x + 4) = 0$	**2.** $(2x - 3)(x + 5) = 0$	**3.** $(3x - 2)(2x + 5) = 0$
4. $x(2x - 3)$	**5.** $x(x + 2) = 0$	**6.** $(3x - 2)(3x + 2) = 0$
7. $2x^2 - 11x + 5 = 0$	**8.** $2x^2 + 7x + 3 = 0$	**9.** $3x^2 + 2x - 5 = 0$
10. $5x^2 + 4x - 1 = 0$	**11.** $3x^2 + 5x - 12 = 0$	**12.** $2x^2 + x - 3 = 0$

13.	$7x^2 + 29x + 4 = 0$	**14.**	$3x^2 + 10x = 8$	**15.**	$5x^2 + 3x = 2$
16.	$x(x-4) = 21$	**17.**	$x(x-6) = 16$	**18.**	$(x+3)(x-5) = 9$
19.	$x^2 + 3x = 0$	**20.**	$x^2 - 2x = 0$	**21.**	$x^2 - 5x = 0$
22.	$2x^2 + 5x = 0$	**23.**	$3x^2 = 2x$	**24.**	$5x^2 = 4x$
25.	$x^2 - 4 = 0$	**26.**	$x^2 - 25 = 0$	**27.**	$x^2 - 1 = 0$
28.	$9x^2 - 4 = 0$	**29.**	$4x^2 - 25 = 0$	**30.**	$4x^2 - 1 = 0$
31.	$4x^2 - 11x - 3 = 0$	**32.**	$6x^2 + 13x - 5 = 0$	**33.**	$8x^2 - 14x + 3 = 0$
34.	$x^2 - 2x + 1 = 0$	**35.**	$4x^2 + 4x + 1 = 0$	**36.**	$9x^2 - 12x + 4 = 0$
37.	$4x^2 - 29x + 7 = 0$	**38.**	$6x^2 + 20 = 29x$	**39.**	$4x^2 + 5 = 12x$
40.	$x(2x+7) + 6 = 0$	**41.**	$6x(x-1) + 2 = x(3-4x)$	**42.**	$x^2 + 3 = (2x+1)(x+3)$
43.	$(2x-3)^2 = 4$	**44.**	$(x+1)^2 + (x-2)^2 = 9$	**45.**	$(3x-1)^2 = (x+2)^2$
46.	$(5x-2)(3x+1) = (3x+1)(2x-3)$		**47.**	$(2x+3)(x+1) = (x+3)^2$	

Quadratic equations in fractional form

Quadratic equations in fractional form are solved with the following steps:

1. Multiply each part of the equation by the LCM of the expressions on the bottom.
2. Simplify both sides (no fractions left).
3. Proceed as in the previous section.

Example ▼

Solve for x: $5 = \dfrac{6}{x} + \dfrac{8}{x^2}$

Solution:

$$5 = \frac{6}{x} + \frac{8}{x^2} \qquad \text{(the LCM is } x^2\text{)}$$

$$x^2(5) = x^2\left(\frac{6}{x}\right) + x^2\left(\frac{8}{x^2}\right) \qquad \text{(multiply each part by } x^2\text{)}$$

$$5x^2 = 6x + 8 \qquad \text{(simplify both sides)}$$

$$5x^2 - 6x - 8 = 0 \qquad \text{(every term on the left-hand side)}$$

$$(5x+4)(x-2) = 0 \qquad \text{(factorise the left-hand side)}$$

$$5x + 4 = 0 \quad \text{or} \quad x - 2 = 0 \qquad \text{(let each factor} = 0\text{)}$$

$$5x = -4 \quad \text{or} \quad x = 2$$

$$x = -\tfrac{4}{5} \quad \text{or} \quad x = 2 \qquad \text{(solve each simple equation)}$$

Solve for x: $\dfrac{3}{4} - \dfrac{1}{x+2} = \dfrac{1}{x}$

Solution:

We will use two methods to solve this equation.

Method 1:

Multiply each part by the LCM of the expressions on the bottom.

$$\dfrac{3}{4} - \dfrac{1}{(x+2)} = \dfrac{1}{x} \qquad \text{(put brackets on } x+2\text{)}$$

$$4x(x+2)\left(\dfrac{3}{4}\right) - 4x(x+2)\dfrac{1}{(x+2)} = 4x(x+2)\left(\dfrac{1}{x}\right) \qquad \begin{array}{l}\text{(the LCM is } 4x(x+2)\text{)}\\ \text{(multiply each part by } 4x(x+2)\text{)}\end{array}$$

$3x(x+2) - 4x = 4(x+2)$	(simplify both sides)
$3x^2 + 6x - 4x = 4x + 8$	(remove the brackets)
$3x^2 + 6x - 4x - 4x - 8 = 0$	(every term on the left-hand side)
$3x^2 - 2x - 8 = 0$	(simplify the left-hand side)
$(3x+4)(x-2) = 0$	(factorise the left-hand side)
$3x + 4 = 0 \qquad \text{or} \qquad x - 2 = 0$	(let each factor $= 0$)
$3x = -4 \qquad \text{or} \qquad x = 2$	
$x = -\frac{4}{3} \qquad \text{or} \qquad x = 2$	(solve each simple equation)

Method 2:

Write each part of the equation in terms of the LCM and then remove the LCM.

$$\dfrac{3}{4} - \dfrac{1}{(x+2)} = \dfrac{1}{x} \qquad \text{(put brackets on } x+2\text{)}$$

$\dfrac{3x(x+2) - 4x = 4(x+2)}{4x(x+2)}$	(the LCM is $4x(x+2)$)
	(each part in terms of the LCM)
$3x(x+2) - 4x = 4(x+2)$	(remove the LCM)
$3x^2 + 6x - 4x = 4x + 8$	(remove the brackets)
$3x^2 + 6x - 4x - 4x - 8 = 0$	(every term on the left-hand side)
$3x^2 - 2x - 8 = 0$	(simplify the left-hand side)
$(3x+4)(x-2) = 0$	(factorise the left-hand side)
$3x + 4 = 0 \qquad \text{or} \qquad x - 2 = 0$	(let each factor $= 0$)
$3x = -4 \qquad \text{or} \qquad x = 2$	
$x = -\frac{4}{3} \qquad \text{or} \qquad x = 2$	(solve each simple equation)

Solve each of the following equations:

1. $1 + \dfrac{6}{x} + \dfrac{8}{x^2} = 0$

2. $1 - \dfrac{5}{x} + \dfrac{6}{x^2} = 0$

3. $x - 2 = \dfrac{15}{x}$

4. $x - \dfrac{2}{x} = 1$

5. $4x = 5 - \dfrac{1}{x}$

6. $x - \dfrac{4}{x} = 0$

7. $1 = \dfrac{25}{x^2}$

8. $3 = \dfrac{2}{x} + \dfrac{5}{x^2}$

9. $5x = \dfrac{9}{x} - 12$

10. $\dfrac{2}{x} = 13 - 6x$

11. $4 - \dfrac{12}{x} + \dfrac{5}{x^2} = 0$

12. $\dfrac{x}{2} = \dfrac{2}{x} + \dfrac{x + 10}{x}$

13. $\dfrac{1}{2} = \dfrac{1}{x - 1} - \dfrac{1}{x}$

14. $3 = \dfrac{1}{x} - \dfrac{2}{x - 2}$

15. $\dfrac{1}{x} = \dfrac{1}{x + 2} + \dfrac{1}{4}$

16. $\dfrac{1}{x} = \dfrac{1}{x + 1} + \dfrac{1}{20}$

17. $\dfrac{3}{2} - \dfrac{1}{x} = \dfrac{1}{x - 1}$

18. $3 = \dfrac{1}{x} - \dfrac{2}{x - 2}$

19. $1 = \dfrac{3}{x - 1} - \dfrac{2}{x + 1}$

20. $\dfrac{2}{x - 1} - \dfrac{1}{x + 2} = \dfrac{1}{2}$

21. $\dfrac{7}{x} + \dfrac{6}{x + 5} = 2$

22. $\dfrac{5}{4} = \dfrac{1}{x} + \dfrac{1}{x - 3}$

23. $\dfrac{3}{x + 1} + \dfrac{1}{x - 1} = 2$

24. $\dfrac{6}{x + 1} - \dfrac{5}{x + 2} = 2$

25. $\dfrac{12}{x - 3} + \dfrac{7}{x + 1} = 5$

26. $5 + \dfrac{4}{x - 2} = \dfrac{8}{x + 4}$

27. $\dfrac{10}{x - 1} = \dfrac{7}{2} - \dfrac{12}{x + 2}$

28. $\dfrac{4}{2x - 3} - \dfrac{2}{x} = \dfrac{1}{9}$

29. $\dfrac{60}{x - 2} = \dfrac{60}{x} + \dfrac{1}{3}$

30. $\dfrac{5}{2} = \dfrac{1}{x - 1} + \dfrac{3}{x + 2}$

31. **(i)** Express as one fraction $\quad \dfrac{1}{2} - \dfrac{1}{x} - \dfrac{1}{x + 3}$

  (ii) Hence, or othewise, solve $\quad \dfrac{1}{2} - \dfrac{1}{x} - \dfrac{1}{x + 3} = 0$

Quadratic formula

In many quadratic equations $ax^2 + bx + c$ cannot be resolved into factors. When this happens the formula **must** be used. To save time trying to look for factors, a clue that you must use the formula is often given in the question. When the question requires an approximate answer, e.g., 'correct to two decimal places', 'correct to three significant figures', 'correct to the nearest integer', or 'express your answer in surd form', then the formula must be used.

> The roots of the quadratic equation $ax^2 + bx + c = 0$, are given by the formula:
>
> $$x = \frac{-b \pm \sqrt{b^2 - 4ac}}{2a}$$
>
> **Notes: 1.** The whole of the top of the right-hand side, including $-b$, is divided by $2a$.
>   **2.** It is often called the '$-b$' or 'quadratic' formula.
>   **3.** Before using the formula, make sure every term is on the left-hand side, i.e. write the equation in the form $ax^2 + bx + c = 0$.

Note: If $\sqrt{b^2 - 4ac}$ is a whole number then $ax^2 + bx + c$ can be factorised.

The formula can still be used even if $ax^2 + bx + c$ can be factorised.

Example ▼

Solve the equation, $3x^2 - 8x - 2 = 0$, giving your solutions correct to two decimal places.

Solution:

$3x^2 - 8x - 2 = 0$ (two decimal places $\therefore$ use formula)

$a = 3,\ b = -8,\ c = -2$

$$x = \frac{-b \pm \sqrt{b^2 - 4ac}}{2a}$$

$$x = \frac{8 \pm \sqrt{(-8)^2 - 4(3)(-2)}}{2(3)}$$

$$x = \frac{8 \pm \sqrt{64 + 24}}{6}$$

$$x = \frac{8 \pm \sqrt{88}}{6}$$

$$x = \frac{8 \pm 9.3808}{6} \qquad (\sqrt{88} = 9.3808 \text{ correct to four decimal places})$$

$$x = \frac{8 + 9.3808}{6} \quad \text{or} \quad x = \frac{8 - 9.3808}{6}$$

$$x = \frac{17.3808}{6} \quad \text{or} \quad x = \frac{-1.3808}{6}$$

$$x = 2.8968 \quad \text{or} \quad x = -0.2301$$

$\therefore x = 2.90$ or $x = -0.23$, correct to two decimal places.

Exercise 5.3 ▼

In questions 1 to 6, solve the equations   **(i)** by resolving into factors   **(ii)** by formula:

1. $x^2 - 5x + 4 = 0$ **2.** $x^2 + 8x + 12 = 0$ **3.** $2x^2 - 3x - 2 = 0$

4. $3x^2 + 5x - 12 = 0$ **5.** $3x^2 - 10x - 8 = 0$ **6.** $5x^2 + 7x - 6 = 0$

Solve, correct to two places of decimals, each of the following equations:

7. $2x^2 - 3x - 7 = 0$ **8.** $x^2 + 7x - 3 = 0$ **9.** $2x^2 + 3x - 4 = 0$

10. $3x^2 - 7x - 2 = 0$ **11.** $3x^2 + 5x - 7 = 0$ **12.** $5x^2 + 6x - 3 = 0$

13. $4x^2 + x - 1 = 0$ **14.** $5x^2 + 7x - 4 = 0$ **15.** $7x^2 + 8x - 2 = 0$

16. $2x^2 - 11x + 4 = 0$ **17.** $3x^2 + 10x + 4 = 0$ **18.** $4x^2 + 2x - 5 = 0$

Express each of the following equations in the form $ax^2 + bx + c = 0$, and hence, solve each equation, giving your solutions correct to one place of decimals.

19. $x^2 + \dfrac{x}{2} = \dfrac{5}{2}$ **20.** $x + \dfrac{1}{x} = 3$ **21.** $2 + \dfrac{3}{x} = \dfrac{8}{x^2}$

22. $4 = \dfrac{1}{x+1} + \dfrac{2}{x}$ **23.** $2 + \dfrac{1}{x} = \dfrac{12}{x+2}$ **24.** $\dfrac{1}{x+2} - \dfrac{1}{x} = 3$

25. $\dfrac{1}{x-1} + \dfrac{2}{x} = \dfrac{1}{2}$ **26.** $\dfrac{5}{2x-1} - \dfrac{2}{x} = \dfrac{1}{9}$ **27.** $\dfrac{1}{x} + \dfrac{1}{x+1} = \dfrac{2}{3}$

28. **(i)** Write $\dfrac{1}{x+1} + \dfrac{2}{x-3}$ as a single fraction.

     (ii) Hence, or otherwise, find, correct to one place of decimals, the two solutions of:

$$\frac{1}{x+1} + \frac{2}{x-3} = 1$$

Sometimes we are asked to give the solutions in surd form:

Example ▼

Solve the equation, $x^2 - 6x + 1 = 0$, giving your solutions in surd form.

Solution:

$$x^2 - 6x + 1 = 0 \qquad \text{[surd form} \therefore \text{ use formula]}$$
$$a = 1, \ b = -6, \ c = 1$$

$$x = \frac{-b \pm \sqrt{b^2 - 4ac}}{2a}$$

$$= \frac{6 \pm \sqrt{(-6)^2 - 4(1)(1)}}{2(1)}$$

$$= \frac{6 \pm \sqrt{36 - 4}}{2}$$

$$= \frac{6 \pm \sqrt{32}}{2}$$

$$= \frac{6 \pm 4\sqrt{2}}{2}$$

$$= 3 \pm 2\sqrt{2} \qquad \text{[divide both parts on top by 2]}$$

$$\therefore \text{ the roots are } 3 + 2\sqrt{2} \quad \text{or} \quad 3 - 2\sqrt{2}.$$

$$\sqrt{32}$$
$$= \sqrt{16 \times 2}$$
$$= \sqrt{16}\sqrt{2}$$
$$= 4\sqrt{2}$$

Note: $x^2 = 1x^2$ and therefore $a = 1$.

Express each of the following in the form $a\sqrt{b}$, where b is a prime number:

29. $\sqrt{12}$ **30.** $\sqrt{18}$ **31.** $\sqrt{32}$ **32.** $\sqrt{50}$ **33.** $\sqrt{27}$ **34.** $\sqrt{80}$

Solve each of the following, giving your solutions in surd form:

35. $x^2 - 2x - 4 = 0$	**36.** $x^2 - 2x - 2 = 0$	**37.** $x^2 - 4x + 1 = 0$
38. $x^2 + 6x + 7 = 0$	**39.** $x^2 + 4x - 8 = 0$	**40.** $x^2 - 4x - 14 = 0$
41. $x^2 - 8x + 4 = 0$	**42.** $2x^2 - 2x - 1 = 0$	**43.** $4x^2 + 2x - 1 = 0$

Express each of the following equations in the form $ax^2 + bx + c = 0$, and hence, solve each equation, giving your solutions in surd form:

44. $1 - \dfrac{2}{x} - \dfrac{1}{x^2} = 0$

45. $x + 2 = \dfrac{2}{x}$

46. $1 + \dfrac{22}{x^2} = \dfrac{10}{x}$

47. $\dfrac{1}{x+1} + \dfrac{1}{x-1} = \dfrac{1}{2}$

48. $\dfrac{2}{x} - \dfrac{1}{x+1} = \dfrac{1}{3}$

49. $2 = \dfrac{1}{x} + \dfrac{1}{x+2}$

50. **(i)** Write $\dfrac{1}{4} - \dfrac{1}{x+2} - \dfrac{1}{x-2}$ as a single fraction.

 (ii) Hence, or otherwise, solve the equation $\dfrac{1}{4} - \dfrac{1}{x+2} - \dfrac{1}{x-2} = 0$ giving your solutions in surd form.

51. Verify that $1 + \sqrt{7}$ is a solution of the equation $x^2 - 2x - 6 = 0$.

52. Verify that $-2 + \sqrt{5}$ is a solution of the equation $x^2 + 4x - 1 = 0$.

Quadratic equations solved by substitution

In some questions we can use the roots of one quadratic equation to help us to solve another quadratic equation by using a substitution.

Example ▼

Solve $x^2 - 9x + 20 = 0$ and hence, solve $\left(t + \dfrac{4}{t}\right)^2 - 9\left(t + \dfrac{4}{t}\right) + 20 = 0$.

Solution:

$$x^2 - 9x + 20 = 0$$
$$\Rightarrow \quad (x - 5)(x - 4) = 0$$
$$\Rightarrow \quad x - 5 = 0 \quad \text{or} \quad x - 4 = 0$$
$$\Rightarrow \quad x = 5 \quad \text{or} \quad x = 4$$

$$\text{let} \left(t + \dfrac{4}{t}\right) = x \qquad \text{(this is the substitution)}$$

$t + \dfrac{4}{t} = 5$ or $t + \dfrac{4}{t} = 4$

$\Rightarrow \quad t^2 + 4 = 5t$ $\Rightarrow \quad t^2 + 4 = 4t$

(multiply across by t)   (multiply across by t)

$$\Rightarrow \quad t^2 - 5t + 4 = 0 \qquad\qquad\qquad \Rightarrow \quad t^2 - 4t + 4 = 0$$
$$\Rightarrow \quad (t+4)(t-1) = 0 \qquad\qquad \Rightarrow \quad (t-2)(t-2) = 0$$
$$\Rightarrow \quad t - 4 = 0 \quad \text{or} \quad t - 1 = 0 \qquad \Rightarrow \quad t - 2 = 0 \quad \text{or} \quad t - 2 = 0$$
$$\Rightarrow \quad t = 4 \quad \text{or} \quad t = 1 \qquad\qquad \Rightarrow \quad t = 2 \quad \text{or} \quad t = 2$$
$$\therefore \ t = 4, 1, 2, 2$$

Exercise 5.4 ▼

1. Solve the equation $x^2 - 2x - 8 = 0$.
   Hence, or otherwise, find the values of y for which $(y-3)^2 - 2(y-3) - 8 = 0$.

2. Solve the equation $x^2 - 8x + 15 = 0$.
   Hence, or otherwise, find the values of t for which $(2t-1)^2 - 8(2t-1) + 15 = 0$.

3. Solve the equation $x^2 - 4x - 21 = 0$.
   Hence, or otherwise, solve $(5t+2)^2 - 4(5t+2) - 21 = 0$.

4. Solve the equation $4x^2 - 12x + 5 = 0$.

   Hence, or otherwise, solve $\quad 4\left(\dfrac{t}{2}-1\right)^2 - 12\left(\dfrac{t}{2}-1\right) + 5 = 0$.

5. Solve the equation $x^2 - 8x + 12 = 0$.
   Hence, use your solutions to find the four values of y for which
   $$(y^2 + y)^2 - 8(y^2 + y) - 12 = 0.$$

6. Solve the equation $x^2 - 8x - 84 = 0$.
   Hence, solve $(t^2 - 5t)^2 - 8(t^2 - 5t) - 84 = 0$.

7. Solve the equation $y^2 - 7y + 10 = 0$.
   Hence, solve $(x^2 + 1)^2 - 7(x^2 + 1) + 10 = 0$.

8. Solve the equation $20 + 8x - x^2 = 0$.
   Hence, solve $(x^2 - 3x)^2 - 8(x^2 - 3x) - 20 = 0$.

9. Solve the equation $x^2 - 6x + 5 = 0$.

   Hence, find the four values of k for which $\left(k - \dfrac{6}{k}\right)^2 - 6\left(k - \dfrac{6}{k}\right) + 5 = 0$.

10. Solve the equation $x^2 + 3x - 54 = 0$.

    Hence, solve $\left(y + \dfrac{8}{y}\right)^2 + 3\left(y + \dfrac{8}{y}\right) - 54 = 0$.

11. Solve the equation $20 + x - x^2 = 0$.

    Hence, solve $\left(2y + \dfrac{2}{y}\right)^2 - \left(2y + \dfrac{2}{y}\right) - 20 = 0$.

12. Solve the equation $4x^2 - 5x + 1 = 0$.

Hence, solve $4\left(\dfrac{1}{y^2}\right)^2 - 5\left(\dfrac{1}{y^2}\right) + 1 = 0$.

13. **(i)** Solve, correct to one decimal place, the equation $x^2 + 3x - 5 = 0$.
   (ii) Using your answers to part **(i)**, or otherwise, find, correct to one decimal place, the two values of y for which $(2y + 1)^2 + 3(2y + 1) - 5 = 0$.

14. Solve, correct to two places of decimals, the equation $3x^2 - 2x - 2 = 0$.
   Hence, or otherwise, find, correct to one place of decimals, the values of x for which
   $$3(2x - 1)^2 - 2(2x - 1) - 2 = 0.$$

15. Solve, correct to one place of decimals, the equation, $5x^2 - 7x - 10 = 0$.

   Hence, or otherwise, find the values of y for which $5\left(\dfrac{1}{y}\right)^2 - 7\left(\dfrac{1}{y}\right) - 10 = 0$,

   and give your answers correct to one place of decimals.

16. Solve the equation $x - 11 + \dfrac{24}{x} = 0$.

   Hence, solve $(x^2 - 2x) - 11 + \dfrac{24}{(x^2 - 2x)} = 0$.

Constructing a quadratic equation when given its roots

This is the reverse process to solving a quadratic equation by using factors.

Example ▼

Find a quadratic equation with roots   **(i)** -2 and 3 **(ii)** $\frac{2}{3}$ and $-\frac{1}{5}$

Write your answers in the form $ax^2 + bx + c = 0$, $a, b, c \in \mathbf{Z}$

Solution:

   (i) roots -2 and 3
   Let $x = -2$ and $x = 3$
   $\Rightarrow$ $x + 2 = 0$ and $x - 3 = 0$
   $\Rightarrow$ $(x + 2)(x - 3) = 0$
   $\Rightarrow$ $x^2 - 3x + 2x - 6 = 0$
   $\Rightarrow$ $x^2 - x - 6 = 0$

   (ii) roots $\frac{2}{3}$ and $-\frac{1}{5}$
   Let $x = \frac{2}{3}$ and $x = -\frac{1}{5}$
   $\Rightarrow$ $3x = 2$ and $5x = -1$
   $\Rightarrow$ $3x - 2 = 0$ and $5x + 1 = 0$
   $\Rightarrow$ $(3x - 2)(5x + 1) = 0$
   $\Rightarrow$ $15x^2 + 3x - 10x - 2 = 0$
   $\Rightarrow$ $15x^2 - 7x - 2 = 0$

Construct a quadratic equation with roots:
(In each case, write your answer in the form $ax^2 + bx + c = 0, \quad a, b, c \in \mathbf{Z}$)

1. 2, 3	**2.** $-1, 2$	**3.** $-2, 5$	**4.** $-1, 4$	**5.** $-3, -2$
6. 4, 5	**7.** $-3, 4$	**8.** $-8, 3$	**9.** $-3, 3$	**10.** 2, 2
11. $-2, 0$	**12.** 0, 5	**13.** $-1, 1$	**14.** $\frac{1}{2}, 3$	**15.** $-\frac{1}{3}, 2$
16. $-3, \frac{1}{2}$	**17.** $-1, \frac{5}{2}$	**18.** $\frac{1}{3}, \frac{1}{2}$	**19.** $\frac{1}{3}, -\frac{2}{3}$	**20.** $\frac{1}{2}, \frac{3}{4}$

21. The equation $x^2 + mx + n = 0$ has roots -3 and 5, find the values of m and n.

22. The equation $ax^2 + bx + c = 0$ has roots $-\frac{1}{2}$ and $\frac{2}{5}$.
Find one set of values of a, b, and c, $\quad a, b, c \in \mathbf{Z}$.

Chapter test

Solve each of the following equations:

1. $2x^2 - x - 10 = 0$ **2.** $3x^2 - 5x = 0$ **3.** $x^2 - 4 = 0$

4. $3x^2 - 10 = 13x$ **5.** $x^2 = 4x$ **6.** $x^2 - 25 = 0$

7. $3(x-1)^2 - 2(x-1) - 1 = 0$ **8.** $2(x-2)^2 - 2 = 3(6-x)$

9. $(x+1)^2 = 4$ **10.** $(5x+2)(3x-1) = (3x-1)(2x+3)$

11. $x + \dfrac{5}{x} = 6$ **12.** $2 = \dfrac{3}{x} + \dfrac{2}{x^2}$

13. $2 = \dfrac{3}{x} + \dfrac{4}{x+1}$ **14.** $\dfrac{3}{x-1} = \dfrac{5}{x} - \dfrac{1}{6}$

15. $\dfrac{1}{x-3} - \dfrac{3}{x+2} = \dfrac{1}{2}$ **16.** $\dfrac{2}{9} = \dfrac{1}{x-5} - \dfrac{1}{x+1}$

In questions 17 – 22, give your solutions correct to two decimal places:

17. $x^2 - 5x - 3 = 0$ **18.** $3x^2 - x - 1 = 0$

19. $7 + \dfrac{8}{x} - \dfrac{2}{x^2} = 0$ **20.** $2 - \dfrac{3}{x} = \dfrac{8}{x^2}$

21. $3 = \dfrac{2}{1-x} - \dfrac{4}{x}$ **22.** $\dfrac{2}{x-1} - \dfrac{1}{x+1} = \dfrac{1}{4}$

In questions 23 – 28, give your solutions in surd form:

23. $x^2 - 2x - 1 = 0$

24. $x^2 + 2x - 6 = 0$

25. $x + 6 + \dfrac{4}{x} = 0$

26. $1 + \dfrac{4}{x} + \dfrac{1}{x^2} = 0$

27. $\dfrac{1}{x} - \dfrac{1}{x+2} = \dfrac{1}{2}$

28. $\dfrac{1}{x+3} = \dfrac{1}{2} - \dfrac{1}{x+1}$

29. Verify that $2 - \sqrt{3}$ is a solution of the equation $x^2 - 4x + 1 = 0$.

30. Verify that $-5 + \sqrt{2}$ is a solution of the equation $x^2 + 10x + 23 = 0$.

31. Solve the equation $5x^2 + 9x - 2 = 0$.
Hence, or otherwise, find the values of y for which $5(2y - 1)^2 + 9(2y - 1) - 2 = 0$.

32. Solve the equation $2x^2 - 5x - 12 = 0$.

Hence, solve the equation $\quad 2\left(\dfrac{t}{2} + 1\right)^2 = 5\left(\dfrac{t}{2} + 1\right) + 12 = 0$.

33. Solve the equation $x^2 - 4x - 5 = 0$.
Hence, find the four values of y for which $(2y^2 + 3y)^2 - 4(2y^2 + 3y) - 5 = 0$.

34. Solve the equation $3x^2 + 16x - 12 = 0$.

Hence, find the four values of t for which $\quad 3\left(t - \dfrac{7}{t}\right)^2 + 16\left(t - \dfrac{7}{t}\right) - 12 = 0$.

35. Solve the equation $4x^2 + 7x - 2 = 0$.
Hence, or otherwise, find the four values of y for which $2 - 7(y^2 - 6) - 4(y^2 - 6)^2 = 0$.

36. **(i)** Solve, correct to one decimal place, the equation $2x^2 - 3x - 4 = 0$.
(ii) Using your answers to part **(i)**, or otherwise, find, correct to one decimal place, the two values of a for which $2(a + 3)^2 - 3(a + 3) - 4 = 0$.

37. Solve, correct to two places of decimals, the equation $2x^2 - 5x - 2 = 0$.
Hence, or otherwise, find the values of x for which $2(3x - 1)^2 - 5(3x - 1) - 2 = 0$,
and give your answers correct to one place of decimals.

38. Construct a quadratic equation with roots

(i) -1 and 8 **(ii)** $-\frac{1}{2}$ and 3 **(iii)** $\frac{1}{2}$ and $\frac{2}{3}$.

39. The equation $px^2 + qx + r = 0$ has roots $-\frac{1}{3}$ and 2.
Find one set of values of p, q, and r, p, q and $r \in \mathbf{Z}$.

40. If $x = 2$ is one root of the equation $2x^2 + kx + 2 = 0$,
find: **(i)** the value of k **(ii)** the other root.

LINEAR INEQUALITIES IN ONE VARIABLE

Inequalities

The four inequality symbols:

> $>$ means   'greater than'
> $\geqslant$ means   'greater than or equal to'
> $<$ means   'less than'
> $\leqslant$ means   'less than or equal to'

Algebraic expressions that are linked by one of the four inequality symbols are called **'inequalities'**.

For example, $3x - 1 \leqslant 11$ and $-3 < 2x - 1 \leqslant 7$ are inequalities.

Solving inequalities is exactly the same as solving equations, with the following exception:

> Multiplying or dividing both sides of an inequality by a **negative** number **reverses** the direction of the inequality.
> That is:
> $>$ changes to $<$ $\geqslant$ changes to $\leqslant$
> $<$ changes to $>$ $\leqslant$ changes to $\geqslant$

For example, $4 > -7$ is true. If we multiply both sides by -1, it gives $-4 > 7$, which is **not** true.

Thus, $-4 < 7$ is true, multiplying both sides by -1 and reversing the direction of the inequality keeps the inequality true.

Note: Inequalities can be turned around. For example:

$$5 \leqslant x \text{ means the same as } x \geqslant 5$$
$$8 \geqslant x \geqslant 3 \text{ means the same as } 3 \leqslant x \leqslant 8$$

Solving an inequality means finding the values of x that make the inequality true.

The following rules apply to graphing inequalities on a number line:

> Number line for $x \in \boldsymbol{N}$ or $x \in \boldsymbol{Z}$, use dots.
> Number line for $x \in \boldsymbol{R}$, use a 'full' heavy line.

Simple inequalities

Example ▼

Find the range of values of $x \in \mathbf{R}$ for which $4(x-2) > 5(2x-1) - 9$ and graph your solution on the number line.

Solution:

$$4(x-2) > 5(2x-1) - 9$$

$4x - 8 > 10x - 5 - 9$	(remove the brackets)
$4x - 10x > -5 - 9 + 8$	(letters to the left, numbers to the right)
$-6x > -6$	(simplify both sides)
$6x < 6$	(multiply both sides by -1 and reverse the inequality, i.e., turn $>$ into $<$)
$x < 1$	(divide both sides by 6)

Number line:

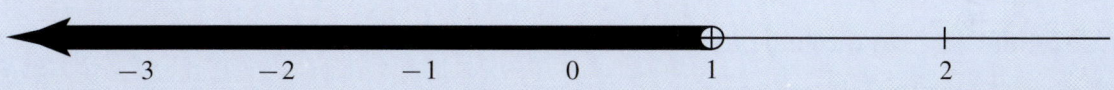

A circle is put around 1 to indicate that 1 is **not** included in the solution.

Example ▼

Find the values of x for which $7x - 11 < 2x + 9$, $x \in \mathbf{N}$.
Graph your solution on the number line.

Solution:

$7x - 11 < 2x + 9$	
$7x - 2x < 9 + 11$	(letters to the left, numbers to the right)
$5x < 20$	(simplify both sides)
$x < 4$	(divide both sides by 5)

This is the set of natural numbers less than 4.
Therefore, the values are 0, 1, 2 and 3 (4 is **not** included).

Number line:

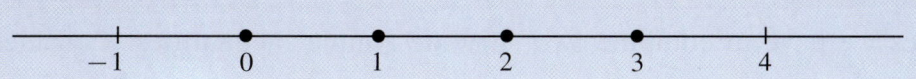

Double inequalities

A double inequality is one like $-3 \leqslant 2x + 1 \leqslant 7$.
There are two methods for solving double inequalities.

Method 1:

> Whatever we do to one part we do the same to all three parts.

Method 2:

> 1. Write the double inequality as two separate simple inequalities.
> 2. Solve each simple inequality and combine their solutions.

Example ▼

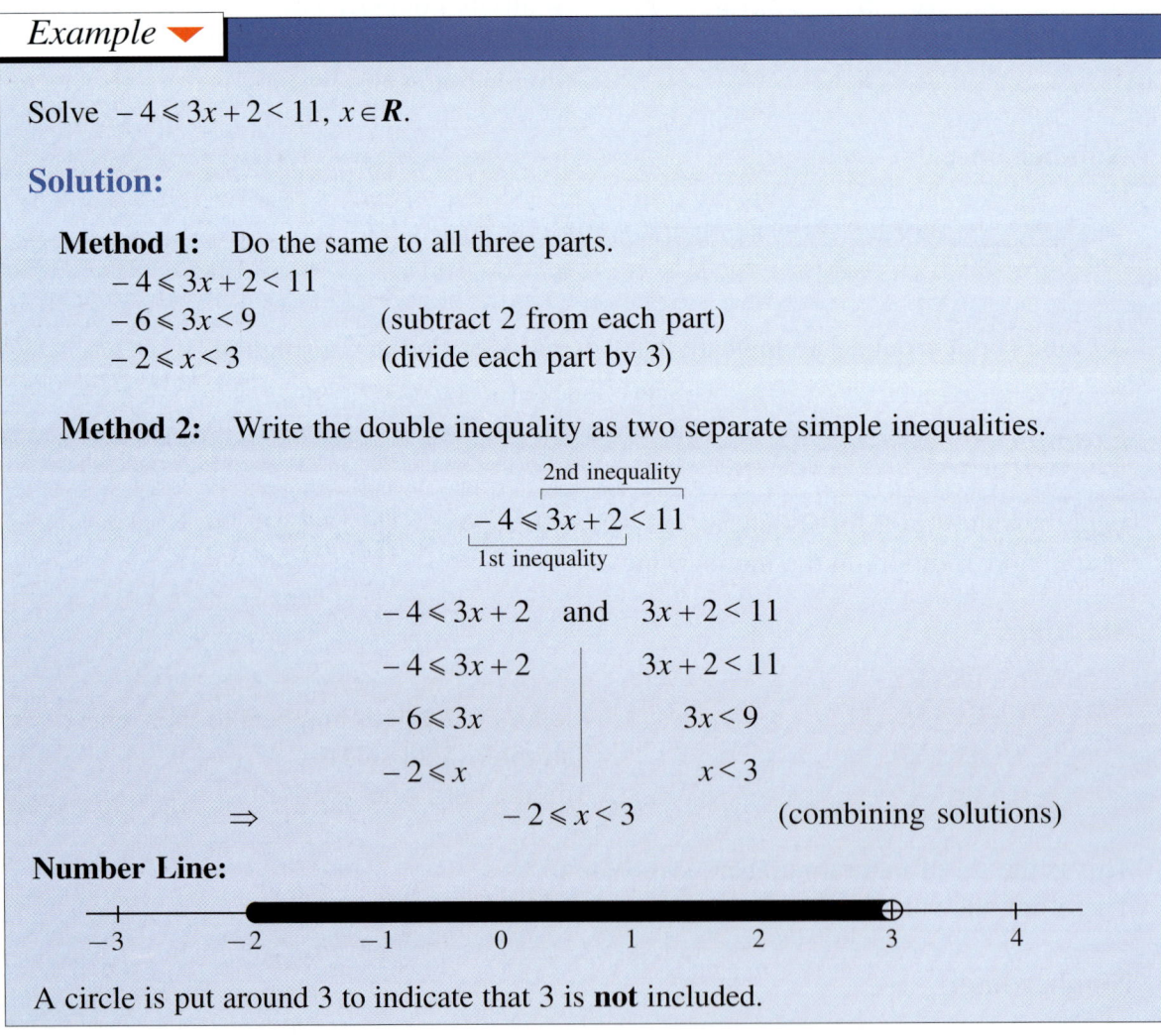

Solve $-4 \leqslant 3x + 2 < 11$, $x \in \mathbf{R}$.

Solution:

Method 1: Do the same to all three parts.
$$-4 \leqslant 3x + 2 < 11$$
$$-6 \leqslant 3x < 9 \qquad \text{(subtract 2 from each part)}$$
$$-2 \leqslant x < 3 \qquad \text{(divide each part by 3)}$$

Method 2: Write the double inequality as two separate simple inequalities.

2nd inequality

$$-4 \leqslant 3x + 2 < 11$$

1st inequality

$$-4 \leqslant 3x + 2 \quad \text{and} \quad 3x + 2 < 11$$

$-4 \leqslant 3x + 2$	$3x + 2 < 11$
$-6 \leqslant 3x$	$3x < 9$
$-2 \leqslant x$	$x < 3$

$\Rightarrow \qquad -2 \leqslant x < 3 \qquad \text{(combining solutions)}$

Number Line:

A circle is put around 3 to indicate that 3 is **not** included.

Sometimes we have to combine two separate simple inequalities. Consider the next example.

(i) Find the solution set E of $2x + 7 < 11$, $x \in \textbf{\textit{R}}$.

(ii) Find the solution set H of $3 - 2x < 10$, $x \in \textbf{\textit{R}}$.

(iii) Find $E \cap H$ and graph your solution on the number line.

Solution:

We solve each inequality separately and then combine the solutions.

(i) $E: \ 2x + 7 < 11$

$$2x < 11 - 7$$
$$2x < 4$$
$$x < 2$$

(ii) $H: \ 3 - 2x < 10$

$$-2x < 10 - 3$$
$$-2x < 7$$
$$2x > -7$$
$$x > -\tfrac{7}{2}$$

(iii) Combining the two inequalities gives:

$$E \cap H: \ -\tfrac{7}{2} < x < 2$$

Number line:

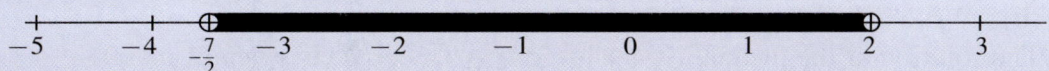

A circle is put around $-\tfrac{7}{2}$ and 2 to indicate that $-\tfrac{7}{2}$ and 2 are **not** included in the solution.

Solve each of the following inequalities, and in each case graph your solution on the number line:

1. $2x - 1 \geqslant 5, \quad x \in \mathbf{R}$
2. $3x + 2 \leqslant 5, \quad x \in \mathbf{R}$
3. $5x + 3 \geqslant 3x + 7, \quad x \in \mathbf{R}$
4. $7x - 6 \geqslant 2x + 9, \quad x \in \mathbf{N}$
5. $9x - 1 \leqslant 5x + 3, \quad x \in \mathbf{Z}$
6. $9x - 5 > 5x - 1, \quad x \in \mathbf{R}$
7. $3x - 8 < x + 2, \quad x \in \mathbf{N}$
8. $2x - 3 \geqslant 4x - 9, \quad x \in \mathbf{N}$
9. $3(x - 4) \leqslant 2(x - 3), \quad x \in \mathbf{Z}$
10. $5(x + 2) \geqslant 2(x - 1), \quad x \in \mathbf{R}$
11. $5(x - 2) - 7 \geqslant 3(x - 4), \quad x \in \mathbf{R}$
12. $2(x + 3) < 6(x + 2), \quad x \in \mathbf{R}$
13. $2(x + 4) < 2 - x, \quad x \in \mathbf{R}$
14. $9(x + 1) - 1 \geqslant 2(5x + 6), \quad x \in \mathbf{Z}$
15. $-6 \leqslant 2x \leqslant 4, \quad x \in \mathbf{R}$
16. $-10 < 5x \leqslant 20, \quad x \in \mathbf{R}$
17. $-1 \leqslant 2x + 1 \leqslant 9, \quad x \in \mathbf{R}$
18. $-13 < 4x - 1 < 19, \quad x \in \mathbf{R}$
19. $-4 \leqslant 3x + 2 < 11, \quad x \in \mathbf{Z}$
20. $-3 < 2x + 1 < 5, \quad x \in \mathbf{Z}$
21. $-5 \leqslant 2x - 3 \leqslant -1, \quad x \in \mathbf{R}$
22. $-2 \leqslant 5x - 2 \leqslant 13, \quad x \in \mathbf{R}$
23. $-13 \leqslant 4x - 1 \leqslant 3, \quad x \in \mathbf{R}$
24. $-5 \leqslant 2x - 3 < 7, \quad x \in \mathbf{R}$
25. $-1 \leqslant 6x + 5 < 17, \quad x \in \mathbf{R}$
26. $-33 \leqslant 7x - 5 \leqslant -12, \quad x \in \mathbf{R}$
27. $2 \geqslant -x \geqslant -3, \quad x \in \mathbf{R}$
28. $2 > -2x > -8, \quad x \in \mathbf{Z}$
29. $3 \geqslant 1 - 2x > -5, \quad x \in \mathbf{Z}$
30. $-1 > -2x - 3 \geqslant -7, \quad x \in \mathbf{R}$
31. $3 > 2x - 7 \geqslant -5, \quad x \in \mathbf{R}$
32. $-9 < 1 - 5x < 6, \quad x \in \mathbf{R}$

33. **(i)** The solution of the inequality, $-3 \leqslant 2x - 1 \leqslant 7, \quad x \in \mathbf{R}$, is given as $a \leqslant x \leqslant b$. Find the value of a and the value of b.
    (ii) Write down the values of $x \in \mathbf{Z}$ for which $-3 \leqslant 2x + 5 < 11$.

34. The solution of the inequality, $4 \geqslant 1 - 3x \geqslant -5, \quad x \in \mathbf{R}$, is given as $p \leqslant x \leqslant q$.

    Find the value of p and the value of q. Hence, evaluate $\sqrt{\dfrac{1}{q^2} - 6p}$

35. Find the values of x for which $4x - 11 \leqslant 2x - 5, \quad x \in \mathbf{N}$.

36. The solution of the inequality $11 - 2x \geqslant 3, \quad x \in \mathbf{N}$ is given as $\{a, b, c, d, e\}$. Write down the values of a, b, c, d and e where $a < b < c < d < e$.

    Hence, evaluate $\sqrt{\dfrac{b}{0.c} + de - 1}$

37. Find the solution set of **(i)** $A: x + 2 \leqslant 5, \quad x \in \mathbf{R}$ **(ii)** $B: x + 3 \geqslant 1, \quad x \in \mathbf{R}$. Find $A \cap B$ and graph your solution on the number line.

38. Find the solution set of **(i)** $H: 2x - 3 \leqslant 5, \quad x \in \mathbf{R}$ **(ii)** $K: 3x + 2 \geqslant -1, \quad x \in \mathbf{R}$. Find $H \cap K$ and graph your solution on the number line.

39. **(i)** Find the solution set P of $4x - 1 \leqslant 3, \quad x \in \mathbf{R}$.
    (ii) Find the solution set Q of $5 - x \leqslant 8, \quad x \in \mathbf{R}$.
    (iii) Find $P \cap Q$ and graph your solution on the number line.

40. **(i)** Find the solution set G of $3x - 1 \leqslant 9 - 2x$, $x \in \mathbf{R}$.

    (ii) Find the solution set H of $1 - 3x \leqslant 8 - x$, $x \in \mathbf{R}$.

    (iii) Find $G \cap H$ and graph your solution on the number line.

41. **(i)** Find the solution set M of $4 - x \leqslant 6$, $x \in \mathbf{R}$.

    (ii) Find the solution set N of $3x - 1 \leqslant x + 9$, $x \in \mathbf{R}$.

    (iii) If $M \cap N = a \leqslant x \leqslant b$, write down the value of a and the value of b.

42. Find the solution set H of $9 - 2x \geqslant 7$, $x \in \mathbf{N}$.

Find the solution set K of $3x - 4 \leqslant 5$, $x \in \mathbf{N}$.

Write down the elements of the set $K \backslash H$.

43. Write down an inequality to represent each of the following shaded sections of the number line:

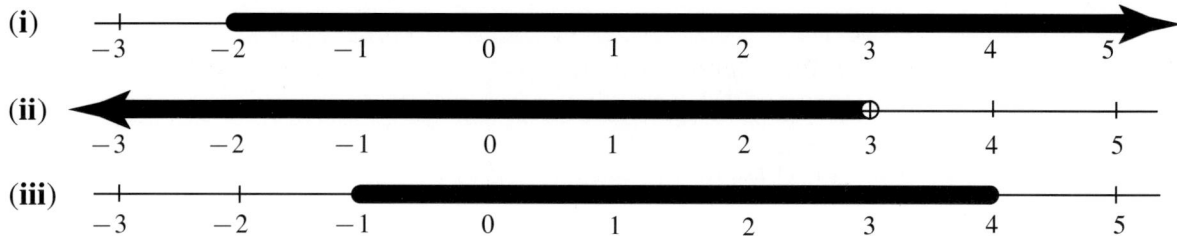

CHANGING THE SUBJECT OF A FORMULA

Changing the subject of a formula

When we rearrange a formula so that one of the variables is given in terms of the others we are said to be '**changing the subject of the formula**'. The rules in changing the subject of a formula are the same as when solving an equation, that is we can:

1. **Add** or **subtract** the same quantity to both sides.
   (In practice this involves moving a term from one side to another and changing its sign)
2. **Multiply** or **divide** both sides by the same quantity.
3. **Square** both sides.
4. Take the **square root** of both sides.

Note: Whatever letter comes after the word 'express' is to be on its own.

Example ▼

If $r = \dfrac{1}{p} + \dfrac{1}{q}$, express p in terms of q and r.

Solution:

$$r = \frac{1}{p} + \frac{1}{q}$$

$$pqr = pq\frac{1}{p} + pq\frac{1}{q} \qquad \text{[multiply each part by } pq]$$

$$pqr = q + p \qquad \text{[simplify right-hand side]}$$

$$pqr - p = q \qquad \text{[terms with } p \text{ on the left-hand side]}$$

$$p(qr - 1) = q \qquad \text{[take out common factor } p \text{ on the left-hand side]}$$

$$p = \frac{q}{qr - 1} \qquad \text{[divide both sides by } (qr - 1)]$$

Example ▼

If $a = \dfrac{3bc}{b+c}$, express c in terms of a and b.

Solution:

$$a = \frac{3bc}{b+c}$$

$a(b+c) = 3bc$	[multiply both sides by $(b+c)$]
$ab + ac = 3bc$	[remove brackets on the left-hand side]
$-3bc + ac = -ab$	[terms with c on the left-hand side]
$3bc - ac = ab$	[multiply each term by -1]
$c(3b - a) = ab$	[take out common factor c on the left-hand side]
$c = \dfrac{ab}{3b - a}$	[divide both sides by $(3b - a)$]

Example ▼

If $v = \sqrt{\dfrac{u-s}{ut}}$, express t in terms of u, v and s.

Solution:

$$v = \sqrt{\frac{u-s}{ut}}$$

$(v)^2 = \left(\sqrt{\dfrac{u-s}{ut}}\right)^2$	[square both sides]
$v^2 = \dfrac{u-s}{ut}$	[square root sign disappears]
$v^2 ut = u - s$	[multiply both sides by ut]
$t = \dfrac{u-s}{v^2 u}$	[divide both sides by $v^2 u$]

If $\dfrac{8-q^2}{2a^2} = m$, express a in terms of m and q.

Find the **values** of a when $q = 2$ and $m = 4.5$.

Solution:

$$\frac{8-q^2}{2a^2} = m$$

$$8 - q^2 = 2a^2 m \qquad \text{[multiply both sides by } 2a^2]$$

$$2a^2 m = 8 - q^2 \qquad \text{[swap sides to have '}a\text{' on the left-hand side]}$$

$$a^2 = \frac{8-q^2}{2m} \qquad \text{[divide both sides by } 2m]$$

$$a = \pm\sqrt{\frac{8-q^2}{2m}} \qquad \text{[take the square root of both sides]}$$

$$q = 2, \quad m = 4.5$$

$$a = \pm\sqrt{\frac{8-q^2}{2m}} = \pm\sqrt{\frac{8-2^2}{2(4.5)}} = \pm\sqrt{\frac{8-4}{9}} = \pm\sqrt{\frac{4}{9}} = \pm\frac{\sqrt{4}}{\sqrt{9}} = \pm\frac{2}{3}$$

Note: If $x^2 = k$, then $x = \pm\sqrt{k}$, always include both the positive and negative solutions.

Exercise 7.1 ▼

1. If $2a - b = c$, express a in terms of b and c.
2. If $3p + q = r$, express p in terms of q and r.
3. If $ab - c = d$, express b in terms of a, c and d.
4. If $u + at = v$, express t in terms of a, u and v.
5. If $3p + 2q = 5r$, express p in terms of q and r.
6. If $3a - 4b = 2c$, express b in terms of a and c.
7. If $2(p - r) = q$, express p in terms of q and r.
8. If $y(x - a) = t$, express x in terms of a, t and y.
9. If $\dfrac{a+b}{2} = c$, express a in terms of b and c.
10. If $p = \dfrac{q-2r}{3}$, express r in terms of p and q.
11. If $x = \frac{1}{2}(y - z)$, express z in terms of x and y.

12. If $a = \dfrac{b}{3} - c$, express c in terms of a and b.

13. If $\dfrac{p}{3} + \dfrac{q}{2} = r$, express p in terms of q and r.

14. If $\dfrac{ap}{4} + \dfrac{bp}{2} = c$, express p in terms of a, b and c.

15. If $r = \dfrac{1}{s} + t$, express s in terms of r and t.

16. If $p + \dfrac{t}{q} = r$, express q in terms of p, t and r.

17. If $\dfrac{a}{b} = \dfrac{b}{c} + d$, express c in terms of a, b and d.

18. If $\dfrac{1}{b} = \dfrac{3}{p} - \dfrac{4}{a}$, express p in terms of a and b.

19. If $\dfrac{1}{u} + \dfrac{1}{v} = \dfrac{1}{f}$, express f in terms of u and v.

20. If $p = \dfrac{q}{r-s}$, express s in terms of p, q and r.

21. If $c = \dfrac{2ab}{a+b}$, express b in terms of a and c.

Hence, or otherwise, find the value of b when $a = 4$ and $c = 6$.

22. **(i)** If $x = \dfrac{p+q}{p-q}$, express p in terms of q and x.

(ii) If $\dfrac{p}{p-x} = \dfrac{q}{q+x}$, express p in terms of q.

23. If $r = \dfrac{q^2 - pr}{q+p}$, express p in terms of q and r.

24. If $p^2 q = r$, express p in terms of q and r.

25. If $\frac{1}{2}at^2 = s$, express t in terms of a and s.

26. If $c = \dfrac{b}{a^2}$, express a in terms of b and c.

27. If $m^2 = \dfrac{1}{h^2} - 8p$, express h in terms of p and m.

Hence, determine the values of h when $m = 9$ and $p = -7$.

28. If $\sqrt{x} = y$, express x in terms of y.

29. If $\sqrt{pq} = r$, express p in terms of q and r.

30. If $a = \sqrt{\dfrac{p}{q}}$, express q in terms of a and p.

31. If $3\sqrt{xy} = z$, express y in terms of x and z.

32. If $\frac{1}{2}\sqrt{ut} = s$, express u in terms of t and s.

33. If $\sqrt{2x - 3} = y$, express x in terms of y.

34. If $\sqrt{pq - r} = s$, express p in terms of q, r and s.

35. If $t = k\sqrt{\dfrac{l}{g}}$, express l in terms of t, k and g.

36. If $t = \sqrt{\dfrac{x}{y - 2}}$, express y in terms of t and x.
Hence, determine the value of y if $x = 25$ and $t = 5$.

37. If $\dfrac{p}{2} = \sqrt{\dfrac{1}{x^2 - 4}}$, express x^2 in terms of p.

If $p = 2$ and $x = \sqrt{k}$, determine the value of k.

38. $y = ax - 2a^2, \quad x = 2 + 3a$
    (i) express y in terms of a **(ii)** evaluate y when $a = -2$

39. $y = ax + a^3, \quad x = 3 - 2a^2$
    (i) express y in terms of a **(ii)** evaluate y when $a = 1$

40. $z + 3 = 2x, \quad y = 2z - 3(x - 2)$
    (i) express z in terms of x **(ii)** express y in terms of x

41. If $\frac{1}{3}(a - 2b) = \frac{1}{4}$, express a in terms of b.
If $z + 3a = 2b$ and $w - 2a = 4b$, show that $2z + w = -3$.

42. **(i)** If $q^2 x = p + 2q^2$, express x in terms of p and q.

    (ii) If $y = q(x - 4)$, show that $y = \dfrac{p - 2q^2}{q}$.
Hence, evaluate y when $p = 30$ and $q = 3$.

43. If $px - b = a - qx$, express x in terms of a, b, p and q.

If $\sqrt{2p} = 4a$ and $q = -8b^2$, show that $8x = \dfrac{1}{a - b}$.

UNDETERMINED COEFFICIENTS

Undetermined coefficients

When two expressions in x (or any other variable) are equal to one another for all values of x, we can equate the coefficients of the same powers of x in the two expressions. This is known as the '**principle of undetermined coefficient**'.

Method:

1. Remove all fractions and brackets.
2. Form equations by equating coefficients of like terms.
3. Solve the equations to find the coefficients.

Example ▼

(i) If $x^2 - 2x + q = (x - p)^2 + 5$ for all values of x, find the value of p and the value of q.

(ii) $2(x + 4) = a(x + 1) + b(x - 1)$ for all values of x. Write two equations in a and b. Hence, or otherwise, calculate the value of a and the value of b.

Solution:

(i) $x^2 - 2x + q = (x - p)^2 + 5$

$x^2 - 2x + q = x^2 - 2px + p^2 + 5$ (remove brackets)

$x^2 - 2x + q = x^2 - 2px + (p^2 + 5)$ (group constants together)

① $\quad -2 = -2p \quad$ and $\quad$ ② $\quad q = p^2 + 5$ (equate coefficients of like terms)

① $\quad -2 = -2p \qquad\qquad$ ② $\quad q = p^2 + 5$

$\qquad 2 = 2p \qquad\qquad\qquad\qquad q = (1)^2 + 5$ (put in $p = 1$ into ②)

$\qquad 1 = p \qquad\qquad\qquad\qquad\quad q = 1 + 5$

$\qquad\qquad\qquad\qquad\qquad\qquad\qquad q = 6$

(ii) $2(x + 4) = a(x + 1) + b(x - 1)$

$2x + 8 = ax + a + bx - b$ (remove brackets)

$2x + 8 = (a + b)x + (a - b)$ (group like terms together)

① $\quad 2 = a + b \quad$ and $\quad$ ② $\quad 8 = a - b$ (equate coefficients of like terms)

We now solve the simultaneous equations ① and ②:

$$a + b = 2 \qquad ①$$
$$\underline{a - b = 8} \qquad ②$$
$$2a = 10$$
$$a = 5$$

$$a + b = 2 \qquad ①$$
$$5 + b = 2$$
$$b = 2 - 5$$
$$b = -3$$

Put $a = 5$ into ① or ②.

$\therefore a = 5$ and $b = -3$

Exercise 8.1 ▼

1. If $2ax + 3by = 6x + 15y$ for all values of x and y, find the value of a and b.
2. If $(x + 3)(x + 2) = x^2 + px + q$ for all values of x, find the value of p and q.
3. $a(x + 2) + b(x - 1) = 3(x + 1)$ for all values of x. Write two equations in a and b. Hence, or otherwise, find the value of a and the value of b.
4. $7x + 4 = a(x + 2) - b(x - 3)$ for all values of x. Write two equations in a and b. Hence, or otherwise, find the value of a and the value of b.
5. $a(2x + 1) + 3b(x - 2) = 3(x + 8)$ for all values of x. Write two equations in a and b. Hence, or otherwise, find the value of a and the value of b.
6. If $a(2x + 3y) + b(4x - y) = -2x + 11y$ for all values of x and y, find the value of a and the value of b.
7. (i) If $a(x^2 - 3x) + b(x^2 + x) = 5x^2 - 3x$ for all values of x, find the value of a and the value of b.
   (ii) If $p(x^2 - 2x + 1) + q(2x^2 - 6x + 4) = x^2 - 6x + 5$, for all values of x, find the value of p and the value of q.
8. If $x^2 - a^2 = (x - 2)(x + 2)$ for all values of x, find the values of a.
9. If $x^2 - 4x + q = (x - p)^2 + 3$ for all values of x, find the value of p and the value of q.
10. If $px(x + 2) + qx = 3x^2 + 8x$ for all values of x, find the value of p and q.
11. If $ax(x + 1) + bx + c = 2x^2 + 5x + 4$ for all values of x, find the value of a, the value of b and the value of c.
12. If $(x + 2)(2x^2 + kx + h) = 2x^3 - x^2 - 13x - 6$ for all values of x, find h and k.
13. If $\frac{1}{3}x + y - 4 = 0$, express x in terms of y.

    If $x = 4a + 3by$, find the value of a and the value of b.
14. If $x^2y + 2xy - 1 = 0$, express y in terms of x.

    Find the value of a for which $\dfrac{1}{y} = (x + a)^2 - a$, $\qquad a \in \mathbf{N}$.
15. $6xy - x^2y - 5 = 0$, express y in terms of x.

    Find the value of q for which $\dfrac{5}{y} = q^2 - (x - q)^2$.

STATISTICS

Averages

There are many types of averages. Three that we will meet on our course are:

1. The mean   **2. The mode**   **3. The median**

They are also known as measures of central tendency.

Mean

The **mean** is the proper name for what most people call the average.

> The mean of a set of values is the sum of all the values divided by the number of values.

That is,

$$\text{mean} = \frac{\text{sum of all the values}}{\text{number of values}}$$

The formula is often written as: $\bar{x} = \dfrac{\Sigma x}{n}$

$\bar{x}$, pronounced 'x bar' is the symbol for the mean.
Σx, pronounced 'sigma x' is the symbol for 'the sum of the values'.
n is the number of values.

Mode

> The **mode** is the value that occurs most often.

In other words, the mode is the value with the highest frequency, or the most popular value.

Median

When the values are arranged in ascending, or descending, order of size, then the median is the middle value. If the number of values is even, then the median is the average of the two middle values.

Note: Half the values lie below the median and half the values lie above the median.

Example ▼

Find **(i)** the mean **(ii)** the median **(iii)** the mode of the following array of numbers:
$$8, 9, 2, 6, 2, 7, 8, 10, 2$$

Solution:

(i) Mean $= \bar{x} = \dfrac{\sum x}{n} = \dfrac{8+9+2+6+2+7+8+10+2}{9} = \dfrac{54}{9} = 6$

(ii) Median: First write the numbers in ascending order.
2, 2, 2, 6, ⑦, 8, 8, 9, 10.
The middle number is 7, $\therefore$ the median is 7.

(iii) The number which occurs most often is 2, $\therefore$ the mode is 2.

Example ▼

Find the median of the following array of numbers: 12, 2, 8, 2, 10, 5.

Solution:

First write the numbers in ascending order: 2, 2, 5, 8, 10, 12
Since there is an even number of numbers we take the average of the two middle ones, 5 and 8.

$$\therefore \text{the median } = \frac{5+8}{2} = \frac{13}{2} = 6.5$$

Find **(i)** the mean **(ii)** the median **(iii)** the mode of each of the following arrays of numbers:

1. 3, 2, 7, 3, 5   **2.** 2, 3, 2, 5, 4, 2, 3   **3.** 12, 4, 5, 4, 2, 4, 8, 5, 10

4. 2, 8, 6, 8   **5.** 3, 7, 10, 5, 7, 4   **6.** 14, 1, 7, 8, 7, 10, 13, 12

7. 5, 0, 7, 8, 0   **8.** 6, 1, 0, 4, 0, 3, 2, 6, 0, 8   **9.** 2.3, 4.1, 5.4, 0.3, 5.4

10. $-2, 5, 0, 4, -1, -5, -1$ **11.** $1\frac{1}{2}, 2\frac{3}{4}, 5\frac{2}{3}, 1\frac{1}{2}, \frac{7}{12}$ **12.** $\frac{1}{3}, \frac{1}{2}, \frac{1}{3}, \frac{3}{4}, \frac{1}{3}, \frac{3}{4}$

13. The table below shows the percentages which a girl received in her summer exams:

Subject	Irish	English	Maths	French	History	Geography
Percentage	69	74	87	62	79	67

Calculate her mean percentage.

14. Two dice were thrown together six times and the upward-facing results are shown below:

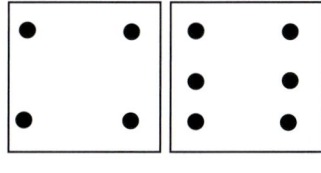 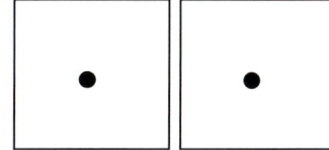 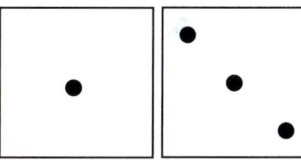

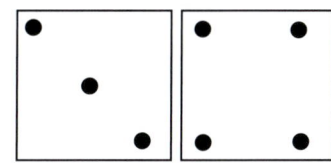 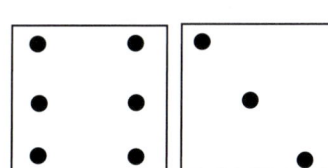 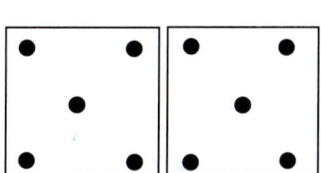

A score is obtained by adding the two values on the dice each time.

Find   **(i)** the mean   **(ii)** the median   **(iii)** the mode of these scores.

15. Consider the array of numbers 8, 5, 7, 2, 5, 8, 9, 2, 8.

If a = the mean, b = the median and c = the mode,

calculate the value of $\dfrac{a+b+c}{3}$.

16. Calculate the mean, in terms of x, of each of the following:

   (i) $x, 2x, 3x, 4x, 5x$ **(ii)** $x+3, 2x-5, 3x+1, 2x+1$

   (iii) $4x+1, 2x-3, 6x+5$ **(iv)** $4x+6, x-3, 7x+12, 3-x, 4x+7$

17. The median of 10, x, 3, 5, 9, 4 is 6. Calculate x.

Given the mean 1

Often we are given the mean and we need to find one of the values. Essentially, we are given an equation in disguise and by solving this equation we can calculate the missing value.

Example ▼

The mean of the five numbers 7, x, 8, $2x$ and 2 is 7. Calculate the value of x.

Solution:

Method 1:

Equation given in disguise: mean = 7

$$\therefore \frac{7 + x + 8 + 2x + 2}{5} = 7$$

$$\frac{3x + 17}{5} = 7$$

$$3x + 17 = 35$$

$$3x = 18$$

$$x = 6$$

Method 2:

The mean of the five numbers is 7.

$\therefore$ the numbers must add up to 35

$$\left(\text{because } 5 \times 7 = 35 \quad \text{or} \quad \frac{35}{5} = 7 \right)$$

$$\therefore 7 + x + 8 + 2x + 2 = 35$$

$$3x + 17 = 35$$

$$3x = 18$$

$$x = 6$$

Example ▼

The mean of ten numbers is 6. When four of these numbers are removed the mean is increased by 1. Find the sum of the four numbers that have been removed.

Solution:

Old situation (ten numbers):

The mean of the 10 numbers is 6.

$\therefore$ the numbers must add up to 60

$$\left(\text{because } 10 \times 6 = 60 \quad \text{or} \quad \frac{60}{10} = 6 \right)$$

New situation (six numbers):

The mean of the remaining 6 numbers is 7.

$\therefore$ the numbers must add up to 42

$$\left(\text{because } 6 \times 7 = 42 \quad \text{or} \quad \frac{42}{6} = 7 \right)$$

The sum of the four numbers removed = 60 − 42 = 18

1. The mean of 8 numbers is 7. Find the sum of the numbers.
2. The mean of 9 numbers is 8. Find the sum of the numbers.
3. The mean of the three numbers 7, 9 and x is 10. Calculate the value of x.
4. The mean of the four numbers 5, x, 7 and 10 is 6. Calculate the value of x.
5. The mean of the five numbers $2x$, 5, x, 7 and 10 is 8. Calculate the value of x.
6. The mean of the six numbers 7, $2x + 1$, $3x$, 8, 4 and 2 is 7. Calculate the value of x.
7. The mean of the six numbers 3, $6 + x$, 11, $5x + 7$, -1 and 4 is 8.
   Calculate the value of x.
8. The mean of the five numbers $2x + 2$, 8, $3x + 1$, 11 and $x - 2$ is 10.
   Calculate the value of x.
9. The mean of four numbers is 5. When another number $3x$ is added on, the mean is doubled. Calculate the value of x.
10. The mean of the five numbers 2, x, 3, 4, 7 is 4.4. Calculate the value of x.
11. The mean of the six numbers 2, x, 2, 4, 4, 10 is 4. Calculate the value of x.
    Hence, write down the value of **(i)** the median **(ii)** the mode.
12. The mean of eight numbers is 9. When one of the numbers is removed the mean is increased by 1. Find the number that was removed.
13. The mean of seven numbers is 8. When one of the numbers is removed the mean is decreased by 1. Find the number that was removed.
14. The mean of six numbers is 15. When one extra number is added the mean is decreased by 2. Find the number that was added.
15. The mean of 10 numbers is 12. When three of these numbers are removed the mean is increased by 4. Find the sum of the three numbers that have been removed.
16. The mean of seven numbers is 8. The mean of four of these numbers is 5.
    What is the mean of the remaining three numbers?
17. The mean of fifteen numbers is 4. The mean of ten of these numbers is 2.
    What is the mean of the remaining five numbers?
18. Four people have a meal in a restaurant. The average cost of the meal per person is €37.50. What is the total bill for the four people if a 12% service charge is added?
19. A basketball player had an average of eight points per game in her last seven games. How many points must she score in her next game if she is to increase her average to nine points per game?
20. A set of four odd numbers have a mode 5, a median of 6 and a mean of $6\frac{1}{2}$.
    What are these four numbers?
21. The mean of p, q and r is 4. Find the mean of $p + 2$, $q + 2$ and $r + 2$.

Frequency distribution

> If the values in a distribution are arranged in ascending, or descending order, showing their corresponding frequencies, the distribution is called a **frequency distribution**.

Note: If the values and frequencies are given in a table, it is called a **frequency distribution table**.

Mean, median and mode of a frequency distribution

Mean

To find the mean of a frequency distribution, do the following:

> 1. Multiply each value by its corresponding frequency.
> 2. Sum all these products.
> 3. Divide this sum by the total number of frequencies.

That is:

$$\bar{x} = \frac{\Sigma fx}{\Sigma f}$$

(i) x is the value of each measurement

(ii) f is the frequency of each measurement

(iii) Σfx is the sum of all the fx values

(iv) Σf is the sum of all the frequencies.

Median

As the values are arranged in order of size, the median can be read directly from a frequency distribution table by looking for the middle value or the average of the two middle values if there is an even number of values.

Mode

The mode can be read directly from the table. The mode is the value with the highest frequency (most common value).

Note: Remember that the mode is the value, **not** the frequency.

A test consisted of six questions. 1 mark was awarded per question for a correct solution and no marks for an incorrect solution. The following frequency distribution table shows how a class of students scored in the test:

Mark	0	1	2	3	4	5	6
Number of students	1	7	6	5	2	6	3

Calculate **(i)** the mean **(ii)** the median and **(iii)** the modal mark.

Solution:

(i) Mean

$$\text{Mean} = \bar{x} = \frac{\sum fx}{\sum f} = \frac{1(0) + 7(1) + 6(2) + 5(3) + 2(4) + 6(5) + 3(6)}{1 + 7 + 6 + 5 + 2 + 6 + 3}$$

$$= \frac{0 + 7 + 12 + 15 + 8 + 30 + 18}{30} = \frac{90}{30} = 3$$

$$\therefore \text{ the mean} = 3 \text{ marks.}$$

(ii) Median

There are 30 values altogether. Therefore, the median is the average of the 15th and 16th mark. The first mark is 0, the next 7 are each 1 mark, the next 6 are 2 marks each. The next 5 are 3 marks each and these include 15th and 16th mark.

$$\therefore \text{ the median} = \frac{3 + 3}{2} = 3 \text{ marks.}$$

(iii) Mode

From the table it is clear that there are more 1's than any other value.

$$\therefore \text{ the mode} = 1 \text{ mark.}$$

Find **(i)** the mean **(ii)** the median **(iii)** the mode of each of the following frequency distributions:

1.

Number	1	2	3	4
Frequency	8	6	4	2

2.

Number	3	4	5	6	7
Frequency	8	4	3	6	7

3.

Number	0	2	4	6
Frequency	7	2	8	5

4.

Number	10	15	20	25	30
Frequency	2	6	3	3	11

5.

Number	0	1	2	3	4	5	6	7
Frequency	9	4	8	14	15	6	0	4

6.

Number	1	2	3	4	5	6	7	8	9	10
Frequency	1	3	6	8	3	7	4	5	2	1

7. The table below shows the results of a survey which recorded the number of absences of 30 students during a certain week in a school:

Number of days missed	0	1	2	3	4	5
Number of students	6	10	4	3	2	5

   (i) Calculate the mean number of days missed.
   (ii) Write down the modal number of days missed.
   (iii) What was **(a)** the greatest **(b)** the least number of pupils that could have been present on any one of the days?
   (iv) Represent the data with a pie chart.

8. The frequency distribution table below shows the number of goals scored by 50 teams in 25 matches, each team playing only once:

Number of goals scored	0	1	2	3	4	5	6
Number of teams	1	8	12	11	9	5	4

   (i) Write down the modal number of goals scored per team.
   (ii) Calculate the mean number of goals scored **(a)** per team **(b)** per match.
   (iii) Find the greatest number of matches that could have ended in a draw.

9. A test, consisting of 8 questions, was given to 40 pupils. One mark was awarded per question for a correct solution and no marks for an incorrect solution.
The results were as follows:

$$3, 2, 5, 6, 1, 3, 5, 7, 1, 4$$
$$2, 4, 3, 7, 4, 8, 6, 3, 2, 3$$
$$6, 5, 6, 1, 5, 5, 2, 4, 5, 4$$
$$5, 4, 2, 3, 4, 3, 4, 5, 3, 5$$

   (i)   Represent the information on a frequency distribution table.
   (ii) Calculate the mean mark per pupil.
   (iii) Calculate the median mark.
   (iv) If the pass mark was 4, what percentage of the pupils failed the test?
   (v)   10 other pupils did the same test. The mean mark then for the 50 pupils was unchanged. Calculate the sum of the marks for the 50 pupils.
   (vi) A different 50 pupils did the same test and the mean for the 100 pupils was increased by one mark. Calculate the mean mark for the second set of 50 pupils.

10. A die was thrown 40 times and the frequency of each score was as follows:

Score	1	2	3	4	5	6
Frequency	7	7	8	9	5	4

   (i)   Write down the modal score.
   (ii) Find the median score.
   (iii) Calculate the mean of these scores.
   The die was then thrown another 10 times. The mean of these 10 throws was 3.5.
   (iv) Calculate the overall mean for all 50 throws.

Grouped frequency distribution

Sometimes the range of the values is very wide and it is not suitable to show all the values individually. When this happens we arrange the values into suitable groups called **class intervals**, such as 0 – 10, 10 – 20 etc. When the information is arranged in class intervals it is not possible to calculate the exact value of the mean. However, it is possible to estimate it by using the **mid-interval value** of each class interval. The easiest way to find the mid-interval value is to add the two extreme values and divide by 2.

For example, in the class interval 30 – 50, add 30 and 50 and divide by 2.

i.e., $\dfrac{30+50}{2} = \dfrac{80}{2} = 40$ $\therefore$ 40 is the mid-interval value.

Otherwise, the procedure for estimating the mean is the same as the previous section.

Example ▼

20 pupils were given a problem to solve. The following grouped frequency distribution table gives the number of pupils who solved the problem in the given time interval.

Time (minutes)	0 – 4	4 – 12	12 – 24	24 – 40
Frequency	3	8	7	2

(i) By taking the data at mid-interval values, calculate the mean number of minutes taken per pupil to solve the problem.

(ii) In which class interval does the median lie?

Solution:

(i) The table can be re-written using the mid-interval values.

Time (minutes)	2	8	18	32
Frequency	3	8	7	2

$$\text{Mean} = \bar{x} = \frac{\sum fx}{\sum f} = \frac{3(2) + 8(8) + 7(18) + 2(32)}{3 + 8 + 7 + 2}$$

$$= \frac{6 + 64 + 126 + 64}{20} = \frac{260}{20} = 13 \text{ minutes}$$

(ii) There are 20 pupils altogether. The two middle values are the 10th and 11th. We require the class interval in which the 10th and 11th values lie.

By looking at the grouped frequency distribution table the 10th and 11th values lie in the 4 – 12 minutes class interval.

$\therefore$ the median lies in the 4 – 12 minutes class interval.

By taking the data at mid-interval values, calculate the mean of each of the following grouped frequency distributions. In each case state in which class interval the median lies:

1.

Number	0 – 2	2 – 6	6 – 12
Frequency	5	4	6

2.

Number	0 – 10	10 – 30	30 – 60
Frequency	10	5	10

3.

Number	1 – 3	3 – 5	5 – 7	7 – 9
Frequency	4	3	0	2

4.

Number	0 – 20	20 – 40	40 – 60	60 – 80
Frequency	5	6	9	10

5.

Number	0 – 30	30 – 60	60 – 100	100 – 150	150 – 250
Frequency	12	13	5	7	3

6.

Number	0 – 5	5 – 10	10 – 20	20 – 35	35 – 40	40 – 50
Frequency	3	5	6	9	5	2

7. The frequency distribution below shows the number of hours per week spent watching television by 37 people.

No. of hours	0 – 2	2 – 6	6 – 12	12 – 20	20 – 30
No. of people	5	9	12	6	5

Note: 0 – 2 means 0 is included but 2 is not and so on.

(i) Estimate the mean number of hours spent per week watching television.
(ii) In which class interval does the median lie?

8. The table shows the distribution of ages of a group of 100 people.

Age (in years)	0 – 10	10 – 20	20 – 30	30 – 50	50 – 80
Number of people	10	19	25	30	16

Note: 10 – 20 means that 10 is included but 20 is not and so on.

Taking 5, 15, etc. as mid-interval values, estimate the mean age of the people in the group.

9. The following table shows the sizes, in hectares, of 20 farms in a particular area:

Number of hectares	15 – 45	45 – 75	75 – 105	105 – 195
Number of farms	1	4	8	7

By taking the data at mid-interval values, calculate the mean number of hectares per farm.

10. A department store carried out a survey on the length of time a number of people spent shopping in their store. The table shows the length of time shopping in 10 minute intervals.

Time interval in minutes	0 – 10	10 – 20	20 – 30	30 – 40	40 – 50	50 – 60	60 – 70
Number of shoppers	30	x	24	30	40	20	10

Note: 0 – 10 means 0 or more but less than 10, etc.

(i) If the average number of shoppers for the first, second and third interval was 30, calculate the value of x.

(ii) Using mid-interval values, calculate the average shopping time in the store.

(iii) What is the least number of shoppers who completed their shopping within 35 minutes?

Given the mean 2

Often we are given the mean of a frequency distribution and we need to find one of the values or frequencies. Essentially, we are given an equation in disguise and by solving this equation we can calculate the missing value or frequency.

The frequency distribution below shows the frequency of 0, 1, 2 or 3 goals scored in a number of football matches:

Number of goals scored	0	1	2	3
Number of matches	1	x	1	5

If the mean number of goals scored per match is 2, find the value of x.

Solution:

Equation given in disguise: Mean = 2

$$\therefore \quad \frac{1(0) + x(1) + 1(2) + 5(3)}{1 + x + 1 + 5} = 2$$

$$\frac{0 + x + 2 + 15}{x + 7} = 2$$

$$\frac{x + 17}{x + 7} = 2$$

$$x + 17 = 2(x + 7) \qquad \text{[Multiply both sides by } (x + 7)\text{]}$$

$$x + 17 = 2x + 14$$

$$x - 2x = 14 - 17$$

$$-x = -3$$

$$x = 3$$

Exercise 9.5 ▼

1. In the following frequency distribution the mean is 8. Find the value of x.

Number	2	6	9	x	13
Frequency	3	4	6	5	2

2. In the following frequency distribution the mean is 6. Find the value of x.

Number	4	5	6	7	8
Frequency	3	6	15	2	x

3. In the following frequency distribution the mean is 5. Find the value of x.

Number	1	5	6	8	11
Frequency	7	4	7	3	x

4. In the following frequency distribution the mean is 3. Find the value of x.

Number	1	2	3	4	5	6
Frequency	3	x	8	4	2	1

5. In the following frequency distribution the mean is 8. Find the value of x.

Number	2	6	9	10	13
Frequency	x	4	$2x$	5	2

6. The frequency distribution below shows the number of goals in a number of football matches:

Number of goals scored	0	1	2	3	4	5
Number of matches	1	4	3	8	4	x

If the mean number of goals scored per match is 3, find the value of x.

7. The frequency distribution below shows the contributions, in euros, of a number of people to a charity:

Amount in €	1	2	3	4	5
Number of people	$x+1$	x	7	1	5

If the mean contribution was €3, calculate the value of x.

8. The following frequency table shows the marks awarded to a class of students in a test:

Marks	1	2	3	4	5	6	7
No. of students	5	8	x	$x+2$	7	4	2

If the mean mark for the class was 3.6, find the value of x.

9. People attending a course were asked to choose one of the whole numbers from 1 to 12. The results were recorded as follows:

Number	1 − 3	4 − 6	7 − 9	10 − 12
No. of people	3	x	2	8

Using mid-interval values, 6.5 was calculated as the mean of the numbers chosen. Find the value of x.

10. The following grouped frequency distribution shows the sizes, in hectares, of a number of farms in a particular area:

Number of hectares	0 – 2	2 – 6	6 – 12	12 – 20	20 – 30
Number of farms	$m + 1$	4	2	m	1

Note: 0 – 2 means 0 is included but 2 is not, etc.
Using mid-interval values the mean size of a farm was calculated to be 8 hectares.
Find the value of m.

11. In the following frequency distribution the mean is 5.
Calculate the two possible values of p.

Number	1	5	$p - 1$	8	11
Frequency	p	4	p	3	2

Histogram

A histogram is often used to display information contained in a frequency distribution. It is similar to a bar chart with no gaps between the bars, and the two are often confused. The essential characteristic of a histogram is that the **area of each rectangle represents the frequency** and the sum of the areas of the rectangles is equal to the sum of the frequencies. The drawing of a histogram is straightforward. However, be careful when the class intervals are unequal.

Procedure for constructing a histogram

A histogram is constructed with the following steps:

1. Let the base of the rectangle which represents the class interval of smallest width have a length of 1 unit.
2. Express the bases of the other rectangles, depending on the width of the class intervals, in terms of this base (i.e. are they one and a half times the base? double it? treble it? etc.)
3. Divide each frequency by its corresponding base in Step 2 to find the height of each rectangle.

   That is: $\text{Height} = \dfrac{\text{Frequency}}{\text{Base}}$

4. With the values on the horizontal axis and the frequencies on the vertical axis, construct the rectangles beside each other.

When given a grouped frequency distribution and asked to represent the distribution with a histogram it is good practice to rewrite the table again with extra rows to show the base and height of each rectangle.

The following frequency distribution gives the marks obtained, out of 120, by students in an examination.

Marks	0 – 30	30 – 40	40 – 60	60 – 100	100 – 120
Number of students	21	8	12	20	8

Note: 0 – 30 means 0 is included but 30 is not, etc.
Represent the data with a histogram.

Solution:

The smallest interval is the 30 – 40, i.e. it has a range of 10 marks. The rectangle that represents this interval will have a base of 1. The bases of the other rectangles are expressed in terms of this.

The rectangle representing the 0 – 30 interval will have a base of 3 (range 30).
The rectangle representing the 40 – 60 interval will have a base of 2 (range 20).
The rectangle representing the 60 – 100 interval will have a base of 4 (range 40).
The rectangle representing the 100 – 120 interval will have a base of 2 (range 20).

New table:

Marks	0 – 30	30 – 40	40 – 60	60 – 100	100 – 120
No. of students	21	8	12	20	8
Base	3	1	2	4	2
Height	7	8	6	5	4

On the last row, the height is found by dividing the base into the number of students.

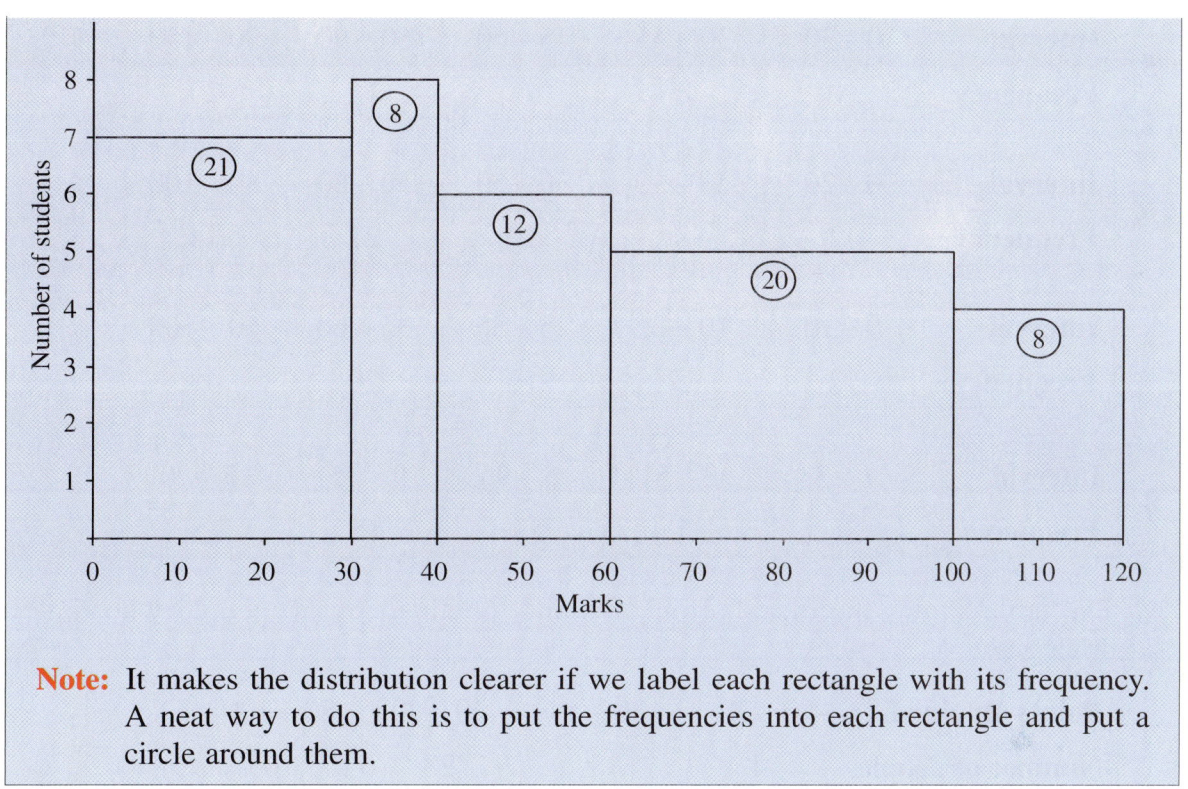

Note: It makes the distribution clearer if we label each rectangle with its frequency. A neat way to do this is to put the frequencies into each rectangle and put a circle around them.

Note: The horizontal axis is marked in units of the smallest class interval.

Exercise 9.6 ▼

Draw a histogram to represent each of the following grouped frequency distributions:

1.

Interval	0 – 20	20 – 50	50 – 60	60 – 80	80 – 120
Frequency	8	21	8	10	24

2.

Interval	0 – 4	4 – 12	12 – 16	16 – 28	28 – 32
Frequency	7	18	8	30	6

3.

Interval	0 – 10	10 – 30	30 – 60	60 – 100	100 – 150
Frequency	10	16	27	24	30

4.

Interval	0 – 2	2 – 10	10 – 14	14 – 16	16 – 20
Frequency	8	24	10	6	18

5.

Interval	0 – 30	30 – 45	45 – 60	60 – 90	90 – 150
Frequency	10	8	6	16	20

6.

Interval	0 – 20	20 – 30	30 – 50	50 – 80	80 – 100
Frequency	12	8	10	27	14

7.

Interval	0 – 10	10 – 25	25 – 35	35 – 60	60 – 100
Frequency	12	12	16	20	48

8.

Interval	1 – 3	3 – 5	5 – 9	9 – 15	15 – 20
Frequency	6	5	14	15	15

9. The table shows the distribution of points obtained by 50 people who took a driving test.

Points obtained	0 – 20	20 – 40	40 – 80	80 – 100
Number of people	4	8	28	10

(i) Draw a histogram to illustrate the data.
(ii) To pass the driving test a person must obtain 65 points or more.
What is the greatest possible number of people who passed the test?
(iii) By taking the data at the mid-interval values, estimate the mean number of points per person.

10. The distribution of the ages of people attending a meeting is shown in the following grouped frequency distribution table:

Age (years)	20 – 25	25 – 35	35 – 50	50 – 70
Frequency	7	14	33	16

(i) Represent the data with a histogram.
(ii) By taking the data at the mid-interval values, verify that the mean age is 42 years.
(iii) What is the greatest possible number of people who are below the mean age?

Given the histogram

Sometimes we are given the histogram already drawn and we need to calculate the frequencies represented by the rectangles. We are usually given the area of one of the rectangles (which represents the frequency) and its height (read directly from the diagram). From this we can work out the width of the base of the rectangle whose area we are given. We can then calculate the width of the bases of the other rectangles. The heights of the other rectangles can be read directly from the diagram.

> We then use the formula: Frequency = Area of rectangle = base × height

We use the following steps:

1. Divide the area of the rectangle whose area we are given by its height. This gives the base of the rectangle.

$$\text{Base} = \frac{\text{Area}}{\text{Height}}$$

2. Express the base of each of the other rectangles in terms of this base. (i.e. is it half this base, double it, treble it, etc.)
3. Multiply the given height of each rectangle by its base to find its area. The area of a rectangle is equal to the frequency it represents.

The histogram shows the distribution of the distances, in km, that some students have to travel to school:

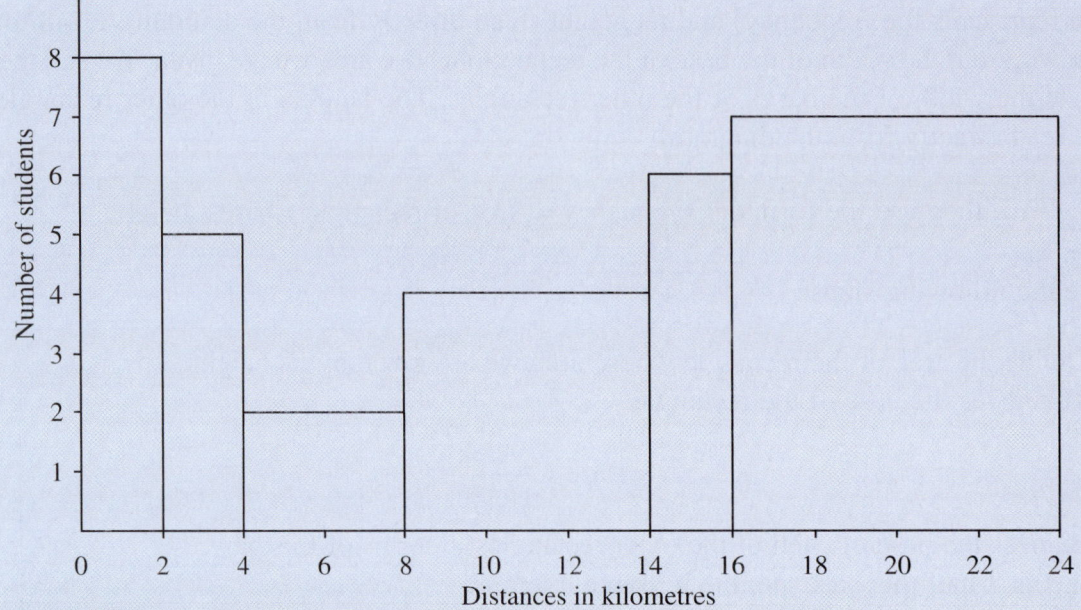

Distances in kilometres

Complete the corresponding frequency distribution table:

Distances (km)	0 – 2	2 – 4	4 – 8	8 – 14	14 – 16	16 – 24
No. of students				24		

Calculate the total number of students.

Solution:

1. Given: Area of the rectangle representing the distances between 8 and 14 km = 24

   The height of this rectangle = 4

   $$(\text{base}).(\text{height}) = \text{area}$$
   $$\Rightarrow \quad (\text{base})(4) = 24$$
   $$\Rightarrow \quad (\text{base}) = \frac{24}{4} = 6$$

   This rectangle uses three marked units on the horizontal axis.
   ∴ each marked unit on the horizontal axis has a measurement of 2 (i.e. 6 ÷ 3 = 2).

2. Thus, the base of the other rectangles can be worked out.

0 – 2 km: base = 2   2 – 4 km: base = 2   4 – 8 km: base = 4

14 – 16 km: base = 2   16 – 24 km: base = 8

3. Area of each rectangle = base × height = frequency

0 – 2 km: Area = frequency = base × height = 2 × 8 = 16

2 – 4 km: Area = frequency = base × height = 2 × 5 = 10

4 – 8 km: Area = frequency = base × height = 4 × 2 = 8

14 – 16 km: Area = frequency = base × height = 2 × 6 = 12

16 – 24 km: Area = frequency = base × height = 8 × 7 = 56

We could also work out the frequencies from the given histogram.

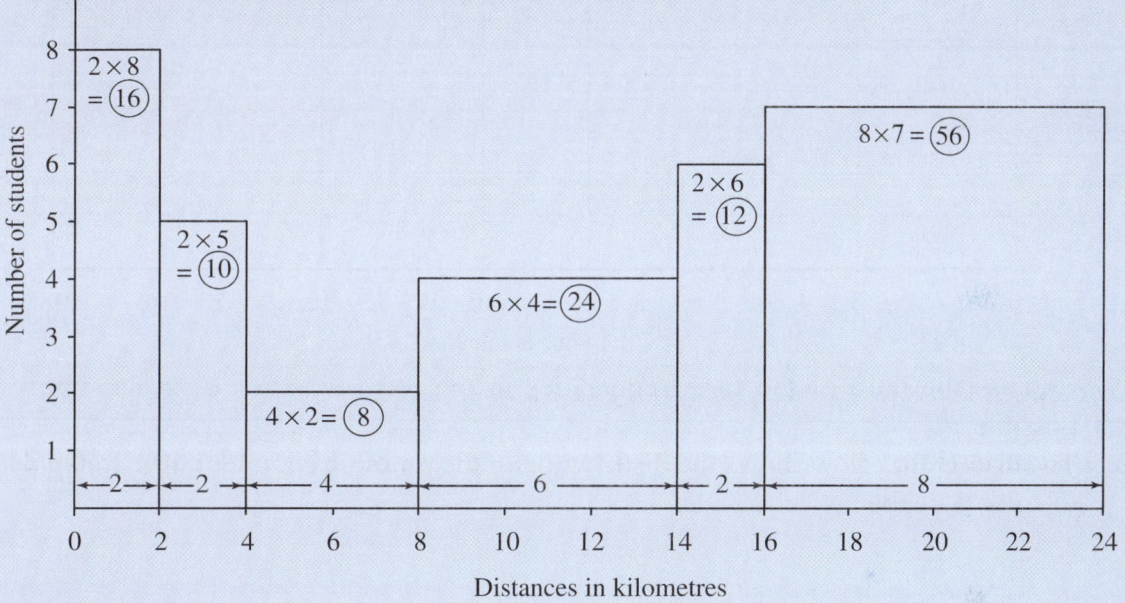

The areas (frequencies) are circled in each rectangle.

Completed table:

Distances (km)	0 – 2	2 – 4	4 – 8	8 – 14	14 – 16	16 – 24
No. of students	16	10	8	24	12	56

Total number of students = 16 + 10 + 8 + 24 + 12 + 56 = 126

1. The histogram below shows the distribution of the times taken, in minutes, for a group of people to complete a crossword:

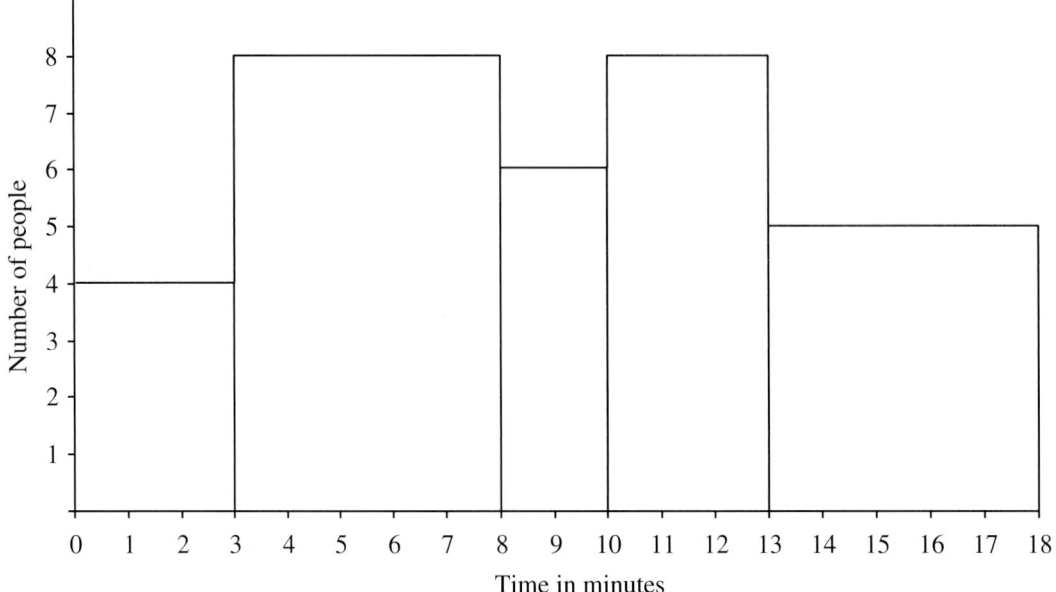

Express the ratio of the five frequencies in the form $a : b : c : d : e$, as simply as possible.

2. The histogram below shows the distribution of the times taken, in minutes, for students to solve a mathematical puzzle:

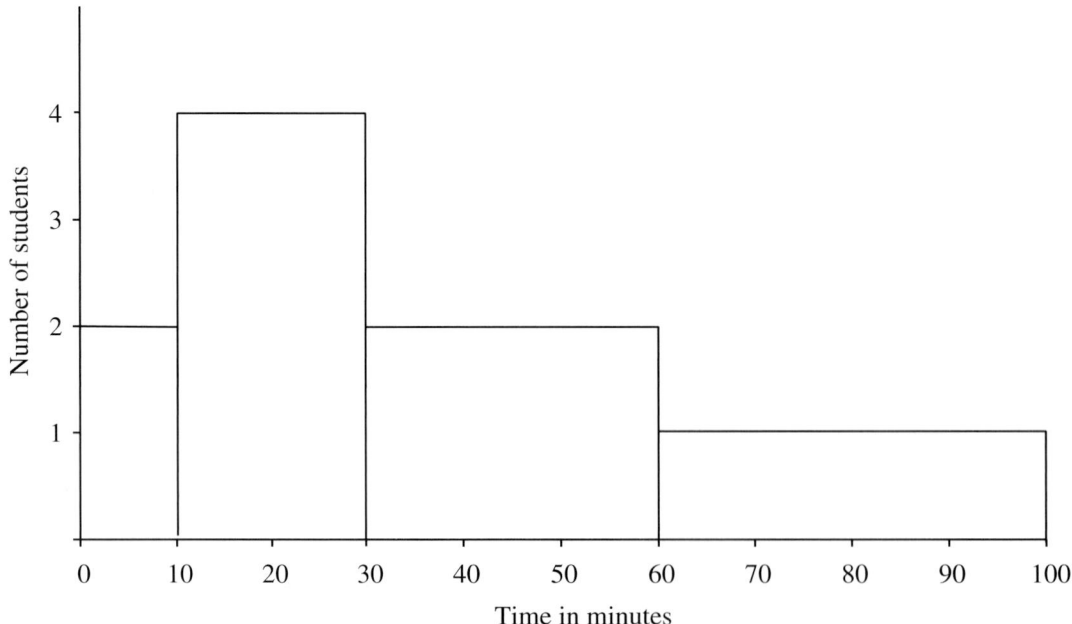

Express the ratio of the four frequencies in the form $a : b : c : d$, as simply as possible.

3. The distribution of the ages of people at a meeting is shown in the histogram below:

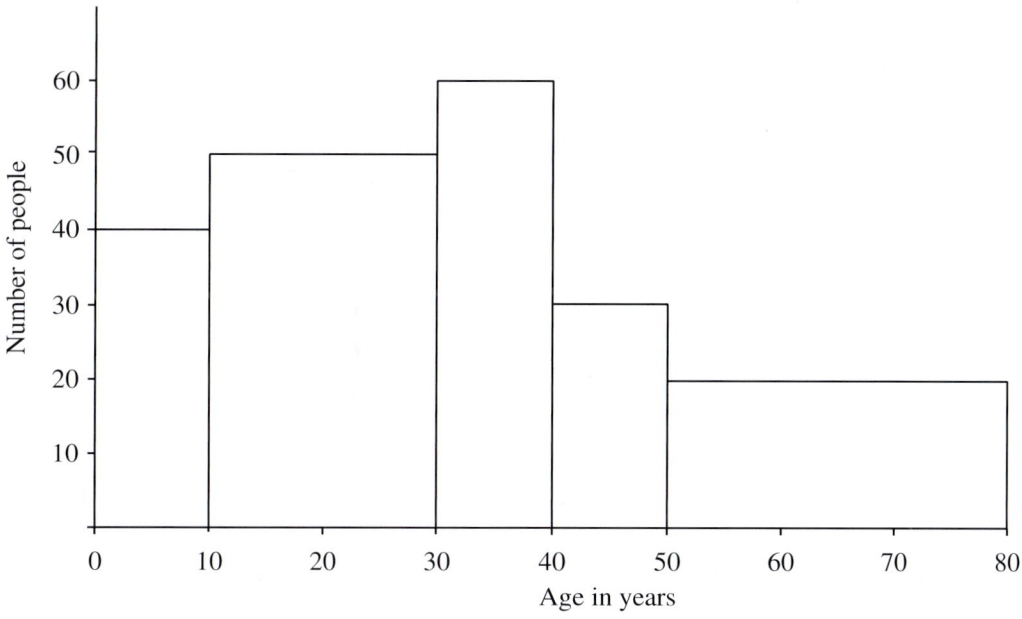

Complete the corresponding frequency distribution table:

Age (years)	0 – 10	10 – 30	30 – 40	40 – 50	50 – 80
No. of people			60		

How many people were at the meeting?

4. The distribution of the distances, in km, that a group of people have to travel to work each day is shown in the histogram below:

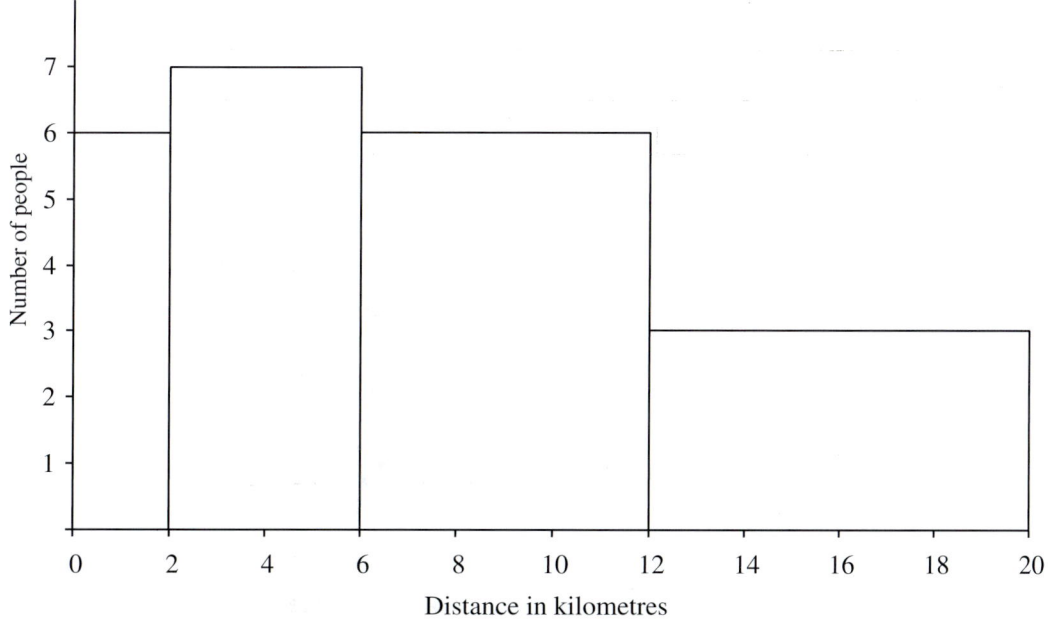

Complete the corresponding frequency distribution table:

Distances (km)	0 – 2	2 – 6	6 – 12	12 – 20
No. of people		28		

By taking the data at the mid-interval values, verify that the mean is 8.32 km.

5. The distribution of contributions, in euros, given to a charity by a number of people is shown in the histogram below:

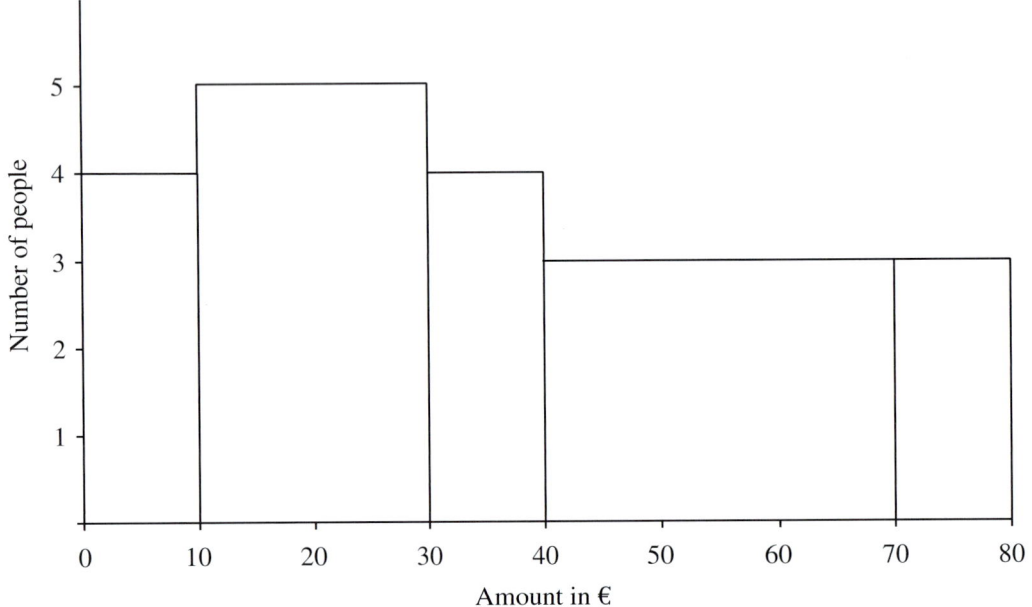

Complete the corresponding frequency distribution table:

Amount in €	0 – 10	10 – 30	30 – 40	40 – 70	70 – 80
Number of people		30			

By taking the data at the mid-interval values, calculate the mean contribution.

6. A random selection of claims, in €1000's, made against an insurance company for a certain year is shown in the histogram below:

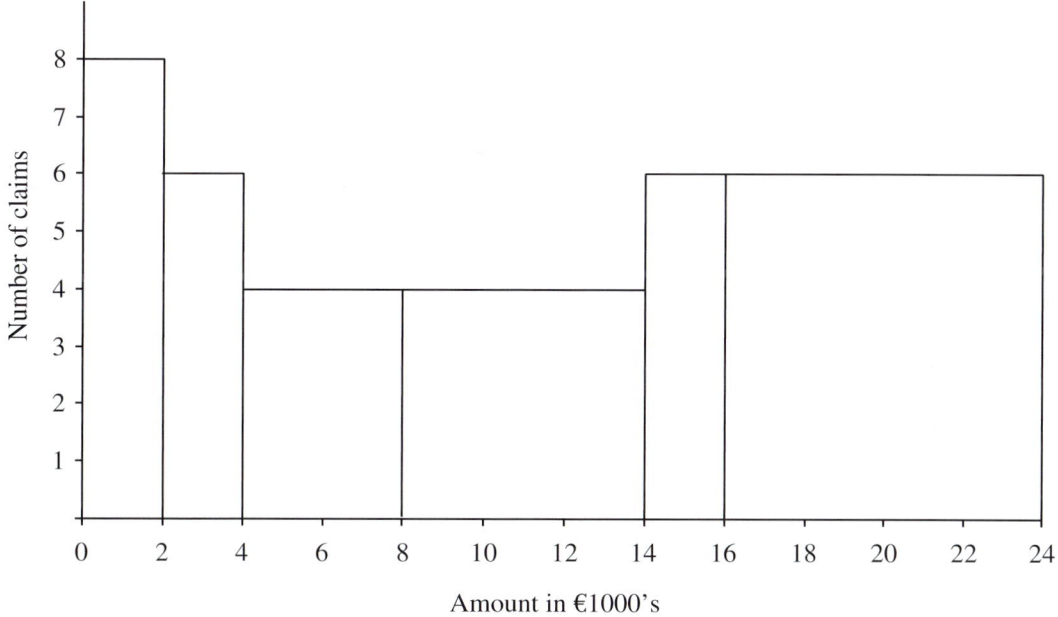

Complete the corresponding frequency distribution table:

Amount in (€1000's)	0 – 2	2 – 4	4 – 8	8 – 14	14 – 16	16 – 20
Number of claims					24	

(i) Calculate the number of claims in this random sample.
(ii) By taking the data at the mid-interval values, calculate the mean claim against the insurance company, from this sample.

Cumulative frequency

In a cumulative frequency the frequencies are accumulated. Each accumulated frequency is the combined total of all the previous frequencies up to that particular value. If we fill in the accumulated frequencies in tabular form we have what is called a **cumulative frequency table**. The graph of a cumulative frequency is called a **cumulative frequency curve** or **ogive**. It has a distinctively lopsided S-shape.

To draw a cumulative frequency curve do the following:

1. Construct a cumulative frequency table (if not given).

2. Put the values on the horizontal axis and cumulative frequency on the vertical axis.

3. Plot the points (value, cumulative frequency).

4. Join the points with a smooth curve.

Note: If the data is given as a grouped frequency distribution always make sure that in step 3 the **upper class limits** (not the mid-interval value or lower class limit) are plotted against the cumulative frequencies.

Median and interquartile range

How to calculate the median and the interquartile range from a cumulative frequency curve is shown below:

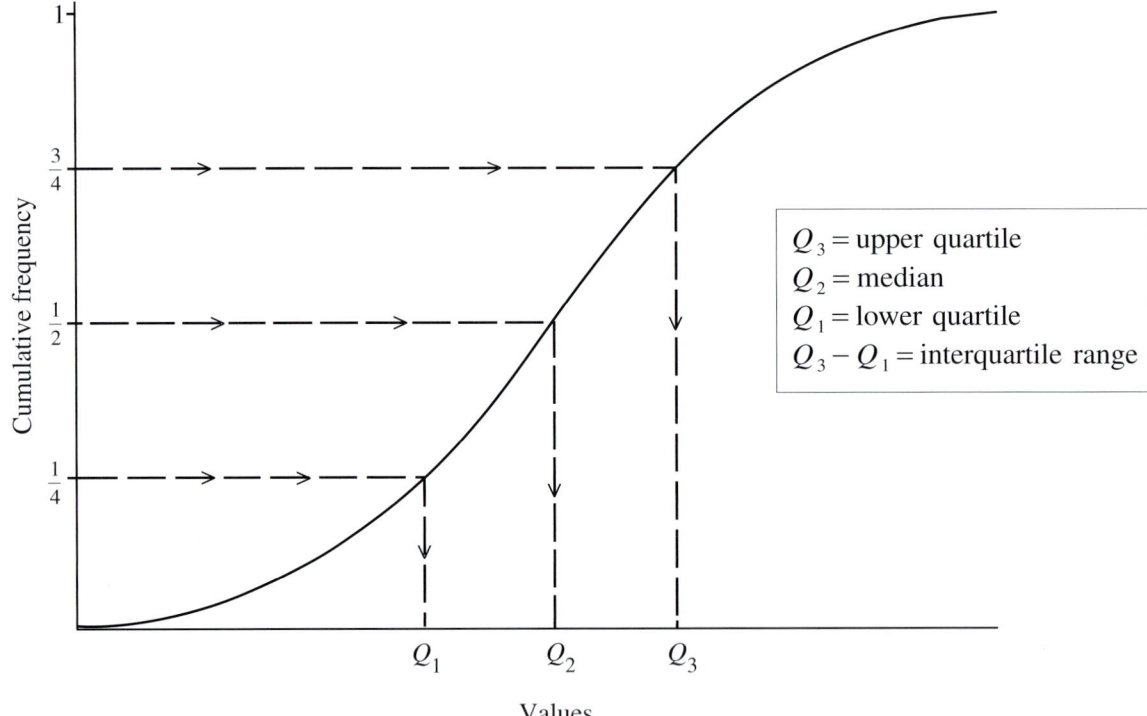

$Q_3 = $ upper quartile
$Q_2 = $ median
$Q_1 = $ lower quartile
$Q_3 - Q_1 = $ interquartile range

Note: Readings from a cumulative frequency curve are only estimates.
The interquartile range is a single number.

80 students took an exam and their marks are shown in the table:

Marks	30 – 40	40 – 50	50 – 60	60 – 70	70 – 80	80 – 90	90 – 100
Number of students	2	5	10	20	27	13	3

Note: 30 – 40 means 30 is included and 40 is not, etc.

(i) Construct a cumulative frequency table.
(ii) Draw a cumulative frequency curve (ogive).
    Use the curve to estimate:
(iii) the median
(iv) the upper quartile
(v) the lower quartile
(vi) the interquartile range.

Solution:

(i) Cumulative frequency table:

Marks	< 30	< 40	< 50	< 60	< 70	< 80	< 90	< 100
Number of students	0	2	7	17	37	64	77	80

(ii) Cumulative frequency curve:
    Plot the points, (30, 0), (40, 2), (50, 7), (60, 17), (70, 37), (80, 64), (90, 77), (100, 80) and join them with a smooth curve.

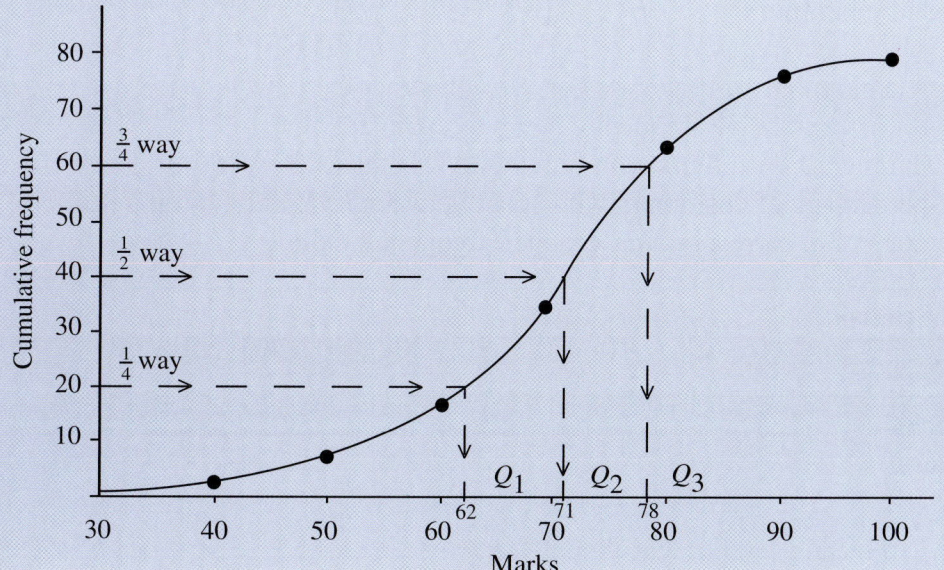

(iii) Median:
   The middle value on the cumulative frequency axis is 40.
   Draw a horizontal line from 40 to meet the curve and then straight down.
   The median $= Q_2 = 71$.

(iv) Upper quartile:
   The three-quarter way value on the cumulative frequency axis is 60.
   Draw a horizontal line from 60 to meet the curve and then straight down.
   The upper quartile $= Q_3 = 78$.

(v) Lower quartile:
   The quarter way value on the cumulative frequency axis is 20.
   Draw a horizontal line from 20 to meet the curve and then straight down.
   The lower quartile $= Q_1 = 62$.

(vi) Interquartile range:
   The interquartile range $= Q_3 - Q_1 = 78 - 62 = 16$.

Using cumulative frequency curves

A cumulative frequency curve can be used to estimate the number of values that lie **below**, or **above**, a particular value or to estimate the number of values that lie **between** two values.

Example ▼

A garage owner recorded the amount of money spent by customers on petrol on a certain day in the following cumulative frequency table:

Value of petrol sales, €s	< 10	< 20	< 30	< 40	< 60
Number of customers	6	18	47	93	120

(i)   Draw a cumulative frequency curve to illustrate the data.
      Use your cumulative frequency curve to estimate:
(ii) the number of customers who purchased less than €26 worth of petrol.
(iii) the percentage of customers who spent between €34 and €46 on petrol.
(iv) Complete the corresponding grouped frequency table:

Value of petrol sales, €s	0 – 10	10 – 20	20 – 30	30 – 40	40 – 60
Number of customers					

Note: 0 – 10 means $\geqslant 0$ but less than 10, etc.

Solution:

(i) Plot the points (0, 0), (10, 6), (20, 18), (30, 47), (40, 93), (60, 120) and join them with a smooth curve.

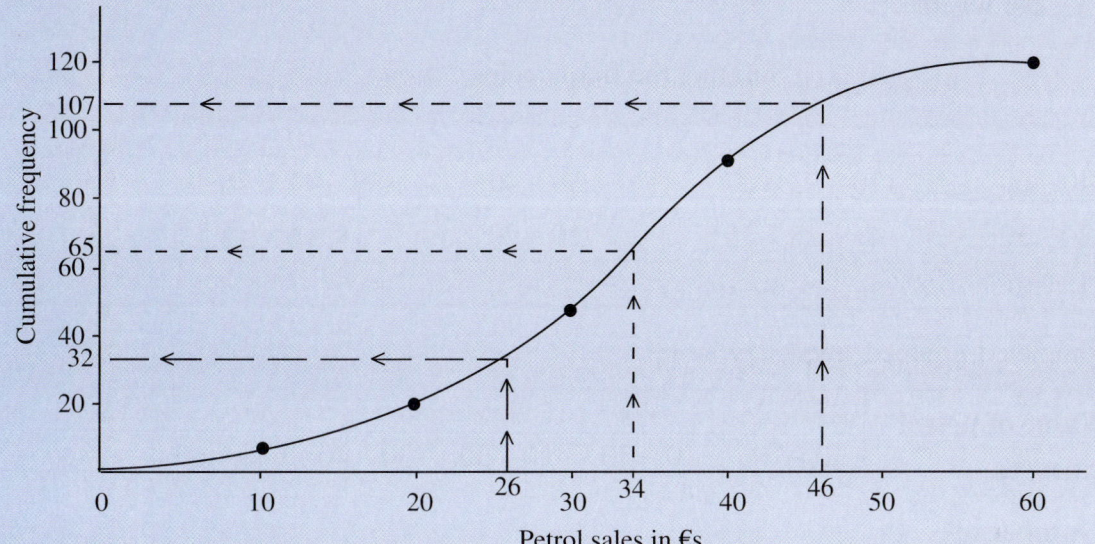

Note: (0, 0) is plotted even though this is not a value in the cumulative frequency table.

(ii) **Number of customers who purchased less than €26 worth of petrol.**
From 26 on the horizontal axis draw a vertical line to meet the curve and then straight across to the vertical axis.
This line meets the vertical axis at 32.
Thus we estimate that 32 people purchased less than €26 worth of petrol.

(iii) **The percentage of customers who spent between €34 and €46 on petrol.**
First work out the numbers.
From 34 and 46 on the horizontal axis draw vertical lines to meet the curve and then straight across to the vertical axis.
These lines meet the vertical axis at 65 and 107.
107 − 65 = 42

42 as a percentage of $120 = \dfrac{42}{120} \times \dfrac{100}{1}\% = 35\%$

Thus we estimate that 35% of the customers spent between €34 and €46 on petrol.

(iv) Corresponding grouped frequency table

When the cumulative frequency table was constructed the frequencies were added. Therefore, to construct a corresponding grouped frequency table we simply do the reverse:

Subtract the frequencies

40 – 60	120 – 93 = 27
20 – 30	47 – 18 = 29
0 – 10	= 6 (remains the same)

30 – 40	93 – 47 = 46
10 – 20	18 – 6 = 12

Completed grouped frequency table:

Value of petrol sales, €s	0 – 10	10 – 20	20 – 30	30 – 40	40 – 60
Number of customers	6	12	29	46	27

Exercise 9.8 ▼

In the following cumulative frequency curves (ogives), estimate:
(i) the median **(ii)** the upper quartile **(iii)** the lower quartile **(iv)** the interquartile range.

1.

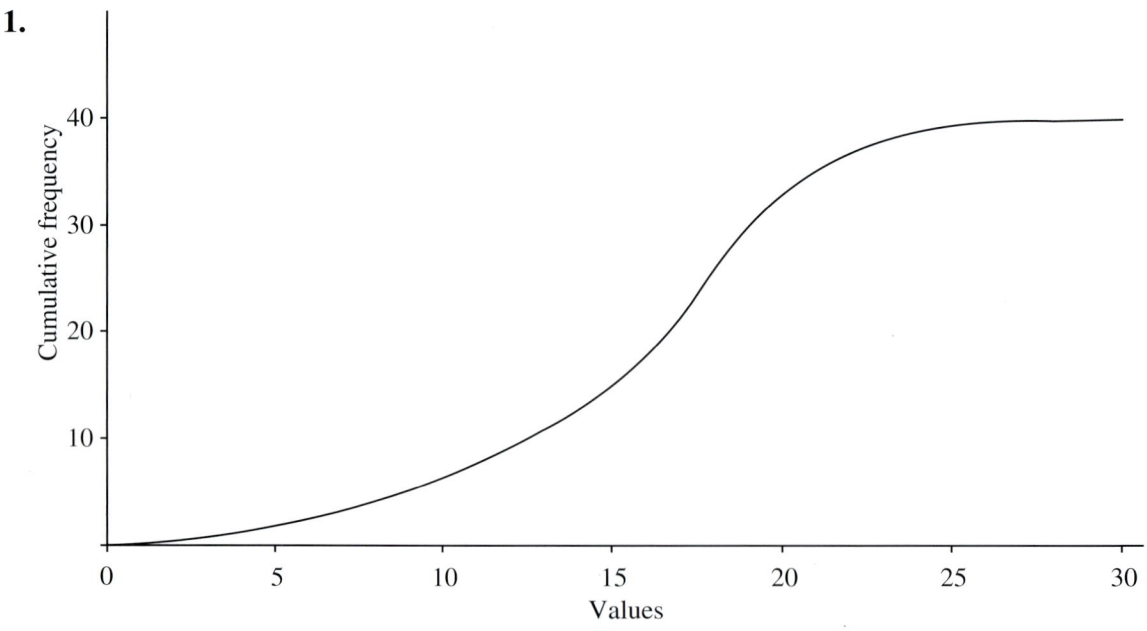

2.

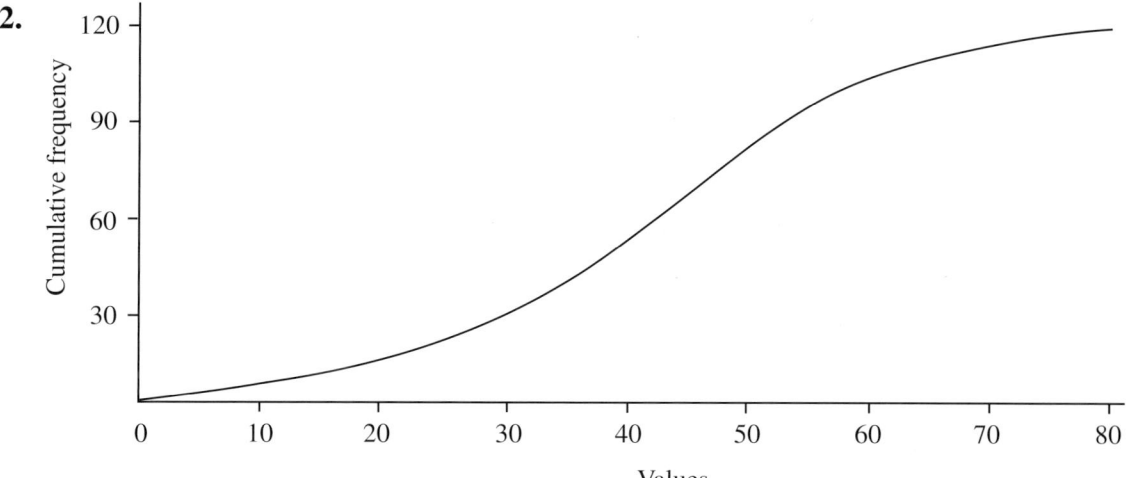

3.

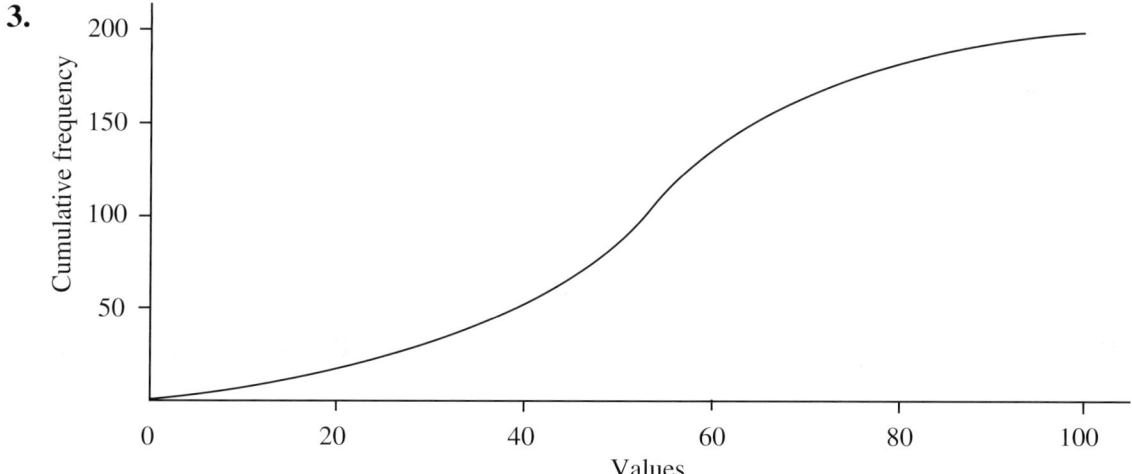

4.

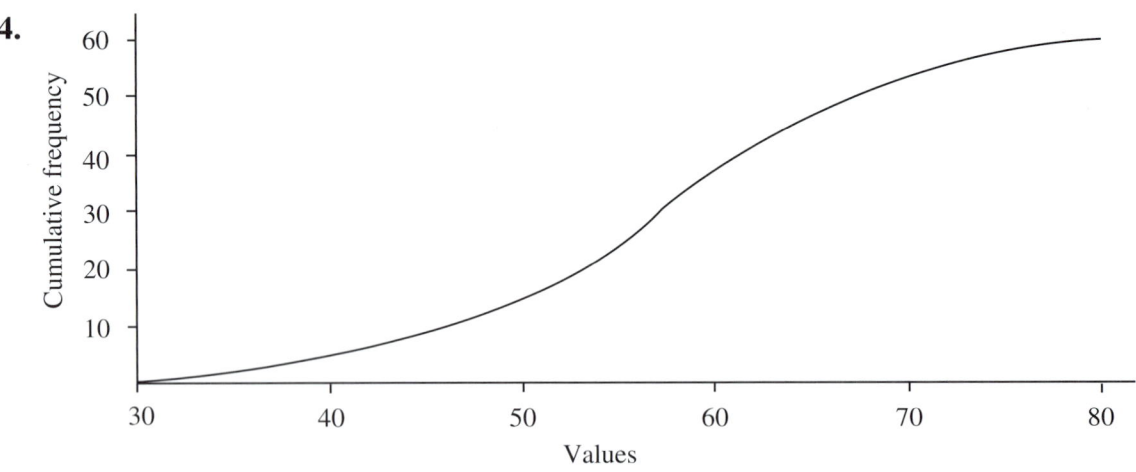

5. The times spent waiting at the checkout by 40 customers at a supermarket are represented by the cumulative frequency curve (ogive) shown.
Use the curve to estimate:

(i) the median waiting time

(ii) the interquartile range of waiting times

(iii) how many customers managed to get through in less than $2\frac{1}{2}$ minutes

(iv) how many customers took longer than $6\frac{1}{2}$ minutes to get through.

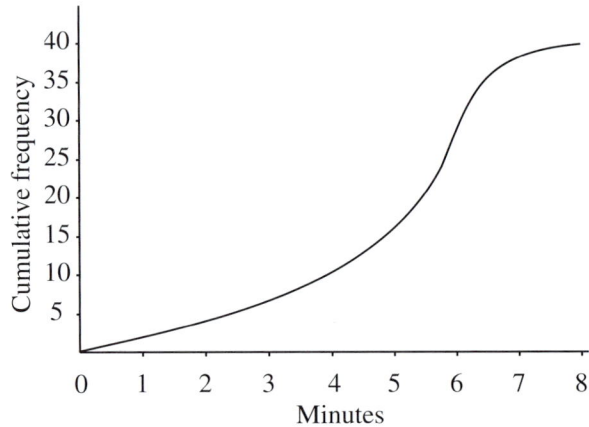

6. The marks of 200 candidates in an examination were as follows:

Marks	0 – 10	10 – 20	20 – 30	30 – 40	40 – 50	50 – 60	60 – 70	70 – 80	80 – 90	90 – 100
No. of students	4	6	10	14	26	30	60	34	10	6

Note: 0 – 10 means 0 but less than 10, 10 – 20 means 10 but less than 20, etc.
Complete the corresponding cumulative frequency table:

Marks	< 0	< 10	< 20	< 30	< 40	< 50	< 60	< 70	< 80	< 90	< 100
No. of students	0	4	10								

Represent the data on a cumulative frequency curve. Use your curve to estimate:

(i) the median mark

(ii) the interquartile range of marks

(iii) the number of candidates who scored 75 or more

(iv) the pass mark if 70 pupils failed.

7. A garage owner recorded the amount of money spent by customers on petrol on a certain day in the following cumulative frequency table:

Value of petrol sales, €s	< 5	< 10	< 15	< 20	< 25	< 30	< 40
Number of customers	4	10	18	30	52	88	100

Draw a cumulative frequency curve to illustrate the data.
Use the curve to estimate:
(i) the number of customers who purchased less than €14 worth of petrol
(ii) the number of customers who spent between €18 and €26 on petrol.
(iii) Complete the corresponding frequency table:

Value of petrol sales, €s	0 – 5	5 – 10	10 – 15	15 – 20	20 – 25	25 – 30	30 – 40
Number of customers					22		

Note: 0 – 5 means ⩾ 0 but less than 5, etc.
(iv) By taking the sales at the mid-interval values, verify that the mean sale was €22.70.

8. The following table shows the distribution of the arrival times at school by a group of 120 students:

Arrival time	08.20 – 08.30	08.30 – 08.40	08.40 – 08.50	08.50 – 09.00	09.00 – 09.10
No. of students	9	15	35	53	8

Complete the corresponding cumulative frequency table:

Arrival time	< 08.20	< 08.30	< 08.40	< 08.50	< 09.00	< 09.10
No. of students	0					120

Draw a cumulative frequency curve to illustrate the data. Use your curve to estimate:
(i) the median arrival time
(ii) the number of students who arrived between 08.35 and 08.45
(iii) the percentage of students who were late for school if arriving after 08.55 is considered as late.

9. The cumulative frequency table shows the number of people who entered a super-market in the time intervals indicated:

Time interval	10.00 – 10.30	10.30 – 11.00	11.00 – 11.30	11.30 – 12.00	12.00 – 12.30	12.30 – 13.00
No. of people	25	60	125	250	450	500

Draw a cumulative frequency curve to represent the data and use the curve to estimate:
(i) the number of people who had entered the supermarket between 10.00 and 11.15
(ii) the time by which 70 percent of the total number of people had entered the supermarket
(iii) the time interval, beginning at 11.30, during which 275 people had entered
(iv) the interquartile range of times people entered.

10. The cumulative frequency table below shows the marks obtained by 100 students in a school test.

Marks	⩽ 20	⩽ 40	⩽ 60	⩽ 80	⩽ 100
Cumulative frequency	6	18	46	93	100

Draw a cumulative frequency curve to represent the data.
(i) Use the curve to estimate the number of students who got less than 50 marks.
(ii) The school decides that the 15 highest marked students will each receive a prize. Use the curve to estimate the least mark a student must obtain in order to qualify for a prize.

11. A group of people form a club and over a period of time contribute to a fund to purchase equipment.
The records showed the contributions as follows:

Contributions, €s	0 – 10	10 – 20	20 – 30	30 – 40	40 – 60
Number of club members	5	10	25	40	20

Note: 0 – 10 means 0 is included but 10 is not etc.

(i) Taking the contributions at the mid-interval values, calculate the mean contribution.

(ii) Represent the data with a histogram.

(iii) Complete the corresponding cumulative frequency table:

Contributions, €s	< 0	< 10	< 20	< 30	< 40	< 60
Number of club members	0					100

(iv) Represent the data with a cumulative frequency curve (ogive).
Use your curve to estimate:

(v) the median contribution

(vi) the interquartile range of contributions

(vii) the number of contributions less than €18

(viii) the number of contributions between €45 and €55.

Exercise 9.9 ▼

Chapter test

1. **(a)** The mean of the six numbers 5, x, 3, 9, 8 and 7 is 7. Find the value of x.

(b) The grouped frequency table below shows the time, in minutes, that 100 students took to solve a maths problem:

Time (minutes)	0 – 20	20 – 40	40 – 60	60 – 80	80 – 100
No. of students	8	10	21	46	15

Note: 0 – 20 means 0 is included but 20 is not, etc.

(i) By taking the mid-interval values, verify that the mean time taken to solve the problem is 1 hour.

(ii) Complete the corresponding cumulative frequency table:

Time (minutes)	< 0	< 20	< 40	< 60	< 80	< 100
No. of students	0	8				

(iii) Represent the data with a cumulative frequency curve (ogive) putting the number of students on the vertical axis.
Use your curve to estimate:

(iv) the median time

(v) the interquartile range of times.

2. (a) Find the median of the array of numbers 2, 3, 10, 8, 7, 3, 2, 5.

(b) The distribution of the marks students received after an exam are recorded in the following histogram:

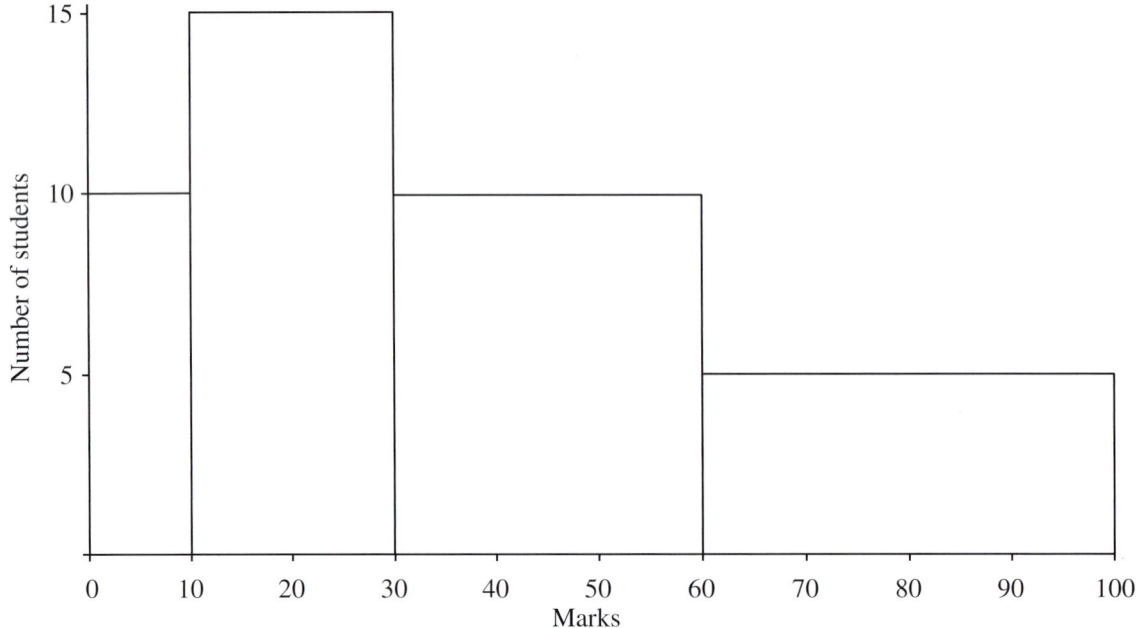

Complete the corresponding frequency distribution table for this histogram:

Marks	0 – 10	10 – 30	30 – 60	60 – 100
Number of people			30	

   (i) How many students took the exam?

   (ii) In which interval does the median lie?

   (iii) By taking the mid-interval values, calculate the mean mark.

(c) The cumulative frequency table below shows the distribution of ages of 110 people living in an estate.

Age in years	⩽ 5	⩽ 10	⩽ 20	⩽ 35	⩽ 50	⩽ 60
Number of people	5	15	40	90	105	110

   (i) Draw the cumulative frequency curve, putting number of people on the vertical axis.

   (ii) Use your curve to estimate the median age.

   (iii) Use your curve to estimate the number of people who are more than 15 years of age.

3. **(a)** Four people have a meal in a restaurant. The average cost of the meal per person is €21.50, excluding the service charge.
What is the total bill for the four people if a 10% service charge is added?

(b) Draw a histogram to represent the following frequency distribution:

Values	0 – 2	2 – 6	6 – 12	12 – 20
Frequency	16	16	24	44

Note: 0 – 2 means $\geqslant$ 0 but less than 2, etc.
By taking the mid-interval values, calculate the mean of the distribution.

(c) In the following frequency distribution the mean is 3. Find the value of x.

Number	1	2	3	4	5	6
Frequency	3	5	10	x	2	1

4. **(a)** A pie chart is drawn to represent the numbers
$x + 2$, 7, 11
Calculate the value of x.

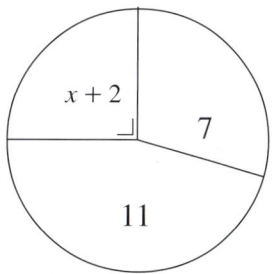

(b) One hundred students took a maths exam and their results are in the cumulative frequency table below:

Marks	< 20	< 40	< 50	< 70	< 100
Number of students	5	15	45	85	100

    (i) Represent the data on a cumulative frequency curve (ogive) putting the number of students on the vertical axis.
Estimate from your graph:

    (ii) the median

    (iii) the interquartile range

    (iv) the pass mark, given that 90 of the students passed.

    (v) Complete the corresponding grouped frequency table:

Marks	0 – 20	20 – 40	40 – 50	50 – 70	70 – 100
Number of students		10			

    (vi) By taking the mid-interval values, calculate the mean mark.

    (vii) Represent the data with a histogram.

5. (a) The number of apples yielded by each of 50 trees in an orchard was recorded and the following cumulative frequency table was drawn up:

Number of apples per tree	⩽ 10	⩽ 20	⩽ 30	⩽ 40	⩽ 50	⩽ 60	⩽ 70
Number of trees	2	6	15	28	45	48	50

Draw the ogive (cumulative frequency curve), putting the number of trees on the vertical axis.
Use your graph to estimate:
(i) the number of trees which yielded 25 apples or less
(ii) the median number of apples per tree
(iii) the interquartile range.

(b) The mean of the following frequency distribution table is 4.
Find the value of k, $k > 0$.

Number	2	$k - 2$	k	7	8
Frequency	7	10	$k + 3$	4	1

6. (a) The following table shows the distribution of the time in minutes taken by a group of 40 students to complete a test:

Time in minutes	0 – 10	10 – 30	30 – 40	40 – 60	60 – 100
Number of students	2	2	4	12	20

Note: 0 – 10 means 0 or more but less than 10, etc.
(i) Taking the data at mid-interval values, verify that mean time is 59 minutes 45 seconds.
(ii) Draw a histogram to illustrate the above data.
(iii) Copy and complete the corresponding cumulative frequency table:

Time in minutes	< 10	< 30	< 40	< 60	< 100
Number of students					

(iv) Draw the ogive (cumulative frequency curve), putting the number of students on the vertical axis.
Use your graph to estimate:
(v) the median time
(vi) the interquartile range of times.

(b) The mean of the following frequency distribution is 13. Find the value of x.

Number	10	12	14	16
Frequency	5	6	x	4

7. (a) The incomplete table and pie chart show the number of seats in a theatre and their respective cost:

Price per seat, €s	10	26	30	40
Number of seats	135	x	390	y

Calculate:
(i) the value of x and the value of y
(ii) the total number of seats sold
(iii) the mean price per seat.
(iv) Complete the pie chart.

(b) The mean of the following frequency distribution is 8.
Find the value of x.

Number	2	5	8	11	14
Frequency	2	x	$x+1$	5	2

(c) The cumulative frequency table below shows the ages of people attending a swimming pool on a particular day:

Ages of people (years)	< 10	< 20	< 40	< 50	< 70
Number of people	2	4	19	39	50

(i) Represent the data with a cumulative frequency curve (ogive) putting the number of people on the vertical axis.
Use your graph to estimate:
(ii) the median age
(iii) the number of people aged less than 34
(iv) the number of people between the ages of 48 and 59.
(v) Complete the corresponding grouped frequency distribution:

Ages of people (years)	0 – 10	10 – 20	20 – 40	40 – 50	50 – 70
Number of people		2	15		

(vi) Using the mid-interval values, calculate the mean age of these swimmers.

8. (a) 100 pupils were given a problem to solve. The following grouped frequency distribution table gives the numbers of pupils who solved the problem in the given time interval.

Time (minutes)	0 – 10	10 – 30	30 – 50	50 – 100
No. of pupils	10	21	47	22

Note: 0 – 10 means 0 is included but 10 is not, etc.

(i)   Verify, using the mid-interval time values, that the average time taken per pupil to solve the problem is 40 minutes.

(ii) Complete the corresponding cumulative frequency table:

Time (minutes)	< 0	< 10	< 30	< 50	< 100
No. of pupils	0				

(iii) Represent the data on a cumulative frequency curve (ogive) putting the number of pupils on the vertical axis.
Use your graph to estimate:

(iv) the number of pupils who solved the problem between 85 and 100 minutes

(v)   the time by which half the total number of pupils had solved the problem

(vi) the interquartile range

(vii) the time taken, beginning after 15 minutes, during which 60 pupils had solved the problem.

(b) The mean mark using mid-interval values from the following table is 10.

Class	0 – 5	5 – 10	10 – 20
Frequency	1	x	4

Calculate the value of x.

9. (a) A number of students took a test and the grades are shown in the table below. A pie chart was drawn to illustrate the data.

Grade	A	B	C	D
Number of students	18	48	36	x
Angle of pie chart			90°	

(i)   Calculate the value of x.

(ii) Complete the table and draw the pie chart.

(b) The following cumulative frequency table shows the results of a test given to a group of 50 students:

Mark	⩽ 20	⩽ 50	⩽ 70	⩽ 80	⩽ 90	⩽ 100
No. of students	4	15	31	45	49	50

(i) Draw the cumulative frequency curve (ogive), putting the number of students on the vertical axis.

(ii) Estimate the median mark.

(iii) Use the cumulative frequency curve to estimate the number of students who scored between 40 marks and 85 marks.

(iv) If 60% of the students passed this test, estimate the lowest mark that a student who passed the test could have obtained.

(c) People attending a course were asked to choose one of the whole numbers from 1 to 20. The results were recorded as follows:

Number	1 − 5	6 − 10	11 − 15	16 − 20
No. of people	5	x	7	2

Using mid-interval values, 9.5 was calculated as the mean of the numbers chosen. Find the value of x.

10. (a) The mean of 14 numbers is 5. The mean of 8 of these numbers is 3.5. What is the mean of the remaining 6 numbers?

(b) A new shop opened at 0900 hours. During the first hour of trading, customers were counted as they entered the shop. The following cumulative frequency table shows the number of customers who had entered before the given times:

Time	Before 0910 hours	Before 0920 hours	Before 0930 hours	Before 0940 hours	Before 0950 hours	Before 1000 hours
No. of customers who had entered	10	30	70	150	240	250

(i) Draw a cumulative frequency curve.

(ii) A photograph was taken of the 100th customer as he or she entered the shop. Use your curve to estimate the time at which the photograph was taken.

(iii) Use your curve to estimate the number of customers who entered the shop during the 15 minutes immediately after the photograph was taken.

(c) A survey of 50 students gave the amount of money spent monthly in the school canteen as follows:

Amount in €	0 – 10	10 – 40	40 – 50	50 – 70	70 – 100
No. of students	4	12	x	14	12

Note: 0 – 10 means 0 is included but 10 is not, etc.

(i) Calculate the value of x.

(ii) Illustrate the above data by a histogram.

(iii) Calculate the mean amount of money spent per student, taking the amounts at the mid-interval values.

The survey was repeated six months later. It was found that half the number of students in each interval, except the (0 – 10) interval, had spent less than before in such a way that each of these students moved into the previous class interval.

Complete the new frequency distribution table:

Amount in €	0 – 10	10 – 40	40 – 50	50 – 70	70 – 100
No. of students					

(iv) Calculate the mean amount of money spent per student in this new survey, assuming the data can be taken at the mid-interval amounts.

COORDINATE GEOMETRY

Distance between two points

If (x_1, y_1) and (x_2, y_2) are two points, the distance d between them is given by the formula:

$$d = \sqrt{(x_2 - x_1)^2 + (y_2 - y_1)^2}$$

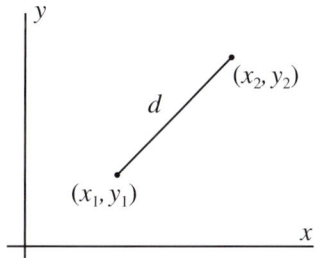

Note: Always decide which point is (x_1, y_1) and which point is (x_2, y_2) before you use the formula. The distance between the points a and b is written $|ab|$.

Example ▼

$a(4, 1)$, $b(7, 5)$, $c(2, 5)$ and $d(-2, 6)$ are four points.
Calculate   **(i)** $|ab|$ **(ii)** $|cd|$

Solution:

(i) $a(4, 1)$ and $b(7, 5)$
     (x_1, y_1) (x_2, y_2)
     $x_1 = 4, y_1 = 1$ $x_2 = 7, y_2 = 5$

$$|ab| = \sqrt{(x_2 - x_1)^2 + (y_2 - y_1)^2}$$
$$= \sqrt{(7 - 4)^2 + (5 - 1)^2}$$
$$= \sqrt{(3)^2 + (4)^2}$$
$$= \sqrt{9 + 16}$$
$$= \sqrt{25}$$
$$= 5$$

(ii) $c(2, 5)$ and $d(-2, 6)$
     (x_1, y_1) (x_2, y_2)
     $x_1 = 2, y_1 = 5$ $x_2 = -2, y_2 = 6$

$$|cd| = \sqrt{(x_2 - x_1)^2 + (y_2 - y_1)^2}$$
$$= \sqrt{(-2 - 2)^2 + (6 - 5)^2}$$
$$= \sqrt{(-4)^2 + (1)^2}$$
$$= \sqrt{16 + 1}$$
$$= \sqrt{17}$$

(leave your answer as $\sqrt{17}$)

Find the distance between each of the following pairs of points:

1. (5, 2) and (8, 6)
2. $(-1, 1)$ and (5, 9)
3. $(1, -3)$ and (2, 5)
4. (2, 0) and (0, 4)
5. $(-2, 2)$ and $(-7, -3)$
6. $(-7, -2)$ and $(-1, -4)$
7. (3, 0) and $(0, -2)$
8. $\left(\frac{1}{2}, \frac{1}{2}\right)$ and (2, 1)
9. $\left(\frac{3}{2}, -\frac{1}{2}\right)$ and (0, 1)

10. If $a(1, -3)$, $b(-4, -2)$ and $c(0, 5)$ are the vertices of $\triangle abc$, verify that $|ac| = |bc|$.
11. Verify that the triangle with vertices $p(4, -3)$, $q(-1, 0)$ and $r(2, 5)$ is isosceles.
12. $x(2, 3)$, $y(-1, 6)$ and $z(1, 8)$ are the vertices of $\triangle xyz$.
    Verify that $|xz|^2 = |xy|^2 + |yz|^2$.
13. Find the radius of a circle with centre (2, 2) and passing through the point (5, 6).

Midpoint of a line segment

If (x_1, y_1) and (x_2, y_2) are two points, their midpoint is given by the formula:

$$\text{Midpoint} = \left(\frac{x_1 + x_2}{2}, \frac{y_1 + y_2}{2}\right)$$

In words: $\left(\dfrac{\text{add the } x\text{'s}}{2}, \dfrac{\text{add the } y\text{'s}}{2}\right)$

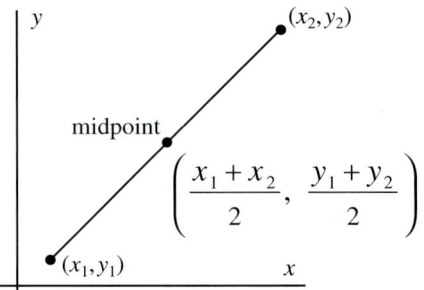

Example ▼

$a(3, -1)$ and $b(5, -5)$ are two points. Find the midpoint of $[ab]$.

Solution:

$$a(3, -1) \qquad b(5, -5) \qquad x_1 = 3 \qquad y_1 = -1$$
$$(x_1, y_1) \qquad (x_2, y_2) \qquad x_2 = 5 \qquad y_2 = -5$$

$$\text{Midpoint} = \left(\frac{x_1 + x_2}{2}, \frac{y_1 + y_2}{2}\right) = \left(\frac{3+5}{2}, \frac{-1-5}{2}\right) = \left(\frac{8}{2}, \frac{-6}{2}\right) = (4, -3)$$

In some questions we will be given the midpoint and one end point of a line segment and be asked to find the other end point. To find the other end point use the following method:

1. Make a rough diagram.
2. Find the translation that maps (moves) the given end point to the midpoint.
3. Apply the same translation to the midpoint to find the other end point.

The point $m(1, -3)$ is the midpoint of $[pq]$. If the coordinates of p are $(6, -7)$, find the coordinates of q.

Solution:

1. Rough diagram:

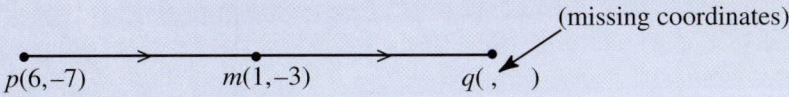

(missing coordinates)

$p(6,-7)$ $m(1,-3)$ $q(\ ,\ )$

2. Translation from p to m: Rule 'subtract 5 from x, add 4 to y'.
3. Apply this rule to m:
   $m(1, -3)$ ® $(1-5, -3+4) = q(-4, 1)$
   ∴ the coordinates of q are $(-4, 1)$

Exercise 10.2 ▼

Find the midpoint of the line segment joining each of the pairs of points:

1. $(3, 1)$ and $(5, 5)$
2. $(1, -1)$ and $(3, 7)$
3. $(5, 1)$ and $(-3, 7)$
4. $(0, -1)$ and $(-2, -3)$
5. $(-5, -3)$ and $(-1, 1)$
6. $(-4, -7)$ and $(6, 3)$
7. $\left(1\frac{1}{2}, 1\frac{1}{3}\right)$ and $\left(\frac{1}{2}, \frac{2}{3}\right)$
8. $(5, 4)$ and $(2, 1)$
9. $(0, -2)$ and $(-1, -1)$
10. Find the coordinates of m, the midpoint of the line segment joining $a(5, 2)$ and $b(1, -6)$. Show that $|am| = |mb|$.
11. The point $m(-4, 3)$ is the midpoint of $[pq]$. If the coordinates of p are $(-5, 4)$, find the coordinates of q.
12. The point $b(-1, 1)$ is the midpoint of $[ac]$. If the coordinates of a are $(3, -1)$, find the coordinates of c.
13. The point $q(-3, 2)$ is the midpoint of $[pr]$. If the coordinates of p are $(-5, -1)$, find the coordinates of r. Calculate $|pr|$.
14. The point $m(2, 7)$ is the midpoint of the line segment joining (a, b) and $(5, 8)$. Find the value of a and the value of b.
15. If the midpoint of $(4, -3)$ and $(-2, 7)$ is the same as the midpoint of (p, q) and $(-4, 7)$, find the value of p and the value of q.
16. $a(6, 2)$, $b(-4, -4)$ and $c(4, -10)$ are the coordinates of the $\triangle abc$.
    Find   **(i)** the coordinates of p, the midpoint of $[a,b]$.
           (ii) the coordinates of q, the midpoint of $[a,c]$.

    Verify that $|pq| = \frac{1}{2}|bc|$.
17. Verify that the midpoint of the line segment joining $(1, -2)$ and $(7, 2)$ is on the x axis.

Slope of a line when given two points on the line

If a line contains the two points (x_1, y_1) and (x_2, y_2),
then the slope of the line is given by the formula:

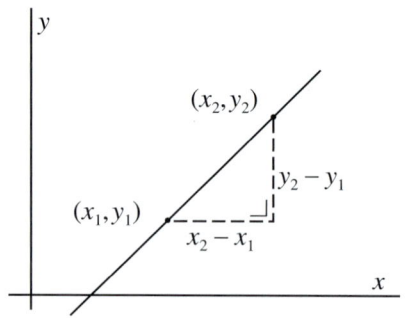

$$m = \frac{y_2 - y_1}{x_2 - x_1}$$

Example ▼

Find the slope of the line containing the points $(-2, 4)$ and $(3, 2)$.

Solution:

$$
\begin{array}{llll}
(-2, 4) & (3, 2) & x_1 = -2 & y_1 = 4 \\
(x_1, y_1) & (x_2, y_2) & x_2 = 3 & y_2 = 2
\end{array}
$$

$$\text{Slope} = m = \frac{y_2 - y_1}{x_2 - x_1} = \frac{2 - 4}{3 + 2} = \frac{-2}{5} = -\frac{2}{5}$$

Parallel lines

> If two lines are parallel they have equal slopes (and vice versa).

Consider the parallel lines L_1 and L_2.
Let m_1 be the slope of L_1 and m_2 be the slope of L_2.
As $L_1 \parallel L_2$, then $m_1 = m_2$

Perpendicular lines

> If two lines are perpendicular, when we multiply their slopes we always get -1 (and vice versa).

Consider the perpendicular lines L_1 and L_2.
Let m_1 be the slope of L_1 and m_2 be the slope of L_2.
As $L_1 \perp L_2$, then $m_1 . m_2 = -1$

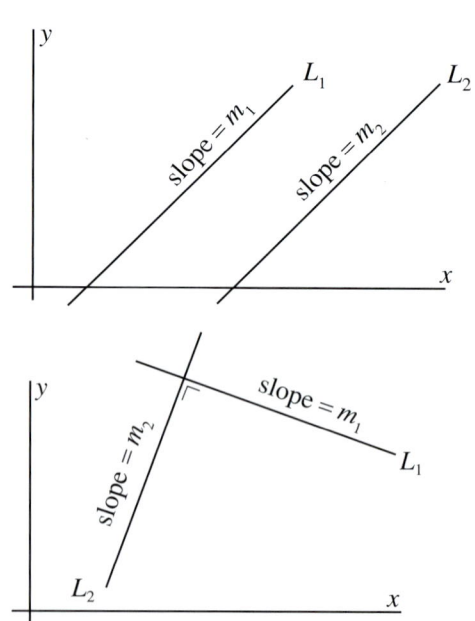

Note: If we know the slope of a line and we need to find the slope of a line perpendicular to it, simply do the following:

Turn the known slope upside down and change its sign.

For example, if a line has a slope of $-\frac{3}{4}$, then the slope of a line perpendicular to it has a slope of $\frac{4}{3}$ (turn upside down and change its sign), because $-\frac{3}{4} \times \frac{4}{3} = -1$.

Example ▼

$a(3, 4)$, $b(5, 7)$, $c(-1, 1)$ and $d(-4, 3)$ are four points. Show that $ab \perp cd$.

Solution:

Let m_1 = the slope of ab and m_2 = the slope of cd.

$$a(3, 4) \quad b(5, 7) \qquad x_1 = 3$$
$$(x_1, y_1) \quad (x_2, y_2) \qquad y_1 = 4$$
$$x_2 = 5$$
$$m_1 = \frac{y_2 - y_1}{x_2 - x_1} \qquad y_2 = 7$$
$$= \frac{7 - 4}{5 - 3}$$
$$= \frac{3}{2}$$

$$c(-1, 1) \quad d(-4, 3) \qquad x_1 = -1$$
$$(x_1, y_1) \quad (x_2, y_2) \qquad y_1 = 1$$
$$x_2 = -4$$
$$m_2 = \frac{y_2 - y_1}{x_2 - x_1} \qquad y_2 = 3$$
$$= \frac{3 - 1}{-4 + 1}$$
$$= -\frac{2}{3}$$

$$m_1 \times m_2 = \tfrac{3}{2} \times -\tfrac{2}{3} = -1$$
$$\therefore ab \perp cd$$

Example ▼

The slope of the line through the points $(2, 1)$ and $(6, k)$, is $\frac{7}{2}$. Find the value of k.

Solution:

$$(2, 1) \quad \text{and} \quad (6, k)$$
$$(x_1, y_1) \qquad (x_2, y_2)$$

$$m = \frac{y_2 - y_1}{x_2 - x_1}$$
$$= \frac{k - 1}{6 - 2}$$
$$= \frac{k - 1}{4}$$
$$\therefore \text{Slope} = \frac{k - 1}{4}$$

Given: Slope $= \dfrac{7}{2}$

$$\therefore \quad \frac{k - 1}{4} = \frac{7}{2}$$
$$2k - 2 = 28$$

(multiply both sides by 8)

$$2k = 28 + 2$$
$$2k = 30$$
$$k = 15$$

Thus, the value of k is 15.

Find the slope of the line containing each of the given pairs of points:

1. $(1, 3)$ and $(4, 8)$ **2.** $(2, 7)$ and $(4, 10)$ **3.** $(5, 2)$ and $(8, 6)$

4. $(2, 5)$ and $(4, 7)$ **5.** $(4, 3)$ and $(7, 9)$ **6.** $(3, 5)$ and $(7, -3)$

7. $(3, -3)$ and $(7, -2)$ **8.** $(-3, -6)$ and $(-5, -4)$ **9.** $(0, -3)$ and $(-1, 0)$

10. $a(-3, -2)$, $b(0, 2)$, $c(3, 3)$ and $d(6, 7)$ are four points. Verify that $ab \parallel cd$.

11. $p(-2, -1)$, $q(3, 3)$, $r(-1, -5)$ and $s(4, -1)$ are four points. Show that $pq \parallel rs$.

12. $a(-1, 3)$, $b(1, 0)$, $c(-2, 1)$ and $d(1, 3)$ are four points. Verify that $ab \perp cd$.

13. $p(3, 3)$, $q(7, 1)$ and $r(1, -1)$ are three points. Verify that $pq \perp pr$.

14. $x(-5, 3)$, $y(-1, 2)$ and $z(1, 10)$ are the vertices of $\triangle xyz$. Prove $|\angle xyz| = 90°$.

15. The line L has slope $-\frac{3}{5}$. Find the slope of K if **(i)** $K \parallel L$ **(ii)** $K \perp L$.

16. The line M has slope $\frac{1}{2}$. Find the slope of N if **(i)** $M \parallel N$ **(ii)** $M \perp N$.

17. The slope of the line through the points $(1, 3)$ and $(3, k)$ is 2. Find the value of k.

18. The slope of the line through the points $(3, -2)$ and $(5, k)$ is 3. Find the value of k.

19. The slope of the line through the points $(2, k)$ and $(7, 2k)$ is $\frac{3}{5}$. Find the value of k.

20. The slope of the line through the points $(2, k)$ and $(6, 3)$ is $-\frac{1}{2}$. Find the value of k.

21. $a(-2, -2)$, $b(4, 1)$, $c(2, -3)$ and $d(k, -1)$ are four points.
If $ab \parallel cd$, find the value of k.

22. $p(2, -3)$, $q(3, 1)$ and $r(-1, k)$ are three points. If $pq \perp qr$, find the value of k.

Equation of a line 1

Let us plot the points $(-1, 8)$, $(0, 6)$, $(1, 4)$, $(2, 2)$, $(3, 0)$ and $(4, -2)$.
The points all lie on the same straight line. In this set of points there is the same relationship (connection, link) between the x coordinate and the y coordinate for **each** point.

If we double the x coordinate and add the y coordinate the result is always 6.

That is : $\boxed{2x + y = 6}$

This result will hold for every other point on the line. We say '$2x + y = 6$' is the equation of the line.

Note: $2x + y - 6 = 0$ is also the equation of the line.

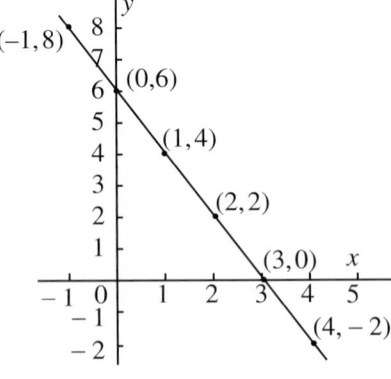

To verify that a point belongs to a line

Once we have an equation of a line we can determine if a point is on the line or not on the line. If a point belongs to a line, its coordinates will satisfy the equation of the line. We substitute the coordinates of the point in the equation of the line. If they satisfy the equation, then the point is **on** the line. Otherwise, the point is **not** on the line.

Example ▼

Investigate if the points $(2, -1)$ and $(6, 1)$ are on the line $2x - 5y - 9 = 0$.

Solution:

$$2x - 5y - 9 = 0$$
Substitute $x = 2$ and $y = -1$
$(2, -1)$: $2(2) - 5(-1) - 9$
$$= 4 + 5 - 9$$
$$= 9 - 9$$
$$= 0$$
Satisfies the equation
Thus, $(2, -1)$ is on the line

$$2x - 5y - 9 = 0$$
Substitute $x = 6$ and $y = 1$
$(6, 1)$: $2(6) - 5(1) - 9$
$$= 12 - 5 - 9$$
$$= 12 - 14$$
$$= -2 \neq 0$$
Does not satisfy the equation
Thus, $(6, 1)$ is not on the line

Example ▼

The equation of the line L is $5x + 4y + 3 = 0$ and the equation of the line K is $3x + ty - 8 = 0$. The point $(-3, k)$ is on L and the point $(2, -1)$ is on the line K. Find the value of k and the value of t.

Solution:

$$5x + 4y + 3 = 0$$
Substitute $x = -3$ and $y = k$
$(-3, k)$: $5(-3) + 4(k) + 3 = 0$
$$-15 + 4k + 3 = 0$$
$$4k - 12 = 0$$
$$4k = 12$$
$$k = 3$$

$$3x + ty - 8 = 0$$
Substitute $x = 2$ and $y = -1$
$(2, -1)$: $3(2) + t(-1) - 8 = 0$
$$6 - t - 8 = 0$$
$$-t - 2 = 0$$
$$-t = 2$$
$$t = -2$$

Find whether the given point is on the corresponding line:

1. $(2,3)$; $x + y - 5 = 0$
2. $(3,1)$; $2x + 3y - 9 = 0$
3. $(1, -2)$; $2x + y - 1 = 0$
4. $(-1, -5)$; $3x - y + 8 = 0$
5. $(-2, -3)$; $5x - 3y + 1 = 0$
6. $(-4, 3)$; $2x + y - 6 = 0$
7. $(5, -4)$; $x + 2y + 1 = 0$
8. $(-2, 0)$; $3x + y + 6 = 0$
9. $(2, \frac{1}{2})$; $x - 4y = 0$
10. $(\frac{2}{3}, \frac{7}{3})$; $6x + 3y - 11 = 0$

11. Verify that the point $(3, -2)$ is on the line $2x - y - 8 = 0$.
12. Verify that the point $(-5, -1)$ is on the line $x - 3y + 2 = 0$.
13. The point $(3, 1)$ is on the line $2x + 3y = k$. Find the value of k.
14. The point $(t, 2)$ is on the line $x - 3y + 1 = 0$. Find the value of t.
15. The point $(-3, k)$ is on the line $5x + 4y + 3 = 0$. Find the value of k.
16. The point $(2, -3)$ is on the line $3x + ky - 12 = 0$. Find the value of k.
17. The point $(-4, 7)$ is on the line $tx + 5y - 19 = 0$. Find the value of t.
18. The point $(1, -2)$ is on the line $5x + ky + 1 = 0$. Find the value of k.

Equation of a line 2

To find the equation of a line we need:

1. The slope of the line, m 2. A point on the line, (x_1, y_1)

Then use the formula: $(y - y_1) = m(x - x_1)$

In short: we need the **slope** and a **point** on the line.

Find the equation of the line:

(i)   containing the point $(3, -4)$ with slope 2.

(ii) containing the point $(-2, 1)$ with slope $-\frac{3}{5}$.

Solution:

(i) Containing $(3, -4)$ with slope 2

$$x_1 = 3, \quad y_1 = -4, \quad m = 2$$
$$(y - y_1) = m(x - x_1)$$
$$(y + 4) = 2(x - 3)$$
$$y + 4 = 2x - 6$$
$$-2x + y + 4 + 6 = 0$$
$$-2x + y + 10 = 0$$
$$2x - y - 10 = 0$$

(ii) Containing $(-2, 1)$ with a slope $-\frac{3}{5}$

$$x_1 = -2, \quad y_1 = 1, \quad m = -\frac{3}{5}$$
$$(y - y_1) = m(x - x_1)$$
$$(y - 1) = -\frac{3}{5}(x + 2)$$
$$5(y - 1) = -3(x + 2)$$
(multiply both sides by 5)
$$5y - 5 = -3x - 6$$
$$3x + 5y - 5 + 6 = 0$$
$$3x + 5y + 1 = 0$$

Find the equation of each of the following lines:

1.   Containing $(3, 1)$ with slope -2

2.   Containing $(2, 5)$ with slope -3

3.   Containing $(5, 1)$ with slope 4

4.   Containing $(1, 4)$ with slope 1

5.   Containing $(2, 3)$ with slope -5

6.   Containing $(-2, 4)$ with slope -1

7.   Containing $(-4, 1)$ with slope $-\frac{1}{2}$

8.   Containing $(-4, -3)$ with slope $\frac{2}{3}$

9.   Containing $(-2, 5)$ with slope $-\frac{2}{5}$

10. Containing $(0, 0)$ with slope $\frac{5}{4}$

11. Containing $(-1, 0)$ with slope $\frac{1}{3}$

12. Containing $(0, -3)$ with slope $-\frac{1}{4}$

13.   A line L has slope 3 and contains the point $(-2, 3)$. Find the equation of L.

14.   A line K has slope $-\frac{1}{5}$ and contains the point $(-1, -4)$. Find the equation of K.

Equation of a line 3

To find the equation of a line we need the **slope** and one point on the line.
However, in many questions one or both of these are missing.

Find the equation of the line that contains the points $(-2, 3)$ and $(4, -7)$.

Solution:

The slope is missing. We first find the slope and use **either one** of the two points to find the equation.

$(-2, 3)$ $(4, -7)$ $x_1 = -2$

(x_1, y_1) (x_2, y_2) $y_1 = 3$

$\qquad\qquad\qquad x_2 = 4$

$m = \dfrac{y_2 - y_1}{x_2 - x_1}$ $y_2 = -7$

$\quad = \dfrac{-7 - 3}{4 + 2}$

$\quad = \dfrac{-10}{6}$

$\quad = -\dfrac{5}{3}$

Containing $(-2, 3)$ with slope $-\frac{5}{3}$

$x_1 = -2, \quad y_1 = 3, \quad m = -\frac{5}{3}$

$(y - y_1) = m(x - x_1)$

$(y - 3) = -\frac{5}{3}(x + 2)$

$3(y - 3) = -5(x + 2)$

(multiply both sides by 3)

$3y - 9 = -5x - 10$

$5x + 3y - 9 + 10 = 0$

$5x + 3y + 1 = 0$

Exercise 10.6 ▼

Find the equation of the line containing the given pair of points:

1. $(1, 4)$ and $(5, 8)$ **2.** $(2, 10)$ and $(4, 6)$ **3.** $(2, 2)$ and $(3, 5)$

4. $(-1, 5)$ and $(1, 3)$ **5.** $(-1, -2)$ and $(2, 4)$ **6.** $(0, 3)$ and $(2, 11)$

7. $(2, 7)$ and $(4, 6)$ **8.** $(-1, 5)$ and $(4, 7)$ **9.** $(-2, 2)$ and $(1, 4)$

10. $(-2, 2)$ and $(-1, 6)$ **11.** $(-3, -5)$ and $(-5, 0)$ **12.** $(2, -2)$ and $(-6, -8)$

13. $a(3, -2)$, $b(2, 3)$ and $c(5, 7)$ are three points.
  (i)   find the slope of bc.
  (ii) find the equation of the line L containing the point a and parallel to bc.

14. $p(1, 5)$, $q(4, 7)$ and $r(-2, 1)$ are three points.
  (i)   find the slope of pq.
  (ii) find the equation of the line K containing the point r and perpendicular to pq.

15. $a(6, 3)$ and $b(-2, -1)$ are two points. Find the equation of the line L containing the point $(5, -1)$ and the midpoint of $[ab]$.

16. The line L contains the points $(3, 4)$ and $(0, 5)$.
  The line K contains the points $(-3, 2)$. If $K \perp L$, find the equation of the line K.

17. $a(2, 3)$ and $b(6, 1)$ are two points.
  (i)   find the midpoint of $[ab]$
  (ii) find the slope of ab
  (iii) find the equation of the perpendicular bisector of $[ab]$.

Slope of a line when given its equation

To find the slope of a line when given its equation, do the following:

Method 1

> Get y on its own and the number in front of x is the slope.

Note: The number in front of x is called the **coefficient** of x.

In short, write the line in the form:

$y = mx \qquad + c$

$y = (\text{slope})\, x + (\text{where the line cuts the } y \text{ axis})$

Method 2

> If the line is in the form $ax + by + c = 0$, then $-\dfrac{a}{b}$ is the slope.

In words: $\text{slope} = -\dfrac{\text{number in front of } x}{\text{number in front of } y}$

Note: When using this method, make sure every term is on the left-hand side in the given equation of the line.

Example ▼

Find the slope of the line   **(i)** $2x - y + 3 = 0$ **(ii)** $3x + 4y - 5 = 0$

Solution:

(i) **Method 1**

$2x - y + 3 = 0$

$-y = -2x - 3$

$y = 2x + 3$

compare to $y = mx + c$

Thus, the slope $= 2$

(ii) **Method 1**

$3x + 4y - 5 = 0$

$4y = -3x + 5$

$y = -\tfrac{3}{4}x + \tfrac{5}{4}$

compare to $y = mx + c$

Thus, the slope $= -\tfrac{3}{4}$

(i) Method 2

$2x - y + 3 = 0$

$a = 2, \quad b = -1$

$\text{Slope} = -\dfrac{a}{b}$

$= -\dfrac{2}{-1}$

$= 2$

(ii) Method 2

$3x + 4y - 5 = 0$

$a = 3, \quad b = 4$

$\text{Slope} = -\dfrac{a}{b}$

$= -\dfrac{3}{4}$

Example ▼

L: $5x + 3y - 7 = 0$ and K: $3x - 5y - 4 = 0$ are two lines. Prove $L \perp K$.

Solution:

Find the slope of L

$5x + 3y - 7 = 0$

$\text{Slope of } L = -\dfrac{a}{b} = -\dfrac{5}{3}$

Find the slope of K

$3x - 5y - 4 = 0$

$\text{Slope of } K = -\dfrac{a}{b} = -\dfrac{3}{-5} = \dfrac{3}{5}$

$$(\text{Slope of } L) \times (\text{Slope of } K) = -\dfrac{5}{3} \times \dfrac{3}{5} = -1$$

$$\therefore L \perp K$$

Example ▼

The line $kx + 2y - 5 = 0$ is perpendicular to the line $2x - 3y - 1 = 0$.
Find the value of k.

Solution:

$kx + 2y - 5 = 0$

$\text{Slope} = m_1 = -\dfrac{a}{b} = -\dfrac{k}{2}$

$2x - 3y - 1 = 0$

$\text{Slope} = m_2 = -\dfrac{a}{b} = -\dfrac{2}{-3} = \dfrac{2}{3}$

lines are perpendicular

$$\therefore \quad m_1 \times m_2 = -1$$

$$\Rightarrow \quad -\frac{k}{2} \times \frac{2}{3} = -1$$

$$\Rightarrow \quad -\frac{k}{3} = -1$$

$$\Rightarrow \quad \frac{k}{3} = 1 \qquad \text{(multiply both sides by } -1\text{)}$$

$$\Rightarrow \quad k = 3 \qquad \text{(multiply both sides by 3)}$$

Exercise 10.7 ▼

Find the slope of each of the following lines:

1. $2x + y + 3 = 0$ **2.** $3x - y - 1 = 0$ **3.** $2x + 3y - 6 = 0$

4. $4x - 5y + 4 = 0$ **5.** $x + 2y - 3 = 0$ **6.** $x + y - 4 = 0$

7. $x - 3y - 4 = 0$ **8.** $x + 4y - 2 = 0$ **9.** $x - y - 1 = 0$

10. $4x + 3y = 0$ **11.** $2x - 5y - 1 = 0$ **12.** $7x - 2y - 11 = 0$

13. L: $3x + 2y - 4 = 0$ and K: $6x + 3y + 1 = 0$ are two lines. Prove $L \parallel K$.

14. L: $3x - 2y - 6 = 0$ and K: $2x + 3y + 12 = 0$ are two lines. Prove $L \perp K$.

15. L: $2x - y + 2 = 0$ and K: $x + 2y - 3 = 0$ are two lines. Prove $L \perp K$.

16. L: $4x + 5y - 10 = 0$ and K: $10x - 8y - 5 = 0$ are two lines. Prove $L \perp K$.

17. L: $x + y - 1 = 0$ and K: $x - y + 2 = 0$ are two lines. Prove $L \perp K$.

18. Show that the lines $x + 3y - 1 = 0$ and $3x + 9y + 1 = 0$ are parallel.

19. L: $3x + 2y - 10 = 0$ and K: $tx + 2y - 8 = 0$ are two lines. If $L \parallel K$, find the value of t.

20. L: $5x - 3y - 1 = 0$ and K: $10x + by - 3 = 0$ are two lines. If $L \parallel K$, find the value of b.

21. L: $5x - 4y - 20 = 0$ and K: $ax + 5y - 10 = 0$ are two lines. If $L \perp K$, find the value of a.

22. L: $2x - 3y - 4 = 0$ and K: $6x + ty + 1 = 0$ are two lines. If $L \perp K$, find the value of t.

23. If the lines $3x + y - 2 = 0$ and $x + ky + 1 = 0$ are perpendicular, find the value of k.

24. L is the line $5x + 2y - 10 = 0$. Find the slope of L.

K is the line $ax + 10y + 3 = 0$. Find the slope of K in terms of a.

Find the value of a if   **(i)** $K \parallel L$ **(ii)** $K \perp L$.

Equation of a line, parallel or perpendicular to a given line

In some questions we need to find the equation of a line containing a particular point which is parallel to or perpendicular to a given line.

When this happens do the following:

1. Find the slope of the given line.
2. (a) if parallel, use the slope in step 1.
   (b) if perpendicular, turn the slope in step1 upside down and change sign.
3. Use the slope in step 2 with the point in the formula:
$$(y - y_1) = m(x - x_1)$$

Example ▼

L is the line $5x - 3y - 2 = 0$. The line K contains the point $(3, -1)$ and $K \perp L$. Find the equation of K.

Solution:

We have a point, $(3, -1)$. The slope is missing.

1: Find slope of L.

$$5x - 3y - 2 = 0$$

$$\text{Slope of } L = -\frac{5}{-3}$$

$$= \frac{5}{3}$$

2: Find slope of K.

Perpendicular to L.

$$\therefore \text{ slope of } K = -\tfrac{3}{5}$$

(turn upside down and change sign)

3: Containing $(3, -1)$ with slope $-\tfrac{3}{5}$

$$x_1 = 3, \ y_1 = -1, \ m = -\tfrac{3}{5}$$

$$(y - y_1) = m(x - x_1)$$

$$\Rightarrow \quad (y + 1) = -\tfrac{3}{5}(x - 3)$$

$$\Rightarrow \quad 5(y + 1) = -3(x - 3)$$

(multiply both sides by 5)

$$\Rightarrow \quad 5y + 5 = -3x + 9$$

$$\Rightarrow 3x + 5y + 5 - 9 = 0$$

$$\Rightarrow \quad 3x + 5y - 4 = 0$$

The equation of the line K is $3x + 5y - 4 = 0$.

Exercise 10.8 ▼

1. Find the equation of the line containing $(2, 1)$ and parallel to $2x - y + 1 = 0$.
2. Find the equation of the line containing $(-2, 5)$ and perpendicular to $3x - 2y + 1 = 0$.
3. Find the equation of the line containing $(-3, -1)$ and parallel to $4x + 3y - 8 = 0$.
4. Find the equation of the line containing $(1, -4)$ and perpendicular to $5x + 4y - 11 = 0$.
5. L is the line $3x + 2y - 4 = 0$. The line K contains the point $(1, -2)$.
   If $L \perp K$, find the equation of K.

6. *M* is the line $x + 2y + 4 = 0$. The line *L* contains the point $(-3, 4)$.
If $L \parallel M$, find the equation of *L*.

7. $a(3, -6)$ and $b(-1, -2)$ are two points. *c* is the midpoint of $[ab]$ and *K* is the line $2x + 5y - 5 = 0$. The line *L* contains the point *c* and $L \perp K$. Find the equation of *L*.

Point of intersection of two lines

Use the method of solving simultaneous equations to find the point of intersection of two lines.

1. When the point of intersection contains whole numbers only

Example ▼

L is the line $2x - 5y - 9 = 0$ and *K* is the line $3x - 2y - 8 = 0$.
Find the coordinates of *q*, the point of intersection of *L* and *K*.

Solution:

Write both equations in the form $ax + by = k$.

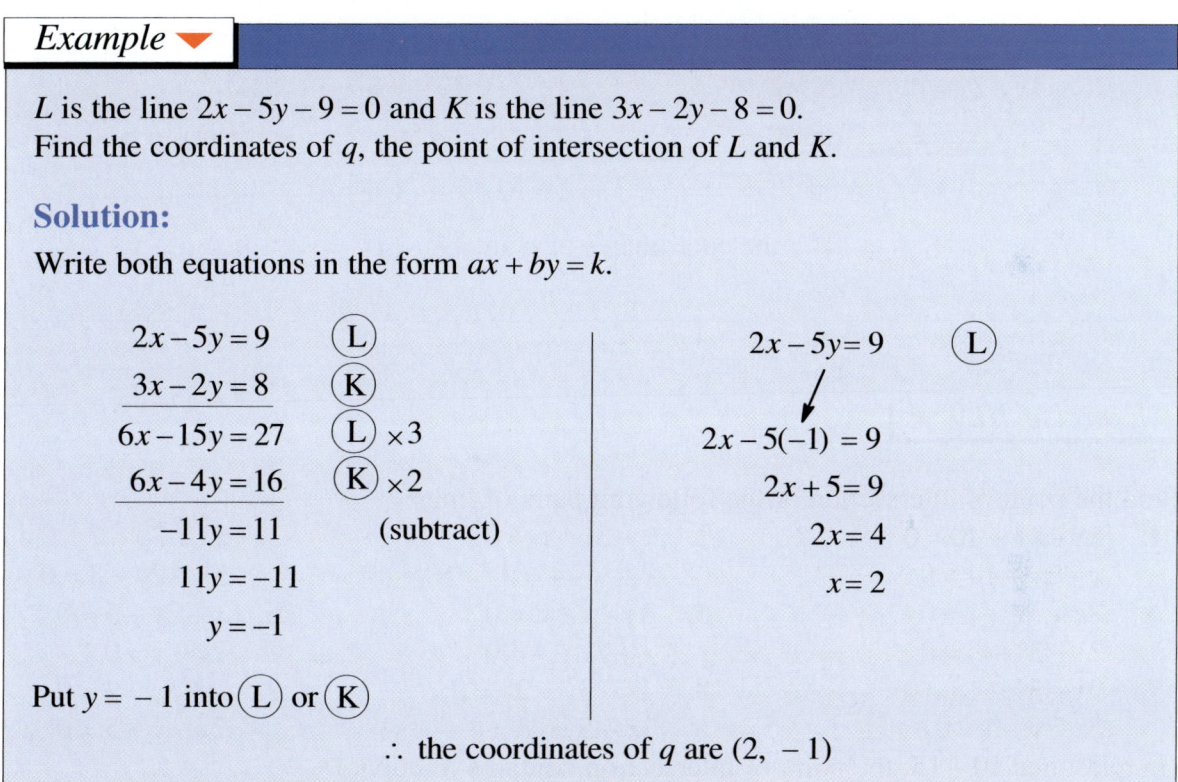

$$2x - 5y = 9 \quad \textcircled{L}$$
$$3x - 2y = 8 \quad \textcircled{K}$$
$$6x - 15y = 27 \quad \textcircled{L} \times 3$$
$$6x - 4y = 16 \quad \textcircled{K} \times 2$$
$$-11y = 11 \quad \text{(subtract)}$$
$$11y = -11$$
$$y = -1$$

$$2x - 5y = 9 \quad \textcircled{L}$$
$$2x - 5(-1) = 9$$
$$2x + 5 = 9$$
$$2x = 4$$
$$x = 2$$

Put $y = -1$ into $\textcircled{L}$ or $\textcircled{K}$

∴ the coordinates of *q* are $(2, -1)$

2. When the point of intersection contains fractions
If the point of intersection contains fractions, a very useful method is to:

> **Step 1:** Remove the *y*'s and get a value for *x*.
> **Step 2:** Remove the *x*'s and get a value for *y*.

Note: This method can be used even if the point of intersection contains whole numbers only.

The equation of the line M is $x + 2y - 2 = 0$ and the equation of the line N is $2x - y - 2 = 0$. If $M \cap N = \{p\}$, find the coordinates of p.

Solution:

Write both equations in the form $ax + by = k$.

Remove the y's		Remove the x's	
$x + 2y = 2$	Ⓜ	$x + 2y = 2$	Ⓜ
$2x - y = 2$	Ⓝ	$2x - y = 2$	Ⓝ
$x + 2y = 2$	Ⓜ	$2x + 4y = 4$	Ⓜ ×2
$4x - 2y = 4$	Ⓝ ×2	$2x - y = 2$	Ⓝ
$5x = 6$	(add)	$5y = 2$	(subtract)
$x = \frac{6}{5}$		$y = \frac{2}{5}$	

$\therefore$ the coordinates of p are $\left(\frac{6}{5}, \frac{2}{5} \right)$

Find the point of intersection of the following pairs of lines:

1. $5x + 4y - 40 = 0$
$x + 2y - 14 = 0$

2. $x + 3y - 6 = 0$
$x + y - 4 = 0$

3. $2x + 3y - 7 = 0$
$5x - 2y - 8 = 0$

4. $3x + 4y - 1 = 0$
$2x - 3y + 5 = 0$

5. $3x - y + 8 = 0$
$x - 7y - 4 = 0$

6. $x + 2y - 5 = 0$
$2x - y = 0$

7. $2x - 3y - 15 = 0$
$5x - y - 5 = 0$

8. $4x - 3y + 25 = 0$
$3x + 5y - 3 = 0$

9. $x + 5y - 3 = 0$
$2x - y + 5 = 0$

(In questions $10 - 15$, the point of intersection contains fractions)

10. $3x - y - 6 = 0$
$x - 7y - 12 = 0$

11. $2x - 3y + 2 = 0$
$4x - y - 2 = 0$

12. $4x + 2y - 11 = 0$
$3x - y - 7 = 0$

13. $3x + y = 0$
$2x + 2y - 1 = 0$

14. $2x + 3y - 8 = 0$
$2x - 3y - 2 = 0$

15. $6x + 3y - 11 = 0$
$5x + 2y - 8 = 0$

16. $L: 3x + y + 4 = 0$ and $K: 3x - 2y + 10 = 0$ are the equations of two lines.
If $L \cap K = \{p\}$, find the coordinates of p.

17. The equation of the line M is $4x - y - 1 = 0$ and the equation of the line N is $3x + 2y - 9 = 0$. If $M \cap N = \{q\}$, find the coordinates of q.

18. $L: 3x - 2y - 4 = 0$ and $K: 5x + 2y - 12 = 0$ are the equations of two lines.
$M: x + 3y + 8 = 0$ and $N: 3x + 4y + 9 = 0$ are also the equations of two lines.
$L \cap K = \{p\}$ and $M \cap N = \{q\}$.
Find **(i)** the coordinates of p and the coordinates of q
(ii) the equation of the line pq.

19. The equation of the line L is $ax + 5y - 11 = 0$ and the equation of the line K is $7x + by + 2 = 0$. The coordinates of the point of intersection of L and K is $(-2, 3)$. Find the value of a and the value of b.

Graphing lines

To draw a line, only two points are needed. The easiest points to find are those where lines cut the x and y axes.

This is known as the **intercept method**. We use the following fact:

> On the x axis $y = 0$.   On the y axis $x = 0$.

To draw a line do the following:

> **1.** Let $y = 0$ and find x.
> **2.** Let $x = 0$ and find y.
> **3.** Plot these two points.
> **4.** Draw the line through these points.

Note: Any two points on the line will do, it is not necessary to use the points where the line cuts the x and y axes.

Example ▼

Graph the line $2x - 3y + 12 = 0$.

Solution:

1 and 2. $2x - 3y = -12$

$y = 0$	$x = 0$
$2x = -12$	$-3y = -12$
$x = -6$	$3y = 12$
$(-6, 0)$	$y = 4$
	$(0, 4)$

$2x - 3y + 12 = 0$

3. Plot the points $(-6, 0)$ and $(0, 4)$.
4. Draw the line through these points.

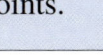

Graph each of the following lines:

1. $3x + 2y - 12 = 0$ **2.** $2x + 5y - 10 = 0$ **3.** $4x + 3y + 12 = 0$

4. $3x - 5y + 15 = 0$ **5.** $2x - y + 4 = 0$ **6.** $x + y - 3 = 0$

7. $x - y + 4 = 0$ **8.** $x + 3y - 6 = 0$ **9.** $4x - y + 8 = 0$

10. $3x + 4y + 24 = 0$ **11.** $2x + y + 6 = 0$ **12.** $x + 2y - 3 = 0$

13. The equation of the line L is $2x + y - 8 = 0$ and the equation of the line K is $x - y + 2 = 0$.

     (i) On the same axes and scales, graph the lines L and K.

     (ii) From your graph, write down the coordinates of $L \cap K$.

     (iii) Verify your answer to part **(ii)** by solving algebraically the simultaneous equations

$$2x + y = 8$$
$$x - y = -2$$

14. The equation of the line L is $2x + 3y - 12 = 0$.

     L cuts the x axis at p and the y axis at q.

     (i) Find the coordinates of p and the coordinates of q.

     (ii) Graph the line L.

     (iii) Calculate the area of $\triangle opq$, where o is the origin.

15. The equation of the line K is $x + 2y + 8 = 0$.

     K cuts the x axis at a and the y axis at b.

     (i) Find the coordinates of a and the coordinates of b.

     (ii) Calculate $|ab|$.

     (iii) Calculate the area of the triangular region enclosed by K, the x axis and the y axis.

Lines that contain the origin

If the constant in the equation of a line is zero, e.g. $3x - 5y = 0$, or $4x = 3y$, then the line will pass through the origin, $(0, 0)$. In this case the **intercept method** will not work. To draw a line that contains the origin, $(0, 0)$, do the following:

> **1.** Choose a suitable value for x and find the corresponding value for y (or vice versa).
> **2.** Plot this point.
> **3.** A line drawn through this point and the origin is the required line.

Note: A very suitable value is to let x equal the number in front of y and then find the corresponding value for x (or vice versa).

Graph the line $2x + 3y = 0$.

Solution:

1. Let $x = 3$ (number in front of y)

$$2x + 3y = 0$$

$$2(3) + 3y = 0$$
$$6 + 3y = 0$$
$$3y = -6$$
$$y = -2$$

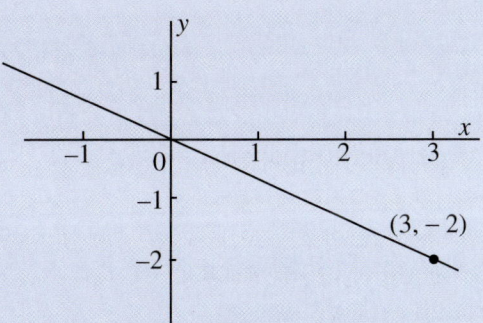

2. Plot the point $(3, -2)$.
3. Draw the line through the points $(0, 0)$ and $(3, -2)$.

Graph each of the following lines:

1.	$3x + 4y = 0$	**2.**	$2x - 3y = 0$	**3.**	$5x + 2y = 0$
4.	$2x - y = 0$	**5.**	$5x + 3y = 0$	**6.**	$x + 2y = 0$
7.	$x + y = 0$	**8.**	$x - y = 0$	**9.**	$3x - 4y = 0$
10.	$3x + y = 0$	**11.**	$x - 5y = 0$	**12.**	$4x + y = 0$

Lines parallel to the axes

Some lines are parallel to the x or y axis.

$x = 5$ is a line parallel to the y axis through 5 on the x axis.

$y = -3$ is a line parallel to the x axis through -3 on the y axis.

Note:
> $y = 0$, is the equation of the x axis.
> $x = 0$, is the equation of the y axis.

On the same axes and scales, graph the lines
$x = 2$ and $y = -1$.

Solution:

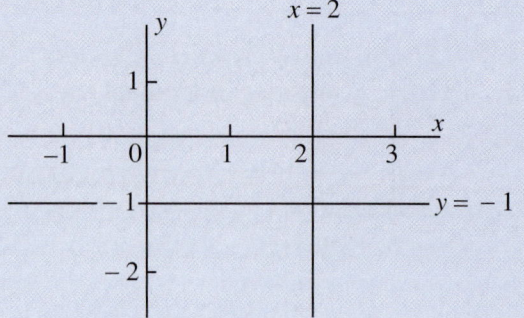

(i) $x = 2$

Line parallel to the y axis
through 2 on the x axis.

(ii) $y = -1$

Line parallel to the x axis
through -1 on the y axis.

Exercise 10.12 ▼

Graph each of the following lines:

1.	$x = 1$	**2.**	$y = 3$	**3.**	$x = -2$
4.	$y = -3$	**5.**	$x = 5$	**6.**	$y = 1$
7.	$x + 3 = 0$	**8.**	$y - 2 = 0$	**9.**	$x + 4 = 0$

10. $x - 4 = 0$ is the equation of the line L and $y + 2 = 0$ is the equation of the line K.

   (i) on the same axes and scales, graph the lines L and K.

   (ii) write down the coordinates of q, the point of intersection of L and K.

11. Write down the equation of the line containing the point (2, 3) which is:

   (i) parallel to the x axis   **(ii)** perpendicular to the x axis.

Transformations of the plane

Translation

A translation moves a point in a straight line.

> ### Example ▼
>
> $p(-1, 5)$ and $q(1, 1)$ are two points. Find the image of the point $(7, 1)$ under the translation $\overrightarrow{pq}$.
>
> **Solution:**
>
> Under the translation $\overrightarrow{pq}$, $(-1, 5) \rightarrow (1, 1)$
>
> Rule: add 2 to x, subtract 4 from y.
>
> $\therefore (7, 1) \rightarrow (7+2, 1-4) = (9, -3)$
>
> $\therefore$ the image of $(7, 1)$ is $(9, -3)$

Translations are very useful in finding the missing coordinates of one of the vertices of a parallelogram when given the other three.

> ### Example ▼
>
> $a(-6, 1)$, $b(-4, 3)$ and $c(1, 0)$ are three vertices of the parallelogram $abcd$. Find the coordinates of the fourth vertex d.
>
> **Solution:**
>
> Make a rough diagram (keep cyclic order).
>
> Since $abcd$ is a parallelogram $\overrightarrow{bc} = \overrightarrow{ad}$.
> (i.e. the movement from b to c is the same as the movement from a to d.)
>
> We find the rule that moves b to c.
> Then apply this rule to a to find d.
>
> $\overrightarrow{bc} : (-4, 3) \rightarrow (1, 0)$
>
> **Rule:** Add 5 to x, subtract 3 from y.
>
> $\overrightarrow{ad} : (-6, 1) \rightarrow (-6+5, 1-3) = (-1, -2)$
>
> $\therefore$ the coordinates of d are $(-1, -2)$

Note: By cyclic order we mean that the points are taken in clockwise, or anti-clockwise, order.

Central symmetry

Central symmetry is a reflection in a point.
The image of a point under a central symmetry in another point can be found with a translation.

Example ▼

Find the image of the point $a(1, -2)$ under the central symmetry in the point $b(-2, 2)$.

Solution:

Rough diagram:

$a(1, -2)$ $b(-2, 2)$ $a'(-5, 6)$

Translation from a to b: Rule 'subtract 3 from x, add 4 to y'.
Apply this rule to b:

$$b(-2, 2) \rightarrow (-2 - 3, 2 + 4) = a'(-5, 6)$$

Therefore, the image of $a(1, -2)$ is $a'(-5, 6)$.

Axial symmetry in the axes and central symmetry in the origin

Note:

> S_x means 'axial symmetry in the x axis'
> S_y means 'axial symmetry in the y axis'
> S_o means 'central symmetry in the origin'

We will look at two methods of finding the images of points under axial symmetry in the axes and central symmetry in the origin.

1. **Mathematical method.**
   The following three patterns emerge, and it is worth memorising them:

> 1. Axial symmetry in the x axis → **change the sign of y.**
> 2. Axial symmetry in the y axis → **change the sign of x.**
> 3. Central symmetry in the origin, $(0, 0)$ → **change the sign of both x and y.**

2. **Graphical method.**

> Plot the point on the coordinated plane and use your knowledge of axial symmetry and central symmetry to find the image.

Example ▼

Find the image of (3, 2) under: **(i)** S_x **(ii)** S_y **(iii)** S_o

Solution:

1. Mathematical method

(i) S_x (3, 2) = (3, −2)   (change the sign of y)

(ii) S_y (3, 2) = (−3, 2)   (change the sign of x)

(iii) S_o (3, 2) = (−3, −2)   (change the sign of both x and y)

2. Graphical method

From the graph it can be seen that

(i) S_x (3, 2) = (3, −2)

(ii) S_y (3, 2) = (−3, 2)

(iii) S_o (3, 2) = (−3, −2)

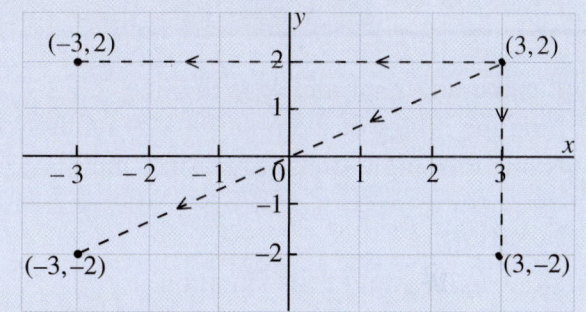

Axial symmetry in lines parallel to the *x* or *y* axis

Example ▼

Find the image of the point (−1, 3) under axial symmetry in the line $x = 1$.

Solution:

A diagram is particularly useful
in this type of question.

Draw the line $x = 1$ and plot the point (−1, 3).
From the diagram the point (−1, 3)
is mapped onto (3, 3) under the axial
symmetry in the line $x = 1$.

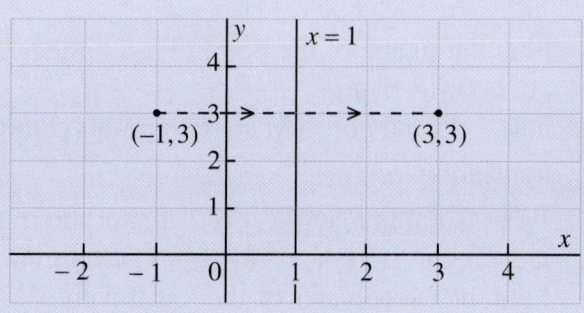

Composition of transformations

Often we need to find the images of points under a composition of transformations.

Notation:

$S_x \circ S_y$ means 'axial symmetry in the x axis **after** axial symmetry in the y axis'.
$S_L \circ S_a$ means 'axial symmetry in the line L **after** central symmetry in the point a'.

$S_o \circ \overrightarrow{ab}$ means 'central symmetry in the origin **after** the translation $\overrightarrow{ab}$'.
The procedure is illustrated with an example.

Note: The symbol for after is $\circ$.

Example ▼

L is the line $y = 1$ and M is the line $x = 2$.
Find the image of the point $p(3, 2)$ under $S_L \circ S_M$ (i.e. axial symmetry in L after M).
Name the single transformation which is equivalent to $S_L \circ S_M$.

Solution:

Draw a diagram of the situation.

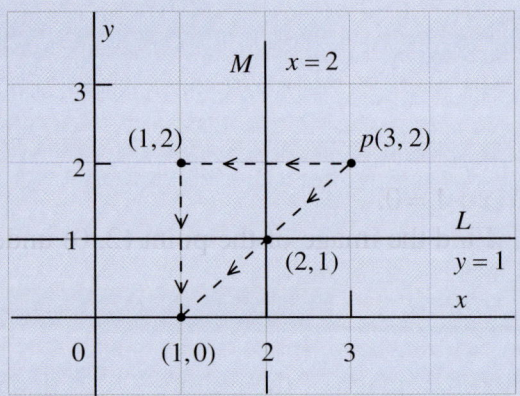

$S_M(3, 2) = (1, 2)$ $S_L(1, 2) = (1, 0)$
∴ the image of $(3, 2)$ under $S_L \circ S_M = (1, 0)$
$S_L \circ S_M$ is equal to a central symmetry in the point of intersection of L and M.
$$L \cap M = (2, 1)$$
∴ $S_L \circ S_M = S_{(2, 1)}$, i.e. a central symmetry in the point $(2, 1)$.

Exercise 10.13 ▼

1. Find the image of the point $(3, -2)$ under the translation which maps
   $(1, 1) \rightarrow (-1, 5)$.
2. $a(1, -3)$ and $b(4, -5)$ are two points. Find the image of the point $(-4, 3)$ under the
   translation $\overrightarrow{ab}$.

   What is the image of $(-1, 2)$ under the translation $\overrightarrow{ba}$?
3. $p(3, 2)$, $q(-1, 1)$ and $r(-3, -5)$ are three vertices of the parallelogram $pqrs$.
   Find the coordinates of the fourth vertex s.

4. $a(1, -2)$, $b(-3, 1)$, $c(2, 3)$ are three vertices of the parallelogram $abcd$.
   Find the coordinates of the fourth vertex d.

5. $p(-1, -2)$, $q(5, k)$, $r(8, 2)$ $s(h, 1)$ are the four vertices of the parallelogram $pqrs$.
   Find the value of h and the value of k.

6. $(2, -2)$ is the image of (p, q) under the translation $(2, -3) \rightarrow (0, -4)$.
   Find (p, q).

7. Find the image of the point $(-2, 1)$ under the central symmetry in the point $(1, -4)$.

8. Find the image of the point $(2, 4)$ under the central symmetry in the point $(-4, 6)$.

9. $a(2, 1)$ and $b(x, y)$ are two points. The image of a under the central symmetry in b is $(8, -3)$.
   Find the coordinates of b.

10. $a(1, 1)$, $b(9, 2)$, $c(h, k)$ and $d(p, q)$ are the vertices of parallelogram $abcd$.
    $x(6, 3)$ is the point of intersection of the diagonals $[ac]$ and $[bd]$.
    Find the coordinates of c and d.

11. Find the image of the point $(2, -1)$ under:
    (i) the central symmetry in the origin, $(0, 0)$
    (ii) the axial symmetry in the x axis
    (iii) the axial symmetry in the y axis
    (iv) the axial symmetry in the line $x = 1$
    (v) the axial symmetry in the line $y = 1$.

12. Find the image of the point $(-3, -2)$ under the axial symmetry in the line
    $x + 1 = 0$.

13. Find the image of the point $(2, 0)$ under the axial symmetry in the line $y - 1 = 0$.

14. The image of the point $(-1, 4)$ under the axial symmetry in the line $x = 2$ is (h, k).
    Find (h, k).

15. The equation of the line L is $x + 3y - 12 = 0$.
    The equation of the line K is $3x - y + 14 = 0$.
    (i) Verify that the point $p(-2, 8)$ is on K.
    (ii) Find the coordinates of q, the point
    of intersection of L and K.
    (iii) Prove that $L \perp K$.
    (iv) Find the coordinates of t, the image
    of p under the axial symmetry in L.
    Given that s is the point $(0, 3)$ and that $pqsr$
    is a parallelogram, find:
    (v) the coordinates of r
    (vi) the equation of the line rs.

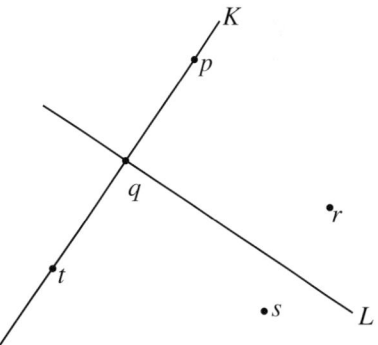

16. The equation of the line L is $2x - 3y - 1 = 0$ and the equation of the line K is
    $3x + 2y - 8 = 0$.
    (i) Verify that the point $p(-4, -3)$ is on L.
    (ii) Find the coordinates of q, the point of intersection of L and K.
    (iii) Verify that $L \perp K$.

(iv) Find the coordinates of r, the image of p under the axial symmetry in K.

(v) Name another transformation that maps p to r.

17. Find the image of the point $(1, 2)$ under $S_y \circ S_x$ (i.e. axial symmetry in the y axis after axial symmetry in the x axis).

18. Find the image of the point $(3, -2)$ under $S_o \circ S_x$ (i.e. central symmetry in the origin after axial symmetry in the x axis).

19. $a(4, 3)$ and $b(1, 2)$ are two points.

Find the image of a under $S_o \circ S_b$ (i.e. central symmetry in the origin after central symmetry in the point b).

20. N is the line $y = 2$ and M is the line $x = 3$.

Find the image of $p(2, 1)$ under $S_M \circ S_N$ (i.e. axial symmetry in M after N).

Name the single transformation which is equivalent to $S_M \circ S_N$.

21. A is the line $y = -1$ and B is the line $x = -2$.

Find the image of $q(-4, 1)$ under $S_B \circ S_A$ (i.e. axial symmetry in B after A).

Name the single transformation which is equivalent to $S_B \circ S_A$.

22. $a(2, 1)$ and $b(5, -1)$ are two points.

Find the image of the point $c(-4, 5)$ under $S_o \circ \overrightarrow{ab}$ (i.e. central symmetry in origin after the translation $\overrightarrow{ab}$).

23. **(i)** Verify that the points $a(2, 1)$ and $b(-1, -3)$ are on the line $4x - 3y - 5 = 0$.

Under the translation $(7, 5) \rightarrow (4, 6)$, a is mapped to p and b is mapped to q.

(ii) Find the coordinates of p and the coordinates of q.

(iii) Find the equation of the line pq.

(iv) Is $ab \parallel pq$? Give a reason for your answer.

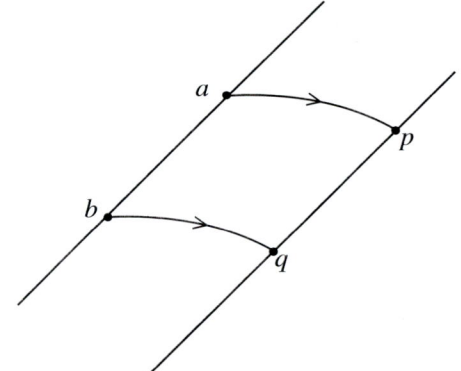

Exercise 10.14 ▼

Chapter test

1. $a(1, 2)$ and $b(7, 10)$ are two points.

Find **(i)** $|ab|$ **(ii)** the coordinates of m, the midpoint of $[ab]$.

2. The point $q(2, -1)$ is the midpoint of $[pr]$.

If the coordinates of p are $(-1, 1)$, find the coordinates of r.

3. Find the equation of the line through the point $(3, -2)$ with slope $-\frac{2}{5}$.

4. $p(1, -2)$ and $q(5, 1)$ are two points. Find:
   (i) the slope of pq **(ii)** the equation of the line pq.

5. $a(3, 3)$, $b(2, 1)$, $c(-2, 3)$, $d(5, -2)$ and $e(7, -1)$ are five points.
   Verify   **(i)** $bd \parallel ae$ **(ii)** $ab \perp bc$

6. Verify that the point $(3, -2)$ is on the line $2x - 5y - 16 = 0$.

7. $L : 3x + 2y - 7 = 0$ and $K: 2x - 3y - 1 = 0$ are the equations of two lines. Prove $L \perp K$.

8. L is the line $x + 2y - 1 = 0$. The line K contains the point $(-1, 4)$ and $K \perp L$.
   Find the equation of K.

9. L is the line $3x + y - 1 = 0$ and K is the line $2x - 3y - 8 = 0$.
   Find the coordinates of p, the point of intersection of L and K.

10. The equation of the line K is $3x - 2y - 12 = 0$.
   K intersects the x axis at a and the y axis at b.
   (i)   Find the coordinates of a and the coordinates of b.
   (ii)   Graph the line K.
   (iii)   Calculate the area of triangle aob where o is the origin.

11. Find the image of the point $(-1, 2)$ under the central symmetry in the point $(3, -1)$.

12. Find the image of the point $(2, -3)$ under the translation $(1, -1) \rightarrow (-2, 1)$.

13. $p(-3, -2)$, $q(1, -1)$ and $r(3, 5)$ are three vertices of the parallelogram $pqrs$.
   Find the coordinates of the fourth vertex s.

14. Find the image of the point $(-1, -2)$ under the axial symmetry in the y axis.

15. Find the image of the point $(3, 5)$ under the axial symmetry in the line $y = 2$.

16. The point $(1, -2)$ is on the line $3x - 4y + k = 0$. Find the value of k.

17. The point $(t, 3)$ is on the line $4x - 5y + 23 = 0$. Find the value of t.

18. The slope of the line containing the points $(4, -3)$ and $(t + 3, t - 2)$ is $\frac{3}{2}$.
   Find the value of t.

19. The line joining $a(2, 4)$ and $b(-5, 6)$ is parallel to the line $2x + ky - 4 = 0$.
   Find the value of k.

20. L is the line $ax + 3y - 2 = 0$ and K is the line $3x - 5y - 4 = 0$. If $L \perp K$, find the value of a.

21. The line $2x + y - 6 = 0$ is perpendicular to the line $2x + ky + 14 = 0$. Find the value of k.

22. The lines $ax + 4y + 5 = 0$ and $8x - by - 3 = 0$ are perpendicular.
   Calculate the ratio $a : b$.

23. $a(-2, 3)$ and $b(6, -1)$ are two points. Find:

   (i) $|ab|$

   (ii) the coordinates of the point c, the midpoint of $[ab]$

   (iii) the slope of ab

   (iv) the equation of ab

   (v) verify that the point $c(8, -2)$ is on the line ab

   (vi) the slope of a line perpendicular to ab

   (vii) the equation of the line L, through the point $d(3, 3)$ and perpendicular to ab

   (viii) verify that $c(2, 1)$ is the point of intersection of the lines ab and L

   (ix) the image of the point d under the axial symmetry in the line ab

   (x) the coordinates of p and q, the points where the line ab cuts the x and y axes respectively.

24. **(a)** Find the distance between the points $(-1, 3)$ and $(3, 0)$.

   (b) L is the line $x - 2y + 2 = 0$ and K is the line $3x + y - 8 = 0$.

   (i) Find the coordinates of p, the point of intersection of L and K.

   (ii) L cuts the x axis at q and M cuts the y axis at r.
   Find the coordinates of q and the coordinates of r.

   (iii) Calculate the area of triangle oqr, where o is the origin.

   (c) K is the line which contains the points $a(0, 4)$ and $b(3, 0)$.
   Find the equation of K.
   N is the line which is perpendicular to K and which contains the origin.
   Find the equation of N.
   Investigate if b is the image of a under the axial symmetry in N.

25. **(a)** The point $(k, 1)$ lies on the line $4x - 3y + 15 = 0$. Find the value of k.

   (b) $a(5, 3)$ and $b(-1, -1)$ are two points on a line. Find:

   (i) the slope of ab

   (ii) the equation of the line ab

   (iii) the coordinates of c, the midpoint of $[ab]$

   (iv) the equation of the line K which passes through c and which is perpendicular to ab.

   (v) The line K cuts the y axis at (o, h). Find the value of h.

   (c) Show that the points $p(4, 3)$, $q(3, 1)$ and $r(2, -1)$ are collinear.

26. **(a)** The point $(1, 2)$ is on the line M whose equation is $4x + ty - 10 = 0$.
   (i) Find the value of t **(ii)** Find the coordinates of the point where M cuts the y axis.

   (b) $a(1, -2)$, $b(-2, 3)$ and $c(3, 6)$ are three points.

   (i) Find the coordinates of p, the midpoint of $[ac]$.

   (ii) Show that $bp \perp ac$.

   (iii) Show that $|ab| = |bc|$.

   (iv) If $abcd$ is a parallelogram, find the coordinates of d.

   (c) The image of the point $(1, 3)$ under the axial symmetry in the line L is the point $(3, 7)$. Find the equation of L.

27. **(a)** Find the image of the point $(1, -2)$ under the central symmetry in the point $(-2, 2)$.

    (b) The equation of the line L is $3x + 4y = 24$.

        L cuts the x-axis at a and the y-axis at b.

        Find:

        (i) the coordinates of a and the coordinates of b

        (ii) the slope of the line L

        (iii) the equation of the line K through $q(7, 7)$ which is perpendicular to L

        (iv) the coordinates of p, the point of intersection of L and K

        (v) $|pq|$

        (vi) the area of the triangle aob, where o is the origin.

        (vii) Write down the equation of the line through q which is parallel to the x axis.

28. **(a)** Find the equation of the line containing the point $(5, 1)$ and which is parallel to the line containing $(0, 0)$ and $(2, 4)$.

    (b) $a(-4, 0)$ and $b(2, 8)$ are two points and o is the origin.

        (i) Find the slope of ab.

        (ii) Find the coordinates of m the midpoint of $[ab]$.

        (iii) Find the equation of the line P which passes through m and which is perpendicular to ab.

        (iv) Show that $|ob| = 2|om|$.

    (c) The line $2x + y - 6 = 0$ is perpendicular to the line $kx + 4y - 14 = 0$.

        Find the value of k.

29. **(a)** Find the coordinates of the midpoint of the line segment which joins the points $(2, -3)$ and $(-8, -6)$.

    (b) $a(-2, -1)$, $b(1, 0)$ and $c(-5, 2)$ are three points.

        (i) Show that $|ab| = \sqrt{10}$.

        (ii) Find $|bc|$.

        (iii) Hence, find the ratio $|ab|:|ab|$.

        Give your answer in the form $m : n$ where m and n are whole numbers.

    (c) The line L has equation $x + 2y - 6 = 0$.

        K is the line through $t(3, 4)$ which is perpendicular to L.

        (i) Find the equation of K.

        (ii) Find the coordinates of p, the point of intersection of L and K.

        L cuts the y axis at q and K cuts the y axis at r.

        (iii) Calculate the area of triangle pqr.

30. **(a)** The point $(-3, 4)$ is on the line whose equation is $5x + y + k = 0$.

        Find the value of k.

    (b) $a(2, -1)$, $b(-2, 3)$, $c(-1, -1)$ and $d(4, -6)$ are points.

        (i) Show that ab is parallel to cd.

        (ii) Investigate if $abcd$ is a parallelogram.

        Give a reason for your answer.

(c) The equation of the line L is $x - 2y + 10 = 0$.
- **(i)** Verify that the point $t(2, 6)$ is on L.
- **(ii)** Find the equation of the line N which passes through t and which is perpendicular to L.
- **(iii)** The line N cuts the x-axis at r and it cuts the y-axis at s.
  Calculate the ratio

$$\frac{|rt|}{|ts|}.$$

Give your answer in the form $\dfrac{p}{q}$, where p and q are whole numbers.

31. **(a)** L is a line through the origin. Under the axial symmetry in L, $(4, -6)$ is the image of $(6, 4)$. Find the equation of L.

(b) The equation of the line M is $y - 4x - c = 0$.
M contains the point $p(1, 6)$.
- **(i)** Find the value of c.
- **(ii)** The origin is the midpoint of $[pq]$.
  Find the equation of the line K if K is parallel to M and K contains the point q.
- **(iii)** Find the equation of the line L if L is perpendicular to M and L contains the point q.

(c) $pqrs$ is a parallelogram in which the opposite vertices are $p(2, 1)$ and $r(4, 4)$.
If the slope of pq is $\frac{1}{3}$ and the slope of $ps = -2$, find:
- **(i)** the equation of pq
- **(ii)** the equation of qr.
- **(iii)** Hence, or otherwise, find the coordinates of q and s.

32. **(a)** $p(4, -1)$ and $q(-6, 5)$ are two points.
Find the equation of the perpendicular bisector of $[pq]$.

(b) The equation of the line L is $2x - y + 4 = 0$.
L intersects the x axis at p and the y axis at q.
Find the coordinates of p and the coordinates of q. Show L on a diagram.
The line K passes through $(1, 1)$ and is perpendicular to L.
Find the equation of K.
Find the coordinates of the point where K cuts the x axis.
Find the coordinates of r, the point of intersection of L and K.
Find the area of the triangle enclosed by L, K and the x axis.

(c) $x(1, 6)$, $y(-3, -1)$ and $z(2, k)$ are three points.
If $|xy|^2 = |xz|^2$, find the two possible values of k.

ARITHMETIC

Significant figures

The most significant figure in a number is the figure which has the greatest value. In other words, the first figure on the left (except 0) is called the first significant figure, the next figure is called the second significant figure and so on.

To round a number to a given number of significant figures do the following:

1. Start at the most significant figure and count the required number of figures.
2. Look at the next figure to the right.
   (i) If it is 5 or more, increase the previous figure by 1.
   (ii) If it is less than 5, leave the previous figure as it is.
3. Add zeros, as necessary, to preserve place value.

Note: On our course, significant figures are for integer values (whole numbers) only.
'Significant figures' is often shortened to sig. fig.

It is always good practice to find an estimate for any calculation before using your calculator.

Example ▼

Write **(a)** 248,300 **(b)** 65,397.68 correct to **(i)** 1 **(ii)** 2 **(iii)** 3 significant figures.

Solution:

(a) 2 4 8 300
①②③

(i) 200,000 correct to 1 sig. fig.
4 < 5 ∴ round down

(ii) 250,000 correct to 2 sig. fig.
8 > 5 ∴ round up

(iii) 248,000 correct to 3 sig. fig.
3 < 5 ∴ round down

(b) 6 5 397.68
①②③

(i) 70,000 correct to 1 sig. fig.
5 = 5 ∴ round up

(ii) 65,000 correct to 2 sig. fig.
3 < 5 ∴ round down

(iii) 65,400 correct to 3 sig. fig.
9 > 5 ∴ round up

1. Complete the following tables by writing the given number correct to the required number of significant figures:

Number	Sig. fig.	Answer
4,827	1	5,000
354,000	2	
59,640	3	
6,854	1	
1,391	2	

Number	Sig. fig.	Answer
27,041	3	
77.387	1	
37.437	2	
183.691	3	
4,358,194	4	

2. Evaluate **(a)** $\sqrt{\dfrac{538.24}{0.01-(0.06)^2}}$ **(b)** $\sqrt{\dfrac{1}{(0.025)^2}+18\sqrt{20.25}}$

giving your answers **(i)** exactly **(ii)** correct to one significant figure.

In questions 3 – 8, round off each number correct to one significant figure and calculate an approximate answer. Then, using your calculator, or otherwise, find the exact answer:

3. 4.8×8.3

4. $4.15(11.2 - 4.4)$

5. $69 \times \sqrt{104.04}$

6. $\dfrac{9.269}{\sqrt{8.9401}}$

7. $\dfrac{199.98}{\sqrt{392.04}}$

8. $\dfrac{61.6502}{\sqrt{24.7009}+(5.1)^2}$

9. Evaluate $\sqrt{62.41} + 11.8 \times 2.5 + 3.2 \div 2$ correct to one significant figure.

10. Evaluate $(8.4)^2 + \dfrac{12}{\sqrt{0.0625}} + \dfrac{\sqrt{72.25}}{0.5}$ correct to two significant figures.

11. Evaluate $(4.38)^2 + \dfrac{\sqrt{50.8}}{2.04}$ correct to two significant figures.

Ratio and proportion

Ratios are used to compare quantities. We can be asked to divide quantities in a given ratio (proportional part) and solve problems on direct and inverse proportion.

Example ▼

(i) Express as a ratio of whole numbers $\frac{1}{2} : \frac{2}{3} : \frac{3}{4}$

(ii) Hence, or otherwise, divide €920 in the ratio $\frac{1}{2} : \frac{2}{3} : \frac{3}{4}$

Solution:

(i) $\frac{1}{2} : \frac{2}{3} : \frac{3}{4}$
   $= 6 : 8 : 9$

   multiply each fraction by 12
   (i.e. the LCM of 2, 3 and 4)

(ii) $\frac{1}{2} : \frac{2}{3} : \frac{3}{4} = 6 : 8 : 9$
   $6 + 8 + 9 = 23$
   there are 23 parts altogether

   $$1 \text{ part} = \frac{€920}{23} = €40$$

   6 parts $= €40 \times 6 = €\ 240$
   8 parts $= €40 \times 8 = €\ 320$
   9 parts $= €40 \times 9 = €\ 360$

   ∴ €920 in the ratio $\frac{1}{2} : \frac{2}{3} : \frac{3}{4}$
   $= €240, €320, €360$

Sometimes we are given an equation in disguise.

Example ▼

A glass rod falls and breaks into 3 pieces whose lengths are in the ratio 8 : 9 : 5. If the sum of the lengths of the two larger pieces is 119 cm, find the length of the third piece.

Solution:

$8 + 9 + 5 = 22$
∴ there are 22 parts altogether
Given: sum of two larger lengths is 119 cm
      (8 + 9) parts $= 119$ cm
      17 parts $= 119$ cm
      1 part $= 7$ cm

   third piece
   $=$ smallest piece
   $= 5$ parts
   $= 5 \times 7$ cm
   $= 35$ cm

If $a : b = 4 : 5$ and $b : c = 6 : 7$, find the ratio $a : b : c$.

Solution:

$a : b = 4 : 5$ and $b : c = 6 : 7$
The method we use is to make the b's the same in each ratio.
$a : b = 4 : 5 = 24 : 30$ (multiply both by 6)
$b : c = 6 : 7 = 30 : 35$ (multiply both by 5)
b is now 30 in both ratios.
  $\therefore a : b : c = 24 : 30 : 35$

Sometimes we have to solve problems involving inverse proportion.

6 men can build a wall in 24 days.
(i) How long would it take 8 men to build the same wall?
(ii) How many men are required to build the wall in 16 days?

Solution:

(i) We are looking for the number of days, so days go on the right-hand side.
     6 men = 24 days   (given)
   $\therefore$ 1 man = 144 days   (1 man takes 6 times as long as 6 men)
   $\therefore$ 8 men = 18 days   (8 men take $\frac{1}{8}$ of the time it takes 1 man)
   $\therefore$ 8 men could build the wall in 18 days.

(ii) We are looking for the number of men, so men go on the right-hand side.
    24 days = 6 men   (given)
   $\therefore$ 1 day = 144 men   (1 day requires 24 times the number of men
                                required by 24 days)

  $\therefore$ 16 days = 9 men   (16 days requires $\frac{1}{16}$ the number of men

                                required by 1 day)
   $\therefore$ 9 men are required to build the wall in 16 days.

Note: Strictly speaking, these are not equations, but using equations makes the working
       easier.

1. €40 is divided between two pupils in the ratio 7 : 3. How much does each pupil get?
2. €58.50 is divided between A and B in the ratio 8 : 5. How much does each receive?
3. Divide 238 in the ratio 2 : 5 : 7.
4. A prize fund of €18,000 is divided as follows:
   the first prize is half the fund, the second prize is two-thirds the first prize, and the third prize is what remains. How much is the third prize?

Express each of the following ratios in their simplest form:

5. $1\frac{1}{2}:2$ **6.** $1\frac{1}{4}:1$ **7.** $\frac{1}{3}:1$ **8.** $\frac{1}{2}:\frac{1}{4}:\frac{1}{3}$ **9.** $\frac{3}{4}:\frac{1}{2}:1$

10. €105 was shared among three people in the ratio $1:2:\frac{1}{2}$. Calculate the smallest share.

11. Divide 462 g in the ratio $\frac{1}{2}:\frac{3}{5}:1$.

12. €546 was shared among three people in the ratio $1:\frac{2}{3}:\frac{1}{2}$.

    How much did each person receive?

13. €140 is divided between A, B and C so that A gets twice as much as B and C gets twice as much as A.
    (i) Who receives the smallest share?
    (ii) How much does each receive?

14. A, B, C and D shared €493. B and C each received twice as much as A while D received 350% of what A received. Calculate how much each received.

15. €450 is divided between A, B and C such that A's share is twice that of B, and C's share is 50% of A and B's share together. Calculate A's share.

16. If $a:b=2:3$ and $b:c=6:7$, find the ratio $a:b:c$.

17. If $p:q=1:2$ and $q:r=5:7$, find the ratio $p:q:r$.

18. If $a:b=4:5$ and $b:c=3:2$, find the ratio $a:c$.

19. If $p:q=\frac{2}{3}:\frac{5}{6}$ and $q:r=\frac{1}{2}:\frac{7}{12}$, find the ratio $p:q:r$.

20. $x:y:z=2:4:5$. If $z=15$, evaluate $x+y+z$.

21. $a:b:c=3:5:6$. If $a=21$, evaluate $3a+2b+5c$.

22. A and B share a sum of money in the ratio 2 : 3. If A's share is €80, calculate B's share.

23. P, Q and R share a sum of money in the ratio 2 : 4 : 5, respectively.
    If Q's share is €60, find (i) P's share (ii) the total sum of money shared.

24. The ratio of the speeds of two cars is 4 : 5. If the faster car is travelling at 85 km/h, calculate the speed of the slower car.

25. The profits of a business owned by A, B, and C are shared in the ratio of their investments, €32,000, €16,000 and €20,000 respectively. If C received €6,350, how much did A receive?

26. A woman gave some money to her 4 children in the ratio 2 : 3 : 5 : 9. If the difference between the largest and the smallest share is €87.50, how much money did she give altogether?

27. The speeds of a train and a motorbike are in the ratio $1\frac{1}{2} : 2$, respectively. If the speed of the train is 84 km/h, find the speed of the motorbike in km/h.

The next four problems involve inverse proportion.

28. 12 men can build a wall in 10 days.
  (i) How many days would it take one man to build the same wall?
  (ii) How many days would it take 15 men to build the same wall?
  (iii) How many men are required to build the wall in 5 days?

29. 20 people take 15 hours to count the votes after an election.
  (i) How long would it take if 25 people were used to do the counting?
  (ii) How many people would be required to count the votes in 6 hours?

30. 14 girls can set up a tent in 30 minutes. How long would it take 20 girls to set up the same tent?

31. 5 men can complete a certain task in 16 days. If conditions change and the task must be completed in 10 days, how many **extra** men are required?

Distance, speed and time

There are three formulas to remember when dealing with problems involving distance (D), speed (S), and time (T). It can be difficult to remember these formulas; however, the work can be made easier using a triangle and the memory aid 'Dad's Silly Triangle'.

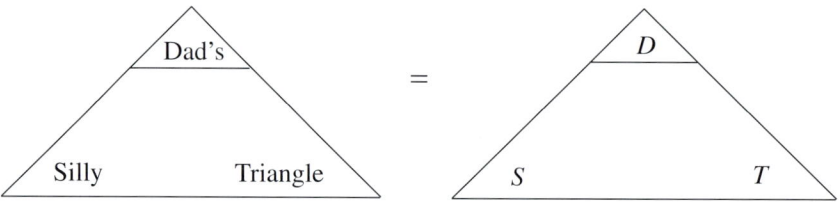

1. $\text{Speed} = \dfrac{\text{Distance}}{\text{Time}}$ **2.** $\text{Time} = \dfrac{\text{Distance}}{\text{Speed}}$ **3.** $\text{Distance} = \text{Speed} \times \text{Time}$

Consider the triangle on the right. By covering the quantity required, D, S or T, any of the three formulas above can be found by inspection.

Note: It is important to be able to change minutes into hours:

  e.g.   40 minutes $= \frac{40}{60}$ hours $= \frac{2}{3}$ hour

  12 minutes $= \frac{12}{60}$ hours $= \frac{1}{5}$ hour

Example ▼

(i) A journey of 18 km took 40 minutes. Find the average speed in metres per second.
(ii) A journey of 276 km began at 10:40 and ended on the same day at 14:30.
Find the average speed in km/h.

Solution:

(i) 18 km $= 18,000$ m

40 minutes $= 40 \times 60 = 2,400$ seconds

$$\text{Speed} = \frac{\text{Distance}}{\text{Time}}$$

$$= \frac{18,000}{2,400}$$

$$= 7\tfrac{1}{2}\,\text{m/s}$$

(ii) Time $= 14{:}30$ hrs $- 10{:}40$ hrs

$$= 3 \text{ hours } 50 \text{ minutes} = 3\tfrac{5}{6} \text{ hours}$$

$$\text{Speed} = \frac{\text{Distance}}{\text{Time}}$$

$$= \frac{276}{3\tfrac{5}{6}}$$

$$= 72 \text{ km/h}$$

Two-part problems

Two-part questions on distance, speed and time involve two separate journeys. In these questions we need the total distance travelled for both journeys and the total time for both journeys. We then use the formula:

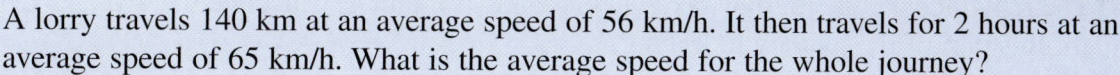

$$\begin{matrix}\text{Overall average speed} \\ \text{for both journeys}\end{matrix} = \frac{\text{Total distance for both journeys}}{\text{Total time for both journeys}}$$

Example ▼

A lorry travels 140 km at an average speed of 56 km/h. It then travels for 2 hours at an average speed of 65 km/h. What is the average speed for the whole journey?

Solution:

In the first journey the time is required

$$\text{Time} = \frac{\text{Distance}}{\text{Speed}}$$

$$= \frac{140}{56}$$

$$= 2\tfrac{1}{2} \text{ hours}$$

In the second journey the distance is required

$$\text{Distance} = \text{Speed} \times \text{Time}$$

$$= 65 \times 2$$

$$= 130 \text{ km}$$

$$\text{Average speed for the whole journey} = \frac{\text{Total distance travelled}}{\text{Total time taken}}$$

$$= \frac{140 + 130}{2\frac{1}{2} + 2} = \frac{270}{4\frac{1}{2}} = 60 \text{ km/h}$$

Exercise 11.3 ▼

1. **(a)** A train takes 3 hours and 30 minutes to travel a distance of 315 km. Calculate the average speed of the train in km/h.
   (b) A cyclist travels $6\frac{3}{4}$ km at an average speed of 5 m/s. How long does the journey take?
   (c) A car travels for 2 hours and 20 minutes at an average speed of 81 km/h. How far does it travel?

2. An athlete ran 1,500 m in 4 minutes. Find the average speed of the athlete in metres per second.

3. A journey of 170 km began at 11:45 and ended on the same day at 14:35. Find the average speed in km/h.

4. Express a speed of 30 km/h in m/s.

5. A journey of 900 m took 40 seconds. Find the average speed in km/h.

6. A distance of 375 metres is travelled in 25 seconds. Find the average speed in km/h.

7. The distance between two railway stations is 253 km. If the train leaves one station at 08:40 and travels at an average speed of 69 km/h, calculate the arrival time at the other station.

8. A motorist travels a journey of 185 km. The motorist travels the first 80 km at an average speed of 75 km/h. How many hours and minutes does it take the motorist to travel the first 80 km?
   The remainder of the journey takes 1 hour and 45 minutes. Calculate the average speed for this part of the journey in km/h.

9. Anne walks a distance of 1.7 km to school from home. She walks at an average speed of 5.1 km/h. What is the latest time she can leave home to be in school at 08:55?

10. It takes 4 hours and 20 minutes to travel a journey at an average speed of 120 km/h. How many hours and minutes will it take to travel the same journey if the average speed is reduced to 100 km/h?

11. In a journey of 235 km a man drives for two hours at an average speed of 80 km/h. How long does the journey take if he travels the remainder of the journey at an average speed of 50 km/h?

12. A car travels 200 km at 50 km/h and then travels 360 km at 60 km/h. Calculate:
  - **(i)** the total distance travelled
  - **(ii)** the total time taken
  - **(iii)** the overall average speed.

13. A bus travelled a distance of 300 km at 75 km/h. It then travelled for 2 hours at 72 km/h. Calculate:
  - **(i)** the time taken for the first journey
  - **(ii)** the distance travelled in the second journey
  - **(iii)** the total distance travelled
  - **(iv)** the total time taken
  - **(v)** the overall average speed.

14. A train travelled 168 km at an average speed of 112 km/h. It then travelled for 45 minutes at an average speed of 100 km/h. Calculate:
  - **(i)** the total distance travelled
  - **(ii)** the total time taken
  - **(iii)** the average speed for the whole journey.

15. In a 160 km road race, a cyclist cycled the first 120 km at a steady speed of 30 km/h and completed the race at a steady speed of 40 km/h. Calculate the time taken by the cyclist for:
  - **(i)** the first 120 km
  - **(ii)** the rest of the race.

A second cyclist started the race at the same time as the first cyclist. At what steady speed must the second cyclist travel the 160 km so as to finish level with the first cyclist?

Percentages

In many questions dealing with percentages we will be given an equation in disguise. The best way to tackle this type of problem is to write down the equation given in disguise. From this we can find 1%, and, hence, any percentage we like.

A solicitor's fee for the sale of a house is $1\frac{1}{2}$ % of the selling price.
If the fee is €3,480 calculate the selling price.

Solution:

Given: Solicitor's fee is €3,480

$\Rightarrow \qquad 1\frac{1}{2}\% = €3,480$ (equation given in disguise)

$\Rightarrow \qquad 3\% = €6,960$ (multiply both sides by 2)

$\Rightarrow \qquad 1\% = €2,320$ (divide both sides by 3)

$\Rightarrow \qquad 100\% = €232,000$ (multiply both sides by 100)

$\therefore$ the selling price of the house was €232,000.

A bill for €94.08 includes VAT at 12%. Calculate the amount of the bill before VAT is added.

Solution:

Think of the bill before VAT is added on as 100%.

Given: $112\% = €94.08$ (equation given in disguise, $100\% + 12\% = 112\%$)

                $1\% = €0.84$ (divide both sides by 112)

             $100\% = €84$ (multiply both sides by 100)

$\therefore$ the bill before VAT is added is €84.

Exercise 11.4 ▼

In each of the following, express the first quantity as a percentage of the second:

1. 28, 140   **2.** 165, 250   **3.** 644 m, 560 m   **4.** 75 mm, 2 m

5. 25 ml, 1 litre   **6.** 390 g, 3 kg   **7.** 0.245, 0.35   **8.** $\frac{5}{8}$, 2.5

9. One litre of water is added to four litres of milk in a container.
Calculate the percentage of water in the container.

10. A tank contains 125 litres of petrol. 50 litres are removed.
What percentage of the petrol remains in the tank?

11. Find   **(i)** 19% of €250   **(ii)** $6\frac{1}{2}$ % of €370   **(iii)** $2\frac{1}{4}$ % of €164

12. Find   **(i)** 80% of 90% of 100   **(ii)** the sum of 50% of 20 and 60% of 30

13. A bill for €96.76 includes VAT at 18%. Calculate the amount of the bill before VAT is added.

14. A bill for €60.75 includes VAT at $12\frac{1}{2}\%$. Calculate the amount of VAT in the bill.

15. When a woman bought a television set in a shop, VAT at 23% was added on. If the VAT on the cost of the set was €195.50, what was the price of the television set before VAT was added? What was the price including VAT?

16. A boy bought a calculator for €73.80, which included VAT at 23%. Find the price of the calculator if VAT was reduced to 15%.

17. When the rate of VAT was increased from 18% to 23%, the price of a guitar increased by €60. Calculate the price of the guitar, inclusive of the VAT at 23%.

18. When 9% of the pupils in a school are absent, 637 are present. How many pupils are on the school roll?

19. A salesperson's income for a year was €70,000. This was made up of a basic pay of €40,000 plus a commission of 5% of sales. Calculate the amount of the sales for the year.

20. A fuel mixture consists of 94% petrol and 6% oil. If the mixture contains 37.6 litres of petrol, calculate the volume of oil.

21. In a sale the price of a piece of furniture was reduced by 10%. The sale price was €1,125. What was the price before the sale?

22. A salesperson's commission for selling a car is $1\frac{1}{4}\%$ of the selling price. If the commission for selling a car was €350, calculate the selling price.

23. 15% of a number is 96. Calculate 25% of the number.

24. When a number is reduced by 35% the result is 41.6. What is the number?

25. 27% of a number is 24. Calculate 18% of this number.

26. $k\%$ of a number is 86.4, while 5% of the same number is 18. Calculate k.

27. 20% of a number is x. Find, in terms of x, 60% of this number.

28. 15% of a number is x. Find, in terms of x, 12% of this number.

Foreign exchange

Currency is another name for money. In the European Union the unit of currency is called the euro (€). The method of direct proportion is used to convert one currency into another currency.

Note: Write down the equation given in disguise, putting the currency we want to find on the right-hand side.

Example ▼

(i) On a certain day, €1 = US$1.12. How many euros would you get for US$840?

(ii) A person buys 1,242 South African rand, R, when the exchange rate is €1 = R2.3. A charge is made for this service. How much, in euros, is this charge if the person pays €548.10?

Solution:

(i) Given:

$$US\$1.12 = €1 \quad \text{(euros on the right, because we want our answer in euros)}$$

$$US\$1 = €\frac{1}{1.12} \quad \text{(divide both sides by 1.12)}$$

$$US\$840 = €\frac{1}{1.12} \times 840 \quad \text{(multiply both sides by 840)}$$

$$US\$840 = €750 \quad \text{(simplify the right-hand side)}$$

(ii) Given:

$$R2.3 = €1 \quad \text{(euros on the right, because we want our answer in euros)}$$

$$R1 = €\frac{1}{2.3} \quad \text{(divide both sides by 2.3)}$$

$$R1{,}242 = €\frac{1}{2.3} \times 1{,}242 \quad \text{(multiply both sides by 1,242)}$$

$$R1{,}242 = €540 \quad \text{(simplify the right-hand side)}$$

Thus, R1,242 is worth €540 when the exchange rate is €1 = R2.3.

The person paid €548.10.

Therefore the charge = €548.10 – €540 = €8.10.

1. If €1 = $1.08, find the value of **(i)** €150 in dollars **(ii)** $918 in euros.
2. An airline ticket costs $598. If €1 = $1.15, calculate the cost of the ticket in euros.
3. If €1 = ¥280 (Japanese Yen), how many:
   (i) yen would you receive for €110?
   (ii) euros would you receive for ¥126,000?
4. A part for a tractor costs €400 in France and the same part costs R 912 in South Africa. If €1 = R 2.4, in which country is it cheaper, and by how much (in euros)?
5. When the exchange rate is €1 = $1.18, a person buys 2,950 dollars from a bank. If the bank charges a commission of $2\frac{1}{4}$%, calculate the total cost in €.
6. A person buys 2,640 Canadian dollars when the exchange rate is €1 = $2.2. A charge (commission) is made for this service. How much, in €, is this charge if the person pays €1,221? Calculate the percentage commission on the transaction.
7. If €1 = $1.20 and €1 = R2.25, how many dollars can be exchanged for 480 rand?
8. A tourist changed €2,000 on board ship into South African rand, at a rate of €1 = R2.4. How many rand did she receive? When she came ashore she found that the rate was €1 = R2.48. How much did she lose, in rands, by not changing her money ashore?
9. Dollars were bought for €800 when the exchange rate was €1 = $1.20. A commission is charged for this service. If the person received $936, calculate the percentage commission charged.
10. A supplier agrees to buy 100 computers for $600 each. He plans to sell them for a total of €62,400.
    (i) Calculate the percentage profit, on the cost price, he will make if the exchange rate is €1 = $1.25.
    (ii) Calculate the percentage profit, on the cost price, if the exchange rate changes to €1 = $1.20.

Income tax

The amount of income tax payable depends on:
1. Rates of tax.
2. Standard rate cut-off point.
3. Tax credits.

The tax office will notify each individual of their standard rate cut-off point and their tax credit, which can vary each year. They will also be notified of the tax rates on gross income, which can also vary from year to year.

The following is called the '**income tax equation**':

Gross tax – Tax credits = Tax payable

Gross tax is calculated as follows:

| Standard rate on all income up to the standard rate cut-off point | + | A higher rate on all income above the standard rate cut-off point |

Note: If a person earns **less** than their standard rate cut-off point then they only pay tax at one rate, the standard rate, on all income.

Net income is the amount of income left after all deductions have been taken away.

Example

A woman has a gross yearly income of €37,800. She has a standard rate cut-off point of €26,500 and a tax credit of €2,099. The standard rate of tax is 17% of income up to the standard rate cut-off point and 38% on all income above the standard rate cut-off point. Calculate:

(i) the amount of gross tax for the year
(ii) the amount of tax paid for the year.

Solution:

(i) Gross tax = 17% of €26,500 + 38% of €11,300
$$= €26,500 \times 0.17 + €11,300 \times 0.38$$
$$= €4,505 + €4,294$$
$$= €8,799$$

| Income above the standard rate cut-off point |
| $= €37,800 - €26,500$ |
| $= €11,300$ |

(ii) Income tax equation: Gross tax − Tax credits = Tax payable
$$€8,799 \quad - €2,099 \quad = €6,700$$

Therefore, she paid €6,700 in tax.

Example

A man paid €6,030 in tax for the year. He had a tax credit of €2,150 and a standard rate cut-off point of €27,500. The standard rate of tax is 18% of income up to the standard rate cut-off point and 38% on all income above the standard rate cut-off point. Calculate:

(i) the amount of income taxed at the rate of 38%
(ii) the man's gross income for the year.

Solution:

(i) Income tax equation: Gross tax − Tax credits = Tax payable

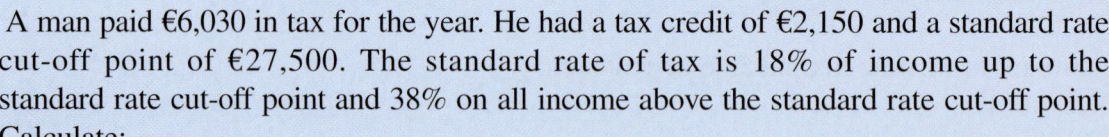

18% of €27,500 + 38% of (income above cut-off point) − €2,150 = €6,030
€4,950 + 38% of (income above cut-off point) − €2,150 = €6,030
38% of (income above cut-off point) + €2,800 = €6,030

$$38\% \text{ of (income above cut-off point)} = €3,230$$
$$1\% \text{ of (income above cut-off point)} = €85$$
divide both sides by 38
$$100\% \text{ of (income above cut-off point)} = €8,500$$
multiply both sides by 100

Therefore, the amount of income taxed at the higher rate of 38% was €8,500.

(ii) Gross income = standard rate cut-off point + income above the standard rate cut-off point
$$= €27,500 + €8,500 = €36,000$$

Exercise 11.6 ▼

1. A man has a gross yearly income of €24,000. He has a standard rate cut-off point of €27,000 and a tax credit of €2,880. The standard rate of tax is 20% of income up to the standard rate cut-off point. Calculate:
   (i) the amount of gross tax for the year
   (ii) the amount of tax paid for the year
   (iii) net income for the year.
   Express tax paid for the year as a percentage of gross income for the year.

2. A woman has a gross yearly income of €26,500. She has a standard rate cut-off point of €29,400 and a tax credit of €1,431. The standard rate of tax is 18% of income up to the standard cut-off point. Calculate:
   (i) the amount of gross tax for the year
   (ii) the amount of tax paid for the year
   (iii) net income for the year.
   Express tax paid for the year as a percentage of gross tax for the year.

3. A man has a gross yearly income of €28,700. He has a standard rate cut-off point of €29,700 and a tax credit of €2,009. The standard rate of tax is 19% of income up to the standard rate cut-off point. Calculate:
   (i) the amount of gross tax for the year
   (ii) the amount of tax paid for the year
   (iii) net income for the year.
   Express tax paid for the year as a percentage of gross income for the year.

4. A person has a gross yearly income of €28,620, with a standard rate cut-off point of €29,450 and a tax credit of €2,673. The standard rate of tax is 15% of income up to the standard cut-off point. Calculate:
   (i) the amount of gross tax for the year
   (ii) the amount of tax paid for the year
   (iii) net income for the year.
   Express tax paid for the year as a percentage of net income for the year.

5. A person has a gross yearly income of €42,000, with a standard rate cut-off point of €29,000 and a tax credit of €2,440. The standard rate of tax is 18% of income up to the standard rate cut-off point and 40% on all income above the standard cut-off point. Calculate:
   (i) the amount of gross tax for the year
   (ii) the amount of tax paid for the year.
   Express the amount of tax paid as a percentage of gross income.

6. A person has a gross yearly income of €38,400, with a standard rate cut-off point of €27,300 and a tax credit of €1,596. The standard rate of tax is 15% of income up to the standard rate cut-off point and 35% on all income above the standard cut-off point. Calculate:
   (i) the amount of gross tax for the year
   (ii) the amount of tax paid for the year.
   Express the amount of tax paid as a percentage of gross income.

7. A man has a gross yearly income of €24,500. He has a standard rate cut-off point of €27,200 and a tax credit of €1,980. If he pays tax of €2,430, calculate the standard rate of tax.

8. A woman has a gross yearly income of €28,200. She has a standard rate cut-off point of €29,500 and a tax credit of €1,875. If she pays tax of €2,919, calculate the standard rate of tax.

9. When the standard rate of tax is 20c in the euro, a man with a tax credit of €1,820 pays €3,140 in tax. If his gross income for the year was below his standard rate cut-off point, calculate his gross income for the year.

10. When the standard rate of tax is 18c in the euro, a woman with a tax credit of €1,786 pays €3,020 in tax. If her gross income for the year was below her standard rate cut-off point, calculate her gross income for the year.

11. A woman paid €9,350 in tax for the year. She had a tax credit of €1,860 and a standard rate cut-off point of €28,500. The standard rate of tax is 18% of income up to the standard rate cut-off point and 38% on all income above the standard rate cut-off point. Calculate:
    (i) the amount of income taxed at the rate of 38%
    (ii) the woman's gross income for the year.

12. A man paid €8,720 in tax for the year. He had a tax credit of €2,760 and a standard rate cut-off point of €25,900. The standard rate of tax is 15% of income up to the standard rate cut-off point and 35% on all income above the standard rate cut-off point. Calculate:
    (i) the amount of income taxed at the rate of 35%
    (ii) the man's gross income for the year.

13. A woman has an annual gross salary of €48,000. She has a standard rate cut-off point of €28,000 and a tax credit of €1,960. The standard rate of tax is 16% of her salary up to the standard rate cut-off point and $r\%$ on all income above the standard rate cut-off point.
    (i) Calculate the amount of tax paid at the standard rate.
    (ii) If the total tax bill for the year is €9,520, calculate the value of r.
    (iii) The woman's tax can be calculated by a simpler method under which the tax credit is increased and tax is paid at 27% on all her annual gross salary. She pays the same amount of tax. Calculate the amount by which her tax credit is increased.

14. A man has a gross yearly income of €x. He has a standard rate cut-off point of €28,000 and a tax credit of €1,760. The standard rate of tax is 18% of income up to the standard cut-off point and 40% of all income above the standard rate cut-off point. If he pays €9,680 in tax for the year, calculate:

    (i) the amount of income taxed at the rate of 40%

    (ii) the value of x

    (iii) The man's tax can be calculated by a simpler method under which the tax credit remains the same and gross tax is calculated on all his gross yearly income at r%. The man pays the same amount of tax. Calculate r.

Compound interest

Very often when a sum of money earns interest this interest is added to the principal to form a new principal. This new principal earns interest in the next year and so on. This is called '**compound interest**'.

When calculating compound interest, do the following:

Method 1:

Calculate the interest for the **first** year and add this to the principal to form the new principal for the next year. Calculate the interest for **one** year on this new principal and add it on to form the principal for the next year, and so on. The easiest way to calculate each stage is to multiply the principal at the beginning of each year by the factor

$$\left(1 + \frac{R}{100}\right)$$

This will give the principal for the next year, and so on.

Method 2:

Use the formula: $A = P\left(1 + \dfrac{R}{100}\right)^T$, where T = the number of years.

It is not necessary to memorise the formula, as compound interest problems are best solved a year at a time (as described in method 1). The examination questions will not require you to calculate compound interest beyond **three** years. Besides, the formula does not work if

(a) the interest rate, R, is changed during the three years, or

(b) money is added or subtracted during the three years.

In the next examples,

P_1 = principal at the beginning of year 1; A_1 = amount at the end of year 1.

P_2 = principal at the beginning of year 2; A_2 = amount at the end of year 2.

P_3 = principal at the beginning of year 3; A_3 = amount at the end of year 3.

Calculate the compound interest on €25,000 for three years at 8% per annum.

Solution:

$$1 + \frac{R}{100} = 1 + \frac{8}{100} = 1.08$$

Method 1:

$P_1 = 25{,}000$	(principal for the first year)
$A_1 = 25{,}000 \times 1.08 = 27{,}000$	(amount at the end of the first year)
$P_2 = 27{,}000$	(principal for the second year)
$A_2 = 27{,}000 \times 1.08 = 29{,}160$	(amount at the end of the second year)
$P_3 = 29{,}160$	(principal for the third year)
$A_3 = 29{,}160 \times 1.08 = 31{,}492.80$	(amount at the end of the third year)

Compound interest $= A_3 - P_1 = €31{,}492.80 - €25{,}000 = €6{,}492.80$

The working can also be shown using a table:

Year	Principal	Amount
1	25,000	$25{,}000 \times 1.08 = 27{,}000$
2	27,000	$27{,}000 \times 1.08 = 29{,}160$
3	29,160	$29{,}160 \times 1.08 = 31{,}492.80$

Compound interest $= A_3 - P_1 = €31{,}492.80 - €25{,}000 = €6{,}492.80$

Method 2:

Given : $P = 25{,}000$, $R = 8$, $T = 3$

$$A = P\left(1 + \frac{R}{100}\right)^T$$

$A = 25{,}000(1.08)^3$

$A = 31{,}492.80$ ▦ $25{,}000$ $\boxed{\times}$ 1.08 $\boxed{y^x}$ 3 $\boxed{=}$

Compound interest $= A - P = €31{,}492.80 - €25{,}000 = €6{,}492.80$

Repayments / further investments

In some questions money is repaid at the end of a year or a further investment is made at the beginning of the next year. It is important to remember that in these cases the **formula does not work**.

In the next example, $F_1 =$ a further investment at the beginning of the second year, $F_2 =$ a further investment at the beginning of the third year.

A person invested €20,000 in a building society. The rate of interest for the first year was $2\frac{1}{2}\%$.

At the end of the first year the person invested a further €2,000. The rate of interest for the second year was 2%.

Calculate the value of the investment at the end of the second year.

At the end of the second year a further sum of €1,050 was invested. At the end of the third year the total value of the investment was €24,720.

Calculate the rate of interest for the third year.

Solution:

$P_1 = 20,000$

$A_1 = 20,000 \times 1.025$ $\quad\left(\left(1 + \dfrac{R}{100}\right) = \left(1 + \dfrac{2\frac{1}{2}}{100}\right) = 1.025\right)$

$A_1 = 20,500$ (amount at the end of the first year)

$F_1 = 2,000$ (further investment of €2,000)

$\overline{P_2 = 22,500}$ ($A_1 + F_1 = P_2 =$ principal for the second year)

$A_2 = 22,500 \times 1.02$ $\quad\left(\left(1 + \dfrac{R}{100}\right) = \left(1 + \dfrac{2}{100}\right) = 1.02\right)$

$A_2 = 22,950$ (amount at the end of the second year)

Therefore, the value of the investment at the end of the second year = €22,950

$F_2 = 1,050$ (further investment of €1,050)

$P_3 = A_2 + F_2$ ($A_2 + F_2 = P_3 =$ principal for the third year)

$P_3 = 22,950 + 1,050 = 24,000$

Given: $A_3 = 24,720$ (amount at the end of the third year)

Interest for the third year $= A_3 - P_3 = 24,720 - 24,000 = 720$

Interest rate for the third year $= \dfrac{\text{Interest for the third year}}{\text{Principal for the third year}} \times \dfrac{100}{1}$

$= \dfrac{720}{24,000} \times \dfrac{100}{1}$

$= 3\%$

Given the final amount

Sometimes we are given the final amount and asked to find the original principal. We will use two methods to solve this type of problem.

Example ▼

A sum of money was invested at compound interest. The interest rate for the first year was 10%, for the second year the rate was 8% and the rate was 5% for the third year. After three years this sum amounted to € 24,948. Find the sum invested.

Solution:

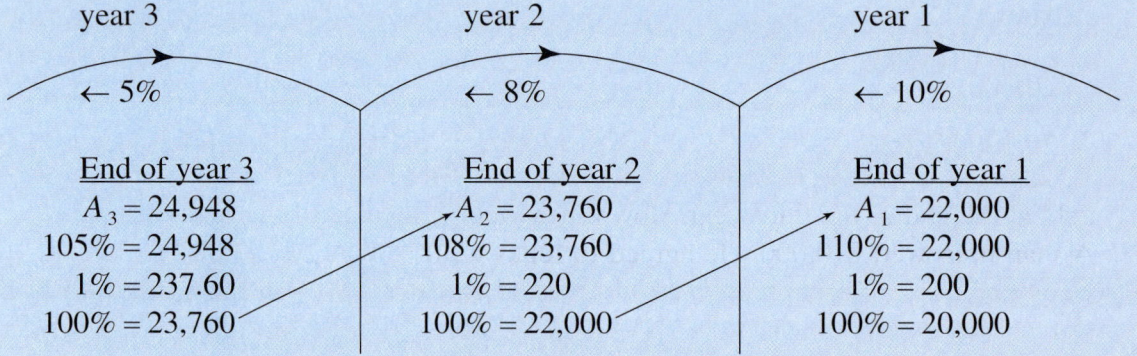

year 3	year 2	year 1
← 5%	← 8%	← 10%

End of year 3	End of year 2	End of year 1
$A_3 = 24,948$	$A_2 = 23,760$	$A_1 = 22,000$
$105\% = 24,948$	$108\% = 23,760$	$110\% = 22,000$
$1\% = 237.60$	$1\% = 220$	$1\% = 200$
$100\% = 23,760$	$100\% = 22,000$	$100\% = 20,000$

Thus, the original sum invested was €20,000

Method 2:
Calculate what €1,000 (or €100, €10,000, etc) will amount to and divide this into €24,948 and multiply this answer by €1,000.

$P_1 = 1,000$
$A_1 = 1,000 \times 1.1 = 1,100$
$A_2 = 1,100 \times 1.08 = 1,188$
$A_3 = 1,188 \times 1.05 = 1,247.40$

$$\frac{A_3}{P_1} = \frac{24,948}{1,247.40} = 20$$

Therefore the original sum invested = €1,000 × 20 = €20,000

Calculate the compound interest on each of the following investments:

1. €15,000 for 2 years at 8% per annum.
2. €12,000 for 2 years at 7% per annum.
3. €18,000 for 3 years at 5% per annum.
4. €25,000 for 3 years at 6% per annum.
5. €10,000 for 3 years at 3% per annum.
6. €20,000 for 3 years at 4% per annum.
7. €750 for 3 years at 10% per annum.
8. €5,000 for 3 years at 2% per annum.
9. €8,000 was invested for two years at compound interest. The interest rate for the first year was 4% and for the second was 5%. Calculate the total interest earned.
10. €6,500 was invested for three years at compound interest. The interest rate for the first year was 5%, for the second year 8%, and for the third year 12%. Calculate the total interest earned.
11. €2,500 was invested for three years at compound interest. The rate for the first year was 4%, the rate for the second year was 3%, and the rate for the third year was $2\frac{1}{2}$%. Calculate the amount after three years.
12. A woman borrowed €35,000 at 6% per annum compound interest. She agreed to repay €5,000 at the end of the first year, €5,000 at the end of the second year and to clear the debt at the end of the third year. How much was paid to clear the debt?
13. A man borrowed €10,000. He agreed to repay €2,000 after one year, €3,000 after two years and the balance at the end of the third year. If interest was charged at 8% in the first year, 5% in the second year and 6% in the third year, how much was paid at the end of the third year to clear the debt?
14. €7,500 amounts to €8,100 after one year. Calculate the interest rate.
15. €8,000 was invested for two years at compound interest.
    (i) The interest at the end of the first year was €320. Calculate the rate of interest for the first year.
    (ii) At the end of the second year the investment was worth €8,819.20. Calculate the rate of interest for the second year.
16. €20,000 is borrowed for two years. Interest for the first year is charged at 6% per annum.
    (i) Calculate the amount owed at the end of first year.
        €5,600 is then repaid.
        Interest is charged at x% per annum for the second year. The amount owed at the end of the second year is €16,146. Calculate the value of x.
17. €50,000 was invested for three years at compound interest. The rate of interest was 4% per annum for the first year and 3% per annum for the second year.
    (i) Calculate the amount of the investment after two years.
        Then a further €6,440 was invested.
    (ii) If the investment amounted to €61,500 at the end of the third year, calculate the rate of interest for the third year.

18. A person invested €25,000 in a building society. The rate of interest for the first year was $3\frac{1}{2}\%$. At the end of the first year the person invested a further €4,125. The rate of interest for the second year was 3%.

    (i) Calculate the value of the investment at the end of the second year.
    At the end of the second year a further sum of €2,100 was invested. At the end of the third year the total value of the investment was €34,485.

    (ii) Calculate the rate of interest for the third year.

19. A sum of money invested at compound interest amounts to €2,809 at 6% per annum for two years. Calculate the sum invested.

20. A sum of money invested at compound interest amounts to €12,597.12 at 8% per annum for three years. Calculate the sum invested.

21. A sum of money was invested at compound interest. The interest rate for the first year was 8% per annum, for the second year the interest rate was 5% per annum and the interest rate was 4% per annum for the third year. After three years this sum amounted to €53,071.20. Find the sum invested.

22. A sum of money was invested at compound interest. The interest rate for the first year was 10% per annum, for the second year the interest rate was 8% per annum and the interest rate was 5% per annum for the third year. After three years this sum amounted to €27,442.80. Find the sum invested.

In questions 23 to 25 it may make the working easier to calculate the amount after two years, then work backwards from the end of the third year and equate these amounts to find the sum of money withdrawn.

23. A person invested €20,000 for three years at 6% per annum compound interest.
    (i) Calculate the amount after two years.
    After two years a sum of money was withdrawn. The money which remained amounted to €22,260 at the end of the third year.
    (ii) Calculate the amount of money withdrawn after two years.

24. A person invested €50,000 for three years at 8% per annum compound interest.
    At the end of the first year, €9,000 was withdrawn.
    At the end of the second year, another sum of money was withdrawn.
    At the end of the third year, the person's investment was worth €39,960.
    Calculate the amount of money withdrawn after two years.

25. €42,000 was invested for three years at compound interest. The interest rate for the first year was 6% per annum, the interest rate for the second year was 4% per annum and the interest rate for the third year was 3% per annum. At the end of the first year €1,520 was withdrawn. At the end of the second year €w was withdrawn. At the end of the third year the investment was worth €41,200. Find the value of w.

26. €12,000 was invested for one year. It earned interest at the rate of 8% per annum.

   (i) Calculate the amount of the investment at the end of the year.

      A charge of €x was then deducted from this amount. The money which remained was converted into dollars, $, and the dollars were invested for a year at a rate of interest of 5% per annum. At the end of the year, the invested dollars amounted to $16,128.

   (ii) If the exchange rate was €1 = $1.20 on the day the euros were exchanged for dollars, calculate the value of x.

Exercise 11.8 ▼

Chapter test

1. (a) The ratio of boys to girls in a class of 35 pupils is 2:3. Find the ratio when two boys and one girl are absent.

   (b) A journey of 12 km took 40 minutes. Find the average speed in metres per second.

   (c) In a sale the price of a piece of furniture was reduced by 15%. The sale price was €1,105. What was the price before the sale?

   (d) $8\frac{1}{2}\%$ of a number is 59.5. Find $4\frac{1}{2}\%$ of the number.

   (e) A person buys 1,380 dollars when the exchange rate is €1 = $1.15. A charge is made for this service. How much, in euros, is this charge if the person pays €1,230?

   (f) A new machine costing €12,000 depreciates at a compound rate of 15% annually. Find the value of the machine at the end of the third year.

2. (a) Express 300 g as a fraction of 2 kg. Give your answer in its lowest terms.

   (b) Petrol cost 89.1c per litre after a budget rise of 8%. Calculate the cost of a litre of petrol before the budget.

   (c) A holiday complex consists of three different types of chalet.

Chart Type	Number of chalets	Number of people per chalet	Weekly rent per chalet
Type A	12	5	€300
Type B	20	6	€350
Type C	14	8	€450

During one week in July all chalets are fully occupied.

   (i) Calculate the number of people staying in the chalets at the holiday complex that week.

   (ii) Calculate the total amount of rent paid for that week.

   (iii) Calculate the average amount of rent paid per person during the week, giving your answer correct to 2 significant figures.

(d) (i) A car starts its journey at 11:51 and arrives at its destination at 15:06. The distance covered is 273 km. What is the average speed of the car in km/h.

(ii) A man drives from his house to visit a friend who lives 240 km away at an average speed of 120 km/h. He returns at an average speed of 80 km/h. What is his average speed for the whole journey?

3. (a) If $a : b = 3 : 5$ and $b : c = 4 : 7$, find $a : b : c$.

(b) A girl had €x pocket money to spend. She spent $\frac{2}{3}$ of her pocket money on a book and $\frac{2}{5}$ of the remainder of her pocket money on a card. She then had €1.20 left. Calcualte the value of x.

(c) At the beginning of each year for three consecutive years a person invested €560 at 5% compound interest per annum. Calculate the total value of the three investments at the end of the third year.

(d) A machine cost €15,000 when new. In the first year it depreciates by 10%. In the second year it depreciates by 8% of its value at the end of the first year. In the third year it depreciates by 5% of its value at the end of the second year. By completing the table, calculate its value after three years. Calculate its total depreciation after three years.

New price	€15,000
Value after 1 year	
Value after 2 years	
Value after 3 years	

4. (a) When a cyclist had travelled a distance of 12.6 km he had completed $\frac{3}{7}$ of his journey. What was the length of the journey?

(b) An estate agent charges a commission for selling a property as follows:
3% of the first €120,000 of the value of a property and 2% on the remainder.

(i) Calculate the fee charged on a property sold for €160,000.

(ii) If the estate agent received a fee of €5,400 for selling a property, how much was the property sold for?

(c) A person borrows a sum of money for two years at 8% per annum compound interest. She agrees to pay back half the amount outstanding, including interest, at the end of the first year and to clear the debt at the end of the second year. If she pays €8,748 to clear the debt at the end of two years, how much did she borrow?

5. (a) Divide €4,000 in the ratio $\frac{1}{2} : 1\frac{1}{2} : 3$

(b) A tanker delivered heating oil to a school. Before the delivery the meter reading showed 11,360 litres of oil in the tanker. After the delivery, the meter reading was 7,160 litres. Calculate the cost of the oil delivered if 1 litre of oil cost 36.5c.
When VAT was added to the cost of the oil delivered, the bill to the school amounted to €1,808.94. Calculate the rate of VAT added.

(c) A sum of money invested for one year earned interest at 4% per annum on the first €5,000 and 5% per annum on any amounts over €5,000. How much was invested if the interest earned was €350?

(d) A man has an annual gross salary of €52,000. He has a standard rate cut-off point of €29,000 and a tax credit of €1,560. The standard rate of tax is 18% of his salary up to the standard rate cut-off point and $r\%$ on all income above the standard rate cut-off point.

   (i)   Calculate the amount of tax paid at the standard rate.

  (ii) If the total tax bill for the year is €12,400, calculate the value of r.

 (iii) The man's tax can be calculated by a simpler method under which the tax credit is decreased and tax is paid at 25% on all his annual gross salary. He pays the same amount of tax. Calculate the amount by which his tax credit is decreased.

6. (a) The scale on a map is 1:25,000. The length of a wall on the map is 2.8 mm. Calculate the actual length in metres.

(b) A certain task takes 18 people 4 days to complete.
How many people would be required to complete the task in 3 days?

(c) Find the value of r for which

$$\left(1+\frac{r}{100}\right)^2 = 1.44, \quad r \in N.$$

(d) An antique dealer bought three chairs at an auction. He sold them later for €301.60, making a profit of 16% on their total cost. Calculate the total cost of the chairs. The first chair cost €72 and it was sold at a profit of 15%.
Calculate its selling price.
The second chair cost €98 and it was sold for €91.
Find the percentage profit made on the sale of the third chair.

(e) €30,000 was invested for a number of years at 10% per annum compound interest. At the end of the first year €5,400 was withdrawn.
At the end of the second year, another sum of money was withdrawn from the account. At the end of the third year, 88% of the original amount remained in the account.
How much money was withdrawn at the end of the second year?

PERIMETER, AREA AND VOLUME

Perimeter and area

Formulas required:

1. Rectangle

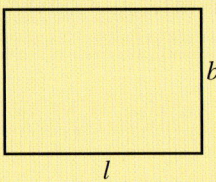

$$\text{Area} = lb$$
$$\text{Perimeter} = 2l + 2b = 2(l + b)$$

2. Square

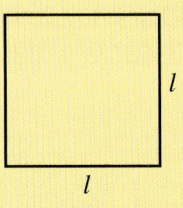

$$\text{Area} = l^2$$
$$\text{Perimeter} = 4l$$

3. Triangle

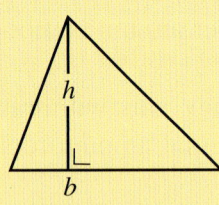

$$\text{Area} = \tfrac{1}{2}bh$$

4. Parallelogram

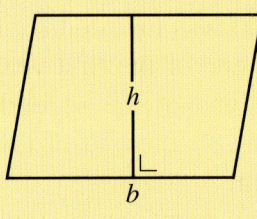

$$\text{Area} = bh$$

5. Circle (Disc)

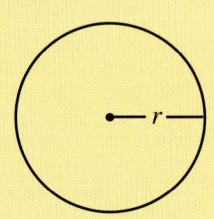

$$\text{Area} = \pi r^2$$
$$\text{Circumference} = 2\pi r$$

6. Sector of a circle

$$\text{Area} = \frac{\theta}{360} \times \pi r^2$$

$$\text{Length of arc} = \frac{\theta}{360} \times 2\pi r$$

$$\left(\text{Similar to circle with } \frac{\theta}{360} \text{ in front of formulas} \right)$$

The figure is made up of a semicircle, a rectangle and a triangle (all dimensions in cm). Find the area of the figure in cm^2.

$\left(\text{Assume } \pi = \frac{22}{7}\right)$

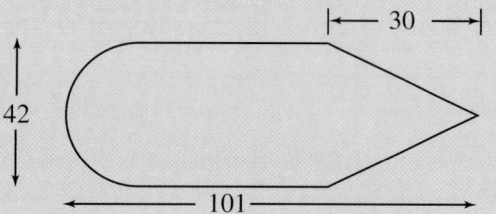

Solution:

Split the figure up into regular shapes, for which we have formulas to calculate the area. Find the area of each shape separately and add these results together.

1. Area of semicircle

$= \frac{1}{2}\pi r^2$

$= \frac{1}{2} \times \frac{22}{7} \times \frac{21}{1} \times \frac{21}{1}$

$= 693 \text{ cm}^2$

radius

$= \dfrac{42}{2} = 21 \text{ cm}$

2. Area of rectangle

$= l \times b$

$= 50 \times 42$

$= 2{,}100 \text{ cm}^2$

length

$= 101 - 21 - 30$

$= 50 \text{ cm}$

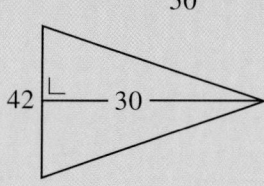

3. Area of triangle

$= \frac{1}{2}bh$

$= \frac{1}{2} \times 42 \times 30$

$= 630$

Area of figure = Area of semicircle + Area of rectangle + Area of triangle

$= 693 + 2{,}100 + 630 = 3{,}423 \text{ cm}^2$

Example ▼

The diagram represents a sector of a circle of radius 15 cm. $|\angle poq| = 72°$.
Find:

(i) the area of the sector *opq*, in terms of π.
(ii) the perimeter of the sector, assume $\pi = 3.14$.

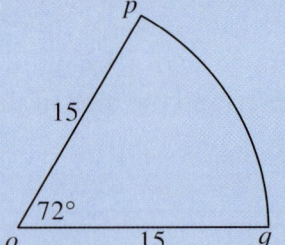

Solution:

(i) Area of sector

$$= \frac{\theta}{360} \times \pi r^2$$

$$= \frac{72}{360} \times \pi \times 15 \times 15$$

$$= \tfrac{1}{5} \times \pi \times 15 \times 15$$

$$= 45\pi \text{ cm}^2$$

(ii) Length of arc *pq*

$$= \frac{\theta}{360} \times 2\pi r$$

$$= \frac{72}{360} \times 2 \times 3.14 \times 15$$

$$= \tfrac{1}{5} \times 2 \times 3.14 \times 15$$

$$= 18.84 \text{ cm}$$

Perimeter $= 15 + 15 + 18.84 = 48.84$ cm

Notes: **1.** When using $\pi = \tfrac{22}{7}$, it is good practice to write the radius as a fraction.

For example, $21 = \tfrac{21}{1}$ or $10.5 = \tfrac{21}{2}$.

2. If a question says 'give your answer in terms of π,' then leave π in the answer: do **not** use 3.14 or $\tfrac{22}{7}$ for π.

Exercise 12.1 ▼

Unless otherwise stated, all dimensions are in cm and take $\pi = 3.14$. All curved lines represent the circumference, or parts of the circumference, of a circle. Where necessary give answers correct to two decimal places.

Find **(i)** the perimeter and **(ii)** the area of each of the following shapes:

1.

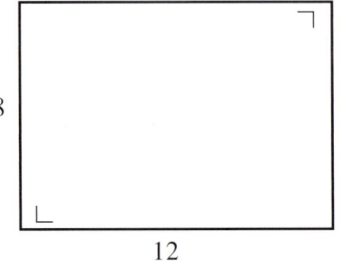

2.

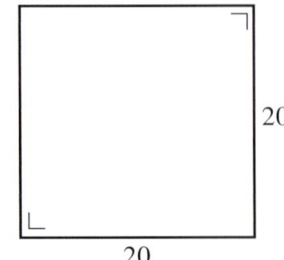

3.

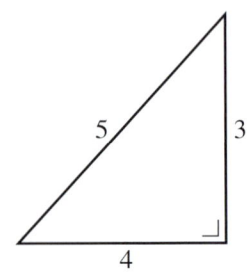

4.

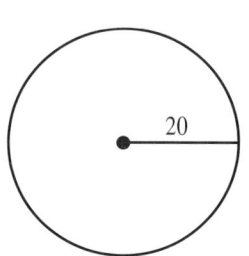

5.

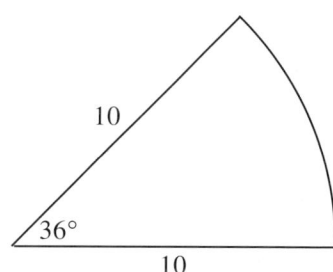

6.

7.

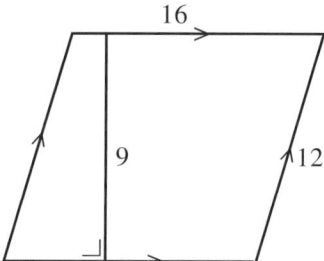

8.

9.

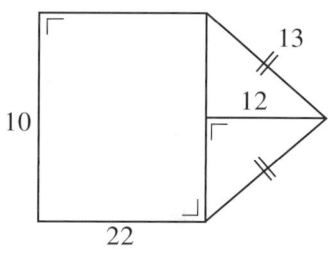

Find the area of each of the following:

10.

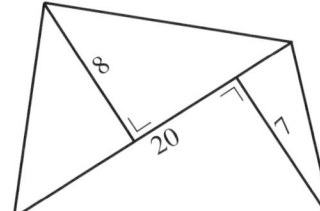

11.

12.

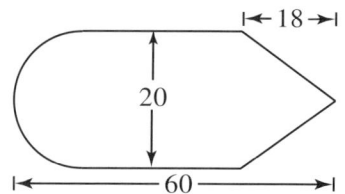

Calculate the area of the shaded region, where *abcd* is a rectangle and *pqrs* is a square:

13.

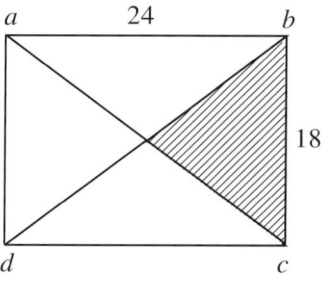

14.

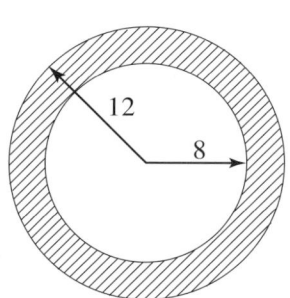

15.

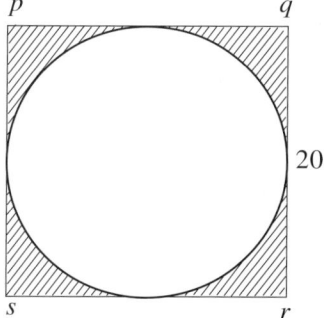

In questions 16 – 20, assume $\pi = \frac{22}{7}$.

16.

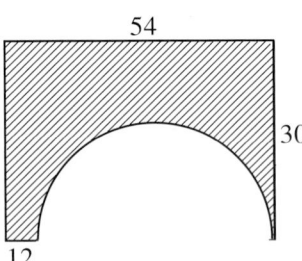

17.

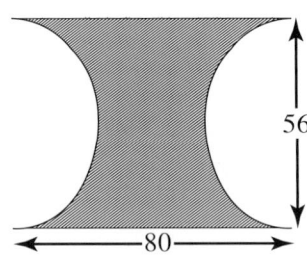

18.

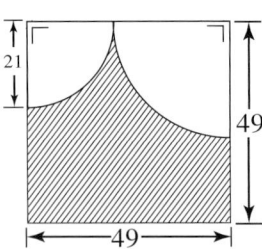

19.

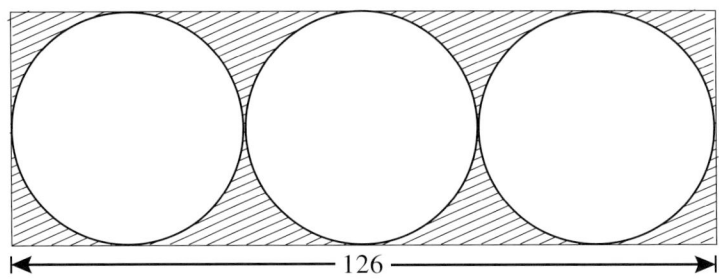

20.

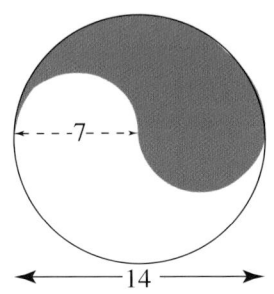

21. Two squares have sides of length 3 cm and 12 cm, respectively.
Find, in its simplest form, the ratio of their areas.

22. A square is inscribed in a circle.
The radius of the circle is 10 cm.
Find the area of the square.

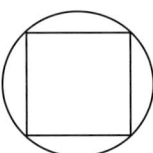

23. A square is inscribed in a circle as shown in the diagram.
The length of the radius of the circle is 7 cm.
Calculate the area of the shaded region.

$\left(\text{Assume } \pi = \frac{22}{7} \right)$

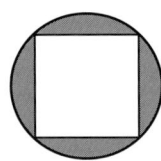

24. A bicycle wheel, including the tyre, has a diameter of 56 cm. How far will it have travelled when it has made 200 revolutions? How many revolutions will the wheel complete in a journey of 924 m?

$\left(\text{Assume } \pi = \frac{22}{7} \right)$

25. A running track is in the shape of a rectangle with semicircular ends as shown:

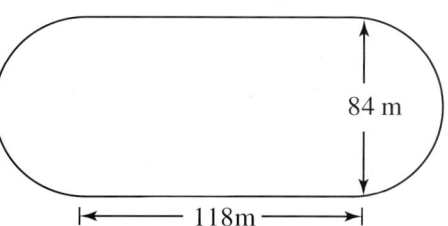

   (a) Calculate the length of the track.

   (b) Calculate the number of laps an athlete
      would have to complete in a 10 km race.

   (c) Another athlete ran 3 laps in 5 minutes.
      Calculate her speed in km/h.

   $\left(\text{Assume } \pi = \frac{22}{7}\right)$

Given the perimeter or area

In some questions we are given the perimeter, the circumference, or the area and asked to find missing lengths. Basically we are given '**an equation in disguise**' and we solve this equation to find the missing length.

Example ▼

The perimeter of a rectangle is 200 m. If length : breadth = 7 : 3, find the area of the rectangle.

Solution:

Let the length = $7x$ and the breadth = $3x$.

Equation given in disguise:

$$\text{Perimeter} = 200$$
$$\Rightarrow \quad 7x + 3x + 7x + 3x = 200$$
$$\Rightarrow \quad 20x = 200$$
$$\Rightarrow \quad x = 10$$
$$\therefore \text{ length} = 7x = 7(10) = 70 \text{ m}$$
$$\text{and breadth} = 3x = 3(10) = 30 \text{ m}$$

$$\text{Area} = l \times b$$
$$= 70 \times 30$$
$$= 2{,}100$$
$$\therefore \text{ Area} = 2{,}100 \text{ m}^2$$

Example ▼

The circumference of a circle is 50.24 cm. Calculate its area (assume $\pi = 3.14$).

Solution:

Equation given in disguise:

Circumference = 50.24 cm
$$\Rightarrow \quad 2\pi r = 50.24$$
$$\Rightarrow \quad 2(3.14)r = 50.24$$
$$\Rightarrow \quad 6.28r = 50.24$$
$$\Rightarrow \quad r = \frac{50.24}{6.28} = 8 \text{ cm}$$

$$\text{Area} = \pi r^2$$
$$= 3.14 \times 8 \times 8$$
$$= 200.96$$
$$\therefore \text{ Area of circle} = 200.96 \text{ cm}^2$$

1. The area of a rectangle is 240 cm². If its length is 20 cm, calculate **(i)** its breadth **(ii)** its perimeter.
2. **(i)** The perimeter of a square is 60 cm. Calculate its area.
    (ii) The area of a square is 81 cm². Calculate its perimeter.
3. The area of a triangle with base 15 cm is 60 cm². Find its perpendicular height.
4. The triangle and the rectangle have equal area. Find *h*.

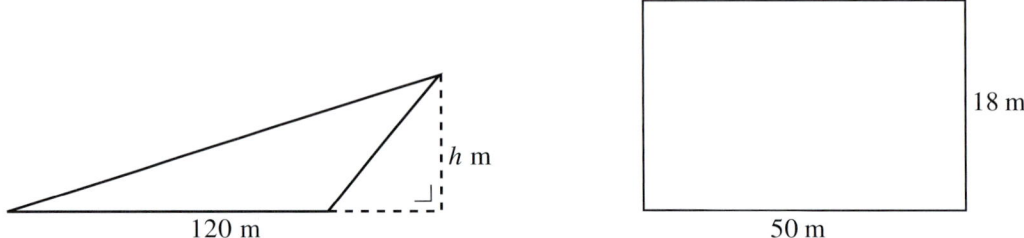

5. The perimeter of a rectangle is 450 m.
    If length : breadth = 5 : 4, find the area of the rectangle.
6. The area of a rectangle is 500 m².
    If length : breadth = 5 : 1, find the length and the breadth of the rectangle.
7. The length and breadth of a rectangle are in the ratio 9 : 5, respectively.
    The length of the rectangle is 22.5 cm. Find its breadth.

The table below shows certain information on circles, including the value of π to be used. In each case write down the equation given in disguise and use this to find the radius and complete the table.

	π	Circumference	Area	Radius
8.	π	20 π cm		
9.	π		16 π m²	
10.	π		6.25 π cm²	
11.	$\frac{22}{7}$	264 cm		
12.	$\frac{22}{7}$		616 m²	
13.	3.14	157 mm		
14.	3.14		2,826 m²	
15.	π		72.25 π cm²	
16.	$\frac{22}{7}$		346.5 m²	
17.	3.14		5,024 cm²	

18. The length of circle A is 6π cm. The length of circle B is 10π cm. Calculate the ratio, area of circle A : area of circle B.

19. A piece of wire of length 154 cm is in the shape of a semicircle, as shown. Find the radius length of the semicircle.

    $\left(\text{assume } \pi = \frac{22}{7}\right)$

    154 cm

20. A piece of wire is 198 cm in length.

198 cm

    The wire is bent into the shape of a circle.

    Calculate the radius of the circle.

    $\left(\text{assume } \pi = \frac{22}{7}\right)$

21. The diagram shows a small circle drawn inside a larger circle. The small circle has an area of 25π cm^2. The larger circle has a circumference of 16π cm. Calculate the area of the shaded region, in terms of π.

22. The diagram shows a small circle drawn inside a larger circle. The shaded area is 65π cm^2. The small circle has a radius of 4 cm. Calculate the radius of the larger circle.

Volume and surface area

The **volume** of a solid is the amount of space it occupies.
Volume is measured in cubic units, such as cubic metres (m^3) or cubic centimetres (cm^3).
Capacity is the volume of a liquid or gas and is usually measured in litres.

Note: 1 litre = 1,000 cm^3 = 1,000 ml

The **surface area** of a solid is the '**total area of its outer surface**'.
It is measured in square units such as square metres or square centimetres.
To calculate the surface area of a solid you have to find the area of each face and add them together (often called the 'total surface area'). With some objects, such as a sphere, the surface area is called the 'curved surface area'.

Note: It is usual to denote volume by V and surface area by SA.

Formulas required:

1. Rectangular solid (cuboid)

$$V = lbh$$

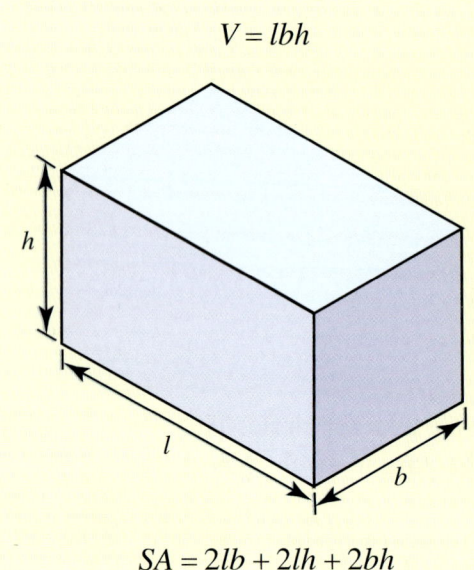

$$SA = 2lb + 2lh + 2bh$$

2. Cube

$$V = l^3$$

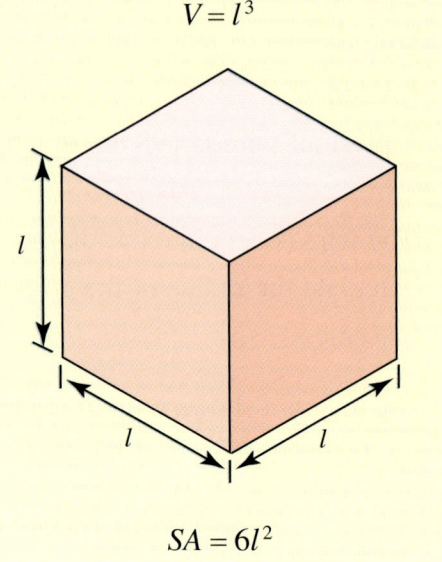

$$SA = 6l^2$$

Example ▼

An open rectangular tank (no top) is full of water.
The volume of water in the tank is 2.4 litres.
If its length is 20 cm and its breadth is 15 cm, find
(i) its height and   **(ii)** its surface area.

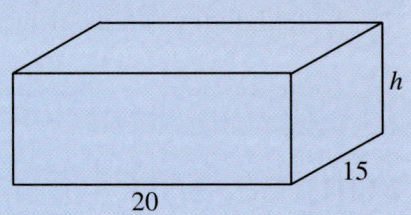

Solution:

1 litre = 1,000 cm^3, $\therefore$ 2.4 litres = 2.4(1,000) = 2,400 cm^3

(i)   Equation given in disguise:
    Volume = 2,400 cm^3
$\Rightarrow$ $l \times b \times h = 2,400$
$\Rightarrow$ $(20)(15)h = 2,400$
$\Rightarrow$ $300h = 2,400$
$\Rightarrow$ $h = 8$ cm

(ii)   Surface area
    $= lb + 2lh + 2bh$ (no top)
    $= (20)(15) + 2(20)(8) + 2(15)(8)$
    $= 300 + 320 + 240$
    $= 860$ cm^2

The surface area of a cube is 54 cm^2.
Calculate its volume.

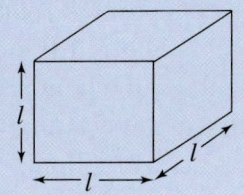

Solution:

Let the length of one side of the cube be l cm.
Equation given in disguise :

	Surface area = 54 cm^2	Volume = l^3
$\Rightarrow$	$6l^2 = 54$	$= 3^3$
$\Rightarrow$	$l^2 = 9$	$= 27$ cm^3
$\Rightarrow$	$l = 3$ cm	Thus, the volume of the cube is 27 cm^3

Exercise 12.3 ▼

Find **(i)** the volume and **(ii)** the surface area of a solid rectangular block with dimensions:

1. 6 cm, 5 cm, 4 cm   **2.** 12 m, 8 m, 6 m   **3.** 20 mm, 9 mm, 7 mm
4. The volume of a rectangular block is 720 cm^3. If its length is 10 cm and its breadth is 9 cm, find: **(i)** its height   **(ii)** its surface area.
5. An open rectangular tank (no top) is full of oil. The volume of oil in the tank is 60 litres. If its length is 50 cm and its height is 30 cm, find:
   (i) its breadth   **(ii)** its surface area.
6. The volume of a cube is 64 cm^3. Calculate its surface area.
7. The volume of a cube is 343 cm^3. Calculate its surface area.
8. The surface area of a cube is 24 cm^2. Calculate its volume.
9. The surface area of a cube is 150 cm^2. Calculate its volume.
10. The volume of a cube is 216 cm^3 and its surface area is $6k^2$ cm^2. Calculate k.
11. The lengths of the sides of a rectangular tank are in the ratio $2:3:5$. If the volume of the tank is $3\frac{3}{4}$ litres, calculate the dimensions of the tank.
12. The dimensions of a rectangular tank are 10 cm, 8 cm and 5 cm. The length of each side is increased by 1 cm. Calculate the percentage increase in capacity.
13. The ratio of the volumes of two cubes is $8:125$. Find the ratio of:
    (i) the lengths of their sides   **(ii)** their surface areas.
14. The diagram shows a steel girder. Calculate:
    (i) the area of its cross-section
    (ii) the volume, in cm^3, of steel used to manufacture it.

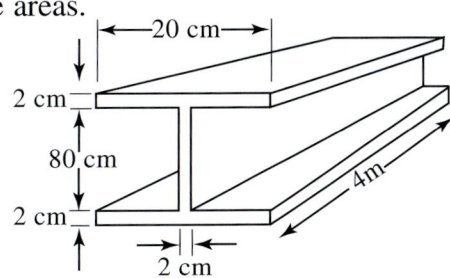

15. Five rectangular shaped concrete steps are constructed as shown.
Each step measures 1.2 m by 0.4 m and the total height is 1.0 m with each step having the same height of 0.2 m.
Calculate the volume of this solid concrete construction.

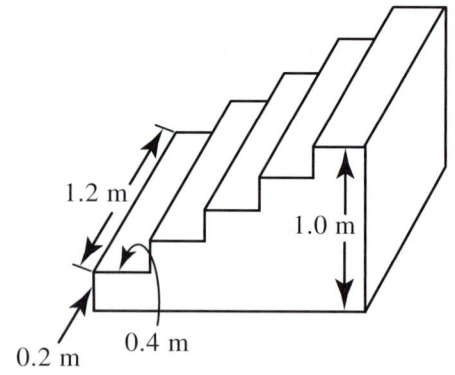

Cylinder, sphere and hemisphere

Formulas required :

Cylinder:

$$\text{Volume, } V = \pi r^2 h$$
$$\text{Curved Surface Area, } CSA = 2\pi rh$$
$$\text{Total Surface Area, } TSA = 2\pi rh + 2\pi r^2$$

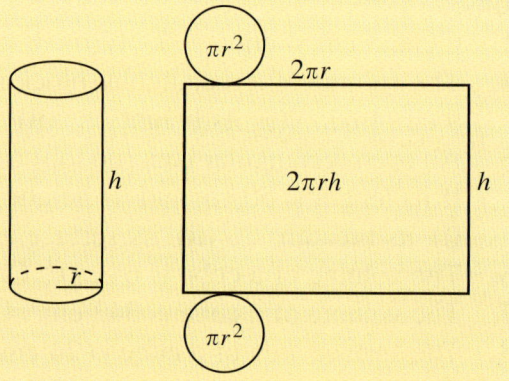

Sphere:

$$\text{Volume, } V = \tfrac{4}{3}\pi r^3$$
$$\text{Curved Surface Area, } CSA = 4\pi r^2$$

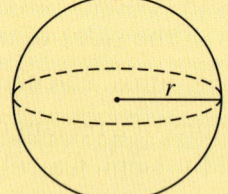

Hemisphere:

$$\text{Volume, } V = \tfrac{2}{3}\pi r^3$$
$$\text{Curved Surface Area, } CSA = 2\pi r^2$$
$$\text{Total Surface Area, } TSA = 2\pi r^2 + \pi r^2 = 3\pi r^2$$

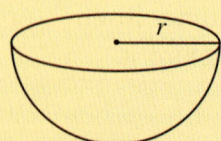

Example ▼

Find **(i)** the volume and **(ii)** the total surface area of a closed cylindrical can of radius 7 cm and height 10 cm $\left(\text{assume } \pi = \frac{22}{7}\right)$.

Solution:

(i) $V = \pi r^2 h$

$V = \frac{22}{7} \times \frac{7}{1} \times \frac{7}{1} \times \frac{10}{1}$

$V = 1{,}540 \text{ cm}^3$

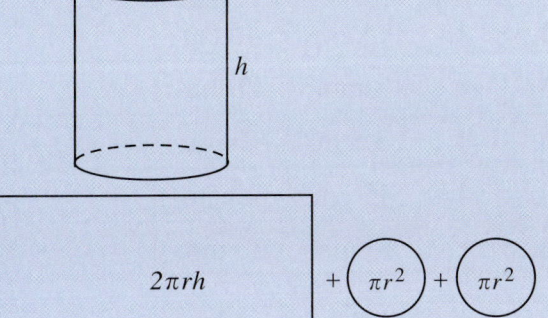

(ii) $TSA = 2\pi rh + 2\pi r^2$

$= \frac{2}{1} \times \frac{22}{7} \times \frac{7}{1} \times \frac{10}{1} + \frac{2}{1} \times \frac{22}{7} \times \frac{7}{1} \times \frac{7}{1}$

$= 440 + 308$

$= 748 \text{ cm}^2$

Example ▼

A solid sphere has a radius of 6 cm. Calculate **(i)** its volume and **(ii)** its curved surface area.

$\left(\text{Assume } \pi = 3.14.\right)$

Solution:

(i) $V = \frac{4}{3}\pi r^3$

$= \frac{4}{3} \times 3.14 \times 6 \times 6 \times 6$

$= 904.32 \text{ cm}^3$

(ii) $CSA = 4\pi r^2$

$= 4 \times 3.14 \times 6 \times 6$

$= 452.16 \text{ cm}^2$

Complete the following table, which gives certain information about various closed **cylinders**:

	π	Radius	Height	Volume	Curved Surface Area	Total Surface Area
1.	$\frac{22}{7}$	7 cm	12 cm			
2.	3.14	15 cm	40 cm			
3.	π	8 mm	11 mm			
4.	$\frac{22}{7}$	3.5 m	10 m			
5.	3.14	12 cm	40 cm			
6.	π	13 mm	30 mm			

Complete the following table, which gives certain information about various **spheres**:

	π	Radius	Volume	Curved Surface Area
7.	$\frac{22}{7}$	21 cm		
8.	3.14	9 m		
9.	π	6 mm		
10.	$\frac{22}{7}$	10.5 cm		
11.	3.14	7.5 cm		
12.	π	1.5 m		

Complete the following table, which gives certain information about various **hemispheres**:

	π	Radius	Volume	Curved Surface Area	Total Surface Area
13.	π	15 mm			
14.	π	$1\frac{1}{2}$ cm			
15.	$\frac{22}{7}$	42 cm			
16.	3.14	12 m			

17. A hollow plastic pipe has an external diameter 16 cm and an internal diameter 10 cm. Calculate the volume of plastic in 2 m of pipe.

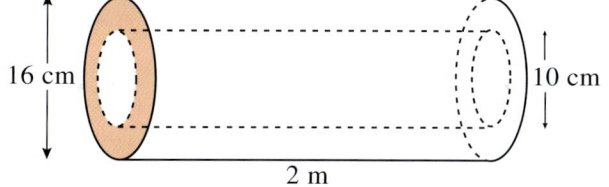

(Assume $\pi = 3.14$)

18. A cylindrical jug has dimensions radius 6 cm and height 40 cm. If the jug is full of lemonade, how many cylindrical tumblers, each with dimensions radius 4 cm and height 10 cm, can be filled from the jug?

19. A machine part consists of a hollow sphere floating in a closed cylinder full of oil. The height of the cylinder is 28 cm; the radius of the cylinder is 15 cm; and the radius of the sphere is $\frac{21}{2}$ cm.

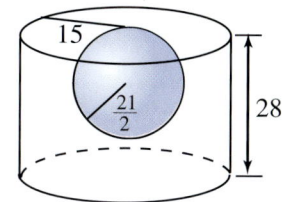

Taking π to be $\frac{22}{7}$, find the volume of

(i)   the cylinder
(ii) the sphere
(iii) the oil.

20. A sphere of diameter 12 cm fits exactly into a cylindrical box. Calculate the ratios:

(i)   curved surface area of cylinder : curved surface area of sphere
(ii) volume of cylinder : volume of sphere

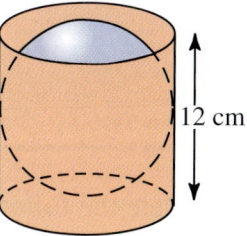

Cone

Formulas required:

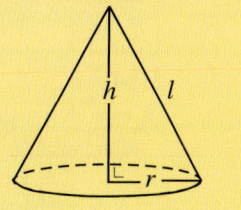

$$\text{Volume, } V = \tfrac{1}{3}\pi r^2 h$$
$$\text{Curved Surface Area, } CSA = \pi r l$$
$$\text{Total Surface Area, } TSA = \pi r l + \pi r^2$$
$$\text{Pythagoras's Theorem} : l^2 = r^2 + h^2$$

Notes: l is called the slant height.

A cone is often called a '**right circular cone**' as its vertex is directly above the centre of the base and its height is at right angles to the base.

A right circular cone has a height of 12 cm and a base radius of 5 cm.
Find **(i)** its volume **(ii)** its curved surface area (assume $\pi = 3.14$).

Solution:

(i) Volume of cone

$= \frac{1}{3}\pi r^2 h$

$= \frac{1}{3} \times 3.14 \times 5 \times 5 \times 12$

$= 314$ cm^3

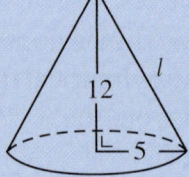

(ii) Slant height is missing.

$l^2 = r^2 + h^2$

$l^2 = 5^2 + 12^2$

$l^2 = 25 + 144$

$l^2 = 169$

$l = 13$ cm

Curved surface area

$= \pi r l$

$= 3.14 \times 5 \times 13$

$= 204.1$ cm^2

Exercise 12.5 ▼

Complete the following table, which gives certain information about various **cones**:

	π	Radius	Height	Slant Height	Volume	Curved Surface Area
1.	π	8 cm	6 cm			
2.	$\frac{22}{7}$		21 mm	29 mm		
3.	3.14	3 cm		5 cm		
4.	π	1.5 m		2.5 m		
5.	3.14		9 cm	41 cm		
6.	π	8 m		17 m		
7.	$\frac{22}{7}$	2.8 cm	4.5 cm			
8.	3.14	4.8 mm		5 mm		
9.	π	12 m	35 m			
10.	3.14	11 cm		61 cm		

11. A cone has a radius length 7 cm and height 2.4 cm.

Calculate **(i)** its volume **(ii)** its total surface area $\left(\text{assume } \pi = \frac{22}{7}\right)$.

12. A cone has a radius length 18 cm and height 16.25 cm.

Calculate **(i)** its volume **(ii)** its total surface area $\left(\text{assume } \pi = 3.14\right)$.

13. A cone with a slant height of 5 cm and a base radius of 3 cm, just fits into a hemisphere, as shown.
Calculate the ratios,
Volume of hemisphere : Volume of cone

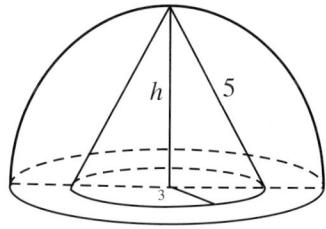

Curved surface area of the hemisphere : Curved surface area of the cone.

The following questions involve compound volumes.
Split the solid up into regular shapes, for which we have formulas to calculate the volume or surface area, and add the results together.

14. A glass container is in the shape of a cone surmounted by a cylinder, as shown. The height of the cylindrical part is 20 cm and the length of its radius is 8 cm. The slant height of the cone is 17 cm.
Show that the volume of the container is $1,600\pi$ cm^3.

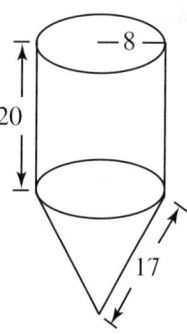

15. A test tube consists of a hemisphere, of diameter 3 cm, surmounted by a cylinder, as shown. The total height of the test tube is $16\frac{1}{2}$ cm.
Calculate, in terms of π, the volume of the test tube.

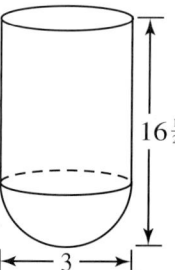

16. A boiler is in the shape of a cylinder with hemispherical ends (as shown in diagram). The total length of the boiler is 30 m and its diameter is 12 m. Find in terms of π:
    (i) its volume
    (ii) its surface area.

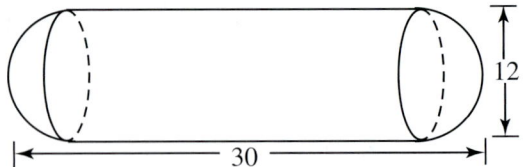

17. A solid object consists of 3 parts, a hemisphere, a cylinder and a cone, as shown, each having a diameter of 18 cm. If the height of the cone is 12 cm and the total height is 35 cm, calculate its volume, and surface area, in terms of π.

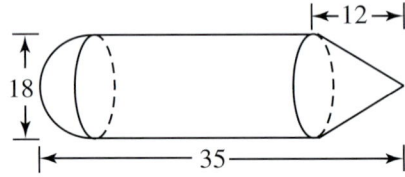

18. A buoy consists of an inverted cone surmounted by a hemisphere, as shown. If the radius of the hemisphere is 6 cm and the height of the cone is 9.1 cm, calculate, assuming $\pi = 3.14$:
    (i) the volume of the buoy
    (ii) the surface area of the buoy.

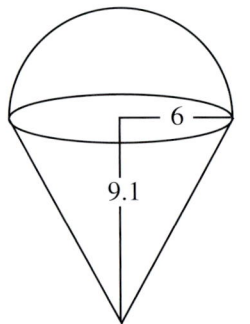

Given the volume or surface area

In some questions we are given the volume or surface area and asked to find a missing dimension. As before, write down the '**equation given in disguise**', and solve this equation to find the missing dimension.

(i) A cylinder has a volume of 192π cm^3. If its radius is 4 cm, calculate its height.

(ii) The volume of a sphere is $\frac{32}{3}\pi$ cm^3. Calculate its radius.

Solution:

(i) Equation given in disguise:

$$\text{Volume of cylinder} = 192\pi \text{ cm}^3$$
$$\pi r^2 h = 192\pi$$
$$r^2 h = 192 \qquad \text{(divide both sides by } \pi)$$
$$16h = 192 \qquad \text{(put in } r = 4)$$
$$h = 12 \text{ cm} \qquad \text{(divide both sides by 16)}$$

(ii) Equation given in disguise:

$$\text{Volume of sphere} = \frac{32}{3}\pi \text{ cm}^3$$
$$\frac{4}{3}\pi r^3 = \frac{32}{3}\pi$$
$$4\pi r^3 = 32\pi \qquad \text{(multiply both sides by 3)}$$
$$4r^3 = 32 \qquad \text{(divide both sides by } \pi)$$
$$r^3 = 8 \qquad \text{(divide both sides by 4)}$$
$$r = 2 \text{ cm} \qquad \text{(take the cubed root of both sides)}$$

Exercise 12.6 ▼

1. A cylinder has a volume of 720π cm^3. If its radius is 6 cm, calculate:
   (i) its height   **(ii)** its curved surface area, in terms of π.
2. The curved surface area of a sphere is 144π cm^2. Calculate:
   (i) its radius   **(ii)** its volume, in terms of π.
3. The volume of a cone is 320π cm^3. If the radius of the base is 8 cm, calculate its height.
4. The volume of a solid sphere is 36π cm^3. Calculate:
   (i) its radius   **(ii)** its surface area, in terms of π.
5. A solid cylinder has a volume of 96π cm^3. If its height is 6 cm, calculate:
   (i) its radius   **(ii)** its total surface area, in terms of π.
6. The curved surface area of a cylinder is 628 cm^2 and its radius is 5 cm.
   Calculate: **(i)** its height   **(ii)** its volume (assume $\pi = 3.14$).
7. A solid cylinder has a volume of 462 m^3. If the height is 12 m, assuming $\pi = \frac{22}{7}$,
   calculate: **(i)** its radius   **(ii)** its total surface area.
8. The curved surface area of a cone is 60π cm^2. If the radius of its base is 6 cm, calculate:
   (i) its slant height   **(ii)** its volume, in terms of π.
9. A cone has a volume of $\frac{160}{3}\pi$ cm^3. If the radius of the base is 4 cm, find its height.

10. The radius of a cylinder is 2.8 cm and its volume is 49.28 cm^3.

Calculate, assuming $\pi = \frac{22}{7}$:   **(i)** its height   **(ii)** its curved surface area.

11. The volume of a solid cylinder is 401.92 m^3. If its height is 8 m, calculate, assuming $\pi = 3.14$:   **(i)** its radius   **(ii)** its total surface area.

Equal volumes

Many questions involve equal volumes with a missing dimension. As before, write down the '**equation given in disguise**' and solve this equation to find the missing dimension.

Notes:

1. Moving liquids

In many questions we have to deal with moving liquid from one container to another container of different dimensions or shape. To help us solve the problem we use the following fact:

> **The volume of the moved liquid does not change**

2. Recasting

Many of the questions we meet require us to solve a recasting problem. What happens is that a certain solid object is melted down and its shape is changed. We use the following fact:

> **The volume remains the same after it is melted down**

3. Displaced liquid

In many questions we have to deal with situations where liquid is displaced by immersing, or removing, a solid object. In all cases the following principle helps us to solve these problems:

> **Volume of displaced liquid = volume of immersed, or removed, solid object**

In problems on moving liquids and recasting or displaced liquids, it is good practice not to put in a value for π (i.e. do **not** put in $\pi = \frac{22}{7}$ or $\pi = 3.14$), as the π's normally cancel when you write down the equation given in disguise.

A sphere of radius 15 cm is made of lead. The sphere is melted down. Some of the lead is used to form a solid cone of radius 10 cm and height 27 cm. The rest of the lead is used to form a cylinder of height 25 cm. Calculate the length of the radius of the cylinder.

Solution:

Equation given in disguise:
Volume of cylinder + Volume of cone = Volume of sphere

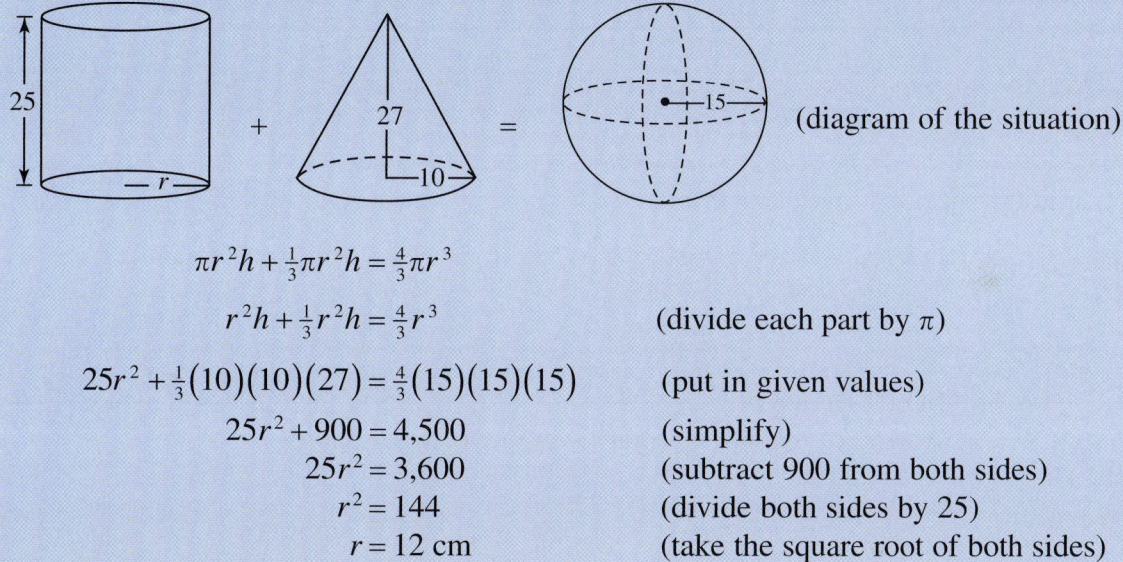

(diagram of the situation)

$$\pi r^2 h + \tfrac{1}{3}\pi r^2 h = \tfrac{4}{3}\pi r^3$$

$$r^2 h + \tfrac{1}{3}r^2 h = \tfrac{4}{3}r^3 \qquad \text{(divide each part by } \pi\text{)}$$

$$25r^2 + \tfrac{1}{3}(10)(10)(27) = \tfrac{4}{3}(15)(15)(15) \qquad \text{(put in given values)}$$

$$25r^2 + 900 = 4{,}500 \qquad \text{(simplify)}$$

$$25r^2 = 3{,}600 \qquad \text{(subtract 900 from both sides)}$$

$$r^2 = 144 \qquad \text{(divide both sides by 25)}$$

$$r = 12 \text{ cm} \qquad \text{(take the square root of both sides)}$$

Therefore, the radius of the cylinder is 12 cm.

(i) Find, in terms of π, the volume of a solid metal sphere of radius 6 cm.

(ii) Five such identical spheres are completely submerged in a cylinder containing water. If the radius of the cylinder is 8 cm, by how much will the level of the water drop if the spheres are removed from the cylinder?

Solution:

(i) Volume of sphere $= \frac{4}{3}\pi r^3 = \frac{4}{3}\pi(6)(6)(6) = 288\pi$ cm^3

(ii) Diagram: Old situation   New situation

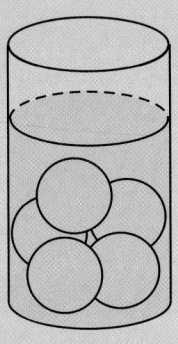
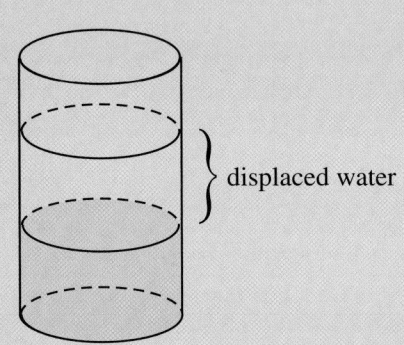

} displaced water

Equation given in disguise:

Volume of displaced water = Volume of five spheres

Diagram: 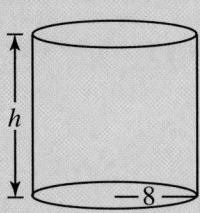 $=$ 5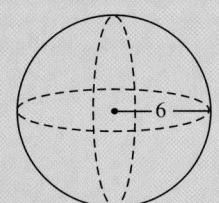

$$\pi r^2 h = 5(288\pi) \qquad \text{(Volume of sphere} = 288\pi)$$
$$\pi r^2 h = 1{,}440\pi$$
$$r^2 h = 1{,}440 \qquad \text{(divide both sides by } \pi)$$
$$64h = 1{,}440 \qquad \text{(put in } r = 8)$$
$$h = 22.5 \qquad \text{(divide both sides by 64)}$$

Thus, the level of water in the cylinder would fall by 22.5 cm.

Find the missing dimension. In each case the volumes are equal (all dimensions in centimetres):

1.

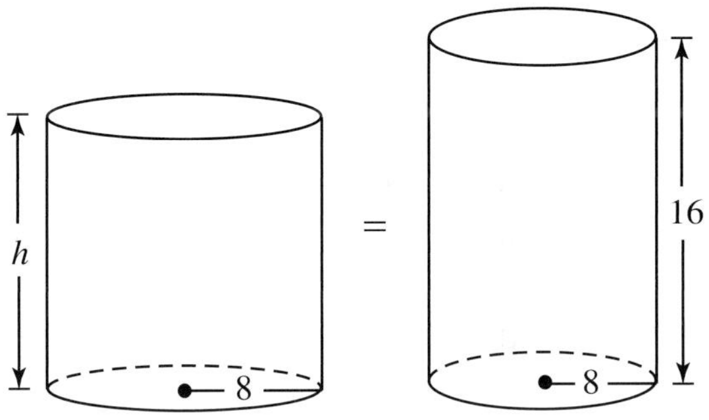

2.

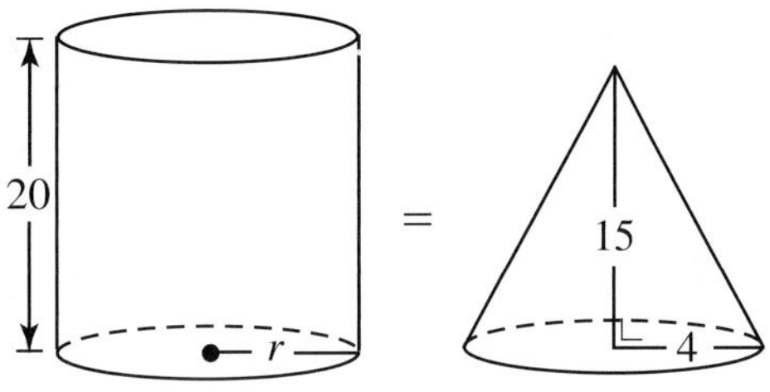

3.

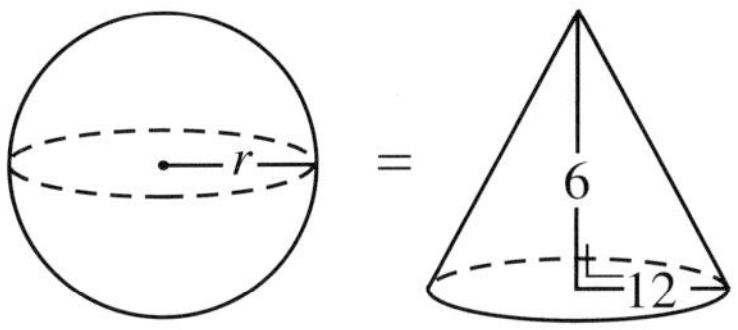

4.

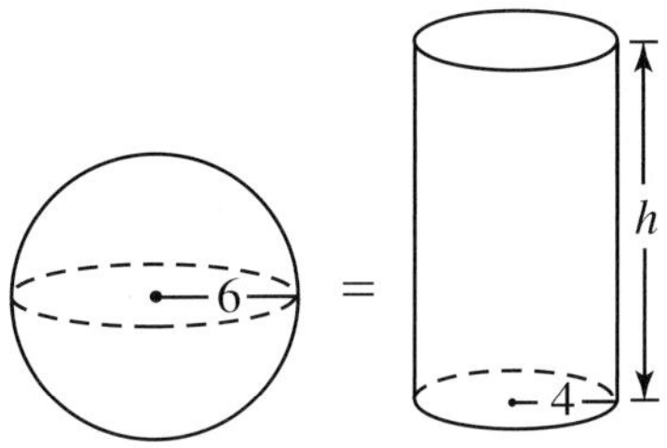

5.

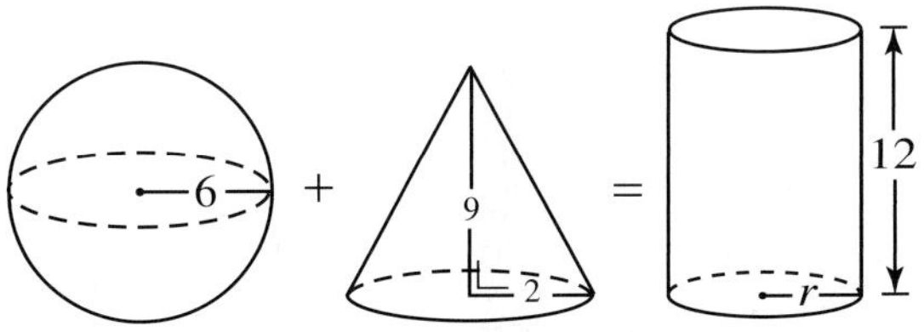

6.

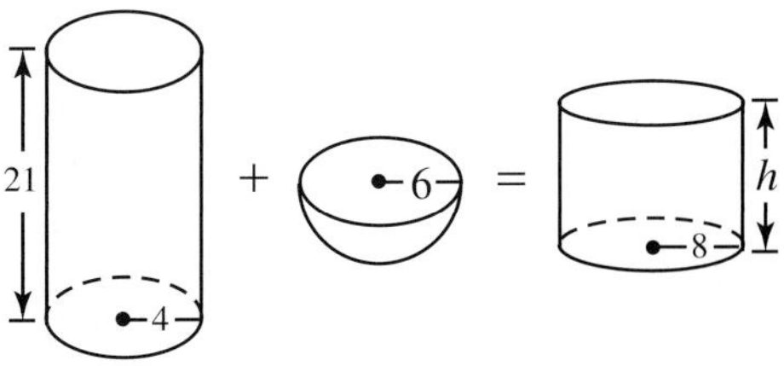

7. A solid lead cylinder of base radius 2 cm and height 15 cm is melted down and recast as a solid cone of base radius 3 cm. Calculate the height of the cone.

8. A cylinder of internal diameter 8 cm and height 18 cm is full of liquid. The liquid is poured into a second cylinder of internal diameter 12 cm. Calculate the depth of the liquid in this second cylinder.

9. A solid metal sphere has a radius of length 3 cm. Express the volume of the sphere in terms of π. A cylindrical container is partly filled with water. The sphere is completely submerged in this container. If the level of water in the container rises by 1 cm, calculate the radius of the base of the cylinder.

10. A solid metal rectangular block 30 cm by 24 cm by 15 cm is melted down and recast into cubes of side 3 cm. How many such cubes were made ?

11. A solid metal hemisphere of radius 4 cm and a cone of height 10 cm and base radius 5 cm are completely immersed in water in a cylindrical can of diameter 12 cm. If both the hemisphere and cone are removed, calculate the drop in height of the water level.

12. A cylinder has diameter of 10 cm and contains water. A metal cone of base diameter 8 cm and height 15 cm is lowered into the cylinder so that it is completely immersed in the water. Find the rise in the level of the water.

13. A solid metal sphere, of radius 9 cm, is completely immersed in a cylinder containing water. The sphere is removed and the level of water drops by 3 cm. Calculate the diameter of the base of the cylinder.

14. A sphere of radius 15 cm is made of lead. The sphere is melted down. Some of the lead is used to form a solid cone of radius 10 cm and height 27 cm. The rest of the lead is used to form a cylinder of base radius 12 cm. Calculate the height of the cylinder.

15. A solid lead cylinder of radius 6 cm and height 24 cm is melted down and recast as 81 spheres. Calculate the radius of one of these spheres.

16. A solid cone is 24 cm in height and the diameter of its base is 12 cm. The cone is completely submerged in water in a cylindrical vessel of internal diameter 30 cm. Calculate the drop in depth of the water in the vessel when the cone is taken out.
A solid sphere is then completely submerged in the same cylindrical vessel and the water rises to the same level as before. Find the radius of the sphere.

17. A ladle in the shape of a hemispherical bowl, attached to a handle, of diameter 24 cm, is full of liquid. Calculate, in terms of π, the volume of liquid in the bowl.
All the liquid is poured from the ladle into a glass cylindrical container with internal radius 8 cm. Calculate the height of liquid in the glass.

18. Find the volume of a solid sphere with a diameter of length 3 cm. Give your answer in terms of π.

A cylindrical vessel with internal diameter of length 15 cm contains water. The surface of the water is 11 cm from the top of the vessel.

How many solid spheres, each with diameter of length 3 cm, must be placed in the vessel in order to bring the surface of the water to 1 cm from the top of the vessel? Assume that all the spheres are submerged in the water.

Algebraic substitution

Some questions require algebraic substitution to be solved.

Example ▼

The volume of a cone is 36π cm^3. If the height is four times the radius of the base, calculate the height of the cone.

Solution:

Equation given in disguise:
Volume of the cone $= 36\pi$ cm^3

$$\tfrac{1}{3}\pi r^2 h = 36\pi$$

$$\tfrac{1}{3}r^2 h = 36 \qquad \text{(divide both sides by } \pi\text{)}$$

$$r^2 h = 108 \qquad \text{(multiply both sides by 3)}$$

$$r^2(4r) = 108 \qquad (h = 4r)$$

$$4r^3 = 108$$

$$r^3 = 27 \qquad \text{(divide both sides by 4)}$$

$$r = 3 \text{ cm} \qquad \text{(take the cubed root of both sides)}$$

$$h = 4r = 4 \times 3 = 12 \text{ cm}$$

Thus, the height of the cone is 12 cm.

1. The volume of a cylinder is 16π cm^3. If the height of the cylinder is twice the length of the radius, calculate the length of the radius.

2. The volume of a cone is 9π cm^3. If the height and the radius of the cone are equal, calculate the height of the cone.

3. The volume of a cylinder is 375π cm^3. The ratio of the height to the length of the radius of the base is 3 : 1. Calculate the height of the cylinder.

4. Two spheres have the lengths of their radii in the ratio 2 : 3.
   Calculate the ratio of their volumes.

5. Two solid cones of equal height have the lengths of the radii of their bases in the ratio 1 : 2. Calculate the ratio of their volumes.

6. A cylinder and a right circular cone have the same radius and the height of the cone is three times the height of the cylinder. Find the ratio of the volume of the cone to the volume of the cylinder.

7. $\dfrac{8\pi}{3}$ cm^3 is the volume of a cone.
   The cone's height and radius length are equal.
   Calculate the length of the radius.

8. Two circles of equal area fit exactly into a rectangle as shown. Calculate the ratio, area of the two circles : area of rectangle
   $\left(\text{assume } \pi = \frac{22}{7}\right)$
   Give your answer in the form $a : b$ where $a, b \in \mathbf{N}$.

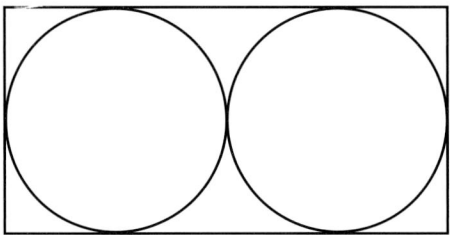

9. When the height of a cylinder is halved and its radius length is doubled the volume is increased k times. Find k.

10. The height of a cylinder is equal to the length of its diameter. The curved surface area of the cylinder is 100π cm^2. Calculate the height.

11. The volume of cone A is 72π cm^3. Another cone B has the same height as cone A but the length of the radius of its base is twice that of cone A. Calculate the volume of cone B, in terms of π.

Chapter test

1. **(a)** The length of the radius of the large circle in the diagram is 8 cm.
   The length of the radius of the small circle is 1 cm.

   Find the area of the shaded region, assuming $\pi = \frac{22}{7}$.

   (b) Three tennis balls fit exactly in a cylindrical container as shown in the diagram. The radius of a tennis ball is 21 mm.

   Find, assuming $\pi = \frac{22}{7}$:

   (i) the volume of a tennis ball
   (ii) the volume of the cylindrical container
   (iii) the difference between the capacity of the container and the capacity of the three tennis balls.

   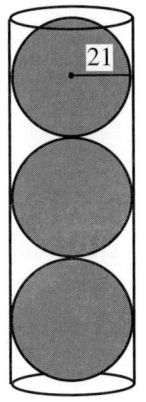

   (c) A toy is made of a cone which fits exactly on top of a hemisphere, as shown in the diagram. The radius length of the hemisphere is 6 cm and the volume of the cone is half the volume of the hemisphere. Calculate, h, the total height of the toy.

   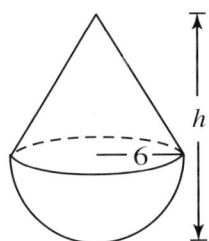

2. (a) Two squares have sides of length 4 cm and 10 cm, respectively. Find, in its simplest form, the ratio of their areas.

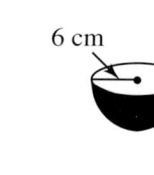

(b) (i) Soup is contained in a cylindrical saucepan which has internal radius 14 cm. The depth of the soup is 20 cm. Calculate, in terms of π, the volume of soup in the saucepan.

(ii) A ladle in the shape of a hemisphere with internal radius of length 6 cm is used to serve the soup. Calculate, in terms of π, the volume of soup contained in one full ladle.

(iii) The soup is served into cylindrical cups each with internal radius of length of 4 cm. One ladleful is placed in each cup. Calculate the depth of the soup in each cup.

(iv) How many cups can be filled from the contents of the saucepan if each cup must contain exactly one full ladle?

3. (a) A bicycle wheel, including the tyre, has a diameter of 70 cm. How many revolutions of the wheel occur in a journey of 11 km $\left(\text{assume } \pi = \frac{22}{7}\right)$?

(b) A container is in the shape of a cone on top of a hemisphere (as shown). The hemisphere has a diameter of 12 cm. Find the volume of the container, in terms of π, given that the height of the cone is $2\frac{1}{2}$ times the length of its radius.

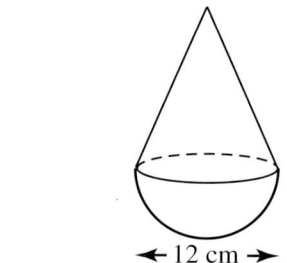

(c) A solid block, as shown, has a height of 12 cm and a base measuring 30 cm by 15.7 cm. Calculate the volume of the block. A solid cylinder is cut out of the block from top to bottom, as in the diagram. If the volume of the cylinder is $\frac{1}{6}$ of the volume of the block, calculate the radius of the cylinder.
(assume $\pi = 3.14$)

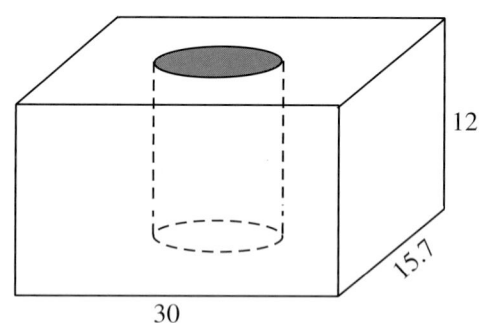

4. (a) Each side of a square is increased in length from 5 cm to 7 cm. Calculate the percentage increase in the area of the square.

(b) A triangle is enclosed in a circle, centre o. The lengths of two of the sides are 8 cm and 6 cm, as shown.

    (i) find the radius of the circle

    (ii) calculate the area of the shaded region. (assume $\pi = 3.14$)

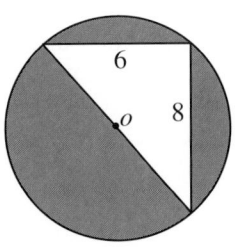

(c) The base of a right circular cone has a radius of length 5 cm. The height of the cone is 12 cm. Calculate the volume in terms of π.

The inverted cone is filled with water. The water then drips from the vertex at the rate $\dfrac{\pi}{5}$ cm^3/s.

Calculate the time in seconds until the cone is empty, assuming the volume of water to be the same as the volume of the cone.

If all the water dripped into a dry cylindrical can of diameter 10 cm in length, calculate the height of water in the can.

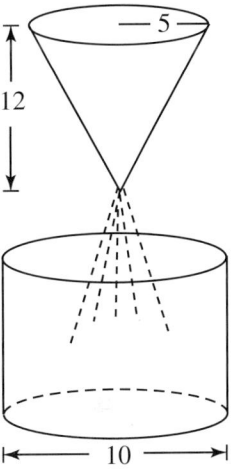

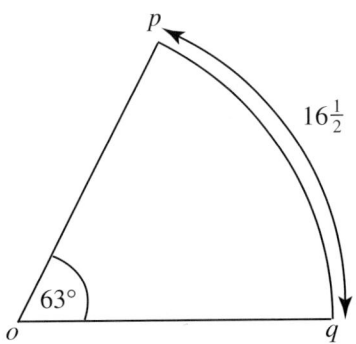

5. (a) A solid rectangular block has a total surface area of 544 cm^2. If the lengths of its sides are in the ratio $1 : 2 : 5$, find its volume.

(b) The diagram shows a sector of a circle, centre o. The length of the arc pq is $16\frac{1}{2}$ cm, and $|\angle poq| = 63°$.

    Find **(i)** the length of the radius

           (ii) the area of the sector opq.

$$\left(\text{assume } \pi = \tfrac{22}{7}\right)$$

(c) Wax in the shape of a cylinder with radius of length 4 cm and height 36 cm is melted down. The resulting wax is formed into cone shaped candles. Each candle has height 6 cm and base of radius length 2 cm.

(i) Calculate the number of candles that can be made, assuming that no wax is lost.

(ii) The candles are placed, base down and in rows of three, in the smallest possible rectangular box. Calculate, in cm^3, the volume (internal capacity) of the box.

(iii) What percentage of the volume of the box is empty? Take $\pi = 3.14$.
Give your answer correct to the nearest whole number.

6. **(a)** A pizza in the shape of a circle has a piece missing from it as shown in the diagram.
The radius of the pizza is 10 cm and $|\angle pqr| = 135°$.
Find the area of the pizza left (assume $\pi = 3.14$).

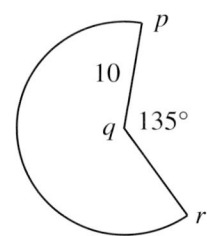

(b) A rectangular reservoir of water has a length of 21 m and width of 10 m.
At present it holds 3,150,000 litres of water.

(i) Calculate the height of water in the reservoir.

(ii) The level of water is raised 3.5 m in 10 minutes by a flow of water into the reservoir. Find the rate of flow into the reservoir in litres per second.
[1 litre = 1,000 cm^3]

(c) A candle is in the shape of a cylinder surmounted by a cone, as in the diagram.

(i) The cone has height 24 cm and the length of the radius of its base is 10 cm.
Find the volume of the cone in terms of π.

(ii) The height of the cylinder is equal to the slant height of the cone. Find the volume of the cylinder in terms of π.

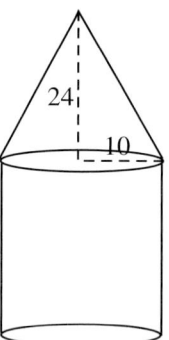

(iii) A solid spherical ball of wax with radius of length r cm was used to make the candle. Calculate r, correct to one decimal place.

7. **(a)** R is the radius of the outer circle. r is the radius of the inner circle. Show that the area of the shaded region is equal to $\pi(R + r)(R - r)$.

(b) Calculate the area of the smaller square in the diagram, given the lengths 3 cm and 7 cm, as shown.

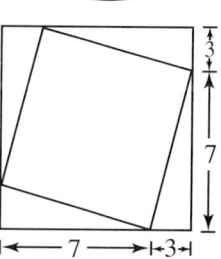

(c) The internal height of a cylinder is 20 cm. 50 identical solid metal cubes, each of edge 2 cm, are placed in the cylinder. Water is then poured into the cylinder until it is full. If the volume of water needed is 1.17 litres, calculate the radius length of the cylinder.
(assume $\pi = 3.14$)

8. **(a)** The radius of the base of a cone and the radius of a sphere are each 4 cm in length. The volume of the cone is equal to the volume of the sphere. Find the height of the cone.

(b) A cylindrical metal pipe is 3 m long. It has external radius of length 11 cm and internal radius of length 10 cm.
  (i) Find, in cm^3, the volume of metal in the pipe in terms of π.
  (ii) A solid cylinder has height 7 cm. Its volume is equal to the volume of metal in the pipe. Calculate its radius length.

(c) The radius of a sphere and the radius of the base of a solid cone are each 5 cm in length.
Write down the surface area of the sphere in terms of π.
The total surface area of the cone is equal to the surface area of the sphere. Calculate the slant height of the cone.
Hence, calculate the vertical height of the cone, correct to one place of decimals.

9. **(a)** A fence joining two opposite corners of a four-sided field is 140 m in length. The perpendicular distances from the other two corners to the fence are 54 m and 46 m.
Calculate the area of the field in m^2.

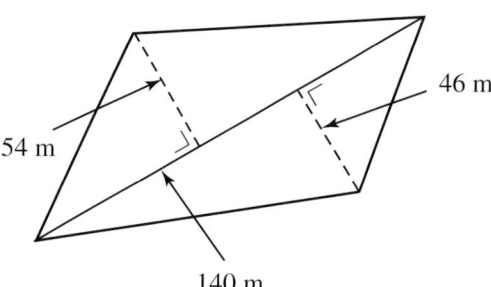

(b) A toy is made of a cone which fits exactly on top of a hemisphere, as shown in the diagram. The radius length of the hemisphere is 6 cm and the total height of the toy is 21 cm.

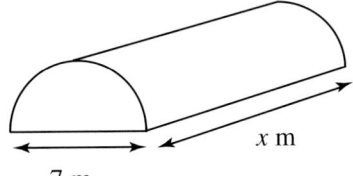

   (i) Write down the height of the cone and hence find the volume of the cone in terms of π.

   (ii) Find the volume of the hemisphere in terms of π.

   (iii) Express the volume of the cone as a percentage of the total volume of the toy. (Give your answer correct to one place of decimals.)

(c) A shed is in the shape of a half-cylinder, closed at both ends, as shown. The diameter length of each semicircular end is 7 m, and the shed is x m long.

   (i) Find the area of each semicircular end.

$$\left(\text{assume } \pi = \tfrac{22}{7}\right)$$

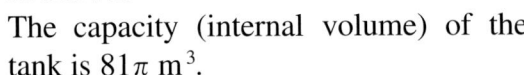

   (ii) The total area of the two ends and the roof is 214.5 m². Find x.

10. (a) The surface area of a cube is 294 cm². Find its volume.

(b) A machine part consists of a solid sphere submerged in a closed cylindrical container full of oil. The radius of the cylinder is 4 cm, the radius of the sphere is 3 cm and the volume of oil contained in the cylinder is 108π cm³. Calculate the height of the cylinder.

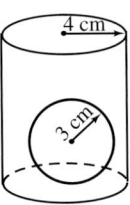

(c) (i) Write down, in terms of π and r, the volume of a hemisphere with radius of length r.

   (ii) A fuel storage tank is in the shape of a cylinder with a hemisphere at each end, as shown.

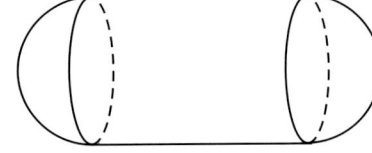

The capacity (internal volume) of the tank is 81π m³.

The ratio of the capacity of the cylindrical section to the sum of the capacities of the hemispherical ends is 5 : 4.

Calculate the internal radius length of the tank.

11. **(a)** A cone of height 21 cm has a capacity of 4.312 litres. Find the radius of the cone.

$\left(\text{assume } \pi = \frac{22}{7}\right)$

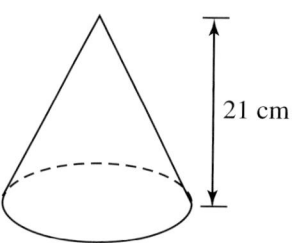

21 cm

(b) A solid cylinder, made of lead, has a radius of length 15 cm and height of 135 cm. Find its volume in terms of π.

The solid cylinder is melted down and recast to make four identical right circular solid cones. The height of each cone is equal to twice the length of its base radius. Calculate the base radius length of the cones.

(c) The mass of a rectangular sheet of metal is 45,000 grammes. The mass of 1 cm^3 of this metal is 7.2 grammes.

The thickness of the sheet of metal is h cm and its length and width are 100 cm and 50 cm, respectively, as in the diagram.

Calculate the value of h.

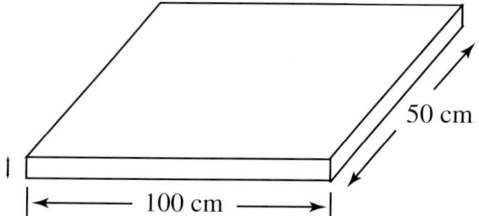

h cm

50 cm

100 cm

12. **(a)** An empty rectangular oil tank has an internal length of 150 cm and an internal width of 50 cm. The price of oil is 24 c per litre. A delivery of oil costing €144 fills half the capacity (internal volume) of the tank.

Calculate:

(i) the number of litres of oil required to fill the tank completely

(ii) the internal height of the tank. [1 litre = 1000 cm^3]

(b) A sphere with radius of length 3 cm has a volume equal to eight times the volume of a smaller sphere with a radius of length r cm. Calculate r.

(c) **(i)** A candle is in the shape of a solid cone of height 6 cm on top of a solid cylinder of height 10 cm.

The cone and the cylinder each have a radius of length 2 cm.

Show that the volume of the candle is 48π cm^3.

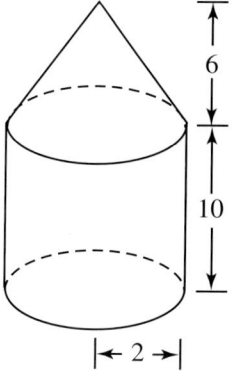

6

10

2

(ii) Four of these candles are packed, cone parts uppermost, into the smallest possible rectangular box.

Find, in cm^3, the volume of empty space in the box.

(assume $\pi = 3.14$)

(iii) A new candle is in the shape of a solid cone of height 3 cm on top of a solid cylinder of height 5 cm.

The cone and the cylinder each have a radius of length r cm.

The volume of the new candle is 6π cm^3.

Find r.

13. **(a)** Find, in terms of π, the volume of a solid metal sphere of diameter 12 cm. 18 such identical spheres are completely submerged in a cylinder containing water. If the radius of the cylinder is 9 cm, calculate by how much the level of the water will drop if the spheres are removed from the cylinder.

(b) Water flows through a circular pipe of internal base diameter 6 cm at a speed of 10 cm/s. Calculate, in terms of π, the rate of flow of water from the pipe. The water flows into a cylindrical container of base diameter 36 cm and height 100 cm. How long will it take to fill the container ?

(c) A small candle is in the shape of a cone which fits exactly on top of a cylinder as shown. The cylinder has a radius of length 2 cm. The slant length of the cone is 2.5 cm.

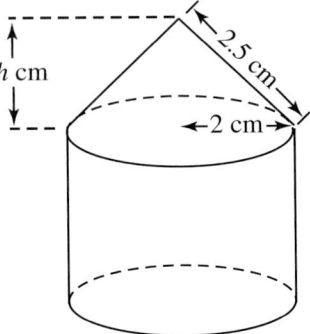

Calculate:
(i) the height, h, of the cone
(ii) the volume of the cone in terms of π.
The volume of the cylinder is 5 times the volume of the cone. Calculate the total height of the candle.

(d) (i) A container is in the shape of a cylinder on top of a hemisphere as shown in the diagram. The cylinder has a radius length of 6 cm and the container has a total height of 22 cm. Calculate the volume of the container in terms of π.

(ii) If two-fifths of the volume of the container is filled with water, calculate the depth, d, of water in the container.

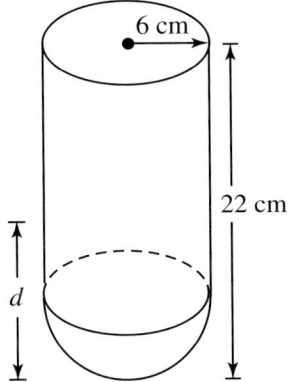

SETS

Numerical problems for two sets

The diagram below indicates the four regions when dealing with the sets *U*, *A* and *B*.

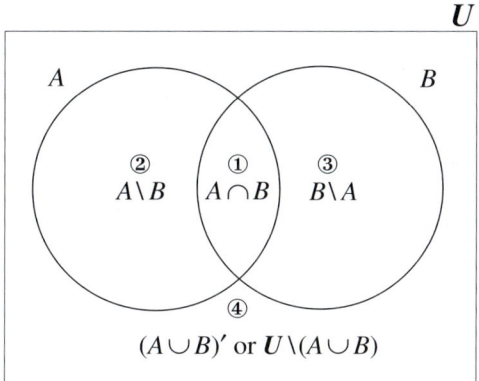

Set notation	Meaning
#(*A*)	number of elements in set *A*
∩	and
∪	or
A ∩ *B*	In *A* and *B*
A ∪ *B*	In *A* or *B*
A \ *B*	In *A* but not in *B* (*A* only)
U	Universal set
A′ = *U* \ *A*	In *U* but not in *A*

Note: If the universal set, *U*, is not involved, there are only three regions.

When putting values into a Venn diagram always work from the centre outwards.
In many problems we introduce a variable *x* to represent the number of elements in a region.
Then we express the number of elements in other regions in terms of *x*. From the question we link the number of elements in the regions to form an equation and solve this equation.

A sports club has 69 members. 37 members play Tennis and 25 play Squash. Some members play Tennis and Squash. Twice as many members play neither of these games as play both.

How many members play **(i)** Tennis and Squash? **(ii)** only one of these games?

Solution:

Draw a Venn diagram showing, U for all the members of the club, T for the members who play Tennis and S for the members who play Squash.

Let the number of members that play both $= x$

Thus, $\#(T \cap S) = x$
$\therefore$ $\#(T \setminus S) = 37 - x$
and $\#(S \setminus T) = 25 - x$
and $\#[U \setminus (S \cup T)] = 2x$

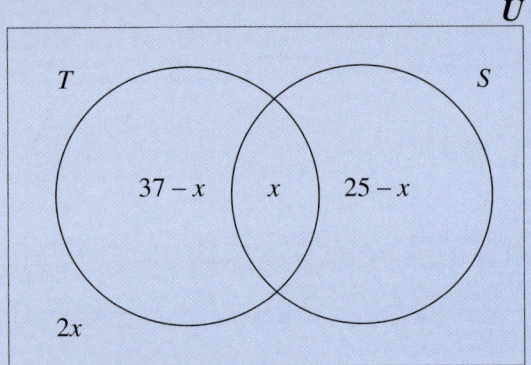

Given: $\#(U) = 69$
$(37 - x) + x + (25 - x) + 2x = 69$
$37 - x + x + 25 - x + 2x = 69$
$x + 62 = 69$
$x = 7$

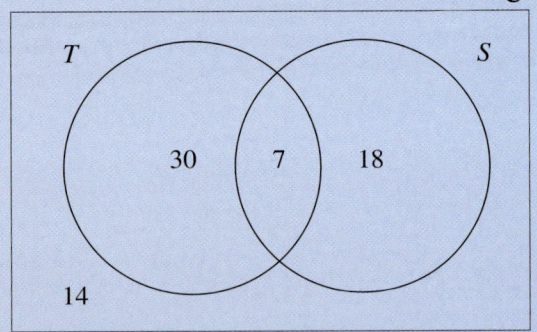

(i)   The number of members who play Tennis and Squash $= 7$
(ii) The number of members who play only one of these games $= 30 + 18 = 48$

Maximising and minimising

The following is very useful when dealing with maximum and minimum problems on two sets.

> **1.** To maximise $\#(A \cup B)$ minimise $\#(A \cap B)$.
> **2.** To minimise $\#(A \cup B)$ maximise $\#(A \cap B)$.

A and B are two sets such that #(A) = 20 and #(B) = 15.
Using a Venn diagram in each case, calculate:
(i) The possible maximum value of #(A∪B).
(ii) The possible minimum value of #(A∪B).

Solution:

(i) The maximum value of #(A∪B)
occurs when #(A∩B) is a minimum.
The minimum value of #(A∩B) = 0
∴ the maximum value of
#(A∪B) = 20 + 0 + 15 = 35

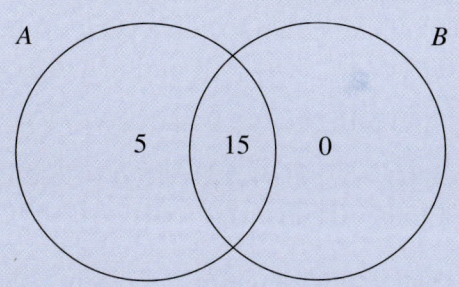

(ii) The minimum value of #(A∪B)
occurs when #(A∩B) is a maximum.
The maximum value of #(A∩B) = 15
(as the #(B) = 15)
∴ the minimum value of
#(A∪B) = 5 + 15 + 0 = 20

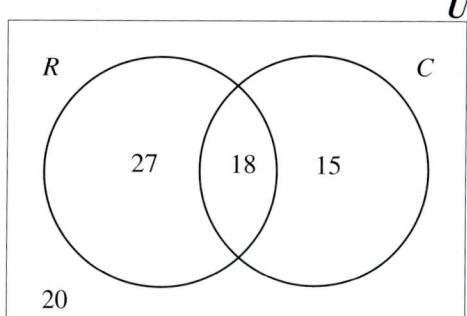

Note: In the example above there was **no** need for a universal set.

1. 80 pupils were asked in a survey whether
they liked rock music, R, or classical
music, C, or neither. The results are
shown in the Venn diagram.
How many said they liked:
(i) both   **(ii)** rock music
(iii) classical music   **(iv)** neither
(v) only one of these types of music?

2. In a class of 34 pupils, 20 play Basketball (*B*), 17 play Football (*F*), and 2 play neither.
Copy the Venn diagram and complete it.
How many pupils in the class play:
  (i) both games
  (ii) only one of these games
  (iii) at least one of these games?

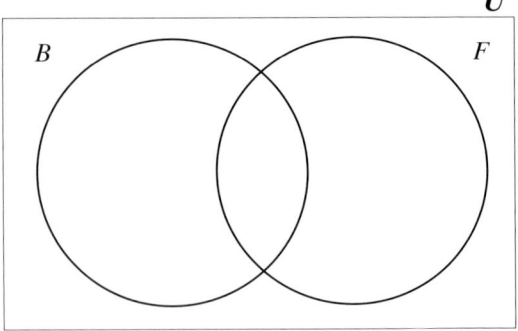

3. A school sports day was attended by 250 pupils.
70 pupils took part in the long jump event.
40 pupils took part in the high jump event.
160 pupils did not take part in either of the two jump events.
Using a Venn diagram, or otherwise, find the number of pupils who took part in the long jump event only.

Use a Venn diagram to solve each of the following:

4. $\#(A) = 13$, $\#(B) = 14$ and $\#(A \cap B) = 6$. Find   **(i)** $\#(A \setminus B)$ **(ii)** $\#(A \cup B)$

5. $\#(X) = 15$, $\#(Y) = 9$ and $\#(X \cup Y) = 19$. Find   **(i)** $\#(X \cap Y)$ **(ii)** $\#(Y \setminus X)$

6. $\#(U) = 57$, $\#(P) = 31$, $\#(Q) = 28$ and $\#(P \cap Q) = 10$.
Find: **(i)** $\#(P \setminus Q)$ **(ii)** $\#[U \setminus (P \cup Q)]$ **(iii)** $\#[(P \cap Q)']$

7. The Venn diagram represents the number of girls in a class of 30 who study French, *F*, Spanish, *S*, or both.
If each girl in the class must study French or Spanish, calculate *x*.
How many girls study:
  (i) French only
  (ii) Spanish only
  (iii) only one of these subjects.

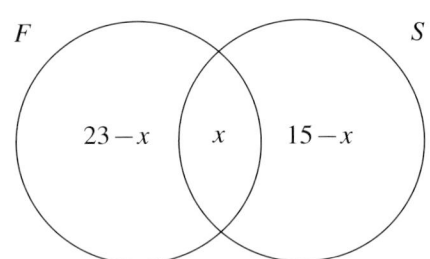

8. The Venn diagram shows the number of elements, in terms of *x*, in the sets *U*, *A* and *B*.
If $\#(B) = 41$, calculate *x*.
Hence, calculate:
  (i) $\#(A \cap B)$ **(ii)** $\#(A \setminus B)$
  (iii) $\#[U \setminus (A \cup B)]$ **(iv)** $\#[(A \cup B) \setminus (A \cap B)]$

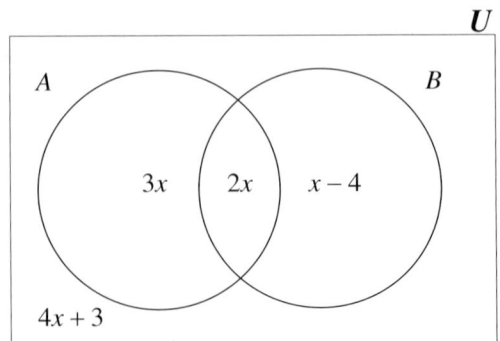

9. *A* and *B* are two sets such that $\#(A \cap B) = 5$ and $\#(A \setminus B) = 3[\#(B \setminus A)]$.
    If $\#(A \cup B) = 21$, calculate $\#(A \setminus B)$. (Hint: let $\#(B \setminus A) = x$)

10. *P* and *Q* are two sets such that $\#(P \cap Q) = 2$ and $\#(P \cup Q) = 32$.
    If $\#(Q \setminus P) = \frac{1}{2}[\#(P \setminus Q)]$, calculate $\#(P)$.

11. A club has 47 members. 18 members play Chess and 13 play Tennis. Some members
    play Chess and Tennis. Three times as many members play neither of these games as
    play both.
    How many members play **(i)** Chess and Tennis? **(ii)** only one of these games?

12. A group of 63 people were asked whether they had a television and/or a computer.
    Four times as many had a television only as had both and 3 people had neither.
    If 24 people said they had a computer, calculate the number who said they had:
    (i) a television and a computer **(ii)** a television or a computer but not both.

13. *A* and *B* are two sets such that $\#(A) = 20$ and $\#(B) = 12$.
    (i) Calculate the maximum possible value of $\#(A \cup B)$.
    (ii) Calculate the minimum possible value of $\#(A \cup B)$.
    (iii) If $\#(A \cap B) \geqslant 3$, calculate the maximum possible value of $\#(A \cup B)$.

14. *P* and *Q* are two sets such that $\#(P) = 10$, $\#(Q) = 11$, $\#(P \cap Q) \geqslant 2$.
    (i) Calculate the maximum possible value of $\#(P \cup Q)$.
    (ii) Calculate the minimum possible value of $\#(P \cup Q)$.

15. *U*, *P* and *Q* are sets such that $\#(U) = 43$, $\#(P) = 20$ and $\#(Q) = 15$.
    $\#(P \cup Q) = x$ and $\#(P \cap Q) = y$.
    If $a \leqslant x \leqslant b$ and $c \leqslant y \leqslant d$, $a, b, c, d \in N$, find the value of *a*, *b*, *c* and *d*.
    Calculate the maximum possible value of $\#[U \setminus (P \cup Q)]$.

Numerical problems for three sets

The diagram below indicates the eight regions when dealing with the sets *U*, *A*, *B* and *C*.

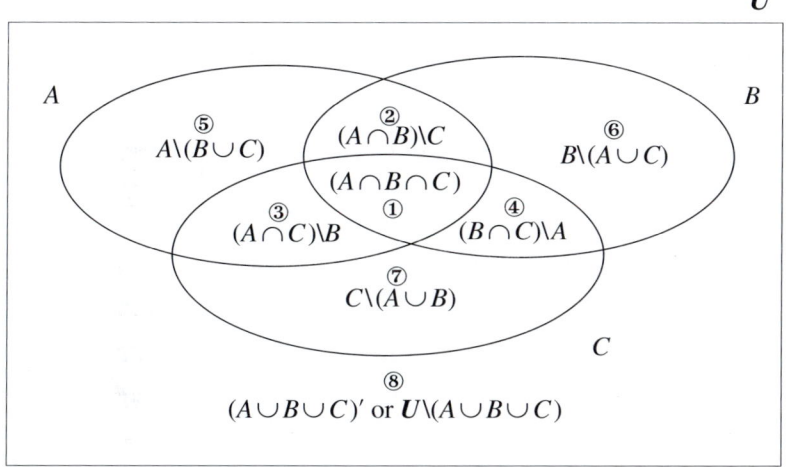

Set notation	Meaning
$A \cup B \cup C$	In A or B or C
$A \cap B \cap C$	In A and B and C
$(A \cup B)\backslash C$	In A or B but not in C
$(A \cap B)\backslash C$	In A and B but not in C
$A\backslash(B \cup C)$	in A but not in B or C (A only)
$(A \cup B \cup C)'$ or $U\backslash(A \cup B \cup C)$	in U but not in A or B or C

Example ▼

Three problems A, B and C were given to a set of students. 31 solved A, 20 solved B and 22 solved C. 4 solved A and B but not C, 10 solved A and C but not B, 5 solved all three problems. Each student solved at least one problem.

(i) How many students solved A only?

(ii) Find the maximum possible number of students that could have solved A or B or C.

(iii) If there were 46 students in all, how many solved C only?

Solution:

Draw a Venn diagram showing A for the set of students who solved problem A, B for the set of students who solved problem B and C for the set of students who solved problem C.

Given: $\#(A) = 31$, $\#(B) = 20$, $\#(C) = 22$,

$\#[(A \cap B)\backslash C] = 4$, $\#[(A \cap C)\backslash B] = 10$,

and $\#(A \cap B \cap C) = 5$

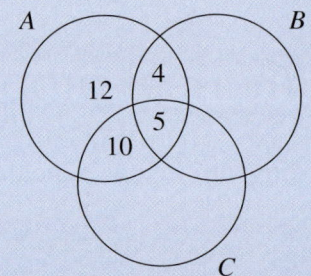

(i) Number who solved A only

$= 31 - 4 - 5 - 10 = 31 - 19 = 12$

(ii) Maximum possible number of students that could have solved A or B or C.

i.e., maximise $\#(A \cup B \cup C)$

The maximum value of $\#(A \cup B \cup C)$ occurs when $\#[(B \cap C)\backslash A]$ is a minimum.

The minimum value of $\#[(B \cap C)\backslash A] = 0$

The number who solved B only $= 20 - 4 - 5 = 11$

The number who solved C only $= 22 - 10 - 5 = 7$

The maximum number that could have solved A or B or C

$= 12 + 4 + 11 + 10 + 5 + 0 + 7 = 49$

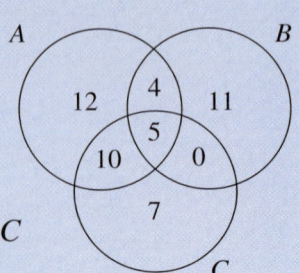

(iii) If there were 46 students in all, how many solved C only?

Let x = the number who solved B and C but not A.

i.e. Let $\#[(B \cap C) \backslash A] = x$

number who solved B only $= 20 - 4 - 5 - x = 11 - x$

number who solved C only $= 22 - 10 - 5 - x = 7 - x$

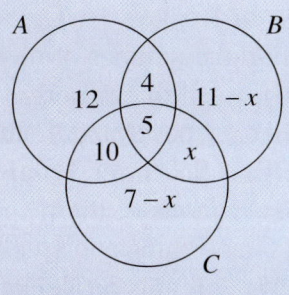

$$\begin{aligned} \text{Given:} \qquad\qquad &46 \text{ students in all} \\ \therefore \qquad\qquad\qquad &\#(A \cup B \cup C) = 46 \\ 12 + 4 + (11 - x) + 10 + 5 + x + (7 - x) &= 46 \\ 12 + 4 + 11 - x + 10 + 5 + x + 7 - x &= 46 \\ 49 - x &= 46 \\ -x &= -3 \\ x &= 3 \end{aligned}$$

The number who solved C only $= 7 - x = 7 - 3 = 4$

Example ▼

After a two hour study period, 160 pupils were asked whether they had studied Mathematics, Science or French. The results were as follows:

13 studied Mathematics only, 7 studied Science only and 10 studied French only. 11 studied none of these subjects. 12 studied Mathematics and Science, 9 studied Mathematics and French, 6 studied Science and French.

How many pupils studied Mathematics and Science and French?

Solution:

Draw a Venn diagram showing U for all 60 pupils, M for Mathematics, S for Science and F for French.

Put in the numbers for Mathematics only, Science only and French only.

Let x = the number of pupils who studied Mathematics and Science and French.

i.e. Let $\#(M \cap S \cap F) = x$

Therefore, the number who studied:

Mathematics and Science but not French $= 12 - x$

Mathematics and French but not Science $= 9 - x$

Science and French but not Mathematics $= 6 - x$

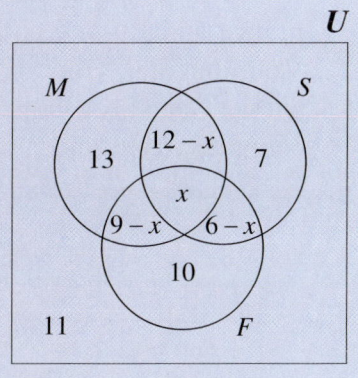

$$\begin{aligned} \text{Given:} \qquad\qquad &60 \text{ pupils surveyed altogether} \\ \therefore \qquad\qquad\qquad &\#(U) = 60 \\ 13 + (12 - x) + 7 + (9 - x) + x + (6 - x) + 10 + 11 &= 60 \\ 13 + 12 - x + 7 + 9 - x + x + 6 - x + 10 + 11 &= 60 \\ 68 - 2x &= 60 \\ -2x &= -8 \\ 2x &= 8 \\ x &= 4 \end{aligned}$$

The number of pupils who studied Mathematics and Science and French $= 4$

1. All 62 members in a youth club were asked in a survey if they played Soccer, *S*, Tennis, *T*, or Hockey, *H*. The results are shown in the Venn diagram. Using the Venn diagram, find the number of members of the youth club who play:
    (i)   all three sports
    (ii)   Soccer and Tennis
    (iii)   Soccer or Tennis
    (iv)   none of these sports
    (v)   Tennis and Hockey but not Soccer
    (vi)   Tennis or Hockey but not Soccer
    (vii)   Soccer
    (viii) Tennis but not Soccer or Hockey
    (ix)   only one of these sports
    (x)   only two of these sports
    (xi)   at least two of these sports.

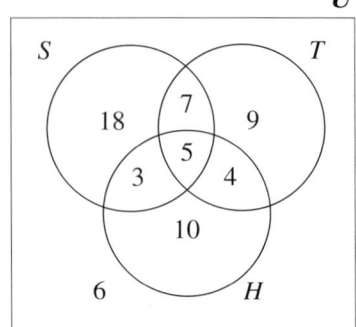

2. The Venn diagram shows the number of elements in the different subsets of *U*, *A*, *B*, and *C*. Evaluate each of the following:

    (i)   #(*U*)   **(ii)**   #(*A*)

    (iii) #(*B*)   **(iv)**   #(*C*)

    (v)   #(*A*∩*B*∩*C*)   **(vi)**   #(*B*∪*C*)

    (vii) #(*A*∪*B*∪*C*)   **(viii)** #[(*A*∪*B*∪*C*)′]

    (ix)   #[(*A*∩*B*)*C*]   **(x)**   #[(*B*∪*C*)*A*]

    (xi)   #[(*B*\(*A*∪*C*)]   **(xii)**   #(*A*∪*B*) − #(*A*∩*B*)

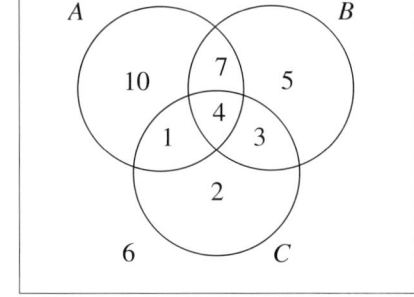

3. 46 people were asked which of the three countries, Canada, France or Russia they had visited last year. They answered as follows: 26 visited Canada, 18 visited France, 17 visited Russia, 9 visited Canada and France, 12 visited Canada and Russia, 8 visited France and Russia, and 5 visited all three countries. Illustrate the information in a Venn diagram. How many people visited **(i)** none of the three countries, **(ii)** Russia but not Canada or France, **(iii)** only one of the three countries, **(iv)** at least one of these countries, **(iv)** Canada or Russia, **(vi)** Canada and France but not Russia?

4. A survey was taken of a group of 44 students, each of whom was studying one or more of the three subjects History, Geography and Art.

28 students studied History.

30 students studied Geography.

22 students studied Art.

6 students studied History only.

15 students studied both History and Geography.

3 students studied all three subjects.

   (i)   Use a Venn diagram to find the number of students who studied History and Geography but not Art.

   (ii)   How many students studied History and Art but not Geography?

   (iii)   Let x represent the number of students who studied Geography and Art but not History.

        Express in terms of x, the number of students who studied:

        (a) Geography only   **(b)** Art only

        Put these expressions for x into your Venn diagram.

        Calculate the value of x.

5. 52 fifth-year students were asked whether they had chosen Accounting, Biology or Chemistry as one of their subjects in school. The results were as follows:

30 chose Accounting, 28 chose Biology and 29 chose Chemistry.

19 chose Accounting and Biology, 3 chose Accounting and Chemistry but not Biology.

12 chose all three subjects and 4 chose not to take any of these subjects.

Let x represent the number of students who chose Biology and Chemistry but not Accounting. Illustrate the above information in a Venn diagram, expressing, in terms of x, the number of students who chose **(a)** Biology only **(b)** Chemistry only.

Calculate the value of x. How many students chose:

   (i) Biology only   **(ii)** Chemistry only   **(iii)** two of these subjects

   (iv) at least two of these subjects.

6. An auctioneer has 60 houses for sale. 6 of these houses have a garage and a conservatory and gas central heating. 10 have a conservatory and gas central heating, 5 have a garage and a conservatory but no gas cental heating, 13 have a garage and gas central heating. 11 have none of these three features. Equal numbers of these houses have only one of the three features. Using x to represent the number of these houses that have only one of these features, illustrate the above information in a Venn diagram.

Calculate the value of x.

How many of these houses do not have a garage or gas central heating?

7. A survey was taken of a group of 33 people, each of whom read one or more of the magazines *P*, *Q* and *R*. The results are shown in the Venn diagram.

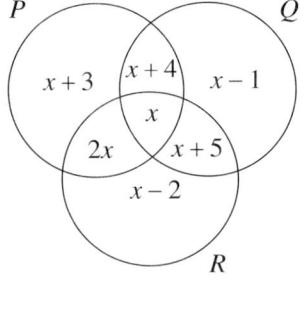

    (i) Calculate the value of *x*.

    (ii) How many of this group read only one of these magazines?

8. All 30 students in a class were asked which of the three modes of transport they used to travel to school, train, *T*, car, *C*, or bus, *B*, in the past year. The results are shown in the Venn diagram.

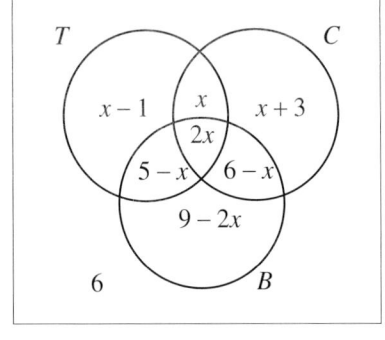

    (i) Calculate the value of *x*.

    (ii) How many of these pupils used two of these modes of transport to travel to school?

9. Three tasks, *A*, *B* and *C* were given to a group of people. Each person completed at least one task. The number who completed *A* and *B* and *C* was *x*.

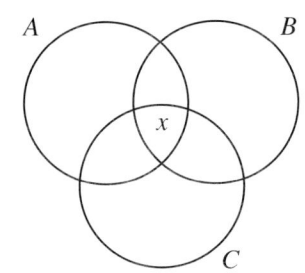

23 completed *A*, 22 completed *B* and 16 completed *C*.

9 completed *A* and *B*, 6 completed *A* and *C*, 7 completed *B* and *C*.

Express, in terms of *x*, the number of people who completed:

A and *B* but not *C*

A and *C* but not *B*

B and *C* but not *A*

A only, *B* only and *C* only.

Hence, complete, in terms of *x*, the Venn diagram.

If there were 43 people in the group, calculate the value of *x*.

10. As 55 people left a fruit market they were asked if they had bought apples or bananas or clementines. The results were as follows:

29 bought apples, 34 bought bananas and 27 bought clementines.

15 bought apples and bananas, 16 bought apples and clementines, 17 bought bananas and clementines. 3 bought none of these fruits.

Using *x* to represent those people who bought all three fruits, illustrate the above information in a Venn diagram.

Calculate the value of *x*.

11. In a club of 46 people, 21 played darts, 22 played chess and 27 played snooker. 11 played both darts and chess, 10 played both darts and snooker, 13 played chess and snooker. 6 did not play any of these three games. Using x to represent the number of people in the club who played all three games, illustrate the above information in a Venn diagram. Calculate the value of x.

Calculate the number of people in the club who played:
(i) only one of these games
(ii) at least two of these games.

12. Three problems P, Q and R were given to a set of pupils. Each pupil solved at least one problem. 25 solved P, 24 solved Q and 18 solved R. 8 solved P and Q and R. 12 solved P and Q, 3 solved P and R but not Q.

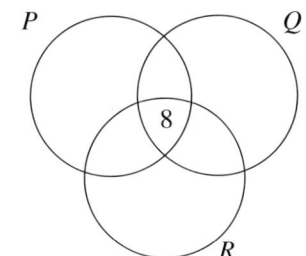

(i) How many pupils solved P and Q but not R?
(ii) How many pupils solved P only?
(iii) Find the **(a)** maximum **(b)** minimum number of pupils that could have solved P or Q or R.
(iv) If there were 39 pupils in all, how many pupils solved Q and R but not P?

(Hint: let $\#[(Q \cap R) \backslash P] = x$)

13. A survey was taken of a number of people as to which of the three forms of exercise, running, R, walking, W or cycling, C, they did to keep fit. Each person used one or more of these exercises.

The results were as follows:
25 run, 16 walk and 22 cycle.
10 run and walk, 11 run and cycle, 8 walk and cycle.
Let x be the number that take all three forms of exercise.

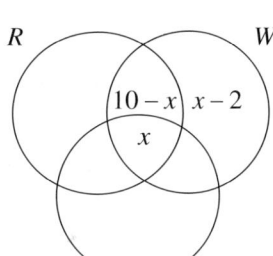

(i) Complete, in terms of x, the Venn diagram.
(ii) Show that the number of people that use at least one of these forms of exercise is $x + 34$.
(iii) Find **(a)** the greatest and **(b)** the least value of x.
(iv) Hence, or otherwise, find the greatest number of people that were in the survey.
(v) If a total of 40 people took part in the survey, calculate the value of x.

14. A survey was taken of 54 students, each of whom was studying one or more of the 3 subjects *A*, *B* and *C*.

6 students studied *B* and *C*.

5 students studied *A* and *C*.

3 times as many students studied *A* and *B* as studied all 3 subjects.

20 students altogether studied *B*.

17 students studied *C* only and 14 students studied *A* only.

Using *x* to represent those students who studied all 3 subjects, illustrate the above information in a Venn diagram.

Calculate the value of *x*.

15. A group of people were asked which of the games, Football, *F*, Badminton, *B*, and Tennis, *T*, they play. The results are shown in the Venn diagram.

11 played Badminton and Tennis.

23 played Badminton.

Write down two equations in *x* and *y*.

Solve your two equations simultaneously.

How many people play:

(i)   all three games

(ii) Badminton and Tennis but not Football

(iii) Tennis   **(iv)** Football and Badminton but not Tennis.

Calculate the total number of people in the group.

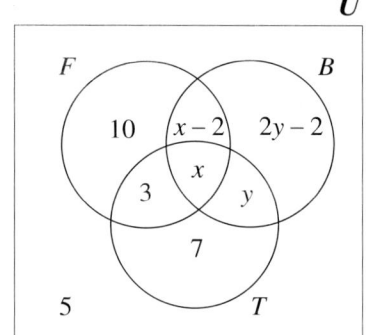

14

FUNCTIONS

Terminology and notation

A function is a rule that changes one number (input) into another number (output). Functions are often represented by the letters f, g, h or k. We can think of a function, f, as a number machine which changes an input, x, into an output, $f(x)$.

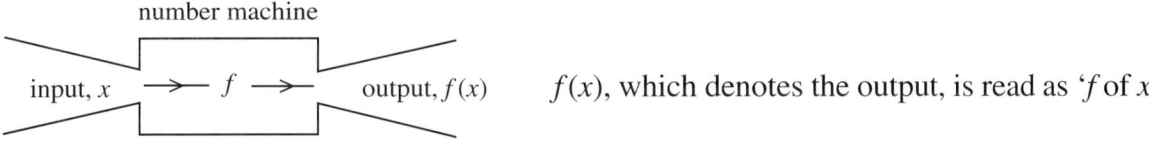

number machine

input, x → f → output, $f(x)$ $f(x)$, which denotes the output, is read as 'f of x'.

For example, let's represent the function 'treble input and then subtract two' by the letter f. This can be written as:

$$f : x \rightarrow 3x - 2 \quad \text{or} \quad f(x) = 3x - 2 \quad \text{or} \quad y = 3x - 2$$
$$(\text{input, output}) = (x, f(x)) = (x, 3x - 2) = (x, y)$$

Note: A **function** is also called a '**mapping**' or simply a '**map**'.

One number is mapped onto another number.
In the above example, x is mapped onto $3x - 2$, usually written $f : x \rightarrow 3x - 2$.

Input number

If $f : x \rightarrow 3x - 2$, then $f(4)$ means input 4 into the function,
i.e. 'it is the result of applying the function f to the number 4'.

$$f(4) = 3(4) - 2 = 12 - 2 = 10 \quad (\text{input} = 4, \text{output} = 10)$$

$$(\text{input, output}) = (4, \ f(4)) = (4, 10)$$

The function *f* is defined as $f: x \to 7 - 3x, \qquad x \in \mathbf{R}.$
- **(a)** Find **(i)** $f(-2)$ **(ii)** $f(24)$.
- **(b)** Find the number *k* such that $kf(-2) = f(24), \qquad k \in \mathbf{R}.$
- **(c)** Find the value of *x* for which $f(x) = -23.$

Solution:

$$f(x) = 7 - 3x$$

(a) (i)
$$\begin{aligned} f(-2) &= 7 - 3(-2) \\ &= 7 + 6 \\ &= 13 \end{aligned}$$

(ii)
$$\begin{aligned} f(24) &= 7 - 3(24) \\ &= 7 - 72 \\ &= -65 \end{aligned}$$

(b)
$$\begin{aligned} kf(-2) &= f(24) \\ k(13) &= -65 \\ 13k &= -65 \\ k &= -5 \end{aligned}$$

(c)
$$\begin{aligned} f(x) &= -23 \\ 7 - 3x &= -23 \\ -3x &= -30 \\ 3x &= 30 \\ x &= 10 \end{aligned}$$

$f: x \to x^2 - 1$ and $g: x \to 1 - 2x$ are two functions defined on $\mathbf{R}$.

(i) Find $f(\sqrt{2})$ and $g(-3k)$ **(ii)** Find the values of *x* for which $3f(x) = 5g(x)$

Solution:

(i)
$$f(x) = x^2 - 1$$

$$\begin{aligned} f(\sqrt{2}) &= (\sqrt{2})^2 - 1 \\ &= 2 - 1 \\ &= 1 \end{aligned}$$

$$g(x) = 1 - 2x$$

$$\begin{aligned} g(-3k) &= 1 - 2(-3k) \\ &= 1 + 6k \end{aligned}$$

(ii)
$$\begin{aligned} 3f(x) &= 5g(x) \\ 3(x^2 - 1) &= 5(1 - 2x) \\ 3x^2 - 3 &= 5 - 10x \\ 3x^2 + 10x - 8 &= 0 \\ (3x - 2)(x + 4) &= 0 \end{aligned}$$

$$3x - 2 = 0 \quad \text{or} \quad x + 4 = 0$$
$$3x = 2 \quad \text{or} \quad x = -4$$
$$x = \tfrac{2}{3} \quad \text{or} \quad x = -4$$

Let $h(x) = x(x - 2)$ for $x \in \mathbf{R}$.
Show that $h(1 + t) = h(1 - t)$ for $t \in \mathbf{R}$.

Solution:

$$h(x) = x(x - 2) = x^2 - 2x$$
$$h(x) = x^2 - 2x$$
$$h(1 + t) = (1 + t)^2 - 2(1 + t)$$
$$= 1 + 2t + t^2 - 2 - 2t$$
$$= t^2 - 1$$

$$h(x) = x^2 - 2x$$
$$h(1 - t) = (1 - t)^2 - 2(1 - t)$$
$$= 1 - 2t + t^2 - 2 + 2t$$
$$= t^2 - 1$$

$$\therefore \ h(1 + t) = h(1 - t)$$

Exercise 14.1 ▼

1. The function f is defined as $f : x \to 2x + 5, \quad x \in \mathbf{R}$.
   Find **(i)** $f(3)$ **(ii)** $f(4)$ **(iii)** $f(1)$ **(iv)** $f(-2)$ **(v)** $f(-3)$

2. The function g is defined as $g : x \to x^2 + 3x, \quad x \in \mathbf{R}$.
   Find **(i)** $f(3)$ **(ii)** $f(1)$ **(iii)** $f(0)$ **(iv)** $f(-2)$ **(v)** $3f(-4)$

3. The function f is defined as $f : x \to x(x + 2), \quad x \in \mathbf{R}$.
   Find **(i)** $f(1)$ **(ii)** $f(-1)$ **(iii)** $f(2) + f(-2)$ **(iv)** $-2f(-3)$
   Find the two values of x for which $f(x) = 15$.

4. The function f is defined as $f : x \to x^2 + 2x - 1, \quad x \in \mathbf{R}$.

   Find the value of **(i)** $f(0)$ **(ii)** $f(-1)$ **(iii)** $f(\tfrac{1}{2})$ **(iv)** $f(\tfrac{3}{5})$

5. The function g is defined as $g : x \to \dfrac{1}{x - 1}, \quad x \in \mathbf{R}, x \neq 1$.

   Evaluate **(i)** $f(2)$ **(ii)** $f(0)$ **(iii)** $f(\tfrac{3}{2})$

6. The function h is defined as $h : x \to 2 - 3x, \quad x \in \mathbf{R}$.
   Solve each of the following:
   (i) $h(x) = -4$ **(ii)** $h(x) = x$ **(iii)** $xh(x) + 1 = 0$ **(iv)** $h(x) \geqslant -1$

7. The function g is defined as $g : x \to 2x - 5$.
   (a) Find the value of **(i)** $g(3)$ **(ii)** $g(0)$ **(iii)** $g(-\tfrac{1}{2})$
   (b) Express, in terms of x, **(i)** $g(3x)$ **(ii)** $g(x + 3)$
   Hence, find the value of x for which $g(3x) + g(x + 3) = g(x) + g(0)$.

8. The function f is defined as $f : x \to 4 - 3x, \quad x \in \mathbf{R}$.

   (a) Find **(i)** $f(-2)$ **(ii)** $f(-\tfrac{1}{3})$

   (b) Find the number k such that $f(-2) = kf(-\tfrac{1}{3})$.

9. The function g is defined as $g : x \to 7 - 4x, \quad x \in \mathbf{R}$.

Find the number k such that $kf(-8) = f(-\frac{3}{2})$.

10. The function f is defined as $f : x \to x^2 - 1, \quad x \in \mathbf{R}$.
    (a) find (i) $f(4)$ (ii) $f(-3)$ (iii) $f(2)$
    (b) for what value of $k \in \mathbf{R}$ is $2k + 1 + f(4) = f(-3)$?
    (c) find the values of x for which $f(x) - f(2) = 0$
    (d) verify that $f(x - 1) = f(1 - x)$.

11. $f : x \to x^2 + 1$ and $g : x \to 2x$ are two functions defined on $\mathbf{R}$.
    (i)   find $f(\sqrt{3})$ and $g(1)$
    (ii) find the value of k for which $f(\sqrt{3}) = kg(1)$
    (iii) find the value of x for which $f(x) = g(x)$
    (iv) verify that $f(x + 2) = g(x^2 + 2x + 1) - f(x) + f(\sqrt{3})$.

12. $f : x \to 2x^2 + 1$ and $g : x \to 5x - 1$ are two functions defined on $\mathbf{R}$.
    (i)   find $f(\sqrt{5})$ and $g(2k + 3)$
    (ii) find the value of k for which $g(2k + 3) = f(\sqrt{5}) - 7$
    (iii) find the two values of m for which $f(m) - g(m) = 0$.

13. h and k are two functions defined by $h : x \to x^2 + 4$ and $k : x \to 2x + 1, \quad x \in \mathbf{R}$.
    (i)   find $k(4), h(2x)$ and $k(3x + 2)$
    (ii) for what values of x is $h(2x) = k(3x + 2) + k(4)$?

14. $g : x \to (x - 1)^2$ is a function defined on $\mathbf{R}$.
    (i)   find $g(1)$ and $g(-1)$
    (ii) find the value of $t \in \mathbf{R}$ for which $tg(-3) = g(9)$
    (iii) verify that $g(1 + k) = g(1 - k)$.

15. The function f is defined as $f : x \to 2x + 5, \quad x \in \mathbf{R}$.
    Find a function g for which $g(x) = f(2x + 3) - f(x)$.
    Hence, or otherwise, find the value of $g(3)$.

16. $f : x \to x^2 - 1$ and $g : x \to (x - 1)^2$ are two functions defined on $\mathbf{R}$.
    (i)   If $9f(x) + 8 = f(kx)$, find two values for $k \in \mathbf{Z}$.
    (ii) Find a function h for which $g(x) = f(x) - 2h(x)$.
    (iii) Express $g(x + 1)$ in terms of $f(x)$.

Functions with missing coefficients

In some questions coefficients of the functions are missing and we are asked to find them. In this type of question we are given equations in disguise and by solving these equations we can calculate the missing coefficients.

Notation

$f(x) = y$

$f(2) = 3$ means when $x = 2$, $y = 3$ or the point $(2, 3)$ is on the graph of the function.

$f(-1) = 0$ means when $x = -1$, $y = 0$ or the point $(-1, 0)$ is on the graph of the function.

Example ▼

$f : x \rightarrow 5x + a$ and $g : x \rightarrow x^2 + bx - 3$ are two functions defined on **R**.

(i) If $f(2) = 7$, find the value of a.

(ii) If $g(-1) = -4$, find the value of b.

Solution:

(i)
$$f(x) = 5x + a$$
$$\text{Given: } f(2) = 7$$
$$\therefore \ 5(2) + a = 7$$
$$10 + a = 7$$
$$a = 7 - 10$$
$$a = -3$$

(ii)
$$g(x) = x^2 + bx - 3$$
$$\text{Given: } g(-1) = -4$$
$$\therefore \ (-1)^2 + b(-1) - 3 = -4$$
$$1 - b - 3 = -4$$
$$-b - 2 = -4$$
$$-b = -4 + 2$$
$$-b = -2$$
$$b = 2$$

Example ▼

$g : x \rightarrow ax^2 + bx + 1$ is a function defined on **R**.
If $g(1) = 0$ and $g(2) = 3$, write down two equations in a and b.
Hence, calculate the value of a and the value of b.

Solution:

$$g(x) = ax^2 + bx + 1$$

$$\text{Given: } g(1) = 0$$
$$\therefore \ a(1)^2 + b(1) + 1 = 0$$
$$a(1) + b(1) + 1 = 0$$
$$a + b + 1 = 0$$
$$a + b = -1 \quad ①$$

$$\text{Given: } g(2) = 3$$
$$\therefore \ a(2)^2 + b(2) + 1 = 3$$
$$a(4) + b(2) + 1 = 3$$
$$4a + 2b + 1 = 3$$
$$4a + 2b = 2$$
$$2a + b = 1 \quad ②$$

We now solve between the equations ① and ②:

$$a + b = -1 \quad ①$$
$$2a + b = 1 \quad ②$$
$$\underline{}$$
$$-a = -2 \quad \text{(subtract)}$$
$$a = 2$$

put in $a = 2$ into ① or ②

Thus, $a = 2$ and $b = -3$

$$a + b = -1 \quad ①$$
$$\downarrow$$
$$2 + b = -1$$
$$b = -1 - 2$$
$$b = -3$$

Example ▼

The graph of the quadratic function
$f : x \rightarrow x^2 + bx + c, \quad x \in \mathbf{R}$, is shown.
Find the value of b and the value of c.
Hence, find the value of k.

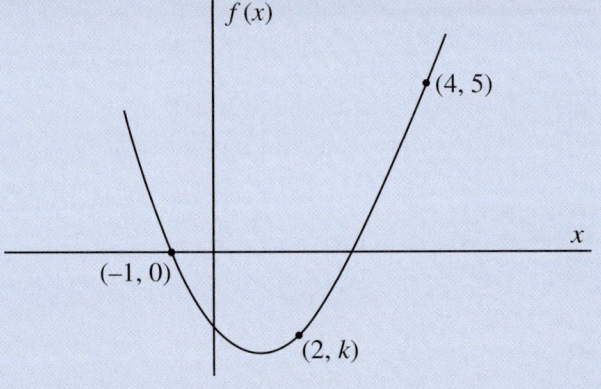

Solution:

$$f(x) = x^2 + bx + c$$

The graph goes through the point $(-1, 0)$

$$\therefore \ f(-1) = 0$$
$$\therefore \ (-1)^2 + b(-1) + c = 0$$
$$1 - b + c = 0$$
$$-b + c = -1$$
$$b - c = 1 \quad ①$$

The graph goes through the point $(4, 5)$

$$\therefore \ f(4) = 5$$
$$\therefore \ (4)^2 + b(4) + c = 5$$
$$16 + 4b + c = 5$$
$$4b + c = -11 \quad ②$$

We now solve between equations ① and ②:

$$b - c = 1 \quad ①$$
$$4b + c = -11 \quad ②$$
$$\underline{}$$
$$5b = -10 \quad \text{(add)}$$
$$b = -2$$

put in $b = -2$ into ① or ②

$$b - c = 1 \quad ①$$
$$\downarrow$$
$$-2 - c = 1$$
$$-c = 1 + 2$$
$$-c = 3$$
$$c = -3$$

Thus, $b = -2$ and $c = -3$
$$f(x) = x^2 + bx + c = x^2 - 2x - 3$$
The graph goes through the point $(2, k)$

$\therefore \qquad\qquad f(2) = k$

$\therefore \qquad (2)^2 - 2(2) - 3 = k$

$\qquad\qquad 4 - 4 - 3 = k$

$\qquad\qquad\qquad -3 = k$

Thus, $k = -3$

Exercise 14.2

1. Let $f(x) = 3x + k$, $x \in \mathbf{R}$. If $f(1) = 5$, find the value of k.
2. Let $g(x) = ax + 5$, $x \in \mathbf{R}$. If $g(2) = 11$, find the value of a.
3. Let $f(x) = x^2 + 3x + h$, $x \in \mathbf{R}$. If $f(1) = -1$, find the value of h.
4. Let $g(x) = 2x^2 + bx + 3$, $x \in \mathbf{R}$. If $g(2) = 3$, find the value of b.
5. Let $h(x) = ax^2 + 3x$, $x \in \mathbf{R}$. If $h(-1) = -5$, find the value of a.
6. Let $f(x) = (x + k)(x - 2)$, $x \in \mathbf{R}$. If $f(3) = 7$, find the value of k.
7. Let $k(x) = (ax)^2 - 7ax + 6$, $x \in \mathbf{R}$. If $k(2) = 0$, find two possible values of a.
8. $f : x \rightarrow 2x + a$ and $g : x \rightarrow 3x + b$
   If $f(2) = 7$ and $g(1) = -1$, find the value of a and the value of b.
9. $h : x \rightarrow 2x + a$ and $k : x \rightarrow b - 5x$ are two functions defined on $\mathbf{R}$.
   If $h(1) = -5$ and $k(-1) = 4$, find the value of a and the value of b.
10. $f : x \rightarrow 3x + a$ and $g : x \rightarrow ax + b$ are two functions defined on $\mathbf{R}$.
    If $f(2) = 8$ and $g(2) = 1$,
    (i) Find the value of a and the value of b.
    (ii) Find $f(-1)$ and $g(4)$.
    (iii) Using your values of a and b from **(i)**, find the two values of x for which:
    $$ax^2 - (a - b)x + 2ab = 0$$
11. $h : x \rightarrow 2x - a$ and $k : x \rightarrow ax + b$ are two functions defined on $\mathbf{R}$, where a and $b \in \mathbf{Z}$.
    $h(3) = 1$ and $k(5) = 8$.
    (i) Find the value of a and the value of b.
    (ii) Hence, list the values of x for which $h(x) \geqslant k(x)$, $x \in \mathbf{N}$.
12. $g : x \rightarrow ax^2 + bx + 1$ is a function defined on $\mathbf{R}$.
    If $g(1) = 2$ and $g(-1) = 6$, write down two equations in a and b.
    Hence, calculate the value of a and the value of b.
13. $g : x \rightarrow px^2 + qx - 3$ is a function defined on $\mathbf{R}$.
    If $g(1) = 4$ and $g(-1) = -6$, write down two equations in p and q.
    Hence, calculate the value of p and the value of q.
    Find the two values of x for which $px^2 + qx - 3 = 0$.

14. (i) $f(x) = ax^2 + bx - 8$, where a and b are real numbers.
If $f(1) = -9$ and $f(2) = 0$, find the value of a and the value of b.

(ii) Using your values of a and b from **(i)**, find the two values of x for which
$ax^2 + bx = bx^2 + ax$.

15. $f : x \rightarrow ax^2 + bx + c$, where a, b and c are real numbers.
If $f(0) = -3$, find the value of c.
If $f(-1) = 6$ and $f(2) = 3$, find the value of a and the value of b.

16. $h : x \rightarrow x^2 + x + q$ is a function defined on $\mathbf{R}$ where $q \in \mathbf{Z}$.
(i) If $h(-3) = 0$, find the value of q.
(ii) Hence, solve the equation $h(x + 5) = 0$.

17. The graph of the quadratic function
$f : x \rightarrow x^2 + bx + c$, $x \in \mathbf{R}$, is shown.
Find the values of b and c.
Hence, find the value of k.

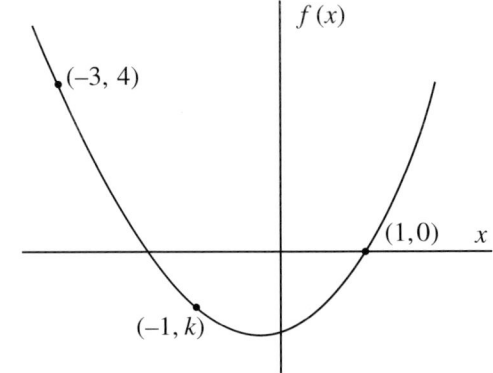

18. The graph of the quadratic function
$g : x \rightarrow ax^2 + bx - 3$, $x \in \mathbf{R}$, is shown.
Find the values of a and b.
Hence, calculate the value of h and k.

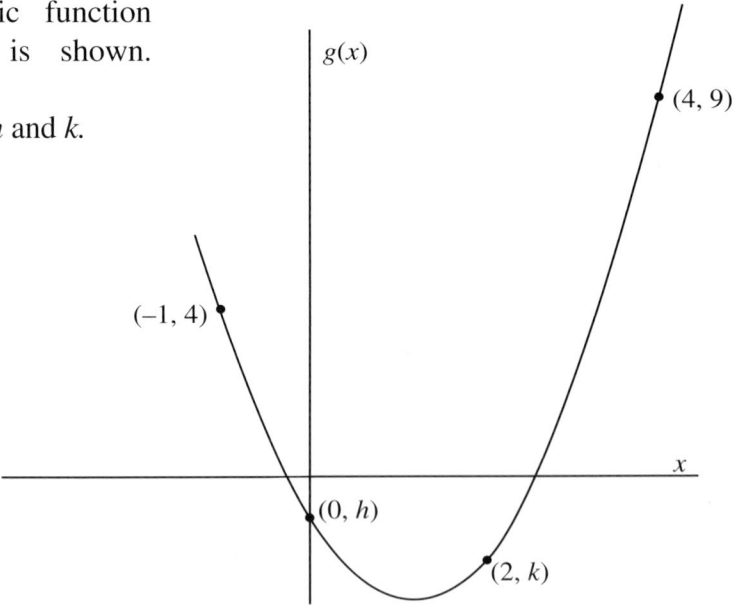

19. The graph of the quadratic function
$h : x \rightarrow c + bx - x^2, \quad x \in \mathbf{R}$, is shown.
Find the value of b and c.
$k : x \rightarrow px + q$ is a function defined on $\mathbf{R}$.
If $k(0) = -1$ and $k(1) = 1$, find the value of
p and the value of q.
Hence, find the two values of x for which
$k(x) = h(x)$.

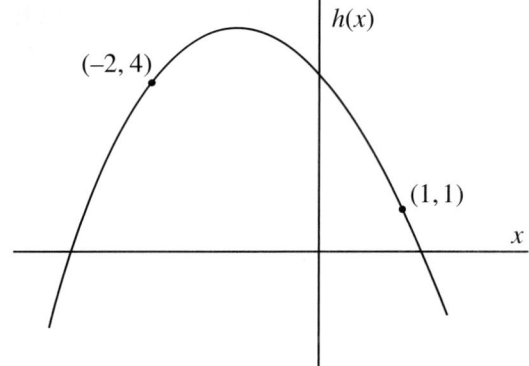

20. Let $f(x) = x^2 + bx + c, \quad x \in \mathbf{R}$.
The solutions of $f(x) = 0$ are -3 and 1.
Find the value of b and the value of c.
If $f(-1) = k$, find the value of k.
Solve the equation $f(x) - k = 0$.

21. Let $g(x) = x^2 + bx + c, \quad x \in \mathbf{R}$.
The solutions of $g(x) = 0$ are symmetrical about the line $x = 1$.
If $x = -3$ is one solution of $g(x) = 0$, find the other solution.
Find the value of b and the value of c.

CHAPTER 15

GRAPHING FUNCTIONS

Notation

The notation $y = f(x)$ means 'the value of the output y depends on the value of the input x, according to some rule called f. Hence, y and $f(x)$ are interchangeable, and the y axis can also be called the $f(x)$ axis.

Note: It is very important not to draw a graph outside the given values of x.

Graphing linear functions

The first four letters in the word '**linear**' spell '**line**'. Therefore the graph of a linear function will be a straight line. A linear function is usually given in the form $f: x \rightarrow ax + b$, where $a \neq 0$ and a, b are constants. For example, $f: x \rightarrow 2x + 5$. As the graph is a straight line, two points are all that is needed to graph it. In the question, you will always be given a set of inputs, x, called the domain.

To graph a linear function do the following:

> 1. Choose two suitable values of x, in the given domain.
>   (Two suitable values are the smallest and largest values of x.)
> 2. Substitute these in the function to find the two corresponding values of y.
> 3. Plot the points and draw the line through them.

Note: $-3 \leqslant x \leqslant 2$ means 'x is between -3 and 2, including -3 and 2'.

Graph the function $g : x \rightarrow 2x - 3$, in the domain $-2 \leqslant x \leqslant 3, \quad x \in \mathbf{R}$.

Solution:

Let $y = g(x) \quad \Rightarrow \quad y = 2x - 3$

x	$2x - 3$	y
-2	$-4 - 3$	-7
3	$6 - 3$	3

Plot the points $(-2, -7)$ and $(3, 3)$ and join them with a straight line.

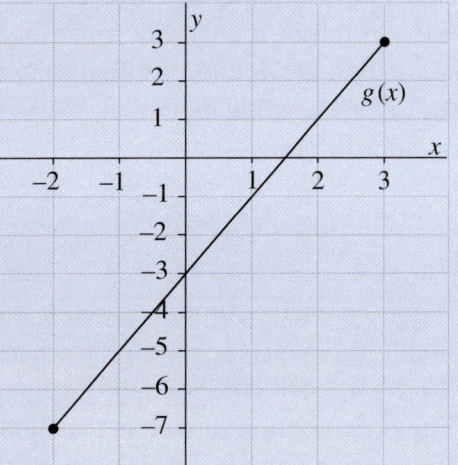

Graph each of the following functions in the given domain:

1.	$f : x \rightarrow 2x + 1$	in the domain	$-2 \leqslant x \leqslant 3, \quad x \in \mathbf{R}$
2.	$g : x \rightarrow 3x + 2$	in the domain	$-1 \leqslant x \leqslant 4, \quad x \in \mathbf{R}$
3.	$f : x \rightarrow 4x - 3$	in the domain	$-3 \leqslant x \leqslant 3, \quad x \in \mathbf{R}$
4.	$g : x \rightarrow 2x - 5$	in the domain	$-1 \leqslant x \leqslant 5, \quad x \in \mathbf{R}$
5.	$h : x \rightarrow x + 2$	in the domain	$-5 \leqslant x \leqslant 3, \quad x \in \mathbf{R}$
6.	$f : x \rightarrow 3x - 1$	in the domain	$-3 \leqslant x \leqslant 3, \quad x \in \mathbf{R}$
7.	$g : x \rightarrow 5x + 2$	in the domain	$-2 \leqslant x \leqslant 4, \quad x \in \mathbf{R}$
8.	$k : x \rightarrow x$	in the domain	$-3 \leqslant x \leqslant 3, \quad x \in \mathbf{R}$
9.	$f : x \rightarrow 2x$	in the domain	$-2 \leqslant x \leqslant 2, \quad x \in \mathbf{R}$
10.	$g : x \rightarrow 3x$	in the domain	$-3 \leqslant x \leqslant 2, \quad x \in \mathbf{R}$
11.	$f : x \rightarrow -x$	in the domain	$-3 \leqslant x \leqslant 3, \quad x \in \mathbf{R}$
12.	$h : x \rightarrow 2 - x$	in the domain	$-4 \leqslant x \leqslant 4, \quad x \in \mathbf{R}$
13.	$k : x \rightarrow 3 - 2x$	in the domain	$-3 \leqslant x \leqslant 4, \quad x \in \mathbf{R}$
14.	$f : x \rightarrow 4 - 3x$	in the domain	$-2 \leqslant x \leqslant 4, \quad x \in \mathbf{R}$
15.	$g : x \rightarrow -1 - x$	in the domain	$-4 \leqslant x \leqslant 3, \quad x \in \mathbf{R}$

Graphing quadratic functions

A **quadratic** function is usually given in the form $f : x \rightarrow ax^2 + bx + c$, $a \neq 0$, and a, b, c are constants. For example, $f : x \rightarrow 2x^2 - x + 3$. Because of its shape, quite a few points are needed to plot the graph of a quadratic function. In the question, you will always be given a set of inputs, x, called the domain. With these inputs, a table is used to find the corresponding set of outputs, y or $f(x)$, called the range. When the table is completed, plot the points and join them with a '**smooth curve**'.

Notes on making out the table

1. Work out each column separately, i.e. all the x^2 values first, then all the x values, and finally the constant. (Watch for patterns in the numbers.)
2. Work out each corresponding value of y.
3. The **only** column that changes sign is the x term (middle) column.
   If the given values of x contain 0, then the x term column will make one sign change, either from $+$ to $-$ or from $-$ to $+$, where $x = 0$.
4. The other two columns **never** change sign. They remain either all pluses or all minuses. These columns keep the sign given in the question.

Note: Decide where to draw the x and y axes by looking at the table to see what the largest and smallest values of x and y are. In general, the units on the x axis are larger than the units on the y axis. Try to make sure that the graph extends almost the whole width and length of the page.

Using the same axes and scales, graph the functions:
$f : x \rightarrow 5 + 2x - x^2$, $g : x \rightarrow 2x - 1$, in the domain $-3 \leqslant x \leqslant 4$, $x \in \mathbf{R}$.

Solution:

Let $y = f(x) \implies y = -x^2 + 2x + 5$ Let $y = g(x) \implies y = 2x - 1$

x	$-x^2 + 2x + 5$	y
-3	$-9 - 6 + 5$	-10
-2	$-4 - 4 + 5$	-3
-1	$-1 - 2 + 5$	2
0	$-0 + 0 + 5$	5
1	$-1 + 2 + 5$	6
2	$-4 + 4 + 5$	5
3	$-9 + 6 + 5$	2
4	$-16 + 8 + 5$	-3

x	$2x - 1$	y
-3	$-6 - 1$	-7
4	$8 - 1$	7

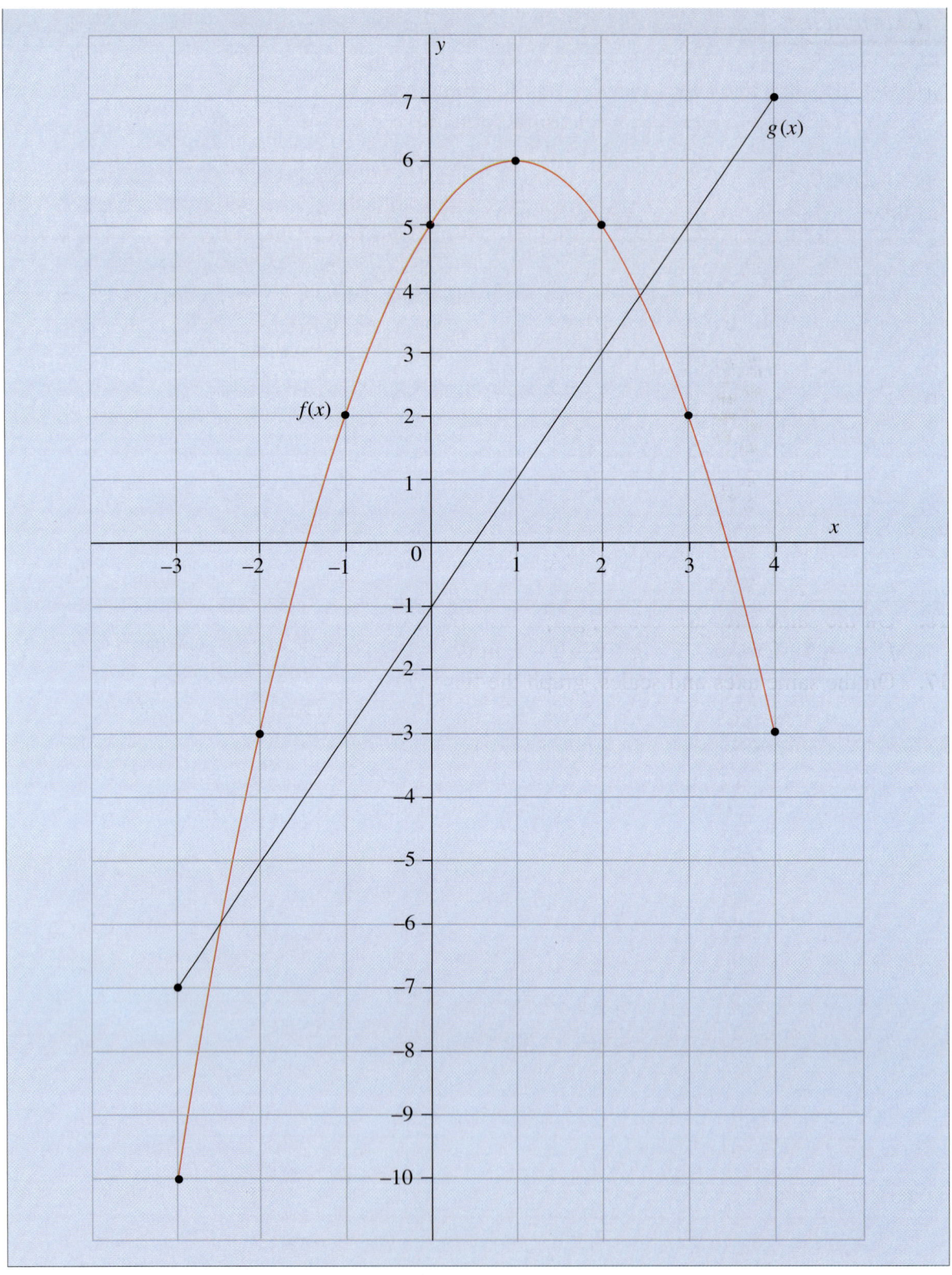

Note: On the same axes and scales means draw both functions on the same diagram.

Graph each of the following functions in the given domain:

1. $f: x \to x^2 + 2x - 8$ in the domain $-5 \leqslant x \leqslant 3,$ $x \in \mathbf{R}$
2. $f: x \to x^2 - 3x - 4$ in the domain $-2 \leqslant x \leqslant 5,$ $x \in \mathbf{R}$
3. $f: x \to x^2 - 2x - 3$ in the domain $-2 \leqslant x \leqslant 4,$ $x \in \mathbf{R}$
4. $f: x \to x^2 - x - 2$ in the domain $-2 \leqslant x \leqslant 3,$ $x \in \mathbf{R}$
5. $f: x \to x^2 + 3x - 2$ in the domain $-5 \leqslant x \leqslant 2,$ $x \in \mathbf{R}$
6. $f: x \to x^2 - 3x$ in the domain $-2 \leqslant x \leqslant 5,$ $x \in \mathbf{R}$
7. $f: x \to 9 + x - x^2$ in the domain $-3 \leqslant x \leqslant 4,$ $x \in \mathbf{R}$
8. $f: x \to 6 - x - x^2$ in the domain $-4 \leqslant x \leqslant 3,$ $x \in \mathbf{R}$
9. $f: x \to 3 + 2x - x^2$ in the domain $-2 \leqslant x \leqslant 4,$ $x \in \mathbf{R}$
10. $f: x \to 2x - x^2$ in the domain $-2 \leqslant x \leqslant 4,$ $x \in \mathbf{R}$
11. $f: x \to 2x^2 + 3x - 2$ in the domain $-3 \leqslant x \leqslant 2,$ $x \in \mathbf{R}$
12. $f: x \to 2x^2 - x - 1$ in the domain $-3 \leqslant x \leqslant 3,$ $x \in \mathbf{R}$
13. $f: x \to 5 + x - 2x^2$ in the domain $-2 \leqslant x \leqslant 3,$ $x \in \mathbf{R}$
14. $f: x \to 3 + 5x - 2x^2$ in the domain $-1 \leqslant x \leqslant 4,$ $x \in \mathbf{R}$
15. On the same axes and scales, graph the functions:
$f: x \to x^2 - 2x - 4,$ $g: x \to 2x + 1,$ in the domain $-3 \leqslant x \leqslant 5,$ $x \in \mathbf{R}.$
16. On the same axes and scales, graph the functions:
$f: x \to 5 + 2x - x^2,$ $g: x \to 2 - x,$ in the domain $-2 \leqslant x \leqslant 4,$ $x \in \mathbf{R}.$
17. On the same axes and scales, graph the functions:
$f: x \to 2x^2 - 3x - 8,$ $g: x \to 3x - 2,$ in the domain $-2 \leqslant x \leqslant 4,$ $x \in \mathbf{R}.$
18. On the same axes and scales, graph the functions:
$f: x \to 6 + x - 2x^2,$ $g: x \to 1 - 2x,$ in the domain $-2 \leqslant x \leqslant 3,$ $x \in \mathbf{R}.$

Using graphs

Once we have drawn the graph, we are usually asked to use the graph to answer some questions. Below are examples of the general type of problems where graphs are used.

Notes: **1.** $y = f(x)$, so $f(x)$ can be replaced by y.
          2. In general, if given x find y, and vice versa.

Examples of the main problems, once the graph is drawn:

1. **Find the values of x for which $f(x) = 0$.**
   This question is asking:
   'Where does the curve meet the x axis?'

   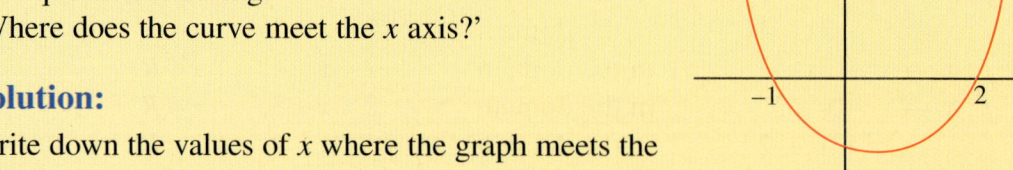

   Solution:

   Write down the values of x where the graph meets the x axis.
   From the graph: $x = -1$ or $x = 2$.

2. **Find the values of x for which $f(x) = 2$.**
   This question is asking:
   'When $y = 2$, what are the values of x?'

   Solution:

   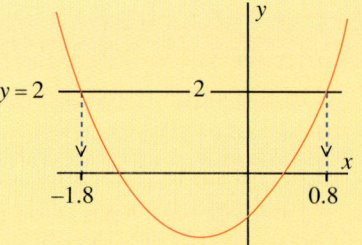

   Draw the line $y = 2$. Where this line meets the curve draw broken perpendicular lines onto the x axis. Write down the values of x where these broken lines meet the x axis.
   From the graph:
   When $y = 2$, $x = -1.8$ or $x = 0.8$.

3. **Find the value of $f(-1.5)$.**
   This question is asking:
   'When $x = -1.5$, what is the value of y?'

   Solution:

   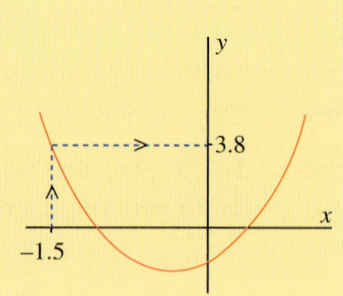

   From $x = -1.5$ on the x axis draw a broken perpendicular line to meet the curve. From this draw a broken horizontal line to meet the y axis. Write down the value of y where this line meets the y axis.
   From the graph:
   $f(-1.5) = 3.8$

4. Maximum point and maximum value.

Solution:

Consider the graph on the right. The maximum point is (2, 4). The maximum value is found by drawing a horizontal line from the maximum point to the y axis and reading the value where this line meets the y axis. The maximum value is 4 (the same as the y coordinate of the maximum point).

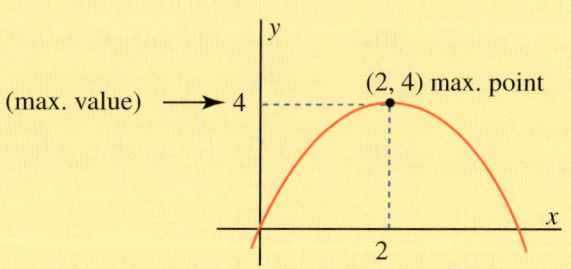

5. Minimum point and minimum value.

Solution:

Consider the graph on the right. The minimum point is $(-1, -3)$. The minimum value is found by drawing a horizontal line from the minimum point to the y axis and reading the value where this line meets the y axis.

The minimum value is -3 (the same as the y coordinate of the minimum point).

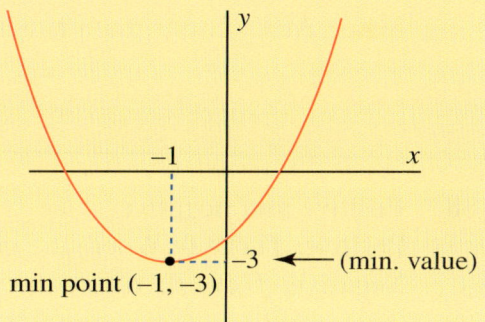

6. Axis of symmetry

Graphs of quadratic functions are symmetrical about a line that passes through the middle of the curve (and also through the maximum and minimum points). The line is called the 'axis of symmetry'.

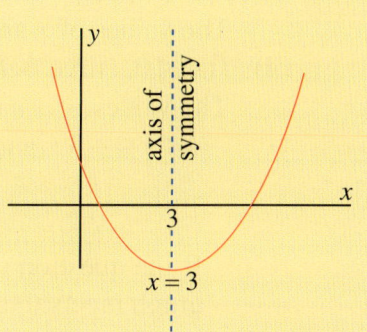

Solution:

From the graph:
The equation of the axis of symmetry is $x = 3$.
3 is where the line meets the x axis.

7. Increasing and decreasing

Graphs are read from left to right.

Increasing: $f(x)$ is increasing where the graph is **rising** as we go from left to right.

Decreasing: $f(x)$ is decreasing where the graph is **falling** as we go from left to right.

The diagram shows the graph of a quadratic function, $f(x)$ in the domain $-2 \leqslant x \leqslant 4$.
Find the values of x for which **(i)** $f(x)$ is decreasing **(ii)** $f(x)$ is increasing.

Solution:

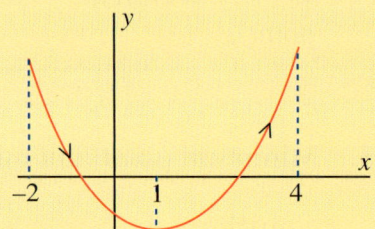

(i) $f(x)$ decreasing, graph falling from left to right.
The values of x are: $-2 \leqslant x < 1$
(ii) $f(x)$ increasing, graph rising from left to right.
The values of x are: $1 < x \leqslant 4$

Note: At $x = 1$, the graph is neither increasing nor decreasing.

8. Positive and negative

Positive, $f(x) > 0$: Where the graph is **above** the x axis.
Negative, $f(x) < 0$: Where the graph is **below** the x axis.

The diagram shows the graph of a quadratic function, $f(x)$, in the domain $-4 \leqslant x \leqslant 2$.
Find the values of x for which **(i)** $f(x) > 0$ **(ii)** $f(x) < 0$.

Solution:

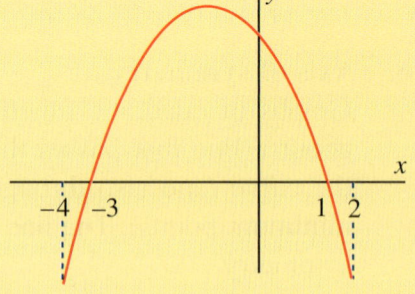

(i) $f(x) > 0$, curve **above** the x axis.
The values of x are: $-3 < x < 1$.
(ii) $f(x) < 0$, curve **below** the x axis.
The values of x are:
$-4 \leqslant x < -3$ and $1 < x \leqslant 2$.

Note: If the question uses $f(x) \geqslant 0$ or $f(x) \leqslant 0$, then the values of x where the graph meets the x axis must also be included.

9. Graph above or below a constant value (an inequality)

The diagram shows the graph of a quadratic function, $f(x)$, in the domain $-2 \leqslant x \leqslant 5$.

Find the values of x for which (i) $f(x) \geqslant 3$ (ii) $f(x) \leqslant 3$.

These questions are asking:

'What are the values of x for which the curve, $f(x)$, is **(i)** 3 or above **(ii)** 3 or below?'

Solution:

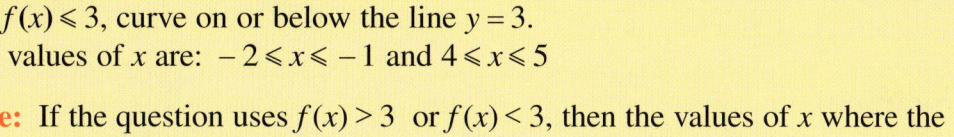

Draw the line $y = 3$.

Write down the values of x for which the curve is:

(i)   on or above the line $y = 3$

(ii)   on or below the line $y = 3$.

(i) $f(x) \geqslant 3$, curve on or above the line $y = 3$.
The values of x are: $-1 \leqslant x \leqslant 4$

(ii) $f(x) \leqslant 3$, curve on or below the line $y = 3$.
The values of x are: $-2 \leqslant x \leqslant -1$ and $4 \leqslant x \leqslant 5$

Note: If the question uses $f(x) > 3$ or $f(x) < 3$, then the values of x where the curve meets the line $y = 3$ (-1 and 4) are not included.

---

10. Two functions graphed on the same axes and scales

The diagram shows the graphs of the functions $f : x \to x^2 - x - 6$ and $g : x \to 2x - 1$ in the domain $-3 \leqslant x \leqslant 5$.

($f(x)$ is a curve, $g(x)$ is a line)

Find the values of x for which:

(i) $f(x) = g(x)$ **(ii)** $f(x) \leqslant g(x)$ **(iii)** $f(x) \geqslant g(x)$

Solution:

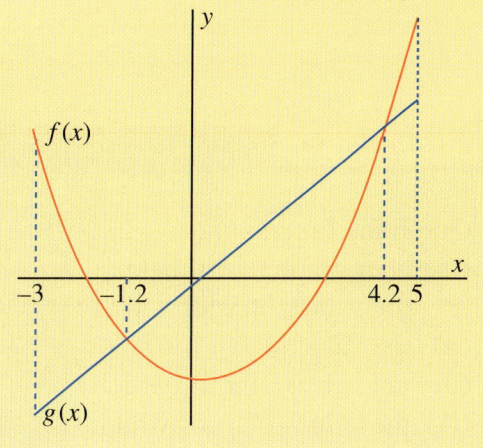

(i) $f(x) = g(x)$
            (curve = line)
            The values of x are: -1.2 and 4.2

(ii) $f(x) \leqslant g(x)$
            (curve equal to and below the line)
            The values of x are: $-1.2 \leqslant x \leqslant 4.2$

(iii) $f(x) \geqslant g(x)$
            (curve equal to and above the line)
            The values of x are:
                $-3 \leqslant x \leqslant -1.2$ and $4.2 \leqslant x \leqslant 5$

11. The number of times a graph meets the x axis gives the number of roots of its equation. Often we need to find a range of values of a constant, which shifts a graph up or down, giving a graph a certain number of roots, e.g.,

For what values of k does the equation $f(x) = k$ have two roots?

Solution:

The equation $f(x) = k$ will have two roots if the line $y = k$ cuts the graph twice.
So we have to draw lines parallel to the x axis that cut the graph twice.
The range of values of k will be in between the lowest and highest values on the y axis that the line $y = k$ cuts the graph twice.

On the right is a graph of the function

$f: x \to x^2 - 2x - 5$, in the domain $-3 \leqslant x \leqslant 4$, $x \in \mathbf{R}$.

Question: Find the range of values of k for which $f(x) = k$ has two roots.

Solution:

The range of values of k are found by finding the range of the equations of the lines, parallel to the x axis, which cut the graph twice.

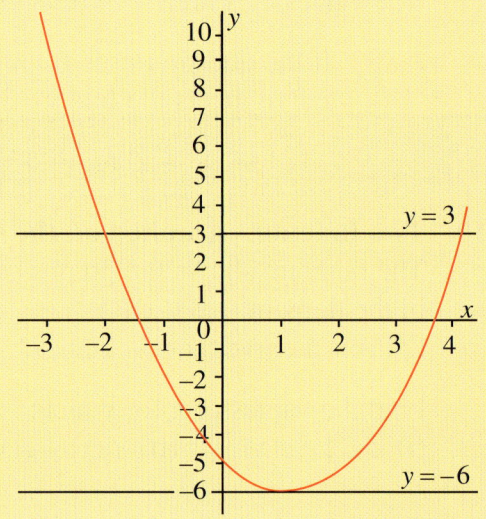

Any lines drawn parallel to the y axis between $y = -6$ and $y = 3$, will cut the graph twice.
∴ k will lie between -6 and 3.
∴ $f(x) = k$ will have two roots for $-6 < k \leqslant 3$ (at $k = -6$ there is only one root).

Example ▼

Graph the function $f: x \to 2x^2 - 3x - 5$ in the domain $-2 \leqslant x \leqslant 3$, $x \in \mathbf{R}$.
Use your graph to estimate:
(i) the values of x for which $f(x) = 0$
(ii) the value of $f(-1.6)$
(iii) the values of x for which $f(x) \geqslant -2$
(iv) the values of x for which $f(x) > 0$ and decreasing.

Solution:

Let $y = f(x) \implies y = 2x^2 - 3x - 5$

x	$2x^2 - 3x - 5$	y
-2	$8 + 6 - 5$	9
-1	$2 + 3 - 5$	0
0	$0 + 0 - 5$	-5
1	$2 - 3 - 5$	-6
2	$8 - 6 - 5$	-3
3	$18 - 9 - 5$	4

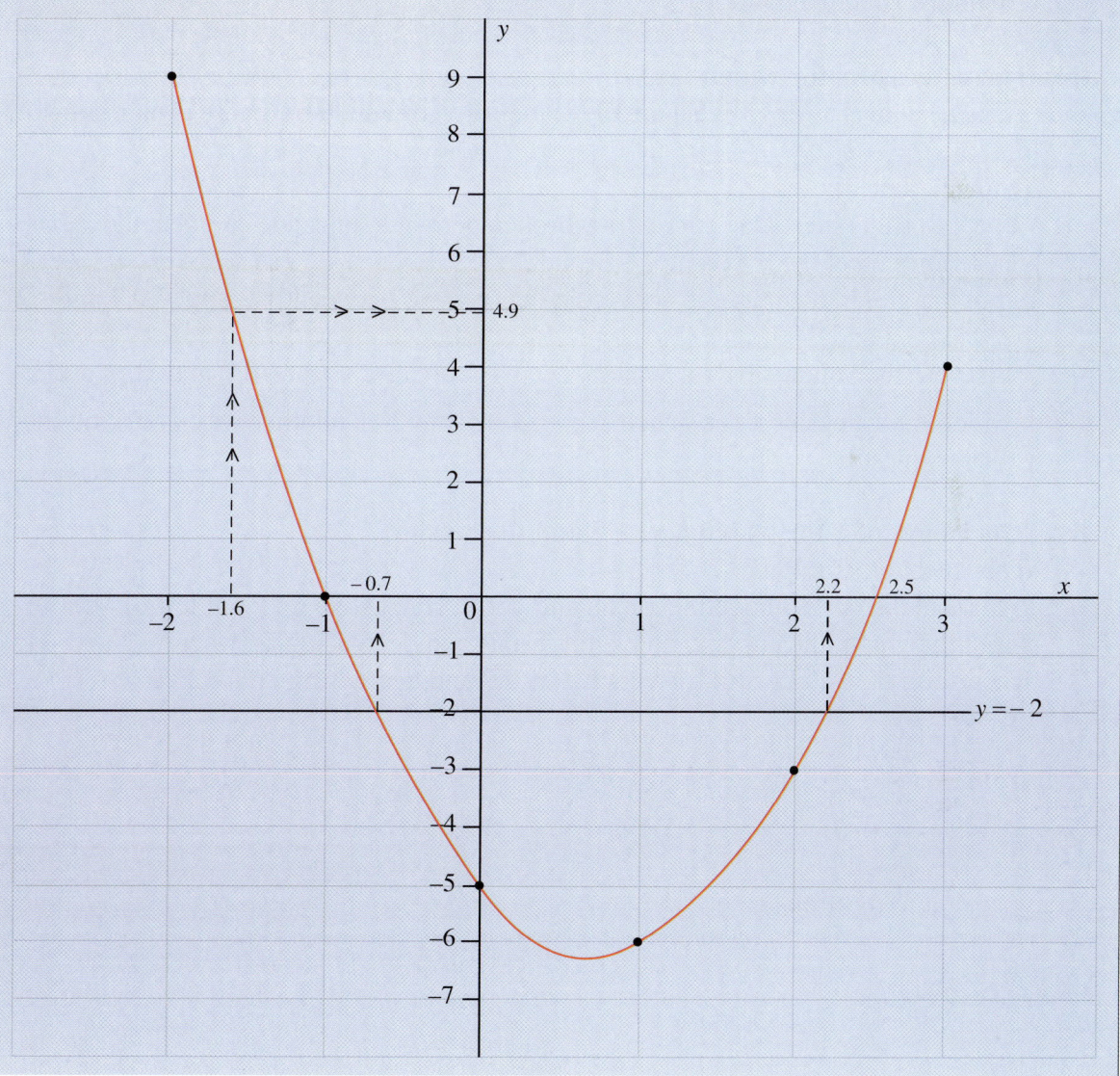

(i) Values of x for which $f(x) = 0$

This question is asking, 'where does the curve meet the x axis?'.

The curve meets the x axis at -1 and 2.5.

Therefore, the values of x for which $f(x) = 0$, are -1 and 2.5.

Note: 'Find the values of x for which $2x^2 - 3x - 5 = 0$, is another way of asking the same question.

(ii) The value of $f(-1.6)$

This question is asking, 'when $x = -1.6$, what is the value of y?'

From $x = -1.6$ on the x axis draw a broken perpendicular line to meet the curve.

From this draw a broken horizontal line to meet the y axis.

This line meets the y axis at 4.9.

Therefore $f(-1.6) = 4.9$.

(iii) The values of x for which $f(x) \geqslant -2$

This question is asking, 'what are the values of x for which the curve is **on** or **above** the line $y = -2$?'.

Draw the line $y = -2$.

Where this line meets the curve draw broken perpendicular lines to meet the x axis.

These lines meet the x axis at -0.7 and 2.2.

From the graph, the curve is above the line $y = -2$ between -2 and -0.7 and between 2.2 and 3.

Therefore the values of x for which $f(x) \geqslant -2$ are $-2 \leqslant x \leqslant -0.7$ and $2.2 \leqslant x \leqslant 3$.

Note: 'Find the values of x for which $2x^2 - 3x - 5 \geqslant -2$' is another way of asking the same question.

(iv) The values of x for which $f(x) > 0$ and decreasing.

This question is asking,

'where is the curve above the x axis and decreasing as we go from left to right?'.

From the graph, the curve is above the x axis and decreasing between -2 and -1.

Therefore, the values of x for which $f(x) > 0$ and decreasing are $-2 \leqslant x < -1$.

Note: $x = -1$ is not included because at $x = -1$, $f(x) = 0$ and is not decreasing.

1. Below is a graph of the function $f: x \rightarrow 2x^2 + x - 6$ in the domain $-3 \leqslant x \leqslant 2$, $x \in \mathbf{R}$.

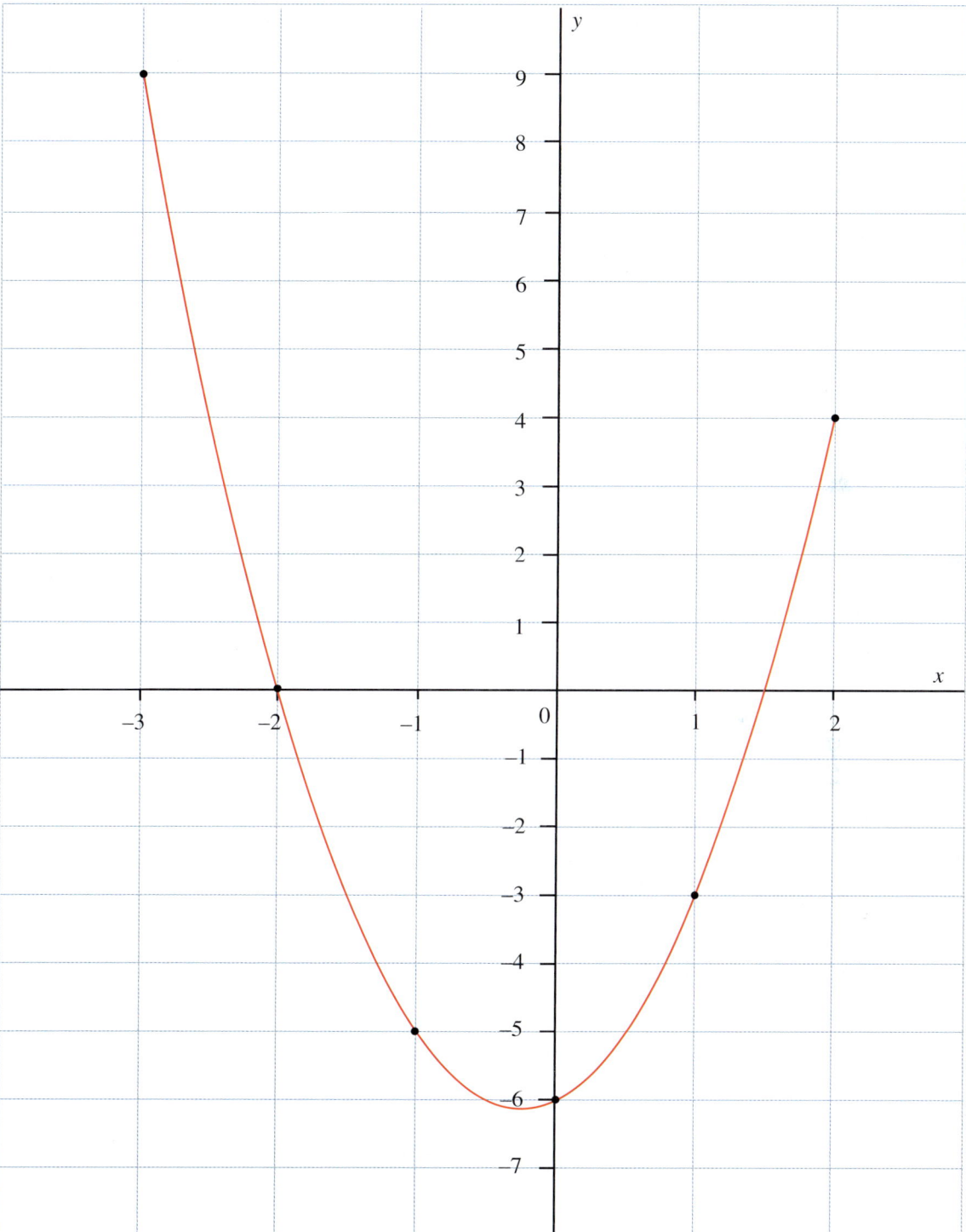

Use the graph to estimate:
- **(i)** the values of x for which $f(x) = 0$
- **(ii)** the minimum value of $f(x)$
- **(iii)** the values of x for which $f(x) = -5$
- **(iv)** the value of $f(-2.8)$
- **(v)** the values of x for which $f(x) \leqslant 0$
- **(vi)** the values of x for which $f(x) > 0$
- **(vii)** the values of x for which $f(x) \leqslant -3$
- **(viii)** the values of x for which $f(x) > 0$ and increasing
- **(ix)** the values of x for which $2x^2 + x - 6 = 4$
- **(x)** the value of k such that $f(k) = f(-2.25), \quad k \neq -2.25$

Draw the axis of symmetry of the graph of $f(x)$.

2. Draw the graph of the function $f : x \to x^2 + 2x - 3$ in the domain $-4 \leqslant x \leqslant 2, \ x \in \mathbf{R}$.
   Use your graph to find:
   - **(i)** the values of x for which $f(x) = 0$
   - **(ii)** the values of x for which $f(x) = -3$
   - **(iii)** the minimum value
   - **(iv)** the minimum point
   - **(v)** the values of x for which $f(x) \leqslant 0$
   - **(vi)** the value of $f(-3.7)$

   The equation of the axis of symmetry is $x = k$. Find the value of k.

3. Draw the graph of the function $f : x \to 4 + 3x - x^2$ in the domain $-2 \leqslant x \leqslant 5, \ x \in \mathbf{R}$.
   Use your graph to:
   - **(i)** find the values of x for which $f(x) = 0$
   - **(ii)** find the values of x for which $f(x) = f(3)$
   - **(iii)** estimate $f(-1.6)$
   - **(iv)** estimate the maximum value of $f(x)$
   - **(v)** find the values of x for which $f(x) \leqslant 0$
   - **(vi)** find the value of k such that $f(k) = f(3.5), \quad k \neq 3.5$.

4. Draw the graph of the function $f : x \to 4x - x^2$ in the domain $-1 \leqslant x \leqslant 5, \ x \in \mathbf{R}$.
   Use your graph to find:
   - **(i)** the maximum point
   - **(ii)** the values of x for which $f(x) \geqslant 3$
   - **(iii)** the values of x for which $f(x) \geqslant 0$ and increasing
   - **(iv)** the values of k for which $f(x) = k$ has two solutions.

5. Graph the function $f : x \to 3x^2 + 2x - 8$ in the domain $-3 \leqslant x \leqslant 2, \ x \in \mathbf{R}$.
   From your graph estimate:
   - **(i)** the values of x for which $f(x) = 0$
   - **(ii)** the values of x for which $3x^2 + 2x - 8 \leqslant 0$
   - **(iii)** the values of x for which $3x^2 + 2x - 8 = 3$
   - **(iv)** the value of $f(1.8)$
   - **(v)** the minimum value of $f(x)$.

6. Graph the function $f : x \rightarrow 2x^2 - 4x - 5$ in the domain $-2 \leqslant x \leqslant 4$, $x \in \mathbf{R}$.
Use your graph to find:

(i) the minimum point of $f(x)$

(ii) the roots of the equation $2x^2 - 4x - 5 = 1$

(iii) the range of values of x for which $2x^2 - 4x - 5 \leqslant -5$

(iv) the range of values of x for which $f(x)$ is decreasing

(v) the value of k for which $f(x) = k$ has only one solution.

7. The function $f : x \rightarrow 3 + 2x - x^2$ is defined in the domain $-2 \leqslant x \leqslant 4$, $x \in \mathbf{R}$.

(i) Complete the table:

x	-2	-1	0	1	2	3	4
$f(x)$	-5				3		

Graph the function f.
Use your graph to find:

(ii) the maximum value of $f(x)$

(iii) the maximum point of $f(x)$

(iv) the value of $f(3.6)$

(v) another value of x such that $f(x) = f(3.6)$

(vi) the values of $f(x)$ for which $-1 \leqslant x \leqslant 3$.

8. Graph the function $f : x \rightarrow 7 + 5x - 2x^2$ in the domain $-2 \leqslant x \leqslant 4$, $x \in \mathbf{R}$.
Use your graph to estimate:

(i) the values of x for which $7 + 5x - 2x^2 = 0$

(ii) the values of x for which $f(x) = f(1) - f(3)$

(iii) the maximum value of $f(x)$

(iv) the values of k for which $f(x) = k$ has no solutions.

Using the same axes and scales graph the functions:

$f : x \rightarrow 5 - x - 2x^2,$ $g : x \rightarrow 1 - 2x,$ in the domain $-3 \leqslant x \leqslant 2,$ $x \in \mathbf{R}.$

Use your graphs to estimate:

(i)   the maximum value of $f(x)$

(ii) the values of x for which $f(x) = g(x)$

(iii) the values of x for which $f(x) > g(x)$

Solution:

Let $y = f(x) \Rightarrow y = -2x^2 - x + 5$

x	$-2x^2 - x + 5$	y
-3	$-18 + 3 + 5$	-10
-2	$-8 + 2 + 5$	-1
-1	$-2 + 1 + 5$	4
0	$-0 + 0 + 5$	5
1	$-2 - 1 + 5$	2
2	$-8 - 2 + 5$	-5

Let $y = g(x) \Rightarrow y = -2x + 1$

x	$-2x + 1$	y
-3	$6 + 1$	7
2	$-4 + 1$	-3

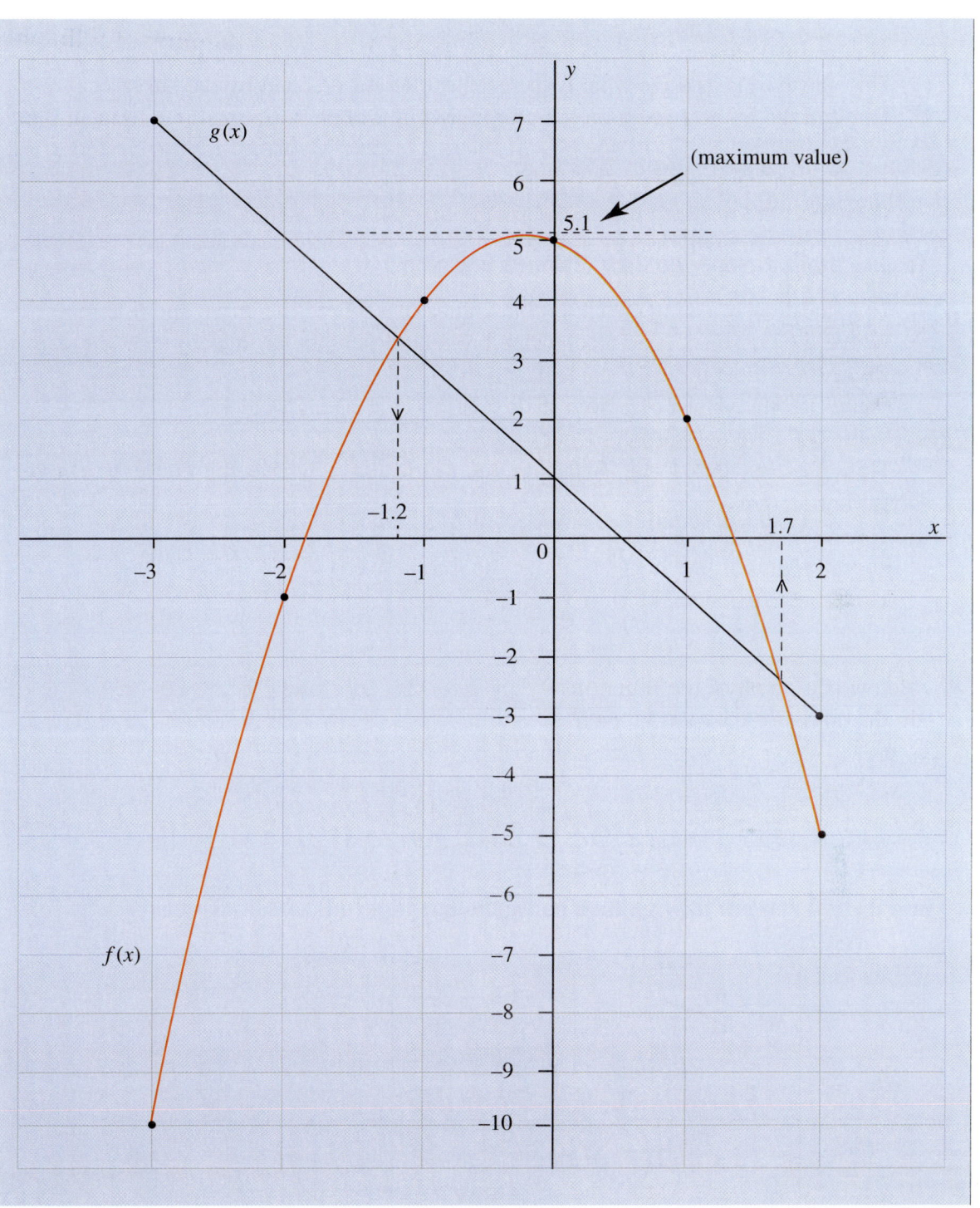

9. Below is a graph of the functions $f : x \rightarrow 8 - 2x - x^2$ and $g : x \rightarrow 6 - x$, in the domain $-5 \leqslant x \leqslant 3$, $x \in \mathbf{R}$.

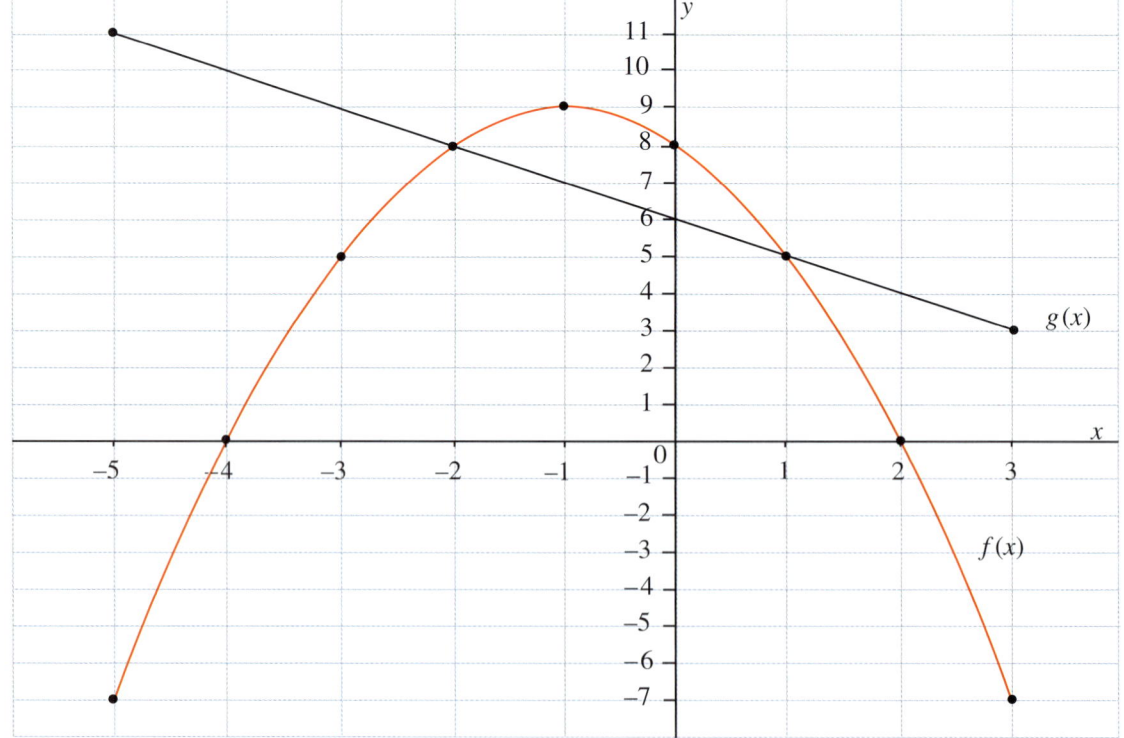

Use the graph to:

(i) find the maximum value of $f(x)$

(ii) find the coordinates of the maximum point of $f(x)$

(iii) find the values of x for which $f(x) = g(x)$

(iv) find the range of values of x for which $f(x) \geqslant g(x)$

(v) find the range of values of x for which $f(x) \leqslant g(x)$

(vi) find the values of x for which $f(x) = g(-2)$

(vii) estimate $f(-4.5)$

(viii) find the area of the rectangle that encloses the graphs of $f(x)$ and $g(x)$ in the domain $-5 \leqslant x \leqslant 3$

(ix) the roots of the equation $8 - 2x - x^2 = 5$

(x) the value of k such that $f(k) = f(1.6)$, $k \neq 1.6$

(xi) the value of x for which $g(x) = 9$

(xii) the equation of the axis of symmetry of $f(x)$ is $x = h$. Write down the value of h.

10. Using the same axes and scales, draw the graphs of:
$$f : x \to x^2 - 2x - 3, \quad g : x \to x - 3, \quad \text{in the domain} \quad -2 \leqslant x \leqslant 4, \quad x \in \mathbf{R}.$$
Use your graphs to find:

(i) the values of x for which $f(x) = 0$

(ii) the minimum point of $f(x)$

(iii) the values of x for which $f(x) = g(x)$

(iv) the values of x for which $g(x) \geqslant f(x)$

(v) the values of x for which $f(x) \geqslant g(x)$

(vi) the values of $f(x)$ for which $0 \leqslant x \leqslant 2$.

11. Using the same axes and scales, draw the graphs of:
$$f : x \to x^2 + x - 2, \quad g : x \to 2 - 2x, \quad \text{in the domain} \quad -4 \leqslant x \leqslant 3, \quad x \in \mathbf{R}.$$
Use your graphs to find:

(i) the values of x for which $f(x) \leqslant 0$

(ii) the value of x for which $g(x) = -4$

(iii) the values of x for which $f(x) = g(x)$

(iv) the values of x for which $f(x) \geqslant g(x)$

(v) the values of x for which $f(x) \leqslant g(x)$.

12. Using the same axes and scales, draw the graphs of:
$$f : x \to 3 + x - 2x^2, \quad g : x \to x + 1, \quad \text{in the domain} \quad -2 \leqslant x \leqslant 2, \quad x \in \mathbf{R}.$$
Use your graphs to estimate:

(i) the maximum value of $f(x)$

(ii) the values of x for which $f(x) = g(x)$

(iii) the values of x for which $f(x) \geqslant g(x)$

(iv) the values of x for which $g(x) \geqslant f(x)$ and $x > 0$.

13. Using the same axes and scales, draw the graphs of:
$f : x \rightarrow 9 - 3x - 2x^2$, $g : x \rightarrow -x$, in the domain $-4 \leqslant x \leqslant 2$, $x \in \mathbf{R}$.
Use your graphs to estimate:
   (i) the values of x for which $f(x) = 0$
   (ii) the maximum value of $f(x)$
   (iii) the values of x for which $f(x) \geqslant g(x)$.

14. Using the same axes and scales, draw the graphs of:
$f : x \rightarrow 7 - x - 2x^2$, $g : x \rightarrow 3 - x$, in the domain $-3 \leqslant x \leqslant 2$, $x \in \mathbf{R}$.
Use your graphs to estimate:
   (i) the values of x for which $f(x) = 0$
   (ii) the values of x for which $f(x) \geqslant 4$
   (iii) the values of x for which $f(x) \geqslant g(x)$.

15. Using the same axes and scales, graph the functions:
$f : x \rightarrow 9 - 4x - 2x^2$, $g : x \rightarrow 1 - 2x$, in the domain $-4 \leqslant x \leqslant 2$, $x \in \mathbf{R}$.
Use your graph to :
   (i) estimate the values of x for which $f(x) = 0$
   (ii) find the value of x for which $g(x) = 0$
   (iii) find the values of x for which $f(x) \geqslant 9$
   (iv) estimate the values of x for which $f(x) = g(x)$
   (v) estimate the values of x for which $f(x) \geqslant g(x)$
   (vi) estimate the values of x for which $f(x) > 0$ and decreasing
   (vii) find the values of k for which $f(x) = k$ has no solution.

16. Using the same axes and scales, graph the functions:
$f : x \rightarrow 6x - x^2$, $g : x \rightarrow 12 + 3x - x^2$, in the domain $0 \leqslant x \leqslant 6$, $x \in \mathbf{R}$.
Use your graph to find:
   (i) the maximum value of $f(x)$
   (ii) the value of x for which $f(x) = g(x)$
   (iii) the coordinates of the point of intersection of $f(x)$ and $g(x)$
   (iv) the values of x for which $f(x) \geqslant g(x)$.

Using graphs to solve real-life problems

Using the same axes and the same scales, graph the two functions:

$f : x \rightarrow 10 + x - 2x^2, \qquad -2 \leqslant x \leqslant 3, \quad x \in \mathbf{R}$

$g : x \rightarrow 3x - x^2, \qquad 0 \leqslant x \leqslant 3, \qquad x \in \mathbf{R}$

$f(x)$ is the height in km reached by an incoming missile launched at 05:00 ($x = -2$).
$g(x)$ is the height in km reached by an intercepting missile launched from the ground
at 05:10 ($x = 0$).

Use your graphs to estimate:

(i) the maximum height reached by the incoming missile

(ii) the height at which the two missiles meet

(iii) the time at which the two missiles meet.

Solution:

$f(x)$

x	$-2x^2 + x + 10$	y
-2	$-8 - 2 + 10$	0
-1	$-2 - 1 + 10$	7
0	$-0 + 0 + 10$	10
1	$-2 + 1 + 10$	9
2	$-8 + 2 + 10$	4
3	$-18 + 3 + 10$	-5

$g(x)$

x	$-x^2 + 3x$	y
0	$-0 + 0$	0
1	$-1 + 3$	2
2	$-4 + 6$	2
3	$-9 + 9$	0

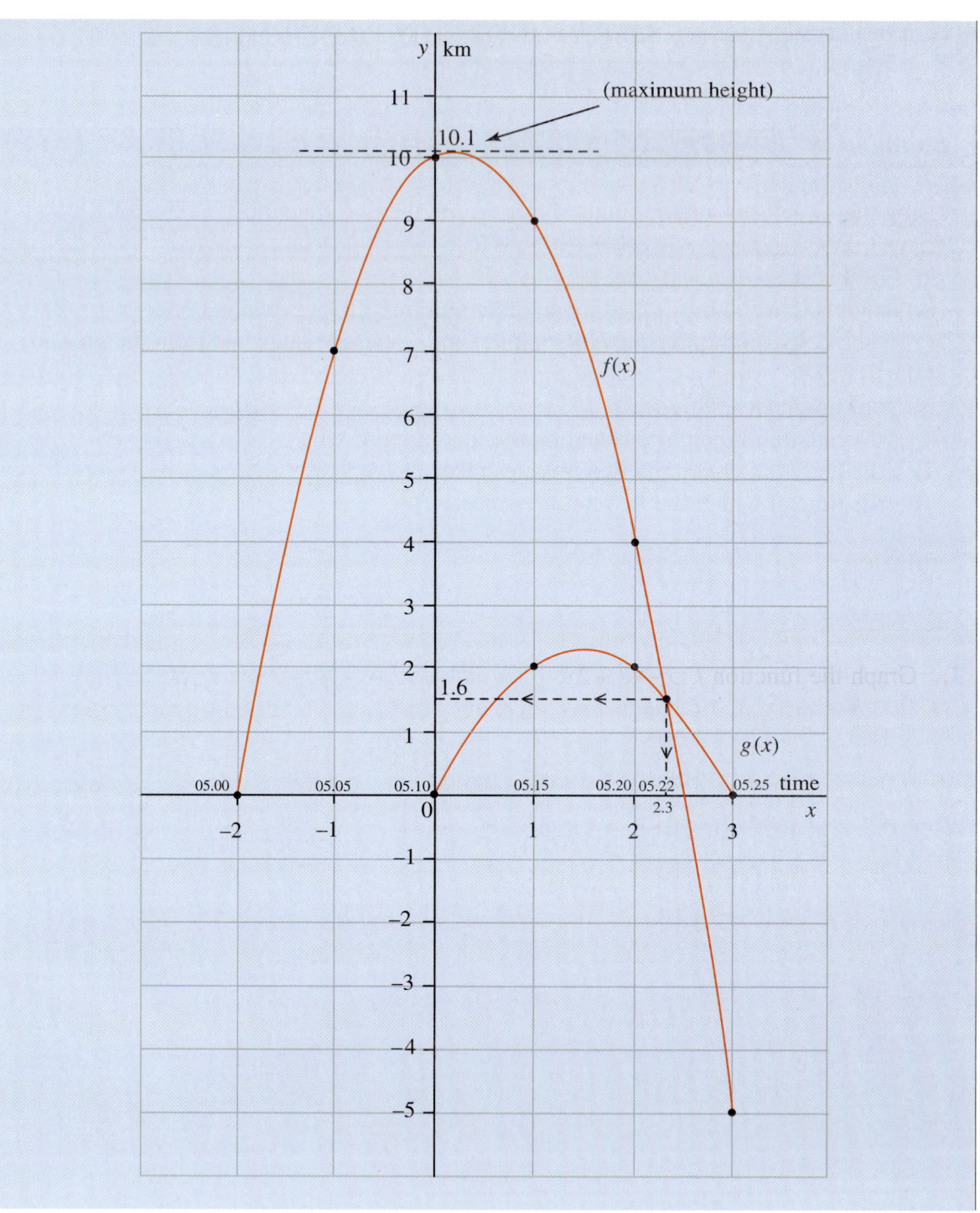

Note: The x axis, time axis, is marked in units of 5 minutes (given in the question)

(i) the maximum height reached by the incoming missile

Through the highest point on the graph of $f(x)$ draw a broken horizontal line to meet the y axis, (height axis). This line meets the y axis at 10.1.

Thus the maximum height reached by the incoming missile is 10.1 km.

(ii) the height at which the two missiles meet

Where the two curves meet draw a broken horizontal line to meet the y axis, (height axis).

This line meets the y axis at 1.6.

Thus the two missiles meet at a height of 1.6 km.

(iii) the time at which the two missiles meet

Where the two curves meet draw a broken vertical line to meet the x axis (time axis).

This line meets the x axis at 2.3 or 05.22 on the time axis.

Thus the two missiles meet at the time 05.22.

Exercise 15.4 ▼

1. Graph the function $f : x \rightarrow 3 + 2x$,   in the domain $0 \leqslant x \leqslant 8$, $x \in \boldsymbol{R}$.

$f(x)$ is the cost, €C, of a taxi journey, the x axis representing the number of kilometres.

Use your graph to find:

(i)   the cost to travel 5 km

(ii)   the cost to travel $6\frac{1}{2}$ km

(iii)   how far is a journey that costs €17

(iv)   the fixed charge on the meter when a journey begins.

2. Draw the graph of the function $f : x \rightarrow x^2 - 6x + 9$ in the domain $0 \leqslant x \leqslant 6$, $x \in \boldsymbol{R}$.

The graph shows the wind speed at hourly intervals.

The x axis shows one-hour intervals:

for example, $x = 0$ means 12:00, $x = 1$ means 13:00, etc.

The y axis shows wind speed in kilometres per hour:

$y = 0$ means 0 km/h, $y = 1$ means 10 km/h, $y = 2$ means 20 km/h, etc.

Use your graph to estimate:

(i)   the times when the wind speed was $22\frac{1}{2}$ km/h

(ii)   the speed of the wind at 17:15

(iii)   the time when there was calm.

3. Graph the function $f : x \rightarrow 7 + 5x - 2x^2$, in the domain $-1 \leqslant x \leqslant 4$, $x \in \mathbf{R}$.

Use your graph, or otherwise, to solve $7 + 5x - 2x^2 = 0$.

$f(x)$ is the height in metres reached by a particle fired from level ground at the point where $x = -1$, the x axis representing the level ground. From the time of firing until it hits the ground again, the particle was in flight for exactly 4.5 seconds.

Use your graph to estimate:

(i) the maximum height reached by the particle

(ii) the height reached by the particle after 1.5 seconds of flight

(iii) the number of seconds the particle is 4 m or more above the ground.

4. A ball is fired upwards from the top of a building.

The height, h metres, reached by the ball after t seconds, is given by $h = 7 + 6t - t^2$.

Graph the function $f : t \rightarrow 7 + 6t - t^2$, in the domain $0 \leqslant t \leqslant 7$, $t \in \mathbf{R}$.

Use your graph to find:

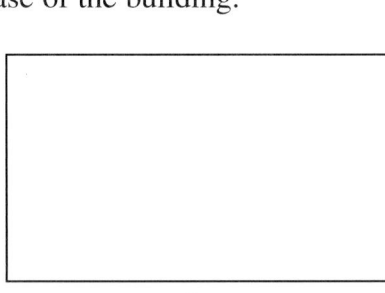

(i) the height of the building

(ii) the maximum height reached by the ball

(iii) the number of seconds taken for the ball to each a height of 15 m above the base of the building for the first time

(iv) the number of seconds the ball is 12 m or higher above the base of the building

(v) how high the ball is after $4\frac{1}{2}$ seconds

(vi) after how many seconds will the ball again reach the height from where it was fired

(vii) after how many seconds will the ball reach the base of the building.

5. The perimeter of a rectangle is 20 m and the length of its base is x m.

Show that the width of the rectangle is $(10 - x)$ m.

Show that the area, A, of the rectangle is given by $A = 10x - x^2$.

Graph the function $f : x \rightarrow 10x - x^2$ in the domain $0 \leqslant x \leqslant 10$, $x \in \mathbf{R}$.

x

Use your graph to find:

(i) the maximum area of the rectangle

(ii) the dimensions of the rectangle that gives this maximum

(iii) the area of the rectangle when the length is 4 m

(iv) the width of the rectangle when its length is 7 m

(v) the length of the rectangle when its area is 12.75 m^2.

6. A farmer has 12 metres of fencing which he uses to make a rectangular plot with a river on one side, as shown.
If the length is x m show that the width is given by $(12 - 2x)$ m.
Explain why the area, A, is given by $A = 12x - 2x^2$.

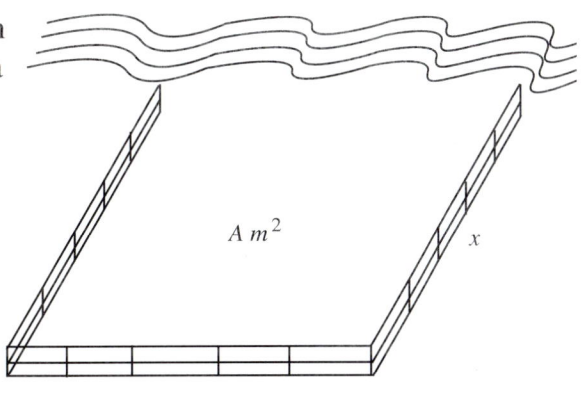

$A\ m^2$

x

Copy and complete the table:

x	0	1	2	3	4	5	6
$A(x)$		10			16		

Graph the function $f : x \to A$ in the domain $0 \leqslant x \leqslant 6$.
Use your graph to find:
- **(i)** the maximum area of the plot
- **(ii)** the dimensions of the plot for this maximum
- **(iii)** the length of the plot when the area is $10\,m^2$
- **(iv)** an estimate for the width when the area is $12\,m^2$, correct to one decimal place
- **(v)** the values of x for which the area is greater than or equal to $16\,m^2$.

7. Using the same axes and scales, draw the functions:
$f : x \to 8x - x^2$, $g : x \to x$, in the domain $0 \leqslant x \leqslant 8$.
$f(x)$ is the flight path of a projectile fired from a point o.
$g(x)$ is the side of a hill, (as shown).
r is the maximum point of the path.
s is directly beneath r and q is directly beneath p.
$x = 1$ represents $5\,m$, $x = 2$ represents $10\,m$, etc.
$y = 1$ represents $10\,m$, $y = 2$ represents $20\,m$, etc.
Use your graphs to find :

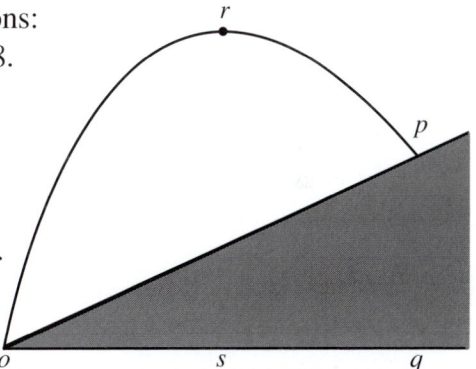

- **(i)** the greatest height reached by the projectile, i.e. $|rs|$
- **(ii)** the height of p above the horizontal, i.e. $|pq|$
- **(iii)** the difference in height between the greatest height and the point p.
Express the distance $|op|$ in the form $a\sqrt{5}$.

SURDS

Irrational numbers and surds

The first five letters in the word **rational** spell **ratio**. A rational number is a number that can be written as a ratio, in other words any number that can be written as a fraction (a whole number over a whole number, e.g. $\frac{3}{5}$). The word **irrational** literally means '**no ratio**'.

There are some numbers, such as $\sqrt{2}, \pi$, which cannot be written as fractions. These numbers are called '**irrational numbers**'.

Irrational numbers such as $\sqrt{2}, \sqrt{3}, \sqrt{5}, \sqrt{7}$ are called '**surds**'.

Note: $\sqrt{a}$ means the positive square root of a. Thus $\sqrt{9} = 3$, not ± 3.

Simplifying surds

Properties of surds

Property	Example
1. $\sqrt{ab} = \sqrt{a}\sqrt{b}$	$\sqrt{20} = \sqrt{4 \times 5} = \sqrt{4}\,\sqrt{5} = 2\sqrt{5}$
2. $\sqrt{\dfrac{a}{b}} = \dfrac{\sqrt{a}}{\sqrt{b}}$	$\sqrt{\dfrac{9}{16}} = \dfrac{\sqrt{9}}{\sqrt{16}} = \dfrac{3}{4}$
3. $\sqrt{a}\sqrt{a} = a$	$\sqrt{3}\sqrt{3} = 3$

When simplifying surds the key idea is to find the largest possible square number bigger than 1 that will divide evenly into the number under the square root symbol.
The square numbers greater than 1 are 4, 9, 16, 25, 36, 49, 64, 81, 100, 121, 144, . . . etc.
You can use your calculator to help you find the largest possible square number that will divide exactly into the number under the square root symbol. Try 4, then try 9, then try 16 and so on until you find the largest possible square number that will divide exactly.

Simplify   **(i)** $\sqrt{18}$ **(ii)** $\sqrt{75}$ **(iii)** $\sqrt{80}$ **(iv)** $\frac{1}{3}\sqrt{108}$ **(v)** $\sqrt{1\frac{7}{9}}$

Solution:

(i) $\sqrt{18} = \sqrt{9 \times 2} = \sqrt{9}\sqrt{2} = 3\sqrt{2}$

(ii) $\sqrt{75} = \sqrt{25 \times 3} = \sqrt{25}\sqrt{3} = 5\sqrt{3}$

(iii) $\sqrt{80} = \sqrt{16 \times 5} = \sqrt{16}\sqrt{5} = 4\sqrt{5}$

(iv) $\frac{1}{3}\sqrt{108} = \frac{1}{3}\sqrt{36 \times 3} = \frac{1}{3}\sqrt{36}\sqrt{3} = \frac{1}{3}.6\sqrt{3} = 2\sqrt{3}$

(v) $\sqrt{1\frac{7}{9}} = \sqrt{\frac{16}{9}} = \frac{\sqrt{16}}{\sqrt{9}} = \frac{4}{3}$

Exercise 16.1 ▼

Simplify each of the following:

1. $\sqrt{8}$ 2. $\sqrt{27}$ 3. $\sqrt{32}$ 4. $\sqrt{125}$ 5. $\sqrt{12}$ 6. $\sqrt{50}$

7. $\sqrt{300}$ 8. $\sqrt{28}$ 9. $\sqrt{45}$ 10. $\sqrt{90}$ 11. $\sqrt{98}$ 12. $\sqrt{24}$

13. $\sqrt{75}$ 14. $\sqrt{54}$ 15. $\sqrt{63}$ 16. $\sqrt{250}$ 17. $\sqrt{150}$ 18. $\sqrt{128}$

19. $3\sqrt{20}$ 20. $2\sqrt{18}$ 21. $5\sqrt{8}$ 22. $\frac{1}{2}\sqrt{40}$ 23. $\frac{2}{5}\sqrt{75}$ 24. $\frac{3}{4}\sqrt{160}$

25. $\sqrt{\frac{4}{9}}$ 26. $\sqrt{\frac{16}{25}}$ 27. $\sqrt{\frac{81}{100}}$ 28. $\sqrt{\frac{36}{49}}$ 29. $\sqrt{\frac{49}{64}}$ 30. $\sqrt{\frac{81}{121}}$

31. $\sqrt{\frac{1}{9}}$ 32. $\sqrt{\frac{1}{64}}$ 33. $\sqrt{2\frac{1}{4}}$ 34. $\sqrt{2\frac{7}{9}}$ 35. $\sqrt{1\frac{9}{16}}$ 36. $\sqrt{4\frac{21}{25}}$

37. Express $\sqrt{72}$ in the form $k\sqrt{2}$.

38. If $\sqrt{48} = k\sqrt{3}$, evaluate $\sqrt{k}$.

Addition and subtraction of surds

Like surds can be added or subtracted.

Express each surd in its simplest form and add or subtract like surds.

Example ▼

Simplify $\sqrt{75} + \sqrt{48} - \sqrt{12}$

Solution

$\sqrt{75} + \sqrt{48} - \sqrt{12}$

$\sqrt{75}$	$\sqrt{48}$	$\sqrt{12}$
$= \sqrt{25 \times 3}$	$= \sqrt{16 \times 3}$	$= \sqrt{4 \times 3}$
$= \sqrt{25}\sqrt{3}$	$= \sqrt{16}\sqrt{3}$	$= \sqrt{4}\sqrt{3}$
$= 5\sqrt{3}$	$= 4\sqrt{3}$	$= 2\sqrt{3}$

$\therefore \sqrt{75} + \sqrt{48} - \sqrt{12}$

$= 5\sqrt{3} + 4\sqrt{3} - 2\sqrt{3}$

$= 9\sqrt{3} - 2\sqrt{3}$

$= 7\sqrt{3}$

Exercise 16.2 ▼

Simplify each of the following:

1. $5\sqrt{2} + 4\sqrt{2}$
2. $4\sqrt{3} + 2\sqrt{3}$
3. $7\sqrt{5} - 4\sqrt{5}$
4. $5\sqrt{3} - \sqrt{3}$
5. $10\sqrt{2} - 7\sqrt{2} + \sqrt{2}$
6. $8\sqrt{5} - 10\sqrt{5}$
7. $\sqrt{18} + \sqrt{8}$
8. $\sqrt{27} + \sqrt{12} + \sqrt{3}$
9. $\sqrt{32} + \sqrt{2}$
10. $\sqrt{20} + \sqrt{45} + \sqrt{80}$
11. $\sqrt{75} + \sqrt{12} - \sqrt{48}$
12. $\sqrt{200} - \sqrt{50} - \sqrt{18}$

13. $\sqrt{20} - \sqrt{5} + \sqrt{45}$

14. $\sqrt{48} - \sqrt{75} + \sqrt{12}$

15. $\sqrt{99} - \sqrt{44} + \sqrt{11}$

16. $2\sqrt{18} - 4\sqrt{2} + \sqrt{2}$

17. $5\sqrt{40} - 3\sqrt{90}$

18. $2\sqrt{63} + 4\sqrt{7} - 5\sqrt{28}$

19. If $5\sqrt{3} + \sqrt{48} - \sqrt{27} = k\sqrt{3}$, find the value of k.

20. If $\sqrt{200} + \sqrt{72} - \sqrt{32} = k\sqrt{2}$, express $\sqrt{k}$ in the form $a\sqrt{3}$.

21. Express $\sqrt{72} + \sqrt{48} + \sqrt{8} - \sqrt{12}$ in the form $a\sqrt{2} + b\sqrt{3}$.

22. Express $\sqrt{20} + \sqrt{45} + \sqrt{18} - \sqrt{50}$ in the form $p\sqrt{p} - q\sqrt{q}$, $p, q \in N$.

Multiplication

> **Example** ▼
>
> Simplify each of the following:
>
> **(i)** $\sqrt{5}\sqrt{5}$ **(ii)** $\sqrt{3}\sqrt{12}$ **(iii)** $3\sqrt{2} \times 4\sqrt{2}$ **(iv)** $4\left(1 + \sqrt{3}\right) - \sqrt{3}\left(2 + \sqrt{3}\right)$
>
> **Solution:**
>
> **(i)** $\sqrt{5}\sqrt{5} = 5$ or $\sqrt{5}\sqrt{5} = \sqrt{5 \times 5} = \sqrt{25} = 5$
>
> **(ii)** $\sqrt{3}\sqrt{12} = \sqrt{3 \times 12} = \sqrt{36} = 6$
>
> **(iii)** $3\sqrt{2} \times 4\sqrt{2} = 3 \times 4 \times \sqrt{2} \times \sqrt{2} = 12 \times 2 = 24$
>
> **(iv)** $4\left(1 + \sqrt{3}\right) - \sqrt{3}\left(2 + \sqrt{3}\right)$
>
> $= 4 + 4\sqrt{3} - 2\sqrt{3} - 3$ (remove brackets)
>
> $= 1 + 2\sqrt{3}$ (simplify like terms)

(i) Express $(\sqrt{2}+3)^2$ in the form $a+b\sqrt{c}$, where $a, b, c \in N$.

(ii) If $k\left(5-\sqrt{2}\right)\left(5+\sqrt{2}\right)=46$, find the value of k.

Solution:

(i) $(\sqrt{2}+3)^2$

$= (\sqrt{2}+3)(\sqrt{2}+3)$

$= \sqrt{2}\sqrt{2}+3\sqrt{2}+3\sqrt{2}+9$

$= 2+3\sqrt{2}+3\sqrt{2}+9$

$= 11+6\sqrt{2}$

(ii) $k(5-\sqrt{2})(5+\sqrt{2})=46$

$k(25+5\sqrt{2}-5\sqrt{2}-2)=46$

$k(23)=46$

$23k=46$

$k=2$

Exercise 16.3 ▼

Simplify each of the following:

1. $\sqrt{3}\sqrt{3}$
2. $\sqrt{5}\sqrt{5}$
3. $\sqrt{2}\sqrt{8}$
4. $\sqrt{2}\sqrt{50}$
5. $\sqrt{3}\sqrt{27}$

6. $2\sqrt{3}\times\sqrt{3}$
7. $5\sqrt{2}\times\sqrt{2}$
8. $2\sqrt{5}\times2\sqrt{5}$
9. $\left(3\sqrt{2}\right)^2$

10. $3\sqrt{5}\times2\sqrt{5}$
11. $4\sqrt{3}\times5\sqrt{3}$
12. $2\sqrt{6}\times\sqrt{6}$
13. $\sqrt{7}\times2\sqrt{7}$

14. $\left(\sqrt{3}\times\sqrt{2}\right)^2$
15. $\sqrt{8}\sqrt{18}$
16. $2\sqrt{2}\times3\sqrt{8}$
17. $3\sqrt{2}\times\sqrt{18}$

18. $3\left(3+\sqrt{2}\right)+2\left(4+\sqrt{2}\right)$
19. $4\left(2-\sqrt{5}\right)-2\left(1-\sqrt{5}\right)$

20. $\sqrt{3}\left(\sqrt{3}+5\right)-2\left(1+2\sqrt{3}\right)$
21. $\sqrt{5}\left(2\sqrt{5}-3\right)-\left(7-2\sqrt{5}\right)$

22. $\left(3+\sqrt{2}\right)\left(3-\sqrt{2}\right)$
23. $\left(5-\sqrt{3}\right)\left(5+\sqrt{3}\right)$
24. $\left(\sqrt{2}+1\right)\left(\sqrt{2}-1\right)$

25. $\left(3-\sqrt{7}\right)\left(3+\sqrt{7}\right)$
26. $\left(\sqrt{6}+\sqrt{2}\right)\left(\sqrt{6}-\sqrt{2}\right)$
27. $\left(3\sqrt{2}+2\sqrt{3}\right)\left(3\sqrt{2}-2\sqrt{3}\right)$

28. $\left(5-\sqrt{3}\right)\left(2+\sqrt{3}\right)$
29. $\left(5+\sqrt{3}\right)^2$
30. $\left(\sqrt{3}-2\right)^2$

31. $\left(3+\sqrt{5}\right)^2+\left(3-\sqrt{5}\right)^2$
32. $\left(\sqrt{3}+\sqrt{2}\right)^2+\left(\sqrt{3}-\sqrt{2}\right)^2$

33. Express $\sqrt{8}$ in the form $k\sqrt{k}$. Hence, or otherwise, simplify $2\left(3-\sqrt{2}\right)-\left(4-\sqrt{8}\right)$.

34. Find the value of $k \in \mathbf{N}$ such that:

   (i) $k\left(5+\sqrt{3}\right)\left(5-\sqrt{3}\right)=66$ **(ii)** $k\left(2\sqrt{2}-3\right)\left(2\sqrt{2}+3\right)+1=0$

35. Find the value of q if $\left(3-\sqrt{5}\right)\left(3+\sqrt{5}\right)=\dfrac{1}{q}$.

36. Find the value of $k \in \mathbf{N}$ such that $k^2=\left(5+\sqrt{7}\right)^2+\left(5-\sqrt{7}\right)^2$.

37. Express $\left(2+\sqrt{\dfrac{3}{2}}\right)\left(2-\sqrt{\dfrac{3}{2}}\right)$ in the form $\dfrac{a}{b}$, $a, b \in \mathbf{N}$.

Further simplification with surds

> ## Example ▼
>
> **(i)** Simplify $\dfrac{\sqrt{32}}{4}$ **(ii)** Express $\dfrac{12}{\sqrt{3}}$ in the form $k\sqrt{3}$.
>
> **Solution:**
>
> **(i)** $\dfrac{\sqrt{32}}{4}=\dfrac{\sqrt{16\times 2}}{4}=\dfrac{\sqrt{16}\sqrt{2}}{4}=\dfrac{4\sqrt{2}}{4}=\sqrt{2}$
>
> Alternatively, $\dfrac{\sqrt{32}}{4}=\dfrac{\sqrt{32}}{\sqrt{16}}=\sqrt{\dfrac{32}{16}}=\sqrt{2}$
>
> **(ii)** $\dfrac{12}{\sqrt{3}}=\dfrac{12}{\sqrt{3}}\times\dfrac{\sqrt{3}}{\sqrt{3}}=\dfrac{12\sqrt{3}}{3}=4\sqrt{3}$
>
> (multiply top and bottom by $\sqrt{3}$)

Note: $\dfrac{\sqrt{3}}{\sqrt{3}}=1$, thus we are effectively multiplying by 1.

Express each of the following in the form $a\sqrt{b}$, where b is a prime number:

1. $\dfrac{8}{\sqrt{2}}$ **2.** $\dfrac{6}{\sqrt{3}}$ **3.** $\dfrac{15}{\sqrt{5}}$ **4.** $\dfrac{4}{\sqrt{2}}$ **5.** $\dfrac{9}{\sqrt{3}}$ **6.** $\dfrac{16}{\sqrt{8}}$

Express each of the following in the form $\dfrac{a\sqrt{b}}{c}$, where b is a prime number:

7. $\dfrac{5}{\sqrt{3}}$ **8.** $\dfrac{3}{\sqrt{2}}$ **9.** $\dfrac{10}{\sqrt{8}}$ **10.** $\dfrac{15}{2\sqrt{5}}$ **11.** $\dfrac{8}{\sqrt{18}}$ **12.** $\dfrac{20}{\sqrt{45}}$

Simplify each of the following:

13. $\dfrac{\sqrt{12}}{\sqrt{3}}$ **14.** $\dfrac{\sqrt{27}}{\sqrt{3}}$ **15.** $\dfrac{\sqrt{80}}{\sqrt{5}}$ **16.** $\dfrac{\sqrt{108}}{6}$ **17.** $\dfrac{\sqrt{128}}{\sqrt{8}}$ **18.** $\dfrac{\sqrt{45}}{3}$

19. $\dfrac{\sqrt{8}}{2}$ **20.** $\dfrac{4\sqrt{3}}{\sqrt{12}}$ **21.** $\dfrac{12\sqrt{2}}{\sqrt{32}}$ **22.** $\dfrac{\sqrt{5}}{\sqrt{20}}$ **23.** $\dfrac{\sqrt{27}}{\sqrt{12}}$ **24.** $\dfrac{\sqrt{50}}{\sqrt{18}}$

Chapter test

1. Express $\sqrt{108}$ in the form $k\sqrt{3}$.

2. If $\sqrt{200} = k\sqrt{2}$, evaluate k.

3. Express $\sqrt{3\dfrac{1}{16}}$ in the form $\dfrac{a}{b}$, $a, b \in \mathbf{N}$.

4. **(a)** Express $\sqrt{48}$ in the form $a\sqrt{b}$ where b is a prime number.

    (b) Simplify $2(4 - 2\sqrt{3}) - (6 - \sqrt{48})$.

5. $\sqrt{50} - \sqrt{200} + \sqrt{98} = k\sqrt{2}$. Find the value of k^2.

6. $\sqrt{3}(4\sqrt{3} + \sqrt{27} - \sqrt{75}) = a$. Find the value of a.

7. Express $(7 + \sqrt{5})^2 - (7 - \sqrt{5})^2$ in the form $k\sqrt{5}$.

8. Express $(5 - \sqrt{3})^2$ in the form $a + b\sqrt{c}$, where $a, b, c \in \mathbf{Z}$.

9. Find the value of $k \in \mathbf{N}$ such that $k\left(7 - \sqrt{3}\right)\left(7 + \sqrt{3}\right) = 92$.

10. $\left(\dfrac{3}{2} + \dfrac{\sqrt{5}}{2}\right)\left(\dfrac{3}{2} - \dfrac{\sqrt{5}}{2}\right) = k$. Find the value of k.

11. Express **(i)** $\dfrac{8}{\sqrt{2}}$ **(ii)** $\dfrac{15}{\sqrt{3}}$ in the form $a\sqrt{b}$, where b is a prime number.

12. $\dfrac{\sqrt{72} + \sqrt{128}}{2\sqrt{2}} = p$. Find the value of p.

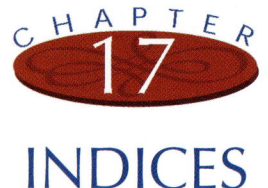

INDICES

Notation for indices

We use a shorthand called '**index notation**' to indicate repeated multiplication.

For example, we write $2 \times 2 \times 2 \times 2 \times 2$ as 2^5.
This is read as '2 to the power of 5'.

2 is the **base**.
5 is the **index** or **power**.

The power or index simply tells you how many times a number is multiplied by itself.

Rules of indices

1. $a^m . a^n = a^{m+n}$ Example: $2^4 . 2^3 = 2^{4+3} = 2^7$
   Multiplying powers of the same number, **add** the indices.

2. $\dfrac{a^m}{a^n} = a^{m-n}$ Example: $\dfrac{3^9}{3^5} = 3^{9-5} = 3^4$

   Dividing powers of the same number, **subtract** the index on the bottom from the index on top.

3. $(a^m)^n = a^{mn}$ Example: $(4^5)^3 = 4^{5 \times 3} = 4^{15}$
   Raising the power of a number to a power, **multiply** the indices.

4. $(ab)^m = a^m b^m$ Example: $(2 \times 3)^5 = 2^5 \times 3^5$
   Raising a product to a power, every factor is raised to the power.

5. $\left(\dfrac{a}{b}\right)^m = \dfrac{a^m}{b^m}$ Example: $\left(\dfrac{2}{5}\right)^3 = \dfrac{2^3}{5^3}$

   Raising a fraction to a power, **both** top and bottom are raised to the power.

6. $a^0 = 1$ Example: $4^0 = 1$
   Any number to the power of zero is 1.

7. $a^{-m} = \dfrac{1}{a^m}$ **Example:** $5^{-2} = \dfrac{1}{5^2}$

A number with a negative index is equal to its reciprocal with a positive index.

Note: If a term is brought from the top to the bottom of a fraction (or vice versa), the sign of its index is changed.

8. $a^{\frac{m}{n}} = \left(a^{\frac{1}{n}}\right)^m$ **Example:** $32^{\frac{3}{5}} = \left(32^{\frac{1}{5}}\right)^3$

Take the root first and then raise to the power (or vice versa).

$8^{\frac{1}{3}}$ means, what number multiplied by itself three times will equal 8.

Thus, $8^{\frac{1}{3}} = 2$ as $2 \times 2 \times 2 = 8$

Similarly, $25^{\frac{1}{2}} = 5$ as $5 \times 5 = 25$ and $81^{\frac{1}{4}} = 3$ as $3 \times 3 \times 3 \times 3 = 81$.

Note: $\sqrt{a} = a^{\frac{1}{2}}$, for example, $\sqrt{16} = 16^{\frac{1}{2}} = 4$.

Also, $\sqrt{a}\sqrt{a} = a^{\frac{1}{2}} \cdot a^{\frac{1}{2}} = a^{\frac{1}{2}+\frac{1}{2}} = a^1 = a$

Alternative notation: $a^{\frac{1}{n}} = \sqrt[n]{a}$, example $8^{\frac{1}{3}} = \sqrt[3]{8}$

$$a^{\frac{m}{n}} = \sqrt[n]{a^m}, \quad \text{example } 32^{\frac{2}{5}} = \sqrt[5]{32^2}$$

When dealing with fractional indices, the calculations are simpler if the root is taken first and the result is raised to the power.

For example, $16^{\frac{3}{4}} = \left(16^{\frac{1}{4}}\right)^3 = (2)^3 = 8$

(root first)   (power next)

Using a calculator

A calculator can be used to evaluate an expression such as $32^{\frac{3}{5}}$.

▦ 32 $\boxed{y^x}$ 3 $\boxed{a\frac{b}{c}}$ 5 $\boxed{=}$

The calculator will give an answer 8.

However, there are problems when dealing with negative indices or raising a fraction to a power, as the calculator can give the answer as a decimal.

241

For example,

$$8^{-\frac{2}{3}} = \frac{1}{8^{\frac{2}{3}}} = \frac{1}{\left(8^{\frac{1}{3}}\right)^2} = \frac{1}{(2)^2} = \frac{1}{4}$$

Using a calculator,

 8 $\boxed{y^x}$ $\boxed{+/-}$ 2 $\boxed{a\frac{b}{c}}$ 3 $\boxed{=}$ gives an answer 0.25

Note: $\frac{1}{4} = 0.25$

Also, $\left(\dfrac{8}{27}\right)^{\frac{2}{3}} = \dfrac{8^{\frac{2}{3}}}{27^{\frac{2}{3}}} = \dfrac{\left(8^{\frac{1}{3}}\right)^2}{\left(27^{\frac{1}{3}}\right)^2} = \dfrac{(2)^2}{(3)^2} = \dfrac{4}{9}$

Using a calculator,

 $\boxed{(}$ 8 $\boxed{a\frac{b}{c}}$ 27 $\boxed{)}$ $\boxed{y^x}$ 2 $\boxed{a\frac{b}{c}}$ 3 $\boxed{=}$ gives an answer 0.444444444....

Note: $\frac{4}{9} = 0.444444444.....$

So avoid using a calculator with negative indices or raising a fraction to a power.

Example ▼

Simplify each of the following:

(i) $32^{\frac{3}{5}}$ **(ii)** $27^{\frac{4}{3}}$ **(iii)** $64^{-\frac{2}{3}}$ **(iv)** $16^{\frac{3}{4}} \cdot 27^{-\frac{2}{3}}$ **(v)** $\left(2\frac{1}{4}\right)^{1\frac{1}{2}}$ **(vi)** $\left(\dfrac{25}{16}\right)^{-\frac{3}{2}}$

Solution:

(i) $32^{\frac{3}{5}} = \left(32^{\frac{1}{5}}\right)^3 = (2)^3 = 8$

(ii) $27^{\frac{4}{3}} = \left(27^{\frac{1}{3}}\right)^4 = (3)^4 = 81$

(iii) $64^{-\frac{2}{3}} = \dfrac{1}{64^{\frac{2}{3}}} = \dfrac{1}{\left(64^{\frac{1}{3}}\right)^2} = \dfrac{1}{(4)^2} = \dfrac{1}{16}$

(iv) $16^{\frac{3}{4}} \cdot 27^{-\frac{2}{3}} = \dfrac{16^{\frac{3}{4}}}{27^{\frac{2}{3}}} = \dfrac{\left(16^{\frac{1}{4}}\right)^3}{\left(27^{\frac{1}{3}}\right)^2} = \dfrac{(2)^3}{(3)^2} = \dfrac{8}{9}$

(v) $\left(2\frac{1}{4}\right)^{1\frac{1}{2}} = \left(\frac{9}{4}\right)^{\frac{3}{2}} = \frac{9^{\frac{3}{2}}}{4^{\frac{3}{2}}} = \frac{\left(9^{\frac{1}{2}}\right)^3}{\left(4^{\frac{1}{2}}\right)^3} = \frac{(3)^3}{(2)^3} = \frac{27}{8}$

(vi) $\left(\frac{25}{16}\right)^{-\frac{3}{2}} = \frac{25^{-\frac{3}{2}}}{16^{-\frac{3}{2}}} = \frac{16^{\frac{3}{2}}}{25^{\frac{3}{2}}} = \frac{\left(16^{\frac{1}{2}}\right)^3}{\left(25^{\frac{1}{2}}\right)^3} = \frac{(4)^3}{(5)^2} = \frac{64}{125}$

Example ▼

(i) Express   **(a)** 243   **(b)** $\sqrt{27}$ in the form 3^n.

(ii) Express $\dfrac{\sqrt{3} \times \sqrt{27}}{3 \times 243}$ in the form 3^n.

Solution:

(i) **(a)** $243 = 3 \times 3 \times 3 \times 3 \times 3 = 3^5$

    (b) $\sqrt{27} = \left(27\right)^{\frac{1}{2}} = \left(3^3\right)^{\frac{1}{2}} = 3^{3 \times \frac{1}{2}} = 3^{\frac{3}{2}}$

(ii) $\dfrac{\sqrt{3} \times \sqrt{27}}{3 \times 243} = \dfrac{3^{\frac{1}{2}} \times 3^{\frac{3}{2}}}{3^1 \times 3^5} = \dfrac{3^{\frac{1}{2} + \frac{3}{2}}}{3^{1+5}} = \dfrac{3^2}{3^6} = 3^{2-6} = 3^{-4}$

Exercise 17.1 ▼

In each of the following write down the value of n:

1. $2^3 \times 2^4 = 2^n$ **2.** $5^4 \times 5^6 = 5^n$ **3.** $7 \times 7^3 = 7^n$

4. $\dfrac{3^7}{3^5} = 3^n$ **5.** $\dfrac{4^{10}}{4^7} = 4^n$ **6.** $\dfrac{6^4}{6^6} = 6^n$

7. $5 \times 5^2 \times 5^3 = 5^n$ **8.** $\left(3^2\right)^5 = 3^n$ **9.** $\left(7^3\right)^6 = 7^n$

10. $3^n = \dfrac{1}{3^2}$ **11.** $4^n = \dfrac{1}{4^3}$ **12.** $5^{-2} = \dfrac{1}{5^n}$

13. $\sqrt{3} = 3^n$ **14.** $\left(\sqrt{5}\right)^4 = 5^n$ **15.** $\left(\sqrt{7}\right)^3 = 7^n$

Evaluate each of the following:

16. $9^{\frac{1}{2}}$ **17.** $25^{\frac{1}{2}}$ **18.** $100^{\frac{1}{2}}$ **19.** $8^{\frac{1}{3}}$ **20.** $27^{\frac{1}{3}}$

21. $64^{\frac{1}{3}}$ **22.** $125^{\frac{1}{3}}$ **23.** $32^{\frac{1}{5}}$ **24.** $81^{\frac{1}{4}}$ **25.** $1000^{\frac{1}{3}}$

26. $16^{\frac{3}{4}}$ **27.** $8^{\frac{2}{3}}$ **28.** $25^{\frac{3}{2}}$ **29.** $32^{\frac{3}{5}}$ **30.** $125^{\frac{2}{3}}$

31. $8^{\frac{4}{3}}$ **32.** $64^{\frac{2}{3}}$ **33.** $4^{\frac{3}{2}}$ **34.** $9^{\frac{5}{2}}$ **35.** $16^{\frac{5}{4}}$

Express each of the following in the form $\dfrac{a}{b}$, $a, b \in N$:

36. $4^{-\frac{1}{2}}$ **37.** $9^{-\frac{1}{2}}$ **38.** $27^{-\frac{2}{3}}$ **39.** $32^{-\frac{4}{5}}$ **40.** $64^{-\frac{2}{3}}$

41. $\left(\dfrac{8}{27}\right)^{\frac{1}{3}}$ **42.** $\left(\dfrac{8}{125}\right)^{\frac{2}{3}}$ **43.** $\left(\dfrac{27}{64}\right)^{-\frac{2}{3}}$ **44.** $\left(\dfrac{16}{81}\right)^{-\frac{1}{4}}$ **45.** $\left(\dfrac{16}{9}\right)^{-\frac{3}{2}}$

46. $\left(27^{-\frac{1}{3}}\right)^{2}$ **47.** $\dfrac{16^{-\frac{3}{4}}}{81^{-\frac{1}{2}}}$ **48.** $\dfrac{27^{-\frac{1}{3}}}{8^{-\frac{2}{3}}}$ **49.** $\left(\dfrac{1}{25}\right)^{\frac{3}{2}}$ **50.** $\dfrac{4^{-\frac{1}{2}}}{64^{\frac{2}{3}}}$

51. If $2^{-3} + 3^{-2} = \dfrac{p}{q}$, $p, q \in N_{0}$, find the value of p and the value of q.

52. If $9^{-\frac{1}{2}} + 8^{-\frac{2}{3}} = \dfrac{a}{b}$, $a, b \in N_{0}$, find the value of a and the value of b.

53. Express $\dfrac{2^{5} \times 2^{6}}{2^{3} \times 2^{4}}$ in the form 2^{n}.

54. **(a)** Express   **(i)** 9   **(ii)** 27   **(iii)** 81   **(iv)** 243 in the form 3^{n}.

   (b) Express $\dfrac{9 \times 27 \times 243}{81}$ in the form 3^{n}.

55. Express $\dfrac{4}{\sqrt{2}}$ in the form 2^{n}.

56. Express $\dfrac{125}{\sqrt{5}}$ in the form 5^{n}.

57. Express $\dfrac{\sqrt{2}}{8}$ in the form 2^{n}.

58. **(a)** Express   **(i)** $25^{\frac{1}{2}}$ **(ii)** $125^{\frac{2}{3}}$ in the form 5^{n}.

   (b) Hence, or otherwise, express $\dfrac{5^{2} \times 25^{\frac{1}{2}}}{125 \times 5^{3}}$ in the form 5^{n}.

59. Express $\dfrac{\sqrt{3} \times 81^{\frac{3}{4}}}{9}$ in the form 3^n.

60. Express $\dfrac{8^{\frac{2}{3}} \times 32^{\frac{4}{5}}}{2 \times 16^{\frac{1}{2}}}$ in the form 2^n.

Exponential equations

Exponent is another name for power or index.
An equation involving the variable in the power is called an '**exponential equation**'.
For example, $3^{2x+3} = 9$ is an exponential equation.

Exponential equations are solved with the following steps:

> **1.** Write all the numbers as powers of the same number (usually a prime number).
> **2.** Write both sides as one power of the same number, using the laws of indices.
> **3.** Equate these powers and solve this equation.

Example ▼

Find the value of x for which:

(i) $9^{x+1} = \dfrac{1}{27}$ **(ii)** $\dfrac{2^{3x+1}}{2^{x+2}} = 32$

Solution:

(i) $9^{x+1} = \dfrac{1}{27}$ (9 and 27 can be written as powers of 3)

$\left(3^2\right)^{x+1} = \dfrac{1}{3^3}$ $\left(9 = 3^2,\ 27 = 3^3\right)$

$3^{2x+2} = 3^{-3}$ $\left(\left(a^m\right)^n = a^{m \times n} \quad \text{and} \quad \dfrac{1}{a^m} = a^{-m}\right)$

$2x + 2 = -3$ (equate the powers)

$2x = -5$

$x = -\dfrac{5}{2}$

(ii)

$$\frac{2^{3x+1}}{2^{x+2}} = 32 \qquad \text{(32 can be written as a power of 2)}$$

$$\frac{2^{3x+1}}{2^{x+2}} = 2^5 \qquad \left(32 = 2^5\right)$$

$$2^{(3x+1)-(x+2)} = 2^5 \qquad \left(\frac{a^m}{a^n} = a^{m-n}\right)$$

$$2^{3x+1-x-2} = 2^5 \qquad \text{(remove brackets on the left-hand side)}$$

$$2^{2x-1} = 2^5 \qquad \text{(simplify powers on the left-hand side)}$$

$$2x - 1 = 5 \qquad \text{(equate the powers)}$$

$$2x = 6$$

$$x = 3$$

Exercise 17.2 ▼

Express each of the following in the form a^n, where a is a prime number:

1. 8   **2.** 9   **3.** 32   **4.** 27   **5.** 125   **6.** 81

7. 49   **8.** 64   **9.** 625   **10.** 243   **11.** 128   **12.** 343

13. $\dfrac{1}{16}$ **14.** $\dfrac{1}{32}$ **15.** $\dfrac{1}{243}$ **16.** $\dfrac{27}{\sqrt{3}}$ **17.** $\dfrac{\sqrt{5}}{25}$ **18.** $32^{\frac{3}{5}}$

Solve each of the following equations for x:

19. $5^{2x} = 5^{10}$ **20.** $7^{2x+1} = 7^7$ **21.** $3^{3x-1} = 3^5$

22. $2^x = 8$ **23.** $2^{x-1} = 16$ **24.** $3^{2x-1} = 27$

25. $9^{x+1} = 81$ **26.** $4^{x-1} = 32$ **27.** $16^{x+1} = 32$

28. $2^{2x-2} = \dfrac{1}{16}$ **29.** $3^{x-1} = \dfrac{1}{81}$ **30.** $25^{x-2} = \dfrac{1}{125}$

31. $\dfrac{2^{2n+3}}{2^{n+1}} = 32$ **32.** $\dfrac{3^{3n-1}}{3^{n+1}} = 9$ **33.** $\dfrac{5^{4x-1}}{25} = 5$

34. Express $32^{\frac{4}{5}}$ in the form 4^n. Hence, or otherwise, solve $4^{2x-1} = 32^{\frac{4}{5}}$.

35. Find the two values of x for which $\dfrac{2^{x^2}}{2^x} = 4$.

36. Express **(i)** 81   **(ii)** $\sqrt{3}$ **(iii)** $\dfrac{81}{\sqrt{3}}$ in the form 3^n.

Hence, or otherwise, find the value of x for which $3^{x+1} = \dfrac{81}{\sqrt{3}}$.

37. Solve for x, $2^{2x+1} = \dfrac{4}{\sqrt{2}}$.

Exercise 17.3 ▼

Chapter test

Simplify each of the following:

1. $8^{\frac{1}{3}}$ **2.** $27^{\frac{2}{3}}$ **3.** $18°$ **4.** $32^{\frac{2}{5}}$ **5.** $49^{\frac{3}{2}}$ **6.** $64^{\frac{4}{3}}$

Express each of the following in the form $\dfrac{a}{b}$, $a, b \in N_0$:

7. 3^{-2} **8.** $\left(\dfrac{9}{16}\right)^{-\frac{3}{2}}$ **9.** $\left(64^{-\frac{1}{3}}\right)^2$ **10.** $\left(\dfrac{8}{27}\right)^{-\frac{2}{3}}$ **11.** $\dfrac{27^{-\frac{1}{3}}}{16^{-\frac{3}{4}}}$ **12.** $\dfrac{25^{-\frac{1}{2}}}{8^{\frac{2}{3}}}$

13. If $\dfrac{1}{64^{\frac{1}{3}}} + \dfrac{1}{25^{\frac{1}{2}}} = \dfrac{p}{q}$, $p, q \in N_0$, find the value of p and the value of q.

14. Express $\left(32^{-\frac{1}{5}}\right)^3$ in the form $\dfrac{1}{q}$, $q \in N_0$.

15. If $4^{-\frac{1}{2}} + 64^{-\frac{2}{3}} = \dfrac{a}{b}$, $a, b \in N_0$, find the value of a and the value of b.

16. If $p = 16$ and $q = 9$, find the value of $\left(p^{\frac{1}{2}} + q^{\frac{1}{2}}\right)(p+q)^{\frac{1}{2}}$.

17. Express $\dfrac{\sqrt{5} \times \sqrt{125}}{5 \times 25}$ in the form $5^n, n \in Z$.

18. Express $\dfrac{9^{\frac{3}{2}} \times 81^{\frac{3}{4}}}{9^{\frac{1}{2}} \times 27^{\frac{2}{3}}}$ in the form $3^n, n \in N$.

19. Express $8^{-\frac{2}{3}} \times 4^{\frac{1}{2}} \times 16$ in the form $2^n, n \in N$.

20. **(a)** Express   **(i)** 4   and   **(ii)** 32 in the form 2^n.

     (b) If $4^{x+1} = 32$, find the value of x.

21. Find the value of n for which $3^{2n+1} = 243$.

22. Express **(i)** $\sqrt{2}$ **(ii)** 8 **(iii)** $8\sqrt{2}$ in the form 2^n, $n \in Q$.

Solve for x the equation $2^{3x-1} = 8\sqrt{2}$.

23. Find the value of n if $\dfrac{3^{2n+1}}{3^{n+1}} = 9$.

24. If $8^x = 4^3 - 2^5$, find the value of x.

25. Express 1 in the form 3^n, $n \in Z$.

Find the two values of x for which $\dfrac{3^{2x^2}}{3^{x+1}} = 1$.

26. $f(x) = 4^x$.

Find **(i)** $f(2)$ **(ii)** $f\left(\frac{1}{2}\right)$ **(iii)** $f(0)$ **(iv)** $f\left(\frac{3}{2}\right)$ **(v)** $f\left(\frac{5}{2}\right)$

27. $f(x) = 81^x$.

Find **(i)** $f\left(\frac{1}{2}\right)$ **(ii)** $f\left(-\frac{1}{2}\right)$ **(iii)** $f\left(\frac{1}{4}\right)$ **(iv)** $f\left(\frac{3}{4}\right)$ **(v)** $f\left(-\frac{5}{4}\right)$

INDEX NOTATION

Index notation

Index notation is a shorthand way of writing very large or very small numbers.
For example, try this multiplication on your calculator: $8,000,000 \times 7,000,000$.
The answer is $56,000,000,000,000$.
It has fourteen digits, which is too many to show on most calculator displays.

Your calculator will display your answer as $\boxed{5.6^{13}}$ or $\boxed{5.6\ 13}$ or $\boxed{5.6E13}$.

This tells you that the 5.6 is multiplied by 10^{13}.
This is written:

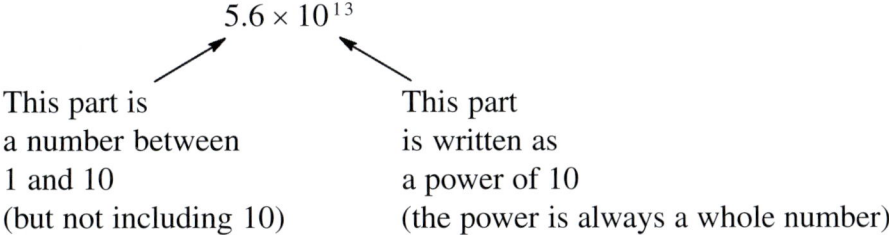

$$5.6 \times 10^{13}$$

This part is
a number between
1 and 10
(but not including 10)

This part
is written as
a power of 10
(the power is always a whole number)

This way of writing a number is called **index notation** or **exponential notation**, or
sometimes **standard form**. (It was formerly called '**scientific notation**'.)
Index notation gives a number in two parts:

| Number between 1 and 10 (but not 10) | × | power of 10 |

This is often written as $a \times 10^n$, where $1 \leqslant a < 10$ and $n \in \mathbf{Z}$.

Example ▼

Express the numbers   **(i)** 8,400,000   **(ii)** 0.000258
in the form $a \times 10^n$, where $1 \leqslant a < 10$, $n \in \mathbf{Z}$.

Solution:

(i)   8,400 000.   (put in the decimal point)
       8.400 000   (move the decimal point six places to the left to give a number
                  between 1 and 10)
     $\therefore 8,400\ 000 = 8.4 \times 10^6$

(ii)   0.000258   (decimal point already there)

     2.58   (move the decimal point four places to the right to give a number between 1 and 10)

     $\therefore 0.000258 = 2.58 \times 10^{-4}$

Example ▼

(i) Express $\dfrac{1,512}{0.36}$ in the form $a \times 10^n$, where $1 \leqslant a < 10$, $n \in \mathbf{Z}$.

(ii) Find x if $\dfrac{624}{0.008} = 7.8 \times 10^x$.

Solution:

(i) $\dfrac{1,512}{0.36} = 4,200 = 4.2 \times 10^3$

(ii) $\dfrac{624}{0.008} = 78,000 = 7.8 \times 10^4$

By comparing 7.8×10^x to 7.8×10^4, $\quad x = 4$.

Exercise 18.1 ▼

Express each of the following in the form $a \times 10^n$, where $1 \leqslant a < 10$ and $n \in \mathbf{Z}$:

1. 7,000	**2.** 83,000	**3.** 428,000	**4.** 520
5. 6,800	**6.** 3,800,000	**7.** 486	**8.** 27
9. 0.004	**10.** 0.0006	**11.** 0.087	**12.** 0.000283

13. $\dfrac{896}{0.32}$ **14.** $\dfrac{51,300}{0.09}$ **15.** $\dfrac{0.00525}{0.15}$ **16.** $\dfrac{0.01752}{2.4}$

In each of the following calculate the value of n:

17. $\dfrac{4,482}{5.4} = 8.3 \times 10^n$ **18.** $\dfrac{36,540}{0.87} = 4.2 \times 10^n$ **19.** $\dfrac{0.01764}{4.9} = 3.6 \times 10^n$.

20. $55,000 \times 0.6 = a \times 10^n$, where $1 \leqslant a < 10$ and $n \in \mathbf{Z}$. Write down the value of a and n.

21. $1,200 \times 1.5^2 = a \times 10^n$, where $1 \leqslant a < 10$ and $n \in \mathbf{Z}$. Write down the value of a and n.

Addition and subtraction

Numbers given in index notation can be keyed into your calculator by using the 'exponent key'. It is marked $\boxed{\text{EXP}}$ or $\boxed{\text{EE}}$ or $\boxed{\text{E}}$.

To key in a number in index notation do the following:

> **1.** Key in 'a', the 'number part', first.
> **2.** Press the exponent key next.
> **3.** Key in the index of the power of 10.

To enter 3.4×10^6, for example, you key in 3.4 $\boxed{\text{EXP}}$ 6.

Note: If you press $\boxed{=}$ at the end, the calculator will write the number as a natural number, provided the index of the power of 10 is not too large.

To add or subtract two numbers in index notation, do the following:

> **1.** Write each number as a natural number.
> **2.** Add or subtract these numbers.
> **3.** Write your answer in index notation.
> Alternatively, you can use your calculator by keying in the numbers in index notation and adding or subtracting as required.

Example ▼

Express **(i)** $4.37 \times 10^4 - 5.4 \times 10^3$ **(ii)** $3.91 \times 10^{-2} + 1.9 \times 10^{-3}$
in the form $a \times 10^n$, where $1 \leqslant a < 10$ and $n \in \mathbf{Z}$.

Solution:

(i) $4.37 \times 10^4 - 5.4 \times 10^3$

$4.37 \times 10^4 = 43{,}700$
$5.4 \times 10^3 = \underline{5{,}400}$
$ 38{,}300 \quad \text{(subtract)}$
$ = 3.83 \times 10^4$

4.37 $\boxed{\text{EXP}}$ 4 $\boxed{-}$ 5.4 $\boxed{\text{EXP}}$ 3 $\boxed{=}$

$= 38300 \quad \text{(on the display)}$
$= 3.83 \times 10^4$

(ii) $3.91 \times 10^{-2} + 1.9 \times 10^{-3}$

$3.91 \times 10^{-2} = 0.0391$
$1.9 \times 10^{-3} = \underline{0.0019}$
$\phantom{1.9 \times 10^{-3} = } 0.0410 \quad \text{(add)}$
$\phantom{1.9 \times 10^{-3} } = 4.1 \times 10^{-2}$

3.91 $\boxed{\text{EXP}}$ $\boxed{+/-}$ 2 $\boxed{+}$ 1.9 $\boxed{\text{EXP}}$ $\boxed{+/-}$ 3 $\boxed{=}$

$= 0.041 \quad \text{(on the display)}$
$= 4.1 \times 10^{-2}$

Multiplication and division

To multiply or divide two numbers in index notation, do the following:

1. Multiply or divide the 'a' parts (the number parts).
2. Multiply or divide the powers of 10 (add or subtract the indices).
3. Write your answer in index notation.

Alternatively, you can use your calculator by keying in the numbers in index notation and multiplying or dividing as required.

Example ▼

Express **(i)** $(4.5 \times 10^2) \times (3.2 \times 10^3)$ **(ii)** $(8.64 \times 10^4) \div (2.4 \times 10^7)$
in the form $a \times 10^n$, where $1 \leqslant a < 10$ and $n \in \mathbf{Z}$.

Solution:

(i) $(4.5 \times 10^2) \times (3.2 \times 10^3)$
$= 4.5 \times 10^2 \times 3.2 \times 10^3$
$= 4.5 \times 3.2 \times 10^2 \times 10^3$
$= 14.4 \times 10^{2+3}$ (add the indices)
$= 14.4 \times 10^5$
$= 1.44 \times 10 \times 10^5$
$= 1.44 \times 10^6$

(ii) $(8.64 \times 10^4) \div (2.4 \times 10^7)$
$= \dfrac{8.64 \times 10^4}{2.4 \times 10^7}$
$= \dfrac{8.64}{2.4} \times \dfrac{10^4}{10^7}$
$= 3.6 \times 10^{4-7}$ (subtract the indices)
$= 3.6 \times 10^{-3}$

4.5 $\boxed{\text{EXP}}$ 2 $\times$ 3.2 $\boxed{\text{EXP}}$ 3 $\boxed{=}$
$= 1440000$ (on the display)
$= 1.44 \times 10^6$

8.64 $\boxed{\text{EXP}}$ 4 $\div$ 2.4 $\boxed{\text{EXP}}$ 7 $\boxed{=}$
$= 0.0036$ (on the display)
$= 3.6 \times 10^{-3}$

Exercise 18.2 ▼

Express each of the following in the form $a \times 10^n$ where $1 \leqslant a < 10$ and $n \in \mathbf{Z}$:

1. $2.4 \times 10^3 + 8 \times 10^2$
2. $3.52 \times 10^6 + 2.8 \times 10^5$
3. $5.48 \times 10^4 - 2.8 \times 10^3$
4. $2.348 \times 10^6 - 4.8 \times 10^4$
5. $8.45 \times 10^{-3} - 6.5 \times 10^{-4}$
6. $3.48 \times 10^{-4} - 5.4 \times 10^{-5}$
7. $(2.2 \times 10^3) \times (3.4 \times 10^2)$
8. $(5.3 \times 10^3) \times (1.8 \times 10^4)$
9. $(8.4 \times 10^7) \div (3.5 \times 10^3)$
10. $(7.56 \times 10^6) \div (2.1 \times 10^2)$
11. $(3 \times 10^3) \div (2 \times 10^{-2})$
12. $(3.91 \times 10^5) \div (1.7 \times 10^8)$
13. $(5.4 \times 10^2) \times (6.5 \times 10^3)$
14. $(1.35 \times 10^7) \div (2.5 \times 10^3)$
15. $(1.5 \times 10^3)^2$
16. $(2.4 \times 10^2)^2 + 1.4 \times 10^3$

17. $\dfrac{(2.4\times10^{4})\times(1.5\times10^{2})}{1.2\times10^{3}}$

18. $\dfrac{3.2\times10^{5}+8.5\times10^{4}}{8.1\times10^{2}}$

19. $\dfrac{2.45\times10^{6}-1.8\times10^{4}}{0.16\times10^{5}}$

20. $\dfrac{1.4\times10^{3}+5.6\times10^{2}}{7\times10^{-1}}$

21. $\dfrac{3.5\times10^{3}-8.4\times10^{2}}{0.07}$

22. $\dfrac{(4\times10^{3})^{3}}{8\times10^{-3}}$

23. $(0.02)^{4}\times10^{5}$

24. $\sqrt{144\times10^{4}}$

25. $(2.89\times10^{-4})^{\frac{1}{2}}$

26. $\dfrac{3.4\times10^{3}}{\sqrt{0.0025}}$

27. $\dfrac{\sqrt{2.89\times10^{4}}}{2\times10^{-2}}$

28. $\sqrt{\dfrac{(3.63\times10^{12})\times(1.2\times10^{-4})}{3.6\times10^{4}}}$

29. The weight of an oxygen atom is 2.7×10^{-23} g and the weight of an electron is 9×10^{-28} g.

If $k=\dfrac{\text{weight of an oxygen atom}}{\text{weight of an electron}}$, calculate the value of k,

expressing your answer in the form $a\times10^{n}$, where $1\leqslant a<10$ and $n\in\mathbf{Z}$.

30. The surface area of the Earth is approximately 5.2×10^{14} m^{2}. Approximately 30% of the surface area of the Earth is land. What area of the Earth is covered by water, approximately?

Give your answer in the form $a\times10^{n}$, where $1\leqslant a<10$ and $n\in\mathbf{Z}$.

TRIGONOMETRY

Trigonometric ratios and right-angled triangles

In a right-angled triangle, special ratios exist between the angles and the lengths of the sides. We look at three of these ratios.

Consider the right-angled triangle below with the acute angle θ:

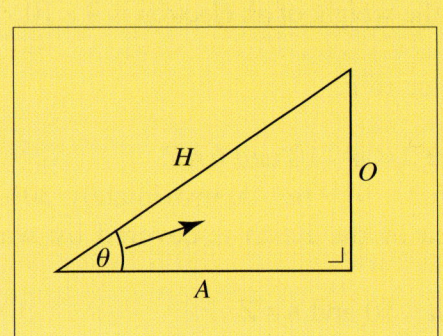

Ratios

$$\sin \theta = \frac{\text{opposite}}{\text{hypotenuse}} = \frac{O}{H}$$

$$\cos \theta = \frac{\text{adjacent}}{\text{hypotenuse}} = \frac{A}{H}$$

$$\tan \theta = \frac{\text{opposite}}{\text{adjacent}} = \frac{O}{A}$$

Memory Aid: <u>Oh</u>, <u>h</u>ell, another <u>h</u>our <u>of</u> <u>a</u>lgebra, sin, cos, and tan.
Each trigonometric ratio links two sides and an angle in a right-angled triangle.

Notes:

1. The side opposite the right angle is called the **hypotenuse**, **H**. The side opposite the angle θ is called the **opposite**, **O**. The other side near the angle θ is called the **adjacent**, **A**.
2. If the lengths of any two sides are known, the third side can be found using Pythagoras's theorem: $A^2 + O^2 = H^2$, where A, O and H are the lengths of the sides.
3. The three angles of a triangle add up to $180°$.
4. Sin, cos and tan are short for sine, cosine, and tangent, respectively.
5. The arrow points to the side opposite the angle under consideration.
6. θ is a Greek letter, pronounced theta, often used to indicate an angle.

We can write trigonometric ratios for the two acute angles in a right-angled triangle. Make sure you know which angle you are using and which sides are the opposite and adjacent (the hypotenuse is always opposite the right angle). A good idea is to draw an arrow from the angle under consideration to indicate the opposite side to the angle.

Example ▼

Consider the right-angled triangle with sides of 1, 2 and $\sqrt{5}$ and angles P and Q, as shown:

Write down the ratios:

(i) $\sin P$ **(ii)** $\cos P$ **(iii)** $\tan P$

(iv) $\sin Q$ **(v)** $\cos Q$ **(vi)** $\tan Q$

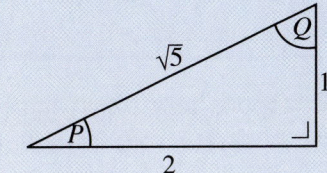

Solution:

Angle P

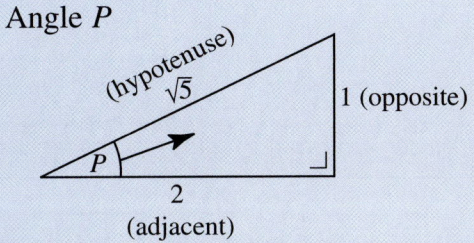

Angle Q

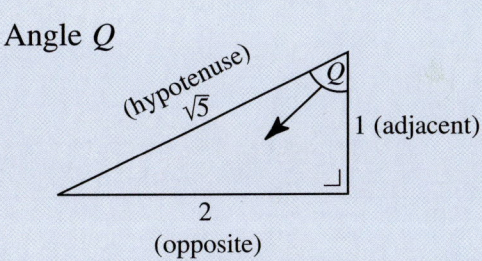

(i) $\sin P = \dfrac{O}{H} = \dfrac{1}{\sqrt{5}}$

(ii) $\cos P = \dfrac{A}{H} = \dfrac{2}{\sqrt{5}}$

(iii) $\tan P = \dfrac{O}{A} = \dfrac{1}{2}$

(vi) $\sin Q = \dfrac{O}{H} = \dfrac{2}{\sqrt{5}}$

(v) $\cos Q = \dfrac{A}{H} = \dfrac{1}{\sqrt{5}}$

(vi) $\tan Q = \dfrac{O}{A} = \dfrac{2}{1} = 2$

Example ▼

θ is an acute angle such that $\tan \theta = \dfrac{20}{21}$.

(i) Find, as fractions, the value of $\cos \theta$ and the value of $\sin \theta$.

(ii) Show that $\cos^2 \theta + \sin^2 \theta = 1$.

Solution:

(i) From the trigonometric ratio given, sketch a right-angled triangle to represent the situation and use Pythagoras's theorem to find the missing side.

Given: $\tan \theta = \dfrac{20}{21}$

Opposite $= 20$, Adjacent $= 21$, let the Hypotenuse $= x$.

$x^2 = 21^2 + 20^2$ (Pythagoras's theorem)

$x^2 = 441 + 400$

$x^2 = 841$

$x = \sqrt{841} = 29$

$\cos \theta = \dfrac{A}{H} = \dfrac{21}{29}$

$\sin \theta = \dfrac{O}{H} = \dfrac{20}{29}$

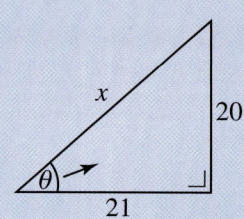

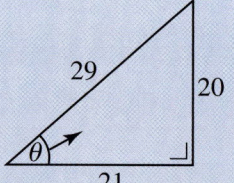

(ii) $\cos^2 \theta + \sin^2 \theta = \left(\dfrac{21}{29}\right)^2 + \left(\dfrac{20}{29}\right)^2 = \dfrac{441}{841} + \dfrac{400}{841} = \dfrac{841}{841} = 1$

Note: $\cos^2 \theta = (\cos \theta)^2$ and $\sin^2 \theta = (\sin \theta)^2$.

Exercise 19.1 ▼

In each of the right-angled triangles, write down the value of the ratios:

(i) $\sin A$ **(ii)** $\cos A$ **(iii)** $\tan A$ **(iv)** $\sin B$ **(v)** $\cos B$ **(vi)** $\tan B$

1.

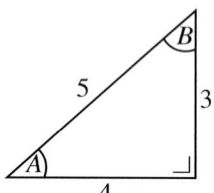

2.

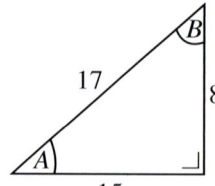

3.

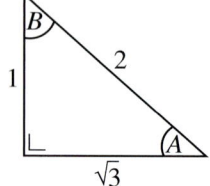

Evaluate each of the following:

4. $\left(\sqrt{3}\right)^2 + 1^2$ **5.** $\left(\sqrt{7}\right)^2 + 3^2$ **6.** $\left(\sqrt{5}\right)^2 + \left(\sqrt{3}\right)^2$ **7.** $\left(\sqrt{2}\right)^2 + \left(\sqrt{7}\right)^2$

Use Pythagoras's theorem to find x, the length of the missing side, in surd form where necessary, and express $\sin\theta$, $\cos\theta$ and $\tan\theta$ as a simple fraction or as a surd fraction in each of the following:

8.

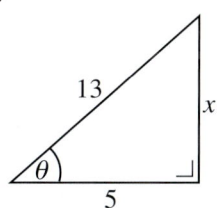

9.

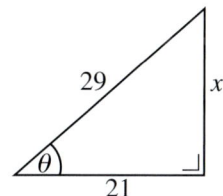

10.

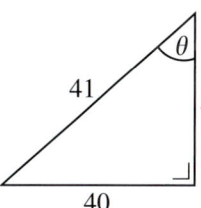

11.

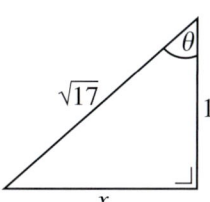

12.

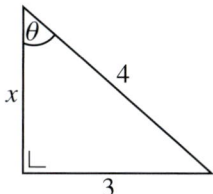

13.

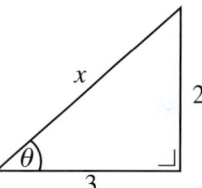

14. A is an acute angle such that $\sin A = \dfrac{4}{5}$.

    (i) Find, as fractions, the value of $\cos A$ and the value of $\tan A$.
    (ii) Verify that $\sin^2 A + \cos^2 A = 1$.

15. θ is an acute angle such that $\cos\theta = \dfrac{24}{25}$.

    (i) Find, as fractions, the value of $\sin\theta$ and the value of $\tan\theta$.
    (ii) Verify that $\cos^2\theta + \sin^2\theta = 1$.

16. A is an acute angle such that $\tan A = 3$.
    Find, as surds, the value of $\sin A$ and the value of $\cos A$.

    Note: $3 = \frac{3}{1}$

17. **(i)** Express 0.4 as a fraction.
    (ii) θ is an acute angle such that $\tan\theta = 0.4$.
        Find, as surds, the value of $\sin\theta$ and the value of $\cos\theta$.

18. B is an acute angle such that $\sin B = \dfrac{\sqrt{3}}{2}$.

    Express, as a fraction, the value of $\cos B$.

19. θ is an acute angle such that $29 \cos \theta = 20$.

If $\sin \theta = \dfrac{k}{29}$, find the value of k.

20. The diagram shows triangle pqr.
   (i) Find $|qr|$.
   (ii) Express $\cos P$ and $\tan P$ as surds.

   (iii) Evaluate $\sqrt{\dfrac{3}{\cos P \tan P}}$

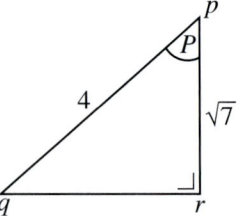

21. The diagram shows a triangle with lengths of sides 3, 4 and 5.

Verify that $\dfrac{\sin B}{\cos B} = \tan B$.

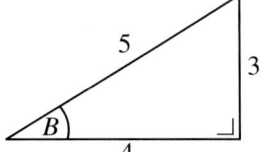

Constructing angles

Often we have to construct an angle θ, when given one of the ratios, $\sin \theta$, $\cos \theta$ or $\tan \theta$. To do this we construct a right-angled triangle using the given ratio.

Note: A rough diagram is useful before attempting to construct an accurate diagram.

> ### *Example* ▼

(i) Construct the angle A such that $7 \cos A = 4$.
(ii) Construct the angle B such that $\tan B = 3$.

Solution:

(i) $7 \cos A = 4$

$\cos A = \dfrac{4}{7}$

Adjacent = 4, Hypotenuse = 7

Rough diagram

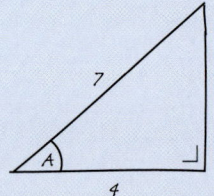

(ii) $\tan B = 3$

$\tan B = \dfrac{3}{1}$

Opposite = 3, Adjacent = 1

Rough diagram

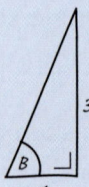

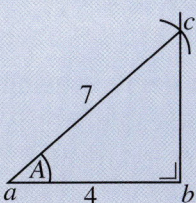

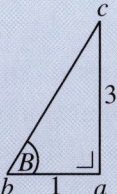

Draw a horizontal line segment [ab],
4 cm in length.
Draw a line through b perpendicular to [ab].
With a compass, centre a and radius 7 cm,
draw an arc to meet the perpendicular line at c.
Join a to c.

$$\cos A = \frac{4}{7}$$

Draw a horizontal line segment [ba],
1 cm in length.
Draw a line through a perpendicular
to [ba].
Mark point c such that |ac| = 3 cm.
Join b to c.

$$\tan B = \frac{3}{1} = 3$$

Exercise 19.2 ▼

Construct the angle represented by a letter in each of the following:

1. $\tan \theta = \frac{3}{4}$ **2.** $\tan \theta = \frac{2}{5}$ **3.** $\tan A = 4$ **4.** $\cos B = \frac{1}{3}$

5. $\sin \theta = \frac{4}{7}$ **6.** $\cos C = 0.6$ **7.** $\sin \theta = \frac{2}{5}$ **8.** $3 \tan A = 5$

9. $5 \tan B = 6$ **10.** $7 \cos A = 3$ **11.** $\tan \theta = 1.2$ **12.** $\cos A = 0.8$

13. θ is an acute angle such that $\sin \theta = \frac{2}{\sqrt{13}}$.

     (i) Write, as a fraction, the value of $\tan \theta$.
     (ii) Construct the angle θ.

14. A is an acute angle such that $\sqrt{5} \cos A = 1$.

     (i) Write, as a fraction, the value of $\tan A$.
     (ii) Construct the angle A.

Use of a calculator

You can find values of sin, cos and tan for angles measured in degrees using a calculator. Before entering angles in degrees you must make certain that the calculator is in 'degree mode'. You will usually see DEG or D at the top of the liquid crystal display (LCD).

The sin, cos and tan keys

Example ▼

Use your calculator to evaluate, correct to four decimal places, where necessary:
(i) cos 120°   (ii) sin 35°24′   (iii) 72°15′

Solution:

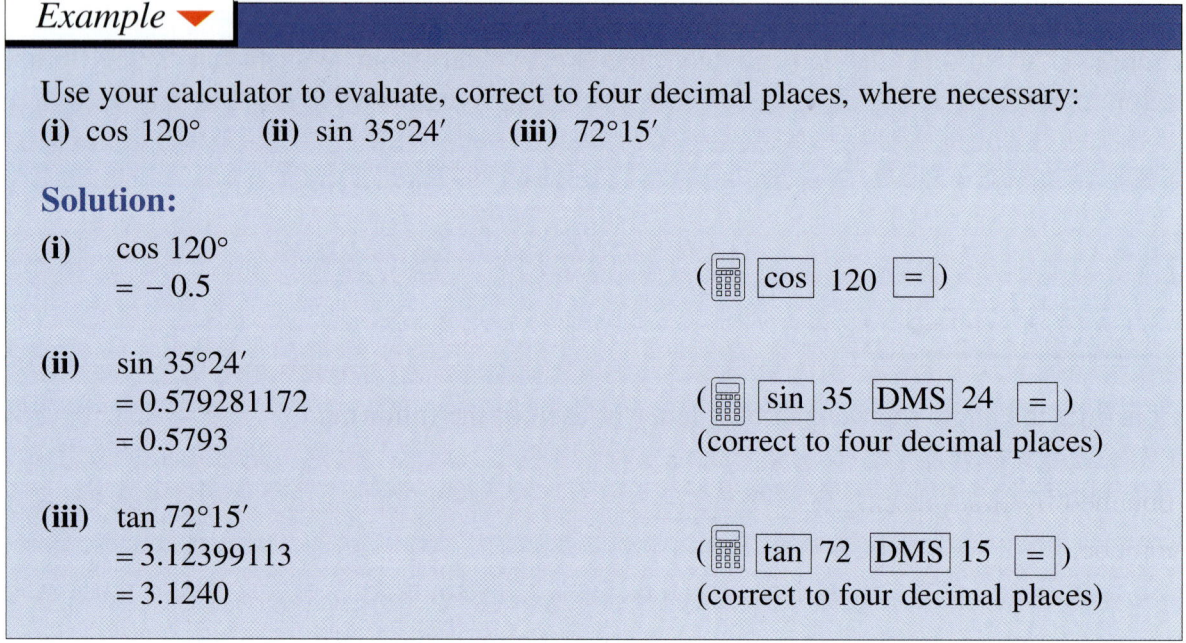

(i)   cos 120°
        = −0.5

$\left(\boxed{\text{cos}}\ 120\ \boxed{=}\ \right)$

(ii)   sin 35°24′
        = 0.579281172
        = 0.5793

$\left(\boxed{\text{sin}}\ 35\ \boxed{\text{DMS}}\ 24\ \boxed{=}\ \right)$
(correct to four decimal places)

(iii)   tan 72°15′
        = 3.12399113
        = 3.1240

$\left(\boxed{\text{tan}}\ 72\ \boxed{\text{DMS}}\ 15\ \boxed{=}\ \right)$
(correct to four decimal places)

Note: On some calculators the DMS (degrees, minutes, seconds) key is ° ′ ″ .
If you are using a non DAL (direct algebraic logic) calculator, then the keys are used slightly differently, for example tan 72°15′ is keyed in:
72 DMS 15 DMS tan =

Exercise 19.3 ▼

Use your calculator to evaluate each of the following, correct to four decimal places:

1.	sin 51°	**2.**	cos 73°	**3.**	tan 47°
4.	cos 10°30′	**5.**	sin 59°15′	**6.**	tan 31°54′
7.	sin 47°42′	**8.**	sin 26°8′	**9.**	tan 31°9′
10.	cos 75°41′	**11.**	sin 83°37′	**12.**	tan 25°18′
13.	10 sin 28°	**14.**	40 cos 37°36′	**15.**	45 tan 75°26′

16. $120 \sin 40°54'$ **17.** $\dfrac{30}{\sin 50°}$ **18.** $\dfrac{120}{\sin 53°8'}$

19. $\dfrac{20 \sin 42°18'}{\sin 48°40'}$ **20.** $\dfrac{18 \sin 16°28'}{\sin 24°54'}$ **21.** $\frac{1}{2}(5)(8) \sin 80°$

22. $\left(\frac{1}{2}\right)(20)(40) \sin 40°28'$ **23.** $\left(\frac{1}{2}\right)(7)(3) \sin 18°30'$

Calculate exactly:

24. $\tan 45°$ **25.** $\tan 135°$ **26.** $\cos 60°$

27. $\sin 330°$ **28.** $\cos^2 120°$ **29.** $\left(\frac{1}{2}\right)(10)(6) \sin 30°$

30. $\left(\frac{1}{2}\right)(20)(7) \sin 150°$

Show that:

31. $2 \sin 30° \neq \sin 60°$ **32.** $\cos 30° + \cos 60° \neq \cos 90°$

The $\boxed{\sin^{-1}}$, $\boxed{\cos^{-1}}$ and $\boxed{\tan^{-1}}$ keys

Given a value of $\sin \theta$, $\cos \theta$, or $\tan \theta$, we can find the value of the angle θ using the $\boxed{\sin^{-1}}$, $\boxed{\cos^{-1}}$ or $\boxed{\tan^{-1}}$ key, respectively. On most calculators, $\boxed{\sin^{-1}}$, $\boxed{\cos^{-1}}$ and $\boxed{\tan^{-1}}$ are obtained by first pressing $\boxed{\text{INV}}$ or $\boxed{\text{2nd F}}$ and then pressing $\boxed{\sin}$, $\boxed{\cos}$ or $\boxed{\tan}$, as the case may be.

Example ▼

Find the value of θ, $0 \leqslant \theta \leqslant 90°$, to the nearest minute, given that:

(i) $\sin \theta = 0.38$ **(ii)** $\cos \theta = \frac{3}{5}$ **(iii)** $4 \tan 2\theta = 1$

Solution:

(i) $\sin \theta = 0.38$

$\theta = \sin^{-1} 0.38$

$\theta = 22.33368266°$ (▦ $\boxed{\text{2nd F}}$ $\boxed{\sin}$ 0.38)

$\theta = 22°20'01.26''$ (▦ $\boxed{\text{2nd F}}$ $\boxed{\text{DMS}}$)

$\theta = 22°20'$ (nearest minute)

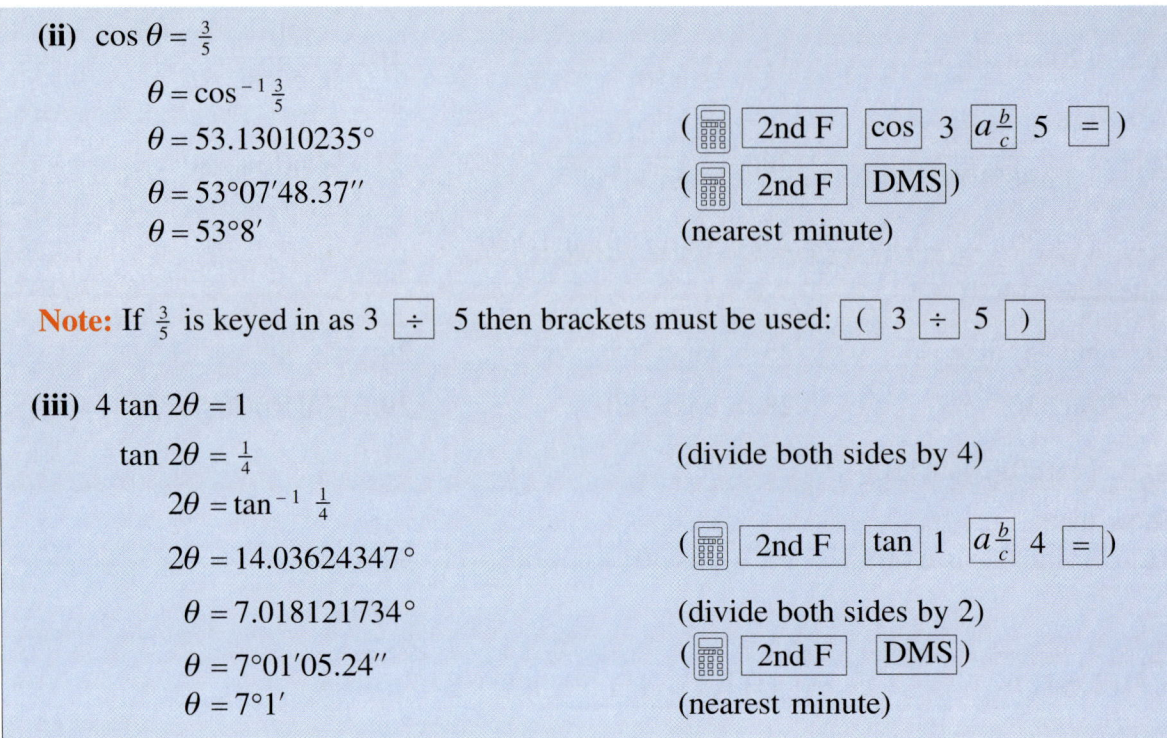

(ii) $\cos \theta = \frac{3}{5}$

$\qquad \theta = \cos^{-1} \frac{3}{5}$

$\qquad \theta = 53.13010235°$ ([2nd F] [cos] 3 [$a\frac{b}{c}$] 5 [=])

$\qquad \theta = 53°07'48.37''$ ([2nd F] [DMS])

$\qquad \theta = 53°8'$ (nearest minute)

Note: If $\frac{3}{5}$ is keyed in as 3 [÷] 5 then brackets must be used: [(] 3 [÷] 5 [)]

(iii) $4 \tan 2\theta = 1$

$\qquad \tan 2\theta = \frac{1}{4}$ (divide both sides by 4)

$\qquad\qquad 2\theta = \tan^{-1} \frac{1}{4}$

$\qquad\qquad 2\theta = 14.03624347°$ ([2nd F] [tan] 1 [$a\frac{b}{c}$] 4 [=])

$\qquad\qquad\quad \theta = 7.018121734°$ (divide both sides by 2)

$\qquad\qquad\quad \theta = 7°01'05.24''$ ([2nd F] [DMS])

$\qquad\qquad\quad \theta = 7°1'$ (nearest minute)

Note: We use the fact that 1 minute = 60 seconds (like the clock) to round off the answer to the nearest minute.

Exercise 19.4 ▼

Use your calculator to find each of the following angles, correct to the nearest minute, where each angle is between 0° and 90°:

1. $\sin A = 0.3$ **2.** $\cos B = 0.35$ **3.** $\tan C = 1.5$

4. $\cos \theta = 0.7835$ **5.** $\tan P = 2.4532$ **6.** $\sin Q = 0.6528$

7. $\tan A = 5$ **8.** $\cos B = 0.38$ **9.** $\sin C = 0.4073$

10. $\sin \angle abc = \frac{1}{3}$ **11.** $\cos \angle qpr = \frac{2}{5}$ **12.** $\tan \angle zxy = \sqrt{5}$

13. $4 \tan A = 3$ **14.** $5 \sin B = 1$ **15.** $3 \cos C = 2$

Note: $\frac{1}{\sqrt{10}}$ must be keyed in as: [(] 1 [÷] [$\sqrt{}$] 10 [)] , brackets are essential.

16. $\sin A = \frac{1}{\sqrt{10}}$ **17.** $\cos B = \frac{2}{\sqrt{7}}$ **18.** $\tan C = \frac{\sqrt{3}}{5}$

19. $\tan 2A = \frac{1}{3}$ **20.** $\cos 2A = \frac{1}{10}$ **21.** $\sin 5A = \frac{5}{7}$

22. $\sin 2A = \frac{1}{5}$ **23.** $\cos \frac{A}{2} = \frac{91}{100}$ **24.** $\tan \frac{A}{2} = \frac{1}{5}$

Find each angle exactly:

25. $\cos Q = \frac{1}{2}$ **26.** $\tan A = \frac{1}{\sqrt{3}}$ **27.** $\sin B = \frac{1}{\sqrt{2}}$

Notation

The diagram shows the **usual notation**
for a triangle in trigonometry:
Vertices: a, b, c
Angles: A, B, C
Length of sides: a, b, c

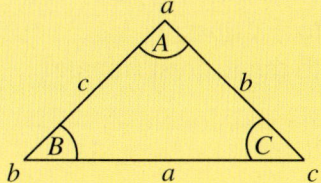

The lengths of the sides are denoted by a lower case letter, and named after the angle
they are opposite, i.e., a is opposite angle A, b is opposite angle B, and c is opposite
angle C.

Using the terminology we also have the following:

$$A = |\angle bac|, \qquad B = |\angle abc|, \qquad C = |\angle acb|$$

$$a = |bc|, \qquad b = |ac|, \qquad c = |ab|$$

Solving right-angled triangles

We can use a trigonometric ratio to calculate the length of a side in a right-angled triangle if
we know the length of one side and one angle (other than the right angle). We can also find
the size of an angle in a right-angled triangle if we know the lengths of two of its sides.

Summary of which trigonometric ratio to choose linking the given sides and angles:

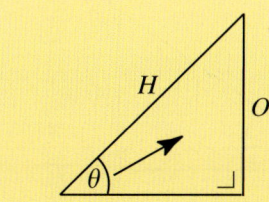

$$\sin \theta = \frac{O}{H}$$

$$\theta = \sin^{-1} \frac{O}{H}$$

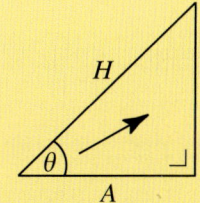

$$\cos \theta = \frac{A}{H}$$

$$\theta = \cos^{-1} \frac{A}{H}$$

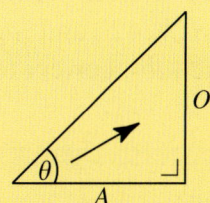

$$\tan \theta = \frac{O}{A}$$

$$\theta = \tan^{-1} \frac{O}{A}$$

In △*pqr*, $|\angle pqr| = 90°$,
$|pq| = 17$ cm and $|pr| = 20$ cm.
Calculate, $|\angle qpr|$,
correct to the nearest minute.

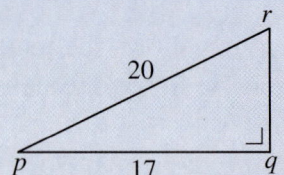

Solution:

Let $P = |\angle qpr|$.
adjacent = 17 cm, hypotenuse = 20 cm
We know adjacent and hypotenuse,
therefore use the cosine ratio.

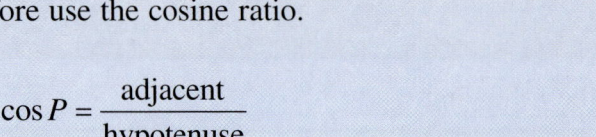

$$\cos P = \frac{\text{adjacent}}{\text{hypotenuse}}$$

$\cos P = \frac{17}{20}$ (put in known values)

$P = \cos^{-1} \frac{17}{20}$

$P = 31.78833062°$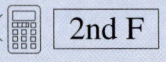

$P = 31°47'17.99''$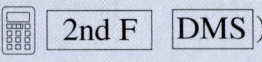

$P = 31°47'$ (nearest minute)

$\therefore \ |\angle qpr| = 31°47'$, correct to the nearest minute.

In △*abc*, $|\angle bca| = 90°$,
$|\angle abc| = 28°42'$, and $|ac| = 10$ m.
Calculate $|ab|$, correct to one decimal place.

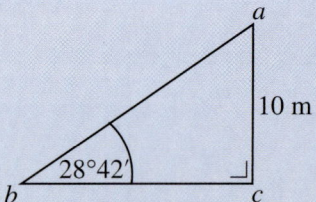

Solution:

Let $B = |\angle abc|$ and $c = |ab|$.
We require the hypotenuse and know the opposite.
Therefore use the sine ratio.

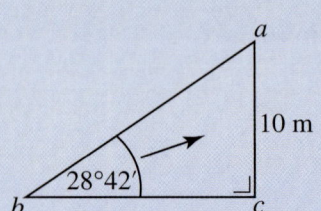

$$\sin B = \frac{\text{opposite}}{\text{hypotenuse}}$$

$\sin 28°42' = \dfrac{10}{c}$ (put in known values)

$c \sin 28°42' = 10$ (multiply both sides by c)

$$c = \frac{10}{\sin 28°42'}$$ (divide both sides by $\sin 28°42'$)

$c = 20.82363744$ (🔢 $10 \div$ sin 28 DMS 42 =)

$c = 20.8$ m (correct to one decimal place)

$\therefore |ab| = 20.8$ m, correct to one decimal place.

Exercise 19.5 ▼

Calculate, to the nearest minute, the angles marked with a letter:

1.

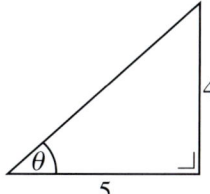

2.

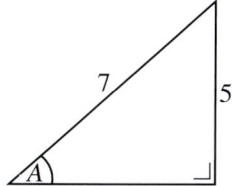

3.

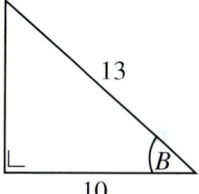

4.

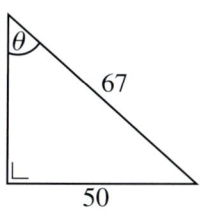

5.

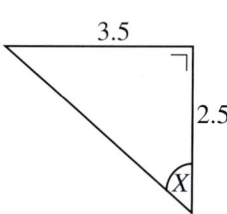

6.

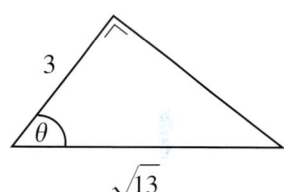

In each of the following calculate the length of the sides marked with a letter, correct to two decimal places:

7.

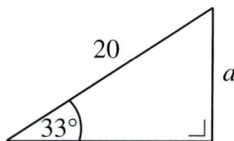

8.

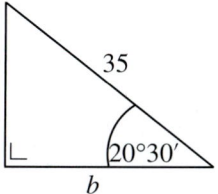

9.

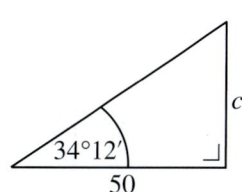

10.

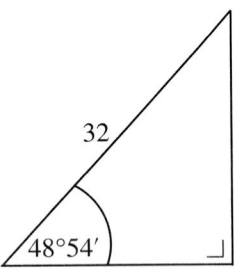

11.

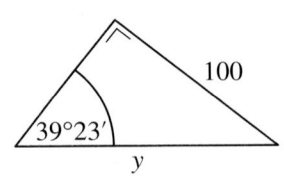

12.

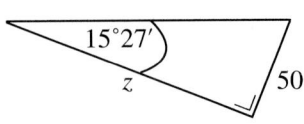

13.

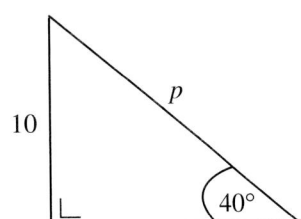

14.

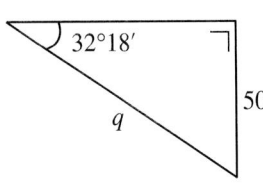

15.

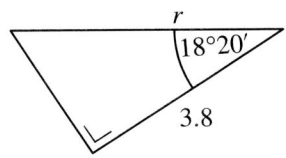

16. In $\triangle abc$, $|\angle abc| = 90°$, $|ab| = 2$, and $|bc| = 1.5$.
Find:
(i) $|ac|$
(ii) $|\angle bac|$, correct to the nearest degree.

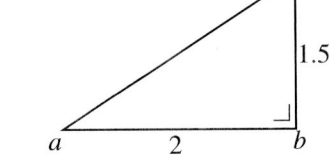

17. In the diagram, $xw \perp yz$,
$|xy| = 10$, $|\angle xyw| = 30°$ and $|wz| = \frac{2}{5}|xy|$.
Calculate:
(i) $|xw|$
(ii) $|\angle wxz|$, correct to the nearest minute.

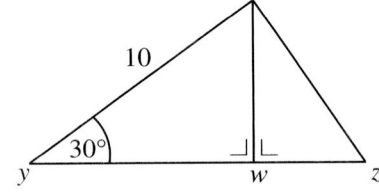

18. In $\triangle abc$, $|ab| = 16$ cm, and $|\angle abc| = 90°$.
The point d is on $[bc]$.
$|bd| = 30$ cm and $|ad| = |dc|$

Find: **(i)** $|ad|$
(ii) $|\angle acb|$, correct to the nearest minute.

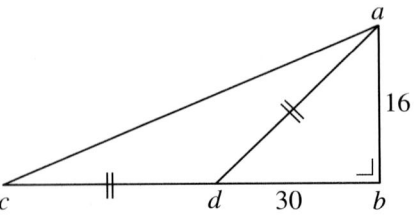

Practical applications

Many practical problems in navigation, surveying, engineering and geography involve solving a triangle. In this section we will restrict the problems to those that involve right-angled triangles. When solving practical problems, using trigonometry, in this section represent each situation with a right-angled triangle.

Mark on your triangle the angles and lengths you know, and label what you need to calculate, using the correct ratio to link the angle or length required with the known angle or length.

Angles of elevation, depression and compass directions

Angle of elevation

The **angle of elevation** of an object as seen by an observer is the angle between the horizontal line from the object to the observer's eye (upwards from the horizontal).

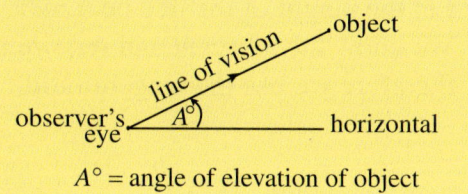

$A° =$ angle of elevation of object

Angle of depression

If the object is below the level of the observer, the angle between the horizontal and the observer's line of vision is called the **angle of depression** (downwards from the horizontal).

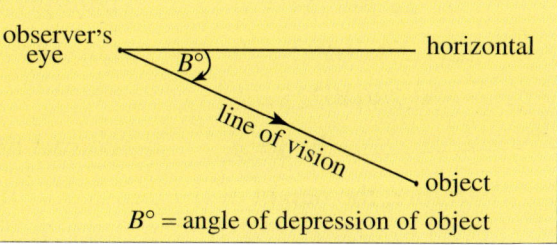

$B° =$ angle of depression of object

Note: An angle of elevation has an equal angle of depression. The angle of elevation from a to b is equal to the angle of depression from b to a. The angles are alternate angles, as the horizontal lines are parallel.

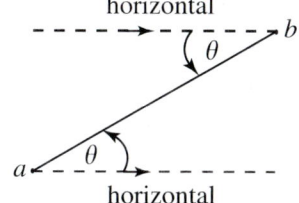

Compass directions

The direction of a point is stated as a number of degrees East or West of North and South.

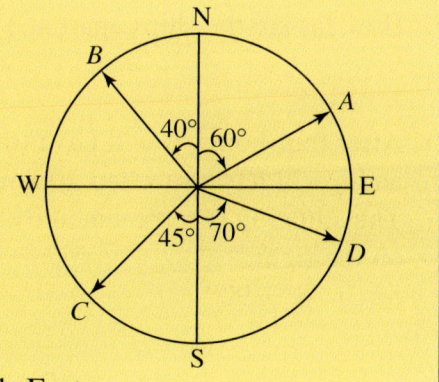

A is N60°E

B is N40°W

C is S45°W (or SW)

D is S70°E

Note: N60°E means start at North and turn 60° towards East.

From a point on the ground 22 m from
the base of a tree, the angle of elevation
of the top of the tree is 54°.
Calculate the height of the tree,
correct to one decimal place.

Solution:

Represent the situation with a right-angled triangle.
Let the height of the tree be h m.
We know the adjacent and require the opposite,
therefore we use the tangent ratio.

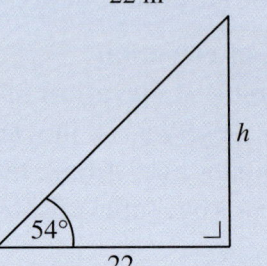

$$\tan 54° = \frac{h}{22} \qquad \left(\frac{\text{opposite}}{\text{adjacent}}\right)$$

$$22 \tan 54° = h \qquad \text{(multiply both sides by 22)}$$

$$22(1.37638192) = h \qquad (\tan 54° = 1.37638192)$$

$$30.28040225 = h$$

$$30.3 = h \qquad \text{(correct to one decimal place)}$$

Therefore, the height of the tree is 30.3 m (correct to one decimal place).

Two ships p and q leave a harbour h at 14:00. p sails in a direction S58°E and q sails in
the direction S32°W. p sails at $5\frac{1}{4}$ km / h and q sails at 5 km / h.
How far are the ships apart at 18:00?

Solution:

After four hours, p will have travelled 21 km
and q will have travelled 20 km.
The situation is represented by the diagram
on the right.
$$32° + 58° = 90°$$

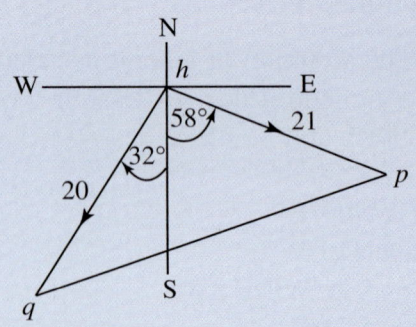

$\therefore |\angle qhp| = 90°$

$\therefore \triangle qhp$ is right-angled.

$|qp|$ = the distance between the ships at 18:00

$|qp|^2 = |qh|^2 + |ph|^2$ (Pythagoras's theorem)

$|qp|^2 = 20^2 + 21^2$

$|qp|^2 = 400 + 441$

$|qp|^2 = 841$

$|qp| = \sqrt{841} = 29$

Therefore, the two ships are 29 km apart at 18:00.

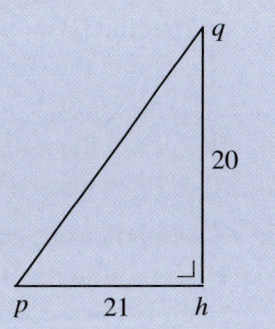

Exercise 19.6 ▼

1. When the angle of elevation of the sun is 23°, an upright flagpole casts a shadow of length 10 m. Calculate the height of the pole, correct to one place of decimals.

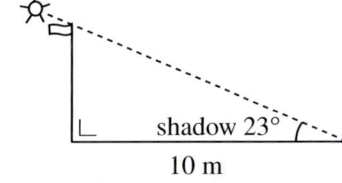

2. [xz] is a vertical television mast such that $|xz| = 12$ m. [xy] is a supporting cable such that $|xy| = 37$ m. Calculate:
   (i) $|yz|$
   (ii) $|\angle xyz|$, correct to the nearest degree.

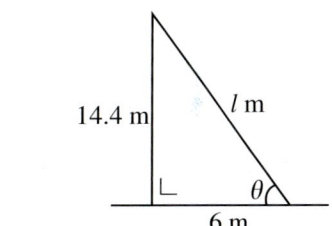

3. A wire is used to support an antenna 14.4 m tall, joining the top of the antenna to a point on the ground 6 m from the base, as shown. Calculate:
   (i) the length, l m, of the wire
   (ii) the angle, θ, that the wire makes with the ground, correct to the nearest degree.

4. [ad] is a vertical mast standing on level ground. Wires join a to the ground at b and at c, as in the diagram. Given that $|ab| = 42$ m, $|dc| = 20$ m, and $|\angle abd| = 30°$, calculate:
   (i) $|ad|$ (ii) $|ac|$
   (iii) $|\angle acd|$, correct to the nearest degree.

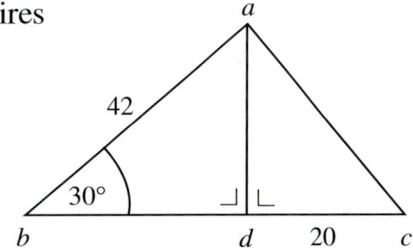

5. A ladder of length 5 m rests against a vertical wall, so that the base of the ladder is 2.5 m from the wall.
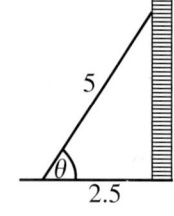
   (i) Find the angle, θ, which the ladder makes with the horizontal.
   (ii) Find the vertical height at which the ladder reaches on the wall, correct to three significant figures.

6. A ramp is to be built to allow wheelchairs enter a building. The step is 42 cm and the ramp is to extend for 4 m as shown. Calculate the angle of inclination, θ, of the ramp, to the level ground.
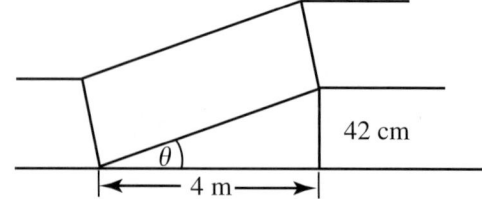

7. An aerial is mounted on top of a building, as shown. From a point on the ground 50 m from the base of the building, the angles of elevation of the top and bottom of the aerial are 28° and 25°, respectively. Find:
   (i) the height of the building
   (ii) the height of the aerial above the building.
 (give answers correct to two decimal places)
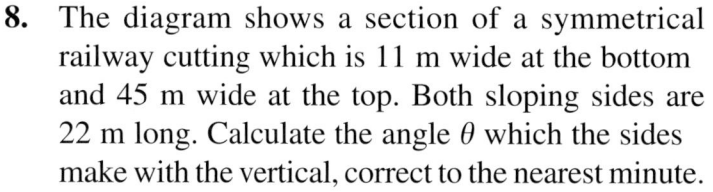

8. The diagram shows a section of a symmetrical railway cutting which is 11 m wide at the bottom and 45 m wide at the top. Both sloping sides are 22 m long. Calculate the angle θ which the sides make with the vertical, correct to the nearest minute.
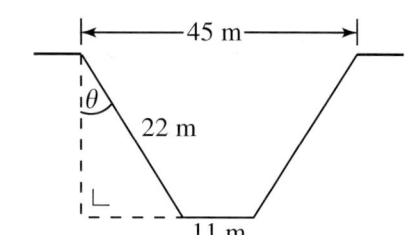

9. The diagram shows a side view of two vertical buildings, A and B.
 $|pq| = 20$ m and $|\angle qpr| = 16°42'$
   (i) Calculate $|qr|$, correct to the nearest m.
     A television cable stretches from s to r, such that $|sr| = 2$ m.
   (ii) Calculate $|\angle srp|$, correct to the nearest minute.
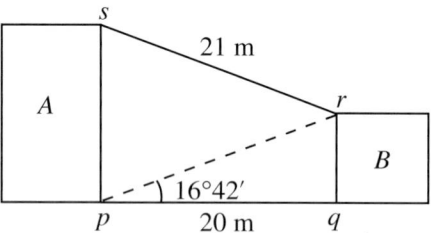

10. From a boat at sea, the angle of elevation to the top of a vertical cliff, 200 m above sea level, is 12°. After the boat has sailed directly towards the cliff, the angle of elevation of the cliff is found to be 24°. How far did the boat sail towards the cliff, correct to the nearest metre?

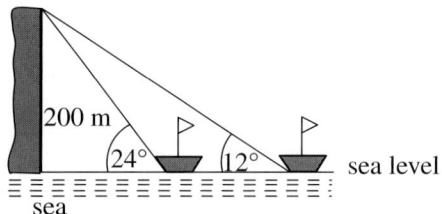

11. Copy the diagram and on it indicate the following directions:

    (i)   N60°E   **(ii)** S20°W

    (iii) S70°E   **(iv)** N50°W

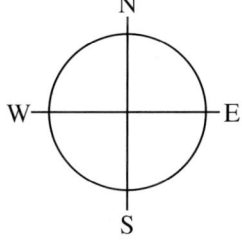

12. Two ships, p and q, leave a harbour h at the same time. p sails in a direction S73°E at $17\frac{1}{2}$ km/h. q sails in the direction S17°W at x km/h. After two hours sailing, the two ships are 37 km apart. Calculate the speed of ship q.

13. Two ships, x and y, leave a harbour o at the same time. x sails in a direction N37°43′W at 8 km/h and y sails in a direction N52°17′E at 15 km/h. After sailing for 3 hours, how far are the ships apart?

14. A boat sails 12 km North and then 9 km West. Find its bearing, to the nearest degree, from its starting point.

15. On leaving a port p, a fishing boat sails in the direction South 30° East for 2 hours at 10 km/h as shown. What distance has the boat then sailed? The boat next sails in the direction North 60° East, at 10 km/h, until it is due East of the port p. Draw a diagram of the boat journey. Calculate how far the boat is from the port p.

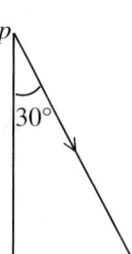

Solving non-right-angled triangles

Area of a triangle

Area of $\triangle abc$

$= \frac{1}{2} ab \sin C = \frac{1}{2} ac \sin B = \frac{1}{2} bc \sin A$

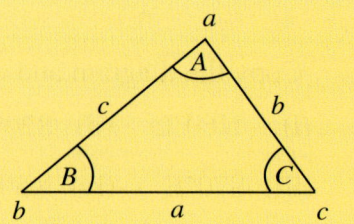

To use this formula to find the area of a triangle we need:
The length of two sides **and** the size of the angle between these sides.

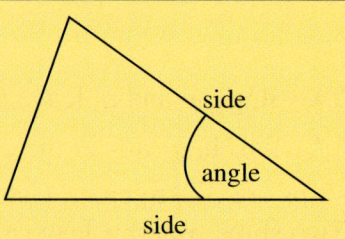

Area of triangle

$= \frac{1}{2}$ (length of side) × (length of side) × (sine of the angle between these sides)

Example ▼

In the triangle abc, $|ab| = 10$ m, $|bc| = 12$ m and $|\angle abc| = 23°42'$.
Calculate the area of the triangle, correct to one place of decimals.

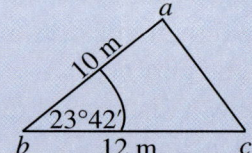

Solution:

Let $B = |\angle abc|$, $a = |bc|$ and $c = |ab|$.

Area of $\triangle abc = \frac{1}{2} ac \sin B$

$\qquad = \frac{1}{2}(12)(10) \sin 23°42'$

$\qquad = \frac{1}{2}(12)(10)(0.401947776)$

$\qquad = 24.1 \text{ m}^2$

(correct to one decimal place)

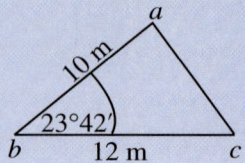

In some questions we are given an equation in disguise.

Example ▼

(i) Calculate sin 125°, correct to two decimal places.

(ii) In triangle pqr, $|pq| = 20$ cm and $|\angle rpq| = 125°$. If the area of triangle $pqr = 147.6$ cm^2, find $|pr|$, using the value of sin 125° obtained in part **(i)**.

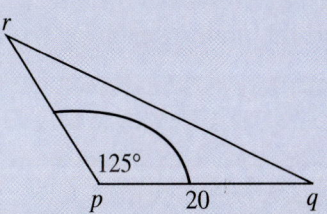

Solution:

(i) sin 125° = 0.819152044 = 0.82 (correct to two decimal places).

(ii) Let $P = |\angle rpq|$, $q = |pr|$ and $r = |pq|$.
Equation given in disguise:

Area of $\triangle pqr = 147.6$

$\frac{1}{2} qr \sin P = 147.6$

$\frac{1}{2}(q)(20)(0.82) = 147.6$ (put in known values)

$8.2q = 147.6$ (simplify left-hand side)

$q = 18$ (divide both sides by 8.2)

$\therefore |pr| = 18$ cm

Example ▼

In the triangle abc, $|ab| = 50$ m and $|ac| = 28$ m.
If the area of the triangle abc is 260 m^2, find $|\angle bac|$, correct to the nearest minute.

Solution:

Let $A = |\angle bac|$, $b = |ac|$ and $c = |ab|$.
Equation given in disguise:

Area of $\triangle abc = 260$

$\frac{1}{2} bc \sin A = 260$

$\frac{1}{2}(28)(50)\sin A = 260$

$700 \sin A = 260$

$\sin A = \frac{260}{700} = \frac{13}{35}$

$A = \sin^{-1} \frac{13}{35}$

$A = 21°48'$ (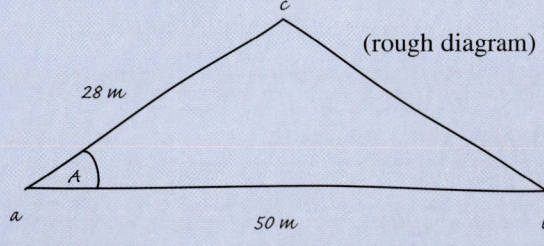)

$\therefore |\angle bac| = 24°48'$, correct to the nearest minute.

273

Unless otherwise stated, where necessary give lengths of sides and areas correct to two decimal places and give angles correct to the nearest minute.

Find the area of each of the following triangles, where the lengths of the sides are in cm:

1.

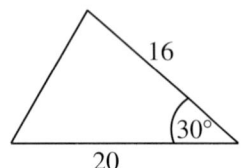

2.

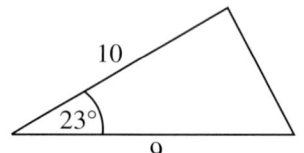

3.

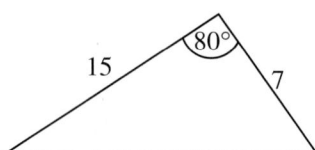

4.

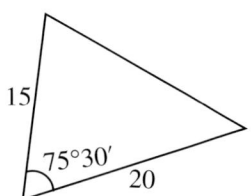

5.

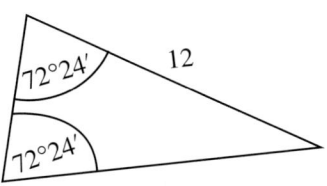

6.

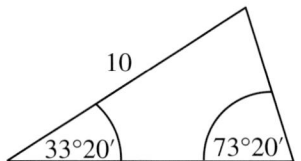

In the following questions a rough diagram may help:

7. In the $\triangle pqr$, $|pr| = 8$ m, $|pq| = 7$ m and $|\angle qpr| = 54°$.
Calculate the area of $\triangle pqr$.

8. In the $\triangle abc$, $|bc| = 10$ cm, $|ac| = 12$ cm and $|\angle acb| = 48°36'$.
Calculate the area of $\triangle abc$.

9. In the $\triangle pqr$, $|qr| = 8$ m, $|pr| = 24$ m, $|\angle rpq| = 40°$ and $|\angle pqr| = 30°$.
Calculate the area of $\triangle pqr$.

10. In the triangle abc, $|ac| = 20$ cm, $|\angle abc| = 70°$ and $|\angle bac| = 40°$.
Calculate the area of triangle abc.

11. The diagram shows the quadrilateral $pqsr$,
$qp \perp pr$, $|pq| = 2.4$ cm, $|pr| = 1.8$ cm,
$|rs| = 2$ cm and $|\angle qrs| = 70°$.
Calculate:
(i) $|qr|$
(ii) Area of $pqsr$.

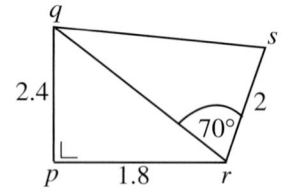

12. $abcd$ is a kite as shown.
$|ab| = |ad|$ and $|cb| = |cd|$,
$|ad| = 40$ cm and $|cd| = 25$ cm,
$|\angle bad| = 42°$ and $|\angle bcd| = 75°$.
Calculate the area of the kite.

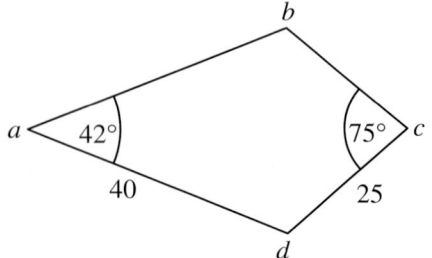

13. (a) *opq* is a sector of a circle with a radius of 10 cm and $|\angle poq| = 36°$.

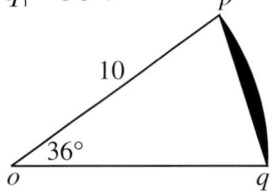

  (i) Calculate the area of the sector *opq*.
  (ii) Calculate the area of triangle *opq*.
  (iii) Calculate the area of the shaded segment.
    (assume $\pi = 3.14$)

(b) *abcd* is a parallelogram with diagonals intersecting at *o*.
$|ac| = 4$, $|bd| = 10$ and $|\angle aob| = 60°$.
Calculate the area of the parallelogram *abcd*,
correct to two decimal places.

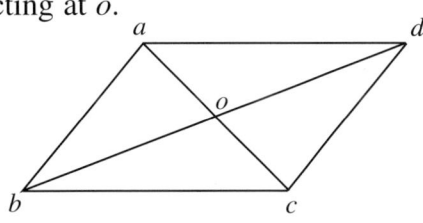

14. In $\triangle pqr$, $|pq| = 8$ cm, $|\angle pqr| = 30°$.
If the area of $\triangle pqr = 48$ cm^2,
calculate $|qr|$.

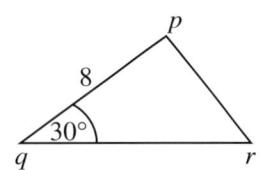

15. (i) Calculate sin 34° correct to two decimal places.
  (ii) In $\triangle abc$, $|ab| = 20$ m, and $|\angle bac| = 34°$.
    If the area of $\triangle abc = 145.6$ m^2, find $|ac|$,
    using the value of sin 34° obtained in part **(i)**.

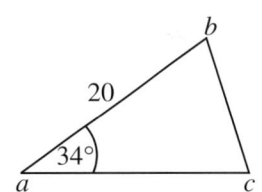

16. (i) Calculate sin 109°57′ correct to two decimal places.
  (ii) In $\triangle pqr$, $|pq| = 80$ m, and $|\angle rpq| = 109°57′$.
    If the area of $\triangle pqr = 2820$ m^2, find $|pr|$,
    using the value of sin 109°57′ obtained in part **(i)**.

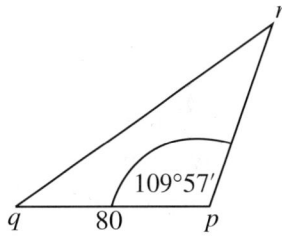

17. In the triangle *pqr*,
$|pq| = |pr|$ and $|\angle qpr| = 30°$.
If the area of triangle *pqr* is 20.25,
calculate $|pq|$.

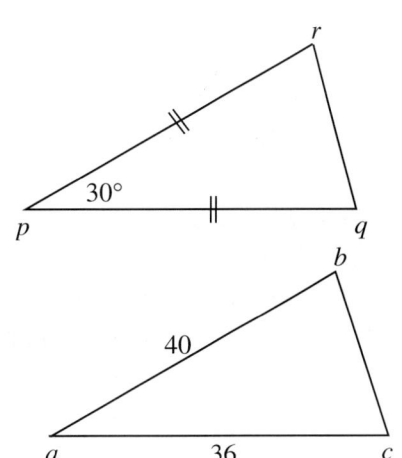

18. In the triangle *abc*,
$|ab| = 40$ cm and $|ac| = 36$ cm.
If the area of triangle *abc* is 420 cm^2,
find $|\angle bac|$, correct to the nearest minute.

19. In the triangle *pqr*,
$|pr| = 14$ m and $|qr| = 10$ m.
If the area of triangle *pqr* is 45 m^2,
calculate $|\angle prq|$.

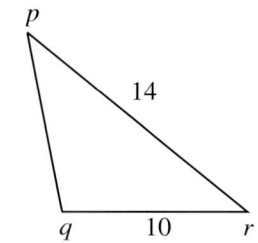

20. In the triangle *xyz*,
$|xz| = 40$ cm and $|yz| = 50$ cm.
If the area of triangle *xyz* is 940 cm^2,
calculate $|\angle xzy|$, correct to the nearest degree.

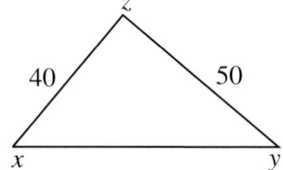

Sine rule

In any $\triangle abc$:

$$\frac{a}{\sin A} = \frac{b}{\sin B} = \frac{c}{\sin C}$$

or:
$$\frac{\sin A}{a} = \frac{\sin B}{b} = \frac{\sin C}{c}$$

(The first form is given on page 9 of the tables)

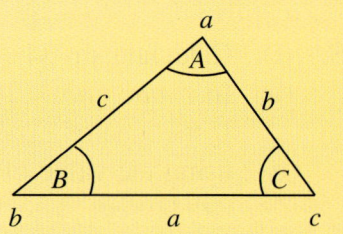

This is known as the '**sine rule**' and it applies to any triangle, including a right-angled triangle.

To find an unknown side *x* using the sine rule we need:	To find an unknown angle, *A*°, using the sine rule we need:
Two angles and one side.	Two sides and the size of one angle opposite one of these sides.
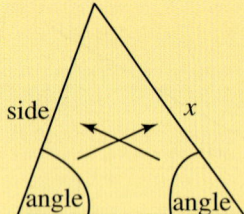	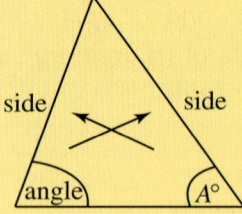
If we know two angles we can calculate the third angle as the three angles add up to 180°.	The unknown angle, *A*°, must be opposite a known side.

The sine rule connects each side with the angle opposite in a triangle.

Note: **1.** In practice we only put two fractions equal to each other, e.g.,

$$\frac{a}{\sin A} = \frac{b}{\sin B}$$

2. Put the required quantity, side or angle, on the top of the first fraction.

To find a, use $\qquad \dfrac{a}{\sin A} = \dfrac{b}{\sin B}$

To find B, use $\qquad \dfrac{\sin B}{b} = \dfrac{\sin A}{a}$

Example ▼

In triangle pqr, $|pr| = 7$ cm, $|\angle pqr| = 35°$ and $|\angle prq| = 75°$.
Find $|pq|$, correct to two decimal places.

Solution:

rough diagram

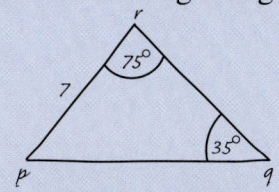

Let:
$q = |pr|$, $\qquad Q = |\angle pqr|$,
$r = |pq|$, $\qquad R = |\angle prq|$,

$$\frac{r}{\sin R} = \frac{q}{\sin Q} \qquad \text{(r is missing, so put that first)}$$

$$\frac{r}{\sin 75°} = \frac{7}{\sin 35°} \qquad \text{(put in known values)}$$

$$r = \frac{7 \sin 75°}{\sin 35°} \qquad \text{(multiply both sides by sin 75°)}$$

$$r = \frac{7(0.965925826)}{0.573576436}$$

$$r = 11.78828201$$

$$\therefore \ |pq| = 11.79 \text{ cm} \qquad \text{(correct to two decimal places)}$$

In triangle abc, $|bc| = 8$ m, $|ac| = 6$ m and $|\angle abc| = 43°$.
Calculate $|\angle bac|$, correct to the nearest minute.

Solution:

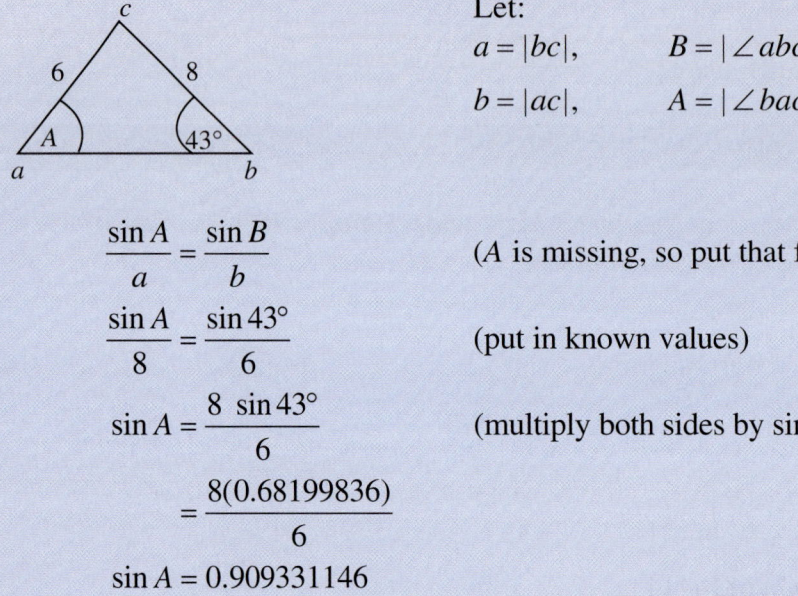

Let:
$$a = |bc|, \qquad B = |\angle abc|$$
$$b = |ac|, \qquad A = |\angle bac|$$

$$\frac{\sin A}{a} = \frac{\sin B}{b}$$

(A is missing, so put that first)

$$\frac{\sin A}{8} = \frac{\sin 43°}{6}$$

(put in known values)

$$\sin A = \frac{8 \sin 43°}{6}$$

(multiply both sides by sin 75o)

$$= \frac{8(0.68199836)}{6}$$

$$\sin A = 0.909331146$$

$$A = \sin^{-1} 0.909331146$$

$$A = 65°25'$$

$$\therefore \quad |\angle bac| = 65°25'$$

If two triangles are linked it is a good idea to draw them separately.

p, s, q and r are points on level ground,
p, s and q in a straight line.
$|\angle qpr| = 39°46'$ and $|\angle pqr| = 68°26'$
$pq \perp rs$ and $|pq| = 95$ m. Calculate:
(i) $|qr|$, correct to two decimal places
(ii) $|rs|$, using your answer for $|qr|$ in part (i).

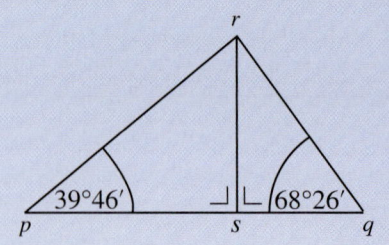

Solution:

Draw triangles *pqr* and *sqr* separately. [*qr*] is common to both triangles.

(i) Consider △*pqr*:

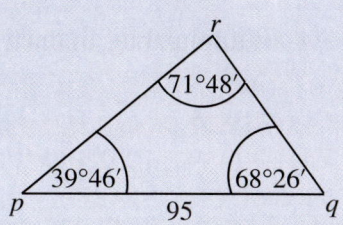

Let:

$r = |pq|,$ $P = |\angle qpr|$

$p = |qr|,$ $Q = |\angle pqr|$

$R = 180° - 39°46' - 68°26' = 71°48'$

$$\frac{p}{\sin P} = \frac{r}{\sin R}$$ (*p* is missing, so put that first)

$$\frac{p}{\sin 39°46'} = \frac{95}{\sin 71°48'}$$ (put in known values)

$$p = \frac{95 \sin 39°46'}{\sin 71°48'}$$ (multiply both sides by sin 39°46′)

$$p = \frac{95(0.639662621)}{0.949972051}$$

$$p = 63.96814414$$

∴ $|qr| = 63.97$ m (correct to two decimal places)

(ii) Consider △*sqr*:

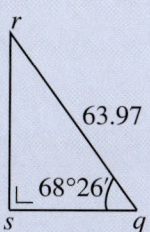

$$\sin 68°26' = \frac{|rs|}{63.97}$$ $\left(\dfrac{\text{opposite}}{\text{hypotenuse}}\right)$

$$63.97 \sin 68°26' = |rs|$$

$$(63.97)(0.929990494) = |rs|$$

$$59.49149195 = |rs|$$

∴ $|rs| = 59.49$ m (correct to two decimal places)

Unless otherwise stated, give lengths of sides correct to two decimal places and give angles correct to the nearest minute.

Find the value of the length of sides marked x or the angle A, as applicable, in each of the following:

1.

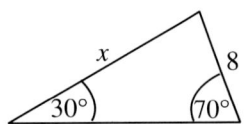

2.

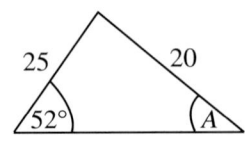

3.

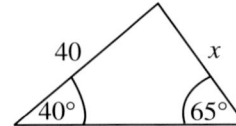

4.

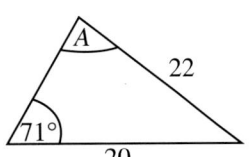

5.

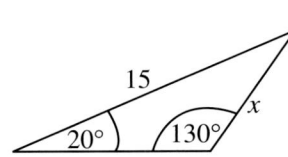

6.

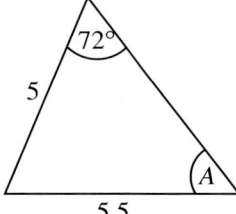

7.

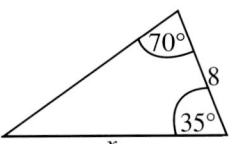

8.

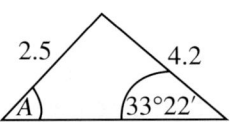

9.

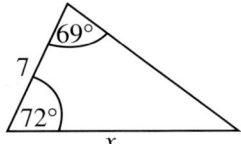

In the following questions, a rough diagram may help:

10. In the triangle pqr, $|qr| = 7$ cm, $|\angle qpr| = 30°$ and $|\angle pqr| = 84°$.
Find **(i)** $|pr|$ **(ii)** $|pq|$.

11. In the triangle abc, $|ac| = 4$ cm, $|ab| = 6$ cm and $|\angle acb| = 36°57'$.
Find $|\angle abc|$.

12. In the triangle xyz, $|xz| = 10$ cm, $|\angle yxz| = 70°$ and $|\angle xyz| = 45°$.
Find **(i)** $|\angle xzy|$ **(ii)** $|yz|$ **(iii)** $|xy|$

13. The diagram shows a triangle pqr.
$pq \perp qr$, $|\angle qpr| = 55°$ and $|pq| = 10$ cm.
$[qs]$ is drawn such that $|rs| = 5$ cm.
Find **(i)** $|qr|$, correct to two decimal places
(ii) area of triangle qrs
(using your answer to part
(i) if necessary).

14. In the diagram, $pq \perp qr$, $|pq| = 8$ m, $|qr| = 15$ m.

    (i)   Find $|pr|$

           $|ps| = |pr|$ and $|\angle psr| = 65°$

    (ii) Find $|\angle spr|$.

    (iii) Find the area of triangle prs, correct to the nearest m^2.

    (iv) Find $|sr|$, correct to two decimal places.

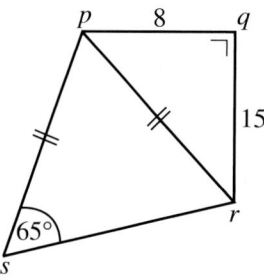

15. In the diagram, $ps \perp qr$.

    $|\angle pqr| = 28°$, $|\angle prq| = 72°$ and $|qr| = 100$ m.

    Calculate   **(i)** $|pq|$, correct to one decimal place

                  (ii) $|ps|$ (using your answer from part **(i)**)

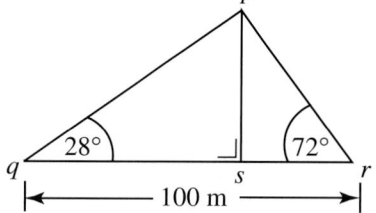

16. In the diagram, $ab \perp ac$, $|ab| = 21$ m and $|ac| = 20$ m.

    Calculate   **(i)** $|bc|$

                  (ii) $|\angle abc|$, to the nearest minute.

    $|bc| = |bd|$, and $|\angle bcd| = 54°$.

    Calculate   **(iii)** $|\angle cbd|$

                  (iv) area of triangle bcd correct to the nearest m^2

                  (v) $|cd|$, correct to the nearest m.

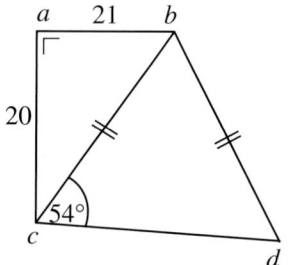

17. In the diagram, $pq \perp sq$, $|sr| = 60$ m, $|\angle psr| = 42°$ and $|\angle prq| = 65°$.

    Calculate   **(i)** $|\angle spr|$

                  (ii) $|pr|$, correct to the nearest m.

    Hence, or otherwise, calculate $|pq|$, correct to the nearest m.

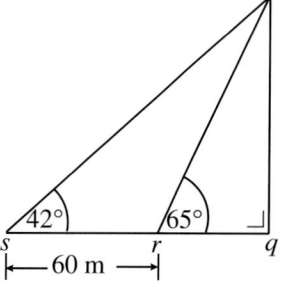

Practical applications

When solving practical problems using trigonometry represent each situation with a triangle. Mark on your triangle the angles and lengths you know and label what you need to calculate. Then use your knowledge of trigonometry to find what you are looking for.

Example ▼

A ship leaves a port p and sails in the direction S42°E for a distance of 9 km. It then changes course and sails in the direction S59°W, for a certain distance and stops. It is then in the direction S24°W, as measured from the port p.
Calculate the distance sailed by the ship, correct to one place of decimals.

Solution:

From the information in the question we construct the triangle pqr.

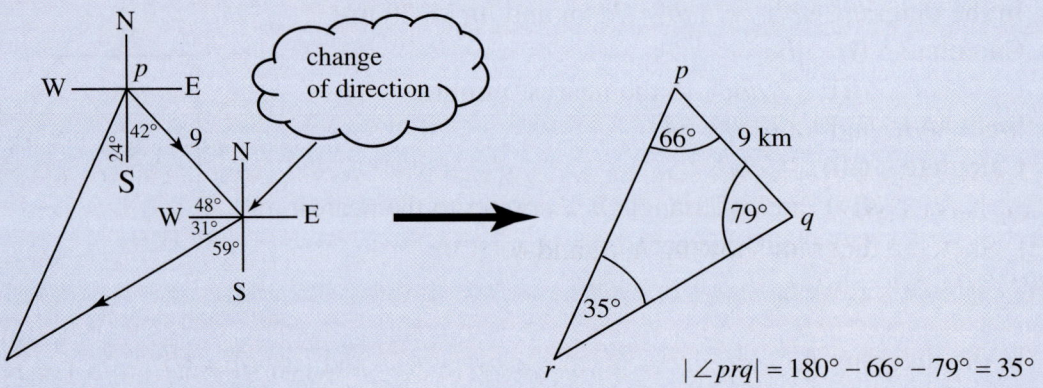

We now use our knowledge of trigonometry on triangle pqr to calculate $|qr|$.
Let $P = |\angle qpr|$, $R = |\angle prq|$, $p = |qr|$ and $r = |pq|$

$$\frac{p}{\sin P} = \frac{r}{\sin R} \qquad (p \text{ is missing, so put that first})$$

$$\frac{p}{\sin 66°} = \frac{9}{\sin 35°} \qquad (\text{put in known values})$$

$$p = \frac{9 \sin 66°}{\sin 35°} \qquad (\text{multiply both sides by } \sin 66°)$$

$$p = \frac{9(0.913545457)}{0.573576436}$$

$$p = 14.3 \qquad (\text{correct to one place of decimals})$$

Therefore the ship sailed $9 + 14.3 = 23.3$ km $\qquad$ (correct to one place of decimals)

---

1. Two ships, p and q, set sail from a harbour, h, at 14:00. p sails in the direction N60°W at 40 km/h. q sails in the direction N40°E at a steady speed. At 16:00 p is directly west of q, as shown. Calculate the speed of q, correct to one place of decimals.

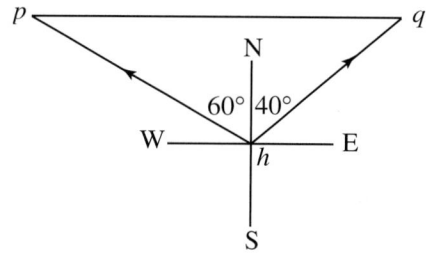

2. x and y are two checkpoints on an orienteering course, and s is the starting point. Colman runs due north from s to x, a distance of 800 m. He knows that y is on a bearing of S70°W from s and on a bearing of S25°W from x.

Calculate   **(i)** $|\angle ysx|$ **(ii)** $|\angle sxy|$ **(iii)** $|\angle xys|$
Colman runs in a straight line from x to y and from y back to s again.
Calculate the total distance run by Colman, correct to the nearest m.

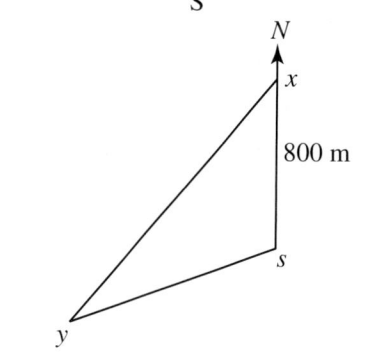

3. A ship leaves a harbour, h, and sails for 30 km in the direction N25°E to a point p. At p it changes course and then sails in the direction N70°W to a point q. From h the bearing of q is N15°W.
(i) Sketch a diagram showing h, p, and q.
(ii) Calculate $|pq|$.

4. A bird leaves a nest, n, and flies 600 m in the direction S46°E to a tree t. It then leaves t and flies in the direction S61°W to a pylon p. It then flies from p back to n. The bearing of n from p is N26°E.
Calculate, to the nearest m, the distance flown by the bird, assuming n, t, and p are the same height above the ground.

5. A surveyor wishes to measure the height of a round tower. Measuring the angle of elevation, he finds that the angle increases from 22° to 36° after walking 25 m towards the base of the tower.
Calculate the height of the tower, correct to the nearest m.

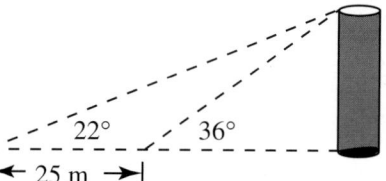

6. A ship which leaves a port, *p*, and travels south-west, with constant speed, observes the flash of a lighthouse, *l*, in a direction S60°W. After travelling for 10 km, to a point, *t*, the ship observes the flash of the same lighthouse, due west.

   (i) Sketch a diagram showing *p*, *t*, and *l*.

   (ii) Find the direction of *p* from *l*.

   (iii) Calculate how far the ship is from the lighthouse at this time i.e. calculate |*tl*|.

   (iv) Calculate how close to the lighthouse will it pass.

   (Answers to **(iii)** and **(iv)**, correct to two places of decimals).

Special angles: 45°, 30° and 60°

There are three special angles whose sines, cosines and tangents ratios can be expressed as simple fractions or surds.

$$\sin 45° = \frac{1}{\sqrt{2}}$$

$$\cos 45° = \frac{1}{\sqrt{2}}$$

$$\tan 45° = 1$$

$$\sin 60° = \frac{\sqrt{3}}{2} \qquad \sin 30° = \frac{1}{2}$$

$$\cos 60° = \frac{1}{2} \qquad \cos 30° = \frac{\sqrt{3}}{2}$$

$$\tan 60° = \sqrt{3} \qquad \tan 30° = \frac{1}{\sqrt{3}}$$

These ratios can be used instead of a calculator.

These ratios are given on page 9 of the maths tables. However, on this page the angles are measured in radians. To use this table we can convert radians to degrees by using the fact that:

$$\pi \text{ radians} = 180°$$

Thus

$\frac{\pi}{2}$ radians = 90°	$\frac{\pi}{3}$ radians = 60°	$\frac{\pi}{4}$ radians = 45°	$\frac{\pi}{6}$ radians = 30°

Without using a calculator, find the value of:

(i) $\tan 45° + \sin 30°$ **(ii)** $\sin^2 60° + \cos^2 45°$

Solution:

(i) $\tan 45° + \sin 30°$

$= 1 + \dfrac{1}{2}$

$= \dfrac{3}{2}$

(ii) $\sin^2 60° + \cos^2 45°$

$= \left(\dfrac{\sqrt{3}}{2}\right)^2 + \left(\dfrac{1}{\sqrt{2}}\right)^2$

$= \dfrac{3}{4} + \dfrac{1}{2} = \dfrac{5}{4}$

Note: $\sin^2 A = (\sin A)^2$, $\cos^2 A = (\cos A)^2$ and $\tan^2 A = (\tan A)^2$

Exercise 19.10 ▼

1. Complete the following tables:

A	30°	45°	60°
$\cos A$			
$\sin A$		$\dfrac{1}{\sqrt{2}}$	
$\tan A$			

A	30°	45°	60°
$\cos^2 A$			
$\sin^2 A$			
$\tan^2 A$		1	

Without using a calculator, evaluate each of the following, exactly:

2. $\cos 60° + \sin 30°$ **3.** $\cos^2 45° + \sin 30°$ **4.** $1 + \tan^2 60°$

5. $\cos^2 45° + \tan 45°$ **6.** $\tan 45° - \tan^2 30°$ **7.** $2 \cos 30° \sin 60°$

8. $1 - \cos^2 30°$ **9.** $\cos^3 60° + \cos^2 45°$ **10.** $3 \tan^2 30° - 2 \cos 60°$

11. Verify that **(i)** $\dfrac{1 + \tan 60° \tan 30°}{\cos^2 45°} = 4$ **(ii)** $\tan^2 30 . \sin^2 60 = \dfrac{1}{4}$

12. If $A = 30°$, verify that:

(i) $\sin 2A = 2 \sin A \cos A$ **(ii)** $\cos 2A = \cos^2 A - \sin^2 A$

13. If $\theta = 60°$, verify that:

(i) $\cos^2 60° + \sin^2 60° = 1$ **(ii)** $\dfrac{\sin \theta}{\cos \theta} = \tan \theta$

Unit circle

The unit circle has its centre at the origin (0, 0) and the length of the radius is 1.
Take any point $p(x, y)$ on the circle, making an angle of θ, from the centre.

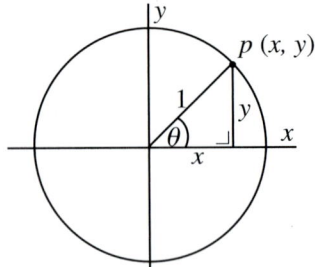

$$\cos \theta = \frac{x}{1} = x$$

$$\sin \theta = \frac{y}{1} = y$$

$$\tan \theta = \frac{y}{x} = \frac{\sin \theta}{\cos \theta}$$

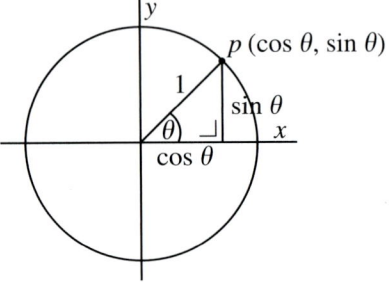

This very important result indicates that the coordinates of any point on the unit circle can be represented by $p(\cos \theta, \sin \theta)$, where θ is any angle.

As the point p rotates, θ changes. These definitions of $\cos \theta$ and $\sin \theta$ in terms of the coordinates of a point rotating around the unit circle apply for **all** values of the angle $\theta°$.
Memory Aid: (christian name, surname) = $(\cos \theta, \sin \theta) = (x, y)$

Note: Using Pythagoras's theorem: $\cos^2 \theta + \sin^2 \theta = 1$

Values of sin, cos and tan for 0°, 90°, 180°, 270° and 360°

Both diagrams below represent the unit circle but using two different notations to describe any point p on the circle.

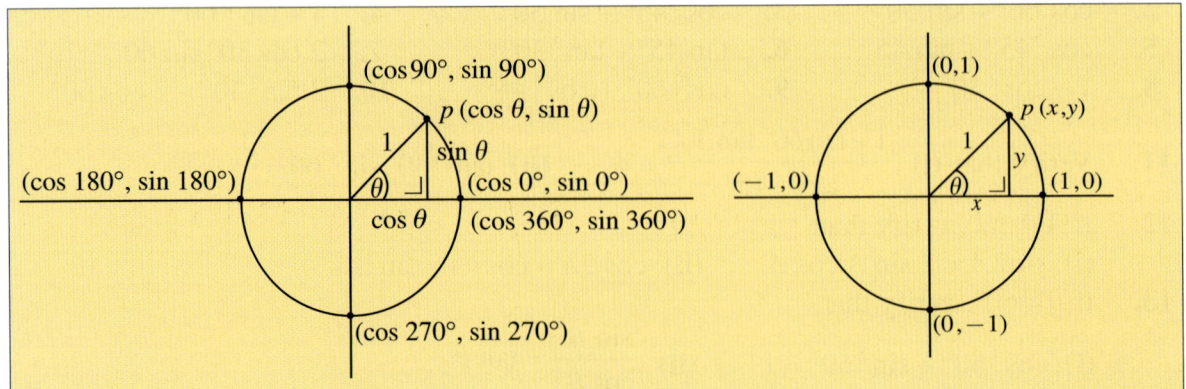

By comparing corresponding points on both unit circles, the values of sin, cos and tan for 0°, 90°, 180°, 270° and 360°, can be read directly.

$(\cos 0°, \sin 0°) = (\cos 360°, \sin 360°) = (1, 0)$ $\cos 0° = \cos 360° = 1$ $\sin 0° = \sin 360° = 0$ $\tan 0° = \tan 360° = \frac{0}{1} = 0$	$(\cos 90°, \sin 90°) = (0, 1)$ $\cos 90° = 0$ $\sin 90° = 1$ $\tan 90° = \frac{1}{0}$ (undefined)
$(\cos 180°, \sin 180°) = (-1, 0)$ $\cos 180° = -1$ $\sin 180° = 0$ $\tan 180° = \frac{0}{-1} = 0$	$(\cos 270°, \sin 270°) = (0, -1)$ $\cos 270° = 0$ $\sin 270° = -1$ $\tan 270° = \frac{-1}{0}$ (undefined)

Note: Division by zero is undefined.

Example ▼

(i) Find the value of A for which $\cos A = -1$, $0° \leqslant A \leqslant 360°$.
(ii) If $0° \leqslant A \leqslant 360°$, find the value of A for which $\sin A = 1$.
(iii) If $0° \leqslant A \leqslant 360°$, find the values of A for which $\cos A = 0$.
(iv) Evaluate $\sin^2 270$.

Solution:

Draw the unit circle.
Remember: (christian name, surname) $= (\cos \theta, \sin \theta) = (x, y)$.

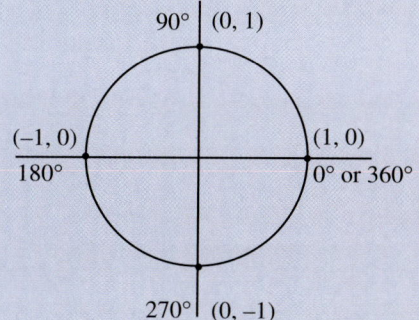

(i) $\cos A = -1$
$\Rightarrow A = 180°$

(ii) $\sin A = 1$
$\Rightarrow A = 90°$

(iii) $\cos A = 0$
$\Rightarrow A = 90°$ or $270°$

(iv) $\sin^2 270$
$= (\sin 270)^2$
$= (-1)^2 = 1$

Evaluate each of the following, without using a calculator:

1. cos 90° **2.** sin 180° **3.** cos 0°
4. sin 90° **5.** cos 180° **6.** sin 270°
7. sin 360° **8.** cos 270° **9.** tan 180°

10. $\dfrac{2\cos 180°}{\sin 90°}$ **11.** $\dfrac{3\sin 270°}{\cos^2 180°}$ **12.** $\dfrac{\sin^2 270° + \cos^2 180°}{2\cos 0°}$

13. sin 180°cos 90° + cos 180° sin 90°   **14.** (sin 90° − cos 180°)^2

Solve for A, where $0° \leqslant A \leqslant 360°$:

15. cos $A = 1$ **16.** sin $A = 1$ **17.** sin $A = -1$
18. cos $A = -1$ **19.** cos $A = 0$ **20.** sin $A = 0$
21. tan $A = 0$
22. If cos $A = 0$, find the two values of sin A, when $0° \leqslant A \leqslant 360°$.

Trigonometric ratios for angles between 0° and 360°

The x and y axes divide the plane into four quadrants.
Consider the unit circle on the right:

$$\cos \theta = x \qquad \sin \theta = y$$

$$\tan \theta = \frac{\sin \theta}{\cos \theta} = \frac{y}{x}$$

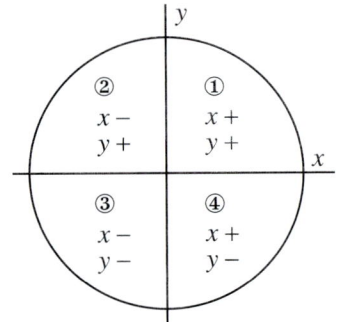

By examining the signs of x and y in the four
quadrants, the signs of sin θ, cos θ, and tan θ
for any value of θ can be found.

Summary of signs

1st quadrant: sin, cos and tan are all positive.
2nd quadrant: sin is positive, cos and tan are negative.
3rd quadrant: tan is positive, sin and cos are negative.
4th quadrant: cos is positive, sin and tan are negative.
A very useful memory aid, *CAST*, in the diagram
on the right, shows the ratios that are positive for the
angles between 0° and 360°.

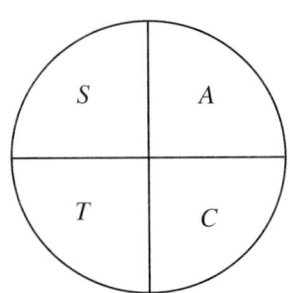

Method for finding the trigonometric ratio for any angle between 0° and 360°.

1. Draw a rough diagram of the angle.
2. Determine in which quadrant the angle lies and use $\boxed{\begin{array}{c|c} S & A \\ \hline T & C \end{array}}$ to find its sign.

3. Find its **related** angle (the acute angle to nearest horizontal).
4. Use the trigonometric ratio of the related angle with the sign in step 2.

Example ▼

Find cos 210°, leaving your answer in surd form.

Solution:

Surd form, ∴ cannot use calculator.
1. The diagram shows the angle 210°.
2. 210° is in the 3rd quadrant.
   cos is negative in the 3rd quadrant.
3. Related angle is 30°.
4. ∴ cos 210°
   $= -\cos 30°$

   $= -\dfrac{\sqrt{3}}{2}$

   (or use tables page 9)

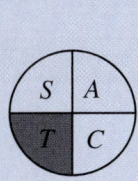

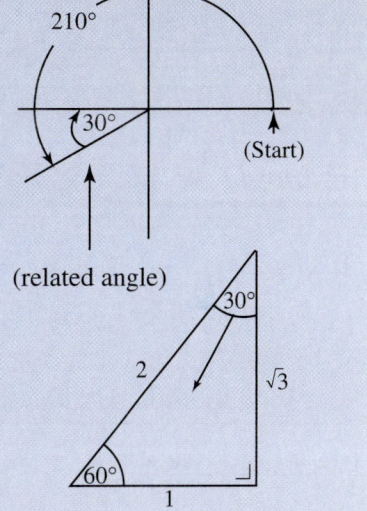

(Start)

(related angle)

Exercise 19.12 ▼

Without using a calculator, evaluate each of the following exactly:

1. sin 150°
2. cos 120°
3. sin 210°
4. tan 240°
5. tan 135°
6. sin 300°
7. cos 135°
8. tan 210°
9. sin 315°
10. tan 330°
11. cos 150°
12. cos 225°
13. tan 315° − sin 330°
14. cos 150° + sin 120°
15. $\cos^2 150° + \tan^2 210°$
16. $\tan^2 225° - 2\cos 240°$
17. If sin 150° = sin A, find A, if 0° ⩽ A ⩽ 90°.
18. If cos 300° = cos A, find A, if 0° ⩽ A ⩽ 90°.
19. If tan 225° = tan A, find A, if 0° ⩽ A ⩽ 90°.
20. If sin 315° = − sin A, find A, if 0° ⩽ A ⩽ 90°.

Solving trigonometric equations

Between $0°$ and $360°$ there may be two angles with the same trigonometric ratio.

For example, $\cos 120° = -\frac{1}{2}$ and $\cos 240° = -\frac{1}{2}$.

To solve a trigonometric equation do the following:

1. Ignore the sign and calculate the related angle.
2. From the sign of the given ratio decide, in which quadrants the angles lie.

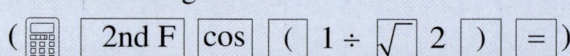

3. Using a rough diagram, state the angles between $0°$ and $360°$.

Example ▼

If $\cos \theta = -\dfrac{1}{\sqrt{2}}$, find two values of θ between $0°$ and $360°$.

Solution:

1. Find the related angle (ignore sign).

   If $\cos \theta = \dfrac{1}{\sqrt{2}}$,

   $\Rightarrow \qquad \theta = 45°$

   The related angle is $45°$.

   (🖩 | 2nd F | cos | (| 1 ÷ | √ | 2 |) | = |)

2. cos is negative in the 2nd and 3rd quadrant.

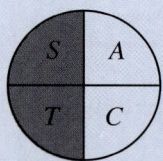

3. Rough diagram.

   θ in the 2nd quadrant θ in the 3rd quadrant

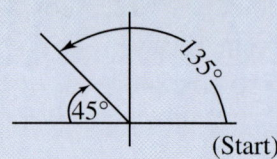

   $\theta = 135°$ $\theta = 225°$

   Thus, if $\cos\theta = -\dfrac{1}{\sqrt{2}}$, $\theta = 135°, 225°$

If $100 \sin A = 43$, find the two values of A in $0° \leqslant A \leqslant 360°$, correct to the nearest minute.

Solution:

1. Find the related angle.

$$100 \sin A = 43$$
$$\sin A = \tfrac{43}{100}$$
$$A = \sin^{-1} \tfrac{43}{100}$$
$$A = 25°28'$$

 (2nd F   sin 43 $a\frac{b}{c}$ 100 = 2nd F   DMS)

2. Sin is positive in the 1st and 2nd quadrant.

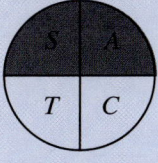

3. Rough diagram

A in the 1st quadrant A in the 2nd quadrant

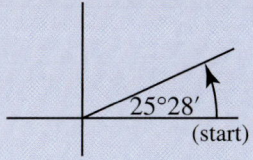   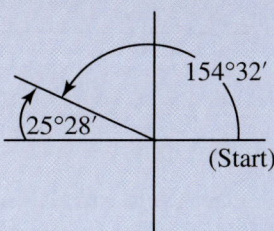

$A = 25°28'$ $A = 154°32'$

Thus, if $100 \sin A = 43$, $A = 25°28'$ or $A = 154°32'$

Find all the values of θ, between $0°$ and $360°$ if:

1. $\sin\theta = \frac{1}{2}$

2. $\cos\theta = \frac{1}{2}$

3. $\sin\theta = -\frac{\sqrt{3}}{2}$

4. $\tan\theta = \frac{1}{\sqrt{3}}$

5. $\tan\theta = -\sqrt{3}$

6. $\sin\theta = \frac{1}{\sqrt{2}}$

7. $\cos\theta = \frac{\sqrt{3}}{2}$

8. $\tan\theta = 1$

9. $\sin\theta = -\frac{1}{2}$

10. $\sin\theta = -\frac{1}{\sqrt{2}}$

11. $\tan\theta = -\frac{1}{\sqrt{3}}$

12. $\tan\theta = -1$

13. $\sqrt{2}\cos\theta = 1$

14. $2\sin\theta - \sqrt{3} = 0$

15. $\tan\theta - \sqrt{3} = 0$

Find all the values of A, between $0°$ and $360°$, correct to the nearest degree, if:

16. $\sin A = 0.342$

17. $\cos A = -0.8192$

18. $\tan A = 1.1106$

Find all the values of A, between $0°$ and $360°$, correct to the nearest minute, if:

19. $\tan A = 2.2251$

20. $\sin A = -0.6074$

21. $\cos A = 0.5925$

22. $4\tan A = 5$

23. $5\sin A = 2$

24. $3\cos A = -1$

Chapter test

1. A is an acute angle such that $\tan A = \frac{3}{4}$.

 (i) Find, as fractions, $\cos A$ and $\sin A$.

 (ii) Show that $\cos^2 A + \sin^2 A = 1$.

 (iii) Construct the angle A.

2. θ is an acute angle such that $\cos\theta = \frac{2}{5}$.

 Construct the angle θ.

3. A is an acute angle such that $\cos A = \frac{1}{2}$.

 Find **(i)** A **(ii)** $\cos\frac{A}{2}$

4. In $\triangle pqr$, $|\angle pqr| = 90°$, $|pq| = 1.5$ and $|qr| = 0.8$.

 Find **(i)** $|pr|$ **(ii)** $|\angle qpr|$, correct to the nearest minute.

5. A tree, 8 m in height, casts a shadow of 12 m on horizontal ground.

 Calculate the angle of elevation of the sun, correct to the nearest minute.

6. A fishing boat is 180 m from the bottom of a vertical cliff. From the top of the cliff the angle of depression to the fishing boat is 32°.

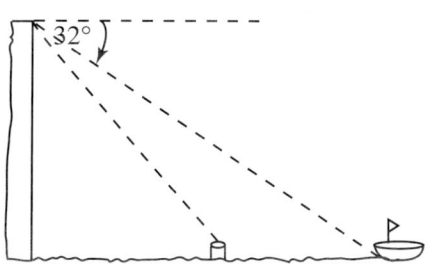

    (i) Calculate the height of the cliff, correct to one place of decimals.

    (ii) A buoy is 90 m from the bottom of the cliff. Calculate the angle of depression to the buoy from the top of the cliff, correct to the nearest minute.

7. Express   **(i)** sin 240°   **(ii)** tan 330° as surds.

8. The area of triangle pqr is 27 cm^2.
Calculate $|\angle pqr|$,
if $|pq| = 9$ cm and $|qr| = 12$ cm.

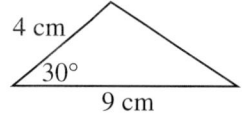

9. Construct an angle A such that tan $A = 0.3$.

10. Two ships G and H sailed from the same port at the same time. G sailed in the direction S32°W while H sailed in the direction S58°E. After a certain time the two ships were 5 km apart and G was then due West of H. How far had the ship H sailed? Give your answer correct to two places of decimals.

11. If sin $A = 0$, find the three values of A in $0° \leqslant A \leqslant 360°$.

12. (a) Calculate the area of the triangle in the diagram.

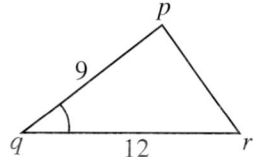

    (b) A ladder which is 6 m long leans against a vertical wall. The foot of the ladder is on level ground at a distance of 1 m from the bottom of the wall.
Find the measure of the angle which the ladder makes with the ground, correct to the nearest minute.

    (c) In the triangle pqr, $|pq| = 3$ m, $|\angle prq| = 23°35'$ and $|\angle qpr| = 35°$.

        (i) Find $|qr|$, correct to one place of decimals.

        (ii) t is a point on the line pq such that $|\angle qrt| = 68°17'$. Find $|qt|$, correct to one place of decimals.

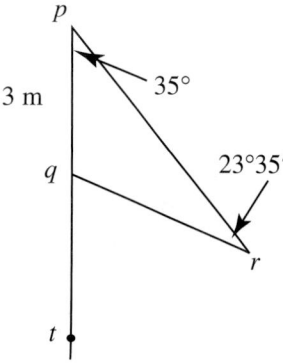

13. (a) If $\tan A = \frac{8}{15}$, $0° \leqslant A \leqslant 90°$, express $\sin A$ and $\cos A$ as fractions.

Verify that $\sin^2 A + \cos^2 A = 1$

(b) In the diagram, o is the centre of the circle with radius length 5 and p and q are points on the circle. $|\angle poq| = 80°$.

Find, correct to two places of decimals

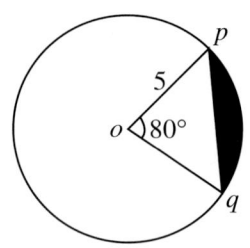

   (i) the area of triangle poq

   (ii) the area of the shaded region, assuming, $\pi = 3.14$.

(c) Construct an angle A, such that $\cos A = \frac{4}{5}$

(d) A hare escaping from a dog ran in a triangular pattern.

The diagram shows the path of the escape.

Calculate, to the nearest metre, the distance run by the hare.

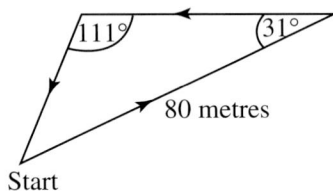

14. (a) In triangle prq, $|\angle pqr| = 90°$, $|pr| = 26$ and $|qr| = 10$.

   (i) Calculate $|pq|$.

   (ii) Express $\tan \angle prq$ as a fraction.

   (iii) Calculate the area of triangle pqr.

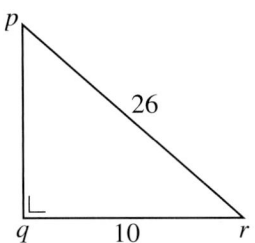

(b) A girl standing on level ground casts a shadow 2.3 metres long.

The angle of elevation of the sun is 27°.

Calculate the girl's height to the nearest centimetre.

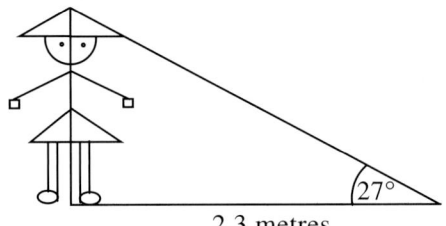

(c) A garden $pqrs$ is in the shape of a quadrilateral.

$|pq| = 22.5$ m, $|ps| = 12$ m, $|rs| = 18$ m and $|\angle srq| = 80°$.

If $|\angle qps| = 90°$,

find the value of :

   (i) $|qs|$

   (ii) $|\angle rqs|$, correct to the nearest degree.

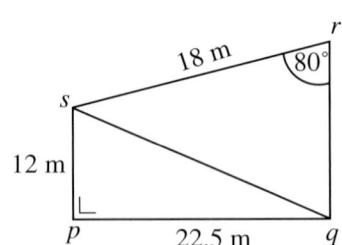

(d) $\cos A = -0.7914$. Find the two values for A in $0° \leqslant A \leqslant 360°$, correct to the nearest minute.

15. (a) In the triangle *abc*, $|ab| = 7$ m, $|bc| = 8$ m and $|\angle abc| = 42°$. Calculate the area of the triangle, correct to one place of decimals.

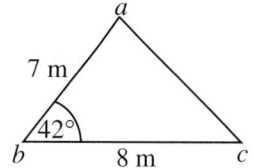

(b) The diagram shows a vertical pole which stands on level ground.
A cable joins the top of the pole to a point on the ground which is 50 m from the base of the pole.
The cable makes an angle of 66° 25′ with the ground.

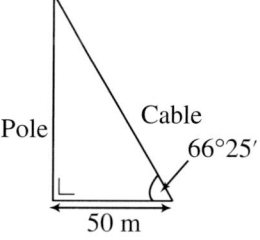

    (i) Find the height of the pole, correct to the nearest metre.
    (ii) Find the length of the cable, correct to the nearest metre.

(c) In the diagram, the triangle *zxy* is right-angled,
$|zx| = 8$ m, $|zy| = 15$ m,
$|xy| = |xw|$ and $xw \parallel zy$.

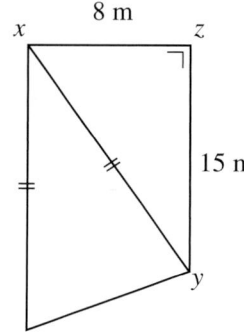

    (i) Find $|xy|$.
    (ii) Express $\sin \angle wxy$ as a fraction.
    (iii) Find the area of triangle *wxy*.
    (iv) Find $|\angle xwy|$, correct to the nearest minute.
    (v) Find $|wy|$, correct to two places of decimals.

16. (a) The isosceles triangle in the diagram has base 6, perpendicular height *h* and perimeter 16.
Find the value of *h*.

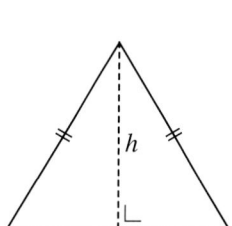

(b) In the triangle *abc*, $|ab| = 5$ cm and $|\angle abc| = 90°$.
The point *d* is on $[bc]$.
$|bd| = 12$ cm and $|ad| = |dc|$.

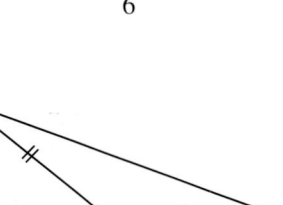

    (i) Find $|ad|$.
    (ii) Find $|\angle acb|$, correct to the nearest minute.

(c) The area of the triangle *pqr* is 9,028 m², |*pq*| = 200 m and |∠*pqr*| = 47°44′.

    (i) Find |*qr*|, correct to the nearest metre. *qt* is perpendicular to *pq*, as shown, and |∠*qtr*| = 37°35′.

    (ii) Find |*rt*|, correct to the nearest metre.

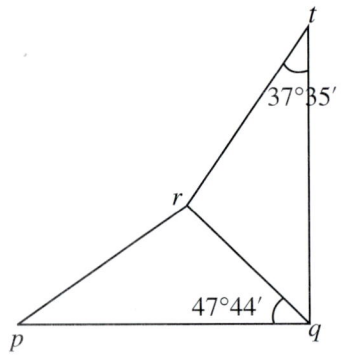

17. (a) Complete the following table:

θ	30°	45°	60°	90°	120°	135°	150°	180°	210°	225°	240°	270°	300°	315°	330°	360°
sin θ			$\frac{\sqrt{3}}{2}$											$-\frac{1}{\sqrt{2}}$		
cos θ								−1					$\frac{1}{2}$			
tan θ				μ												

Note: In this case, μ stands for undefined.

(b) The area of triangle *abc* is 16, |*ac*| = 8, |*bc*| = 10, |*cd*| = 6 and |*ce*| = 5.

    (i) Write sin ∠*bca* as a fraction.

    (ii) Explain why |∠*bca*| = |∠*ecd*|.

    (iii) Hence, or otherwise, calculate the area of triangle *cde*.

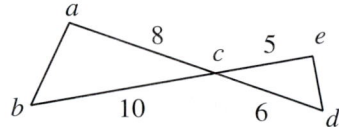

(c) A golfer takes two shots to sink a golf ball into the 3rd hole on a golf course. The distance from the tee to the hole is 380 m. Her first shot is 10° off the line to the hole as shown. The angle between the tee, where the first shot landed and the hole is 140°.

Calculate the distance of:

    (i) the first shot

    (ii) the second shot

        (give both answers correct to the nearest metre).

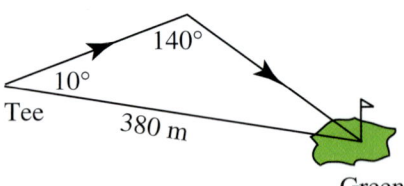

18. (a) In the diagram, $b = 3$, $c = 4$ and $A = 90°$.
Calculate l, the sum of the lengths of the
three sides of the triangle.
Hence, find the value of k if
$k \tan B = l$.

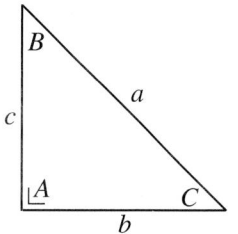

(b) A circle with centre o contains the point p.
pq is a tangent.
$|\angle poq| = 36°52'$ and $|oq| = 5$ cm.

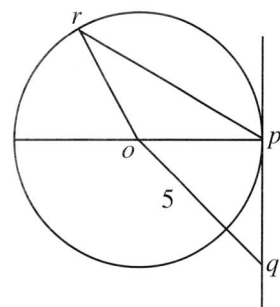

(i) Write down the value of $|\angle opq|$.
(ii) Calculate $\cos 36°52'$, correct to one
decimal place.
(iii) Hence, or otherwise, calculate $|op|$,
the length of the radius of the circle.
(iv) r is another point on the circle and
$\angle rop$ is obtuse as shown. If the area
of triangle rop is 6.48 cm^2,
calculate $|\angle rop|$, correct to the
nearest minute.

(c) x, y and z are three points on level ground.
From x the direction of y is North 45° East.
From x the direction of z is North 22°30′ West.
z is due West of y. $|xy| = 5$ m.
Copy the diagram and indicate on your
diagram the position of z.
Calculate $|xz|$, correct to one place of
decimals.

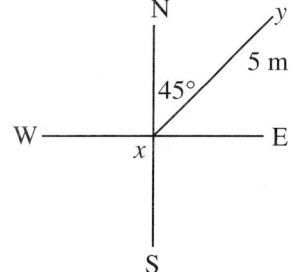

19. (a) If $\sin A = \frac{1}{\sqrt{2}}$, for $0° \leqslant A \leqslant 90°$, find:

    (i) $2 \sin A$

    (ii) $\sin 2A$

(b) pt and qs intersect at r.

    $|\angle pqr| = 90°$, $|pr| = 5$, $|qr| = 4$,

    $|rs| = 2.5$ and area $\triangle pqr =$ area $\triangle rst$.

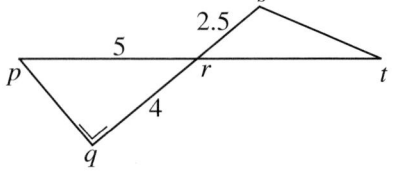

    (i)   Find $|pq|$.

    (ii) Find the area of triangle pqr.

    (iii) Express $\sin \angle prq$ as fraction.

    (iv) Calculate $|rt|$.

(c) In the diagram

    $|\angle krm| = 13°18'$, $|\angle rkm| = 30°$,

    $|\angle kmp| = 68°26'$, $kp \perp mp$ and $|rm| = 10$.

    Calculate $|kp|$, correct to two places of decimals.

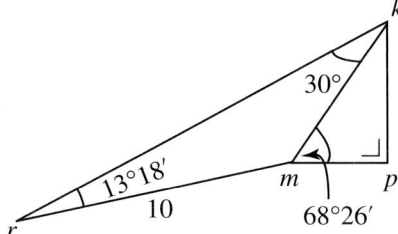

20. (a) (i) If $\sin \theta = \frac{\sqrt{3}}{2}$, find θ, $0° < \theta < 90°$.

    (ii) If $\sin \theta = -\frac{\sqrt{3}}{2}$, find two possible

         values of θ, $0° < \theta < 360°$.

(b) In the right-angled triangle xyz,

    yw bisects $\angle xyz$. $|xw| = 4$ and $|xy| = 6$.

    Calculate:

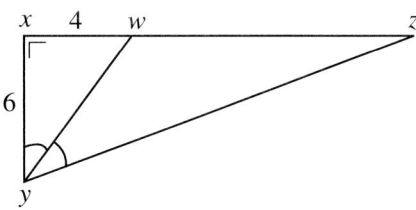

    (i) $|\angle xyw|$, correct to the nearest minute.

    (ii) $|zw|$, correct to one place of decimals.

(c) p, q and r are three boats at rest on a lake.

    $|pq| = 3.2$ km.

    From p, the direction of r is N40°40′E.

    From p, the direction of q is S64°49′E.

    From q, the direction of r is N17°05′E.

    Calculate $|pr|$, correct to two places of decimals.

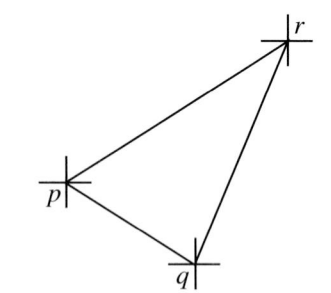

21. (a) From a point p outside the circle, centre o, the tangent pr is drawn and the line po cuts the circle at q.
If $|pq| = 2$ and $|\angle opr| = 30°$ calculate the radius length of the circle.

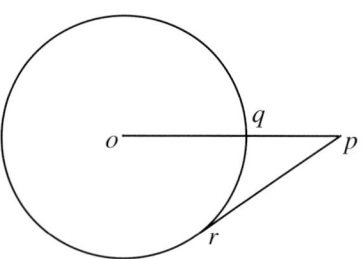

(b) $\cos A = -1$, find the value of A, $0° \leqslant A \leqslant 360°$.

(c) (i) Express $\sin 60°$ in surd form.

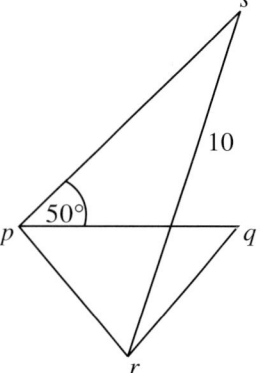

(ii) In triangle pqr,
$|pq| = |qr| = |rp|$.
If the area of triangle pqr is
$4\sqrt{3}$ cm², find $|pq|$.

(iii) If $|\angle spq| = 50°$ and
$|sr| = 10$ cm,
calculate $|\angle psr|$, correct to the nearest minute.

(d) A ship leaves port P and sails S42°E at a steady speed for a distance of 4.5 km.
It then changes course and sails S52°42′W for 0.5 hours at the same steady speed.
It is then in the direction S23°30′W, as measured from the port P.
Calculate the steady speed correct to the nearest km/h.

(e) $\sin \theta = \frac{1}{2}$. Write two values for θ in $0° \leqslant \theta \leqslant 180°$.
Hence write the two corresponding values for $\cos \theta$.

ANGLES, TRIANGLES AND QUADRILATERALS

Types and names of angles

Angles may be considered to be an amount of turning or rotation.
Angles are usually measured in degrees, using the symbol °.

Acute angle	**Right angle**	**Obtuse angle**	**Straight angle**
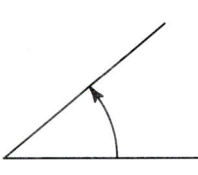	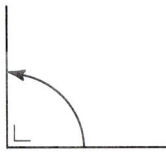	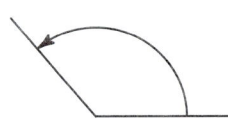	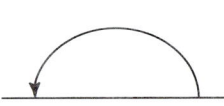
less than 90°	equal to 90°	between 90° and 180°	equal to 180°

Reflex angle	**Complimentary angles**	**Supplementary angles**	**Angles at a point**
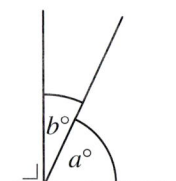		 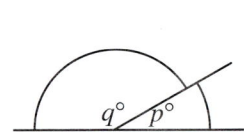	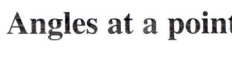
between 180° and 360°	These add up to 90° $a° + b° = 90°$	These add up to 180° $p° + q° = 180°$	These add up to 360° $a° + b° + c° = 360°$

Vertically opposite angles

$a° = c°$ and $b° = d°$

a and c are vertically opposite angles

b and d are vertically opposite angles

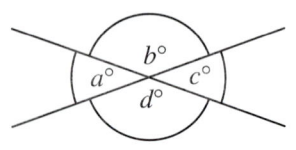

Angles formed by parallel lines

Corresponding angles

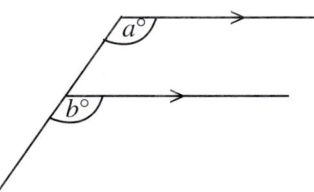

These are equal
$$a° = b°$$

Alternate angles

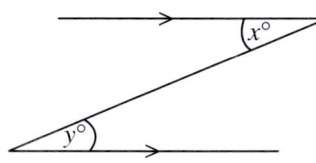

These are equal
$$x° = y°$$

Interior angles

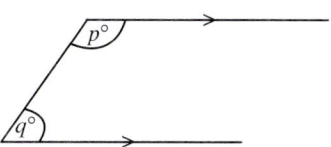

These add up to 180°
$$p° + q° = 180°$$

Angles in triangles

Angle sum of a triangle	**Exterior angle of a triangle**
The three angles of a triangle add up to 180°. 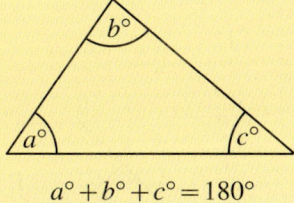 $$a° + b° + c° = 180°$$	If one side is produced, the exterior angle is equal to the sum of the two interior opposite angles. 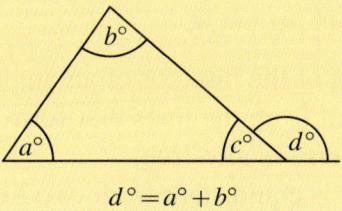 $$d° = a° + b°$$

Special triangles

Equilateral triangle	**Isosceles triangle**	**Right-angled triangle**
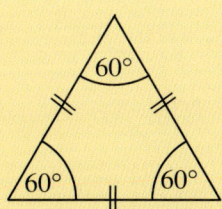 3 sides equal 3 equal angles All angles are equal to 60°	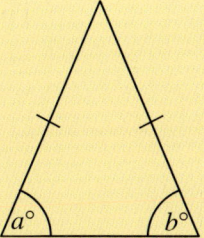 2 sides equal base angles are equal $$a° = b°$$ (base angles are the angles opposite the equal sides)	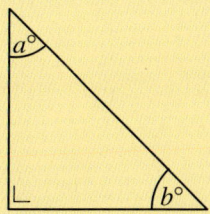 One angle is 90° The other two angles add up to 90°. $$a° + b° = 90°$$

Notes: (i) If two sides of a triangle are of unequal length, then the angles opposite these sides are unequal in measure and the larger angle is opposite the longer side.

(ii) Any two sides of a triangle are together greater than the third side.

Perpendicular bisector of a line segment

Any point on the perpendicular bisector, M, of a line segment, $[a\,b]$, is equidistant from a and b.

The converse is also true.

Any point equidistant from a and b, lies on M, the perpendicular bisector of the line segment $[a\,b]$.

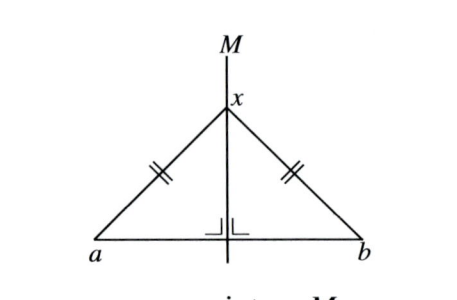

x any point on M,
the perpendicular bisector of $[a\,b]$.
Then $|xa| = |xb|$ and vice versa.

Note: The perpendicular bisector of a line segment is also called the '**mediator**'.

Bisector of an angle

Any point of the bisector of an angle, B, is equidistant from the lines that form the angle.

The converse is also true.

If a point is equidistant from two lines that form an angle, then the point is on the bisector, B, of the angle.

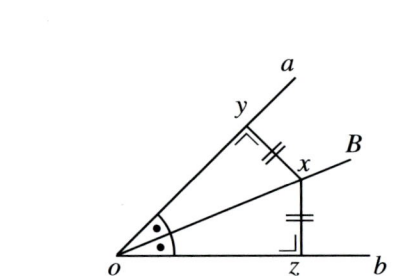

x any point on B, the bisector of $\angle aob$.
Then, $|xy| = |xz|$ and vice versa.

Special quadrilaterals (four sided figures)

Square

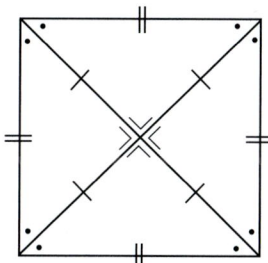

Four equal sides, opposite sides parallel, diagonals bisect each other at 90°.
All interior angles are 90° and diagonals bisect interior angles.

Rectangle

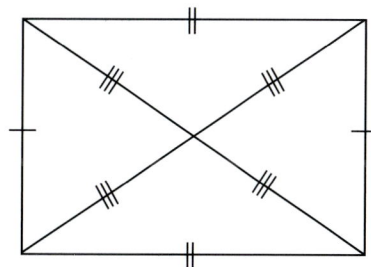

Opposite sides are equal and parallel, all interior angles are 90°, and diagonals bisect each other.

Parallelogram

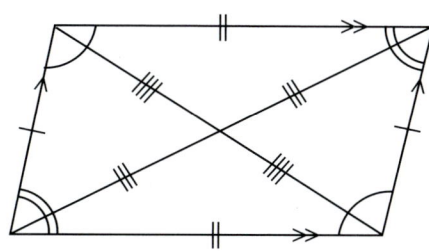

Opposite sides equal and parallel, opposite angles are equal, diagonals bisect each other.

Rhombus

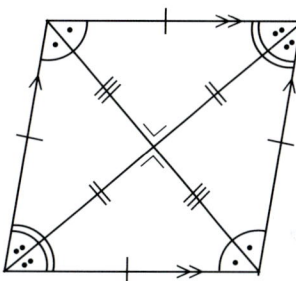

Four equal sides, opposite sides parallel, opposite angles are equal, diagonals bisect each other at right angles, diagonals bisect opposite angles.

In each case the diagonal bisects the area of the figure.

Note: The interior angles of a quadrilateral add up to 360°, as the quadrilateral can be divided into two triangles.

Calculate the value of *x* and the value of *y*.

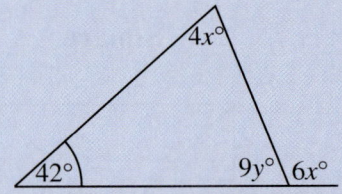

Solution:

$$6x = 4x + 42 \text{ (exterior angle)}$$
$$2x = 42$$
$$x = 21$$

$$6x + 9y = 180 \quad \text{(straight angle)}$$
$$\downarrow$$
$$6(21) + 9y = 180$$
$$126 + 9y = 180$$
$$9y = 54$$
$$y = 6$$

Alternatively, $4x + 9y + 42 = 180$ (three angles in a triangle)

and $6x + 9y = 180$ (straight angle)

Then solve these simultaneous equations, to get $x = 21$ and $y = 6$.

Exercise 20.1 ▼

Calculate the values of the letters representing the angles in each of the following diagrams (arrows indicate parallel lines):

1.

(angles shown: $a°$, $74°$, $62°$, $b°$)

2.

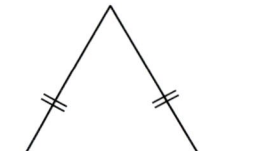

(angles shown: $x°$, $y°$)

3.

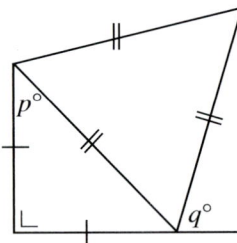

(angles shown: $p°$, $q°$)

4.

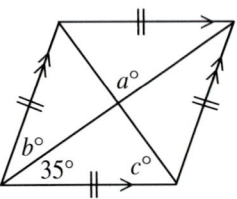

(angles shown: $a°$, $b°$, $35°$, $c°$)

5.

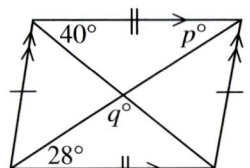

(angles shown: $40°$, $p°$, $q°$, $28°$)

6.

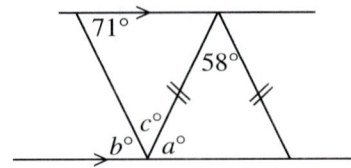

(angles shown: $71°$, $58°$, $b°$, $c°$, $a°$)

7.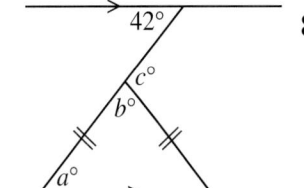

8.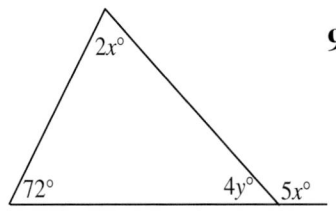

9.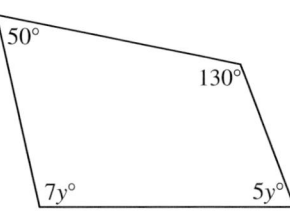

10.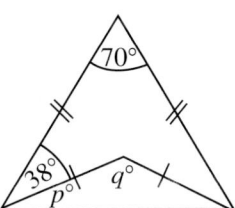

11.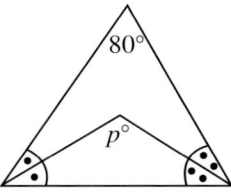

12.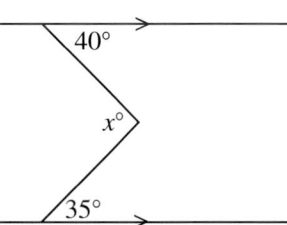

13.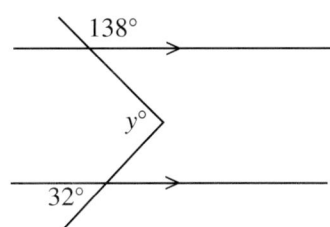

14. The angles in a triangle are in the ratio $3\frac{1}{2}:2:\frac{1}{2}$. Calculate the three angles.

15. The four angles in a quadrilateral are $(3x+10)°$, $x°$, $3x°$ and $(3x+20)°$. Calculate x.

16. *abcd* is a rhombus, *aedf* is a rhombus.
   If $|\angle afd| = 78°$,
   calculate **(i)** $|\angle dbc|$
   (ii) $|\angle bae|$.

17. *pqrs* is a square.
   Calculate the value of x, y and z.

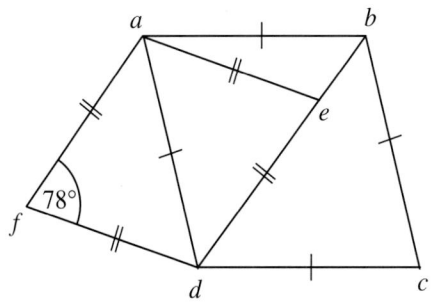

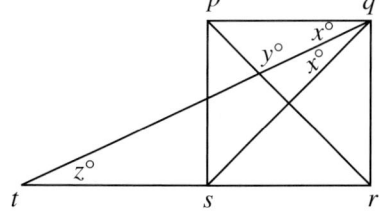

Solve for x and y :

18.

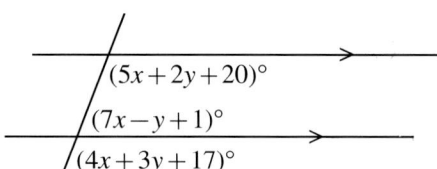

$(5x+2y+20)°$
$(7x-y+1)°$
$(4x+3y+17)°$

19.

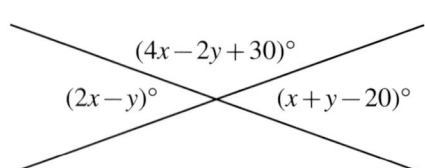

$(4x-2y+30)°$
$(2x-y)°$ $(x+y-20)°$

20.

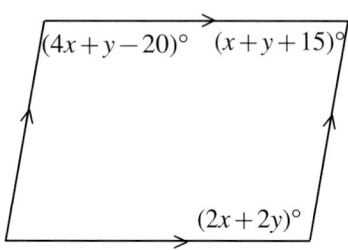

$(4x+y-20)°$ $(x+y+15)°$
$(2x+2y)°$

21.

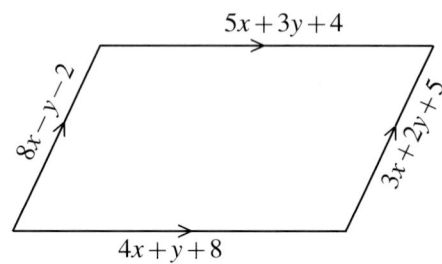

$5x+3y+4$
$8x-y-2$
$3x+2y+5$
$4x+y+8$

22. In the triangle abc, the sides ab, bc and ca are produced to e, f and d respectively, as shown. Write down the value of $|\angle dab| + |\angle bac|$.
Hence, or otherwise, find the value of $|\angle dab| + |\angle ebc| + |\angle fca|$.

23. In the diagram, $|qr| = |qs| = |ps|$ and $|\angle psq| = x°$.
Express in terms of x:
(i) $|\angle pqs|$ **(ii)** $|\angle sqr|$
If $|pq| = |pr|$, calculate the value of x.

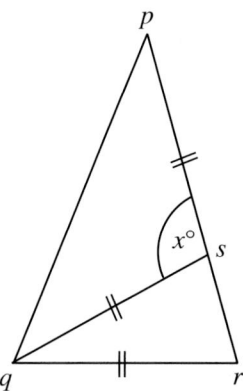

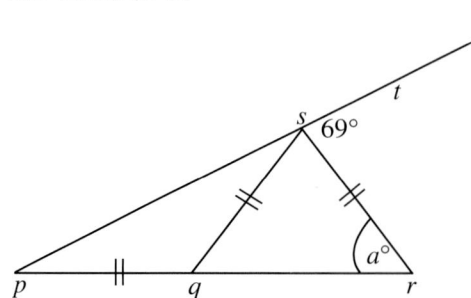

24. In the diagram, $|\angle rst| = 69°$, $|pq| = |qs| = |sr|$.
$|\angle qrs| = a°$, calculate the value of a.

Proofs

A proof in geometry should consist of five steps:

1. **Diagram**
   Draw a clear diagram, if not given, from the information given in the question.
2. **Given**
   State what is given.
3. **To prove**
   State what is to be proved.
4. **Construction**
   If necessary, state any extra lines that have to be added to the diagram to help in the proof.
   Also at this stage, if necessary, it can simplify the work if the angles are labelled with a number.
5. **Proof**
   Set out each line of the proof, justifying each statement made.

Example ▼

The line L bisects $\angle abd$
and the line K bisects $\angle cbd$.
Prove $L \perp K$.

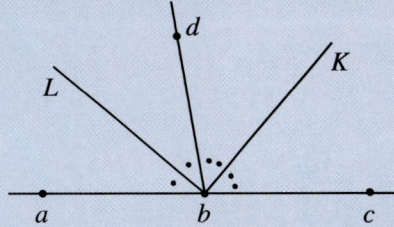

Solution:

Given:	Diagram as shown.
To prove:	$L \perp K$.
Construction:	Label angles 1, 2, 3 and 4.
	Prove $|\angle 2| + |\angle 3| = 90°$

Proof:

$$|\angle 1| + |\angle 2| + |\angle 3| + |\angle 4| = 180° \qquad \text{straight angle}$$
$$\text{but} \quad |\angle 1| = |\angle 2| \text{ and } |\angle 3| = |\angle 4| \qquad \text{given}$$
$$\therefore \quad 2|\angle 2| + 2|\angle 3| = 180°$$
$$\therefore \quad |\angle 2| + |\angle 3| = 90°$$
$$\therefore \quad L \perp K$$

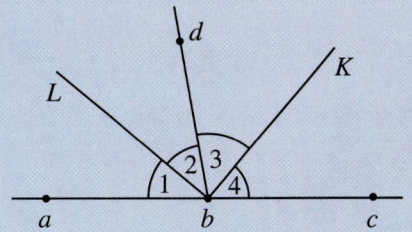

xyz is an isosceles triangle with $|xy| = |xz|$.
Prove that $|\angle xkz| > |\angle xzk|$.

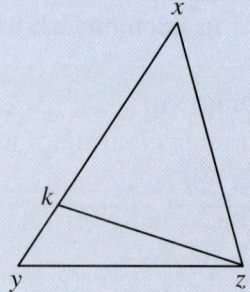

Solution:

Given: Diagram as shown.
To prove: $|\angle xkz| > |\angle xzk|$

Construction: Label angles 1, 2, 3, 4 and 5 and draw triangles *xyz* and *kyz* separately.
                    Prove $|\angle 3| > |\angle 2|$

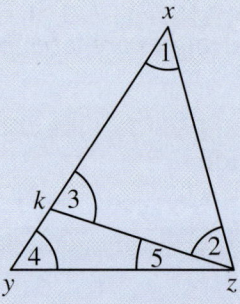 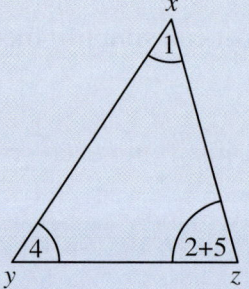 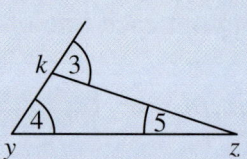

Proof: $|\angle 4| = |\angle 2| + |\angle 5|$ as $|xy| = |xz|$

∴ $|\angle 2| = |\angle 4| - |\angle 5|$

            $|\angle 3| = |\angle 4| + |\angle 5|$ exterior angle of $\triangle kyz$

∴ $|\angle 3| > |\angle 2|$ as $|\angle 4| + |\angle 5| > |\angle 4| - |\angle 5|$

∴ $|\angle xkz| > |\angle xzk|$

1. In the diagram,
$ps \parallel qr$ and $|pq| = |qr|$.
Prove that pr bisects $\angle qps$.

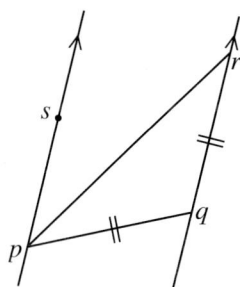

2. In the diagram,
$pq \perp qs$ and $st \parallel pq$.
Prove $|\angle qpr| = |\angle str|$.

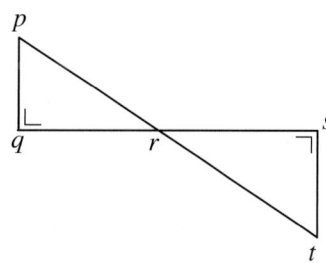

3. In the diagram,
$pr \perp rq$ and $uv \perp pq$.
Prove $|\angle rpq| = |\angle vuq|$.

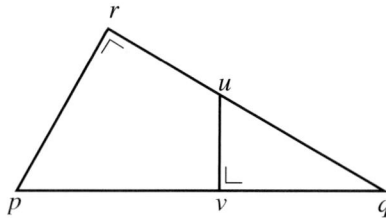

4. $L \parallel K$.
$|\angle spq| = 48°$ and $|\angle trq| = 42°$.
Prove $pq \perp qr$.

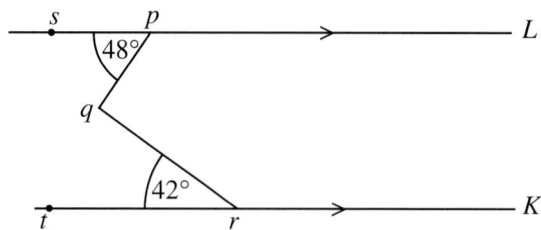

5. $pqrs$ is a parallelogram.
st bisects $\angle psr$ and vq bisects $\angle pqr$.
Prove: **(i)** $st \parallel vq$
        (ii) $|ps| = |pt|$.

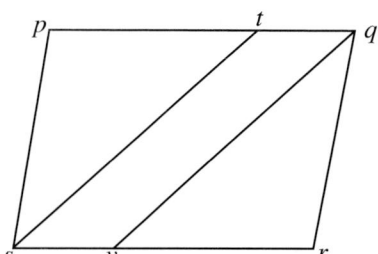

6. $abcd$ is a quadrilateral and p, q, r and s are four points as shown.
  (i) Prove $|\angle abc| + |\angle bcd| + |\angle cda| + |\angle dab| = 360°$.
  (ii) Evaluate $|\angle abc| + |\angle cbq|$.
  (iii) Prove $|\angle pab| + |\angle qbc| + |\angle rcd| + |\angle sda| = 360°$.

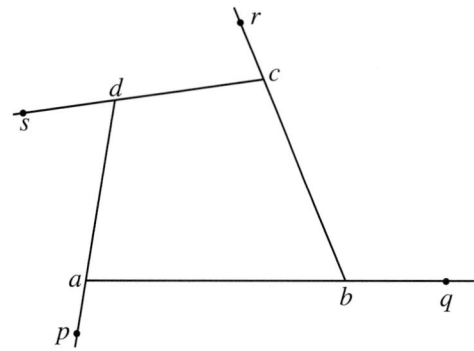

7. *abc* is a triangle with the line *bc* containing the points *d* and *e*.
Prove that
(i) $|\angle ace| > |\angle abc|$
(ii) $|\angle abd| + |\angle ace| > 180°$.

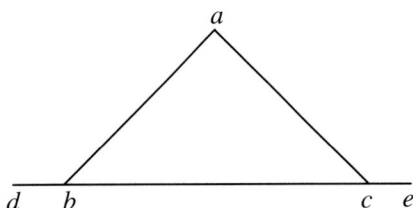

8. In the diagram,
$|\angle qpr| = 2x°$ and
$|\angle pqr| = (90 - x)°$.
Prove that triangle *pqr* is isosceles.

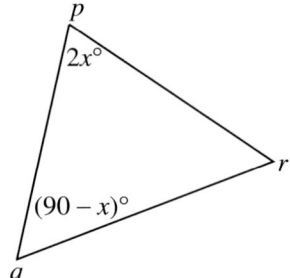

9. *pqr* is an isosceles triangle with $|pq| = |pr|$.
$|\angle srq| = 90°$
and *sq* is a straight line.
Prove that triangle *psr* is isosceles.

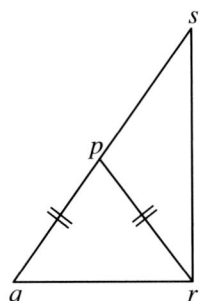

10. (i) *abc* is an isosceles triangle with $|ab| = |ac|$.
[*ba*] is produced to *d*, so that $|ad| = |ab|$.
By joining *d* to *c*, prove that $|\angle bcd| = 90°$.

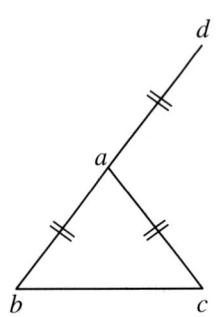

(ii) $L \parallel M$
oa bisects $\angle pab$
ob bisects $\angle qba$
Prove $|\angle aob| = 90°$.

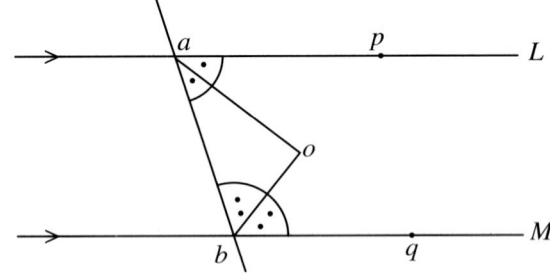

11. In the diagram $qu \perp qp$
and $|\angle quv| = |\angle kpz| = 75°$.
Prove that $vw \perp kw$.

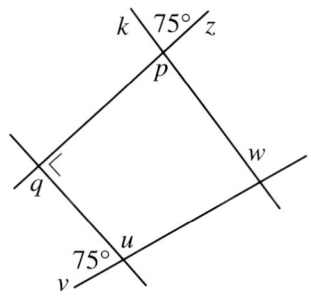

12. $abcd$ is a rectangle in which,
$|ad| = 2|ab|$
ae bisects $\angle bad$
Prove that e is the midpoint of $[bc]$.

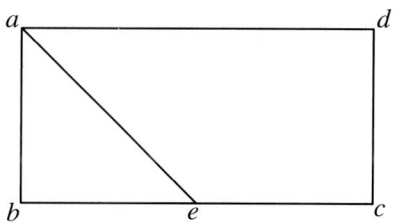

13. L is the perpendicular bisector of $[pq]$
M is the perpendicular bisector of $[qr]$
Prove that $|ps| = |rs|$.

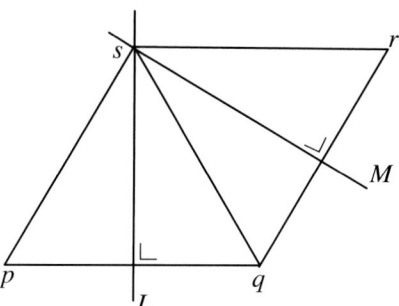

14. The two triangles pqr and abc are
between parallel lines.
$|ac| = 4$ cm and $|pq| = 12$ cm.

Prove $\dfrac{\text{area of the triangle } abc}{\text{area of the triangle } pqr} = \dfrac{1}{3}$.

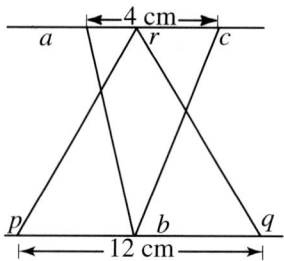

15. In the quadrilateral $wxyz$, $wz \parallel xy$.
Prove that the
area of $\triangle pwx$ = area of $\triangle pzy$.

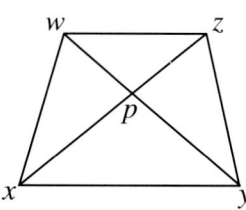

16. $abcd$ is a parallelogram.
The line bg bisects $\angle abc$.
h is an element of the line cd
and of the line bg.
Prove that
(i) $|ab| = |ag|$
(ii) $|dg| = |dh|$
(iii) $|ad| = |ch|$.

17. In the diagram,
$|\angle acx| = |\angle ayc|$.
(i) Prove $|\angle yac| = |\angle ycb|$.
(ii) If $|ab| = |ac|$,
prove $|cy| = |cb|$.

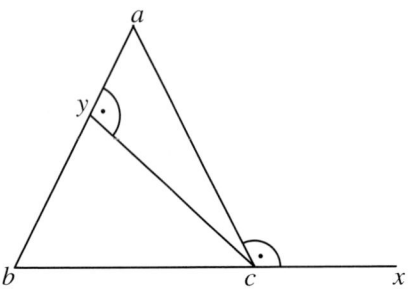

18. In the diagram,
$|ab| = |ad|$.
Prove $|\angle abc| > |\angle acb|$.

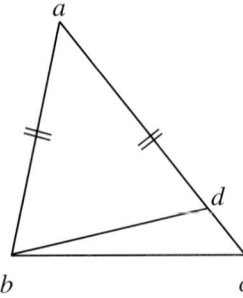

19. *abcd* is a parallelogram in which:
$|ad| = 2|ab|$ and $|bx| = |xc|$.
Prove that $ax \perp xd$.

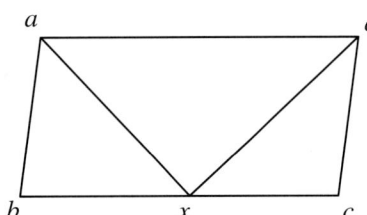

20. In the $\triangle xyz$ the line *xh* bisects $\angle yxz$
and *k* is a point such that:
$|\angle xyk| = |\angle kzy| + |\angle kyz|$
Prove:
(a) $yk \perp xh$
(b) $|xz| > |xy|$
(c) $|\angle xhy| > |\angle yxh|$.

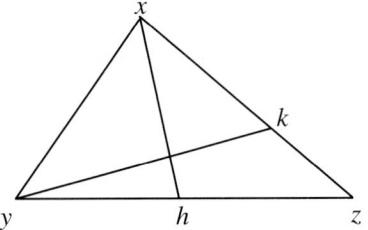

21. In the diagram,
$|xy| = |xc|$ and
$3|\angle acb| + 2|\angle azx| = 180°$.
Prove $|\angle bac| = |\angle cba|$.

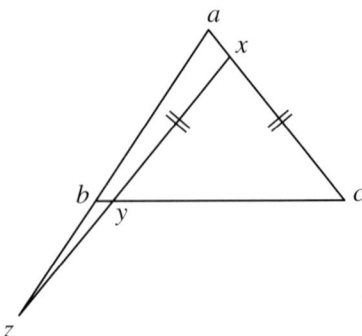

CONGRUENT TRIANGLES

Congruent triangles

Congruent means **identical**. Two triangles are said to be congruent if they are identical in every respect, i.e. they have **equal lengths of sides, equal angles, and equal areas**. In other words, they have the exact same size and shape. One could be placed on top of the other so as to cover it exactly.

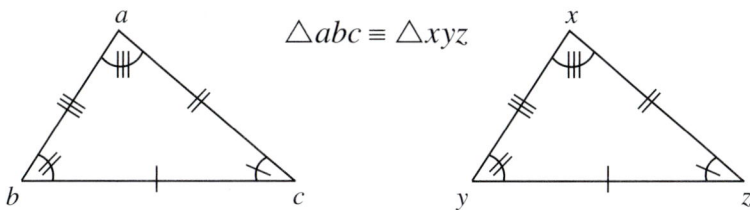

The symbol for congruence is $\equiv$. The fact that $\triangle abc$ is congruent to $\triangle xyz$ is written $\triangle abc \equiv \triangle xyz$. For two triangles to be congruent (identical), the three sides and three angles of one triangle must be equal to the three sides and three angles of the other triangle. However, it is not necessary to prove all six equalities to show that the two triangles are congruent. Any of the following four cases is sufficient to prove that two triangles are congruent. These are often called '**tests for congruency**'.

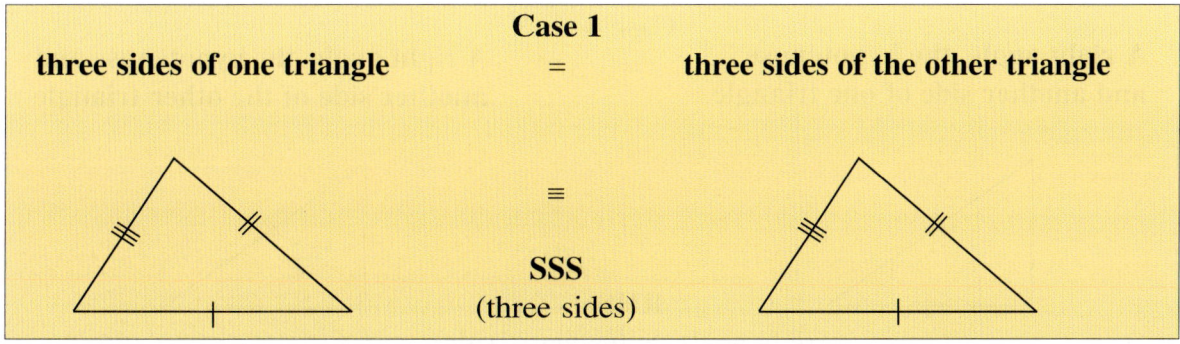

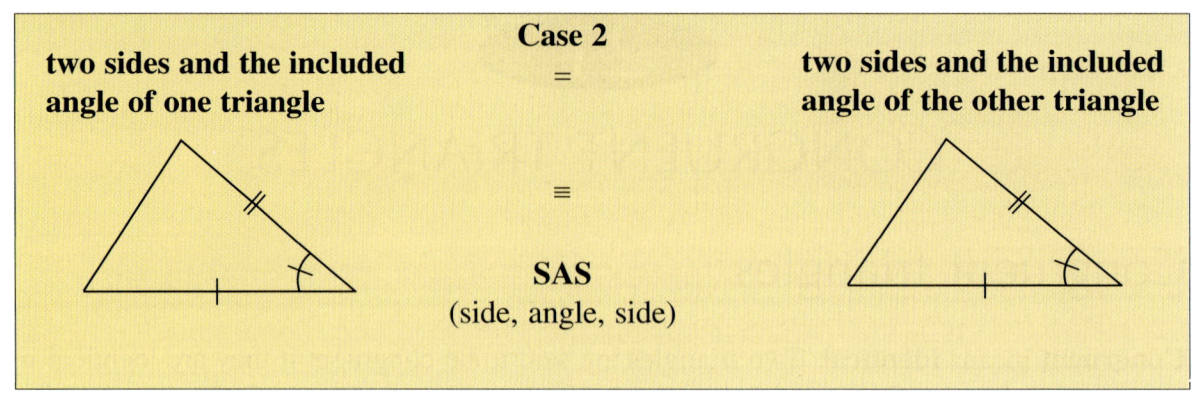

Case 2

two sides and the included
angle of one triangle

=

≡

two sides and the included
angle of the other triangle

SAS
(side, angle, side)

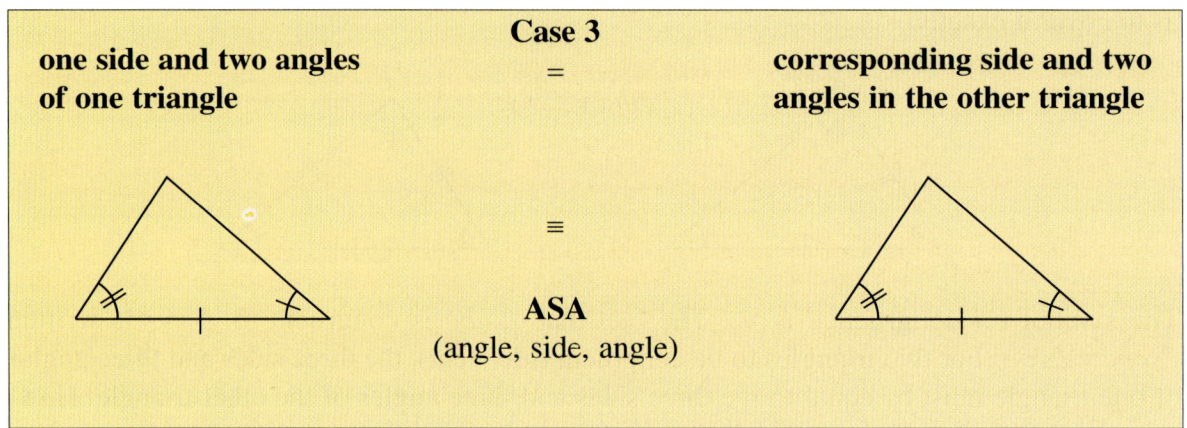

Case 3

one side and two angles
of one triangle

=

≡

corresponding side and two
angles in the other triangle

ASA
(angle, side, angle)

Note: If any two pairs of angles are equal, the third pair of angles must also be equal.
It is essential that the equal sides correspond to each other.

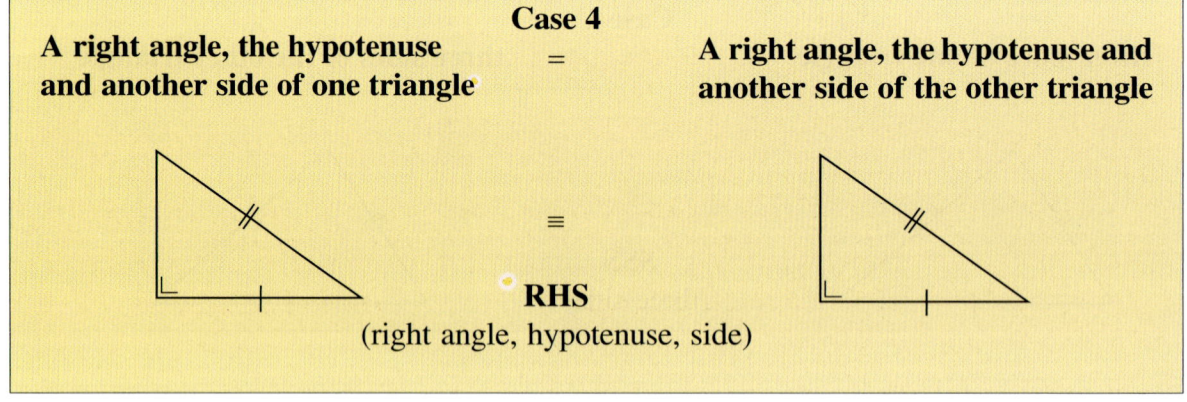

Case 4

A right angle, the hypotenuse
and another side of one triangle

=

≡

A right angle, the hypotenuse and
another side of the other triangle

RHS
(right angle, hypotenuse, side)

If two triangles are congruent then all corresponding sides and angles are equal and the areas of both triangles are equal.

Many geometrical properties can be proved using the four cases of congruent triangles. Always state which case of congruence is used, i.e., whether SSS, SAS, ASA or RHS. Justify each statement made, e.g., common side, opp. sides.

State why angles used are equal, e.g., vertically opposite angles and write down if you are given that two angles are equal or two sides are equal.

It can help to redraw the two triangles separately in a proof, but this is not necessary.

Note: In many situations more than one case of congruence can be used.

Example ▼

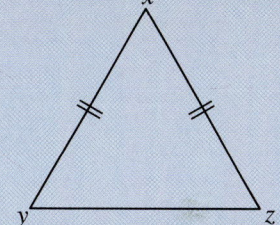

Given $\triangle xyz$ with $|xy| = |xz|$.
Prove that the bisector of $\angle yxz$
bisects $[yz]$ at right angles.

Solution:

Construction:
Draw $[xw]$, the bisector of $\angle yxz$.
Draw $\triangle xyw$ and $\triangle xzw$ separately and label angles 1, 2, 3, 4, 5 and 6 and indicate equal sides.

Proof:

	$|xy| = |xz|$	given
	$|\angle 1| = |\angle 2|$	construction
	$|xw| = |xw|$	common
$\therefore \triangle xyw \equiv \triangle xzw$		S A S
$\therefore |yw| = |wz|$		corresponding sides

Hence, w bisects $|yz|$

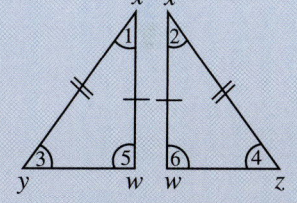

$$|\angle 5| = |\angle 6| \quad \text{corresponding angles}$$
but $|\angle 5| + |\angle 6| = 180°$ straight angle
$\therefore \quad |\angle 5| = |\angle 6| = 90°$
Hence, $[xw] \perp [yz]$
$\therefore [xw]$ bisects $[yz]$ at right angles.

In the diagram, $|pt| = |pr|$,
$st \perp pq$ and $qr \perp ps$.
Prove: **(i)** $\triangle prq \equiv \triangle pts$
  (ii) $|pq| = |ps|$

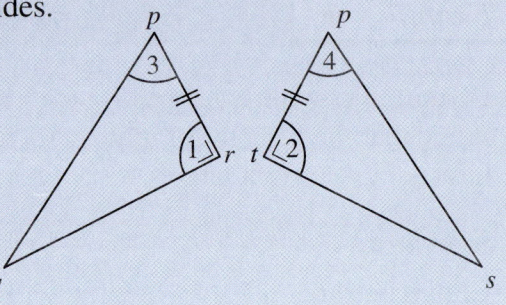

Solution:

Construction:
Draw $\triangle prq$ and $\triangle pts$ separately.
Label angles 1, 2, 3 and 4 and indicate equal sides.

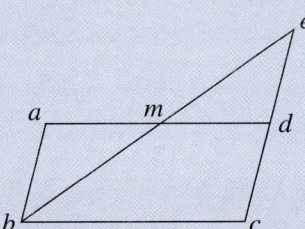

Proof:

$\qquad |\angle 1| = |\angle 2|$ given (as 90°)
$\qquad |pr| = |pt|$ given
$\qquad |\angle 3| = |\angle 4|$ common
$\therefore \triangle prq \equiv \triangle pts$ ASA
$\therefore \quad |pq| = |ps|$ corresponding sides

In the next three examples the triangles are not drawn separately.

$abcd$ is a parallelogram with m the midpoint of $[ad]$.
bm produced meets cd produced at e.
Prove $|bm| = |me|$.

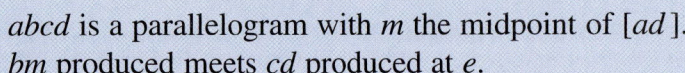

Solution:

Construction:
Label angles 1, 2, 3 and 4 and indicate equal sides.

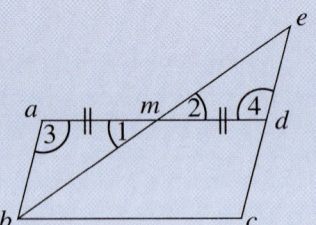

Proof:
Consider $\triangle abm$ and $\triangle dem$.

$\qquad |am| = |md|$ given
$\qquad |\angle 1| = |\angle 2|$ vertically opposite angles
$\qquad |\angle 3| = |\angle 4|$ alternate angles
$\therefore \triangle abm \equiv \triangle dem$ ASA
$\therefore \quad |bm| = |me|$ corresponding sides

pqrs is a parallelogram with diagonal [*qs*].
px bisects ∠*qps* and *ry* bisects ∠*srq*.
Prove **(i)** △*pqx* ≡ △*rsy*
　　　　(ii) |*px*| = |*ry*|

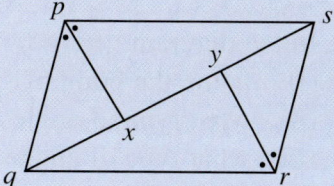

Solution:

Construction:
Label angles 1, 2, 3 and 4 and indicate equal sides.

Proof:
Consider △*pqx* and △*rsy*.

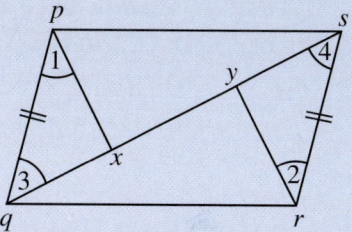

|*pq*| = |*rs*|	opposite sides
|∠1| = |∠2|	given
|∠3| = |∠4|	alternate angles
∴ △*pqx* ≡ △*rsy*	A S A
∴　|*px*| = |*ry*|	corresponding sides

A diameter of a circle is one of the
equal sides of the isosceles △*xyz* where
|*xy*| = |*xz*|.
Prove that the circle bisects [*yz*].

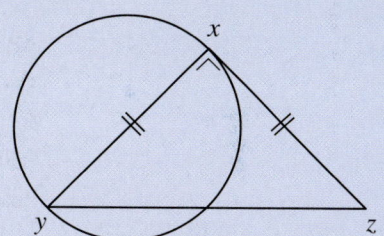

Solution:

Construction:
Join *x* to *w*, the point where [*yz*] meets the circle.
Label angles 1 and 2 and indicate equal sides.

Proof:
Consider △*xyw* and △*xzw*.

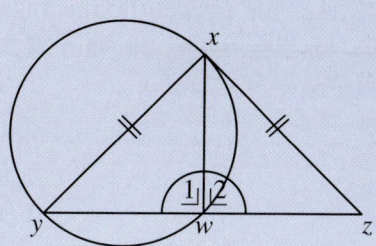

|*xy*| = |*xz*|	given
|*xw*| = |*xw*|	common
|∠1| = 90°	angle in a semi-circle
∴　|∠2| = 90°	as both add to 180°
∴　△*xyw* ≡ △*xzw*	R H S
∴　|*yw*| = |*wz*|	corresponding sides

∴ the circle bisects [*yz*]

1. In the diagram, $|pr| = |rs|$ and $|qr| = |rt|$.
    (i) name the point of symmetry
    (ii) what type of angles are $\angle prq$ and $\angle srt$?
    (iii) what type of angles are $\angle pqr$ and $\angle str$?
    (iv) prove $\triangle prq \equiv \triangle srt$
    (v) prove that *pqst* is a parallelogram.

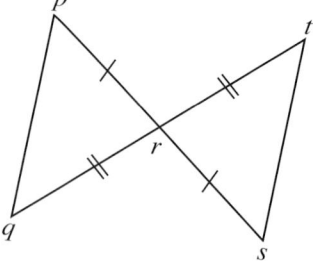

2. In the diagram, $|ad| = |ae|$,
    $|\angle bae| = |\angle cad|$ and $|\angle ade| = |\angle aed|$.
    Prove (i) $\triangle abd \equiv \triangle ace$
        (ii) $|bd| = |ce|$
        (iii) $|be| = |cd|$.

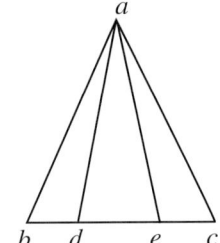

3. In the diagram, $|ab| = |ad|$,
    $ab \perp bc$ and $ad \perp dc$.
    Prove (i) $\triangle abc \equiv \triangle adc$
        (ii) $|bc| = |dc|$.

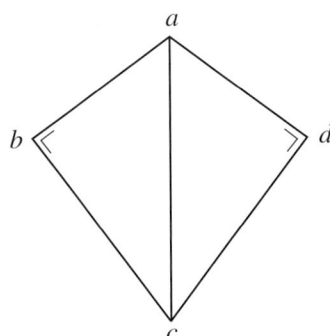

4. *pqrs* is a square.
    tqr is an equilateral triangle inside the square.
    Prove $|pt| = |st|$.

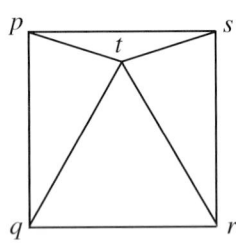

5. *M* is the perpendicular bisector of the line segment [*ab*].
    c is a point on the line *M*.
    Prove $|ac| = |bc|$.

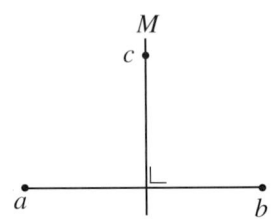

6. *B* is the bisector of $\angle aob$ and *x* is a point on the line *B*.
Prove that *x* is equidistant from *oa* and *ob*.

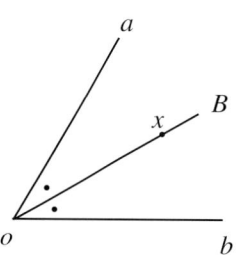

7. *abcd* is a parallelogram with diagonal [*bd*].
$ap \perp bd \perp cq$
Prove: **(i)** $|ap| = |cq|$
　　　　(ii) $|\angle dap| = |\angle bcq|$.

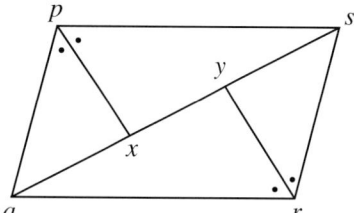

8. *pqrs* is a parallelogram with diagonal [*qs*].
px bisects $\angle qps$ and *ry* bisects $\angle srq$.
Prove: **(i)** $\triangle pqx \equiv \triangle rsy$
　　　　(ii) $|\angle pxq| = |\angle rys|$
　　　　(iii) $|qy| = |sx|$.

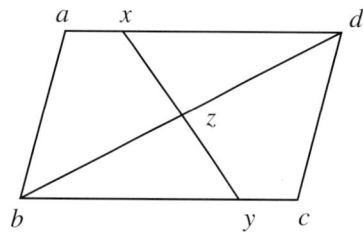

9. *abcd* is a parallelogram with diagonal [*bd*].
z is the midpoint of [*bd*].
Prove: **(i)** $|xz| = |yz|$
　　　　(ii) $|dx| = |by|$
　　　　(iii) $|yc| = |xa|$.

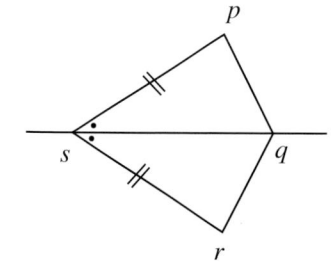

10. *sq* is the bisector of $\angle psr$ and $|ps| = |rs|$.
Prove: **(i)** $|pq| = |rq|$
　　　　(ii) *sq* bisects $\angle pqr$
　　　　(iii) $pr \perp sq$.

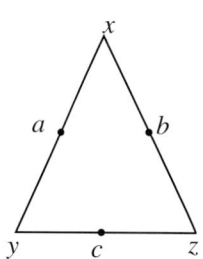

11. Given $\triangle xyz$ with $|xy| = |xz|$.
a, *b* and *c* are the midpoints of the sides, as shown.
Prove: **(i)** $|ac| = |bc|$
　　　　(ii) $|\angle yac| = |\angle yxz|$.
If the area of $\triangle abx = 10$,
find the area of *yabz*.

12. *abcd* is a parallelogram with diagonal *ac*.
x and *y* are points on [*ac*] such that
$|\angle abx| = |\angle cdy|$.
Prove: **(i)** $\triangle abx \equiv \triangle dyc$
  (ii) *bxdy* is a parallelogram.

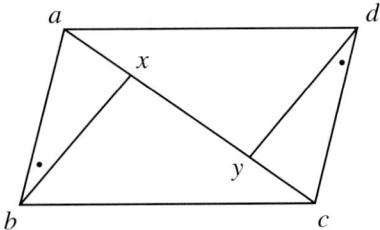

13. *pb* and *pc* bisect the angles shown.
Prove $|px| = |py| = |pz|$.
If *p* is joined to *a*, prove that *pa* bisects the $\angle bac$.

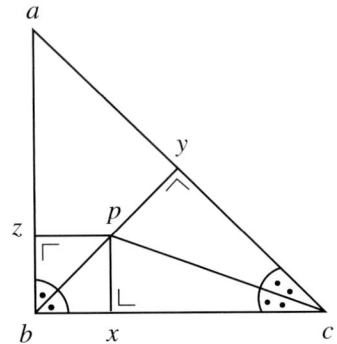

14. *pqrs* is a rectangle, *c* is the midpoint of [*pq*].
With *c* as centre, arcs cut [*ps*] at *a* and [*qr*] at *b*.
Prove: **(i)** $|ap| = |bq|$
  (ii) $|as| = |br|$
  (iii) $|aq| = |pb|$.

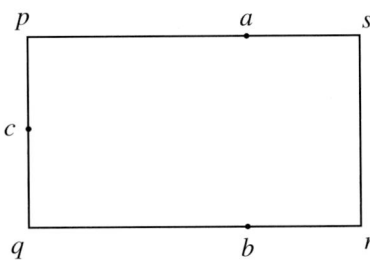

15. In $\triangle pqr$, $|pq| = |pr|$ and $|qs| = |sr|$.
$sx \perp pq$ and $sy \perp pr$
Prove: **(i)** $|sx| = |sy|$
  (ii) $|px| = |py|$
  (iii) $|xq| = |yr|$.

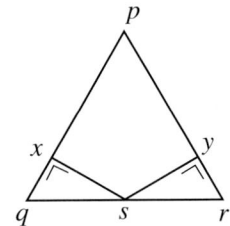

16. *wxyz* is a parallelogram.
The diagonals intersect at *o*, such that $wy \perp xz$.
Prove *wxyz* is a rhombus.

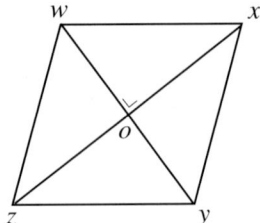

17. In the $\triangle pqr$, $|pq| = |pr|$. Prove $|\angle pqr| = |\angle prq|$.
18. In the $\triangle pqr$, $|\angle pqr| = |\angle prq|$. Prove $|pq| = |pr|$.
19. Prove that the diagonals of a parallelogram bisect its area.

20. Prove that the diagonals of a parallelogram bisect each other.

21. *pqrs* is a parallelogram.

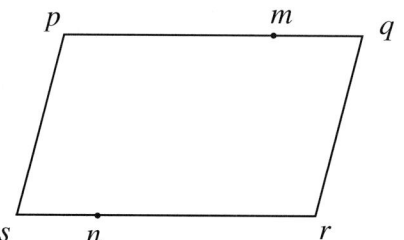

m and n are two points such that
$|pm|:|mq| = 2:1 = |rn|:|ns|$

Prove: **(i)** $|sn| = |qm|$

       (ii) $\triangle psn \equiv \triangle rqm$

       (iii)   *pmrn* is a parallelogram.

Explain why the ratio, Area of $\triangle pnr$: Area of parallelogram *pqrs* = 1 : 6.

CHAPTER 22

CIRCLE THEOREMS

Circle

The diagrams below show some of the terms we use when dealing with a circle:

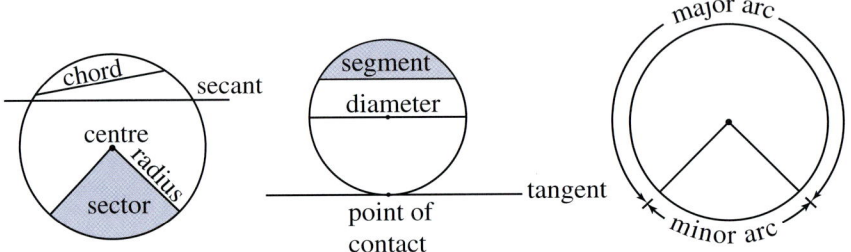

Circle theorems

1. Angle at the centre The measure of the angle at the centre of a circle is twice the measure of the angle at the circumference, standing on the same arc.	 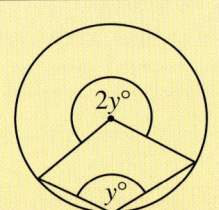
2. Angles on the same arc All angles at the circumference on the same arc are equal in measure.	 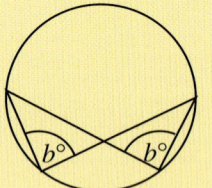
3. Angle in a semicircle An angle subtended by a diameter at the circumference is a right angle.	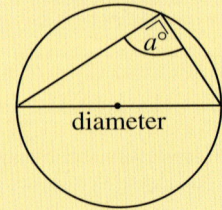 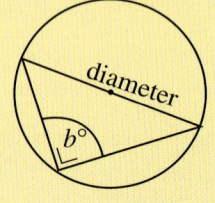 $a = 90$ $b = 90$

4. Cyclic quadrilateral

A cyclic quadrilateral has its four vertices on the circumference of a circle.

> The sum of the opposite angles in a cyclic quadrilateral is 180°.

$a + c = 180$ and $b + d = 180$

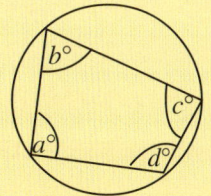

5. Tangent perpendicular to a radius (or diameter)

> A tangent to a circle is perpendicular to a radius (or diameter) at the point of contact.

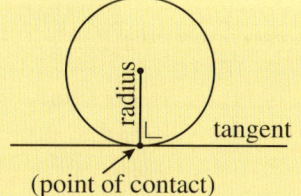

(point of contact)

6. Chord bisector

> A line through the centre of a circle, perpendicular to a chord bisects the chord.

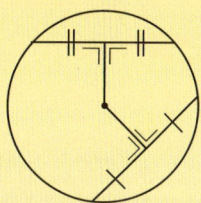

Example ▼

In the diagram, *pqrs* is a cyclic quadrilateral.
o is the centre of the circle.
$|\angle qps| = 61°$ and $|\angle osr| = 72°$,
Find, **(i)** $|\angle qos|$, where $\angle qos$ is obtuse.
  (ii) $|\angle srq|$
  (iii) $|\angle rpo|$

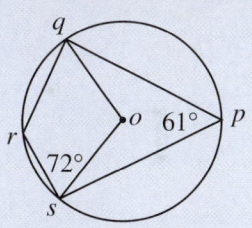

Solution:

(i) $|\angle qos| = 2|\angle qps|$ $\left(\begin{array}{l} \text{angle at the centre} \\ = 2(\text{angle at the circumference}) \end{array} \right)$
$\qquad\quad = 2(61°)$
$\qquad\quad = 122°$

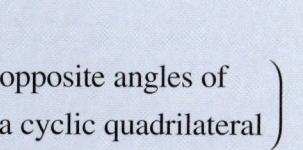

(ii) $|\angle srq| + |\angle qps| = 180°$ $\left(\begin{array}{l} \text{opposite angles of} \\ \text{a cyclic quadrilateral} \end{array} \right)$
$\qquad |\angle srq| + 61° = 180°$
$\qquad\qquad |\angle srq| = 119°$

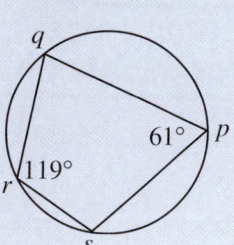

(iii) $|\angle rqo| + 119° + 72° + 122° = 360°$ $\left(\begin{array}{l}\text{four angles in a} \\ \text{quadrilateral add to } 360°\end{array}\right)$
$|\angle rqo| + 313° = 360°$
$|\angle rqo| = 47°$

Example ▼

The circle in the diagram has centre o.
Find the value of x and the value of y.

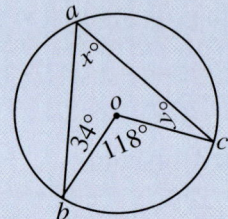

Solution:

$x = \frac{1}{2}(118)$ $\left(\begin{array}{l}\text{angle at the circumference} \\ = \frac{1}{2}(\text{angle at the centre})\end{array}\right)$
$x = 59$

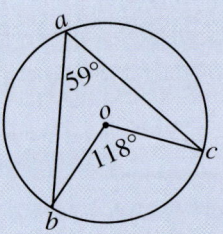

Draw $\triangle obc$ and $\triangle abc$ separately and label angles 1 and 2.
In $\triangle obc$, $|ob| = |oc|$ (both radii)
$|\angle 1| + |\angle 2| + 118° = 180°$ (3 angles in a triangle)
$|\angle 1| + |\angle 2| = 62°$
but $|\angle 1| = |\angle 2|$ (because $|ob| = |oc|$)
$\therefore |\angle 1| = |\angle 2| = 31°$

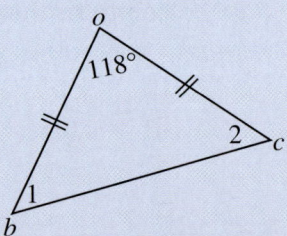

In $\triangle abc$,
$y + 31 + 31 + 34 + 59 = 180$ (3 angles in a triangle)
$y + 155 = 180$
$y = 25$

324

Find the value of the letter representing the angles in each of the following circles.
Where necessary, the centre of the circle is indicated by *o* and the tangents are indicated by
the capital letter *T*:

1.

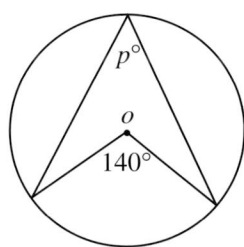

2.

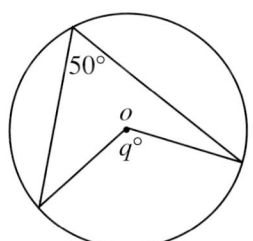

3.

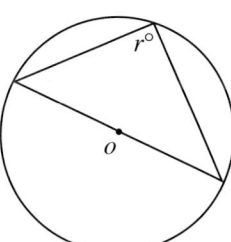

4.

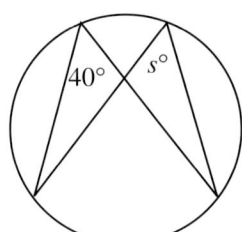

5.

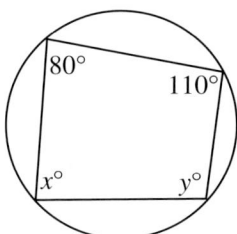

6.

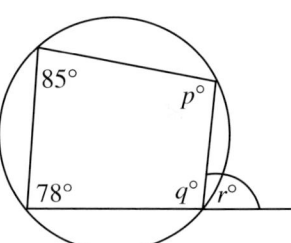

7.

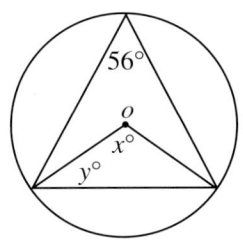

8.

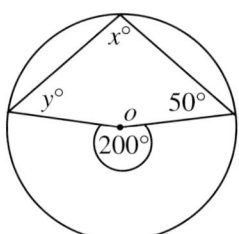

9.

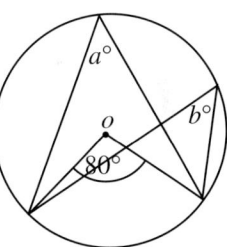

10.

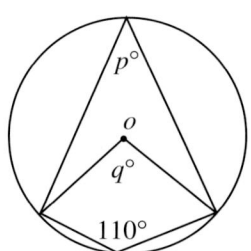

11.

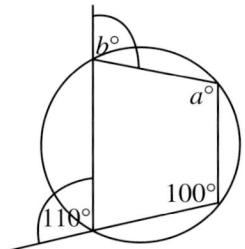

12.

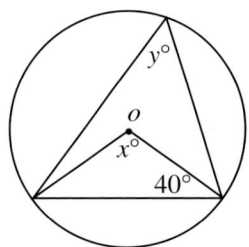

13.

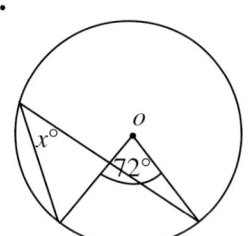

14.

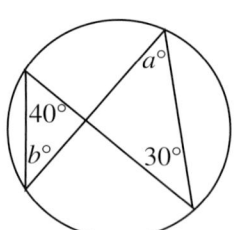

15.

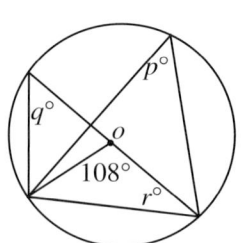

16.

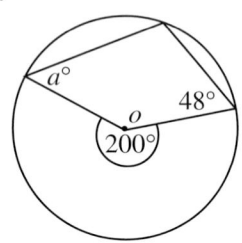

17.

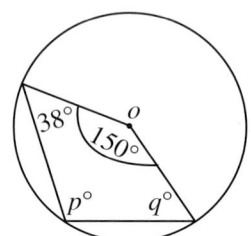

18.

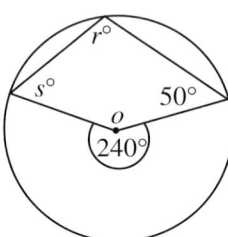

19.

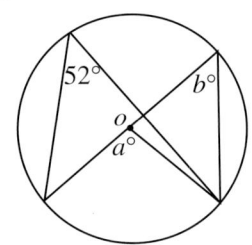

20.

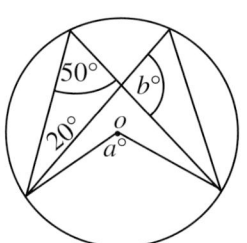

21.

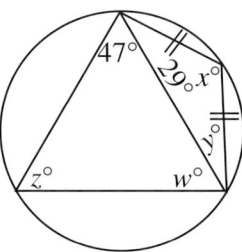

22.

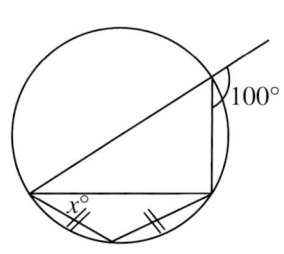

23.

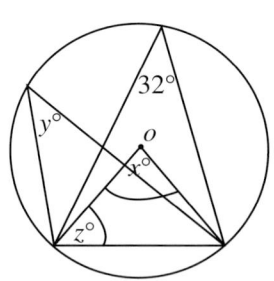

24.

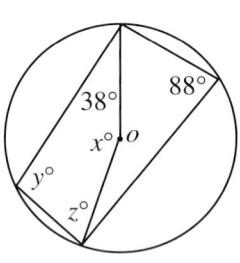

25.

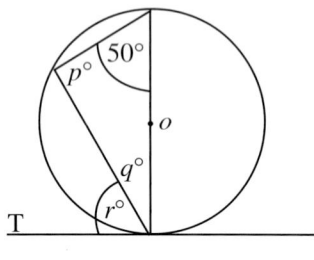

26.

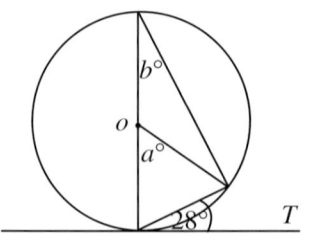

27.

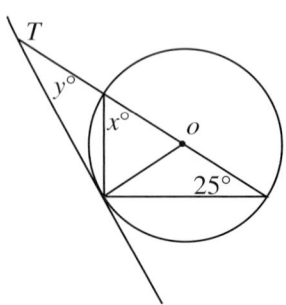

326

28.

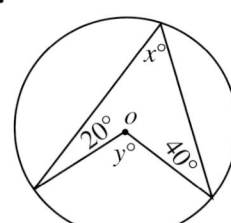

29.

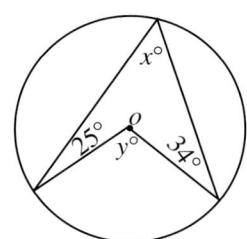

30.

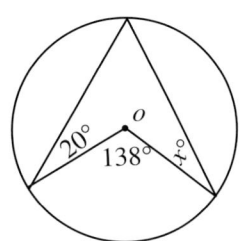

31. In the diagram, o is the centre of the circle. pt is a tangent, $|pq| = |rq|$, $|\angle spt| = 38°$. Calculate $|\angle qrs|$.

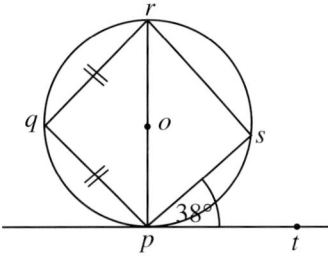

32. In a circle, centre o, oa is parallel to bc. If $|\angle abc| = 23°$, find
  (i) $|\angle aoc|$
  (ii) $|\angle oxb|$
  (iii) $|\angle oca|$.

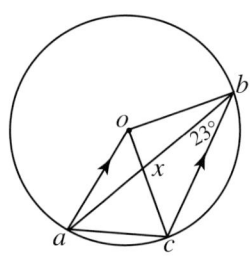

33. In the diagram, $|\angle xcb| = 54°$, o is the centre of the circle. Calculate $|\angle bod|$, where $\angle bod$ is obtuse.

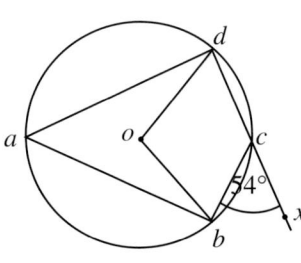

34. The centre of the circle is o. If $|\angle aob| = 130°$ and $|\angle cao| = 15°$, calculate $|\angle obc|$.

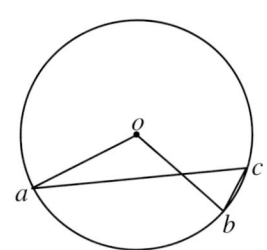

35. p, q, r and s are points of a circle, centre c, as in diagram.
Name an angle equal in measure to
(i) $2|\angle rpq|$ **(ii)** $|\angle qsp|$
(iii) a right angle.
If $|pq| = |pr|$ and $|\angle qsr| = 36°$, calculate $|\angle prs|$.

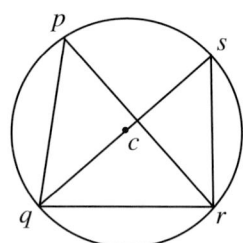

36. In the diagram, ta and tb are tangents at a and b to a circle of centre o.
tc is a line passing through o and $|\angle atb| = 56°$.
Calculate **(i)** $|\angle tao|$
     (ii) $|\angle ato|$
     (iii) $|\angle aob|$
     (iv) $|\angle aco|$.

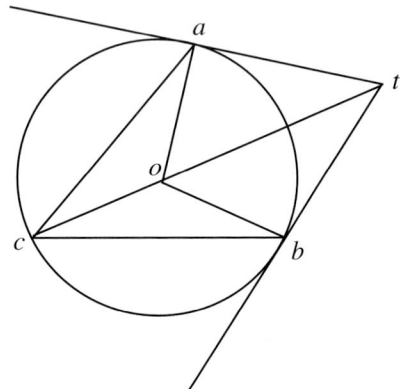

37. In the diagram, o is the centre of the circle. ab is a tangent and $|\angle brq| = 28°$.
Calculate
(i) $|\angle soq|$, where $\angle soq$ is obtuse
(ii) $|\angle soq|$, where $\angle soq$ is reflex
(iii) $|\angle srq|$
(iv) $|\angle ars|$.

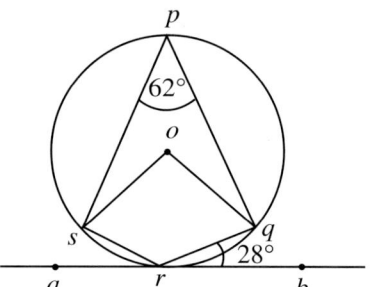

38. In the diagram, $pqrs$ is a cyclic quadrilateral. o is the centre of the circle.
$|\angle qos| = 120°$ and $|\angle osr| = 74°$
Find, **(i)** $|\angle qps|$
     (ii) $|\angle srq|$
     (iii) $|\angle rqo|$.

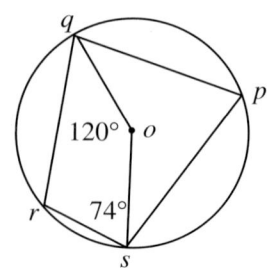

39. r is a point of a circle, centre c, $|\angle cpq| = 40°$.
Calculate **(i)** $|\angle pcq|$ **(ii)** $|\angle prq|$.
If $|\angle pcr| = 200°$, calculate $|\angle crp|$.

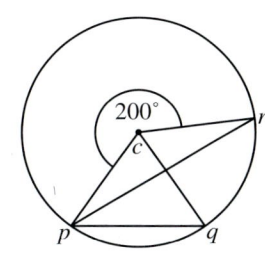

40. Two circles intersect at a and b.
$[ab]$ is a diameter.
c is the centre of the other circle.
Calculate $|\angle bda|$.

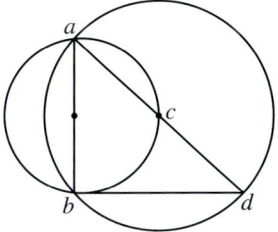

Proofs

If a question says 'prove', 'verify' or 'show', then each statement made must be justified with a comment. Consider the next two examples.

Example ▼

p, t and u are points on a circle K, centre o.
wt is the tangent at t.
$[pt]$ is a diameter.
Prove that $|\angle wtu| = |\angle tpu|$.

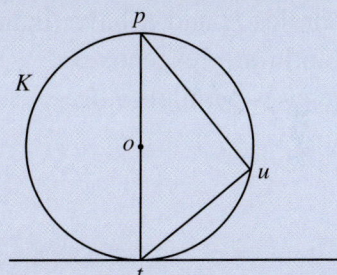

Solution:

Lable angles 1, 2, 3 and 4.

$$|\angle 4| = 90°$$ angle in a semi-circle

∴ $$|\angle 1| + |\angle 2| = 90°$$ remaining angles in $\triangle put$

$$|\angle 3| + |\angle 2| = 90°$$ as wt is a tangent at t

∴ $$|\angle 3| + |\angle 2| = |\angle 1| + |\angle 2|$$

∴ $$|\angle 3| = |\angle 1|$$

i.e. $$|\angle wtu| = |\angle tpu|$$

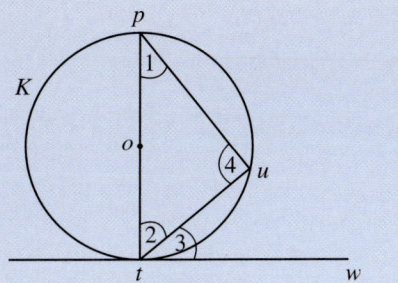

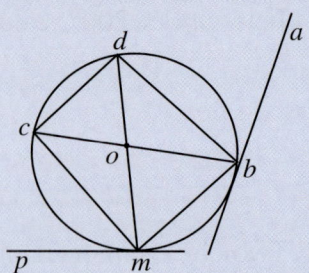

[dm] and [cb] are diameters of a circle, centre o.
ab and pm are tangents at b and m respectively.
Show that $|\angle pmc| = |\angle abd|$.

Solution:

Label angles 1, 2, 3 and 4.

	$|\angle 1| + |\angle 3| = 90°$	as pm is a tangent at m
and	$|\angle 2| + |\angle 4| = 90°$	as ab is a tangent at b
∴	$|\angle 1| + |\angle 3| = |\angle 2| + |\angle 4|$	
but	$|\angle 3| = |\angle 4|$	both standing on arc cd
∴	$|\angle 1| = |\angle 2|$	
i.e.	$|\angle pmc| = |\angle abd|$	

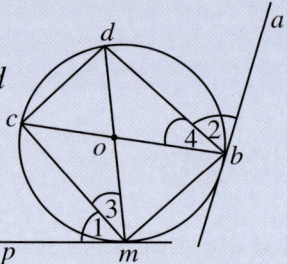

Exercise 22.2 ▼

1. The circles *H* and *K* have diameters
   [ab] and [ac], respectively.
   Prove *eb* is parallel to *dc*.

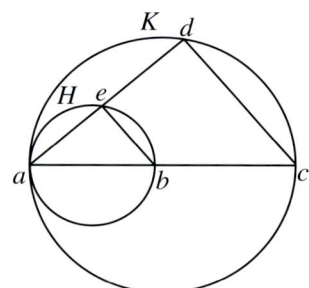

2. *p*, *q*, *r* and *s* are points on a circle.
   If *pq* ∥ *sr*, prove $|\angle psr| = |\angle qrs|$.

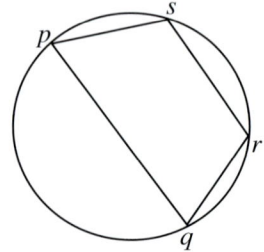

3. p, q, r and s are four points on a circle.
If $|\angle psq| = |\angle rsq|$ and $|\angle pqs| = |\angle rqs|$,
prove that $[sq]$ is a diameter of the circle.

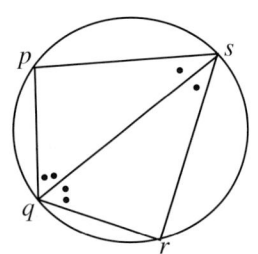

4. (a) $abcd$ is a cyclic quadrilateral.
o is the centre of the circle,
ad is produced to e.
Prove $|\angle abc| = |\angle cde|$.

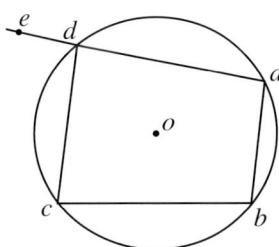

(b) $abcd$ is a parallelogram and
a, b, y, d are points on the circle.
Show that $|dy| = |dc|$.

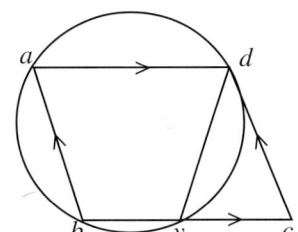

5. (a) In the diagram, pt and ps are
tangents to a circle of centre o,
at t and s, respectively.
Prove:
(i) $\triangle pso \equiv \triangle pto$
(ii) $|\angle tpr| = 2|\angle top|$.

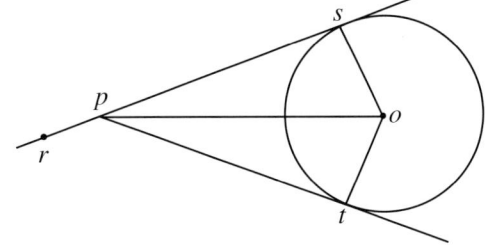

(b) ab and ac are tangents to the
circle at b and c, respectively.
The centre of the circle is o and
d is a point on the circle.
If $|\angle bac| = 30°$ find $|\angle bdc|$.

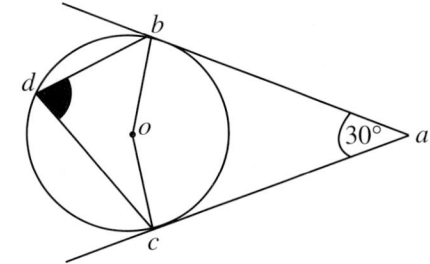

(c) In the diagram, *kp* and *kq* are tangents to a circle of centre *o*, at *p* and *q*, respectively
$|\angle qkp| = 50°$.
Prove $|\angle qkp| = 2|\angle rps|$.

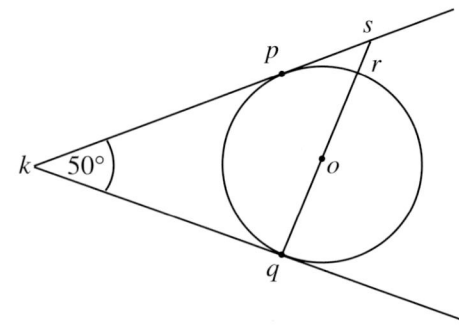

---

6. *abcd* is a cyclic quadrilateral,
$|\angle dab| = 80°$ and $|\angle acb| = 50°$.
Prove $|ad| = |ab|$.

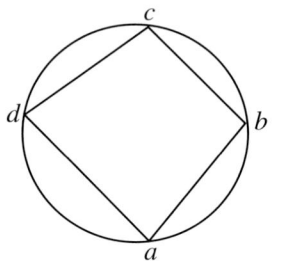

---

7. [*ab*] and [*pq*] are two diameters of a circle, as in diagram.
Prove, **(i)** $|\angle qab| = |\angle qpb|$
      (ii) *aq* ∥ *pb*.

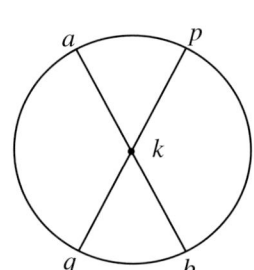

---

8. The diagram shows a circle, centre *o*. *a*, *b*, *c*, *d* and *e* are points on the circle such that:
$|\angle aoe| = 2|\angle eod|$.
Prove $|\angle acd| = 3|\angle ebd|$.

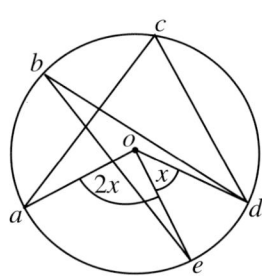

---

9. *k* is the centre of the given circle.
$kp \perp bc$ and $|ab| = |ap|$.
Prove that: **(i)** $|\angle pab| = |\angle pac|$
      (ii) $|\angle abc| = 22\frac{1}{2}°$.

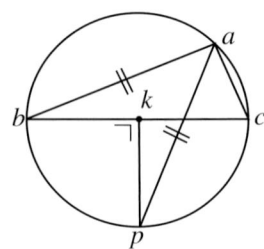

10. *cdts* is a parallelogram and *c* is the centre of the circle.
Prove $|\angle dts| = 120°$.

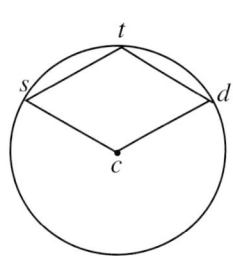

11. *c* is the centre of the circle.
Prove $|\angle cpq| + |\angle qrp| = 90°$.

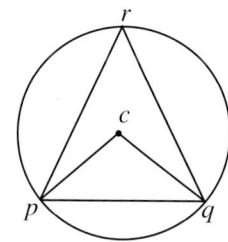

12. *K* is a circle with diameter [*ab*].
S is a circle with diameter [*bc*].
The two circles meet at *b*.
Prove that *d* is on the line *ac*.

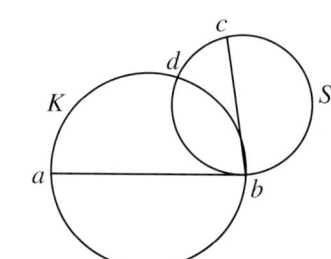

13. *pqrs* is a quadrilateral. $|pq| = |pr| = |ps|$
and $|\angle qps| = 136°$.
Calculate $|\angle qrs|$.
Explain how your answer is obtained.

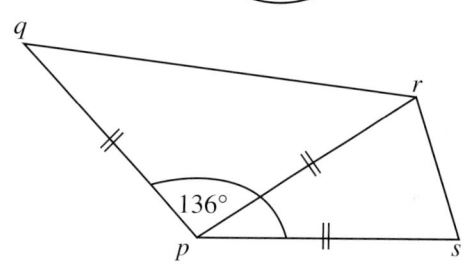

14. *p* is the centre of the circle and $|ab| = |bc|$.
If *k* is the midpoint of [*ab*],
prove that $|\angle apk| = |\angle cab|$.

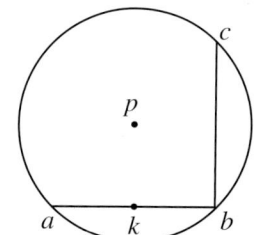

15. *o* is the centre of the circle and *p*, *q* and *r*
are points on the circumference, as shown.
Prove that
$|\angle qpr| = |\angle pqo| + |\angle pro|$.
(**Hint:** Let $|\angle qor| = 2x$).

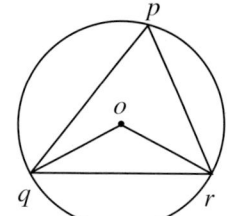

333

SIMILAR TRIANGLES

Similar triangles

Similar triangles have the same shape but one is an enlargement of the other.

Consider the pair of similar triangles *abc* and *xyz*:

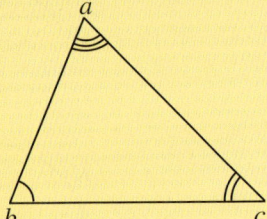 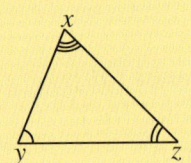

1. The three angles of △*abc* are equal to the three angles of △*xyz*.
  (i.e. the triangles are equiangular)

Note: To prove that two triangles are similar (equiangular) it is only necessary to show
     that two angles in one triangle are each equal to two angles in the other triangle
     (as the other pair of angles must also be equal).

2. The lengths of corresponding sides are in the same proportion (ratio)

$$\frac{|ab|}{|xy|} = \frac{|ac|}{|xz|} = \frac{|bc|}{|yz|}$$

  In practice we only use two of these ratios at any one time.

A line drawn parallel to any one side of a triangle forms two triangles which are similar and divides the other two sides in the same proportion (ratio).

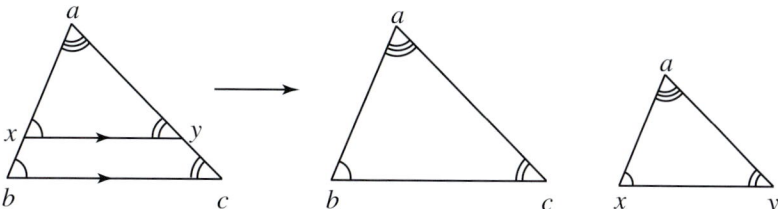

If $xy \parallel bc$ then:

$$\frac{|ax|}{|xb|} = \frac{|ay|}{|yc|} \quad \text{or} \quad \frac{|ab|}{|ax|} = \frac{|ac|}{|ay|} = \frac{|bc|}{|xy|}$$

Note: It helps in solving problems on similar triangles if the two triangles are redrawn so that the corresponding sides, or angles, match each other. It is good practice to put the unknown length on the top of the first fraction.

Example ▼

Find the value of p and q, given the equal angles as shown.

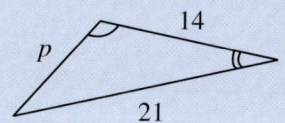
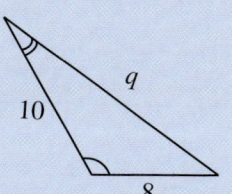

Solution:

As two pairs of angles are equal, the triangles are similar.
Redraw both triangles so that corresponding angles match each other.
Corresponding sides:

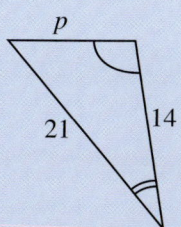
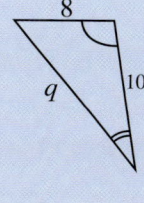

Large triangle	Small triangle
14	10
p	8
21	q

$$\frac{p}{8} = \frac{14}{10}$$

$$10p = 112$$

$$p = \frac{112}{10}$$

$$p = 11\tfrac{1}{5} \text{ or } 11.2$$

$$\frac{q}{21} = \frac{10}{14}$$

$$14q = 210$$

$$q = \frac{210}{14}$$

$$q = 15$$

In the △*abc*, *xy* ∥ *bc*.

Prove that △*abc* and △*axy* are similar.

If |*ax*| = |*bc*| = 6 cm, |*ay*| = $5\frac{1}{2}$ cm and |*ab*| = 9 cm,

find **(i)** |*yc*| **(ii)** |*xy*|.

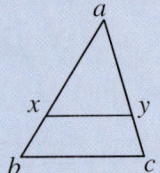

Solution:

Redraw △*abc* and △*axy* separately. Label angles 1, 2, 3 and 4 and put in known lengths.

As *xy* ∥ *bc*, |∠1| = |∠2| and |∠3| = |∠4| corresponding angles

∴ △*abc* and △*axy* are similar.

Large triangle	Small triangle
9	6
|*ac*|	$5\frac{1}{2}$
6	|*xy*|

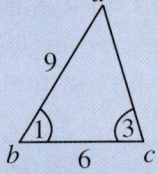 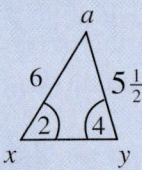

(i)
$$\frac{|ac|}{|ay|} = \frac{|ab|}{|ax|}$$

$$\frac{|ac|}{5\frac{1}{2}} = \frac{9}{6}$$

$$6\,|ac| = 49.5$$

$$12\,|ac| = 99$$

$$|ac| = \frac{99}{12}$$

$$|ac| = 8\frac{1}{4} \text{ cm}$$

$$|yc| = |ac| - |ay|$$

$$= 8\frac{1}{4} - 5\frac{1}{2} = 2\frac{3}{4} \text{ cm}$$

(ii)
$$\frac{|xy|}{|bc|} = \frac{|ax|}{|ab|}$$

$$\frac{|xy|}{6} = \frac{6}{9}$$

$$9\,|xy| = 36$$

$$|xy| = 4 \text{ cm}$$

1. In the diagram, $xy \parallel bc$.

Write down the following ratios, in simplest form:

Prove that $\triangle abc$ and $\triangle axy$ are similar.

(i) $\dfrac{\mid ab \mid}{\mid ax \mid}$ **(ii)** $\dfrac{\mid xy \mid}{\mid bc \mid}$ **(iii)** $\dfrac{\mid yc \mid}{\mid ac \mid}$

Verify **(iv)** $\dfrac{\mid ab \mid}{\mid ax \mid} = \dfrac{\mid ac \mid}{\mid ay \mid} = \dfrac{\mid bc \mid}{\mid xy \mid}$

(v) $\dfrac{\mid xy \mid^2}{\mid bc \mid^2} = \dfrac{\mid ay \mid^2}{\mid ac \mid^2}$

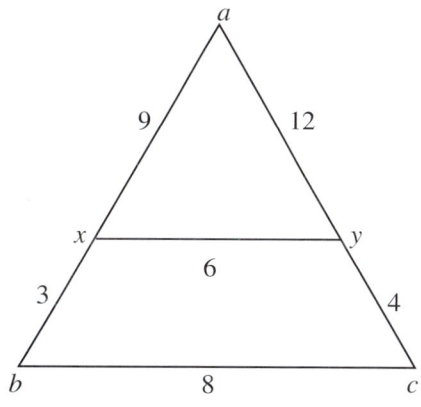

In questions 2 to 9 the triangles are similar with equal angles marked.

In each case, calculate the lengths p and q.

2.

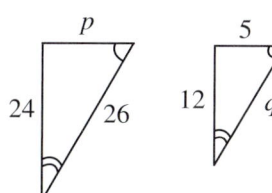

3.

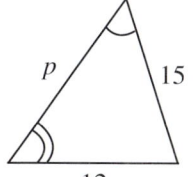

4.

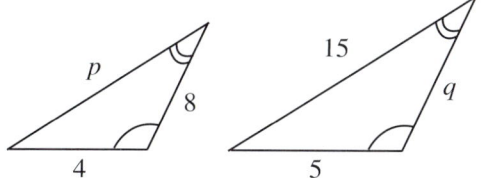

5.

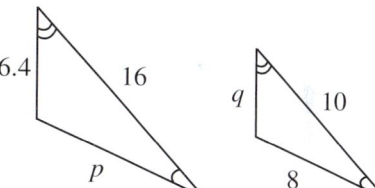

Note: It may help to redraw the triangles so that the positions of corresponding angles, or sides, match each other.

6.

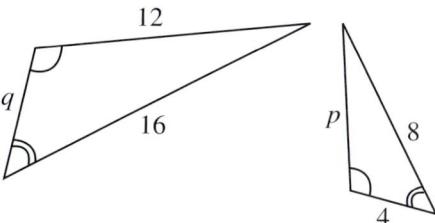

7.

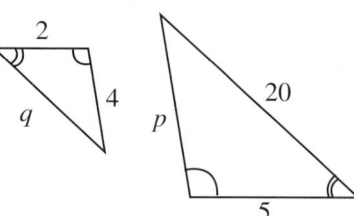

8.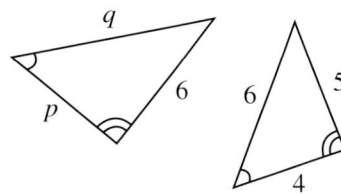

9.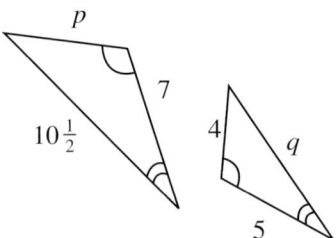

10. In the $\triangle abc$, $xy \parallel bc$.
$|ax| = 4$, $|xb| = 2$,
$|ay| = 6$ and $|bc| = 12$.
Prove $\triangle abc$ and $\triangle axy$ are similar.
Find **(i)** $|yc|$ **(ii)** $|xy|$

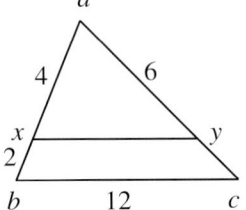

11. In the $\triangle pqr$, $ab \parallel qr$.
$|ap| = 3$, $|pb| = 4$,
$|ab| = 6$ and $|qr| = 15$.
Find **(i)** $|pq|$ **(ii)** $|aq|$
(iii) $|pr|$ **(iv)** $|br|$

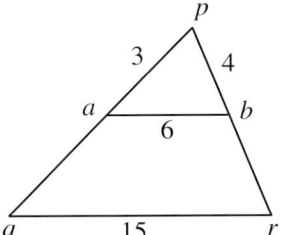

12. In the $\triangle pqr$, $xy \parallel qr$.
$|px| = 4$, $|py| = 5$
$|yr| = 1.25$ and $|qr| = 4.5$
Calculate **(i)** $|xq|$
(ii) $|xy|$

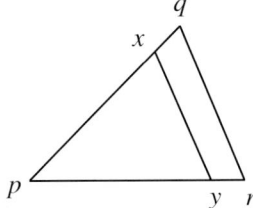

13. In the $\triangle xyz$, $ab \parallel xy$.
Explain why $\triangle xyz$ and $\triangle abz$ are similar.
$|xz| = 48$, $|yz| = 36$,
$|bz| = \frac{1}{3}|yz|$ and $|xy| = 21$.
Calculate **(i)** $|ax|$ **(ii)** $|ab|$

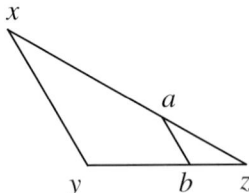

14. In the $\triangle abc$, $pq \parallel ab$.
If $|cp| = 4$, $|pa| = 2$ and
$|cb| = 9$, find $|cq|$.

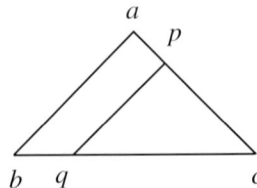

15. In the $\triangle xyz$, $ab \parallel yz$.
$|xa| = 12$, $|ab| = 9$
and $|ay| = \frac{2}{3}|xa|$.
Calculate $|yz|$.

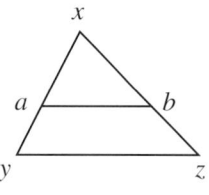

16. In the $\triangle rst$, xy is parallel to st.
If $|xs| = 2$, $|yt| = 3$ and $|rs| = 10$
find $|rt|$.

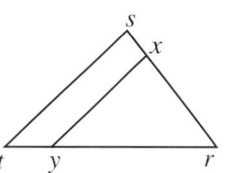

17. In the $\triangle pqr$, $xy \parallel qr$ and $xt \parallel pr$.
$|xt| = |tq| = 5$ cm and $|xy| = 11$ cm.
Find $|pr|$.

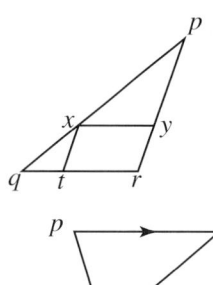

18. In the diagram, $pq \parallel rs$.
$|pq| = 10$ cm, $|rs| = 8$ cm
and $|st| = 6$ cm.
Prove that $\triangle pqt$ and $\triangle srt$ are similar.
Which side in $\triangle srt$ corresponds to $[pt]$?
Calculate $|pt|$.

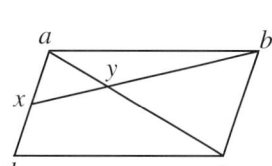

19. $abcd$ is a parallelogram.
ac intersects bx at y, as shown.
Explain why $\triangle axy$ and $\triangle cby$ are similar.
If $|ad| = 9$ cm, $|ay| = 4$ cm
and $|yc| = 6$ cm, calculate $|ax|$.

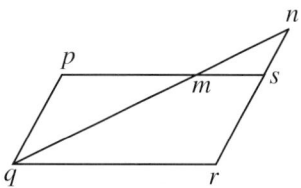

20. $pqrs$ is a parallelogram.
$|pm|:|ms| = 4 : 3$
Prove that $\triangle pqm$ and $\triangle snm$ are similar.
If $|pq| = 24$ and $|mn| = 30$,
calculate   **(i)** $|ns|$ **(ii)** $|qm|$

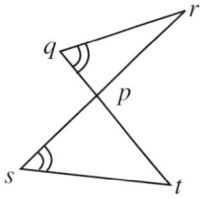

21. In the diagram, $|\angle pqr| = |\angle pst|$.
$|pq| = 6$, $|qr| = 9$,
$|ps| = 8$ and $|pt| = 12$.
Prove that $\triangle pqr$ and $\triangle pst$ are similar.
Calculate   **(i)** $|st|$ **(ii)** $|pr|$

22. In the $\triangle pqr$, mn is drawn
such that $|\angle pqr| = |\angle mnp|$.
Prove that $\triangle pqr$ and $\triangle pnm$ are similar.
If $|pm| = 4$, $|pn| = 5$ and $|mq| = 11$,
calculate $|nr|$.

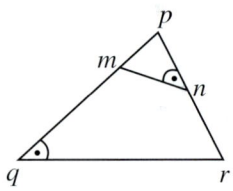

23. In $\triangle pqr$, st is drawn
such that $|\angle pst| = |\angle qrp|$.
Show that $\triangle pts$ and $\triangle pqr$ are similar.
$|ps| = 6$ cm, $|sq| = 4$ cm,
$|qr| = 12$ cm and $|pr| = 8$ cm.
Calculate **(i)** $|st|$ **(ii)** $|tr|$

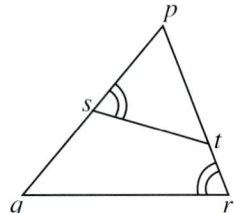

24. In the $\triangle pqr$, s is a point on $[qr]$,
such that $|\angle pqr| = |\angle spr|$.
$|pr| = 8$ cm, $|sr| = 4$ cm and $|ps| = 6$ cm.
Show that $\triangle pqr$ and $\triangle spr$ are similar.
Verify that $\triangle pqr$ is isosceles.

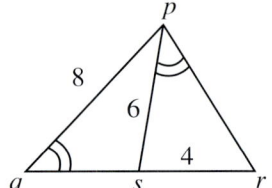

Proofs and similar triangles

> ### Example ▼
>
> $|\angle abc| = |\angle rst| = 40°$
> $|\angle bca| + |\angle str| = 140°$
> Show that $|\angle bac| = |\angle str|$.
> Hence or otherwise show that
> $$\frac{|ab|}{|ts|} = \frac{|bc|}{|rs|}$$
>
> **Solution:**
> Label angles 1, 2, 3, 4, 5 and 6.

$$|\angle 1| = |\angle 2| = 40° \qquad \text{given}$$

∴ $\qquad |\angle 3| + |\angle 5| = 140°$

but $\qquad |\angle 3| + |\angle 4| = 140° \qquad \text{given}$

∴ $\qquad |\angle 3| + |\angle 5| = |\angle 3| + |\angle 4|$

∴ $\qquad |\angle 5| = |\angle 4|$

i.e. $\qquad |\angle bac| = |\angle str|$

∴ $\qquad \triangle abc$ and $\triangle rst$ are similar

as two pairs of angles are equal.

Redraw both triangles so that corresponding angles, or sides, match each other.

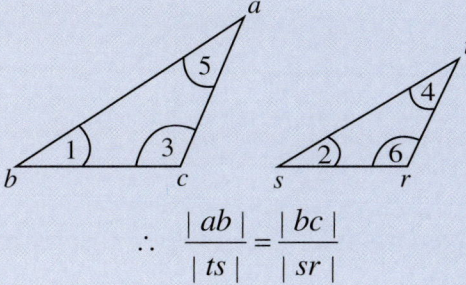

$$\therefore \quad \frac{|ab|}{|ts|} = \frac{|bc|}{|sr|}$$

Example ▼

In the $\triangle abc$, $xy \parallel ac$.

A line through a parallel to xc cuts bc, produced at d.

Prove

$$\frac{|by|}{|yc|} = \frac{|bc|}{|cd|}$$

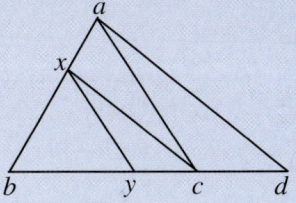

Solution:

Redraw so that corresponding parallel lines match each other.

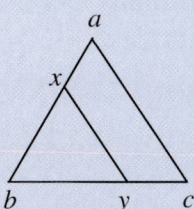

$xy \parallel ac \qquad$ given

$\therefore \dfrac{|bx|}{|xa|} = \dfrac{|by|}{|yc|}$

$xc \parallel ad \qquad$ given

$\therefore \dfrac{|bx|}{|xa|} = \dfrac{|bc|}{|cd|}$

$$\therefore \frac{|by|}{|yc|} = \frac{|bc|}{|cd|} \quad \left(\text{as both are equal to } \frac{|bx|}{|xa|}\right)$$

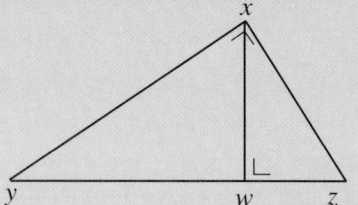

In the diagram, $|\angle yxz| = 90°$ and $xw \perp yz$.
Prove that the $\triangle wyz$ and $\triangle wxz$ are similar.
Deduce that $|xw|^2 = |yw|.|wz|$

Solution:

Label angles 1, 2, 3, 4 and 5.

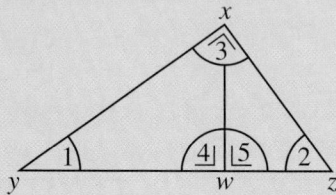

Redraw the three right-angled triangles separately so that corresponding angles, or sides, match each other.

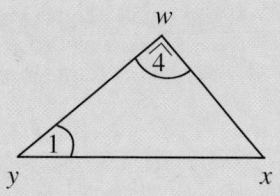 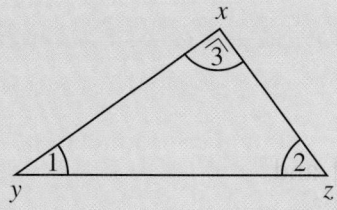 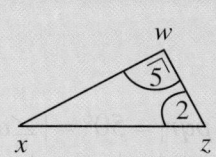

In $\triangle wyx$ and $\triangle xyz$

$|\angle 1| = |\angle 1|$	same angle
$|\angle 4| = |\angle 3| = 90°$	given

$\therefore$ $\triangle wyx$ and $\triangle xyz$ are similar

In $\triangle xyz$ and $\triangle wxz$

$|\angle 2| = |\angle 2|$	same angle
$|\angle 3| = |\angle 5| = 90°$	given

$\therefore$ $\triangle xyz$ and $\triangle wxz$ are similar

(i.e. all three triangles are similar)

$\therefore \triangle wyx$ and $\triangle wxz$ are similar

$$\therefore \quad \frac{|xw|}{|wz|} = \frac{|yw|}{|xw|}$$

(cross multiply)

$$\therefore \quad |xw|^2 = |yw|.|wz|$$

1. In the $\triangle pqr$, mn is drawn
    such that $|\angle pqr| = |\angle pnm|$.
    Prove that $\triangle pqr$ and $\triangle pnm$ are similar.

    Prove that $\dfrac{|pq|}{|pn|} = \dfrac{|pr|}{|pm|}$.

    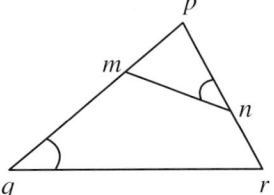

2. In the diagram,
    $ab \parallel yx \parallel dc$ and $ab \perp bc$.

    Prove $\dfrac{|ad|}{|ay|} = \dfrac{|bc|}{|bx|}$.

    Hint: Draw a line through a parallel to bc.

    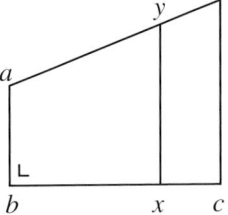

3. In the $\triangle pqr$,
    $bc \parallel qr$ and $ac \parallel br$.

    Prove $\dfrac{|pb|}{|bq|} = \dfrac{|pa|}{|ab|}$.

    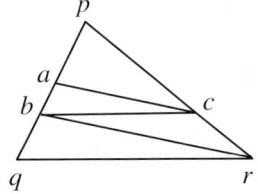

4. $|\angle pqr| = 50° = |\angle abc|$ and
    $|\angle qrp| + |\angle bac| = 130°$
    (i)   evaluate $|\angle qpr| + |\angle bac|$
    (ii) prove $|\angle qpr| = |\angle bac|$

    (iii) Hence, or otherwise, show that $\dfrac{|pq|}{|ab|} = \dfrac{|qr|}{|bc|}$.

    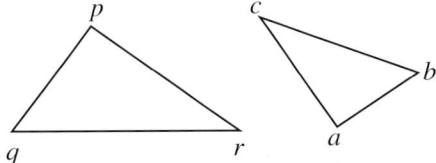

5. In the $\triangle abc$, $xy \parallel bc$ as shown,
    with $|\angle ayx| = |\angle xyb|$.
    (i)   Prove that
    $$|yc| = |yb|$$
    (ii) Hence prove
    $$\dfrac{|ax|}{|ay|} = \dfrac{|by|}{|bx|}.$$

    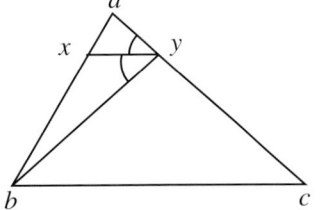

6. *abcd* is a rectangle.

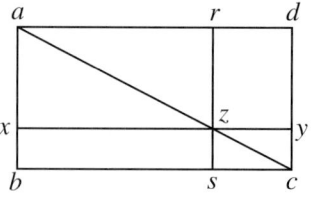

xy and *rs* intersect at *z*, a point on *ac*.

xy ∥ *bc* and *rs* ∥ *dc*.

   (i)   Prove that $|ax|:|xb| = |ar|:|rd|$.

   (ii) Prove that the rectangles *xbsz* and *rzyd* are equal in area.

7. *abcd* is a rectangle. The lines *bc* and *ac* are produced to *e* and *f* respectively, where $|\angle cef| = 90°$.

Prove that $|ab|:|ef| = |bc|:|ce|$.

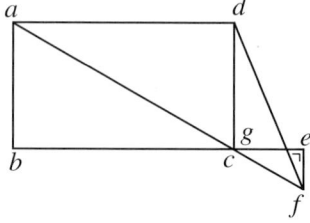

df intersects *ce* at the point *g*.

$|dc| = 8$, $|cg| = 4$ and $|ge| = 1$.

Find $|ef|$ and hence, find $|bc|$.

8. **(i)**   *abcd* is a parallelogram.

Prove that the triangles *adx* and *abe* are equiangular.

If $|dx| = \frac{3}{4}|dc|$, show that $|bc| = \frac{3}{4}|be|$.

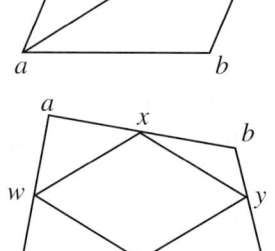

   (ii) *abcd* is a quadrilateral.

xyzw are the midpoints of [*ab*], [*bc*], [*cd*], [*da*], as shown.

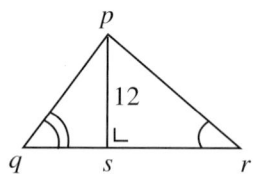
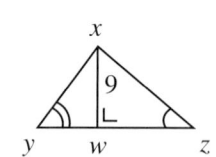

     (a) Prove *wx* is parallel to *db*

     (b) Deduce *xyzw* is a parallelogram.

9. △*pqr* and △*xyz* are similar.

The perpendicular heights are 12 cm and 9 cm, respectively.

If the area of △*xyz* is $67\frac{1}{2}$ cm^2,

prove that the area of △*pqr* is 120 cm^2.

Hence, or otherwise, verify that $\dfrac{\text{Area of } \triangle pqr}{\text{Area of } \triangle xyz} = \dfrac{|ps|^2}{|xw|^2}$.

10. C_1 and C_2 are two circles, *o* is the centre of C_1 and [*oa*] is the diameter of C_2.

The chord [*ab*] intersects C_2 at *x*.

Prove that $|ax| = |xb|$.

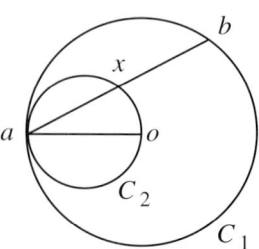

11. $[pq]$ is the diameter of circle K_1.
$[ps]$ is the diameter of circle K_2.
Explain why $|\angle prq| = |\angle pqs|$.
Show that $\triangle pqr$ and $\triangle psq$ are similar.
Redraw $\triangle pqr$ and $\triangle psq$ so that corresponding angles, or sides, match each other.
Prove that $|pq|^2 = |pr|.|ps|$.

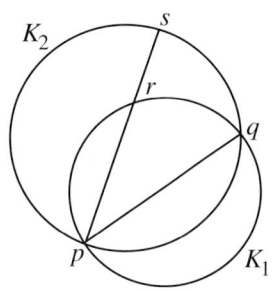

12. In $\triangle abc$, $ba \perp ac$ and $ad \perp bc$.
Prove that $\triangle abc$, $\triangle dba$ and $\triangle dac$ are similar.
Hint: Redraw the three triangles so that corresponding angles, or sides, match each other.
By comparing $\triangle abc$ and $\triangle dba$ prove $|ab|^2 = |bc|.|bd|$.
By comparing $\triangle abc$ and $\triangle dac$ prove $|ac|^2 = |bc|.|dc|$
Hence, prove $|ab|^2 + |ac|^2 = |bc|^2$.

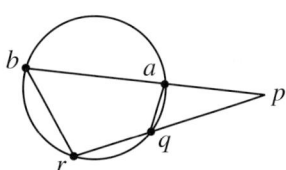

13. Show that the triangles pbr and paq are equiangular (similar).
Deduce that $|pa|.|pb| = |pq|.|pr|$.

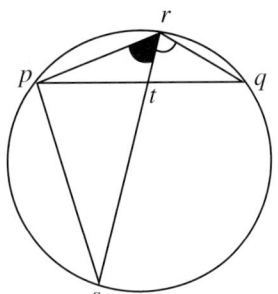

14. Two chords pq, rs of a circle meet in t, such that $|\angle srp| = |\angle qrt|$.
Explain why the triangles srp and qrt are equiangular.

Complete the ratio $\dfrac{|pr|}{|rs|} = \dfrac{|rt|}{|??|}$.

Prove $|pr|.|rq| = |rt|^2 + |pt|.|tq|$.

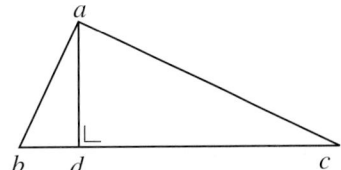

15. In the triangle abc, $|\angle bac| = 90°$ and $ad \perp bc$.
   (i) Using equiangular triangles, or otherwise, prove that
   $$|ab|^2 = |bd|.|bc|.$$
   (ii) Write down two ratios equal to
   $$\frac{|ad|}{|bd|}.$$
   If $|ac| = 2|ab|$ and $|ad| = 4$, find the value of $|ab|$.

16. In $\triangle rst$, $\quad xy \parallel st$, $\quad xu \parallel sy$
and $|ry|:|yt| = |ru|:|xy|$.
Show that $|xy| = |uy|$.
Hence, or otherwise, prove that sy bisects $\angle xyt$.

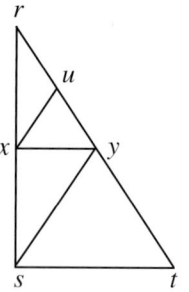

17. kp is parallel to mn and t is the midpoint of $[kp]$.
Prove

$$\frac{|mn|}{|tk|} = \frac{|nh|}{|ht|}.$$

Deduce

$$\frac{|ns|}{|ts|} = \frac{|nh|}{|ht|}.$$

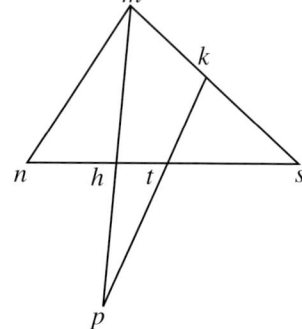

CHAPTER 24

PYTHAGORAS'S THEOREM

Pythagoras's theorem

The longest side in a right-angled triangle is always opposite the right angle and is called the '**hypotenuse**'.

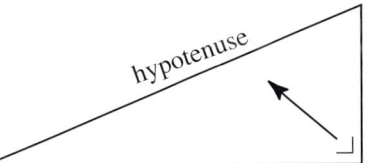

Pythagoras's theorem:

In a right-angled triangle, the square on the hypotenuse is equal to the sum of the squares on the other two sides.

$c^2 = a^2 + b^2$

The converse is also true.

If $c^2 = a^2 + b^2$, then the triangle is right-angled and c is the hypotenuse.

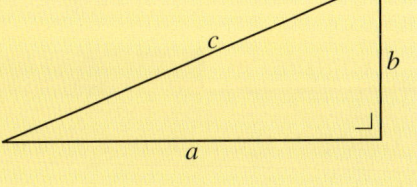

Note: Pythagoras's theorem applies only to right-angled triangles.
We can use Pythagoras's theorem to find the missing length of a side in a right-angled triangle if we know the lengths of the other two sides.

Example ▼

Find the value of x and y.

Solution:

Redraw both right-angled triangles separately and apply Pythagoras's theorem twice.

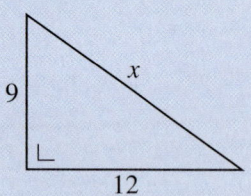

$$x^2 = 9^2 + 12^2$$
$$x^2 = 81 + 144$$
$$x^2 = 225$$
$$x = \sqrt{225}$$
$$x = 15$$

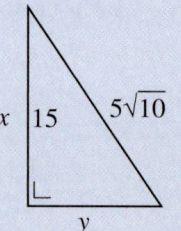

$$x^2 + y^2 = (5\sqrt{10})^2$$
$$15^2 + y^2 = (5\sqrt{10})^2$$
$$225 + y^2 = 250$$
$$y^2 = 25$$
$$y = \sqrt{25} = 5$$

Example ▼

Calculate the value of x.

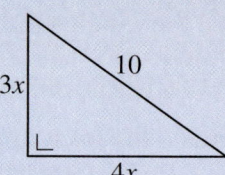

Solution:

$$(3x)^2 + (4x)^2 = (10)^2$$
$$9x^2 + 16x^2 = 100$$
$$25x^2 = 100$$
$$x^2 = 4$$
$$x = \sqrt{4} = 2$$

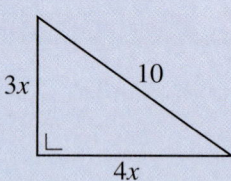

Use Pythagoras's theorem to find the length of the sides indicated by a letter in each of the following diagrams (answers in surd form when necessary):

1.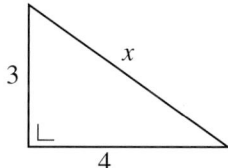

2.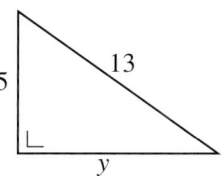

3.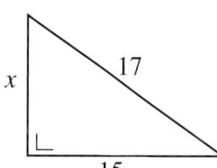

4.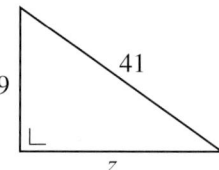

5.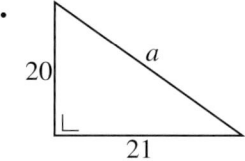

6.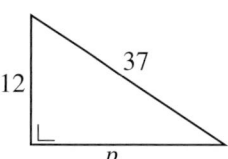

7.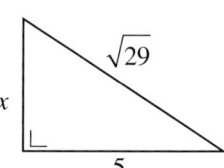

8.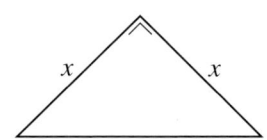

9.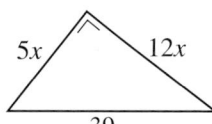

10.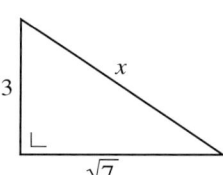

11.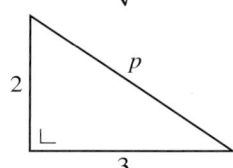

12.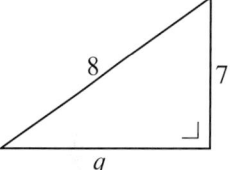

In questions 13–15, the diagrams represent squares:

13.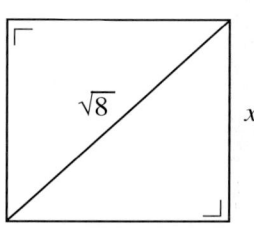

14.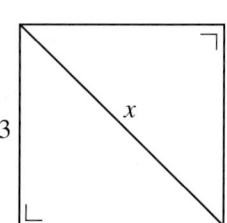

15.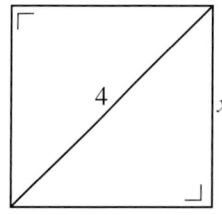

16.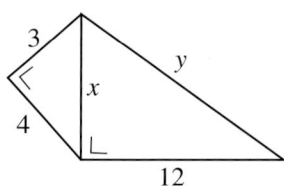

17.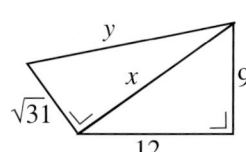

18.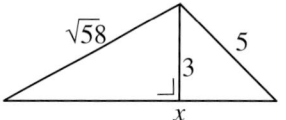

19. In the $\triangle pqr$,
$|\angle pqr| = 90°$.
Calculate the perimeter and area
of the triangle.

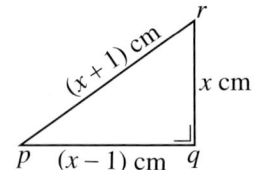

20. The centre of the circle is o,
$|ab| = 6$ and $|bo| = 5$.
Find $|bc|$.

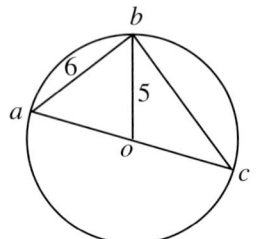

21. pt is a tangent to the circle at t.
The centre of the circle is o.
$|mo| = |np|$.
If $|pt| = 3$, find the radius of the circle.

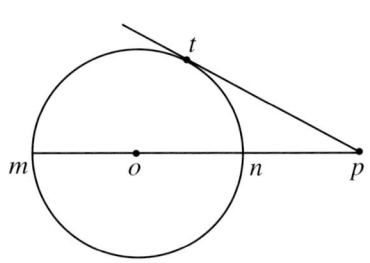

22. The diagram shows the side view of a ramp.
Calculate the length, l, of the sloping part of the
ramp.

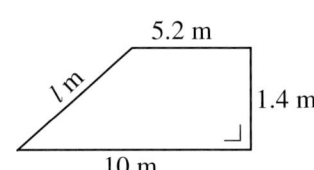

23. The top of a bucket has a diameter of 34 cm.
The bottom of the bucket has a diameter of 20 cm.
The sloping sides have a length of 25 cm.
Calculate the depth, d, of the bucket.

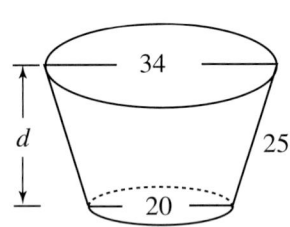

24. A vertical flagpole is held by four wires as shown.
Each wire is fixed to the pole at a height of 1.6 m above
the ground and to the ground at 3 m from the foot of
the pole.
Calculate the total length of the wire used.

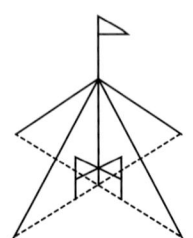

350

25. Find, in terms of π, the area of the circle inscribed in the square *ptwq* given that $|pr| = \sqrt{5}$ cm, $|qr| = 2$ cm and $|\angle qrp| = 90°$.

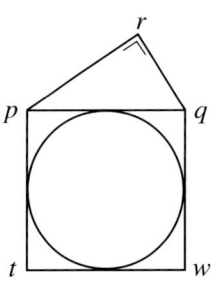

26. The lengths of the sides of a right-angled triangle are *p*, *q* and *r* as shown.
P, *Q* and *R* are semicircles with diameters of length *p*, *q* and *r*, respectively.
Express the area of *P* in terms of *p* and π.
Prove
area of *P* + area of *Q* = area of *R*.

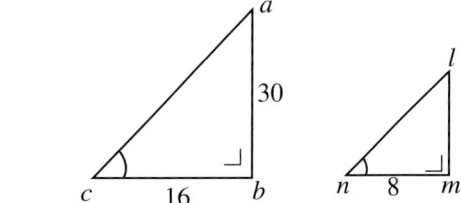

27. An equilateral triangle has sides of length 8 cm.

The perpendicular height of the triangle is $a\sqrt{b}$ cm, where *b* is prime.

Calculate **(i)** the value of *a* and the value of *b*
(ii) the area of the triangle (leave your answer in surd form).

The following problems involve similar right-angled triangles:

28. *abc* and *lmn* are right-angled triangles.
$|\angle acb| = |\angle lnm|$
$|ab| = 30$
$|bc| = 16$
$|mn| = 8$
Calculate:
(i) $|ac|$ **(ii)** $|ln|$ **(iii)** $|lm|$

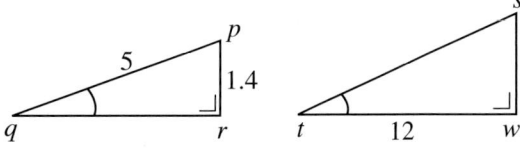

29. *pqr* and *stw* are two triangles.
$|\angle prq| = |\angle swt| = 90°$, and
$|\angle pqr| = |\angle stw|$.
Calculate
(i) $|sw|$ **(ii)** $|ts|$

30. In the triangle *abc*, $|\angle abc| = 90°$,
$|ab| = 9$ cm and $|bc| = 12$ cm.
xy is parallel to *bc* and $|xy| = 8$ cm.
Calculate $|ay|$.

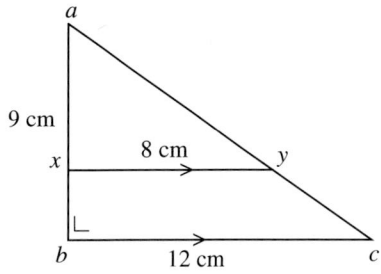

351

31. *abc* is a right-angled triangle
with *de* ∥ *bc*.
|*ab*| = 12, |*bc*| = 9 and
|*de*| = 3. Find |*ae*|.

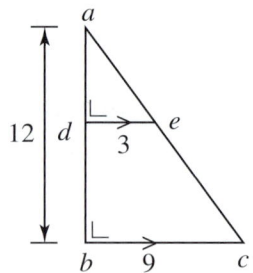

32. In the triangle *abc*,

$$\frac{|ay|}{|yc|} = \frac{2}{3}$$

xy ∥ *bc*

|∠*ayx*| = 90°

Calculate the ratio $\dfrac{\text{Area} \triangle axy}{\text{Area} \triangle abc}$

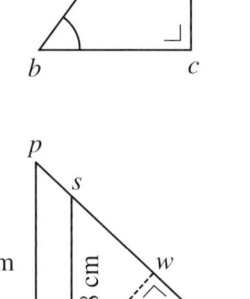

33. **(i)** In the triangle *pqr*, *pq* ⊥ *qr* and *st* ∥ *pq*.
Calculate |*qt*|, if |*pq*| = 12 cm,
|*st*| = 8 cm and |*rt*| = 6 cm.

(ii) If *tw* ⊥ *pr*, calculate |*wr*|.

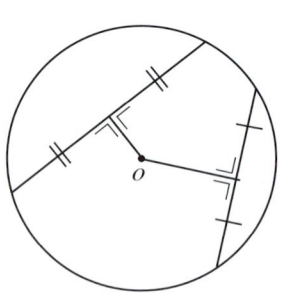

Pythagoras's theorem and bisecting chords

In chapter 22, we learned that:
A line through the centre of a circle, perpendicular to a chord bisects the chord.

Pythagoras's theorem can be used to solve problems involving lines through the centre of a circle which are perpendicular to a chord.

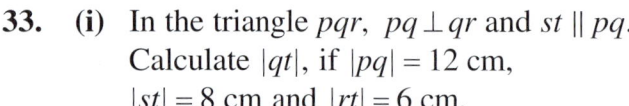

k is the centre of the circle.
If $|ab| = 9.6$ cm and the distance from *k* to
ab is 1.4 cm, calculate the length of the
diameter of the circle.

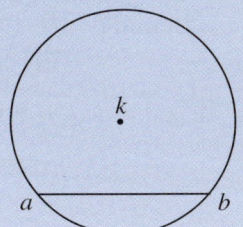

Solution:

Draw $kc \perp ab$, $\therefore |ac| = |cb|$.

$|kc| = 1.4$ cm, $|ac| = \frac{1}{2}(9.6) = 4.8$ cm and $|ak| = $ radius.

Using Pythagoras's theorem:
$|ak|^2 = |ac|^2 + |ck|^2$
$|ak|^2 = 4.8^2 + 1.4^2$
$|ak|^2 = 23.04 + 1.96$
$|ak|^2 = 25$

$|ak| = \sqrt{25} = 5$ cm
Diameter $= 2|ak| = 2(5) = 10$ cm.

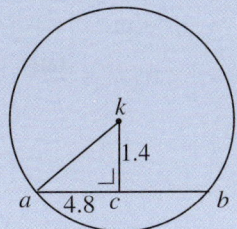

Exercise 24.2 ▼

1. *k* is the centre of the circle. If $|ab| = 30$ cm and the
    distance from *k* to *ab* is 8 cm, calculate the radius
    of the circle.

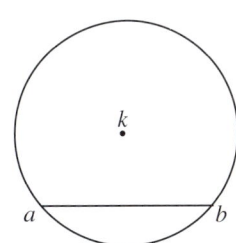

2. Circle, centre *c* and radius 5.
    $|xy| = 8$, $|rs| = 6$ and $xy \parallel rs$.
    Find the distance between *xy* and *rs*.

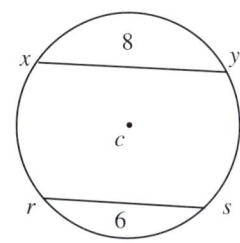

3. [*pq*] is the diameter of a circle, centre *o*.
|*pq*| = 26 cm, |*rs*| = 10 cm and *pq* ⊥ *rs*.
Calculate   **(i)** |*or*| **(ii)** |*rt*|
             (iii) |*ot*| **(iv)** |*pt*|

If |*ps*| = $k\sqrt{26}$ cm, find the value of *k*.

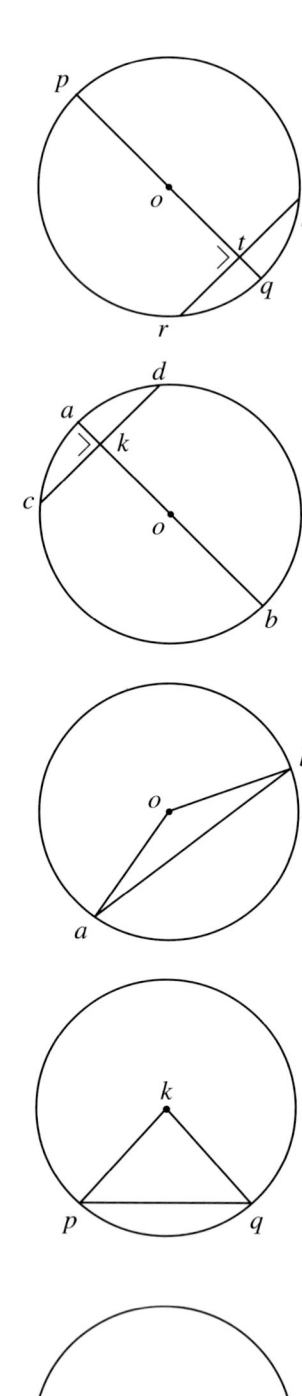

4. The centre of the circle is *o*.
ab ⊥ *cd* and *ab* ∩ *cd* = *k*.
|*ab*| = 22 cm and |*cd*| = 17.6 cm.
Calculate   **(i)** |*od*| **(ii)** |*kd*|
             (iii) |*ok*| **(iv)** |*ka*|

5. *o* is the centre of the circle.
|*ab*| = 48 cm
If the area of △*aob* is 168 cm², calculate:
(i) the distance from *o* to the line *ab*
(ii) the radius of the circle.

6. *k* is the centre of the circle.
|*pq*| = 11 cm.
If the area of △*pkq* is 72.6 cm²,
calculate the radius of the circle.

7. *o* is the centre of the circle
and [*ab*] is a chord.
om ⊥ *ab*.
Prove that *m* is the midpoint of [*ab*].

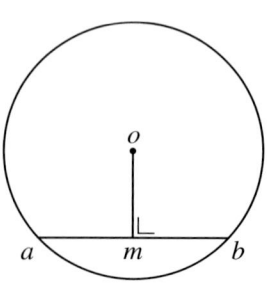

Proofs and Pythagoras's theorem

In many problems the diagram will contain two, or more, right-angled triangles.
It may help to draw the right-angled triangles separately and apply Pythagoras's theorem
to each. Isolating an algebraic expression for **common sides** can also help.

Example ▼

In $\triangle xyz$, $|\angle xzy| = 90°$, k is a point on $[xz]$.
Prove that $|xy|^2 + |kz|^2 = |ky|^2 + |xz|^2$.

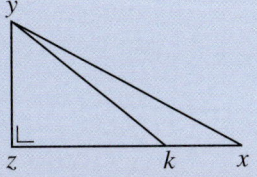

Solution:

Draw $\triangle xyz$ and $\triangle kyz$ separately and apply Pythagoras's theorem to each.
$[yz]$ is a side common to both triangles. Find two different algebraic expressions for $|yz|$ and equate them.

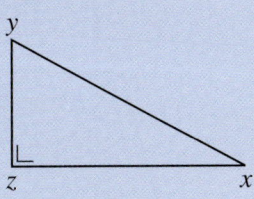

$$|yz|^2 + |xz|^2 = |xy|^2$$
$$|yz|^2 = |xy|^2 - |xz|^2$$

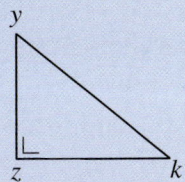

$$|yz|^2 + |kz|^2 = |ky|^2$$
$$|yz|^2 = |ky|^2 - |kz|^2$$

$$|yz|^2 = |yz|^2$$
$$\therefore \quad |xy|^2 - |xz|^2 = |ky|^2 - |kz|^2$$
$$\therefore \quad |xy|^2 + |kz|^2 = |ky|^2 + |xz|^2$$

1. Complete the following table:

a	b	$2ab$	a^2-b^2	a^2+b^2
2	1	4	3	5
3	1			
3	2			
4	1		15	
4	3			
5	2			
6		12		
6				40
7			12	
8				73

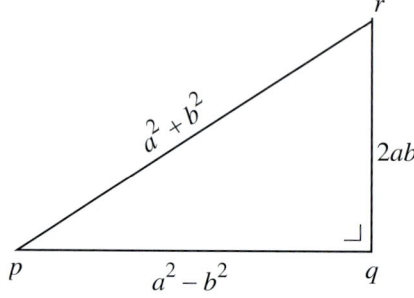

Show algebraically that:
$$(a^2-b^2)^2+(2ab)^2=(a^2+b^2)^2$$
What does this prove about $\triangle pqr$?

2. *pqrs* is a parallelogram, with $pr \perp qs$.
   Prove $|pq|=|ps|$.
   If $|pr|=9.6$ and $|qs|=28$,
   calculate **(i)** $|pq|$ **(ii)** the area of the $\triangle pqr$.

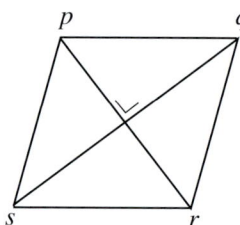

3. *abcd* is a quadrilateral in which ac is perpendicular to bd.
   Why is $|ab|^2=|am|^2+|bm|^2$?
   Hence prove that
   $|ab|^2+|cd|^2=|ad|^2+|bc|^2$.

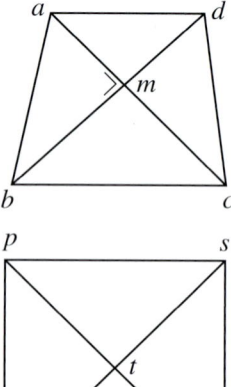

4. *pqrs* is a square.
   The diagonals meet at t.
   Prove $|qr|^2=2|pt|^2$.

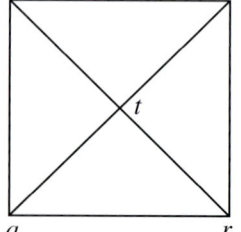

5. In the $\triangle pqr$,
$|pq| = |pr| = |qr|$
and $pq \perp rs$
Prove   **(i)** $\triangle prs \equiv \triangle qrs$
             (ii) $3|pr|^2 = 4|rs|^2$

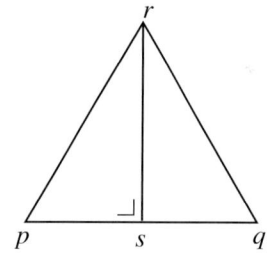

6. The diagram shows a square $pqrs$
and another square $pruv$.

     Prove $\dfrac{\text{area of square } pqrs}{\text{area of square } pruv} = \dfrac{1}{2}$

     Hint: Let $x =$ the length of a side of the
            smaller square.

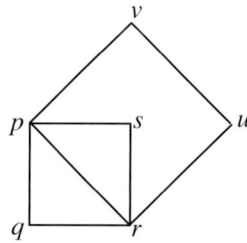

7. In the triangle xyz, $xw \perp yz$.
Prove that
$|xy|^2 + |wz|^2 = |yw|^2 + |xz|^2$.

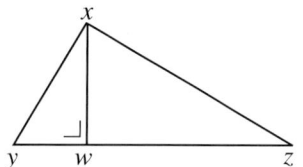

8. In the diagram,
$pq \perp st$ and $ps \perp qr$.
Prove that $\triangle pqr$ and $\triangle pst$ are similar.
If $|st| = |pr| = 8$, find the value of $|qr|.|pt|$.

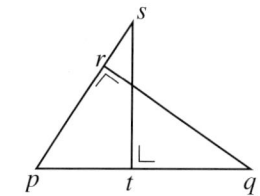

9. In the given diagram,
$|\angle pqr| = 90° = |\angle prs|$,
$|pq| = |qr| = 2|rs|$.
By letting $|rs| = x$, or otherwise,
prove that $|ps| = 3|rs|$.

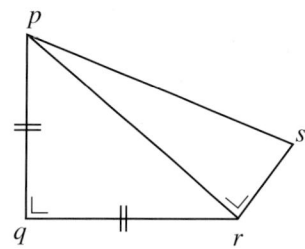

10. **(i)** In the $\triangle abc$, $|\angle acb| = 90°$,
$|ac| = |bc|$ and $ab \perp cd$.
Prove $|ab| = 2|cd|$.

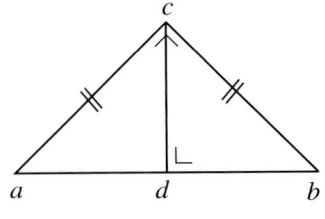

(ii) In the $\triangle pqr$,
$|pq|^2 = |pt|^2 + |tr|^2$
and $qt \perp pr$.
Prove $|\angle qrt| = 45°$.

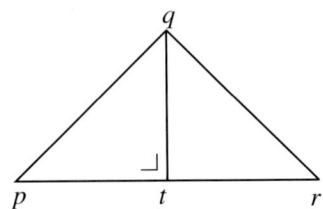

11. In the $\triangle abc$,
$|ac|^2 = |ad|^2 + 3|db|^2$
and $ab \perp cd$.
Prove $|\angle bcd| = 30°$.

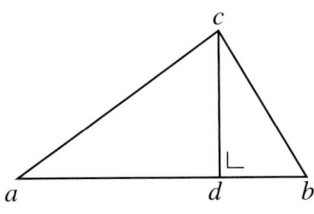

12. In the $\triangle pqr$, $|\angle pqr| = 90°$.
Prove that $|qr|^2 = |sr|^2 - |sq|^2$.
Using $|pq| = |ps| + |sq|$,
prove $|pr|^2 = |ps|^2 + |rs|^2 + 2|ps|.|sq|$.

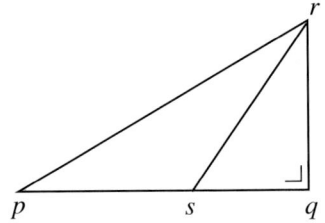

13. In the $\triangle pqr$, $ps \perp rq$.
Use $|rs| = |rq| - |qs|$
to write an expression for $|rs|^2$.
Deduce that
$|rp|^2 = |rq|^2 + |qp|^2 - 2|qr|.|qs|$.

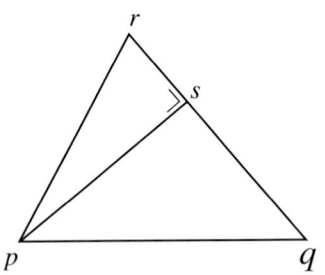

14. o is any point in triangle xyz.
From o, the perpendiculars oa, ob
and oc are drawn to the sides as shown.
Show that:
$|ay|^2 + |bz|^2 + |cx|^2 = |ax|^2 + |cz|^2 + |by|^2$.

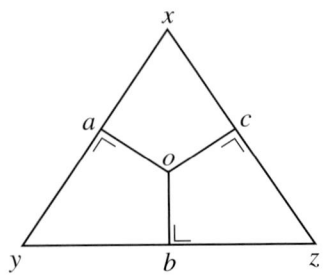

CONSTRUCTIONS

The six constructions

There are six constructions on our course:
1. Perpendicular bisector of a line segment.
2. Circumcircle of a triangle.
3. Bisector of an angle.
4. Incircle of a triangle.
5. Divide a line segment into a given number of parts.
6. Construct a triangle given sufficient information.

Any work involving accurate constructions requires a good pencil, a compass, a ruler, and a protractor. It is very important not to rub out any construction lines or marks you make at any stage during a construction. All construction lines or marks should **always** be left on the diagram.

1. Perpendicular bisector of a line segment

The perpendicular bisector of a line segment, [xy], is constructed with the following steps:

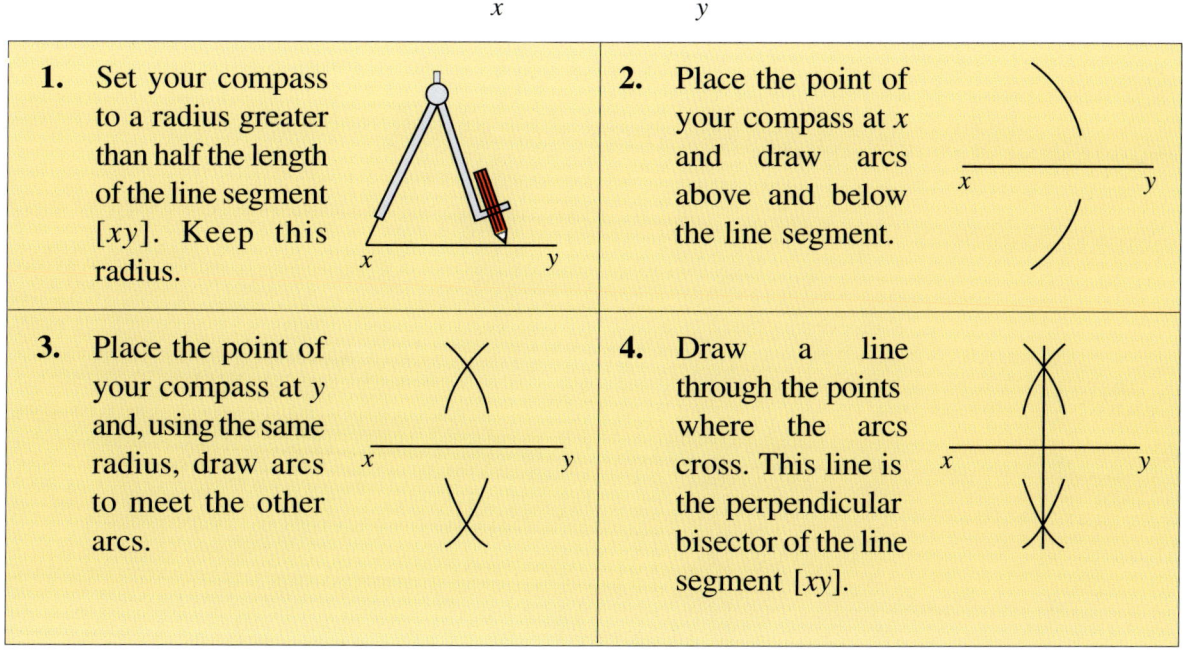

2. Circumcircle of a triangle

The circumcircle of a triangle is constructed with the following steps:

1. Draw the triangle *abc*. 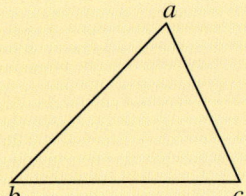	**2.** Construct the perpendicular bisector of [*ab*]. 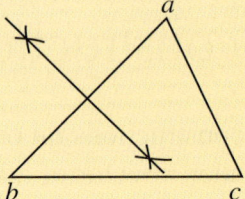
3. Construct the perpendicular bisector of [*ac*], to meet the other perpendicular bisector at *k*. 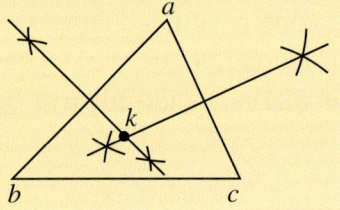	**4.** With *k* as centre and |*ka*| as radius, draw the circumcircle of triangle *abc*. 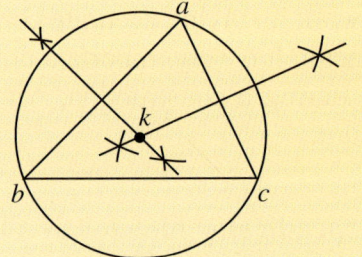

Note: *k* is called the 'circumcentre' of △*abc*.

3. Bisector of an angle

The bisector of an angle is constructed with the following steps:

1. Place the point of your compass on the vertex, *o*, of the angle. Using the same radius, draw two arcs to meet the arms of the angle at *x* and *y*. 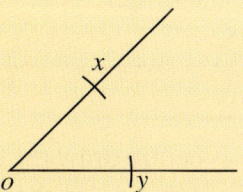	**2.** Place the point of your compass at *x* and draw an arc. 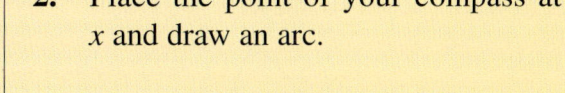
3. Place the point of your compass at *y* and, using the same radius, draw an arc to meet the other arc. 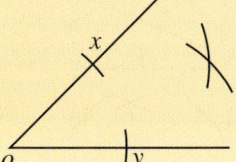	**4.** Draw a line through *o* and the point where the arcs cross. This line is the bisector of the angle. 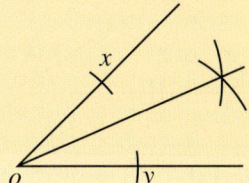

4. Incircle of a triangle

The incircle of a triangle is constructed with the following steps:

1. Draw the triangle *abc*. 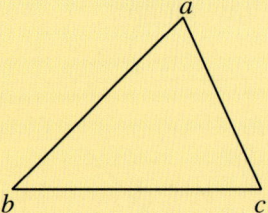	**2.** Construct the bisector of ∠*abc*. 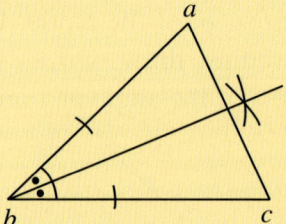
3. Construct the bisector of ∠*acb*, to meet the other angle bisector at *k*. 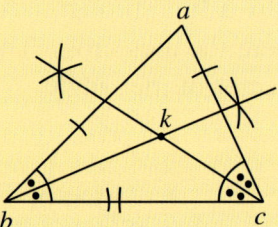	**4.** With *k* as centre draw the circle which touches each side of the triangle. 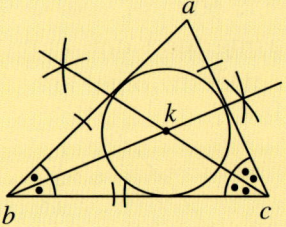

Note: *k* is called the 'incentre' of △*abc*.

5. Divide a line segment into a given number of parts.

A line segment, [xy], is divided into three equal parts with the following steps:

1.	Draw a line through x at an acute angle to xy. 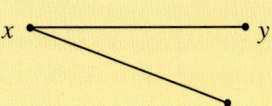
2.	Using a compass, mark off three points a, b and c on this line so that $\|xa\| = \|ab\| = \|bc\|$. 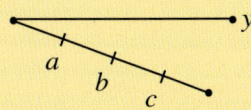
3.	Join c to y. Using a ruler and a set square, draw lines through a and b parallel to cy to meet the line segment at w and z. z and w divide the line segment [xy] into three equal parts. 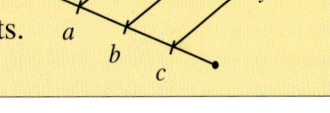

Note: This method can also be used to bisect a line segment or to divide a line segment into any number of equal parts.

6. Constructing triangles given sufficient information

The following hints are helpful when constructing triangles:

1. Draw a rough sketch first (usually freehand). Label it with the information given.
2. Use a pencil (it's easy to rub out if you make a mistake).
3. Leave all your construction lines on your final drawing (do not rub them out).
4. Draw your final diagram as accurately as possible.
5. Label your final drawing clearly.

The method used for drawing a triangle depends on the information you are given. We will look at four cases. A triangle can be drawn if you are given:

1. The length of the three sides (SSS).
2. The length of two sides and the angle between them (SAS).
3. The length of one side and two angles (ASA).
4. A right angle, the length of the hypotenuse, and one other side (RHS).

Note: If you know two angles in a triangle it is possible to calculate the third angle. The four cases above are related to the '**four cases of congruence**' as in Chapter 21.

1. Given the length of the three sides (SSS)

Example ▼

Construct the triangle *abc* so that $|ab| = 6$ cm, $|ac| = 5$ cm, and $|bc| = 4$ cm.

Solution:

A rough sketch, with the given information, is shown on the right.

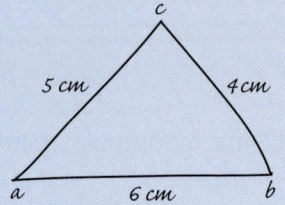

---

1. Using your ruler, draw a horizontal line segment 6 cm in length. Label the end points *a* and *b*.

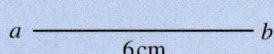

2. Set your compass to a radius of 5 cm. Place the compass point on *a*. Draw an arc above the line.

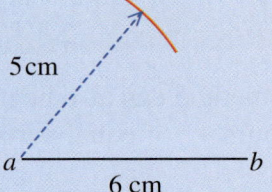

---

3. Set your compass to a radius of 4 cm. Place the compass point at *b*. Draw an arc above the line to meet the other arc. Label this point *c*.

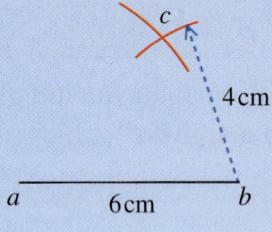

4. Using your ruler, join *a* to *c* and *b* to *c*. The triangle *abc* is now drawn, as required.

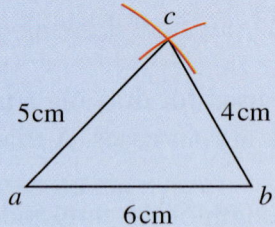

2. Given the length of two sides and the angle between them (SAS)

Construct a triangle *pqr* so that $|pq| = 5$ cm, $|pr| = 4$ cm, and $|\angle qpr| = 60°$.

Solution:

A rough sketch, with the given information, is shown on the right.

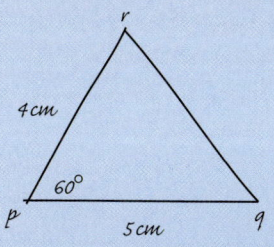

1. Using your ruler, draw a horizontal line segment 5 cm in length. Label the end points *p* and *q*. 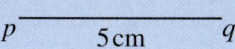	**2.** Use your protractor to draw an angle of 60° at *p*. 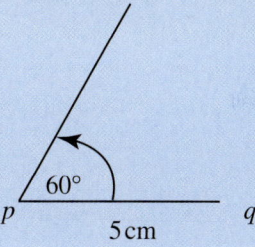
3. Use your ruler, or compass, to mark the point *r*, so that $|pr| = 4$ cm. 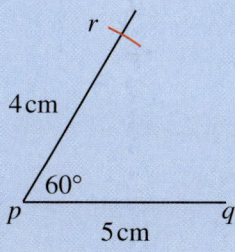	**4.** Using your ruler, join *r* to *q*. The triangle *pqr* is now drawn as required. 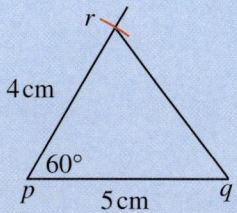

3. Given the length of one side and two angles (ASA)

Construct a triangle xyz so that $|xy| = 7$ cm, $|\angle yxz| = 40°$, and $|\angle xyz| = 70°$.

Solution:

A rough sketch, with the given information, is shown on the right.

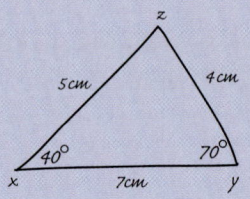

1. Using your ruler, draw a horizontal line segment 7 cm in length. Label the end points x and y.	2. Use your protractor to draw an angle of 40° at x.

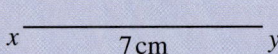

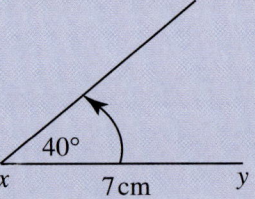

3. Use your protractor to draw an angle of 70° at y.	4. Where these two lines meet, label the point z. The triangle xyz is now drawn as required.

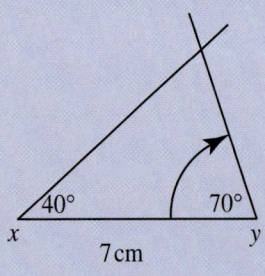

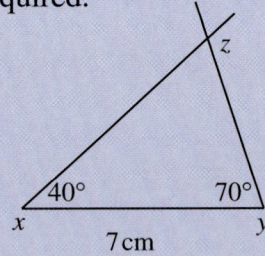

366

4. Given a right angle, the hypotenuse, and another side (RHS)

Example ▼

Construct the triangle *abc* so that $|\angle bac| = 90°$, $|ab| = 7$ cm, and $|bc| = 8$ cm.

Solution:

A rough sketch, with the given information, is shown on the right.

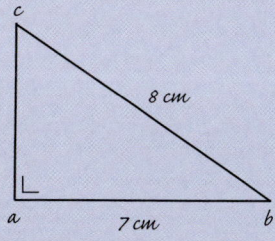

1. Using your ruler, draw a horizontal segment 7 cm in length. Label the end points *a* and *b*. 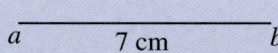	**2.** Using your protractor or set square, draw an angle of 90° at *a*. 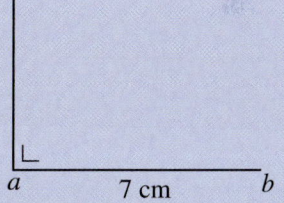
3. Set your compass to a radius of 8 cm. Place the compass point on *b*. Draw an arc to meet the vertical line. Label this point *c*. 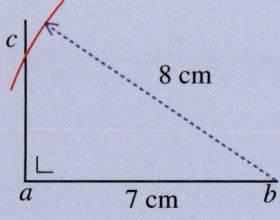	**4.** Using your ruler, join *b* to *c*. The triangle *abc* is now drawn as required. 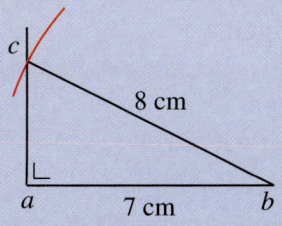

Construct accurately, showing all construction lines, each of the following triangles, with all dimensions in centimetres (the diagrams are not drawn to scale):

1.

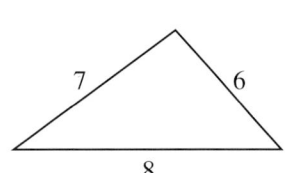

2.

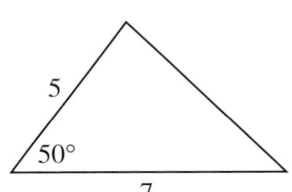

3.

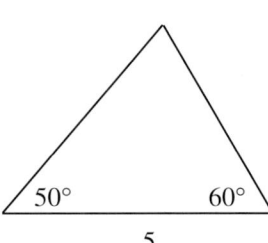

4.

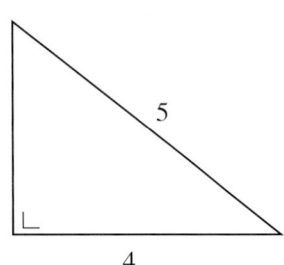

5.

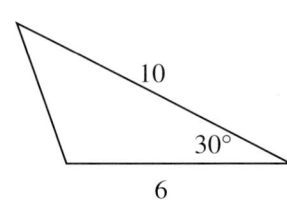

6.

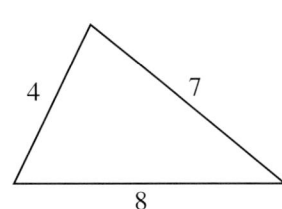

7.

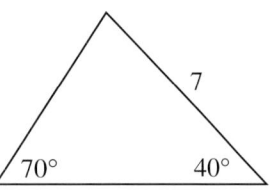

8.

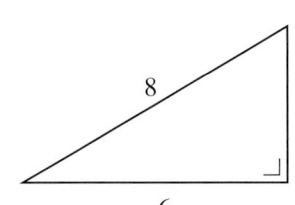

9.

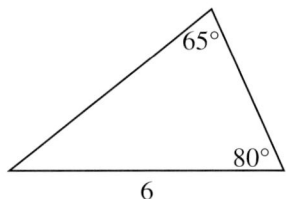

Construct accurately each of the following triangles.

(It is good practice to draw a rough sketch first and to draw one side as a horizontal base at the beginning.)

10. $|pq| = 6$ cm, $|pr| = 5$ cm, and $|\angle qpr| = 50°$.

11. $|ab| = 7$ cm, $|ac| = 6$ cm, and $|bc| = 5$ cm.

12. $|yz| = 8$ cm, $|\angle xyz| = 50°$, and $|\angle xzy| = 30°$.

13. $|ab| = 5$ cm, $|ac| = 7$ cm, and $|\angle abc| = 90°$.

14. $|pq| = 7$ cm, $|\angle pqr| = 80°$ and $|\angle prq| = 75°$.

15. Construct $\triangle pqr$ with $|pq| = 7$ cm, $|pr| = 6$ cm and $|qr| = 5$ cm.
Draw the circumcircle of $\triangle pqr$.

16. **(i)** Construct a triangle abc with $|ab| = 6$ cm, $|\angle bac| = 50°$ and $|ac| = 5$ cm.
Draw the bisector of $\angle acb$, showing all construction lines.

(ii) Construct $\triangle abc$ with $|ab| = 8$ cm, $|ac| = 7$ cm and $|bc| = 6$ cm.
Draw the incircle of $\triangle abc$, showing all construction lines.

17. [pq] is a line segment such that |pq| = 7 cm.
Copy the line segment.

p ——————————————————— q

7 cm

Divide the line segment into 4 equal parts,
showing all construction lines.

18. [ab] is a line segment such that |ab| = 93 mm.
Copy the line segment.

a ——————————————————— b

93 mm

Divide the line segment into 5 equal parts,
showing all construction lines.

19. In the △xyz,
|xy| = 10 cm, |xz| = 9 cm, and |∠yxz| = 55°.
Construct the incircle of △xyz, showing all construction lines.

20. k is the circumcentre of the △pqr.
|∠prq| = 70°, and |∠kpr| = 25°.
Calculate: **(i)** |∠pkq| **(ii)** |∠kqr|.

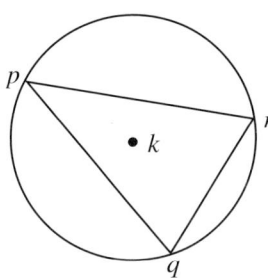

21. k is the incentre of △pqr.
|∠qpr| = 80°.
Calculate |∠qkr|.

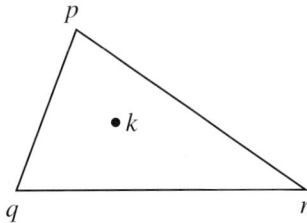

22. In the △pqr, k is the incentre.
|∠pkq| = 110°.
Calculate:
(i) |∠prq| **(ii)** |∠prk|

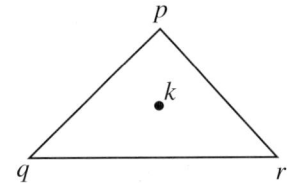

369

23. In the diagram,
$|xy| = 5$ cm, $|\angle xyz| = 120°$ and $|yz| = 4$ cm.
Copy the diagram.
Construct the point k such that $|kx| = |ky| = |kz|$.
With k as centre and radius $|ky|$, draw a circle.
What is the point k called?

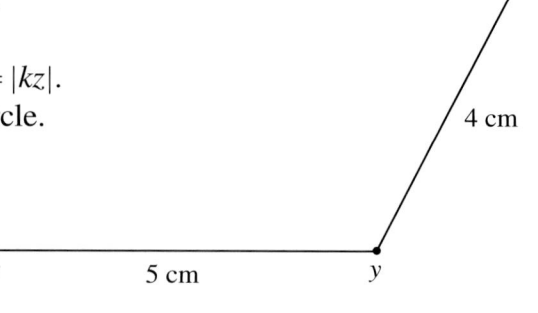

24. The diagram shows a rectangular field $pqrs$ such that
$|pq| = 90$ m and $|ps| = 50$ m.
Copy the diagram using a scale of 1 cm = 10 m.
A gold coin is hidden in the field at the point x.
The point x is equidistant from pq and ps and
$|rx| = 70$ m.
Construct the point x.

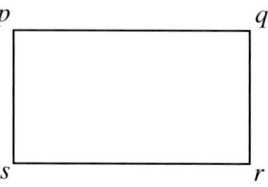

25. k is the incentre of the $\triangle pqr$.
$|kx| = |ky| = |kz| = $ radius of the incircle.
Prove   **(i)** $|px| = |py|$
        (ii) $|pr| + |rq| > |pq|$.

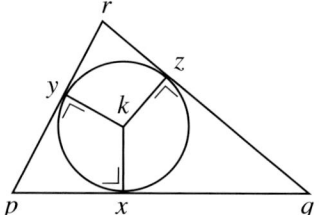

26. In the $\triangle pqr$, k is the circumcentre. The area of the
circumcircle is 25π cm^2 and $|pq| = 8$ cm.
Calculate the distance from k to pq.

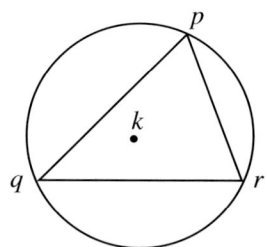

27. Construct a triangle xyz in which $|xy| = 10$ cm, $|yz| = 8$ cm and $|xz| = 6$ cm.
Construct the circumcircle of the triangle, showing all your construction lines clearly.
Explain why the centre of the circumcircle is the midpoint of $[xy]$.
Show that the area of the circle is greater than three times the area of the triangle.
Let $|xy| = a$, $|yz| = b$, and $|xz| = c$.

Verify that the area of the $\triangle xyz$ is given by $A = \sqrt{s(s-a)(s-b)(s-c)}$ cm^2
where $s = \dfrac{a+b+c}{2}$.

28. Construct the $\triangle abc$, with $|bc| = 10$ cm, $|ab| = 9$ cm, and $|ac| = 7$ cm, as shown. Construct the incircle of $\triangle abc$, with centre k.
Show all your construction lines clearly.
If r cm is the length of the radius of the circle, prove:
(i) the area of $\triangle kbc$ is $5r$ cm^2
(ii) the area of $\triangle abc$ is $13r$ cm^2.

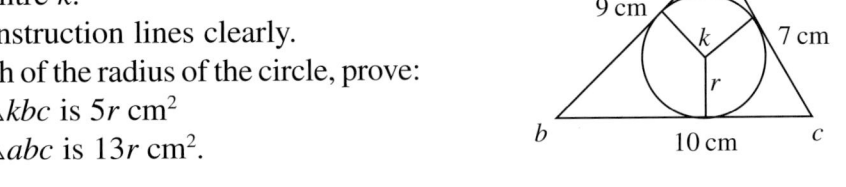

29. In the $\triangle abc$, o is the incentre, r is the radius of the incircle. $|ac| = 3$ cm, $|\angle acb| = 90°$, and $|cb| = 4$ cm.
Construct the $\triangle abc$.
Calculate **(i)** $|ab|$ **(ii)** the area of $\triangle abc$.
Explain why the area of the $\triangle aoc = \frac{3}{2}r$.
Hence, or otherwise, show that r, the radius of the incentre is 1 cm.

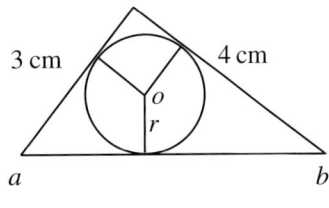

30. Construct the triangle pqr such that:
$|pq| = 5$ cm, $|qr| = 12$ cm, and $|pr| = 13$ cm.
prove: **(i)** $|\angle pqr| = 90°$
(ii) the radius of the circumcircle is $6\frac{1}{2}$ cm
(iii) the area of the triangle is 30 cm^2
(iv) the radius of the incircle is 2 cm.

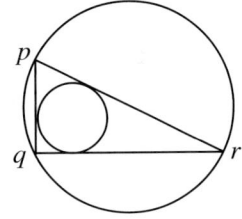

31. In the $\triangle abc$,
$|ab| = |ac| = |bc|$.
Prove that the radius of the circumcircle is twice the radius of the incircle.

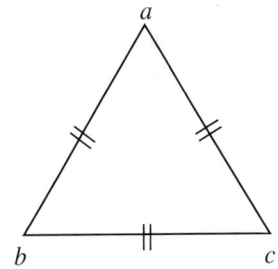

TRANSFORMATIONS OF THE PLANE

Transformations

The word '**transformation**' means change.

Object and image

The original position of a figure is called the '**object**'.
The new position of a figure is called the '**image**'.
In other words, the image is where the object moves to.

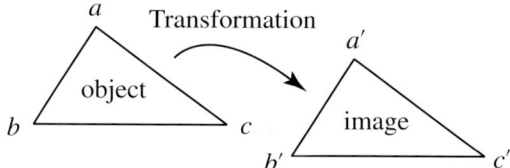

Notice that each letter on the image is dashed. Transformations are sometimes called '**mappings**', and the object is said to be mapped onto the image.
On our course we will look at four types of transformations:
1. Translations   **2.** Axial symmetries   **3.** Central symmetries   **4.** Rotations
Each of these transformations changes the position of a figure but not its size or shape.

Translation

A translation moves a figure in a straight line.

A translation is often called a '**slide**' or '**shift**'.
The figure does not turn or flip over.

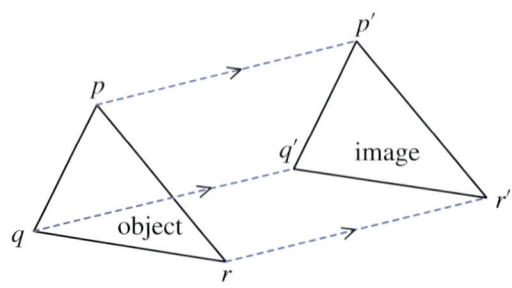

Under a translation, every point (on the figure) moves the **same distance** and in the **same direction**.

To define a translation we must give the distance and the direction moved.

The translation above could be described as $p \rightarrow p'$, written $\overrightarrow{pp'}$ (or $\overrightarrow{qq'}$ or $\overrightarrow{rr'}$)

Notice that under a translation, a line is parallel to the original line.

As can be seen from the diagram, $pr \parallel p'r'$, $pq \parallel p'q'$, and $qr \parallel q'r'$.

All line segments in the image are equal in length and parallel to the corresponding line segments in the object.

Axial symmetry

> Axial symmetry is a reflection in a line.

A reflection in a line, an axial symmetry, gives an image that looks like the reflection of an object in a mirror. The object and the image are the **same distance** on either side of the line. However, under a reflection in a line, a figure flips over.

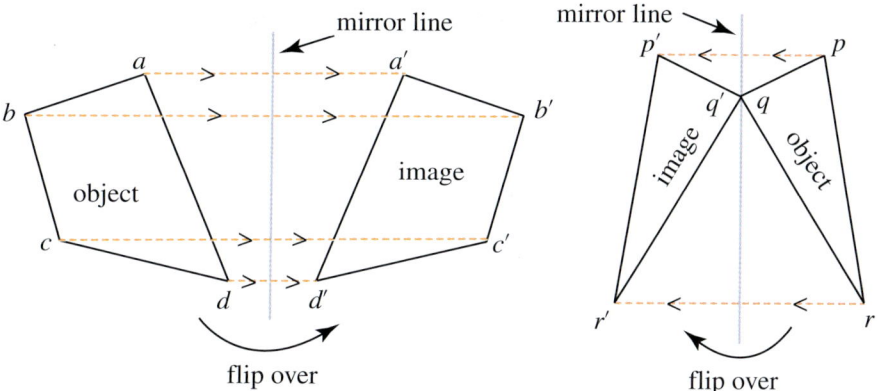

Notes: 1. If a point lies on the mirror line (line of symmetry), its image is the same point. In the second diagram, the image of q is still q.
2. By the same distance on either side of the line we mean the same perpendicular distance.

Central symmetry

> Central symmetry is a reflection in a point.

Consider below the $\triangle abc$ and its image $\triangle a'b'c'$ under a central symmetry in the point o.

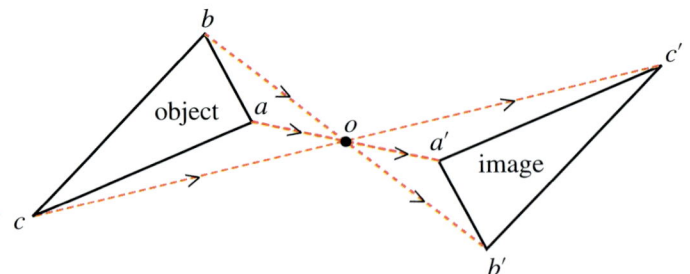

Notice that under a central symmetry, a line is parallel to the original line.
As can be seen from the diagram, $ab \parallel a'b'$, $ac \parallel a'c'$ and $bc \parallel b'c'$.

Note: The image of the point o under a central symmetry in o is the point itself.
We say that o is its own image.

Rotation

> A rotation turns a figure through an angle about a fixed point.

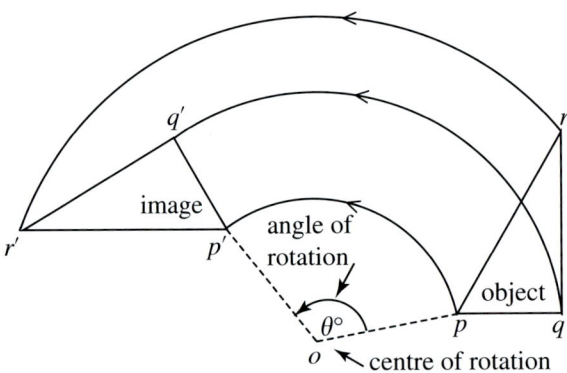

The triangle (object) has been rotated in an anticlockwise direction through an angle θ about the centre of rotation o.
The centre of rotation can be inside, on or outside a figure. Under a rotation the centre of rotation does not change. When a figure is rotated it maintains the same shape but its **orientation** on the page changes.

To describe a rotation we need:

> **1.** The position of the centre of rotation.
> **2.** The angle through which the object is to be rotated.
> **3.** The direction, positive or negative, of the rotation.

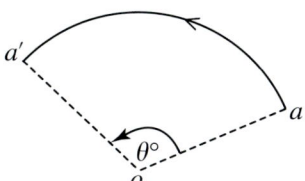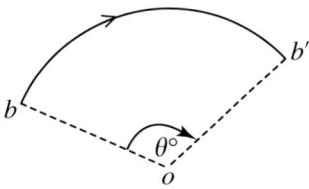
Axis of symmetry

If a figure is **identical** on each side of a line drawn through it then it is said to have 'line symmetry'. A figure with line symmetry is balanced on each side of the line. The line that divides the figure into two identical halves is called an **'axis of symmetry'** (often called a 'line of symmetry' or a 'mirror line').

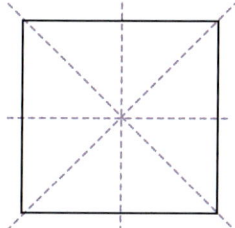

A square has four axes of symmetry.

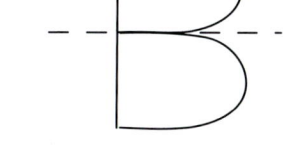

The capital letter B has one axis of symmetry.

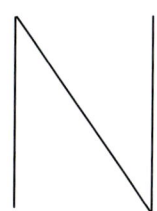

The capital letter N has no axis of symmetry.

Centre of symmetry

Some figures are symmetrical about a point. The point is called the **'centre of symmetry'**. The following figures have a centre of symmetry, indicated by *o*.

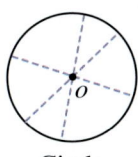

Circle

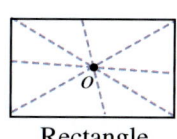

Rectangle

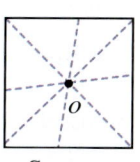

Square

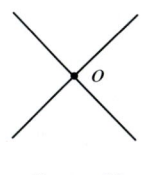

Letter X

In each case, if any point is taken on the figure, its image under a reflection in the point *o* is always another point on the figure.

Not all figures have a centre of symmetry. For example, a triangle has no centre of symmetry.

Rotational symmetry

When a figure can be rotated about its centre to a new position so that it fits exactly over its original position, then the figure is said to have 'rotational symmetry'. The number of different positions a figure fits onto itself in one complete turn is called the 'order of rotational symmetry'.

Equilateral triangle

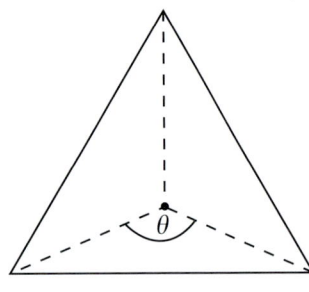

Square

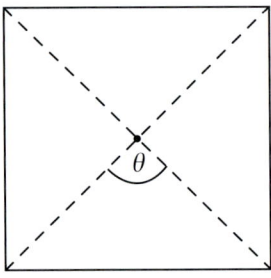

Hexagon

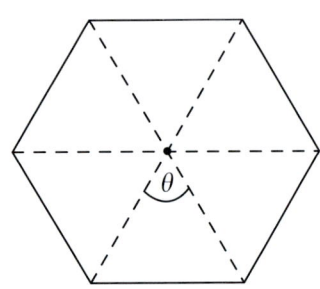

Order 3

$$\theta = \frac{360°}{3} = 120°$$

Order 4

$$\theta = \frac{360°}{4} = 90°$$

Order 6

$$\theta = \frac{360°}{6} = 60°$$

Notes:
1. All figures have a rotational symmetry of at least order 1.
2. A figure can have both axial (line) symmetry and rotational symmetry.

Example ▼

Sketch the image of the figure A under a positive (anticlockwise) rotation of 90° about the point p.

Solution:

The figure A' is the image of the figure A.
A is mapped onto A'.
All points on the figure A are turned through an angle of 90° in an anticlockwise direction about the point p.
The point p is called the **centre of rotation**.
When a figure is rotated it keeps the same shape and size but its **orientation** is changed.

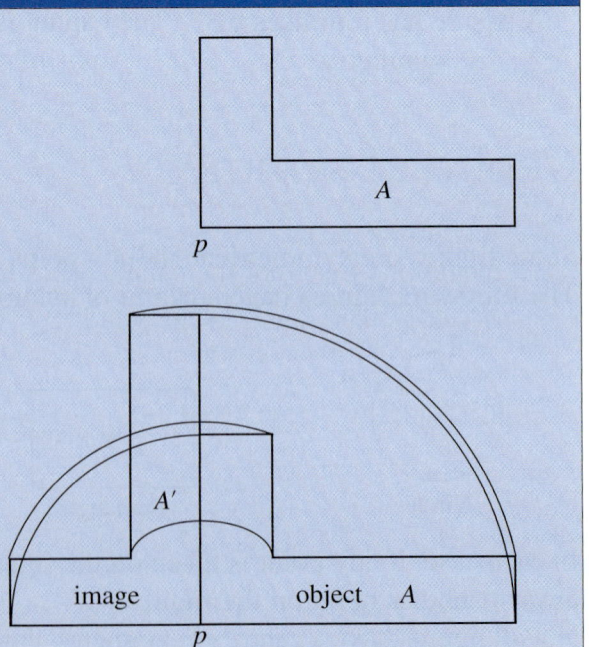

For each figure, state whether it has a centre of symmetry, and indicate where it is:

1. 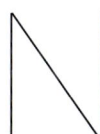 **2.** 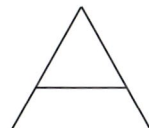 **3.**  **4.**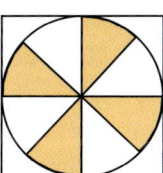

For each figure state:
(i) the number of lines of symmetry **(ii)** the order of its rotational symmetry.

5. 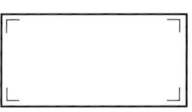 **6.** 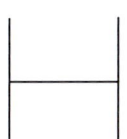 **7.** 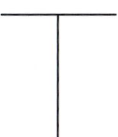 **8.**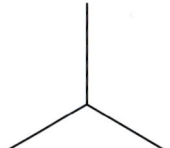

9. 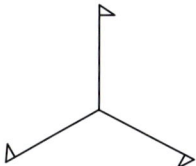 **10.**  **11.** 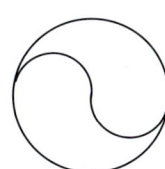 **12.**

13. 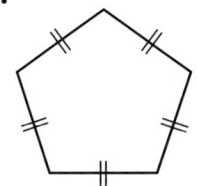 **14.** 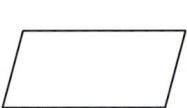 **15.** 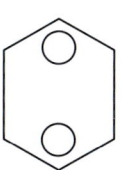 **16.**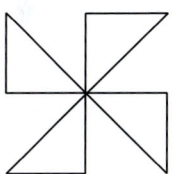

17. Sketch the image of the capital letter F under:

    (i) axial symmetry in the line *L*.   **(ii)** central symmetry in the point *P*.

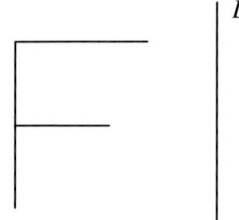

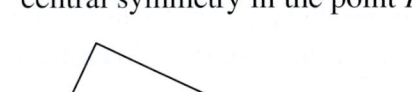

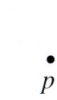

18. Sketch the image of △*abc* under an axial symmetry in the line *K*.

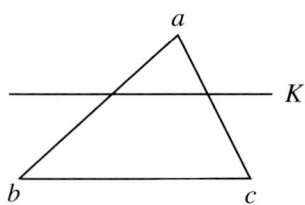

19. Sketch the image of the figure shown under a positive (anticlockwise) rotation of 60° about the point *p*.

20. The diagram shows a regular hexagon *pqrstu* with a centre *o*.
   (i) What is the order of rotational symmetry of the hexagon?
   (ii) Find the smallest angle of rotation, about *o*, which maps *p* to *q*.
   (iii) Describe two rotations which map *p* onto *t*.

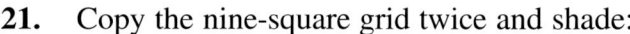

21. Copy the nine-square grid twice and shade:
   (a) three squares so that the resultant figure has two lines of symmetry and rotational symmetry of order two.
     How many different ways can this be done?
   (b) five squares so that the resultant figure has four lines of symmetry and rotational symmetry of order four.
     How many different ways can this be done?

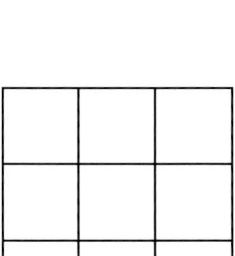

22. In the diagram, *C* represents the cushion of a snooker table. *W*, *P* and *R* represent the white, pink and red balls, respectively. A player wants to play the white ball against the cushion at the point *q* to strike the red ball directly. By using an axial symmetry, show how to find the point *q*.

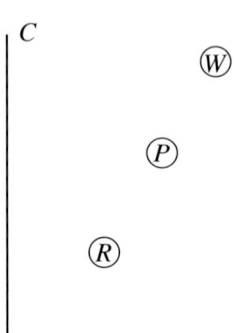

23. x and y represent two houses which require connection to a water main represented by the line L. By using an axial symmetry determine the location of a common connection point on the main supply line which will give the shortest length of pipe required.

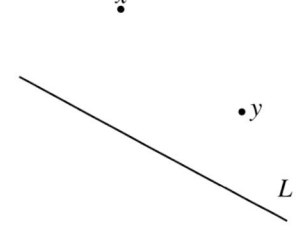

24. $pqrs$ is mapped onto $p'q'r's'$ under an axial symmetry in the line $y = x - 1$.

   (i) Draw and label the image.

   (ii) Write down the coordinates of p', q', r' and s'.

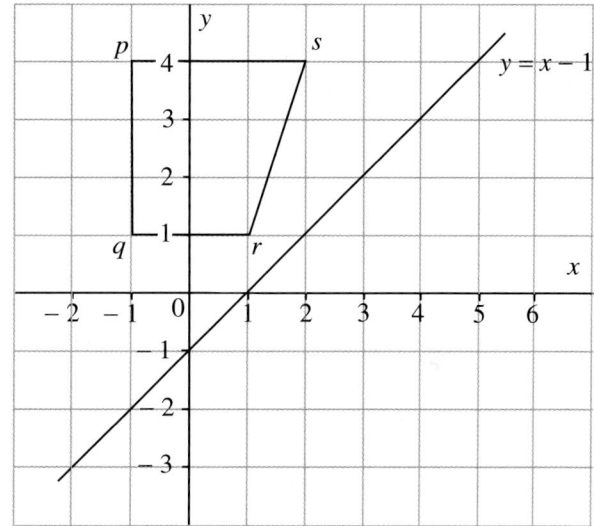

25. $\triangle pqr$ is mapped onto $\triangle p'q'r'$ under a rotation of 90°, anticlockwise, about the point $a(1,1)$.

   (i) Draw and label the image.

   (ii) Write down the coordinates of p', q' and r'.

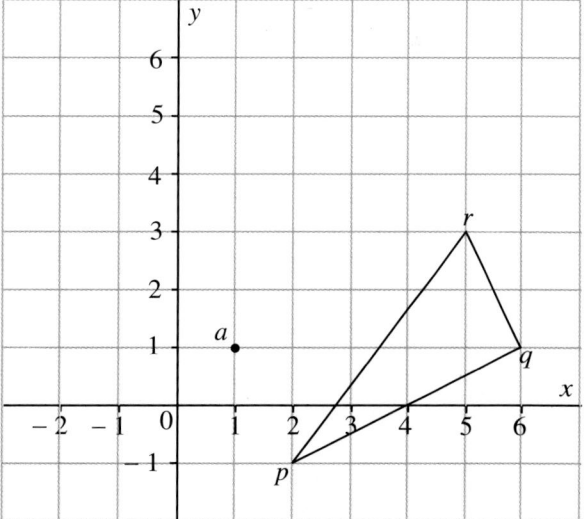

26. $\triangle abc$ is mapped onto $\triangle a'b'c'$ under a rotation of 90°, anticlockwise about the origin, $o(0, 0)$.
   (i) Draw and label the image.
   (ii) Write down the coordinates of a', b' and c'.

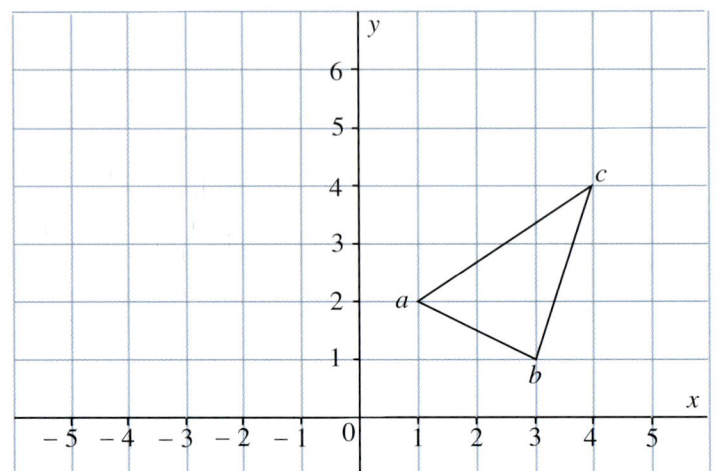

27. $\triangle a'b'c'$ is the image of $\triangle abc$ under an axial symmetry in the x axis and $\triangle a''b''c''$ is the image of $\triangle a'b'c'$ under an axial symmetry in the y-axis. Describe three different **single** transformations which map $\triangle abc$ onto $\triangle a''b''c''$.

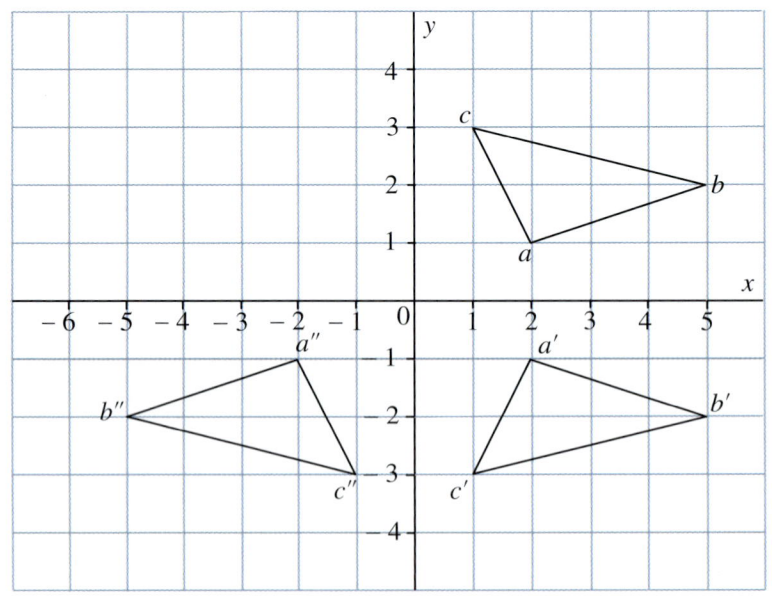

28. Describe fully the transformation which maps figure S onto figure S'.

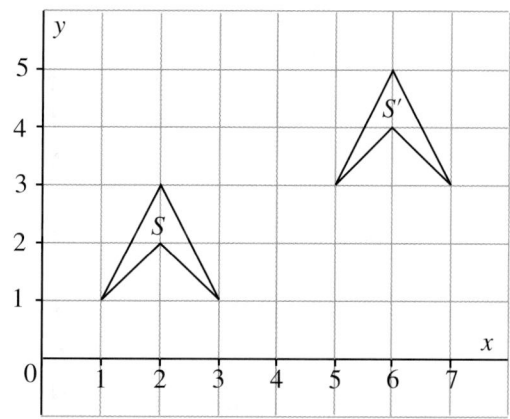

29. Describe fully the transformation which maps figure A onto figure B.

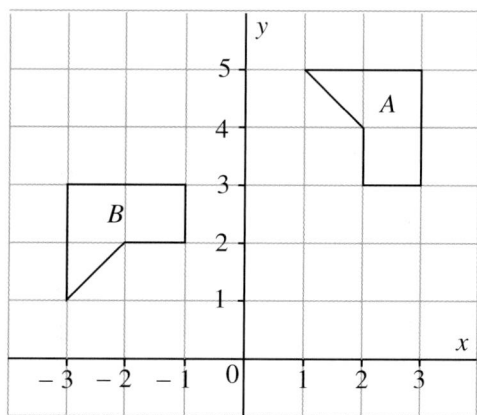

30. Describe fully the single transformation that maps:

    (i) A_1 onto A_2 **(ii)** A_1 onto A_4 **(iii)** A_2 onto A_3

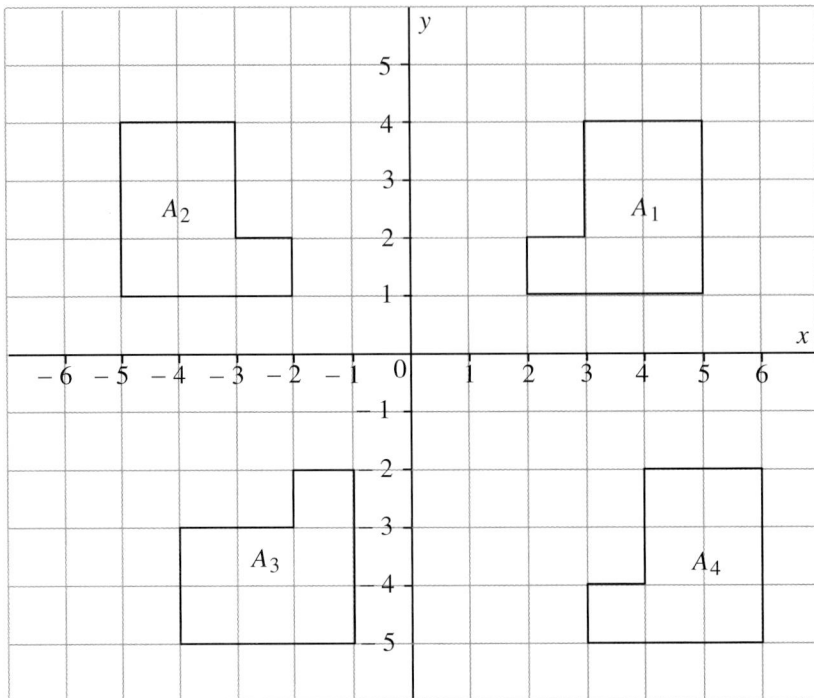

31. The diagram shows six square tiles which are arranged to produce a repeating pattern, as shown.
Describe fully the single transformation which maps:
    (i) the tile *vwrq* onto the tile *xwrs*
    (ii) the tile *abwz* onto the tile *srwx*
    (iii) the tile *rsxw* onto the tile *xsty*.

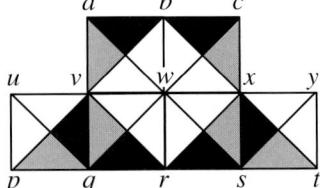

32. L and K are two lines intersecting at the point o, as shown. The angle between L and K is θ.
x' is the image of x under an axial symmetry in L.
x'' is the image of x' under an axial symmetry in K.
x'' is the image of x under a positive (anticlockwise) rotation about the point o.
Explain, or prove, why $|\angle xox''| = 2\theta$.

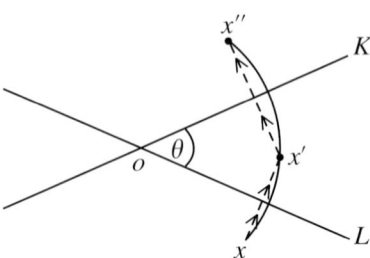

USING EQUATIONS TO SOLVE PROBLEMS

Forming expressions

Statements in words can be translated into algebraic expressions. It is common to let x represent the unknown number, usually the smallest, in a problem given in words. However, any other letter would do.

For example, if x represents an unknown number, then:

Words	Expression
5 more than the number	$(x + 5)$
2 less than the number	$(x - 2)$
3 times the number	$3x$
4 times the number, less 1	$(4x - 1)$
a third of the number	$\frac{1}{3}x \ or \ \frac{x}{3}$
the number subtracted from 6	$6 - x$
the difference between two numbers is 8	x and $(x + 8)$
two numbers add up to 10	x and $(10 - x)$
the number plus 3, then divided by 4	$\dfrac{x + 3}{4}$

Steps in constructing an equation in solving a practical problem

A numerical problem given in words can often be translated into an equation. The solution of this equation will give the answer to the problem. To solve a practical problem by constructing an equation, do the following:

Step 1: Read the question carefully a few times.

Step 2: Let x equal the unknown number that is required.

Step 3: Write each statement in the problem in terms of x. Use a diagram if necessary.

Step 4: Use the information in the problem to link the parts in step 3 to form an equation. Make sure both sides are measured in the same units.

Step 5: Solve the equation (find the unknown number).

Step 6: Test your solution in the problem itself—**not in your equation**, as your equation may be wrong.

Note: If the problem requires simultaneous equations to be solved, then step 2 becomes 'Let x and y equal the unknown numbers that are required.'

When an equation is constructed from a problem given in words, it may lead to any one of three types of equation:

1. simple linear equation   **2.** simultaneous linear equations   **3.** quadratic equation.

1. Using simple equations to solve problems

> ### Example ▼
>
> The sum of three consecutive odd numbers is 87.
>
> **(i)** If the smallest number is x, express the other two numbers in terms of x.
>
> **(ii)** Write an equation in terms of x to represent this information and solve the equation to find the value of x.
>
> **(iii)** Write down the three numbers.
>
> **Solution:**
>
> **(i)** $x =$ the smallest number
>
> The next number is 2 more than x, i.e. $(x + 2)$
>
> The next number is 4 more than x, i.e. $(x + 4)$
>
> **(ii) Link used to form the equation:**
>
> **Given:** Sum of the three numbers is 87.
>
> **Equation:**
> $$x + (x + 2) + (x + 4) = 87$$
> $$x + x + 2 + x + 4 = 87$$
> $$3x + 6 = 87$$
> $$3x = 81$$
> $$x = 27$$

(iii) $x = 27$ is the smallest number.

$x + 2 = 27 + 2 = 29$ is the next number.

$x + 4 = 27 + 4 = 31$ is the other number.

Check: $27 + 29 + 31 = 87$ (correct)

Thus, the three numbers are 27, 29 and 31.

Note: If you are not told that the smallest number is x, then letting the three consecutive odd numbers be $x - 2$, x and $x + 2$ can simplify your equation.

Example ▼

The difference between two numbers is 5.

Half the larger number less one third the smaller number is 4.

Find the numbers.

Solution:

Let $x =$ the smaller number.

Then $(x + 5) =$ the larger number   (5 more than x)

Half the larger number $= \dfrac{(x + 5)}{2}$ $\left(\dfrac{\text{larger number}}{2} \right)$

One third the smaller number $= \dfrac{x}{3}$ $\left(\dfrac{\text{smaller number}}{3} \right)$

Link used to form an equation:

Given: (Half the larger number) $-$ (one third the smaller number) $= 4$

Equation: $\dfrac{(x + 5)}{2} - \dfrac{x}{3} = 4$

$$\dfrac{6(x + 5)}{2} - \dfrac{6(x)}{3} = 6(4) \qquad \text{(multiply both sides by 6)}$$

$$3(x + 5) - 2x = 24 \qquad \text{(divide the bottom into top)}$$

$$3x + 15 - 2x = 24 \qquad \text{(remove the brackets)}$$

$$x + 15 = 24 \qquad \text{(simplify the left-hand side)}$$

$$x = 9 \qquad \text{(subtract 15 from both sides)}$$

$x = 9$ is the smaller number

$x + 5 = 9 + 5 = 14$ is the larger number

Check: $14 - 9 = 5$ (correct)

$\frac{1}{2}(14) - \frac{1}{3}(9) = 7 - 3 = 4$ (correct)

Thus, the numbers are 9 and 14.

Note: This problem could have been solved using simultaneous equations.

Let x = the larger number and y = the smaller number.

Write two equations in x and y and solve these equations simultaneously.

Exercise 27.1 ▼

1. A certain number is multiplied by 5 and then 2 is taken away. The result is 18. Find the number.

2. A certain number is multiplied by 3, and then 4 is taken away. The result is the same as multiplying the number by 2 and then adding on 10. Find the number.

3. One number is 3 more than another number. If 10 times the smaller number is equal to 4 times the larger number, find the numbers.

4. A bar of chocolate costs x cents.
   A bottle of orange juice costs 10 cents more than a bar of chocolate.
   Two bars of chocolate and one bottle of orange juice cost €2.50.
   (i) Write this information as an equation in x.   **(ii)** Solve for x.
   (iii) What is the cost of a bottle of orange juice?

5. The length of a rectangle is 3 cm longer than the breadth.
   If the breadth is x cm, write in terms of x:
   (i) the length of the rectangle   **(ii)** the perimeter of the rectangle.
   If the perimeter of the rectangle is 26 cm,
   (iii) use this information to form an equation
   (iv) solve the equation to find the value of x.
   What is the area of the rectangle?

6. In a bag there are 44 disks, x of which are blue. There are four times as many red disks as blue and two more green than blue. Write down an equation in x to represent this information and solve it to calculate x.

7. If x is an odd number, express in terms of x the next three odd numbers.
   If the sum of three consecutive odd numbers plus twice the next odd number is 73, find the four numbers.

8. The difference between two numbers is 9.
   If the smaller number is x, express the larger number in terms of x.
   One quarter of the larger number less two thirds the smaller number is 1.
   Write down an equation in x to represent this information and solve it to calculate x.
   What is the larger number?

9. A woman's age this year is four times that of her son. In five years' time she will be three times as old as her son.
   (i) If the son's age is x years this year, find, in terms of x, his mother's age now.
   (ii) Write, in terms of x, their ages in five years' time.
   (iii) Form an equation in x.
   (iv) Solve the equation to find the value of x.
   (v) What age is each of them now?

10. A girl bought a coat for €$\frac{x}{3}$ and a dress for €$\frac{x}{5}$.

The total amount of money she spent was €112.
- **(i)** Use this information to form an equation in x.
- **(ii)** Solve the equation to find the value of x.
- **(iii)** Find the cost of her **(a)** coat **(b)** dress.

11. 1500 people attended a concert when the price was €10 per ticket per person. Calculate the total receipts.

For another concert $(1500 - x)$ people attended, but the price was €12 per ticket per person and the receipts were €1200 more.

Form an equation in x and find the value of x.

12. A small firm employs 10 people, x of which are men.
- **(i)** Express in terms of x the number of women.

    Each man earns €20 per hour and each woman earns €18 per hour.
    The total wages per hour amount to €192.
- **(ii)** Use this information to form an equation and use it to calculate x.

13. **(a)** Express distance in terms of time and average speed.
- **(b)** A car travels for 5 hours at an average speed of x km/h.

    Calculate, in terms of x, the distance travelled by the car.
- **(c)** Two trains, one of which travels at an average speed of 10 km/h faster than the other, start towards each other at the same time from two places 320 km apart. They pass each other after two hours. The speed of the slower train is x km/h. Express in terms of x:
  - **(i)** the speed of the faster train
  - **(ii)** the distance travelled by each train.
  - **(iii)** Use this information to form an equation.
  - **(iv)** Solve the equation to find the value of x.
  - **(v)** What is the average speed of the faster train?

14. **(a)** Express time in terms of distance and average speed.
- **(b)** A train travelled x km at an average speed of 60 km/h.

    Express the time, in terms of x, taken by the train to complete the journey.
- **(c)** A girl cycles from her home at an average speed of 15 km/h and immediately boards a train which then travels at an average speed of 45 km/h to her destination. The total distance travelled is 95 km and the total journey takes the girl 3 hours.

    If the distance cycled by the girl was x km, express in terms of x:
  - **(i)** the distance travelled by the girl on the train
  - **(ii)** the time spent cycling **(iii)** the time spent travelling on the train.
  - **(iv)** Write down an equation in x to represent this information and use it to calculate x.
  - **(v)** How long, in hours and minutes, was the girl cycling?

15. (a) Express average speed in terms of distance and time.

(b) A man runs a distance of x km in 3 hours. Express his speed in terms of x.

(c) p and q are two points 100 km apart. A cyclist starts from p and cycles towards q, while at the same time another cyclist, who can cycle at an average speed of 3 km/h faster than the first, sets off from q towards p. They meet each other after four hours. If the slower cyclist travels a distance of x km, express in terms of x:

    (i) the distance travelled by the faster cyclist

    (ii) the average speed of the slower cyclist

    (iii) the average speed of the faster cyclist.

    (iv) Form an equation in x, to express the difference of their average speeds, and solve it to find the value of x.

    (v) What is the average speed of the faster cyclist?

2. Using simultaneous equations to solve problems

Method:

> **1.** Let $x =$ one unknown number and $y =$ the other unknown number.
> **2.** Look for **two** facts that **link** x and y, and form two equations.
> **3.** Solve these simultaneous equations.

Example ▼

300 people came to a school play, each adult paying €10 and each child paying €5. One of the organisers remarked that if each adult had been charged €12 and each child €4 there would have been an extra €240 taken in. How many adults and how many children came to the school play?

Solution:

Let $x =$ the number of adults and $y =$ the number of children.

First fact that links x and y:

Given: The total number of people who came was 300.

Equation: $x + y = 300$ ①

Second fact that links x and y:

Total money paid in;   new situation: €$(12x + 4y)$

Total money paid in;   old situation: €$(10x + 5y)$

Given: (Total money paid in new situation) − (Total money paid in old situation) = €240

Equation: $(12x + 4y) - (10x + 5y) = 240$

$$12x + 4y - 10x - 5y = 240$$
$$2x - y = 240 \qquad ②$$

Now solve the simultaneous equation ① and ②

$$x + y = 300 \quad ①$$
$$2x - y = 240 \quad ②$$
$$3x = 540 \quad \text{(add)}$$
$$x = 180$$

$$x + y = 300 \quad ①$$
$$180 + y = 300$$
$$y = 120$$

Put $x = 180$ into ① or ②

Check: Total number of people who came $= 180 + 120 = 300$ (correct)
(Total money paid in new situation) $-$ (Total money paid in old situation)
$= [180(12) + 120(4)] - [180(10) + 120(5)] = 2640 - 2400 = 240$ (correct)
Thus, the number of adults was 180 and the number of children was 120.

Note: This problem could have been solved using a single variable equation.
Let $x =$ the number of adults, $\therefore$ $(300 - x) =$ the number of children.
Then proceed to set up a single variable equation to find x.

Exercise 27.2 ▼

1. The sum of two numbers is 15. Their difference is 7.
   Let $x =$ the larger number and $y =$ the smaller number.
   Write two equations in x and y to represent this information.
   Solve the simultaneous equations to find the numbers.
2. The sum of four times one number and three times the second number is 61.
   If twice the first number less the second number is 13, find the numbers.
3. Five pens and two pencils cost €2.50. Three pens and two pencils cost €1.70.
   (a) Write **(i)** €2.50 and **(ii)** €1.70 as cents.
      Let x cents be the price of a pen and y cents the price of a pencil.
   (b) Write down an equation in x and y to show the price of
      (i) five pens and two pencils **(ii)** three pens and two pencils.
   (c) Solve your two equations simultaneously.
   (d) What is the price of **(i)** a pen **(ii)** a pencil?
4. A school bought twenty tickets for a show. Some were teachers' tickets, costing €8
   each, and some were pupils' tickets, costing €5 each. The total price of the tickets was
   €118. Let x be the number of teachers' tickets bought and y be the number of pupils'
   tickets bought.
   (a) Write down an equation in x and y for the total **number** of tickets bought.
   (b) Write down an equation in x and y for the total **price** of the tickets.
   (c) Solve your two equations simultaneously.
   (d) How many of each type of ticket did the school buy?

5. Two numbers are such that if 2 is added to the first the answer is twice the second. If 7 is subtracted from the first number the answer is half the second. Find the two numbers.
    (**Hint:** Let $x =$ the first number and $y =$ the second number)

6. A bag contains 20 coins, all of them either 10c or 50c coins. If the value of coins in the bag is €7.60, how many of each coin does the bag contain?
    (**Hint:** Let $x =$ the number of 10c coins and $y =$ the number of 50c coins)

7. A firm exports two types of machine, P and Q. Type P occupies 2 m^3 of space and type Q, 4 m^3. Type P weighs 9 kg and type Q, 6 kg. The machines occupied 160 m^3 of space on a ship and their total weight was 360 kg.
    Letting $x =$ the number of type P exported and $y =$ the number of type Q exported,
    (i)   Write down an equation in x and y for the space occupied by the machines.
    (ii) Write down an equation in x and y for the weight of the machines.
    (iii) Solve your two equations simultaneously.
    (iv) How many of each machine was exported?

8. During a certain day a factory produced two types of bicycles, racing bicycles and mountain bicycles.
    The following table shows the cost and time requirement for each bicycle:

Type	Racing bicycle	Mountain bicycle
Cost of materials	€45	€30
Labour hours	5	4

    The total amount of money spent on materials was €540 and the total labour time was 64 hours. Calculate the number of racing bicycles and the number of mountain bicycles produced.
    (**Hint:** Let $x =$ the number of racing bicycles produced and $y =$ the number of mountain bicycles produced)
    If the profit on each racing bicycle is €60 and the profit on each mountain bicycle is €50, calculate the profit for the day.

9. A holiday campsite caters for caravans and tents. There are x caravans and y tents on the campsite. Each caravan accommodates 8 people and each tent accommodates 5 people. On a particular evening each caravan and each tent is full, and the number of people on the campsite is 400. Each caravan is allotted 60 m^2 and each tent is allotted 50 m^2. The total area available is 3600 m^2 and there is no more room left for a caravan or a tent.
    Write two equations in x and y, one for the number of people on the campsite and the other for the area allotted to a caravan and a tent.
    How many caravans and how many tents are on the site?
    If the charges on the site are €30 for a caravan and €20 for a tent, calculate the income for the campsite owners, for this particular evening.

3. Using quadratic equations to solve problems

When we use an equation to solve a practical problem, the equation often turns out to be a quadratic equation. These equations usually have two solutions. If one of these makes no sense, for example producing a negative number of people, we reject it. Again always look for the link in the question to set up the equation. In many questions there will be an '**old situation**' and a '**new situation**' and we will be given a '**link**' between these situations which we use to set up the equation. Also setting out the information in a table can help to construct the equation.

Note: 'product' means 'the result from multiplying'

Example ▼

210 people attended the first night of a concert. They were seated in rows, each of which contained x people.

(i) Express, in terms of x, the number of rows needed.

(ii) The following night 216 people attended the concert. They were seated in rows, each of which contained $x + 1$ people. Write down an expression in x for the number of rows needed on the second night.

(iii) On the second night, there were 3 fewer rows needed than on the first night. Write down an equation in x to represent this information and use it to calculate x.

Solution:

(i) number of rows needed $= \dfrac{\text{Total number of people}}{\text{number of people per row}} = \dfrac{210}{x}$

(ii) number of rows needed $= \dfrac{\text{Total number of people}}{\text{number of people per row}} = \dfrac{216}{x+1}$

This information can be neatly presented using a table showing the situation on the first night and the second night.

$$= \dfrac{\text{number of people per row}}{}$$
$$= \dfrac{\text{Total number of people}}{\text{number of people per row}}$$

	First night	Second night
Number of people	210	216
Number of people per row	x	$x + 1$
Number of rows	$\dfrac{210}{x}$	$\dfrac{216}{x+1}$

Link used to form the equation:

Given: $\left(\begin{array}{c}\text{number of rows}\\ \text{on the first night}\end{array}\right) - \left(\begin{array}{c}\text{number of rows}\\ \text{on the second night}\end{array}\right) = 3$

Equation:

$$\frac{210}{x} - \frac{216}{(x+1)} = 3$$

$$\frac{x(x+1)210}{x} - \frac{x(x+1)216}{(x+1)} = 3x(x+1)$$

(multiply both sides by $x(x+1)$ the LCM of x and $(x+1)$)

$$210(x+1) - 216x = 3x(x+1)$$

$$210x + 210 - 216x = 3x^2 + 3x$$

$$210 - 6x = 3x^2 + 3x$$

$$-3x^2 - 3x - 6x + 210 = 0$$

$$-3x^2 - 9x + 210 = 0$$

$$3x^2 + 9x - 210 = 0$$

$$x^2 + 3x - 70 = 0$$

$$(x+10)(x-7) = 0$$

$$x + 10 = 0 \qquad \text{or} \quad x - 7 = 0$$

$$x = -10 \quad \text{or} \qquad x = 7$$

The negative value, $x = -10$, is not possible, therefore $x = -10$ is rejected.

Check: $\dfrac{210}{7} - \dfrac{216}{8} = 30 - 27 = 3$ (correct)

Thus, $x = 7$

Example ▼

A person rowed a loaded boat across a lake, a distance of 5 km, and rowed the return journey empty. The total journey took 3 hours.

The boat travelled at a speed of $(x - 4)$ km/h on the outward journey and at a speed of $(x + 4)$ km/h on the return.

Calculate x.

Solution:

This information can be neatly represented in a table.

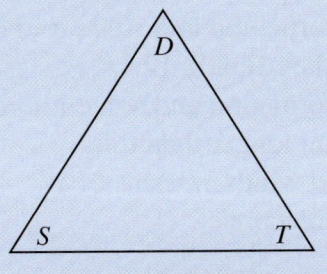

	Loaded	Empty
Distance	5	5
Speed	$x-4$	$x+4$
Time	$\dfrac{5}{x-4}$	$\dfrac{5}{x+4}$

$$\text{Time} = \frac{\text{Distance}}{\text{Speed}}$$

Link used to form the equation:

Given: $\left(\begin{array}{c}\text{Time rowing across}\\\text{the lake loaded}\end{array}\right) + \left(\begin{array}{c}\text{Time rowing back across}\\\text{the lake empty}\end{array}\right) = 3 \text{ hours}$

Equation:

$$\frac{5}{(x-4)} + \frac{5}{(x+4)} = 3$$

$$\frac{5(x-4)(x+4)}{(x-4)} + \frac{5(x-4)(x+4)}{(x+4)} = 3(x-4)(x+4)$$

(multiply both sides by $(x-4)(x+4)$ the LCM of $(x-4)$ and $(x+4)$)

$$5(x+4) + 5(x-4) = 3(x-4)(x+4)$$

$$5x + 20 + 5x - 20 = 3(x^2 - 16)$$

$$10x = 3x^2 - 48$$

$$-3x^2 + 10x + 48 = 0$$

$$3x^2 - 10x - 48 = 0$$

$$(3x+8)(x-6) = 0$$

$$3x + 8 = 0 \quad \text{or} \quad x - 6 = 0$$

$$3x = -8 \quad \text{or} \quad x = 6$$

$$x = -\tfrac{8}{3} \quad \text{or} \quad x = 6$$

The negative value, $x = -\tfrac{8}{3}$, is rejected.

Check: $\dfrac{5}{x-4} + \dfrac{5}{x+4} = \dfrac{5}{6-4} + \dfrac{5}{6+4} = \dfrac{5}{2} + \dfrac{5}{10} = 2\dfrac{1}{2} + \dfrac{1}{2} = 3$ (correct)

Thus, $x = 6$

1. When a number x is added to its square, the total is 30.
   Write down an equation in x to represent this information and solve it to calculate x.

2. When a number x is subtracted from its square, the result is 12.
   Write down an equation in x to represent this information and solve it to calculate x.

3. A rectangle has a width of x cm. Its length is 5 cm longer than this.
   (i) Sketch the rectangle, marking the length and width in terms of x.
   (ii) Write an expression in x for the area of the rectangle.
   If the area of the rectangle is 36 cm^2,
   (iii) use this information to form an equation
   (iv) solve the equation to find the value of x.

4. A mug costs €$(x + 2)$ in a shop. A person bought x of these mugs at this price.
   (i) Write, in terms of x, how much the person spent.
   If the person spent €80,
   (ii) use the information to form an equation
   (iii) solve the equation to find x.
   What is the price of a mug?

5. **(a)** Express distance in terms of average speed and time.
   (b) A girl walked at an average speed of x km/h for $(x - 3)$ hours.
   (i) Write, in terms of x, the distance walked by the girl.
   If the girl walked a distance of 18 km,
   (ii) use this information to form an equation
   (iii) solve the equation to find x.

6. A rectangle of area 72 cm^2 is divided into 4 smaller rectangles. The lengths of the sides are as shown in the diagram.

   Write down an equation in x to represent this information.

   Solve for x.

   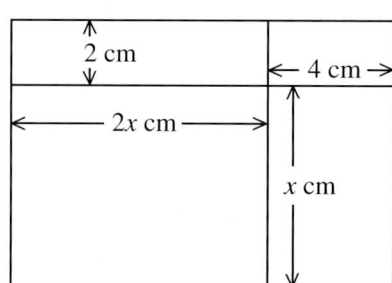

7. A closed rectangular box has a square base of side x cm.
   The height of the box is 5 cm.

   The total surface area of the box is 288 cm^2.

   Write down an equation in x to represent this information and use it to calculate x.

   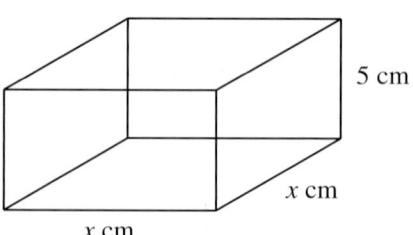

8. In the first week of a draw, x people shared equally in a prize of €200. The following week, $x + 5$ people shared equally in the prize of €200. Each share in the second week was €2 less than each share in the first week.

By completing the table, or otherwise, write an equation in x to represent this

	First week	Second week
Prize	200	
Number of winners		
Share		$\dfrac{200}{x+5}$

information. Solve the equation to find how many shared the prize in the first week.

9. The distance between two places, A and B, is 60 km. A cyclist travels at an average speed of x km/h from A to B and travels back from B to A at an average speed of 2 km/h faster. The return journey took one hour less to complete.

By completing the table, or otherwise, write an equation in x to represent this informa-

	A to B	B to A
Distance		60
Speed	x	
Time	$\dfrac{60}{x}$	

tion. Solve the equation to find the average speed from A to B.

10. A person spent €7.20 in buying x identical pens. Express the price of one pen in terms of x. If each pen had been 4 c cheaper, then an extra 2 pens could have been purchased for €7.20. By completing the table, or otherwise, write an equation in x to represent this information. Solve the equation to find the value of x.

	Old Situation	New Situation
Money	720	
Number		$x + 2$
Price		

11. To promote a school concert a class undertook to make 100 posters, each of the pupils making the same number of posters. If the number of pupils in the class is x, express in terms of x the number of posters made by each pupil.

	Old Situation	New Situation
Number of posters	100	
Number of pupils		$x - 5$
Number of posters made per pupil		

On the day they were making the posters 5 pupils were absent and each pupil present had to make one extra poster.

By completing the table, or otherwise, write an equation in x to represent this information.

Solve this equation to find the number of students in the class.

12. In the first week of a draw, x people shared equally in a prize of €80.
How much was each share, in terms of x?
The following week, $x + 6$ people shared equally in the prize of €80.
How much was each share then, in terms of x?
Each share in the second week was €3 less than each share in the first week.
Write an equation in x to represent all the above information.
Solve the equation to find how many shared the prize in the first week.

13. 150 people attended the first night of a concert.
They were seated in rows, each of which contained x people.
   (i) Express, in terms of x, the number of rows needed.
  (ii) The following evening 156 people attended the concert. They were seated in rows,
      each of which contained $x + 2$ people.
      Express, in terms of x, the number of rows needed on the second night.
 (iii) On the second night, there were 2 fewer rows needed than on the first night.
      Write down an equation in x to represent this information and use it to calulate x.

14. A person rowed a boat across a lake, a distance of 12 km, at an average speed of x km/h.
   (i) Express, in terms of x, the time taken to cross the lake.
  (ii) On the return journey, the average speed was $(x + 1)$ km/h.
      Express, in terms of x, the time taken to cross the lake on the return journey.
 (iii) The total time for both journeys was 7 hours.
      Write down an equation in x to represent this information and use it to calculate x.

15. A cyclist travelled from A to B, a distance of 20 km, at an average speed of x km/h.
   (i) Express, in terms of x, the time taken to travel from A to B.
  (ii) On the return journey, the cyclist travelled at an average speed of $(x + 2)$ km/h.
      Express, in terms of x, the time taken to travel from B to A.
 (iii) Express 20 minutes as a fraction of an hour.
 (iv) The return journey took 20 minutes less.
      Write down an equation in x to represent this information and use it to calculate x.

In the following three questions let $x =$ the unknown number. Use the information in the question to write an equation in x and solve the equation to find the unknown number. Writing the information in a table may help to set up the equation.

16. A prize of €120 is shared between a certain number of people.
If 2 fewer people had shared the prize each would have received €5 more; how many people shared the prize?

17. For a drill display the instructor divided a group of 90 students into an equal number of rows.
Each row had the same number of students.
It was then decided to put 3 fewer students into each row.
As a result 5 more rows were required.
How many students were in each row originally?

18. Two cyclists travel from A to B, a distance of 60 km. If one cycles at an average speed of 3 km/h more than the other, find their speeds if the slower cyclist arrives one hour later than the faster cyclist.

Exercise 27.4 ▼

1. When a number, x, is added to its square, the result is 12. Write down an equation in x to represent this information and use it to find the value of x.

2. x is a positive even number. Express, in terms of x, the next positive even number.
Two consecutive even positive numbers are squared and the results are added to give 164.
Write down an equation to represent this information and use it to calculate both numbers.

3. x and y are two positive whole numbers with $x > y$.
When the smaller of the two numbers is subtracted from three times the larger number the result is 3. When half the larger number is added to a third of the smaller number the result is 5.
Write down two equations in x and y to represent this information.
Solve the simultaneous equations to find the two numbers, x and y.

4. A coffee machine takes 20c or 50c coins. When emptied, it was found to contain 40 coins totalling €15.20 in value. How many of each coin did the machine contain?
(**Hint:** Let $x =$ the number of 20c coins and $y =$ the number of 50c coins and write two equations in x and y.)

5. 300 people came to a school play, each adult paying €10 and each child paying €6. One of the organisers remarked that if each adult had been charged €11 and each child €5 there would have been an extra €100 taken in. Let $x =$ the number of adults and $y =$ the number of children. Write two equations in x and y and solve these equations simultaneously to calculate the number of (**i**) adults   (**ii**) children.

6. (**a**) Express the area of a triangle in terms of its perpendicular height, h, and its base, b.
(**b**) Four isosceles triangles of base x cm and height $(x + 2)$ cm are glued to the edges of a square of side x cm. The tips of the triangles are brought to a point to make a pyramid. If the total surface area of the pyramid, including the base, is 64 cm^2, find the value of x.

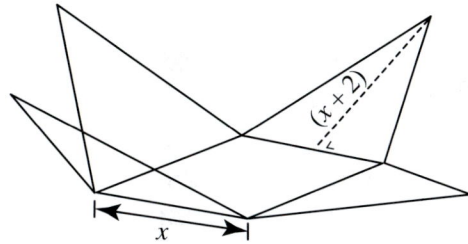
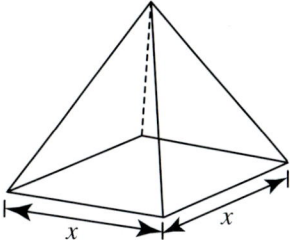

7. A rectangular garden measures 10 m by 8 m. There is a flower bed in the centre of the garden.

The flower bed is surrounded on all sides by a path which is x m wide, as shown in the diagram.

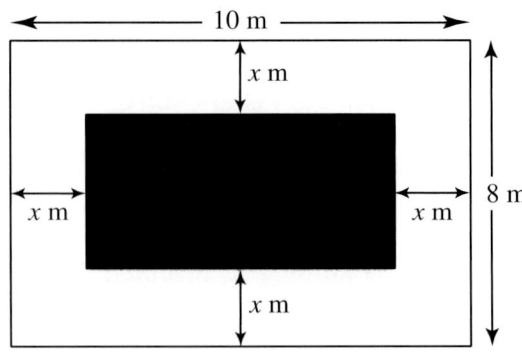

(i) Write down an expression in x which represents the area of the flower bed.

(ii) Calculate the value of x if the path covers 40% of the total area of the garden.

8. In the first week of a draw, x people shared equally in a prize of €360.
  (i) Express, in terms of x, each person's share.
  (ii) The following week, $x - 2$ shared equally in a prize of €360.
  Express, in terms of x, each person's share in the second week.
  (iii) Each share in the second week was €6 more than each share in the first week.
  Write an equation in x to represent all the above information.
  Solve the equation to find how many shared the prize in the first week.

9. Rectangular flagstones are to be laid, edge to edge, in a single line along a straight path which is 60 m long. Each flagstone is x m long.
  (i) Express, in terms of x, the number of flagstones needed.
  (ii) If each flagstone were 1 m longer express, in terms of x, the number of flagstones which would then be needed.
  (iii) If the longer flagstones were used, the total number required would decrease by 5. Write down an equation in x to represent this information and use it to calculate x.

10. 600 people attended the first night of a concert. They were seated in rows, each of which contained x people.
  (i) Express, in terms of x, the number of rows needed.
  (ii) The following night 630 people attended the concert. They were seated in rows, each of which contained $x - 2$ people. Write down an expression in x for the number of rows needed on the second night.
  (iii) On the second night, there were 5 more rows needed than on the first night. Write down an equation in x to represent this information and use it to calculate x.

11. A cyclist travelled from A to B, a distance of 90 km, at an average speed of x km/h.
  (i) Express, in terms of x, the time taken to travel from A to B.
  (ii) On the return journey, the cyclist travelled at an average speed of 3 km/h faster. Express, in terms of x;
    (a) the average speed   and   **(b)** the time taken to travel from B to A.
  (iii) The return journey took 1 hour less. Write down an equation in x to represent this information and use it to calculate x.

12. A farmer wants to fence off part of his garden. He buys 18 metres of fencing and uses it to make three sides of a rectangle, using a fence as the fourth side, as shown. The length of one side of the rectangle is x m and the length of the other side is y m, where $x < y$.

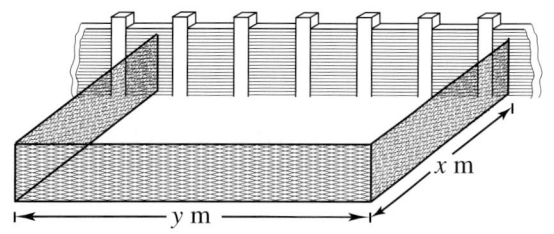

    (i)   Write down an equation in x and y to represent this information.

    (ii) Express y in terms of x.

    (iii) If the area of the rectangle is 40 m^2, explain why $xy = 40$.

    (iv) Using your answer from part (ii) write down an equation in x only to represent the area of the rectangle and solve this equation to find the values of x and y.

13. The total cost of an outing for a group of people is €630. If 2 people drop out of the group, the cost would increase by €20 per person for the remainder of the group. Find the number of people in the original group.

14. 140 students taking part in a drill display were arranged in rows containing equal numbers of students. To facilitate 4 extra students, one extra student was added to each row. It was found that 2 fewer rows were required. How many students were originally in each row?

PROOFS AND THEOREMS

The ten theorems

There are 10 theorems to be proved on our course:

1. Vertically opposite angles are equal in measure.

2. The measures of the three angles of a triangle sum to 180°.

3. An exterior angle of a triangle equals the sum of the two interior opposite angles in measure.

4. If two sides of a triangle are equal in measure, then the angles opposite these sides are equal in measure.

5. Opposite sides and opposite angles of a parallelogram are respectively equal in measure.

6. A diagonal bisects the area of a parallelogram.

7. The measure of the angle at the centre of the circle is twice the measure of the angle at the circumference, standing on the same arc.

   There are three deductions associated with this theorem:

   Deduction 1:
   All angles at the circumference on the same arc are equal in measure.

   Deduction 2:
   An angle subtended by a diameter at the circumference is a right angle.

   Deduction 3:
   The sum of opposite angles of a cyclic quadrilateral is 180°.

8. A line through the centre of a circle perpendicular to a chord bisects the chord.

9. If two triangles are equiangular, the lengths of corresponding sides are in proportion.

10. In a right-angled triangle, the square of the length of the side opposite to the right angle is equal to the sum of the squares of the lengths of the other two sides.

Theorem: | Vertically opposite angles are equal in measure.

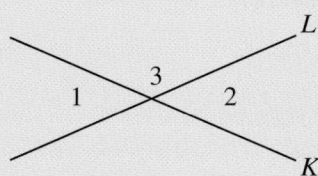

Given: Intersecting lines L and K, with vertically opposite angles 1 and 2.

To prove: $|\angle 1| = |\angle 2|$

Construction: Label angle 3.

Proof:
$|\angle 1| + |\angle 3| = 180°$ straight angle

$|\angle 2| + |\angle 3| = 180°$ straight angle

$\therefore \quad |\angle 1| + |\angle 3| = |\angle 2| + |\angle 3|$

$\therefore \quad\quad\quad |\angle 1| = |\angle 2|$

Theorem: | The measures of the three angles of a triangle sum to 180°.

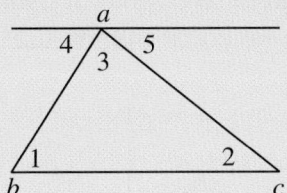

Given: $\triangle abc$ with angles 1, 2 and 3.

To prove: $|\angle 1| + |\angle 2| + |\angle 3| = 180°$.

Construction: Draw a line through a, parallel to bc. Label angles 4 and 5.

Proof:
$|\angle 1| = |\angle 4|$ and $|\angle 2| = |\angle 5|$ alternate angles

$\therefore \quad |\angle 1| + |\angle 2| + |\angle 3| = |\angle 4| + |\angle 5| + |\angle 3|$

but $|\angle 4| + |\angle 5| + |\angle 3| = 180°$.   straight angle

$\therefore \quad |\angle 1| + |\angle 2| + |\angle 3| = 180°$.

Theorem: An exterior angle of a triangle equals the sum of the two interior opposite angles in measure.

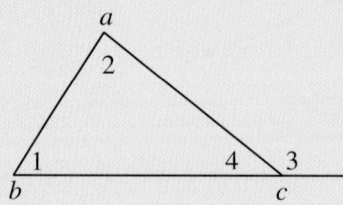

Given: $\triangle abc$ with interior opposite angles 1 and 2 and exterior angle 3.

To prove: $|\angle 1| + |\angle 2| = |\angle 3|$

Construction: Label angle 4.

Proof:

$|\angle 1| + |\angle 2| + |\angle 4| = 180°.$ three angles in a triangle

$|\angle 3| + |\angle 4| = 180°$ straight angle

∴ $|\angle 1| + |\angle 2| + |\angle 4| = |\angle 3| + |\angle 4|$

∴ $|\angle 1| + |\angle 2| = |\angle 3|$

Theorem: If two sides of a triangle are equal in measure, then the angles opposite these sides are equal in measure.

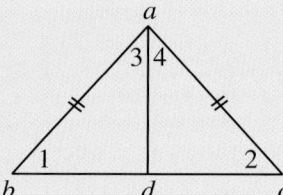

Given: $\triangle abc$, with $|ab| = |ac|$ and base angles 1 and 2.

To prove: $|\angle 1| = |\angle 2|$

Construction: Draw ad, the bisector of $\angle bac$. Label angles 3 and 4.

Proof: Consider $\triangle abd$ and $\triangle acd$:

$|ab| = |ac|$ given

$|\angle 3| = |\angle 4|$ construction

$|ad| = |ad|$ common

∴ $\triangle abd \equiv \triangle acd$ S A S

∴ $|\angle 1| = |\angle 2|$ corresponding angles

Theorem: Opposite sides and opposite angles of a parallelogram are respectively equal in measure.

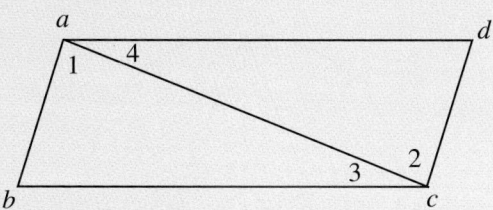

Given: Parallelogram *abcd*

To prove: $|ab| = |dc|$, $|ad| = |bc|$
$|\angle abc| = |\angle adc|$, $|\angle bad| = |\angle bcd|$

Construction: Join *a* to *c*. Label angles 1, 2, 3 and 4.

Proof: Consider $\triangle abc$ and $\triangle adc$:

$|\angle 1| = |\angle 2|$ and $|\angle 3| = |\angle 4|$	alternate angles
$|ac| = |ac|$	common
$\therefore \quad \triangle abc \equiv \triangle adc$	A S A
$\therefore \quad |ab| = |dc|$ and $|ad| = |bc|$	corresponding sides
and $|\angle abc| = |\angle adc|$	corresponding angles

similarly, $|\angle bad| = |\angle bcd|$

Theorem: A diagonal bisects the area of a parallelogram.

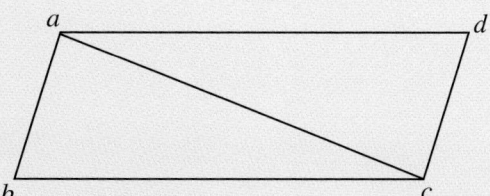

Given: Parallelogram *abcd* with diagonal [*ac*].

To prove: Area of $\triangle abc$ = Area of $\triangle adc$.

Proof: Consider $\triangle abc$ and $\triangle adc$:

$|ab| = |dc|$	opposite sides
$|ad| = |bc|$	opposite sides
$|ac| = |ac|$	common
$\therefore \quad \triangle abc \equiv \triangle adc$	S S S
$\therefore \quad$ Area $\triangle abc$ = Area $\triangle adc$.	

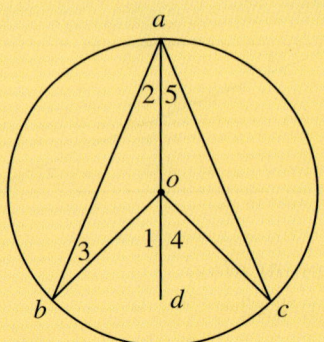

Given: Circle, centre o, containing points a, b and c.

To prove: $|\angle boc| = 2|\angle bac|$

Construction: Join a to o and continue to d. Label angles 1, 2, 3, 4 and 5.

Proof: Consider $\triangle aob$:

$|\angle 1| = |\angle 2| + |\angle 3|$ exterior angle

but $|\angle 2| = |\angle 3|$ $|oa| = |ob|$

$\therefore$ $|\angle 1| = 2|\angle 2|$

similarly, $|\angle 4| = 2|\angle 5|$

$\therefore$ $|\angle 1| + |\angle 4| = 2|\angle 2| + 2|\angle 5|$

$\therefore$ $|\angle 1| + |\angle 4| = 2(|\angle 2| + |\angle 5|)$

i.e. $|\angle boc| = 2|\angle bac|$

Deduction 1: | All angles at the circumference on the same arc are equal in measure.

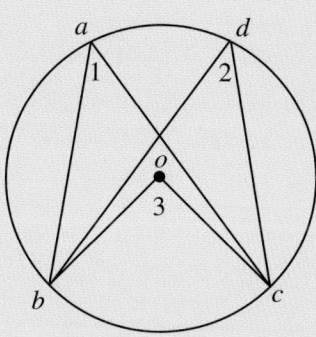

To prove: $|\angle bac| = |\angle bdc|$

Proof:
$$|\angle 3| = 2|\angle 1|$$
angle at the centre is twice the angle on the circumference (both on arc bc)

$$|\angle 3| = 2|\angle 2|$$
angle at the centre is twice the angle on the circumference (both on arc bc)

$$\therefore \quad 2|\angle 1| = 2|\angle 2|$$
$$\therefore \quad |\angle 1| = |\angle 2|$$
i.e. $\quad |\angle bac| = |\angle bdc|$

Deduction 2: | An angle subtended by a diameter at the circumference is a right angle.

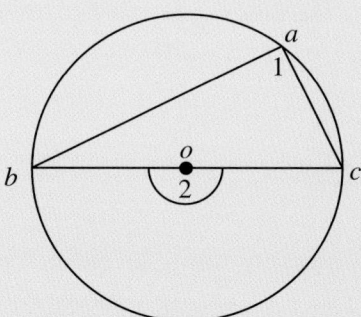

To prove: $|\angle bac| = 90°$

Proof:
$$|\angle 2| = 2|\angle 1|$$
angle at the centre is twice the angle on the circumference (both on arc bc)

but $\quad |\angle 2| = 180°$ straight angle

$$\therefore \quad 2|\angle 1| = 180°$$
$$\therefore \quad |\angle 1| = 90°$$
i.e. $\quad |\angle bac| = 90°$

Deduction 3: The sum of the opposite angles of a cyclic quadrilateral is 180°.

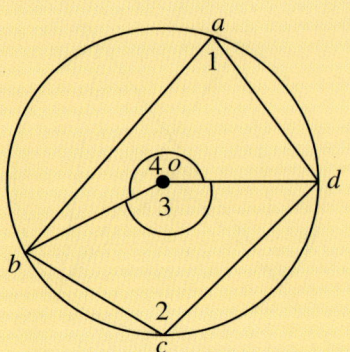

To prove: $|\angle bad| + |\angle bcd| = 180°$

Proof:

$|\angle 3| = 2|\angle 1|$ angle at the centre is twice the angle on the circumference (both on minor arc bd)

$|\angle 4| = 2|\angle 2|$ angle at the centre is twice the angle on the circumference (both on major arc bd)

$\therefore \quad |\angle 3| + |\angle 4| = 2|\angle 1| + 2|\angle 2|$

but $\quad |\angle 3| + |\angle 4| = 360°$ angles at a point

$\therefore \quad 2|\angle 1| + 2|\angle 2| = 360°$

$\therefore \quad |\angle 1| + |\angle 2| = 180°$

i.e. $\quad |\angle bad| + |\angle bcd| = 180°$

Similarly, $|\angle abc| + |\angle adc| = 180°$

| **Theorem:** | A line through the centre of a circle perpendicular to a chord bisects the chord. |

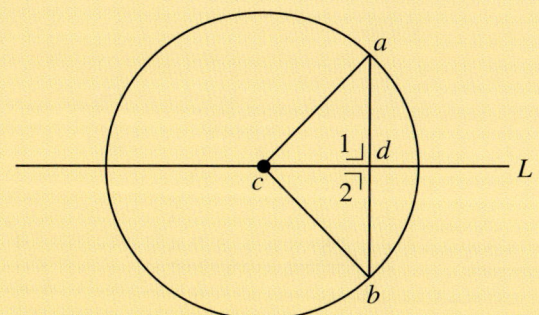

Given:	Circle, centre c, a line L containing c, chord $[ab]$, such that $L \perp ab$ and $L \cap ab = d$.
To prove:	$|ad| = |bd|$
Construction:	Label right angles 1 and 2.
Proof:	Consider $\triangle cda$ and $\triangle cdb$:

$$|\angle 1| = |\angle 2| = 90° \qquad \text{given}$$
$$|ca| = |cb| \qquad \text{both radii}$$
$$|cd| = |cd| \qquad \text{common}$$
$$\therefore \quad \triangle cda \equiv \triangle cdb \qquad \text{R H S}$$
$$\therefore \quad |ad| = |bd| \qquad \text{corresponding sides}$$

Theorem: | If two triangles are equiangular, the lengths of corresponding sides are in proportion.

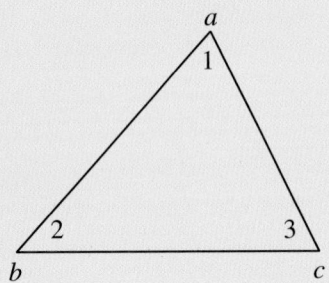 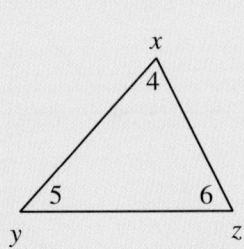 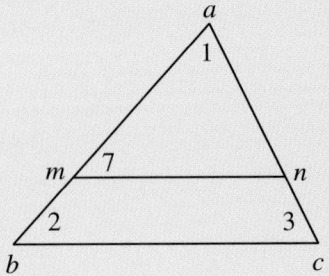

Given: Equiangular triangles abc and xyz in which
$|\angle 1| = |\angle 4|$, $|\angle 2| = |\angle 5|$ and $|\angle 3| = |\angle 6|$.

To prove: $\dfrac{|ab|}{|xy|} = \dfrac{|ac|}{|xz|} = \dfrac{|bc|}{|yz|}$

Construction: Mark the point m on $[ab]$ such that $|am| = |xy|$.
Mark the point n on $[ac]$ such that $|an| = |xz|$.
Join m to n. Label angle 7.

Proof: Consider $\triangle ayz$ and $\triangle xyz$:

$\quad |ay| = |xy|$ and $|az| = |xz|$ construction

$\quad |\angle 1| = |\angle 4|$ given

$\therefore \quad \triangle ayz \equiv \triangle xyz$ S A S

$\therefore \quad |\angle 7| = |\angle 5|$ corresponding angles

but $\quad |\angle 2| = |\angle 5|$ given

$\therefore \quad |\angle 7| = |\angle 2|$

$\therefore \quad\quad yz \parallel bc$

$\therefore \quad \dfrac{|ab|}{|am|} = \dfrac{|ac|}{|an|}$ A line parallel to one side divides the other two sides in the same proportion

$\therefore \quad \dfrac{|ab|}{|xy|} = \dfrac{|ac|}{|xz|}$ $|am| = |xy|$ and $|an| = |xz|$

similarly, $\dfrac{|ab|}{|xy|} = \dfrac{|bc|}{|yz|}$

$\therefore \quad \dfrac{|ab|}{|xy|} = \dfrac{|ac|}{|xz|} = \dfrac{|bc|}{|yz|}$

Theorem:	In a right-angled triangle, the square of the length of the side opposite to the right angle is equal to the sum of the squares of the lengths of the other two sides.

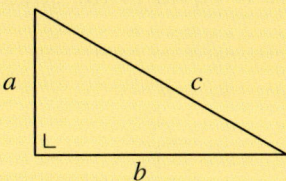

Given:	Right-angled triangle with length of sides a, b and c as shown.
To prove:	$a^2 + b^2 = c^2$
Construction:	Draw a square with sides of length $a + b$.
	Draw four congruent right angled triangles in the square with sides of length a and b and hypotenuse c, as shown.
	Label angles 1, 2, 3 and 4.

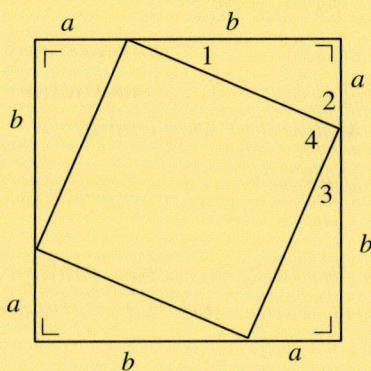

$$|\angle 1| + |\angle 2| = 90° \qquad \text{remaining angles}$$
$$|\angle 1| = |\angle 3| \qquad\qquad \text{corresponding angles}$$
$$\therefore \quad |\angle 2| + |\angle 3| = 90°$$
$$\therefore \quad |\angle 4| = 90°$$
$$\therefore \quad \text{Area of square} = (a + b)^2 = 4(\text{area of one triangle}) + c^2$$
$$\Rightarrow \qquad (a + b)^2 = 4(\tfrac{1}{2}ab) + c^2$$
$$\Rightarrow \quad a^2 + 2ab + b^2 = 2ab + c^2$$
$$\Rightarrow \qquad\quad a^2 + b^2 = c^2$$

Note: A difficulty with the proof is trying to draw the diagram. One way to do this is to let $a = 2$ cm, $b = 5$ cm and draw a square with each side 7 cm in length. Then simply mark off 2 cm on each side in clockwise direction. Join these points to construct the smaller square.

Alternative Proof

Theorem: In a right-angled triangle, the square of the length of the side opposite to the right angle is equal to the sum of the squares of the lengths of the other two sides.

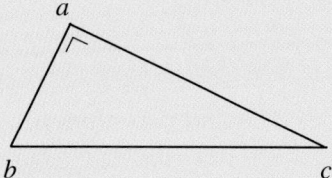 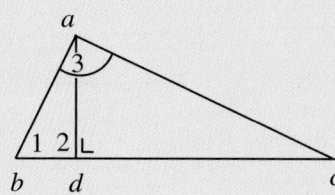 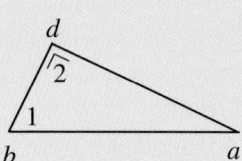

Given:	$\triangle abc$, $|\angle bac| = 90°$.
To prove:	$|bc|^2 = |ab|^2 + |ac|^2$
Construction:	Draw $ad \perp bc$.
	Label angles 1, 2 and 3.
Proof:	In $\triangle$'s abc and dba

$|\angle 1| = |\angle 1|$ common angle

$|\angle 2| = |\angle 3| = 90°$ construction

$\therefore$ $\triangle abc$ and $\triangle dba$ are similar

$\therefore$ $\dfrac{|ab|}{|bc|} = \dfrac{|bd|}{|ab|}$ corresponding sides are in proportion

$|ab|^2 = |bc|.|bd|$ ①   cross multiply

Similarly, $\triangle abc$ and $\triangle dac$ are similar

and $|ac|^2 = |bc|.|dc|$ ②

Adding ① and ②:

$$|ab|^2 + |ac|^2 = |bc|.|bd| + |bc|.|dc|$$
$$= |bc|(|bd| + |dc|)$$
$$= |bc|.|bc|$$
$$= |bc|^2$$

$\therefore$ $|bc|^2 = |ab|^2 + |ac|^2$.

ANSWERS

24. $5(x + 2)$ **25.** $p(q + r)$ **26.** $x(2 + y)$

27. $x(x + 5)$ **28.** $2x(2x + 1)$ **29.** $a(a - 3)$

30. $a(2 - 3b)$ **31.** $3a(b - 2c)$ **32.** $x(x - 1)$

33. $4x(2 - 3x)$ **34.** $x(x - 6)$ **35.** $3c(5b - c)$

36. $4xy(x - 2y)$ **37.** $ax(x + 1)$ **38.** $5p(2 - 3q)$

39. $p(q + r + 1)$ **40.** $ab(1 - 2a + 3b)$ **41.** $4ab(2 - 3b + 4a)$

42. $x^2 - 4x;\ x(x - 4)$ **43.** $3p^2 - 3pq;\ 3p(p - q)$

44. **(i)** $6p(2q - 1)$ **(ii)** $3(2q - 1);\ 2p$

Exercise 1.2 ▼

1. $(a + b)(c + d)$ **2.** $(p - q)(r - s)$ **3.** $(p + 3q)(2x + y)$

4. $(x - 2y)(3a - 2b)$ **5.** $(x + y)(a + b)$ **6.** $(q + r)(p + x)$

7. $(m - n)(a + 4)$ **8.** $(q + r)(p - 3)$ **9.** $(x - 3)(x + y)$

10. $(x - y)(x + z)$ **11.** $(p - 2)(q + p)$ **12.** $(b - c)(a + c)$

13. $(2x - z)(3x + y)$ **14.** $(x - 3y)(x + 2a)$ **23.** $(b + c)(a - 2)$

24. $(x + y)(x - 3)$ **25.** $(p + q)(p - r)$ **26.** $(x + 3)(p - q)$

27. $(a + b)(x + 1)$ **28.** $(p + q)(x - 1)$ **29.** $(x - y)(p - 2)$

30. $(b - c)(a + 1)$ **31.** $(x - 2)(x - y)$ **32.** $(3 - p)(p - q)$

33. $(p - q)(a + x)$ **34.** $(a - b)(5 + 2x)$ **35.** $(x - 3y)(x - 2a)$

36. $(x - y)(p - 1)$ **37.** $(c + d)(a + b)$ **38.** $(q + r)(p + 2)$

39. $(x + w)(y - z)$ **40.** $(x - y)(3 - q)$ **41.** $(a + b)(2x - y)$

42. $(a + 1)(b + 2)$ **43.** $(a + b)(3 - 2a)$ **44.** $(p + 3)(p - 2q)$

45. $(a + b)(n - 5)$ **46.** $(a - 2b)(3x - 2y)$ **47.** $(p + 1)(p - 2q)$

48. $(q + b)(q - 2a)$ **49.** $(x - a)(x - b)$ **50.** $(a - b)(a - 3)$

51. $(2p - q)(5r + p)$ **52.** $(a - y)(a - 2x)$

Exercise 1.3 ▼

1. $(2x + 3)(x + 1)$ **2.** $(3x + 2)(x + 3)$ **3.** $(2x - 3)(x - 2)$

4. $(3x + 7)(x - 1)$ **5.** $(2x + 1)(x - 5)$ **6.** $(3x - 1)(x + 3)$

7. $(5x + 1)(x + 3)$ **8.** $(5x - 1)(x + 2)$ **9.** $(7x - 2)(x + 1)$

10. $(2x - 5)(x + 2)$ **11.** $(3x + 5)(x - 2)$ **12.** $(3x + 2)(x - 1)$

13. $(2x + 1)(x - 3)$ **14.** $(x + 2)(x + 1)$ **15.** $(x + 3)(x + 4)$

16. $(x - 3)(x - 7)$ **17.** $(x - 5)(x + 3)$ **18.** $(x - 6)(x + 2)$

19. $(2x+7)(x+2)$ **20.** $(2x-3)(x+5)$ **21.** $(3x+4)(x-5)$
22. $(7x-2)(x-3)$ **23.** $(11x+3)(x-2)$ **24.** $(13x-1)(x+2)$
25. $(2x+1)(2x+3)$ **26.** $(3x+1)(2x+3)$ **27.** $(4x+1)(x+3)$
28. $(6x-1)(x-2)$ **29.** $(4x+1)(x-3)$ **30.** $(3x-2)(2x+1)$
31. $(4x+5)(2x-1)$ **32.** $(5x-3)(2x+1)$ **33.** $(9x-7)(x+1)$
34. $(6x+5)(x-2)$ **35.** $(4x-3)(x+2)$ **36.** $(3x+4)(3x-2)$
37. $(8x+3)(x-2)$ **38.** $(8x+3)(3x-1)$ **39.** $(5x-4)(3x+2)$
40. $2x^2-x-15;\ (2x+5)(x-3)$ **41.** $x^2-6x-7;\ (x+1)(x-7)$
42. $2x^2+11x+12;\ (2x+3)(x+4)$ **43.** $7x^2+15x+8;\ (7x+8)(x+1)$

Exercise 1.4 ▼

10. $(2p-3q)(2p+3q)$ **11.** $(4a-5b)(4a+5b)$ **12.** $(6x-7y)(6x+7y)$
13. $(8a-9b)(8a+9b)$ **14.** $(10-3a)(10+3a)$ **15.** $(1-5p)(1+5p)$
16. $(4x-1)(4x+1)$ **17.** $(5x-2y)(5x+2y)$ **18.** $(8q-1)(8q+1)$
19. $(q-4)(q+4)$ **20.** $(9a-4b)(9a+4b)$ **21.** $(x-5)(x+5)$
22. $(10-a)(10+a)$ **23.** $(5x-4y)(5x+4y)$ **24.** $(5a-2)(5a+2)$
25. $(7-10m)(7+10m)$ **26.** $(11x-3y)(11x+3y)$ **27.** $(12p-5q)(12p+5q)$
28. $(1-14x)(1+14x)$ **29.** $(10p-9q)(10p+9q)$ **30.** $(ab-2c)(ab+2c)$
31. $4x^2-9;\ (2x-3)(2x+3)$ **32.** $9x^2-y^2;\ (3x-y)(3x+y)$

Exercise 1.5 ▼

1. $3(x-y)(x+y)$ **2.** $2(x-2y)(x+2y)$ **3.** $3(2-3y)(2+3y)$
4. $5(x+1)(x+2)$ **5.** $3(x+2)(x-4)$ **6.** $4(x+1)(x-3)$
7. $3(a+b)(x+2)$ **8.** $5(a+b)(2x-y)$ **9.** $2(a-b)(3-q)$
10. $2a(3x-5y)(3x+5y)$ **11.** $6(2x+1)(x+3)$ **12.** $2q(3x-2)(x+4)$
13. $x(x+y)(x+4)$ **14.** $5q(2p-3q)(2p+3q)$ **15.** $2ab(2p-q)(2p+q)$
16. $2p(q+r)(2p-5)$ **17.** $3a(5a-2b)(5a+2b)$ **18.** $ab(2a-5b)(2a+5b)$
19. $3x(x-2y)(x+2y)$ **20.** $2a(5a-7b)(5a+7b)$ **21.** $2a(4x+1)(x-3)$
22. $2a(x+5)(x-3)$ **23.** $25x^2-30x+5;\ 5(5x-1)(x-1)$
24. $8x^2-18y^2;\ 2(2x-3y)(2x+3y)$

1. $3y(2x + y)$ **2.** $(x - y)(x - z)$ **3.** $(2x + 1)(x + 2)$

4. $(3x - 4)(3x + 4)$ **5.** $2x(2x - 1)$ **6.** $(c - d)(a + 2b)$

7. $(3x - 4)(x + 2)$ **8.** $(5x - 2y)(5x + 2y)$ **9.** $(1 - 3x)(1 + 3x)$

10. $4ab(2a - 1 + 3b)$ **11.** $(7x - 3)(x + 5)$ **12.** $(9a - 11b)(9a + 11b)$

13. $(xy - z)(2x - 3)$ **14.** $(6x - 1)(6x + 1)$ **15.** $(4x + 5)(2x - 3)$

16. $2xy(x - 2y)$ **17.** $(3x - 2)(2x - 5)$ **18.** $(10 - 11q)(10 + 11q)$

19. $3xy(1 - 4y)$ **20.** $(5x - 3)(3x + 2)$ **21.** $(2a + b)(2ab - 3)$

22. $5(x - 2y)(x + 2y)$ **23.** $3(x + 3)(x - 2)$ **24.** $2(x - y)(x + z)$

25. $3p(x - 12)(x - 2)$ **26.** $2(5 - 4a)(5 + 4a)$ **27.** $3(3x - 1)(3x + 1)$

28. $2pq(p - 2q)(p + 2q)$ **29.** $3p(2x - 5y)(2x + 5y)$ **30.** $3q(2x + 1)(2x + 3)$

31. $(2x - 3y)(2x + 3y)$ **32.** $(5x - 2y)(5x + 2y)$ **33.** $(y - 6)(y + 2)$

34. $(3x + 4)(x - 2)$ **35.** $(x + 2)(x - 6)$ **36.** $(a - 3b)(a + 3b)$

37. $5b(2a - b)$ **38.** $8(p - q)(p + q)$ **39.** $2x(x + 2y)$

40. $(3x - 1)(x + 1)$

1. $2x$ **2.** $3a$ **3.** $8b$ **4.** 2 **5.** 1 **6.** 3

7. 2 **8.** $\dfrac{3}{4}$ **9.** $\dfrac{5}{3}$ **10.** 2 **11.** $2x$ **12.** $2ab$

13. $x - 1$ **14.** $x + 3$ **15.** $3x$ **16.** $\dfrac{4}{x + 4}$ **17.** $\dfrac{1}{x - 2}$ **18.** $\dfrac{2}{x + 4}$

19. $\dfrac{x}{x + 3}$ **20.** $\dfrac{x + 3}{2x + 1}$ **21.** $\dfrac{3}{a + b}$ **22.** $\dfrac{2}{3}$ **23.** $\dfrac{2x}{3}$ **24.** 2

25. $\dfrac{x}{2}$ **26.** 2 **27.** $\dfrac{x}{y}$

1. $\dfrac{17x}{12}$

2. $\dfrac{13x}{6}$

3. $\dfrac{x}{15}$

4. $\dfrac{5x+13}{6}$

5. $\dfrac{33x-17}{20}$

6. $\dfrac{2-x}{21}$

7. $\dfrac{x+5}{6}$

8. $\dfrac{1}{12}$

9. $\dfrac{6x+1}{18}$

10. $\dfrac{14x+11}{4}$

11. $\dfrac{43}{12x}$

12. $\dfrac{20x+9}{20x}$

13. $\dfrac{5x+7}{(x+1)(x+2)}$

14. $\dfrac{5x+19}{(x+3)(x+5)}$

15. $\dfrac{3x}{(x+2)(x-4)}$

16. $\dfrac{13x+14}{(2x+1)(3x+4)}$

17. $\dfrac{18x-1}{(2x+1)(2x-1)}$

18. $\dfrac{13x+4}{(3x-2)(2x+5)}$

19. $\dfrac{x+3}{2x(3x-1)}$

20. $\dfrac{11x-29}{(2x-5)(x-3)}$

21. $\dfrac{7-6x}{(3x-1)(2-3x)}$

22. $\dfrac{3x+11}{x+3}$

23. $\dfrac{5x+14}{3(x+4)}$

24. $\dfrac{2x+29}{6(2x-1)}$

25. $\dfrac{x^2+3x+12}{4x(x+3)}$

26. $\dfrac{x^2+10x+3}{3x(x+1)}$

27. $\dfrac{x^2+4x-30}{3x(x-2)}$

28. $\dfrac{11x-4}{30}$

29. $\dfrac{10x-1}{(2x+1)(2x-1)}$

30. (i) $\dfrac{7}{6}$ (ii) $\dfrac{1}{12}$

31. (i) $p=2;\ q=3$ (ii) $a=7,\ b=-2$

32. (i) $\dfrac{3}{x+2}$ (ii) $\dfrac{2}{2x-5}$ (iii) $\dfrac{-3}{3x-1}$ or $\dfrac{3}{1-3x}$ (iv) $\dfrac{1}{x-1}$

33. $\dfrac{2}{x-1}$

34. $\dfrac{3}{x-2}$

35. $\dfrac{10}{x-5}$

36. $\dfrac{8}{2x-3}$

37. $\dfrac{5}{3x-1}$

38. $\dfrac{7}{2-5x}$

39. 0

40. 3

1. x^2
2. $2x$
3. $2x^2$
4. 1
5. $4x$
6. -2
7. $-2x$
8. 1
9. -5
10. $-3x$
11. $x+1$
12. $x+3$
13. $x+2$
14. $x+4$
15. $x+2$
16. $x+5$
17. $x-3$
18. $2x+5$
19. x^2+3x+2
20. x^2+4x+3
21. x^2+3x+1
22. $2x^2+3x+1$
23. x^2+2x+1
24. $2x^2+3x+4$
25. x^2-2x-3
26. x^2+x-3
27. x^2-5x+6
28. x^2-3x-5
29. $2x^2+x-10$
30. x^2-x-6
31. x^2+x-6
32. $x^2-2x-15$
33. $2x^2-3x+5$
34. $4x^2+3x-1$
35. x^2-x+2
36. $x^2+2x+15$
37. x^2-4x+3
38. x^2-2x-1
39. $4x^2+8x+3$

40. $3x^2-8x+4$
41. $x^2+3x+2;\ \dfrac{24}{4}=6$
42. $x^2+x-2;\ \dfrac{30}{3}=10$

43. $2x^2-11x+12;\ (2x-3)(x-4)$
44. $a=1,\ b=4,\ c=3;\ 6;\ (x+3)(x+1)$
45. $a=1,\ b=-5,\ c=6;\ 5;\ (x-3)(x-2)$
46. x^2+4
47. x^2-5
48. $2x^2-7$
49. x^2-4
50. x^2-x+1
51. x^2-2x+4
52. x^2+3x+9
53. $4x^2+2x+1$
54. $4x^2-6x+9$
55. $4x^2+10x+25$

1. $x=2,\ y=1$
2. $x=4,\ y=2$
3. $x=3,\ y=2$
4. $x=2,\ y=4$
5. $x=-1,\ y=3$
6. $x=-2,\ y=-3$
7. $x=2,\ y=2$
8. $x=-2,\ y=4$
9. $x=3,\ y=-1$
10. $x=-3,\ y=5$
11. $x=-1,\ y=1$
12. $x=1,\ y=-4$
13. $x=2,\ y=-3$
14. $x=10,\ y=4$
15. $x=3,\ y=3$
16. $x=15,\ y=4$
17. $x=4,\ y=3$
18. $x=3,\ y=4$
19. $x=-2,\ y=-1$
20. $x=3,\ y=4$
21. $x=2,\ y=-2$
22. $x=5,\ y=-1$
23. $x=2,\ y=-2$
24. $x=-1,\ y=-3$
25. $x=1,\ y=1$
26. $x=2,\ y=1$
27. $x=3,\ y=4$
28. $x=-4,\ y=5$
29. $x=\dfrac{3}{2},\ y=\dfrac{5}{2}$
30. $x=1,\ y=\dfrac{1}{3}$
31. $x=\dfrac{5}{2},\ y=\dfrac{4}{3}$
32. $x=\dfrac{3}{5},\ y=\dfrac{4}{5}$
33. $x=\dfrac{5}{2},\ y=-\dfrac{5}{2}$
34. $x=\dfrac{1}{5},\ y=\dfrac{1}{4}$

1. $-4, 3$ 2. $-5, \frac{3}{2}$ 3. $-\frac{5}{2}, \frac{2}{3}$ 4. $0, \frac{3}{2}$ 5. $-2, 0$

6. $-\frac{2}{3}, \frac{2}{3}$ 7. $\frac{1}{2}, 5$ 8. $-3, -\frac{1}{2}$ 9. $-\frac{5}{3}, 1$ 10. $-1, \frac{1}{5}$

11. $-3, \frac{4}{3}$ 12. $-\frac{3}{2}, 1$ 13. $-4, -\frac{1}{7}$ 14. $-4, \frac{2}{3}$ 15. $-1, \frac{2}{5}$

16. $-3, 7$ 17. $-2, 8$ 18. $-4, 6$ 19. $-3, 0$ 20. $0, 2$

21. $0, 5$ 22. $-\frac{5}{2}, 0$ 23. $0, \frac{2}{3}$ 24. $0, \frac{4}{5}$ 25. $-2, 2$

26. $-5, 5$ 27. $-1, 1$ 28. $-\frac{2}{3}, \frac{2}{3}$ 29. $-\frac{5}{2}, \frac{5}{2}$ 30. $-\frac{1}{2}, \frac{1}{2}$

31. $-\frac{1}{4}, 3$ 32. $-\frac{5}{2}, \frac{1}{3}$ 33. $\frac{1}{4}, \frac{3}{2}$ 34. $1, 1$ 35. $-\frac{1}{2}, -\frac{1}{2}$

36. $\frac{2}{3}, \frac{2}{3}$ 37. $\frac{1}{4}, 7$ 38. $\frac{5}{6}, 4$ 39. $\frac{1}{2}, \frac{5}{2}$ 40. $-2, -\frac{3}{2}$

41. $\frac{2}{5}, \frac{1}{2}$ 42. $-7, 0$ 43. $\frac{1}{2}, \frac{5}{2}$ 44. $-1, 2$ 45. $-\frac{1}{4}, \frac{3}{2}$

46. $-\frac{1}{3}$ 47. $-2, 3$

1. $-4, -2$ 2. $2, 3$ 3. $-3, 5$ 4. $-1, 2$ 5. $\frac{1}{4}, 1$

6. $-2, 2$ 7. $-5, 5$ 8. $-1, \frac{5}{3}$ 9. $-3, \frac{3}{5}$ 10. $\frac{1}{6}, 2$

11. $\frac{1}{2}, \frac{5}{2}$ 12. $-4, 6$ 13. $-1, 2$ 14. $\frac{2}{3}, 1$ 15. $-4, 2$

16. $-5, 4$ 17. $\frac{1}{3}, 2$ 18. $\frac{2}{3}, 1$ 19. $-2, 3$ 20. $-3, 4$

21. $-\frac{7}{2}, 5$ 22. $\frac{3}{5}, 4$ 23. $0, 2$ 24. $-3, \frac{1}{2}$ 25. $-\frac{1}{5}, 6$

26. $-2, \frac{4}{5}$ 27. $-\frac{5}{7}, 6$ 28. $-\frac{9}{2}, 6$ 29. $-18, 20$ 30. $-1, \frac{8}{5}$

31. (i) $\dfrac{x^2 - x - 6}{2x(x+3)}$ (ii) $-2, 3$

1. $1, 4$
2. $-6, -2$
3. $-\frac{1}{2}, 2$
4. $-3, \frac{4}{3}$

5. $-\frac{2}{3}, 4$
6. $-2, \frac{3}{5}$
7. $-1.27, 2.77$
8. $-7.41, 0.41$

9. $-2.35, 0.85$
10. $-0.26, 2.59$
11. $-2.57, 0.91$
12. $-1.58, 0.38$

13. $-0.64, 0.39$
14. $-1.84, 0.44$
15. $-1.35, 0.21$
16. $0.39, 5.11$

17. $-2.87, -0.46$
18. $-1.40, 0.90$
19. $-1.9, 1.4$
20. $0.4, 2.6$

21. $-2.9, 1.4$
22. $-0.8, 0.6$
23. $0.3, 3.2$
24. $-1.6, -0.4$

25. $0.6, 6.4$
26. $-1.6, 6.4$
27. $-0.58, 2.58$

28. (i) $\dfrac{3x-1}{(x+1)(x-3)}$ (ii) $-0.4, 5.4$

29. $2\sqrt{3}$
30. $3\sqrt{2}$
31. $4\sqrt{2}$
32. $5\sqrt{2}$

33. $3\sqrt{3}$
34. $4\sqrt{5}$
35. $1\pm\sqrt{5}$
36. $1\pm\sqrt{3}$

37. $2\pm\sqrt{3}$
38. $-3\pm\sqrt{2}$
39. $-2\pm2\sqrt{3}$
40. $2\pm3\sqrt{2}$

41. $4\pm2\sqrt{3}$
42. $\dfrac{1\pm\sqrt{3}}{2}$
43. $\dfrac{-1\pm\sqrt{5}}{4}$
44. $1\pm\sqrt{2}$

45. $-1\pm\sqrt{3}$
46. $5\pm\sqrt{3}$
47. $2\pm\sqrt{5}$
48. $1\pm\sqrt{7}$

49. $\dfrac{-1\pm\sqrt{5}}{2}$
50. (i) $\dfrac{x^2-8x-4}{4(x-2)(x+2)}$ (ii) $4\pm2\sqrt{5}$

1. $-2, 4; 1, 7$
2. $3, 5; 2, 3$
3. $-3, 7; -1, 1$

4. $\frac{1}{2}, \frac{5}{2}; 3, 7$
5. $2, 6; -3, -2, 1, 2$
6. $-6, 14; -2, 2, 3, 7$

7. $2, 5; -2, -1, 1, 2$
8. $-2, 10; -2, 1, 2, 5$
9. $1, 5; -2, -1, 3, 6$

10. $-9, 6; -8, -1, 2, 4$
11. $-4, 5; -2, \frac{1}{2}, -1, -1$
12. $\frac{1}{4}, 1; -2, -1, 1, 2$

13. $-4.2, 1.2; -2.6, 0.1$
14. $-0.55, 1.22; 0.2, 1.1$
15. $-0.9, 2.3; -1.1, 0.4$

16. $3, 8; -2, -1, 3, 4$

1. $x^2 - 5x + 6 = 0$ **2.** $x^2 - x - 2 = 0$ **3.** $x^2 - 3x - 10 = 0$
4. $x^2 - 3x - 4 = 0$ **5.** $x^2 + 5x + 6 = 0$ **6.** $x^2 - 9x + 20 = 0$
7. $x^2 - x - 12 = 0$ **8.** $x^2 + 5x - 24 = 0$ **9.** $x^2 - 9 = 0$
10. $x^2 - 4x + 4 = 0$ **11.** $x^2 + 2x = 0$ **12.** $x^2 - 5x = 0$
13. $x^2 - 1 = 0$ **14.** $2x^2 - 7x + 3 = 0$ **15.** $3x^2 - 5x - 2 = 0$
16. $2x^2 + 5x - 3 = 0$ **17.** $2x^2 - 3x - 5 = 0$ **18.** $6x^2 - 5x + 1 = 0$
19. $9x^2 + 3x - 2 = 0$ **20.** $8x^2 - 10x + 3 = 0$ **21.** $m = -2,\ n = -15$
22. $a = 10,\ b = 1, c = -2$

1. $-2, \frac{5}{2}$ **2.** $0, \frac{5}{3}$ **3.** $-2, 2$ **4.** $-\frac{2}{3}, 5$

5. $0, 4$ **6.** $-5, 5$ **7.** $\frac{2}{3}, 2$ **8.** $-\frac{3}{2}, 4$

9. $-3, 1$ **10.** $\frac{1}{3}, \frac{1}{3}$ **11.** $1, 5$ **12.** $-\frac{1}{2}, 2$

13. $-\frac{1}{2}, 3$ **14.** $3, 10$ **15.** $-7, 4$ **16.** $-4, 8$
17. $-0.54, 5.54$ **18.** $-0.43, 0.77$ **19.** $-1.35, 0.21$ **20.** $-1.39, 2.89$
21. $-1.76, 0.76$ **22.** $-2.12, 6.12$ **23.** $1 \pm \sqrt{2}$ **24.** $-1 \pm \sqrt{7}$
25. $3 \pm \sqrt{5}$ **26.** $-2 \pm \sqrt{3}$ **27.** $-1 \pm \sqrt{5}$ **28.** $-\sqrt{5}, \sqrt{5}$

31. $-2, \frac{1}{5}; -\frac{1}{2}, \frac{3}{5}$ **32.** $-\frac{3}{2}, 4; -5, 6$ **33.** $-1, 5; -\frac{5}{2}, -1, -\frac{1}{2}, 1$

34. $-6, \frac{2}{3}; -7, -\frac{7}{3}, 1, 3$ **35.** $-2, \frac{1}{4}; -\frac{5}{2}, -2, 2, \frac{5}{2}$
36. $-0.9, 2.4; -3.9, -0.6$ **37.** $-0.35, 2.85; 0.2, 1.3$
38. **(i)** $x^2 - 7x - 8 = 0$ **(ii)** $2x^2 - 5x - 3 = 0$ **(iii)** $6x^2 - 7x + 2 = 0$
39. $p = 3, q = -5, r = -2$ **40.** $k = -5; \frac{1}{2}$

1. $x \geqslant 3$ **2.** $x \leqslant 1$ **3.** $x \geqslant 2$ **4.** $x \geqslant 3$ **5.** $x \leqslant 1$ **6.** $x > 1$

7. $x < 5$ **8.** $x \leqslant 3$ **9.** $x \leqslant 6$ **10.** $x \geqslant -4$ **11.** $x \geqslant \frac{5}{2}$ **12.** $x > -\frac{3}{2}$

13. $x < -2$ **14.** $x \leqslant -4$ **15.** $-3 \leqslant x \leqslant 2$ **16.** $-2 < x \leqslant 4$

17. $-1 \leqslant x < 4$ **18.** $-3 < x < 5$ **19.** $-2 \leqslant x < 3$

20. $-2 < x < 2$ **21.** $-1 \leqslant x \leqslant 1$ **22.** $0 \leqslant x \leqslant 3$

23. $-3 \leqslant x \leqslant 1$ **24.** $-1 \leqslant x < 5$ **25.** $-1 \leqslant x < 2$

26. $-4 \leqslant x \leqslant -1$ **27.** $-2 \leqslant x \leqslant 3$ **28.** $-1 < x < 4$

29. $-1 \leqslant x < 3$ **30.** $-1 < x \leqslant 2$ **31.** $1 \leqslant x < 5$

32. $-1 < x < 2$ **33.** (i) $a = -1, b = 4$ (ii) $-4, -3, -2, -1, 0, 1, 2$

34. $p = -1, q = 2$; $\frac{5}{2}$ or 2.5   **35.** $0, 1, 2, 3$ **36.** $a = 0, b = 1, c = 2, d = 3, e = 4$; 4

37. (i) $x \leqslant 3$ (ii) $x \geqslant -2$; $-2 \leqslant x \leqslant 3$ **38.** (i) $x \leqslant 4$ (ii) $x \geqslant -1$; $-1 \leqslant x \leqslant 4$

39. (i) $x \leqslant 1$ (ii) $x \geqslant -3$ (iii) $-3 \leqslant x \leqslant 1$

40. (i) $x \leqslant 2$ (ii) $x \geqslant -\frac{7}{2}$ (iii) $-\frac{7}{2} \leqslant x \leqslant 2$

41. (i) $x \geqslant -2$ (ii) $x \leqslant 5$ (iii) $a = -2, b = 5$ **42.** $\{0, 1\}$; $\{0, 1, 2, 3\}$; $\{2, 3\}$

1. $\dfrac{b+c}{2}$ **2.** $\dfrac{r-q}{3}$ **3.** $\dfrac{c+d}{a}$ **4.** $\dfrac{v-u}{a}$ **5.** $\dfrac{5r-2q}{3}$

6. $\dfrac{3a-2c}{4}$ **7.** $\dfrac{q+2r}{2}$ **8.** $\dfrac{t+ay}{y}$ **9.** $2c - b$ **10.** $\dfrac{q-3p}{2}$

11. $y - 2x$ **12.** $\dfrac{b-3a}{3}$ **13.** $\dfrac{6r-3q}{2}$ **14.** $\dfrac{4c}{a+2b}$ **15.** $\dfrac{1}{r-t}$

16. $\dfrac{t}{r-p}$ **17.** $\dfrac{b^2}{a-bd}$ **18.** $\dfrac{3ab}{a+4b}$ **19.** $\dfrac{uv}{u+v}$ **20.** $\dfrac{pr-q}{p}$

21. $\dfrac{ac}{2a-c}$; 12   **22.** (i) $\dfrac{qx+q}{x-1}$ (ii) $p = -q$ **23.** $\dfrac{q^2-qr}{2r}$ **24.** $\pm\sqrt{\dfrac{r}{q}}$

25. $\pm\sqrt{\dfrac{2s}{a}}$ **26.** $\pm\sqrt{\dfrac{b}{c}}$ **27.** $\pm\sqrt{\dfrac{1}{m^2+8p}}$; ± 0.2 **28.** y^2

29. $\dfrac{r^2}{q}$ **30.** $\dfrac{p}{a^2}$ **31.** $\dfrac{z^2}{9x}$ **32.** $\dfrac{4s^2}{t}$ **33.** $\dfrac{y^2+3}{2}$

34. $\dfrac{s^2+r}{q}$ **35.** $\dfrac{gt^2}{k^2}$ **36.** $\dfrac{2t^2+x}{t^2}$ **37.** $\dfrac{4+4p^2}{p^2}$; 5

38. **(i)** $2a+a^2$ **(ii)** 0 **39.** **(i)** $3a-a^3$ **(ii)** 2

40. **(i)** $2x-3$ **(ii)** x **41.** $\dfrac{8b+3}{4}$ **42.** **(i)** $\dfrac{p+2q^2}{q^2}$ **(ii)** 4

43. $\dfrac{a+b}{p+q}$

Exercise 8.1 ▼

1. $a=3,\ b=4$ **2.** $p=5,\ q=6$ **3.** $a+b=3,\ 2a-b=3;\ a=2,\ b=1$
4. $a-b=7,\ 2a+3b=4;\ a=5,\ b=-2$
5. $2a+3b=3,\ a-6b=24;\ a=6,\ b=-3$
6. $a=3,\ b=-2$ **7.** **(i)** $a=2,\ b=3$ **(ii)** $p=-3,\ q=2$ **8.** $-2,2$
9. $p=2,\ q=7$ **10.** $p=3,\ q=2$ **11.** $a=2,\ b=3,\ c=4$
12. $k=-5,\ h=-3$ **13.** $12-3y;\ a=3,\ b=-1$

14. $\dfrac{1}{x^2+2x};\ a=1$ **15.** $\dfrac{5}{6x-x^2};\ q=3$

Exercise 9.1 ▼

1. **(i)** 4 **(ii)** 3 **(iii)** 3 **2.** **(i)** 3 **(ii)** 3 **(iii)** 2
3. **(i)** 6 **(ii)** 5 **(iii)** 4 **4.** **(i)** 5 **(ii)** 6 **(iii)** 7
5. **(i)** 6 **(ii)** 6 **(iii)** 7 **6.** **(i)** 9 **(ii)** 9 **(iii)** 7
7. **(i)** 4 **(ii)** 5 **(iii)** 0 **8.** **(i)** 3 **(ii)** 2.5 **(iii)** 0
9. **(i)** 3.5 **(ii)** 4.1 **(iii)** 5.4 **10.** **(i)** 0 **(ii)** -1 **(iii)** -1
11. **(i)** $\frac{12}{5}$ **(ii)** $1\frac{1}{2}$ **(iii)** $1\frac{1}{2}$ **12.** **(i)** $\frac{1}{2}$ **(ii)** $\frac{5}{12}$ **(iii)** $\frac{1}{3}$
13. 73% **14.** **(i)** 7 **(ii)** 8 **(iii)** 10 **15.** 7
16. **(i)** $3x$ **(ii)** $2x$ **(iii)** $4x+1$ **(iv)** $3x+5$ **17.** 7

Exercise 9.2 ▼

1. 56 **2.** 72 **3.** 14 **4.** 2 **5.** 6 **6.** 4 **7.** 3
8. 5 **9.** 10 **10.** 6 **11.** 2 **(i)** 3 **(ii)** 2 **12.** 2
13. 14 **14.** 1 **15.** 8 **16.** 12 **17.** 8 **18.** €168   **19.** 16
20. $5,5,7,9$ **21.** 6

Exercise 9.3

1. **(i)** 2 **(ii)** 2 **(iii)** 1   2. **(i)** 5 **(ii)** 5 **(iii)** 3
3. **(i)** 3 **(ii)** 4 **(iii)** 4   4. **(i)** 23 **(ii)** 25 **(iii)** 30
5. **(i)** 3 **(ii)** 3 **(iii)** 4   6. **(i)** 5.25 **(ii)** 5 **(iii)** 4
7. **(i)** 2 **(ii)** 1 **(iii) (a)** 25 **(b)** 6
8. **(i)** 2 **(ii) (a)** 3 **(b)** 6 **(iii)** 23
9. **(ii)** 4 **(iii)** 4 **(iv)** 40% **(v)** 200 **(vi)** 6
10. **(a)** 4 **(b)** 3 **(c)** 3.25 **(d)** 3.3

Exercise 9.4

1. 5; 2 – 6   2. 24; 10 – 30   3. 4; 3 – 5   4. 46; 40 – 60
5. 66; 30 – 60   6. 22; 20 – 35   7. **(i)** 10 **(ii)** 6 – 12
8. 32   9. 102   10. **(i)** 36 **(ii)** 31 **(iii)** 90

Exercise 9.5

1. 10   2. 5   3. 2   4. 5   5. 3   6. 5
7. 3   8. 6   9. 17   10. 4   11. 3,7

Exercise 9.6

9. **(ii)** 38 **(iii)** 57.2   10. **(iii)** 54

Exercise 9.7

1. 3 : 10 : 3 : 6 : 5   2. 1 : 4 : 3 : 2   3. 290   5. 36
6. **(i)** 256 **(ii)** €11,375

Exercise 9.8

1. **(i)** 17 **(ii)** 19 **(iii)** 12.5 **(iv)** 4.5   2. **(i)** 43 **(ii)** 54 **(iii)** 30 **(iv)** 24
3. **(i)** 53 **(ii)** 64 **(iii)** 39 **(iv)** 25   4. **(i)** 57 **(ii)** 64 **(iii)** 50 **(iv)** 14
5. **(i)** $5\frac{1}{2}$ mins **(ii)** 2 mins **(iii)** 5 **(iv)** 3
6. **(i)** 62 **(ii)** 24 **(iii)** 30 **(iv)** 54
7. **(i)** 16 **(ii)** 21   8. **(i)** 08.51 **(ii)** 23 **(iii)** 25%
9. **(i)** 85 **(ii)** 12.15 **(iii)** 11.30 – 12.24; 56 minutes **(iv)** 50 minutes
10. **(i)** 30 **(ii)** 74
11. **(i)** €32 **(v)** €33 **(vi)** €13 **(vii)** 12 **(viii)** 8

1. **(a)** 10 **(b)** **(iv)** 66 mins **(v)** 29 mins
2. **(a)** 4 **(b)** **(i)** 90 **(ii)** 30 – 60 **(iii)** 40 **(c)** **(ii)** 24 years **(iii)** 85
3. **(a)** €94.60 **(b)** 10 **(c)** 4
4. **(a)** 4 **(b)** **(ii)** 52 **(iii)** 15 **(iv)** 33 **(vi)** 53.75
5. **(a)** **(i)** 10 **(ii)** 37 **(iii)** 17 **(b)** 5
6. **(a)** **(v)** 60 mins **(vi)** 27 mins **(b)** 9
7. **(a)** **(i)** $x = 300; y = 255$ **(ii)** 1080 **(iii)** €28.75 **(b)** 5
   (c) **(ii)** 44 **(iii)** 13 **(iv)** 11 **(vi)** 41
8. **(a)** **(iv)** 2 **(v)** 39 mins **(vi)** 23 mins **(vii)** 32 mins **(b)** 5
9. **(a)** **(i)** 42 **(b)** **(ii)** 65 **(iii)** 39 **(iv)** 59 **(c)** 6
10. **(a)** 7 **(b)** **(ii)** 09.36 **(ii)** 142 **(c)** **(i)** 8 **(iii)** €52 **(iv)** €42.30

1. 5
2. 10
3. $\sqrt{65}$
4. $\sqrt{20}$ or $2\sqrt{5}$
5. $\sqrt{50}$ or $5\sqrt{2}$
6. $\sqrt{40}$ or $2\sqrt{10}$
7. $\sqrt{13}$
8. $\sqrt{\frac{5}{2}}$
9. $\sqrt{\frac{9}{2}}$ or $\frac{3}{\sqrt{2}}$
13. 5

1. (4, 3)
2. (2, 3)
3. (1, 4)
4. (−1, −2)
5. (−3, −1)
6. (1, −2)
7. (1, 1)
8. $\left(\frac{7}{2}, \frac{5}{2}\right)$
9. $\left(-\frac{1}{2}, -\frac{3}{2}\right)$
10. $m(3, −2)$
11. $q(−3, 2)$
12. $c(−5, 3)$
13. $r(−1, 5)$; $\sqrt{52}$ or $2\sqrt{13}$
14. $a = −1, b = 6$
15. $p = 6, q = −3$
16. $p(1, −1), q(5, −4)$; $5 = \frac{1}{2}(10)$
17. (4, 0), on the x axis

1. $\frac{5}{3}$
2. $\frac{3}{2}$
3. $\frac{4}{3}$
4. 1
5. 2
6. −2
7. $\frac{1}{4}$
8. −1
9. −3
17. 7
18. 4
19. 3
20. 5
21. 6
22. 2

13. 9
14. 5
15. 3
16. −2
17. 4
18. 3

1. $2x + y - 7 = 0$ **2.** $3x + y - 11 = 0$ **3.** $4x - y - 19 = 0$
4. $x - y - 3 = 0$ **5.** $5x + y - 13 = 0$ **6.** $x + y - 2 = 0$
7. $x + 2y + 2 = 0$ **8.** $2x - 3y - 1 = 0$ **9.** $2x + 5y - 21 = 0$
10. $5x - 4y = 0$ **11.** $x - 3y + 1 = 0$ **12.** $x + 4y + 12 = 0$
13. $3x - y + 9 = 0$ **14.** $x + 5y + 21 = 0$

1. $x - y + 3 = 0$ **2.** $2x + y - 14 = 0$ **3.** $3x - y - 4 = 0$
4. $x + y - 4 = 0$ **5.** $2x - y = 0$ **6.** $4x - y + 3 = 0$
7. $x + 2y - 16 = 0$ **8.** $2x - 5y + 27 = 0$ **9.** $2x - 3y + 10 = 0$
10. $4x - y + 10 = 0$ **11.** $5x + 2y + 25 = 0$ **12.** $3x - 4y - 14 = 0$
13. **(i)** $\frac{4}{3}$ **(ii)** $4x - 3y - 18 = 0$ **14.** **(i)** $\frac{2}{3}$ **(ii)** $3x + 2y + 4 = 0$
15. $2x + 3y - 7 = 0$ **16.** $3x - y + 11 = 0$
17. **(i)** $(4, 2)$ **(ii)** $-\frac{1}{2}$ **(iii)** $2x - y - 6 = 0$

1. -2 **2.** 3 **3.** $-\frac{2}{3}$ **4.** $\frac{4}{5}$ **5.** $-\frac{1}{2}$ **6.** -1
7. $\frac{1}{3}$ **8.** $-\frac{1}{4}$ **9.** 1 **10.** $-\frac{4}{3}$ **11.** $\frac{2}{5}$ **12.** $\frac{7}{2}$
19. 3 **20.** -6 **21.** 4 **22.** 4 **23.** -3
24. $-\frac{5}{2}$; $-\frac{a}{10}$;   **(i)** 25 **(ii)** -4

1. $2x - y - 3 = 0$ **2.** $2x + 3y - 11 = 0$ **3.** $4x + 3y + 15 = 0$
4. $4x - 5y - 24 = 0$ **5.** $2x - 3y - 8 = 0$ **6.** $x + 2y - 5 = 0$
7. $5x - 2y - 13 = 0$

Exercise 10.9 ▼

1. (4, 5)   **2.** (3, 1)   **3.** (2, 1)   **4.** (−1, 1)   **5.** (−3, −1)

6. (1, 2)   **7.** (0, −5)   **8.** (−4, 3)   **9.** (−2, 1)   **10.** $\left(\frac{3}{2}, -\frac{3}{2}\right)$

11. $\left(\frac{4}{5}, \frac{6}{5}\right)$ **12.** $\left(\frac{5}{2}, \frac{1}{2}\right)$ **13.** $\left(-\frac{1}{4}, \frac{3}{4}\right)$ **14.** $\left(\frac{5}{2}, 1\right)$ **15.** $\left(\frac{2}{3}, \frac{7}{3}\right)$

16. (−2, 2)   **17.** (1, 3)   **18.** (i) $p(2, 1)$, $q(1, −3)$ (ii) $4x − y − 7 = 0$

19. $a = 2$, $b = 4$

Exercise 10.10 ▼

13. (ii) (2, 4)   (iii) (2, 4)   **14.** (i) $p(6, 0)$, $q(0, 4)$ (iii) 12

15. (i) $a(−8, 0)$, $b(0, −4)$ (ii) $\sqrt{80}$ or $4\sqrt{5}$ (iii) 16

Exercise 10.13 ▼

1. (1, 2)   **2.** (−1, 1), (−4, 4)   **3.** $s(1, −4)$ **4.** (6, 0)

5. $h = 2$, $k = −1$ **6.** (4, −1)   **7.** (4, −9)   **8.** (−10, 8)

9. $b(5, −1)$ **10.** $c(11, 5)$, $d(3, 4)$

11. (i) (−2, 1)   (ii) (2, 1)   (iii) (−2, −1)   (iv) (0, −1)   (v) (2, −1)

12. (1, −2)   **13.** (2, 2)   **14.** (5, 4)

15. (ii) $q(−3, 5)$ (iv) $t(−4, 2)$ (v) $r(1, 6)$ (vi) $3x − y + 3 = 0$

16. (ii) (2, 1)   (iv) $r(8, 5)$ **17.** (−1, −2)   **18.** (−3, −2)   **19.** (2, −1)

20. (4, 3), central symmetry in (3, 2)   **21.** (0, −3), central symmetry in (−2, −1)

22. (1, −3)   **23.** (i) $p(−1, 2)$, $q(−4, −2)$ (ii) $4x − 3y + 10 = 0$

(iii) yes, slope of ab = slope of pq.

Exercise 10.14 ▼

1. (i) 10   (ii) (4, 6)   **2.** $r(5, −3)$ **3.** $2x + 5y + 4 = 0$

4. (i) $\frac{3}{4}$ (ii) $3x − 4y − 11 = 0$ **8.** $2x − y + 6 = 0$ **9.** $p(1, −2)$

10. (i) $a(4, 0)$, $b(0, −6)$ (iii) 12   **11.** (7, −4)   **12.** (−1, −1)

13. $s(−1, 4)$ **14.** (1, −2)   **15.** (3, −1)   **16.** −11   **17.** −2

18. 5   **19.** 7   **20.** 5   **21.** −4   **22.** 1 : 2

23. (i) $\sqrt{80}$ or $4\sqrt{5}$ (ii) (2, 1)   (iii) $-\frac{1}{2}$ (iv) $x + 2y − 4 = 0$ (vi) 2

(vii) $2x − y − 3 = 0$ (ix) (1, −1)   (x) $p(4, 0)$, $q(0, 2)$

24. (a) 5   (b) (i) $p(2, 2)$ (ii) $q(−2, 0)$, $r(0, 8)$ (iii) 8

(c) $4x + 3y − 12 = 0$; $3x − 4y = 0$; no

25. **(a)** -3 **(b)** **(i)** $\frac{2}{3}$ **(ii)** $2x - 3y - 1 = 0$ **(iii)** $c(2, 1)$
(iv) $3x + 2y - 8 = 0$ **(v)** 4

26. **(a)** **(i)** $t = 3$ **(ii)** $(0, \frac{10}{3})$ **(b)** **(i)** $p(2, 2)$ **(iv)** $d(6, 1)$
(c) $x + 2y - 12 = 0$

27. **(a)** $(-5, 6)$ **(b)** **(i)** $a(8, 0), b(0, 6)$ **(ii)** $-\frac{3}{4}$ **(iii)** $4x - 3y - 7 = 0$
(iv) $p(4, 3)$ **(v)** 5 **(vi)** 24 **(vii)** $y = 7$

28. **(a)** $2x - y - 9 = 0$ **(b)** **(i)** $\frac{4}{3}$ **(ii)** $m(-1, 4)$ **(iii)** $3x + 4y - 13 = 0$
(iv) $\sqrt{68} = 2\sqrt{17}$ **(c)** $k = -2$

29. **(a)** $\left(-3, -\frac{9}{2}\right)$ **(b)** **(i)** $\sqrt{40}$ or $2\sqrt{10}$ **(ii)** $1 : 2$ **(c)** **(i)** $2x - y - 2 = 0$
(ii) $(2, 2)$ **(iii)** 5

30. **(a)** $k = 11$ **(b)** **(ii)** no; $bc \nparallel ad$ **(c)** **(ii)** $2x + y - 10 = 0$ **(iii)** $\frac{3}{2}$

31. **(a)** $x + 5y = 0$ **(b)** **(i)** $c = 2$ **(ii)** $4x - y - 2 = 0$ **(iii)** $x + 4y + 25 = 0$
(c) **(i)** $x - 3y + 1 = 0$ **(ii)** $2x + y - 12 = 0$ **(iii)** $q(5, 2), s(1, 3)$

32. **(a)** $5x - 3y + 11 = 0$ **(b)** $p(-2, 0), q(0, 4); K : x + 2y - 3 = 0; (3, 0); (-1, 2); 5$
(c) $k = -2$ or 14

Exercise 11.1 ▼

2. **(a) (i)** 290 **(ii)** 300 **(b) (i)** 41 **(ii)** 40 **3.** $40; 39.84$ **4.** $28; 28.22$
5. $700; 703.8$ **6.** $3; 3.1$ **7.** $10; 10.1$ **8.** $2; 1.99$
9. 40 **10.** 140 **11.** 23

Exercise 11.2 ▼

1. €28; €12 **2.** €36; €22.50 **3.** $34; 85; 119$ **4.** €3000
5. $3 : 4$ **6.** $5 : 4$ **7.** $1 : 3$ **8.** $6 : 3 : 4$
9. $3 : 2 : 4$ **10.** €15 **11.** $110g; 132g; 220g$
12. €252; €168; €126
13. **(i)** B **(ii)** A received €40, B received €20, C received €80
14. A received €58, B received €116, C received €116, D received €203 **15.** €200
16. $4 : 6 : 7$ **17.** $5 : 10 : 14$ **18.** $6 : 5$ **19.** $24 : 30 : 35$
20. 33 **21.** 343 **22.** €120
23. **(i)** €30 **(ii)** €165 **24.** 68 km/h
25. €10,160 **26.** €237.50 **27.** 112 km/h
28. **(i)** 120 days **(ii)** 8 days **(iii)** 24 men **29.** **(i)** 12 hours **(ii)** 50 people
30. 21 minutes **31.** 3 men

1. **(a)** 90 km/h   **(b)** 1350 seconds or $22\frac{1}{2}$ minutes   **(c)** 189 km   2. $6\frac{1}{4}$ m/s

3. 60 km/h   4. $8\frac{1}{3}$ m/s   5. 81 km/h   6. 54 km/h

7. 12 : 20   8. 1 hour 4 mins; 60 km/h   9. 08 : 35

10. 5 hours 12 mins   11. $3\frac{1}{2}$ hours

12. **(i)** 560 km   **(ii)** 10 hours   **(iii)** 56 km/h

13. **(i)** 4 hours   **(ii)** 144 km   **(iii)** 444 km   **(iv)** 6 hours   **(v)** 74 km/h

14. **(i)** 243 km   **(ii)** $2\frac{1}{4}$ hours   **(iii)** 108 km/h

15. **(i)** 4 hours   **(ii)** 1 hour; 32 km/h

1. 20%   2. 66%   3. 115%   4. $3\frac{3}{4}$%   5. $2\frac{1}{2}$%

6. 13%   7. 70%   8. 25%   9. 20%   10. 60%

11. **(i)** €47.50   **(ii)** €24.05   **(iii)** €3.69

12. **(i)** 72   **(ii)** 28   13. € 82   14. €6.75   15. €850; €1,045.50

16. €69   17. €1,476   18. 700   19. €600,000   20. 2.4 litres

21. €1,250   22. €28,000   23. 160   24. 64   25. 16

26. $k = 24$ 27. $3x$ 28. $\dfrac{4x}{5}$

1. **(i)** $162   **(ii)** €850   2. €520   3. **(i)** ¥30,800   **(ii)** €450

4. South Africa; €20   5. €2,556.25   6. € 21; 1.75%   7. $256

8. R4,800;   R160   9. $2\frac{1}{2}$%   10. **(i)** 30%   **(ii)** 24.8%

1. **(i)** €4,800   **(ii)** €1,920   **(iii)** €22,080; 8%

2. **(i)** €4,770   **(ii)** €3,339   **(iii)** €23,161; 70%

3. **(i)** €5,453   **(ii)** €3,444   **(iii)** €25,256; 12%

4. **(i)** €4,293   **(ii)** €1,620   **(iii)** €27,000; 6%

5. **(i)** €10,420   **(ii)** €7,980; 19%   6. **(i)** €7,980   **(ii)** €6,384; 80%

7. 18%   8. 17%   9. €24,800   10. €26,700

11. **(i)** €16,000   **(ii)** €44,500   12. **(i)** €21,700   **(ii)** €47,600

13. **(i)** €4,480   **(ii)** $r = 35$ **(iii)** €1,480

14. **(i)** €16,000   **(ii)** €44,000   **(iii)** $r = 26$

1. €2,496
2. €1,738.80
3. €2,837.25
4. €4,775.40
5. €927.27
6. €2,497.28
7. €248.25
8. €306.04
9. €736
10. €1,755.52
11. €2,744.95
12. €30,767.56
13. €6,614.40
14. 8%
15. (i) 4% (ii) 6%
16. (i) €21,200 (ii) $3\frac{1}{2}$
17. (i) €53,560 (ii) $2\frac{1}{2}$%
18. (i) €30,900 (ii) $4\frac{1}{2}$%
19. €2,500
20. €10,000
21. €45,000
22. €22,000
23. (i) €22,472 (ii) €1,472
24. €11,600
25. €4,720
26. (i) €12,960 (ii) €160

1. (a) 3 : 5 (b) 5 m/s (c) €1,300 (d) 31.5 (e) €30 (f) €7,369.50
2. (a) $\frac{3}{20}$ (b) 82.5c (c) (i) 292 (ii) €16,900 (iii) €60
   (d) (i) 84 km/h (ii) 96 km/h
3. (a) 12 : 20 : 35 (b) €6 (c) €1,853.67 (d) €11,799; €3,201
4. (a) 29.4 km (b) (i) €4,400 (ii) €210,000 (c) €15,000
5. (a) €400; €1,200; €2,400 (b) €1,533; 18% (c) €8,000
   (d) (i) €5,220 (ii) 38 (iii) €960
6. (a) 70 m (b) 24 (c) 20 (d) €260; €82.80; 42% (e) €6,360

1. (i) 40 cm (ii) 96 cm^2
2. (i) 80 cm (ii) 40 cm^2
3. (i) 12 cm (ii) 6 cm^2
4. (i) 125.6 cm (ii) 1,256 cm^2
5. (i) 107.1 cm (ii) 706.5 cm^2
6. (i) 26.28 cm (ii) 31.4 cm^2
7. (i) 56 cm (ii) 144 cm^2
8. (i) 68 cm (ii) 290 cm^2
9. (i) 80 cm (ii) 280 cm^2
10. 150 cm^2
11. 2,206.5 cm^2
12. 977 cm^2
13. 108 cm^2
14. 251.2 cm^2
15. 86 cm^2
16. 927 cm^2
17. 2,016 cm^2
18. 1,438.5 cm^2
19. 1,134 cm^2
20. 77 cm^2
21. 1 : 16
22. 200 cm^2
23. 56 cm^2
24. (i) 352 m (ii) 525
25. (a) 500 m (b) 20 (c) 18 km/h

Exercise 12.2

1. **(i)** 12 cm **(ii)** 64 cm
2. **(i)** 225 cm^2 **(ii)** 36 cm
3. 8 cm
4. 15 m
5. 12,500 m^2
6. 50 m; 10 m
7. 12.5 cm
18. 9 : 25
19. 49 cm
20. $31\frac{1}{2}$ cm
21. 39π cm^2
22. 9 cm

Exercise 12.3

1. **(i)** 120 cm^3 **(ii)** 148 cm^2
2. **(i)** 576 m^3 **(ii)** 432 m^2
3. **(i)** 1,260 mm^3 **(ii)** 766 mm^2
4. **(i)** 8 cm **(ii)** 484 cm^2
5. **(i)** 40 cm **(ii)** 7,400 cm^2
6. 96 cm^2
7. 294 cm^2
8. 8 cm^3
9. 125 cm^3
10. 6
11. 10 cm by 15 cm by 25 cm
12. $48\frac{1}{2}\%$
13. **(i)** 2 : 5 **(ii)** 4 : 25
14. **(i)** 240 cm^2 **(ii)** 96,000 cm^3
15. 1.44 m^3

Exercise 12.4

17. 24,492 cm^3
18. 9
19. **(i)** 19,800 cm^3 **(ii)** 4,851 cm^3 **(iii)** 14,949 cm^3
20. **(i)** 1 : 1 **(ii)** 3 : 2

Exercise 12.5

11. **(i)** $123\frac{1}{5}$ cm^3 **(ii)** $316\frac{4}{5}$ cm^2
12. **(i)** 5,510.7 cm^3 **(ii)** 2,387.97 cm^2
13. **(i)** 32 : 9 **(ii)** 32 : 15
15. 36π cm^3
16. **(i)** 936π m^3 **(ii)** 360π m^2
17. $1,944\pi$ cm^3, 549π cm^2
18. **(i)** 795.048 cm^3 **(ii)** 431.436 cm^2

Exercise 12.6

1. **(i)** 20 cm **(ii)** 240π cm^2
2. **(i)** 6 cm **(ii)** 288π cm^3
3. 15 cm
4. **(i)** 3 cm **(ii)** 36π cm^2
5. **(i)** 4 cm **(ii)** 80π cm^2
6. **(i)** 20 cm **(ii)** 1,570 cm^3
7. **(i)** $3\frac{1}{2}$ m **(ii)** 341 m^2
8. **(i)** 10 cm **(ii)** 96π cm^3
9. 10 cm
10. **(i)** 2 cm **(ii)** 35.2 cm^2
11. **(i)** 4 m **(ii)** 301.44 m^2

Exercise 12.7 ▼

1. $h = 9$ cm
2. $r = 2$ cm
3. $r = 6$ cm
4. $h = 18$ cm
5. $r = 5$ cm
6. $h = 7\frac{1}{2}$ cm
7. 20 cm
8. 8 cm
9. 36π cm^3; 6 cm
10. 400
11. $3\frac{1}{2}$ cm
12. 3.2 cm
13. 36 cm
14. 25 cm
15. 2 cm
16. 1.28 cm; 6 cm
17. $1,152\pi$ cm^3; 18 cm
18. $\frac{9}{2}\pi$ cm^3; 125

Exercise 12.8 ▼

1. 2 cm
2. 3 cm
3. 5 cm
4. 8 : 27
5. 1 : 4
6. 1 : 1
7. 2 cm
8. 11 : 14
9. $k = 2$
10. 10 cm
11. 288π cm^3

Exercise 12.9 ▼

1. **(a)** 198 cm^2 **(b) (i)** 38,808 mm^3 **(ii)** 174,636 mm^3 **(iii)** 58,212 mm^3 **(c)** 12 cm
2. **(a)** 4 : 25 **(b) (i)** $3,920\pi$ cm^3 **(ii)** 144π cm^3 **(iii)** 9 cm **(iv)** 27
3. **(a)** 5,000 **(b)** 324π cm^3 **(c)** 5,652 cm^3; 5 cm
4. **(a)** 96% **(b) (i)** 5 cm **(ii)** 54.5 cm^2 **(c)** 100π cm^3; 500 seconds; 4 cm
5. **(a)** 640 cm^3 **(b) (i)** 15 cm **(ii)** $123\frac{3}{4}$ cm^2 **(c) (i)** 72 **(ii)** 288 cm^3 **(iii)** 74%
6. **(a)** 196.25 cm^2 **(b) (i)** 15 m **(ii)** 1,225 litres/s **(c) (i)** 800π cm^3 **(ii)** $2,500\pi$ cm^3
    (iii) 13.5 cm
7. **(b)** 58 cm^2 **(c)** 5 cm
8. **(a)** 16 cm **(b) (i)** $6,300\pi$ cm^3 **(ii)** 30 cm **(c)** 100π cm^2; 20 cm; 19.4 cm
9. **(a)** 7,000 m^2 **(b) (i)** 15 cm; 180π cm^3 **(ii)** 144π cm^3

    (iii) 56% **(c) (i)** $19\frac{1}{4}$ m^2 **(ii)** $x = 16$

10. **(a)** 343 cm^3 **(b)** 9 cm **(c) (i)** $\frac{2}{3}\pi r^3$ **(ii)** 3 cm

11. **(a)** 14 cm **(b)** $30,375\pi$ cm^3; $22\frac{1}{2}$ cm **(c)** 1.25 cm

12. **(a) (i)** 1,200 **(ii)** 160 cm **(b)** $\frac{3}{2}$ cm **(c) (ii)** 421.12 cm^3 **(iii)** 1 cm

13. **(a)** 288π cm^3; 64 cm **(b)** 90π cm^3/s; 6 minutes **(c) (i)** 1.5 cm
    (ii) 2π cm^3; 4 cm **(d) (i)** 720π cm^3 **(ii)** 10 cm

1. (i) 18 **(ii)** 45 **(iii)** 33 **(iv)** 20 **(v)** 42   **2. (i)** 5 **(ii)** 27 **(iii)** 32
3. 50   **4. (i)** 7 **(ii)** 21   **5. (i)** 5 **(ii)** 4   **6. (i)** 21 **(ii)** 8 **(iii)** 47
7. $x = 8$, **(i)** 15 **(ii)** 7 **(iii)** 22   **8.** $x = 15$, **(i)** 30 **(ii)** 45 **(iii)** 63 **(iv)** 56
9. 12   **10.** 22   **11. (i)** 8 **(ii)** 15   **12. (i)** 9 **(ii)** 51
13. (i) 32 **(ii)** 20 **(iii)** 29   **14. (i)** 19 **(ii)** 11   **15.** $a = 20$, $b = 35$, $c = 0$, $d = 15$; 23

1. (i) 5 **(ii)** 12 **(iii)** 46 **(iv)** 6 **(v)** 4 **(vi)** 23 **(vii)** 33 **(viii)** 9 **(ix)** 37
   (x) 14 **(xi)** 19
2. (i) 38 **(ii)** 22 **(iii)** 19 **(iv)** 10 **(v)** 4 **(vi)** 22 **(vii)** 32 **(viii)** 6 **(ix)** 7
   (x) 10 **(xi)** 5 **(xii)** 19
3. (i) 9 **(ii)** 2 **(iii)** 18 **(iv)** 37 **(v)** 31 **(vi)** 4
4. (i) 12 **(ii)** 7 **(iii) (a)** $15 - x$ **(b)** $12 - x$; $x = 11$
5. (a) $9 - x$ **(b)** $14 - x$; $x = 5$ **(i)** 4 **(ii)** 9 **(iii)** 15 **(iv)** 27
6. $x = 9$; 20   **7. (i)** $x = 3$ **(ii)** 9   **8. (i)** $x = 2$ **(ii)** 9
9. $9 - x$; $6 - x$; $7 - x$; $x + 8$; $x + 6$; $x + 3$; $x = 4$
10. $x = 10$ **11.** $x = 4$; **(i)** 14 **(ii)** 26
12. (i) 4 **(ii)** 10 **(iii) (a)** 44 **(b)** 37 **(iv)** 5
13. (iii) (a) 8 **(b)** 2 **(iv)** 42 **(v)** 6   **14.** $x = 2$
15. (i) 6 **(ii)** 5 **(iii)** 21 **(iv)** 4; 48

1. (i) 11 **(ii)** 13 **(iii)** 7 **(iv)** 1 **(v)** -1
2. (i) 18 **(ii)** 4 **(iii)** 0 **(iv)** -2 **(v)** 12
3. (i) 3 **(ii)** -1 **(iii)** 8 **(iv)** -6; $-5, 3$
4. (i) -1 **(ii)** -2 **(iii)** $\frac{1}{4}$ or 0.25 **(iv)** $\frac{14}{25}$ or 0.56
5. (i) 1 **(ii)** -1 **(iii)** 2
6. (i) $x = 2$ **(ii)** $x = \frac{1}{2}$ **(iii)** $x = -\frac{1}{3}$ or 1 **(iv)** $x \leqslant 1$
7. (a) (i) 1 **(ii)** -5 **(iii)** -6 **(b) (i)** $6x - 5$ **(ii)** $2x + 1$; -1
8. (a) (i) 10 **(ii)** 5 **(b)** $k = 2$ **9.** $k = 3$
10. (a) (i) 15 **(ii)** 8 **(iii)** 3 **(b)** $k = -4$ **(c)** $x = \pm 2$
11. (i) 4 ; 2 **(ii)** $k = 2$ **(iii)** 1   **12. (i)** 11; $10k + 14$ **(ii)** $k = -1$ **(iii)** $\frac{1}{2}$, 2
13. (i) 9; $4x^2 + 4$; $6x + 5$ **(ii)** $-1, \frac{5}{2}$ **14. (i)** 0; 4 **(ii)** 4
15. $g(x) = 2x + 6$; 12   **16. (i)** $k = \pm 3$ **(ii)** $h(x) = x - 1$ **(iii)** $f(x) + 1$

1. $k = 2$ **2.** $a = 3$ **3.** $h = -5$ **4.** $b = -4$ **5.** -2

6. $k = 4$ **7.** $\frac{1}{2}$; 3   **8.** $a = 3$; $b = -4$ **9.** $a = -7$; $b = -1$

10. (i) $a = 2$; $b = -3$ (ii) -1; 5   (iii) $-\frac{3}{2}$; 4

11. (i) $a = 5$; $b = -17$ (ii) 0, 1, 2, 3, 4   **12.** $a + b = 1$; $a - b = 5$; $a = 3$; $b = -2$

13. $p + q = 7$; $p - q = -3$; $p = 2$; $q = 5$; $-\frac{1}{2}$, 3

14. (i) $a = 5$; $b = -6$ (ii) 0; 1   **15.** $c = -3$; $a = 4$; $b = -5$

16. (i) $q = -6$ (ii) -8; -3 **17.** $b = 1$; $c = -2$; $k = -2$

18. $a = 2$; $b = -5$; $h = -3$; $k = -5$ **19.** $b = -2$; $c = 4$; $p = 2$; $q = -1$; -5; 1

20. $b = 2$; $c = -3$; $k = -4$; $x = -1$ **21.** $b = -2$; $c = -15$

Exercise 15.3 ▼

1. (i) -2; 1.5   (ii) -6.1 (iii) -1; 0.5   (iv) 7   (v) $-2 \leqslant x \leqslant 1.5$
(vi) $-3 \leqslant x < -2$ and $1.5 < x \leqslant 2$ (vii) $-1.5 \leqslant x \leqslant 1$ (viii) $1.5 < x \leqslant 2$
(ix) -2.5; 2   (x) 1.75

2. (i) -3; 1   (ii) -2; 0   (iii) -4 (iv) $(-1, -4)$ (v) $-3 \leqslant x \leqslant 1$
(vi) 3.3; $k = -1$

3. (i) -1; 4   (ii) 0; 3   (iii) -3.4 (iv) 6.25   (v) $-2 \leqslant x \leqslant -1$ and $4 \leqslant x \leqslant 5$
(vi) -0.5

4. (i) $(2, 4)$ (ii) $1 \leqslant x \leqslant 3$ (iii) $0 \leqslant x \leqslant 2$ (iv) $-5 \leqslant k < 4$

5. (i) -2; 1.3   (ii) $-2 \leqslant x \leqslant 1.3$ (iii) -2.25; 1.6   (iv) 5.3   (v) -8.3

6. (i) $(1, -7)$ (ii) -1; 3   (iii) $0 \leqslant x \leqslant 2$ (iv) $-2 \leqslant x < 1$ (v) $k = -7$

7. (ii) 4   (iii) $(1, 4)$ (iv) -2.75 (v) -1.6 (vi) $0 \leqslant f(x) \leqslant 4$

8. (i) -1; 3.5   (ii) -0.2; 2.7   (iii) 10.1   (iv) $k > 10.1$ and $k < -11$

9. (i) 9   (ii) $(-1, 9)$ (iii) -2; 1   (iv) $-2 \leqslant x \leqslant 1$ (v) $-5 \leqslant x \leqslant -2$ and $1 \leqslant x \leqslant 3$
(vi) -2; 0   (vii) -3.25 (viii) 144   (ix) -3; 1   (x) -3.6 (xi) -3
(xii) $h = -1$

10. (i) -1; 3   (ii) $(1, -4)$ (iii) 0; 3   (iv) $0 \leqslant x \leqslant 3$ (v) $-2 \leqslant x \leqslant 0$ and $3 \leqslant x \leqslant 4$
(vi) $-4 \leqslant f(x) \leqslant -3$

11. (i) $-2 \leqslant x \leqslant 1$ (ii) 3   (iii) -4; 1   (iv) $1 \leqslant x \leqslant 3$ (v) $-4 \leqslant x \leqslant 1$

12. (i) 3.1   (ii) -1; 1   (iii) $-1 \leqslant x \leqslant 1$ (iv) $1 \leqslant x \leqslant 2$

13. (i) -3; 1.5   (ii) 10.1   (iii) $-2.7 \leqslant x \leqslant 1.7$

14. (i) -2.1; 1.6   (ii) $-1.5 \leqslant x \leqslant 1$ (iii) $-1.4 \leqslant x \leqslant 1.4$

15. (i) -3.3; 1.3   (ii) 0.5   (iii) $-2 \leqslant x \leqslant 0$ (iv) -2.6; 1.6   (v) $-2.6 \leqslant x \leqslant 1.6$
(vi) $-1 < x < 1.3$ (vii) $k > 11$

16. (i) 9   (ii) 4   (iii) $(4, 8)$ (iv) $4 \leqslant x \leqslant 6$

1. **(i)** €13 **(ii)** €16 **(iii)** 7 km **(iv)** €3
2. **(i)** 13:30 and 16:30 **(ii)** 50 km/h **(iii)** 15:00
3. -1; 3.5 **(i)** 10.1 m **(ii)** 9 m **(iii)** $3\frac{1}{2}$ seconds
4. **(i)** 7 m **(ii)** 16 m **(iii)** 2 secs **(iv)** 4 secs **(v)** 13.75 m **(vi)** 6 secs **(vii)** 7 secs
5. **(i)** 25 m² **(ii)** 5 m by 5 m **(iii)** 24 m² **(iv)** 3 m **(v)** 8.5 m or 1.5 m
6. **(i)** 18 m² **(ii)** 6 m by 3 m **(iii)** 1 m or 5 m **(iv)** 2.6 m or 9.4 m **(v)** $2 \leqslant x \leqslant 4$
7. **(i)** 160 m **(ii)** 70 m **(iii)** 90 m **(iv)** $35\sqrt{5}$

Exercise 16.1 ▼

1. $2\sqrt{2}$ 2. $3\sqrt{3}$ 3. $4\sqrt{2}$ 4. $5\sqrt{5}$ 5. $2\sqrt{3}$ 6. $5\sqrt{2}$
7. $10\sqrt{3}$ 8. $2\sqrt{7}$ 9. $3\sqrt{5}$ 10. $3\sqrt{10}$ 11. $7\sqrt{2}$ 12. $2\sqrt{6}$
13. $5\sqrt{3}$ 14. $3\sqrt{6}$ 15. $3\sqrt{7}$ 16. $5\sqrt{10}$ 17. $5\sqrt{6}$ 18. $8\sqrt{2}$
19. $6\sqrt{5}$ 20. $6\sqrt{2}$ 21. $10\sqrt{2}$ 22. $\sqrt{10}$ 23. $2\sqrt{3}$ 24. $3\sqrt{10}$
25. $\frac{2}{3}$ 26. $\frac{4}{5}$ 27. $\frac{9}{10}$ 28. $\frac{6}{7}$ 29. $\frac{7}{8}$ 30. $\frac{9}{11}$
31. $\frac{1}{3}$ 32. $\frac{1}{8}$ 33. $\frac{3}{2}$ 34. $\frac{5}{3}$ 35. $\frac{5}{4}$ 36. $\frac{11}{5}$
37. $6\sqrt{2}$ 38. 2

Exercise 16.2 ▼

1. $9\sqrt{2}$ 2. $6\sqrt{3}$ 3. $3\sqrt{5}$ 4. $4\sqrt{3}$ 5. $4\sqrt{2}$ 6. $-2\sqrt{5}$
7. $5\sqrt{2}$ 8. $6\sqrt{3}$ 9. $5\sqrt{2}$ 10. $9\sqrt{5}$ 11. $3\sqrt{3}$ 12. $2\sqrt{2}$
13. $4\sqrt{5}$ 14. $\sqrt{3}$ 15. $2\sqrt{11}$ 16. $3\sqrt{2}$ 17. $\sqrt{10}$ 18. 0
19. 6   20. $2\sqrt{3}$ 21. $8\sqrt{2}+2\sqrt{3}$ 22. $5\sqrt{5}-2\sqrt{2}$

Exercise 16.3 ▼

1. 3   2. 5   3. 4   4. 10   5. 9   6. 6
7. 10   8. 20   9. 18   10. 30   11. 60   12. 12
13. 14   14. 6   15. 12   16. 24   17. 18   18. $17+5\sqrt{2}$
19. $6-2\sqrt{5}$ 20. $1+\sqrt{3}$ 21. $3-\sqrt{5}$ 22. 7   23. 22

24. 1　　**25.** 2　　**26.** 4　　**27.** 6　　**28.** $7+3\sqrt{3}$

29. $28+10\sqrt{3}$　　**30.** $7-4\sqrt{3}$　　**31.** 28　　**32.** 10

33. $2\sqrt{2};\ 2$　　**34.** (i) 3　(ii) 1　　**35.** $\frac{1}{4}$　　**36.** 8　　**37.** $\frac{5}{2}$

Exercise 16.4 ▼

1. $4\sqrt{2}$　**2.** $2\sqrt{3}$　**3.** $3\sqrt{5}$　**4.** $2\sqrt{2}$　**5.** $3\sqrt{3}$　**6.** $4\sqrt{2}$

7. $\frac{5\sqrt{3}}{3}$　**8.** $\frac{3\sqrt{2}}{2}$　**9.** $\frac{5\sqrt{2}}{2}$　**10.** $\frac{3\sqrt{5}}{2}$　**11.** $\frac{4\sqrt{2}}{3}$　**12.** $\frac{4\sqrt{5}}{3}$

13. 2　**14.** 3　**15.** 4　**16.** $\sqrt{3}$　**17.** 4　**18.** $\sqrt{5}$

19. $\sqrt{2}$　**20.** 2　**21.** 3　**22.** $\frac{1}{2}$　**23.** $\frac{3}{2}$　**24.** $\frac{5}{3}$

Exercise 16.5 ▼

1. $6\sqrt{3}$　**2.** 10　**3.** $\frac{7}{4}$　**4.** (a) $4\sqrt{3}$　(b) 2　**5.** 4

6. 6　**7.** $28\sqrt{5}$　**8.** $28-10\sqrt{3}$　　**9.** 2　　**10.** 1

11. (i) $4\sqrt{2}$　(ii) $5\sqrt{3}$　　**12.** 7

Exercise 17.1 ▼

1. 7　**2.** 10　**3.** 4　**4.** 2　**5.** 3　**6.** -2

7. 6　**8.** 10　**9.** 18　**10.** -2　**11.** -3　**12.** 2

13. $\frac{1}{2}$　**14.** 2　**15.** $\frac{3}{2}$　**16.** 3　**17.** 5　**18.** 10

19. 2　**20.** 3　**21.** 4　**22.** 5　**23.** 2　**24.** 3

25. 10　**26.** 8　**27.** 4　**28.** 125　**29.** 8　**30.** 25

31. 16　**32.** 16　**33.** 8　**34.** 243　**35.** 32　**36.** $\frac{1}{2}$

37. $\frac{1}{3}$　**38.** $\frac{1}{9}$　**39.** $\frac{1}{16}$　**40.** $\frac{1}{16}$　**41.** $\frac{2}{3}$　**42.** $\frac{4}{25}$

43. $\frac{16}{9}$　**44.** $\frac{3}{2}$　**45.** $\frac{27}{64}$　**46.** $\frac{1}{9}$　**47.** $\frac{9}{8}$　**48.** $\frac{4}{3}$

49. $\frac{1}{125}$　**50.** $\frac{1}{32}$　**51.** $p=17;\ q=72$　　**52.** $a=7;\ b=12$

53. 2^{4}　**54.** (a) (i) 3^{2}　(ii) 3^{3}　(iii) 3^{4}　(iv) 3^{5}　(b) 3^{6}

55. $2^{\frac{3}{2}}$　**56.** $5^{\frac{5}{2}}$　**57.** $2^{-\frac{5}{2}}$　**58.** (a) (i) 5 or 5^{1}　(ii) 5^{2}　(b) 5^{-3}

59. $3^{\frac{3}{2}}$　**60.** 2^{3}

1. 2^3 **2.** 3^2 **3.** 2^5 **4.** 3^3 **5.** 5^3 **6.** 3^4

7. 7^2 **8.** 2^6 **9.** 5^4 **10.** 3^5 **11.** 2^7 **12.** 7^3

13. 2^{-4} **14.** 2^{-5} **15.** 3^{-5} **16.** $3^{\frac{5}{2}}$ **17.** $5^{-\frac{3}{2}}$ **18.** 2^3

19. 5 **20.** 3 **21.** 2 **22.** 3 **23.** 5 **24.** 2

25. 1 **26.** $\frac{7}{2}$ **27.** $\frac{1}{4}$ **28.** -1 **29.** -3 **30.** $\frac{1}{2}$

31. 3 **32.** 2 **33.** 1 **34.** $4^2; \frac{3}{2}$ **35.** -1 or 2

36. **(i)** 3^4 **(ii)** $3^{\frac{1}{2}}$ **(iii)** $3^{\frac{7}{2}}; \frac{5}{2}$ **37.** $\frac{1}{4}$

1. 2 **2.** 9 **3.** 1 **4.** 4 **5.** 343 **6.** 256

7. $\frac{1}{9}$ **8.** $\frac{64}{27}$ **9.** $\frac{1}{16}$ **10.** $\frac{9}{4}$ **11.** $\frac{8}{3}$ **12.** $\frac{1}{20}$

13. $p = 9; \; q = 20$ **14.** $\frac{1}{8}$ **15.** $a = 9 \; ; \; b = 16$ **16.** 35

17. 5^{-1} **18.** 3^3 **19.** 2^3 **20.** **(a) (i)** 2^2 **(ii)** 2^5 **(b)** $\frac{3}{2}$

21. 2 **22.** **(i)** $2^{\frac{1}{2}}$ **(ii)** 2^3 **(iii)** $2^{\frac{7}{2}}; \frac{3}{2}$ **23.** 2 **24.** $\frac{5}{3}$

25. $3^0; \; -\frac{1}{2}$ or 1 **26.** **(i)** 16 **(ii)** 2 **(iii)** 1 **(iv)** 8 **(v)** 32

27. **(i)** 9 **(ii)** $\frac{1}{9}$ **(iii)** 3 **(iv)** 27 **(v)** $\frac{1}{243}$

1. 7×10^3 **2.** 8.3×10^4 **3.** 4.28×10^5 **4.** 5.2×10^2 **5.** 6.8×10^3

6. 3.8×10^6 **7.** 4.86×10^2 **8.** 2.7×10 **9.** 4×10^{-3} **10.** 6×10^{-4}

11. 8.7×10^{-2} **12.** 2.83×10^{-4} **13.** 2.8×10^3 **14.** 5.7×10^5 **15.** 3.5×10^{-2}

16. 7.3×10^{-3} **17.** 2 **18.** 4 **19.** -3

20. $a = 3.3; \; n = 4$ **21.** $a = 2.7; \; n = 3$

1. 3.2×10^3 **2.** 3.8×10^6 **3.** 5.2×10^4 **4.** 2.3×10^6 **5.** 7.8×10^{-3}
6. 2.94×10^{-4} **7.** 7.48×10^5 **8.** 9.54×10^7 **9.** 2.4×10^4 **10.** 3.6×10^4
11. 1.5×10^5 **12.** 2.3×10^{-3} **13.** 3.51×10^6 **14.** 5.4×10^3 **15.** 2.25×10^6
16. 5.9×10^4 **17.** 3×10^3 **18.** 5×10^2 **19.** 1.52×10^2 **20.** 2.8×10^3
21. 3.8×10^4 **22.** 8×10^{12} **23.** 1.6×10^{-2} **24.** 1.2×10^3 **25.** 1.7×10^{-2}
26. 6.8×10^4 **27.** 8.5×10^3 **28.** 1.1×10^2 **29.** 3×10^4 **30.** $3.64 \times 10^{14} \, \text{m}^2$

1. (i) $\frac{3}{5}$ (ii) $\frac{4}{5}$ (iii) $\frac{3}{4}$ (iv) $\frac{4}{5}$ (v) $\frac{3}{5}$ (vi) $\frac{4}{3}$

2. (i) $\frac{8}{17}$ (ii) $\frac{15}{17}$ (iii) $\frac{8}{15}$ (iv) $\frac{15}{17}$ (v) $\frac{8}{17}$ (vi) $\frac{15}{8}$

3. (i) $\frac{1}{2}$ (ii) $\frac{\sqrt{3}}{2}$ (iii) $\frac{1}{\sqrt{3}}$ (iv) $\frac{\sqrt{3}}{2}$ (v) $\frac{1}{2}$ (vi) $\sqrt{3}$

4. 4   **5.** 16   **6.** 8   **7.** 9

8. $12; \frac{12}{13}; \frac{5}{13}; \frac{12}{5}$ **9.** $20; \frac{20}{29}; \frac{21}{29}; \frac{20}{21}$ **10.** $9; \frac{40}{41}; \frac{9}{41}; \frac{40}{9}$

11. $4; \frac{4}{\sqrt{17}}; \frac{1}{\sqrt{17}}; 4$ **12.** $\sqrt{7}; \frac{3}{4}; \frac{\sqrt{7}}{4}; \frac{3}{\sqrt{7}}$ **13.** $\sqrt{13}; \frac{2}{\sqrt{13}}; \frac{3}{\sqrt{13}}; \frac{2}{3}$

14. (i) $\frac{3}{5}; \frac{4}{3}$ **15.** (i) $\frac{7}{25}; \frac{7}{24}$ **16.** $\frac{3}{\sqrt{10}}; \frac{1}{\sqrt{10}}$

17. (i) $\frac{2}{5}$ (ii) $\frac{2}{\sqrt{29}}; \frac{5}{\sqrt{29}}$ **18.** $\frac{1}{2}$ **19.** 21

20. (i) 3   (ii) $\frac{\sqrt{7}}{4}, \frac{3}{\sqrt{7}}$ (iii) 2

13. (i) $\frac{2}{3}$ **14.** (i) 2

1. 0.7771   **2.** 0.2924   **3.** 1.0724   **4.** 0.9833   **5.** 0.8594
6. 0.6224   **7.** 0.7396   **8.** 0.4405   **9.** 0.6044   **10.** 0.2473
11. 0.9938   **12.** 0.4727   **13.** 4.6947   **14.** 31.6916   **15.** 173.1706
16. 78.5689   **17.** 39.1622   **18.** 149.9937   **19.** 17.9260   **20.** 12.1183
21. 19.6962   **22.** 259.6022   **23.** 3.3317   **24.** 1   **25.** -1
26. $\frac{1}{2}$ **27.** $-\frac{1}{2}$ **28.** $\frac{1}{4}$ **29.** 15   **30.** 35

1. 17°27′   2. 69°31′   3. 56°19′   4. 38°25′   5. 67°49′
6. 40°45′   7. 78°41′   8. 67°40′   9. 24°2′   10. 19°28′
11. 66°25′   12. 65°54′   13. 36°52′   14. 11°32′   15. 48°11′
16. 18°26′   17. 40°54′   18. 19°6′   19. 9°13′   20. 42°8′
21. 9°7′   22. 5°46′   23. 48°59′   24. 22°37′   25. 60°
26. 30°   27. 45°

1. 38°40′   2. 45°35′   3. 39°43′   4. 48°16′   5. 54°28′
6. 33°41′   7. 10.89   8. 32.78   9. 33.98   10. 21.04
11. 157.60   12. 180.91   13. 15.56   14. 93.57   15. 4.00
16. (i) 2.5   (ii) 36°52′   17. (i) 5   (ii) 38°40′
18. (i) 34   (ii) 14°2′

1. 4.2 m   2. (i) 35   (ii) 18°55′   3. (i) 15.6 m   (ii) 67°23′
4. (i) 21 m   (ii) 29 m   (iii) 46°24′   5. (i) 60°   (ii) 4.33
6. 6°   7. (i) 23.32   (ii) 3.27 m   8. 50°36′
9. (i) 6 m   (ii) 34°27′   10. 492 m   12. 6 km/h   13. 51 km
14. N 37° W   15. 20 km; 40 km

1. 80 cm^2 2. 17.58 cm^2 3. 51.70 cm^2 4. 145.22 cm^2 5. 41.50 cm^2
6. 27.48 cm^2 7. 22.65 m^2 8. 45.01 cm^2 9. 90.21 m^2 10. 128.56
11. (i) 3 cm   (ii) 4.98 cm^2 12. 837.16 cm^2
13. (a) (i) 31.40 cm^2 (ii) 29.39 cm^2 (iii) 2.01 cm^2 (b) 17.32
14. 24 cm   15. (i) 0.56   (ii) 26 m   16. (i) 0.94   (ii) 75 m
17. 9   18. 35°41′   19. 40°   20. 70°

Exercise 19.8 ▼

1. 15.04   **2.** 80°4′   **3.** 28.37   **4.** 59°16′
5. 6.70   **6.** 59°50′   **7.** 7.78   **8.** 67°31′
9. 10.38   **10. (i)** 13.92 cm   **(ii)** 12.79 cm   **11.** 23°37′
12. (i) 65°   **(ii)** 13.29 cm   **(iii)** 12.82 cm
13. (i) 14.28 cm   **(ii)** 20.48 cm^2
14. (i) 17 m   **(ii)** 50°   **(iii)** 111 m^2 **(iv)** 14.37 m
15. (i) 96.6   **(ii)** 45.35
16. (i) 29 m   **(ii)** 43°36′   **(iii)** 72°   **(iv)** 400 m^2 **(v)** 34 m
17. (i) 23°   **(ii)** 103 m, 93 m

Exercise 19.9 ▼

1. 26.1 km/h   **2. (i)** 110°   **(ii)** 25°   **(iii)** 45°; 2,341 m
3. (ii) 23.54 km   **4.** 2,595 m   **5.** 23 m
6. (ii) N60°E   **(iii)** 5.18 km   **(iv)** 3.66 km

Exercise 19.10 ▼

2. 1   **3.** 1   **4.** 4   **5.** $\frac{3}{2}$ or $1\frac{1}{2}$ **6.** $\frac{2}{3}$

7. $\frac{3}{2}$ or $1\frac{1}{2}$ **8.** $\frac{1}{4}$ **9.** $\frac{5}{8}$ **10.** 0

Exercise 19.11 ▼

1. 0   **2.** 0   **3.** 1   **4.** 1   **5.** −1
6. −1   **7.** 0   **8.** 0   **9.** 0   **10.** −2
11. −3   **12.** 1   **13.** −1   **14.** 4   **15.** 0° or 360°
16. 90°   **17.** 270°   **18.** 180°   **19.** 90° or 270°
20. 0°, 180°, 360°   **21.** 0°, 180°, 360°   **22.** 1, −1

Exercise 19.12 ▼

1. $\frac{1}{2}$ **2.** $-\frac{1}{2}$ **3.** $-\frac{1}{2}$ **4.** $\sqrt{3}$ **5.** −1

6. $-\frac{\sqrt{3}}{2}$ **7.** $\frac{1}{\sqrt{2}}$ **8.** $\frac{1}{\sqrt{3}}$ **9.** $-\frac{1}{\sqrt{2}}$ **10.** $-\frac{1}{\sqrt{3}}$

11. $-\frac{\sqrt{3}}{2}$ **12.** $-\frac{1}{\sqrt{2}}$ **13.** $-\frac{1}{2}$ **14.** 0   **15.** $\frac{13}{12}$ or $1\frac{1}{12}$

16. 2   **17.** 30°   **18.** 60°   **19.** 45°   **20.** 45°

1. 30°, 150°   2. 60°, 300°   3. 240°, 300°   4. 30°, 210°
5. 120°, 300°   6. 45°, 135°   7. 30°, 330°   8. 45°, 225°
9. 210°, 330°   10. 225°, 315°   11. 150°, 330°   12. 135°, 315°
13. 45°, 315°   14. 60°, 120°   15. 60°, 240°   16. 20°, 160°
17. 145°, 215°   18. 48°, 228°   19. 65°48′, 245° 48′
20. 217°24′, 322°36′   21. 53°40′; 306°20′   22. 51°20′, 231°20′
23. 23°35′, 156°25′   24. 109°28′, 250°32′

1. (i) $\frac{4}{5}, \frac{3}{5}$ 3. (i) 60°   (ii) $\frac{\sqrt{3}}{2}$ 4. (i) 1.7   (ii) 28°4′

5. 33°41′   6. (i) 112.5 m   (ii) 51°20′   7. (i) $-\frac{\sqrt{3}}{2}$ (ii) $-\frac{1}{\sqrt{3}}$

8. 30°   10. 4.24 km   11. 0°, 180°, 360°

12. (a) 9 cm^2 (b) 80°24′   (c) (i) 4.3 m   (ii) 5.0 m

13. (a) $\frac{8}{17}, \frac{15}{17}$ (b) (i) 12.31   (ii) 5.13   (d) 177 m

14. (a) (i) 24   (ii) $\frac{12}{5}$ (iii) 120   (b) 117 cm   (c) (i) 25.5 m   (ii) 52°
    (d) 142°19′, 217°41′

15. (a) 18.7 m^2 (b) (i) 115 m   (ii) 125 m   (c) (i) 17 m
(ii) $\frac{8}{17}$ (iii) 68 m^2 (iv) 75°58′   (v) 8.24 m

16. (a) 4   (b) (i) 13   (ii) 11°19′   (c) (i) 122 m   (ii) 135 m

17. (b) (i) $\frac{2}{5}$ (iii) 6   (c) (i) 296 m   (ii) 103 m

18. (a) 12; 16   (b) (i) 90°   (ii) 0.8   (iii) 4 cm   (iv) 125°54′   (c) 3.8 m

19. (a) (i) $\frac{2}{\sqrt{2}}$ or $\sqrt{2}$ (ii) 1   (b) (i) 3   (ii) 6   (iii) $\frac{3}{5}$ (iv) 8   (c) 4.28

20. (a) (i) 60°   (ii) 240°, 300°   (b) (i) 33°41′   (ii) 10.4 km   (c) 7.92 km

21. (a) 2   (b) 180°   (c) (i) $\frac{\sqrt{3}}{2}$ (ii) 4   (iii) 22°   (d) 17 km/h
    (e) 30°, 150°; $\frac{\sqrt{3}}{2}$, $-\frac{\sqrt{3}}{2}$

1. $a = 44$, $b = 118$ **2.** $x = 60$, $y = 120$ **3.** $p = 45$, $q = 75$
4. $a = 90$, $b = 35$, $c = 55$ **5.** $p = 28$, $q = 112$
6. $a = 61$, $b = 71$, $c = 48$ **7.** $a = 42$, $b = 96$, $c = 84$ **8.** $x = 24$, $y = 15$
9. $y = 15$ **10.** $p = 17$, $q = 146$ **11.** $p = 130$ **12.** $x = 75$ **13.** $y = 74$
14. $105°, 60°, 15°$ **15.** $x = 33$ **16.** (i) $51°$ (ii) $27°$
17. $x = 22\frac{1}{2}$, $y = 112\frac{1}{2}$, $z = 22\frac{1}{2}$ **18.** $x = 12$, $y = 15$ **19.** $x = 40$, $y = 30$
20. $x = 25$, $y = 30$ **21.** $x = 2$, $y = 1$ **22.** $180°, 360°$
23. (i) $\left(\dfrac{180 - x}{2}\right)°$ (ii) $(2x - 180)°$; 108 **24.** $46°$

1. $p = 70$ **2.** $q = 100$ **3.** $r = 90$ **4.** $s = 40$ **5.** $x = 70, y = 100$
6. $p = 102$, $q = 95$, $r = 85$ **7.** $x = 112, y = 34$ **8.** $x = 100$, $y = 160$
9. $a = 40$, $b = 40$ **10.** $p = 70$, $q = 140$ **11.** $a = 110$, $b = 100$
12. $x = 100$, $y = 50$ **13.** $x = 36$ **14.** $a = 40$, $b = 30$
15. $p = q = 54$, $r = 36$ **16.** $a = 52$ **17.** $p = 105$, $q = 67$
18. $r = 120$, $s = 70$ **19.** $a = 104, b = 52$ **20.** $a = 100$, $b = 110$
21. $x = 122$, $y = 29$, $z = 58$, $w = 75$ **22.** $x = 40$ **23.** $x = 64$, $y = 32$, $z = 58$
24. $x = 176$, $y = 92$, $z = 54$ **25.** $p = 90$, $q = 40$, $r = 50$
26. $a = 56$, $b = 28$ **27.** $x = 65$, $y = 40$ **28.** $x = 60, y = 120$
29. $x = 59, y = 118$ **30.** $x = 49$ **31.** $83°$ **32.** (i) $46°$ (ii) $69°$ (iii) $67°$
33. $108°$ **34.** $80°$ **35.** (i) $\angle rcq$ (ii) $\angle qrp$ (iii) $\angle qrs$; $18°$
36. (i) $90°$ (ii) $28°$ (iii) $124°$ (iv) $31°$
37. (i) $124°$ (ii) $236°$ (iii) $118°$ (iv) $34°$
38. (i) $60°$ (ii) $120°$ (iii) $46°$
39. (i) $100°$ (ii) $50°$; $10°$ **40.** $45°$

Exercise 23.1 ▼

1. (i) $\frac{4}{3}$ (ii) $\frac{3}{4}$ (iii) $\frac{1}{4}$ 2. $p=10; q=13$ 3. $p=24; q=10$

4. $p=12; q=10$ 5. $p=12.8; q=4$ 6. $p=6; q=8$

7. $p=10; q=8$ 8. $p=4.8; q=7.2$ 9. $p=\frac{28}{5}; q=\frac{15}{2}$

10. (i) 3   (ii) 8   11. (i) $7\frac{1}{2}$ (ii) $4\frac{1}{2}$ (iii) 10   (iv) 6

12. (i) 1   (ii) 3.6   13. (i) 32   (ii) 7   14. 6   15. 15

16. 15   17. 16 cm   18. $7\frac{1}{2}$ cm   19. 6 cm   20. (i) 18   (ii) 40

21. (i) 12   (ii) 9   22. 7   23. (i) 9 cm   (ii) $\frac{1}{2}$ cm

24. $|pq| = |qs| = 12$ cm

Exercise 23.2 ▼

4. (i) 130°   7. $|ef| = 2; |bc| = 20$

Exercise 24.1 ▼

1. 5   2. 12   3. 8   4. 40   5. 29   6. 35

7. 2   8. 3   9. 3   10. 4   11. $\sqrt{13}$ 12. $\sqrt{15}$

13. 2   14. $\sqrt{18}$ or $3\sqrt{2}$ 15. $\sqrt{8}$ or $2\sqrt{2}$

16. $x=5, y=13$ 17. $x=15, y=16$ 18. 11

19. 12 cm; 6 cm²   20. 8   21. $\sqrt{3}$ 22. 5   23. 24 cm

24. 13.6 m   25. $2\frac{1}{4}\pi$ cm²   26. $\frac{p^2}{2}\pi$ 27. (i) $a=4; b=3$ (ii) $16\sqrt{3}$ cm²

28. (i) 34   (ii) 17   (iii) 15   29. (i) 3.5   (ii) 12.5   30. 10 cm

31. 5   32. $\frac{4}{25}$ 33. (i) 3 cm   (ii) $3\frac{3}{5}$ cm

Exercise 24.2 ▼

1. 17 cm   2. 7
3. (i) 13 cm   (ii) 5 cm   (iii) 12 cm   (iv) 25 cm; $k=5$
4. (i) 11 cm   (ii) 8.8 cm   (iii) 6.6 cm   (iv) 4.4 cm
5. (i) 7 cm   (ii) 25 cm   6. 14.3 cm

2. **(i)** 14.8 **(ii)** 67.2   8.   64

Exercise 25.1 ▼

20. **(i)** 140° **(ii)** 45°   21.   130°   22. **(i)** 40° **(ii)** 20°   26.   3 cm
29. **(i)** 5 cm   **(ii)** 6 cm^2

Exercise 27.1 ▼

1. 4   2.   10   3.   2; 5   4. **(ii)** 80   **(iii)** 90c
5. **(i)** $(x + 3)$ cm   **(ii)** $(4x + 6)$ cm   **(iv)** 5   **(v)** 40 cm^2
6. 7   7.   11, 13, 15, 17   8. $x + 9$; 3, 12
9. **(i)** $4x$ **(ii)** $x + 5$; $4x + 5$ **(iv)** 10   **(v)** 10; 40
10. **(ii)** 210   **(iii) (a)** €70   **(b)** €42   11.   €15,000; $x = 150$
12. **(i)** $10 - x$ **(ii)** $x = 6$ 13.   **(a)** Distance = (Average speed) × (Time)
     (b) $5x$ km   **(c) (i)** $(x + 10)$ km/h   **(ii)** $2x$ km; $(2x + 20)$ km   **(iv)** 75   **(v)** 85 km/h

14. **(a)** $\text{Time} = \dfrac{\text{Distance}}{\text{Average speed}}$ **(b)** $\dfrac{x}{60}$ hours   **(c) (i)** $(95 - x)$ km   **(ii)** $\dfrac{x}{15}$ hours

    (iii) $\dfrac{95 - x}{15}$ hours   **(iv)** $x = 20$ **(v)** 1 hour 20 mins

15. **(a)** $\text{Average speed} = \dfrac{\text{Distance}}{\text{Time}}$ **(b)** $\dfrac{x}{3}$ km/h

    (c) (i) $(100 - x)$ km   **(ii)** $\dfrac{x}{4}$ km/h   **(iii)** $\left(\dfrac{100 - x}{4}\right)$ km/h   **(iv)** 44   **(v)** 14 km/h

Exercise 27.2 ▼

1. 4; 11   2.   7; 10
3. **(b) (i)** $5x + 2y = 250$ **(ii)** $3x + 2y = 170$ **(d) (i)** 40c   **(ii)** 25c
4. **(a)** $x + y = 20$ **(b)** $8x + 5y = 118$ **(c)** $x = 6$; $y = 14$ **(d)** 6@€8 each and 14@€5 each
5. 10; 6   6.   6 10c coins and 14 50c coins   7. **(i)** $x + 2y = 80$ **(ii)** $3x + 2y = 120$
    (iv) 20 of P and 30 of Q 8.   8 racing bicycles and 6 mountain bicycles; €780
9. $8x + 5y = 400$; $6x + 5y = 360$; 20 caravans and 48 tents; €1560

1. −6 or 5 **2.** −3 or 4 **3.** $x = 4$ **4.** €10

5. **(a)** Distance = (Average speed) × (Time) **(b)** $x = 6$ **6.** $x^2 + 4x − 32 = 0$; $x = 4$

7. $x^2 + 10x − 144 = 0$; $x = 8$ **8.** 20 **9.** 10 km/h **10.** $\dfrac{720}{x}$; $x = 18$

11. $\dfrac{100}{x}$; 25 **12.** $\dfrac{80}{x}$; $\dfrac{80}{x+6}$; $x = 10$ **13.** **(i)** $\dfrac{150}{x}$ **(ii)** $\dfrac{156}{x+2}$ **(iii)** $x = 10$

14. **(i)** $\dfrac{12}{x}$ **(ii)** $\dfrac{12}{x+1}$ **(iii)** $x = 3$ **15.** **(i)** $\dfrac{20}{x}$ **(ii)** $\dfrac{20}{x+2}$ **(iii)** $\dfrac{1}{3}$ **(iv)** $x = 10$

16. 8 **17.** 9 **18.** 12 km/h; 15 km/h

1. −4; 3 **2.** $x + 2$; 8; 10 **3.** 4; 9

4. 16 20c coins and 24 50c coins **5.** **(i)** 200 adults **(ii)** 100 children

6. **(a)** $\frac{1}{2}$(base)(perpendicular height) **(b)** $x = 4$

7. **(i)** $4x^2 − 36x + 80$ **(ii)** $x = 1$

8. **(i)** $\dfrac{360}{x}$ **(ii)** $\dfrac{360}{x-2}$ **(iii)** 12 **9.** **(i)** $\dfrac{60}{x}$ **(ii)** $\dfrac{60}{x+1}$ **(iii)** $x = 3$

10. **(i)** $\dfrac{600}{x}$ **(ii)** $\dfrac{630}{x-2}$ **(iii)** 20 **11.** **(i)** $\dfrac{90}{x}$ **(ii)** $\dfrac{90}{x+3}$ **(iii)** 15

12. **(i)** $2x + y = 18$ **(ii)** $y = 18 − 2x$ **(iii)** $x^2 − 9x + 20 = 0$ **(iv)** $x = 5$, $y = 8$ or $x = 4$, $y = 10$

13. 9 **14.** 7